FUNDAMENTAL IDENTITIES

$$\sec x = \frac{1}{\cos x} \qquad\qquad \csc x = \frac{1}{\sin x}$$

$$\tan x = \frac{\sin x}{\cos x} \qquad\qquad \cot x = \frac{1}{\tan x}$$

$$\sin^2 x + \cos^2 x = 1 \qquad 1 + \tan^2 x = \sec^2 x \qquad 1 + \cot^2 x = \csc^2 x$$

$$\sin(-x) = -\sin x \qquad \cos(-x) = \cos x \qquad \tan(-x) = -\tan x$$

COFUNCTION IDENTITIES

$$\sin\left(\frac{\pi}{2} - x\right) = \cos x \qquad\qquad \cos\left(\frac{\pi}{2} - x\right) = \sin x$$

$$\tan\left(\frac{\pi}{2} - x\right) = \cot x \qquad\qquad \cot\left(\frac{\pi}{2} - x\right) = \tan x$$

$$\sec\left(\frac{\pi}{2} - x\right) = \csc x \qquad\qquad \csc\left(\frac{\pi}{2} - x\right) = \sec x$$

REDUCTION IDENTITIES

$$\sin(x + \pi) = -\sin x \qquad\qquad \sin\left(x + \frac{\pi}{2}\right) = \cos x$$

$$\cos(x + \pi) = -\cos x \qquad\qquad \cos\left(x + \frac{\pi}{2}\right) = -\sin x$$

$$\tan(x + \pi) = \tan x \qquad\qquad \tan\left(x + \frac{\pi}{2}\right) = -\cot x$$

ADDITION AND SUBTRACTION FORMULAS

$$\sin(x + y) = \sin x \cos y + \cos x \sin y$$

$$\sin(x - y) = \sin x \cos y - \cos x \sin y$$

$$\cos(x + y) = \cos x \cos y - \sin x \sin y$$

$$\cos(x - y) = \cos x \cos y + \sin x \sin y$$

$$\tan(x + y) = \frac{\tan x + \tan y}{1 - \tan x \tan y} \qquad \tan(x - y) = \frac{\tan x - \tan y}{1 + \tan x \tan y}$$

DOUBLE-ANGLE FORMULAS

$$\sin 2x = 2 \sin x \cos x \qquad\qquad \cos 2x = \cos^2 x - \sin^2 x$$

$$= 2 \cos^2 x - 1$$

$$\tan 2x = \frac{2 \tan x}{1 - \tan^2 x} \qquad\qquad = 1 - \text{~}$$

FORMULAS FOR REDUCING POWERS

$$\sin^2 x = \frac{1 - \cos 2x}{2} \qquad\qquad \cos^2 x = \frac{1 + \cos 2x}{2}$$

$$\tan^2 x = \frac{1 - \cos 2x}{1 + \cos 2x}$$

HALF-ANGLE FORMULAS

$$\sin\frac{u}{2} = \pm\sqrt{\frac{1 - \cos u}{2}} \qquad\qquad \cos\frac{u}{2} = \pm\sqrt{\frac{1 + \cos u}{2}}$$

$$\tan\frac{u}{2} = \frac{1 - \cos u}{\sin u} = \frac{\sin u}{1 + \cos u}$$

PRODUCT-TO-SUM AND SUM-TO-PRODUCT IDENTITIES

$$\sin u \cos v = \tfrac{1}{2}[\sin(u + v) + \sin(u - v)]$$

$$\cos u \sin v = \tfrac{1}{2}[\sin(u + v) - \sin(u - v)]$$

$$\cos u \cos v = \tfrac{1}{2}[\cos(u + v) + \cos(u - v)]$$

$$\sin u \sin v = \tfrac{1}{2}[\cos(u - v) - \cos(u + v)]$$

$$\sin x + \sin y = 2 \sin\frac{x + y}{2} \cos\frac{x - y}{2}$$

$$\sin x - \sin y = 2 \cos\frac{x + y}{2} \sin\frac{x - y}{2}$$

$$\cos x + \cos y = 2 \cos\frac{x + y}{2} \cos\frac{x - y}{2}$$

$$\cos x - \cos y = -2 \sin\frac{x + y}{2} \sin\frac{x - y}{2}$$

THE LAWS OF SINES AND COSINES

The Law of Sines

$$\frac{\sin A}{a} = \frac{\sin B}{b} = \frac{\sin C}{c}$$

The Law of Cosines

$$a^2 = b^2 + c^2 - 2bc \cos A$$

$$b^2 = a^2 + c^2 - 2ac \cos B$$

$$c^2 + b^2 - 2ab \cos C$$

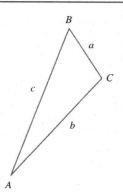

DeMOIVRE'S THEOREM

$$z^n = [r(\cos\theta + i\sin\theta)]^n = r^n(\cos n\theta + i\sin n\theta)$$

$$\sqrt[n]{z} = [r(\cos\theta + i\sin\theta)]^{1/n}$$

$$= r^{1/n}\left(\cos\frac{\theta + 2k\pi}{n} + i\sin\frac{\theta + 2k\pi}{n}\right)$$

where $k = 0, 1, 2, \ldots, n - 1$

ROTATION OF AXES

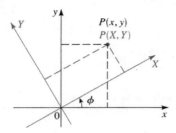

Rotation of axes formulas

$$x = X\cos\phi - Y\sin\phi$$
$$y = X\sin\phi + Y\cos\phi$$

Angle-of-rotation formula for conic sections

$$\cot 2\phi = \frac{A - C}{B}$$

POLAR COORDINATES

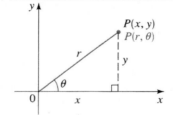

$$x = r\cos\theta$$
$$y = r\sin\theta$$
$$r^2 = x^2 + y^2$$
$$\tan\theta = \frac{y}{x}$$

POLAR EQUATIONS OF CONICS

The graph of a polar equation of the form

$$r = \frac{ed}{1 \pm e\cos\theta}$$

or

$$r = \frac{ed}{1 \pm e\sin\theta}$$

is a conic wth eccentricity e and with one focus at the origin.
The conic is

1. a parabola if $e = 1$.

2. an ellipse if $0 < e < 1$.

3. a hyperbola if $e > 1$.

HARMONIC MOTION

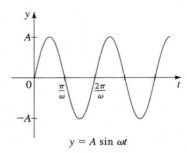

$$y = A\sin\omega t$$

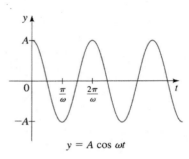

$$y = A\cos\omega t$$

amplitude: A

period: $p = \frac{2\pi}{\omega}$

frequency: $f = \frac{1}{p} = \frac{\omega}{2\pi}$

DAMPED HARMONIC MOTION

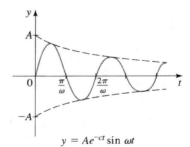

$$y = Ae^{-ct}\sin\omega t$$

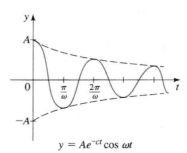

$$y = Ae^{-ct}\cos\omega t$$

damping constant: c

Trigonometry
Anne Arundel Community College

James Stewart
McMaster University

Lothar Redlin
Pennsylvania State University, Ogontz Campus

Saleem Watson
California State University, Long Beach

THOMSON
™
BROOKS/COLE

Australia · Canada · Mexico · Singapore · Spain · United Kingdom · United States

Trigonometry
Stewart / Redlin / Watson

Executive Editors:
Michele Baird, Maureen Staudt &
Michael Stranz

Project Development Manager:
Linda deStefano

Sr. Marketing Coordinators:
Lindsay Annett and Sara Mercurio

Production/Manufacturing Manager:
Donna M. Brown

Production Editorial Manager:
Dan Plofchan

Pre-Media Services Supervisor:
Becki Walker

Rights and Permissions Specialist:
Kalina Ingham Hintz

Cover Image
Getty Images*

The Adaptable Courseware Program
consists of products and additions to
existing Brooks/Cole products that are
produced from camera-ready copy.
Peer review, class testing, and
accuracy are primarily the responsibility
of the author(s).

ISBN: 978-0-495-41474-2
ISBN: 0-495-41474-3

International Divisions List

Asia (Including India):
Thomson Learning
(a division of Thomson Asia Pte Ltd)
5 Shenton Way #01-01
UIC Building
Singapore 068808
Tel: (65) 6410-1200
Fax: (65) 6410-1208

Australia/New Zealand:
Thomson Learning Australia
102 Dodds Street
Southbank, Victoria 3006
Australia

Latin America:
Thomson Learning
Seneca 53
Colonia Polano
11560 Mexico, D.F., Mexico
Tel (525) 281-2906
Fax (525) 281-2656

Canada:
Thomson Nelson
1120 Birchmount Road
Toronto, Ontario
Canada M1K 5G4
Tel (416) 752-9100
Fax (416) 752-8102

UK/Europe/Middle East/Africa:
Thomson Learning
High Holborn House
50-51 Bedford Row
London, WC1R 4LS
United Kingdom
Tel 44 (020) 7067-2500
Fax 44 (020) 7067-2600

Spain (Includes Portugal):
Thomson Paraninfo
Calle Magallanes 25
28015 Madrid
España
Tel 34 (0)91 446-3350
Fax 34 (0)91 445-6218

Preface

The art of teaching is the art of assisting discovery.
MARK VAN DOREN

Trigonometry is an ancient branch of mathematics with exciting modern applications. We have written this book to provide a clear and comprehensive presentation of the concepts of trigonometry, and a view of its practical power in modeling the real world.

The two approaches to defining the trigonometric functions—right triangles and the unit circle—may be taught in either order. Some teachers prefer to begin with the unit circle approach (Chapter 2), thus emphasizing that the trigonometric functions are functions of real numbers. Others prefer to begin with the right triangle approach (Chapter 3), thus building on the foundation of a conventional high-school course in trigonometry. Each order of teaching trigonometry has its merits, and this textbook has been written so that either the unit circle approach or the right triangle approach (Chapter 2 or Chapter 3) may be taught first. More importantly, putting these two approaches in different chapters, each with its relevant applications, helps clarify the purpose of defining the trigonometric functions in different ways. Another way to teach trigonometry is to intertwine the two approaches (for example, Sections 2.1, 2.2, 3.1, 3.2, 3.3, 2.3, 2.4, 3.4, 3.5). Our organization makes it easy to do this without obscuring the fact that the different approaches involve distinct representations of the same functions.

We believe that good teaching comes in different forms, and each instructor brings unique strengths to the classroom; but certainly all instructors are committed to the goal of encouraging conceptual understanding. To implement this goal, some instructors use *technology* to help students become active learners; others use the *rule of four*, "topics should be presented geometrically, numerically, algebraically, and verbally," as well as an expanded emphasis on *applications* to promote conceptual reasoning; still others use *group learning, extended projects*, or *writing exercises* as a way of encouraging students to explore their own understanding of a given concept. In this book we have used all these methods as enhancements to a central core of fundamental skills. These methods are tools to be utilized by instructors and their students to navigate their own course of action toward the goal of conceptual understanding.

■ Special Features

Exercise Sets The most important way to foster conceptual understanding is through the problems that the instructor assigns. To that end we have provided a wide selection of exercises. Each exercise set is carefully graded, progressing from basic conceptual exercises and skill-development problems to more challenging problems requiring synthesis of previously learned material with new concepts.

Graphing Calculators and Computers Calculator and computer technology extends in a powerful way our ability to calculate and visualize mathematics. These capabilities affect not only how a topic is taught but also what is emphasized. We have integrated the use of the graphing calculator throughout the text—to graph and analyze functions, families of functions, to calculate and graph regression curves, and other powerful uses. We also exploit the programming capabilities of the graphing calculator (see pages 84 and 318). The graphing calculator sections, subsections, examples, and exercises, all marked with the special symbol 🖩, are optional and may be omitted without loss of continuity.

The availability of graphing calculators makes it not less important, but far more important to understand the concepts that underlie what the calculator produces. This is particularly true for the trigonometric functions (see for example, pages 139–143). Accordingly, all our calculator-oriented subsections are preceded by sections in which students must graph or calculate by hand, so that they can understand precisely what the calculator is doing when they later use it to simplify the routine, mechanical part of their work.

Focus on Modeling In addition to many applied problems where students are given a model to analyze, we have included several sections and subsections in which students are required to *construct* models of real-life situations. In addition, we have concluded each chapter with a section entitled *Focus on Modeling*. The first such section, after Chapter 1, introduces the basic idea of modeling a real-life situation by fitting lines to data (linear regression). Other sections present ways in which trigonometric, polynomial, exponential, and logarithmic functions can be used to model familiar phenomena from the sciences and from everyday life.

Discovery Projects One way to engage students and make them active learners is to have them work (perhaps in groups) on extended projects that give a feeling of substantial accomplishment when completed. Discovery projects are included in each chapter. For example, in the project *Predator/Prey Models* (page 146), students discover how the trigonometric functions can be used to model population dynamics. In the project *Where to Sit at the Movies* (page 271), students use the trigonometric functions to find where to sit to get the best view of a movie screen. In the project *Fractals* (page 317), students explore an interesting concept from contemporary mathematics.

Mathematical Vignettes Throughout the book we make use of the margins to provide short biographies of interesting mathematicians as well as applications of mathematics to the "real world." The biographies often include a key insight that the mathematician discovered.

(See, for instance, the vignettes on Viète, page 540; Salt Lake City, page 6; and radiocarbon dating, page 464.) They serve to enliven the material and show that mathematics is an important, vital activity, fundamental to everyday life. A series of vignettes, entitled *Mathematics in the Modern World*, emphasizes the central role of mathematics in current advances in technology and the sciences (see, for example, pages 150, 390, and 408).

Discovery, Writing,
and Group Learning

Each exercise set ends with a block of exercises labeled *Discovery•Discussion*. These exercises are designed to encourage the students to experiment, preferably in groups, with the concepts developed in the section, and then to write out what they have learned, rather than simply look for "the answer."

Review Sections
and Chapter Tests

Each chapter ends with an extensive review section, including a *Chapter Test* designed to help the students gauge their progress. Brief answers to odd-numbered exercises in each section (including the review exercises), and to all questions in the Chapter Tests, are given in the back of the book.

The review material in each chapter begins with a *Concept Check*, designed to get the students to think about and explain in their own words the ideas presented in the chapter. These can be used as writing exercises, in a classroom discussion setting, or for personal study.

Appendices

In Appendices A and B, we give a summary of the fundamental concepts of algebra and geometry necessary for the study of trigonometry. Appendix C presents an introduction to using a graphing calculator. All appendices have exercises that students can use to check their readiness for trigonometry or to refresh their memory on these topics.

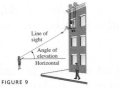

Thales of Miletus (circa 625–547 B.C.) is the legendary founder of Greek geometry. It is said that he calculated the height of a Greek column by comparing the length of the shadow of his staff with that of the column. Using properties of similar triangles, he argued that the ratio of the height h of the column to the height h' of his staff was equal to the ratio of the length s of the column's shadow to the length s' of the staff's shadow:

$$\frac{h}{h'} = \frac{s}{s'}$$

Since three of these quantities are known, Thales was able to calculate the height of the column.

According to legend, Thales used a similar method to find the height of the Great Pyramid in Egypt, a feat that impressed Egypt's king. Plutarch wrote that "although he [the king of Egypt] admired you [Thales] for other things, yet he particularly liked the manner by which you measured the height of the pyramid without any trouble or instrument." The principle Thales used, the fact that ratios of corresponding sides of similar triangles are equal, is the foundation of the subject of trigonometry.

SECTION 3.2   Trigonometry of Right Triangles   **191**

Line of sight
Angle of elevation
Horizontal

Angle of depression
Horizontal
Line of sight

FIGURE 9

The next example gives an important application of trigonometry to the problem of measurement: We measure the height of a tall tree without having to climb it! Although the example is simple, the result is fundamental to the method of applying the trigonometric ratios to such problems.

EXAMPLE 5 ■ Finding the Height of a Tree

A giant redwood tree casts a shadow 532 ft long. Find the height of the tree if the angle of elevation of the sun is 25.7°.

SOLUTION

Let the height of the tree be h. From Figure 10 we see that

$$\frac{h}{532} = \tan 25.7° \qquad \text{Definition of tan}$$

$$h = 532 \tan 25.7° \qquad \text{Multiply by 532}$$

$$\approx 532(0.48127) \approx 256 \qquad \text{Use a calculator}$$

Therefore, the height of the tree is about 256 ft.

25.7°
532 ft

FIGURE 10

◀ Mathematical vignettes provide short biographies of interesting mathematicians, contemporary as well as historical, or describe applications of mathematics to the real world.

◀ Example titles clarify the purpose of examples.

◀ Author notes provide step-by-step comments on solutions.

156   CHAPTER 2   Trigonometric Functions of Real Numbers

Other common examples of periodic behavior involve motion that is caused by vibration or oscillation. A mass suspended from a spring that has been compressed and then allowed to vibrate vertically is a simple example. This same "back and forth" motion also occurs in such diverse phenomena as sound waves, light waves, alternating electrical current, and pulsating stars, to name a few. In this section we consider the problem of modeling periodic behavior.

■ Modeling Periodic Behavior

The trigonometric functions are ideally suited for modeling periodic behavior. A glance at the graphs of the sine and cosine functions, for instance, tells us that these functions themselves exhibit periodic behavior. Figure 1 shows the graph of $y = \sin t$. If we think of t as time, we see that as time goes on, $y = \sin t$ increases and decreases over and over again. Figure 2 shows that the motion of a vibrating mass on a spring is modeled very accurately by $y = \sin t$.

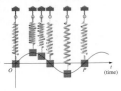

FIGURE 1
$y = \sin t$

FIGURE 2
Motion of a vibrating spring is modeled by $y = \sin t$.

Notice that the mass returns to its original position over and over again. A **cycle** is one complete vibration of an object, so the mass in Figure 2 completes one cycle of its motion between O and P. Our observations about how the sine and cosine functions model periodic behavior are summarized in the following box.

The main difference between the two equations describing simple harmonic motion is the starting point. At $t = 0$, we get

$$y = a \sin \omega \cdot 0 = 0$$

or

$$y = a \cos \omega \cdot 0 = a$$

In other words, in the first case the motion "starts" with zero displacement, while in the second case the motion "starts" with the displacement at maximum (at the amplitude a).

Summary boxes organize and clarify topics ▶ and highlight key ideas.

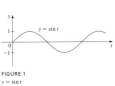

SIMPLE HARMONIC MOTION

If the equation describing the displacement y of an object at time t is

$$y = a \sin \omega t \qquad \text{or} \qquad y = a \cos \omega t$$

then the object is in **simple harmonic motion**. In this case,

$$\text{amplitude} = |a| \qquad \text{Maximum displacement of the object}$$

$$\text{period} = \frac{2\pi}{\omega} \qquad \text{Time required to complete one cycle}$$

$$\text{frequency} = \frac{\omega}{2\pi} \qquad \text{Number of cycles per unit of time}$$

150   CHAPTER 2   Trigonometric Functions of Real Numbers

Error-Correcting Codes
The pictures sent back by the
Pathfinder spacecraft from the surface of Mars on July 4, 1997, were
astoundingly clear. But few watching these pictures were aware of the
complex mathematics used to
accomplish that feat. The distance
to Mars is enormous, and the back-
ground noise (or static) is many
times stronger than the original signal emitted by the spacecraft. So,
when scientists receive the signal, it
is full of errors. To get a clear picture, the errors must be found and
corrected. This same problem of
errors is routinely encountered in
transmitting bank records when you
use an ATM machine, or voice
when you are talking on the
telephone.
   To understand how errors are
found and corrected, we must first
understand that to transmit pictures,
sound, or text we transform them
into bits (the digits 0 or 1; see page
129). To help the receiver recognize
errors, the message is "coded" by
inserting additional bits. For example, suppose you want to transmit
the message "10100." A very
simple-minded code is as follows:
Send each digit a million times. The
person receiving the message reads
(continued)

these values $\sin x = 0$, and $\csc x$ is thus undefined. We see that

$$\csc x \to \infty \quad \text{as} \quad x \to 0^+$$
$$\csc x \to \infty \quad \text{as} \quad x \to \pi^-$$

Thus, the lines $x = 0$ and $x = \pi$ are vertical asymptotes. In the interval $\pi < x < 2\pi$
the graph is sketched in the same way. The values of $\csc x$ in that interval are the
same as those in the interval $0 < x < \pi$ except for sign (see Figure 3). The complete graph in Figure 5(c) is now obtained from the fact that the function cosecant
is periodic with period 2π. Note that the graph has vertical asymptotes at the points
where $\sin x = 0$, that is, at $x = n\pi$, for n an integer.

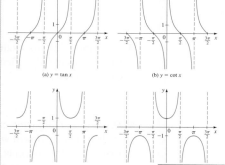

(a) $y = \tan x$

(b) $y = \cot x$

(c) $y = \csc x$

(d

FIGURE 5

   The graph of $y = \sec x$ is sketched in a similar manner. O
of $\sec x$ is the set of all real numbers other than $x = (\pi/2)$
so the graph has vertical asymptotes at those points. The c
in Figure 5(d).
   It is apparent that the graphs of $y = \tan x$, $y = \cot x$, and
ric about the origin, whereas that of $y = \sec x$ is symmetric
because tangent, cotangent, and cosecant are odd function
even function.

140   CHAPTER 2   Trigonometric Functions of Real Numbers

the function. This is especially true for trigonometric functions; Example 6 shows
that, if care is not taken, it's easy to produce a very misleading graph of a trigonometric function.

EXAMPLE 6 ■ Choosing the Viewing Rectangle

Graph the function $f(x) = \sin 50x$ in an appropriate viewing rectangle.

SOLUTION

Figure 15(a) shows the graph of f produced by a graphing calculator using the
viewing rectangle $[-12, 12]$ by $[-1.5, 1.5]$. At first glance the graph appears to be
reasonable. But if we change the viewing rectangle to the ones shown in Figure
15, the graphs look very different. Something strange is happening.

The appearance of the graphs in Figure
15 depends on the machine used. The
graphs you get with your own graphing
device might not look like these
figures, but they will also be quite
inaccurate.

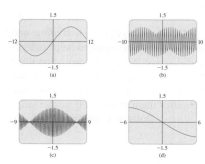

(a)

(b)

(c)

(d)

FIGURE 15
Graphs of $f(x) = \sin 50x$ in
different viewing rectangles

To explain the big differences in appearance of these graphs and to find an
appropriate viewing rectangle, we need to find the period of the function
$y = \sin 50x$:

$$\text{period} = \frac{2\pi}{50} = \frac{\pi}{25} \approx 0.126$$

This suggests that we should deal only with small values of x in order to show just
a few oscillations of the graph. If we choose the viewing rectangle $[-0.25, 0.25]$
by $[-1.5, 1.5]$, we get the graph shown in Figure 16.

◀ Mathematical vignettes provide applications
of mathematics to the real world or give short
biographies of mathematicians, contemporary
as well as historical. A series of vignettes
entitled *Mathematics in the Modern World*
emphasizes the central role of mathematics
in current advances in technology and the
sciences.

Graphing calculator examples, exercises,
and subsections are identified with
the graphing calculator icon. ▶

(b) Find the angle θ of elevation of the sun when the shadow is 20 ft long.

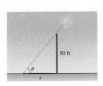

51. A 680-ft rope anchors a hot-air balloon as shown in the figure.

(a) Express the angle θ as a function of the height h of the balloon.

(b) Find the angle θ if the balloon is 500 ft high.

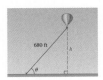

52. The figures indicate that the higher the orbit of a satellite, the more of the earth the satellite can "see." Let θ, s, and h be as in the figure, and assume the earth is a sphere of radius 3960 mi.

(a) Express the angle θ as a function of h.

(b) Express the distance s as a function of θ.

(c) Express the distance s as a function of h. [Find the composition of the functions in parts (a) and (b).]

(d) If the satellite is 100 mi above the earth, what is the distance s that it can see?

(e) How high does the satellite have to be in order to see both Los Angeles and New York, 2450 mi apart?

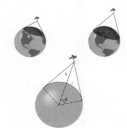

53–54 ■ (a) Graph the function and make a conjecture, and (b) prove that your conjecture is true.

53. $y = \sin^{-1}x + \cos^{-1}x$ **54.** $y = \tan^{-1}x + \tan^{-1}\frac{1}{x}$

55–56 ■ (a) Use a graphing device to find all solutions of the equation, correct to two decimal places, and (b) find the exact solution.

55. $\tan^{-1}x + \tan^{-1}2x = \frac{\pi}{4}$ **56.** $\sin^{-1}x - \cos^{-1}x = 0$

DISCOVERY • DISCUSSION

57. Two Different Compositions   The functions

$$f(x) = \sin(\sin^{-1}x) \qquad \text{and} \qquad g(x) = \sin^{-1}(\sin x)$$

both simplify to just x for suitable values of x. But these functions are not the same for all x. Graph both f and g to show how the functions differ. (Think about the domain and range of $\sin^{-1}$.)

58. Inverse Trigonometric Functions Most calculators do not have keys for $\cot^{-1}$. Prove the following identities and a calculator to find $\sec^{-1}2$,

$$\sec^{-1}x = \cos^{-1}\left(\frac{1}{x}\right)$$

$$\csc^{-1}x = \sin^{-1}\left(\frac{1}{x}\right)$$

$$\cot^{-1}x = \tan^{-1}\left(\frac{1}{x}\right)$$

◀ Real-world applications show the relevance of trigonometry to everyday life and indicate its remarkable problem-solving power.

◀ Graphing calculator examples, exercises, and subsections are identified with the graphing calculator icon.

◀ *Discovery • Discussion* exercises encourage students to experiment with, discuss, and write about the concepts they have learned.

Discovery, Laboratory, Writing, and *Applied Projects* are designed to help students become active learners by providing them with an extended problem, often involving experimentation and a written report, that requires them to use their mathematics skills in a substantial fashion. ▶

Discovery Project

Where to Sit at the Movies

Everyone knows that the apparent size of an object depends on its distance from the viewer. The farther away an object, the smaller its apparent size. The apparent size is determined by the angle the object subtends at the eye of the viewer.

If you are looking at a painting hanging on a wall, how far away should you stand to get the maximum view? If the painting is hung above eye level, then the following figures show that the angle subtended at the eye is small if you are too close or too far away. The same situation occurs when choosing where to sit in a movie theatre.

Small θ Large θ Small θ

1. The screen in a theatre is 22 ft high and is positioned 10 ft above the floor, which is flat. The first row of seats is 7 ft from the screen and the rows are 3 ft apart. You decide to sit in the row where you get the maximum view, that is, where the angle θ subtended by the screen at your eyes is a maximum. Suppose your eyes are 4 ft above the floor, as in the figure, and you sit at a distance x from the screen.

(a) Show that $\theta = \tan^{-1}\left(\frac{28}{x}\right) - \tan^{-1}\left(\frac{6}{x}\right)$.

(b) Use the subtraction formula for tangent to show that

$$\theta = \tan^{-1}\left(\frac{22x}{x^2 + 168}\right)$$

(c) Use a graphing device to graph θ as a function of x. What value of x maximizes θ? In which row should you sit? What is the viewing angle in this row?

2. Now suppose that, starting with the first row of seats, the floor of the seating area is inclined at an angle of $\alpha = 25°$ above the horizontal, and the distance that you sit up the incline is x, as shown in the figure on page 272.

(a) Use the Law of Cosines to show that

$$\theta = \cos^{-1}\left(\frac{a^2 + b^2 - 484}{2ab}\right)$$

230   CHAPTER 3   Trigonometric Functions of Angles

3 TEST

1. Find the radian measures that correspond to the degree measures $300°$ and $-18°$.

2. Find the degree measures that correspond to the radian measures $\frac{5\pi}{6}$ and 2.4.

3. The rotor blades of a helicopter are 25 ft long and are rotating at 200 rpm.
   (a) Find the angular speed of the rotor.
   (b) Find the linear speed of a point on the tip of a blade.

4. Find the exact value of each of the following.
   (a) $\sin 405°$ (b) $\tan(-150°)$
   (c) $\sec \frac{5\pi}{3}$ (d) $\csc \frac{5\pi}{2}$

5. Find $\tan \theta + \sin \theta$ for the angle θ shown.

6. Find the lengths a and b shown in the figure in terms of θ.

7. If $\cos \theta = -\frac{1}{3}$ and θ is in quadrant III, find $\tan \theta \cot \theta + \csc \theta$.

8. If $\sin \theta = \frac{5}{13}$ and $\tan \theta = -\frac{5}{12}$, find $\sec \theta$.

9. Express $\tan \theta$ in terms of $\sec \theta$ for θ in quadrant II.

10. The base of the ladder in the figure is 6 ft from the building, and the angle formed by the ladder and the ground is $73°$. How high up the building does the ladder touch?

◀ Each chapter ends with a review section containing a *Concept Check,* extensive review exercises, and a *Chapter Test.*

Focus on Modeling sections show ▶ how trigonometry is used to model important phenomena from the sciences and from everyday life.

Focus on Modeling
Mapping the World

The method used to survey and map a town (pages 232–235) works well for small areas. But there is a new difficulty in mapping the whole world: How do we represent the *spherical* world by a *flat* map? Several ingenious methods have been developed.

■ Cylindrical Projection

One method is the **cylindrical projection.** In this method we imagine a cylinder "wrapped" around the earth at the equator as in Figure 1. Each point on the earth is projected onto the cylinder by a ray emanating from the center of the earth. The "unwrapped" cylinder is the desired flat map of the world. The process is illustrated in Figure 2.

FIGURE 1
Point P on the earth is projected onto point P' on the cylinder by a ray from the center of the earth C.

FIGURE 2   (a) Cylindrical projection   (b) Cylindrical projection map

Of course, we cannot actually wrap a large piece of paper around the world, so this whole process must be done mathematically, and the tool we need is trigonometry. On the unwrapped cylinder we take the x-axis to correspond to the equator and the y-axis to the meridian through Greenwich, England ($0°$ longitude). Let R be the radius of the earth and let P be the point on the earth at $\alpha°$ E longitude and $\beta°$ N latitude. The point P is projected to the point $P'(x, y)$ on the cylinder (viewed as part of the coordinate plane) where

$$x = \left(\frac{\pi}{180}\right)\alpha R \qquad \text{Formula for length of a circular arc}$$

$$y = R \tan \beta \qquad \text{Definition of tan}$$

354

Acknowledgments

We thank the following reviewers for their thoughtful and constructive comments.

Reviewers   Michelle Benedict, *Augusta State University;* Linda Crawford, *Augusta State University;* Edward Dixon, *Tennessee Technological University;* Richard Dodge, *Jackson Community College;* Floyd Downs, *Arizona State University at Tempe;* Vivian G. Kostyk, *Inver Hills Community College;* Marjorie Kreienbrink, *University of Wisconsin–Waukesha;* Donna Krichiver, *Johnson Community College;* Wayne Lewis, *University of Hawaii* and *Honolulu Community College;* Adam Lutoborski, *Syracuse University;* Heather C. McGilvray, *Seattle University;* Keith Oberlander, *Pasadena City College;* Christine Panoff, *University of Michigan at Flint;* Susan Piliero, *Cornell University;* Gregory St. George, *University of Montana;* Gary Stoudt, *Indiana University of Pennsylvania;* Arnold Vobach, *University of Houston;* Tom Walsh, *City College of San Francisco;* Muserref Wiggins, *University of Akron;* Diane Williams, *Northern Kentucky University;* Suzette Wright, *University of California at Davis;* and Yisong Yang, *Polytech University.*

We have benefited greatly from the suggestions and comments of our colleagues who have used our other books. We extend special thanks in this regard to Linda Byun, Bruce Chaderjian, David Gau, Daniel Hernandez, YongHee Kim-Park, Daniel Martinez, David McKay, Robert Mena, Kent Merryfield, Viet Ngo, Marilyn Oba, Robert Valentini, and Derming Wang, from California State University, Long Beach; to Karen Gold, Betsy Huttenlock, Cecilia McVoy, Mike McVoy, Samir Ouzomgi, and Ralph Rush, of the Pennsylvania State University, Abington College; to Gloria Dion, of Educational Testing Service, Princeton, New Jersey; and to Fred Safier, of the City College of San Francisco.

We especially thank Luana Richards, manager of our production service, for her excellent work and her tireless attention to quality and detail. Her energy, devotion, experience, and intelligence were essential components in the creation of this book. At TECH·arts we thank Brian Betsill for his elegant graphics. At Brooks/Cole, our thanks go to Editorial Production Supervisor Tom Novack, Assistant Editor Stacy Green, Editorial Assistant Jennifer Zimmerman, Marketing Manager Karin Sandberg, National Sales Manager Lucas R. Tomasso, and Art Director Vernon Boes. They have all done an outstanding job.

We are particularly grateful to our editor, Bob Pirtle, for guiding this book through every stage of writing and production. His support and editorial insight when crucial decisions had to be made were invaluable.

ANCILLARIES FOR TRIGONOMETRY

For the Instructor

Instructor's Solutions Manual
by John Banks, San Jose City College and Evergreen Valley College
0-534-39088-9
- Solutions to all even-numbered text exercises

Printed Test Bank
0-534-39089-7
- Text specific
- Contains six sample tests per chapter

TESTING SOFTWARE

Brooks/Cole Assessment Testing
0-534-39095-1
With a balance of efficiency and high performance, simplicity and versatility, Brooks/Cole Assessment (BCA) gives you the power to transform the learning and teaching experience. BCA is a totally integrated testing and course management system accessible by instructors and students anytime, anywhere. Delivered in a browser-based format without the need for any proprietary software or plug-ins, BCA uses correct mathematics notation to provide the drill of basic skills that students need, enabling the instructor to focus more time in higher-level learning activities (that is, concepts and applications). Students can have unlimited practice in questions and problems, building their own confidence and skills. Results flow automatically to a grade book for tracking so that instructors will be better able to assess student understanding of the material, even prior to class or an actual test.

Technical Support
- Toll-free technical support:
  (800) 423-0563 or e-mail: support@kdc.com

For the Student

PRINTED

Student Solutions Manual
by John Banks, San Jose City College and Evergreen Valley College
0-534-38550-8
- Solutions to all odd-numbered text exercises

Study Guide
by John Banks, San Jose City College and Evergreen Valley College
0-534-38551-6
- Detailed explanations
- Worked-out practice problems

ONLINE TUTORIAL

Make the Grade
Every new copy of this text is packaged with Make the Grade. As a part of the Make the Grade package, Brooks/Cole and Elluminate have teamed up to offer vMentor, an ideal solution for homework help, tutoring, classroom projects, and exam preparation. vMentor assists students with live, text-specific, online homework help and tutorial services. It is an efficient way to provide the supplemental assistance that can substantially improve student performance, increase test scores, and enhance technical aptitude. In addition to robust tutorial services, with Make the Grade your students also receive anytime, anywhere access to InfoTrac College Edition. This online library offers the full text of articles from almost 4000 scholarly and popular publications, updated daily and going back as much as 22 years. Both adopters and their students receive unlimited access for four months.

RELATED PRODUCTS

Mastering Mathematics: How to Be a Great Math Student, 3/e © 1998
by Richard Manning Smith, Bryant College
0-534-34947-1

This practical guide will help you
- Avoid mental blocks during math exams
- Identify and improve areas of weakness
- Get the most out of class time
- Study more effectively
- Overcome a perceived low math ability
- Be successful on math tests
- Get back on track when feeling lost

Available to qualified adopters. Please consult your local sales representative for details.

To the Student

This textbook was written for you to use as a guide to mastering trigonometry. Here are some suggestions to help you get the most out of your course.

First of all, you should read the appropriate section of text *before* you attempt your homework problems. Reading a mathematics text is quite different from reading a novel, a newspaper, or even another textbook. You may find that you have to reread a passage several times before you understand it. Pay special attention to the examples, and work them out yourself with pencil and paper as you read. With this kind of preparation you will be able to do your homework much more quickly and with more understanding.

Don't make the mistake of trying to memorize every single rule or fact you may come across. Mathematics doesn't consist simply of memorization. Mathematics is a *problem-solving art*, not just a collection of facts. To master the subject you must solve problems—lots of problems. Do as many of the exercises as you can. Be sure to write your solutions in a logical, step-by-step fashion. Don't give up on a problem if you can't solve it right away. Try to understand the problem more clearly—reread it thoughtfully and relate it to what you have learned from your teacher and from the examples in the text. Struggle with it until you solve it. Once you have done this a few times you will begin to understand what mathematics is really all about.

Answers to the odd-numbered exercises, as well as all the answers to each chapter test, appear at the back of the book. If your answer differs from the one given, don't immediately assume that you are wrong. There may be a calculation that connects the two answers and makes both correct. For example, if you get $1/(\sqrt{2} - 1)$ but the answer given is $1 + \sqrt{2}$, your answer *is* correct, because you can multiply both numerator and denominator of your answer by $\sqrt{2} + 1$ to change it to the given answer.

The symbol ⊘ is used to warn against committing an error. We have placed this symbol in the margin to point out situations where we have found that many of our students make the same mistake.

Student to Student

Hi,

My name is Ellen and I studied trigonometry with Dr. Redlin, one of the coauthors of this textbook. I liked trigonometry very much—especially because of its many uses in explaining things that happen in the real world. I asked if I could add to this book what I've learned about learning trigonometry. I'm happy for the chance to write this and I hope you'll find it useful.

First of all, when you study trigonometry you will find that each element of the course builds upon something you've studied before. If you neglect to do your homework, even once, you will find that you are in danger of falling behind. Not only do I advise you to do your homework, but you may also need to practice extra problems, chosen with the guidance of your teacher.

For many problems you will find that you can't just follow the steps in an example. To solve these problems you will need to really understand the meaning of the trigonometric functions. Take the time to draw diagrams for a problem; if you can sketch to scale you are better off. This is especially true when you get to problems with more than one answer.

If you can form a study group, do so. Frequently a group can succeed at doing the more challenging problems when one person cannot. When you help each other, you learn more. Try to avoid the trap of thinking that a study group is a place to copy problems from one another. Of course, you will learn nothing by just copying.

Your instructor will ask you to remember the sine, cosine, and tangent ratios. Some people find it helpful to remember the made-up word "sohcahtoa." I've always liked my own mnemonic:

Some **O**ld **H**orse	**S**ine = **O**pposite over **H**ypotenuse
Caught **A**nother **H**orse	**C**osine = **A**djacent over **H**ypotenuse
Taking **O**ats **A**way	**T**angent = **O**pposite over **A**djacent

Eventually you will get to the Pythagorean Identities. Learn them. You will use them frequently, not just in this course, but in almost every other math course that you take.

Personally, I loved trigonometry. I thought of it as a great game—a game with real meaning and applications. But like any game, trigonometry has rules. When you learn the rules, you play well. And once you know the rules, you can concentrate on the winning strategy. In this case the winning strategy is problem solving.

Enjoy the course.

Ellen Newman

Dr. Redlin's student at Penn State in Fall 2000.

Calculators and Calculations

Calculators are essential in most mathematics and science subjects. They free us from performing routine tasks, so we can focus more clearly on the concepts we are studying. Calculators are powerful tools but their results need to be interpreted with care. In what follows, we describe the features that a calculator suitable for a trigonometry course should have, and we give guidelines for interpreting the results of its calculations.

Scientific and Graphing Calculators

For this course you will need a *scientific* calculator—one that has, as a minimum, the usual arithmetic operations ($+$, $-$, $\times$, $\div$) and exponential, logarithmic, and trigonometric functions (e^x, 10^x, ln x, log, sin, cos, tan). In addition, a memory and at least some degree of programmability will be useful.

Your instructor may recommend or require that you purchase a *graphing* calculator. This book has optional subsections and exercises that require the use of a graphing calculator or a computer with graphing software. These special subsections and exercises are indicated by the symbol 📈. Besides graphing functions, graphing calculators can also be used to find functions that model real-life data, solve equations, and help you perform other mathematical operations. All these uses are discussed in this book.

It is important to realize that, because of limited resolution, a graphing calculator gives only an *approximation* to the graph of a function. It plots only a finite number of points and then connects them to form a *representation* of the graph. In Appendix C, we give guidelines for using a graphing calculator and interpreting the graphs that it produces.

Calculations and Significant Figures

Most of the applied examples and exercises in this book involve approximate values. For example, one exercise states that the moon has a radius of 1074 miles. This does not mean that the moon's radius is exactly 1074 miles but simply that this is the radius rounded to the nearest mile.

One simple method for specifying the accuracy of a number is to state how many **significant digits** it has. The significant digits in a number are the ones from the first nonzero digit to the last nonzero digit (reading from left to right). Thus, 1074 has four significant digits, 1070 has three, 1100 has two, and 1000 has one significant digit. This rule may sometimes lead to ambiguities. For example, if a distance is 200 km to the nearest kilometer, then the number 200 really has three significant digits, not just one. This ambiguity is avoided if we use scientific notation—that is, if we express the number as a multiple of a power of 10:

$$2.00 \times 10^2$$

When working with approximate values, students often make the mistake of giving a final answer with *more* significant digits than the original data. This is incorrect because you cannot "create" precision by using a calculator. The final result can be no more accurate than the measurements given in the problem. For example, suppose we are told that the two shorter sides of a right triangle are measured to be 1.25 and 2.33 inches long. By the Pythagorean Theorem, we find, using a calculator, that the hypotenuse has length

$$\sqrt{1.25^2 + 2.33^2} \approx 2.644125564 \text{ in.}$$

But since the given lengths were expressed to three significant digits, the answer cannot be any more accurate. We can therefore say only that the hypotenuse is 2.64 in. long, rounding to the nearest hundredth.

In general, the final answer should be expressed with the same accuracy as the *least*-accurate measurement given in the statement of the problem. The following rules make this principle more precise.

RULES FOR WORKING WITH APPROXIMATE DATA

1. When multiplying or dividing, round off the final result so that it has as many *significant digits* as the given value with the fewest number of significant digits.

2. When adding or subtracting, round off the final result so that it has its last significant digit in the *decimal place* in which the least-accurate given value has its last significant digit.

3. When taking powers or roots, round off the final result so that it has the same number of *significant digits* as the given value.

As an example, suppose that a rectangular table top is measured to be 122.64 in. by 37.3 in. We express its area and perimeter as follows:

Area = length × width = $122.64 \times 37.3 \approx 4570 \text{ in}^2$ Three significant digits

Perimeter = 2(length + width) = $2(122.64 + 37.3) \approx 319.9 \text{ in.}$ Tenths digit

 Note that in the formula for the perimeter, the value 2 is an exact value, not an approximate measurement. It therefore does not affect the accuracy of the final result. In general, if a problem involves only exact values, we may express the final answer with as many significant digits as we wish.

Note also that to make the final result as accurate as possible, *you should wait until the last step to round off your answer.* If necessary, use the memory feature of your calculator to retain the results of intermediate calculations.

Abbreviations

cm	centimeter		**MHz**	megahertz
dB	decibel		**mi**	mile
F	farad		**min**	minute
ft	foot		**mL**	milliliter
g	gram		**mm**	millimeter
gal	gallon		**N**	Newton
h	hour		**qt**	quart
H	henry		**oz**	ounce
Hz	Hertz		**s**	second
in.	inch		**Ω**	ohm
J	Joule		**V**	volt
kcal	kilocalorie		**W**	watt
kg	kilogram		**yd**	yard
km	kilometer		**yr**	year
kPa	kilopascal		**°C**	degree Celsius
L	liter		**°F**	degree Fahrenheit
lb	pound		**K**	Kelvin
M	mole of solute per liter of solution		⇒	implies
m	meter		⇔	is equivalent to

Mathematical Vignettes

MATHEMATICS IN THE MODERN WORLD

Contents

6 Analytic Geometry 358

7 Exponential and Logarithmic Functions 430

Appendix A   Algebra Review 511

Trigonometry

1 Functions and Graphs

A function is a rule that describes how one quantity depends on another. For example, the distance traveled by a moving object is a function of time; the population of a species is a function of the available habitat.

Trigonometry is the study of the trigonometric *functions*, so a thorough familiarity with the concept of a function is essential. In this preliminary chapter we review the basic properties of functions and their graphs.

1.1 THE COORDINATE PLANE

In this section we introduce the coordinate plane. In the coordinate plane, we can draw a graph of an equation, thus allowing us to "see" the relationship of the variables in the equation. We can also reverse this process and describe a geometrical figure (such as a circle or a line) by an algebraic equation. Thus, the coordinate plane is the link between algebra and geometry that enables us to use the techniques of algebra to solve geometric problems and the techniques of geometry to solve algebraic problems.

The Coordinate Plane

The Cartesian plane is named in honor of the French mathematician René Descartes (1596–1650), although another Frenchman, Pierre Fermat (1601–1665), also invented the principles of coordinate geometry at the same time. (See their biographies on pages 4 and 255.)

Just as points on a line can be identified with real numbers to form the coordinate line, points in a plane can be identified with ordered pairs of numbers to form the **coordinate plane** or **Cartesian plane**. To do this, we draw two perpendicular real lines that intersect at 0 on each line. Usually one line is horizontal with positive direction to the right and is called the **x-axis**; the other line is vertical with positive direction upward and is called the **y-axis**. The point of intersection of the x-axis and the y-axis is the **origin O**, and the two axes divide the plane into four **quadrants**, labeled I, II, III, and IV in Figure 1. (The points *on* the coordinate axes are not assigned to any quadrant.)

Any point P in the coordinate plane can be located by a unique **ordered pair** of numbers (a, b), as shown in Figure 1. The first number a is called the **x-coordinate**

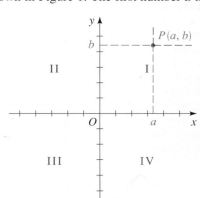

FIGURE 1

3

of P; the second number b is called the **y-coordinate** of P. We can think of the coordinates of P as its "address," because they specify its location in the plane. Several points are labeled with their coordinates in Figure 2.

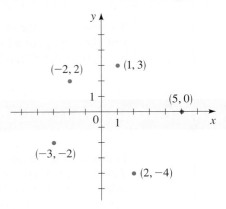

FIGURE 2

René Descartes (1596–1650) was born in the town of La Haye in southern France. From an early age Descartes liked mathematics because of "the certainty of its results and the clarity of its reasoning." He believed that in order to arrive at truth, one must begin by doubting everything, including one's own existence; this led him to formulate perhaps the most well-known sentence in all of philosophy: "I think, therefore I am." In his book *Discourse on Method* he described what is now called the Cartesian plane. This idea of combining algebra and geometry enabled mathematicians for the first time to "see" the equations they were studying. The philosopher John Stuart Mill called this invention "the greatest single step ever made in the progress of the exact sciences." Descartes liked to get up late and spend the morning in bed thinking and writing. He invented the coordinate plane while lying in bed watching a fly crawl on the ceiling, reasoning that he could describe the exact location of the fly by knowing its distance from two perpendicular walls. In 1649 Descartes became the tutor of Queen Christina of Sweden. She liked her lessons at 5 o'clock in the *(continued)*

EXAMPLE 1 ■ **Graphing Regions in the Coordinate Plane**

Describe and sketch the regions given by each set.

(a) $\{(x, y) \mid x \geq 0\}$ (b) $\{(x, y) \mid y = 1\}$ (c) $\{(x, y) \mid |y| < 1\}$

SOLUTION

(a) The points whose x-coordinates are 0 or positive lie on the y-axis or to the right of it, as shown in Figure 3(a).

(b) The set of all points with y-coordinate 1 is a horizontal line one unit above the x-axis, as in Figure 3(b).

(c) Recall that

$$|y| < 1 \qquad \text{if and only if} \qquad -1 < y < 1 \quad \text{(See Appendix A.5, page 549)}$$

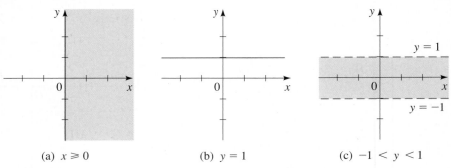

(a) $x \geq 0$ (b) $y = 1$ (c) $-1 < y < 1$

FIGURE 3

morning when, she said, her mind was sharpest. However, the change from his usual habits and the ice-cold library where they studied proved too much for him. In February 1650, after just two months of this, he caught pneumonia and died.

The given region consists of those points in the plane whose y-coordinates lie between -1 and 1. Thus, the region consists of all points that lie between (but not on) the horizontal lines $y = 1$ and $y = -1$. These lines are shown as broken lines in Figure 3(c) to indicate that the points on these lines do not lie in the set. ■

We now find a formula for the distance $d(A, B)$ between two points $A(x_1, y_1)$ and $B(x_2, y_2)$ in the plane. The distance between points a and b on a number line is $d(a, b) = |b - a|$ (see Appendix A.1, page 516). So, from Figure 4 we see that the distance between the points $A(x_1, y_1)$ and $C(x_2, y_1)$ on a horizontal line must be $|x_2 - x_1|$, and the distance between $B(x_2, y_2)$ and $C(x_2, y_1)$ on a vertical line must be $|y_2 - y_1|$. Since triangle ABC is a right triangle, the Pythagorean Theorem gives

$$d(A, B) = \sqrt{|x_2 - x_1|^2 + |y_2 - y_1|^2}$$
$$= \sqrt{(x_2 - x_1)^2 + (y_2 - y_1)^2}$$

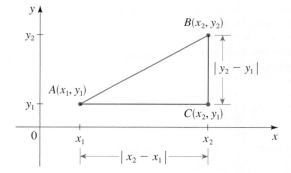

FIGURE 4

DISTANCE FORMULA

The distance between the points $A(x_1, y_1)$ and $B(x_2, y_2)$ in the plane is

$$d(A, B) = \sqrt{(x_2 - x_1)^2 + (y_2 - y_1)^2}$$

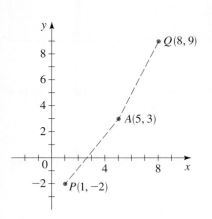

FIGURE 5

EXAMPLE 2 ■ Applying the Distance Formula

Which of the points $P(1, -2)$ or $Q(8, 9)$ is closer to the point $A(5, 3)$?

SOLUTION

By the distance formula, we have

$$d(P, A) = \sqrt{(5 - 1)^2 + [3 - (-2)]^2} = \sqrt{4^2 + 5^2} = \sqrt{41}$$
$$d(Q, A) = \sqrt{(5 - 8)^2 + (3 - 9)^2} = \sqrt{(-3)^2 + (-6)^2} = \sqrt{45}$$

This shows that $d(P, A) < d(Q, A)$, so P is closer to A (see Figure 5). ■

The coordinates of a point in the xy-plane uniquely determine its location. We can think of the coordinates as the "address" of the point. In Salt Lake City, Utah, the addresses of most buildings are in fact expressed as coordinates. The city is divided into quadrants with Main Street as the vertical (North-South) axis and S. Temple Street as the horizontal (East-West) axis. An address such as

1760 W   2100 S

indicates a location 17.6 blocks west of Main Street and 21 blocks south of S. Temple Street. (This is the address of the main post office in Salt Lake City.) With this logical system it is possible for someone unfamiliar with the city to locate any address immediately, as easily as one locates a point in the coordinate plane.

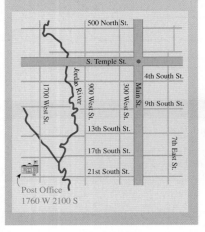

Now let's find the coordinates (x, y) of the midpoint M of the line segment that joins the point $A(x_1, y_1)$ to the point $B(x_2, y_2)$. In Figure 6 notice that triangles APM and MQB are congruent because $d(A, M) = d(M, B)$ and the corresponding angles are equal.

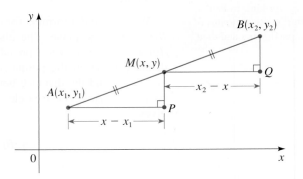

FIGURE 6

It follows that $d(A, P) = d(M, Q)$ and so

$$x - x_1 = x_2 - x$$

Solving this equation for x, we get

$$2x = x_1 + x_2$$

$$x = \frac{x_1 + x_2}{2}$$

Similarly,

$$y = \frac{y_1 + y_2}{2}$$

MIDPOINT FORMULA

The midpoint of the line segment from $A(x_1, y_1)$ to $B(x_2, y_2)$ is

$$\left(\frac{x_1 + x_2}{2}, \frac{y_1 + y_2}{2} \right)$$

EXAMPLE 3 ■ Applying the Midpoint Formula

Show that the quadrilateral with vertices $P(1, 2)$, $Q(4, 4)$, $R(5, 9)$, and $S(2, 7)$ is a parallelogram by proving that its two diagonals bisect each other.

SOLUTION

If the two diagonals have the same midpoint, then they must bisect each other. The midpoint of the diagonal PR is

$$\left(\frac{1 + 5}{2}, \frac{2 + 9}{2} \right) = \left(3, \frac{11}{2} \right)$$

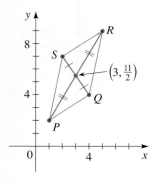

FIGURE 7

Fundamental Principle of Analytic Geometry

A point (x, y) lies on the graph of an equation if and only if its coordinates satisfy the equation.

and the midpoint of the diagonal QS is

$$\left(\frac{4 + 2}{2}, \frac{4 + 7}{2}\right) = \left(3, \frac{11}{2}\right)$$

so each diagonal bisects the other, as shown in Figure 7. (A theorem from elementary geometry states that the quadrilateral is therefore a parallelogram.) ■

Graphs of Equations

Suppose we have an equation involving the variables x and y, such as

$$x^2 + y^2 = 25 \qquad \text{or} \qquad x = y^2 \qquad \text{or} \qquad y = \frac{2}{x}$$

A point (x, y) **satisfies** the equation if the equation is true when the coordinates of the point are substituted into the equation. For example, the point $(3, 4)$ satisfies the first equation, since $3^2 + 4^2 = 25$, but the point $(2, -3)$ does not, since $2^2 + (-3)^2 = 13 \neq 25$.

THE GRAPH OF AN EQUATION

The **graph** of an equation in x and y is the set of all points (x, y) in the coordinate plane that satisfy the equation.

The graphs of most of the equations that we will encounter are curves. For example, we will see later in this section that the first equation, $x^2 + y^2 = 25$, represents a circle; we will determine the shapes represented by the other equations later in this chapter. Graphs help us understand equations because they give us visual representations of the equations.

EXAMPLE 4 ■ **Sketching a Graph by Plotting Points**

Sketch the graph of the equation $2x - y = 3$.

SOLUTION

We first solve the given equation for y to get

$$y = 2x - 3$$

This helps us calculate the y-coordinates in the following table.

x	$y = 2x - 3$	(x, y)
-1	-5	$(-1, -5)$
0	-3	$(0, -3)$
1	-1	$(1, -1)$
2	1	$(2, 1)$
3	3	$(3, 3)$
4	5	$(4, 5)$

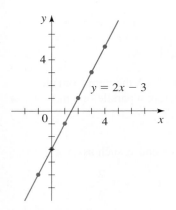

FIGURE 8

A detailed discussion of parabolas and their geometric properties is presented in Chapter 6.

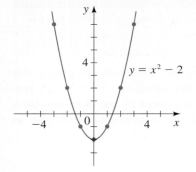

FIGURE 9

Of course, there are infinitely many points on the graph, and it is impossible to plot all of them. But the more points we plot, the better we can imagine what the graph represented by the equation looks like. We plot the points we found in Figure 8; they appear to lie on a line. So, we complete the graph by joining the points by a line. (In Section 1.2 we verify that the graph of this equation is indeed a line.)   ∎

EXAMPLE 5 ■ Sketching a Graph by Plotting Points

Sketch the graph of the equation $y = x^2 - 2$.

SOLUTION

We find some of the points that satisfy the equation in the following table. In Figure 9 we plot these points and then connect them by a smooth curve. A curve with this shape is called a *parabola*.

x	$y = x^2 - 2$	(x, y)
-3	7	$(-3, 7)$
-2	2	$(-2, 2)$
-1	-1	$(-1, -1)$
0	-2	$(0, -2)$
1	-1	$(1, -1)$
2	2	$(2, 2)$
3	7	$(3, 7)$

∎

EXAMPLE 6 ■ Sketching the Graph of an Equation Involving Absolute Value

Sketch the graph of the equation $y = |x|$.

SOLUTION

We make a table of values:

x	$y = |x|$	(x, y)
-3	3	$(-3, 3)$
-2	2	$(-2, 2)$
-1	1	$(-1, 1)$
0	0	$(0, 0)$
1	1	$(1, 1)$
2	2	$(2, 2)$
3	3	$(3, 3)$

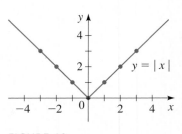

FIGURE 10

In Figure 10 we plot these points and use them to sketch the graph of the equation.   ∎

The x-coordinates of the points where a graph intersects the x-axis are called the **x-intercepts** of the graph and are obtained by setting $y = 0$ in the equation of the graph. The y-coordinates of the points where a graph intersects the y-axis are called the **y-intercepts** of the graph and are obtained by setting $x = 0$ in the equation of the graph.

DEFINITION OF INTERCEPTS

Intercepts	How to find them	Where they are on the graph
x-intercepts: The x-coordinates of points where the graph of an equation intersects the x-axis	Set $y = 0$ and solve for x	
y-intercepts: The y-coordinates of points where the graph of an equation intersects the y-axis	Set $x = 0$ and solve for y	

EXAMPLE 7 ■ Finding Intercepts

Find the x- and y-intercepts of the graph of the equation $y = x^2 - 2$.

SOLUTION

To find the x-intercepts, we set $y = 0$ and solve for x. Thus

$$0 = x^2 - 2 \qquad \text{Set } y = 0$$

$$x^2 = 2 \qquad \text{Add 2 to each side}$$

$$x = \pm\sqrt{2} \qquad \text{Take the square root}$$

The x-intercepts are $\sqrt{2}$ and $-\sqrt{2}$.

To find the y-intercepts, we set $x = 0$ and solve for y. Thus

$$y = 0^2 - 2 \qquad \text{Set } x = 0$$

$$y = -2$$

The y-intercept is -2.

The graph of this equation was sketched in Example 5. It is repeated in Figure 11 with the x- and y-intercepts labeled. ■

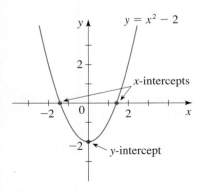

FIGURE 11

■ Circles

So far we have discussed how to find the graph of an equation in x and y. The converse problem is to find an equation of a graph, that is, an equation that represents a given curve in the xy-plane. Such an equation is satisfied by the coordinates of the points on the curve and by no other point. This is the other half of the fundamental principle of analytic geometry as formulated by Descartes and Fermat. The idea is that if a geometric curve can be represented by an algebraic equation, then the rules of algebra can be used to analyze the curve.

As an example of this type of problem, let's find the equation of a circle with radius r and center (h, k). By definition, the circle is the set of all points $P(x, y)$ whose distance from the center $C(h, k)$ is r (see Figure 12). Thus, P is on the circle if and only if $d(P, C) = r$. From the distance formula we have

$$\sqrt{(x - h)^2 + (y - k)^2} = r$$

$$(x - h)^2 + (y - k)^2 = r^2 \qquad \text{Square each side}$$

This is the desired equation.

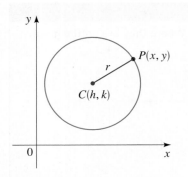

FIGURE 12

EQUATION OF A CIRCLE

An equation of the circle with center (h, k) and radius r is

$$(x - h)^2 + (y - k)^2 = r^2$$

This is called the **standard form** for the equation of the circle.
If the center of the circle is the origin $(0, 0)$, then the equation is

$$x^2 + y^2 = r^2$$

EXAMPLE 8 ■ Graphing a Circle

Graph each equation.

(a) $x^2 + y^2 = 25$

(b) $(x - 2)^2 + (y + 1)^2 = 25$

SOLUTION

(a) Rewriting the equation as $x^2 + y^2 = 5^2$, we see that this is an equation of the circle of radius 5 centered at the origin. Its graph is shown in Figure 13.

(b) Rewriting the equation as $(x - 2)^2 + (y + 1)^2 = 5^2$, we see that this is an equation of the circle of radius 5 centered at $(2, -1)$. Its graph is shown in Figure 14.

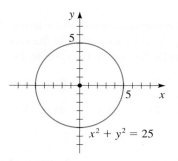

$x^2 + y^2 = 25$

FIGURE 13

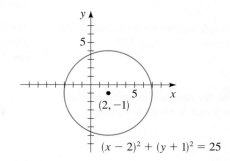

$(2, -1)$

$(x - 2)^2 + (y + 1)^2 = 25$

FIGURE 14

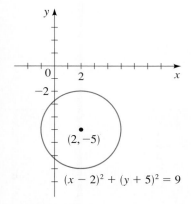

$(2, -5)$

$(x - 2)^2 + (y + 5)^2 = 9$

FIGURE 15

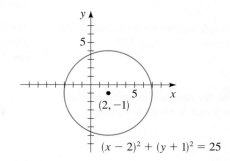

$P(1, 8)$

$(3, 1)$

$Q(5, -6)$

$(x - 3)^2 + (y - 1)^2 = 53$

FIGURE 16

EXAMPLE 9 ■ Finding an Equation of a Circle

(a) Find an equation of the circle with radius 3 and center $(2, -5)$.

(b) Find an equation of the circle that has the points $P(1, 8)$ and $Q(5, -6)$ as the endpoints of a diameter.

SOLUTION

(a) Using the equation of a circle with $r = 3$, $h = 2$, and $k = -5$, we obtain

$$(x - 2)^2 + (y + 5)^2 = 9$$

Its graph is shown in Figure 15.

(b) We first observe that the center is the midpoint of the diameter PQ, so by the Midpoint Formula the center is

$$\left(\frac{1 + 5}{2}, \frac{8 - 6}{2}\right) = (3, 1)$$

The radius r is the distance from P to the center, so by the Distance Formula

$$r^2 = (3 - 1)^2 + (1 - 8)^2 = 2^2 + (-7)^2 = 53$$

Therefore, the equation of the circle is

$$(x - 3)^2 + (y - 1)^2 = 53$$

Its graph is shown in Figure 16.

EXAMPLE 10 ■ Identifying an Equation of a Circle

Sketch the graph of the equation $x^2 + y^2 + 2x - 6y + 7 = 0$ by first showing that it represents a circle and then finding its center and radius.

Completing the square is discussed in Appendix A.4, page 539.

SOLUTION

We first group the x-terms and y-terms. Then we complete the square within each grouping. That is, we complete the square for $x^2 + 2x$ by adding $\left(\frac{1}{2} \cdot 2\right)^2 = 1$, and we complete the square for $y^2 - 6y$ by adding $\left[\frac{1}{2} \cdot (-6)\right]^2 = 9$.

$$(x^2 + 2x \quad\ ) + (y^2 - 6y \quad\ ) = -7 \qquad \text{Group terms}$$

⊘ We must add the same numbers to *each side* to maintain equality.

$$(x^2 + 2x + 1) + (y^2 - 6y + 9) = -7 + 1 + 9 \qquad \begin{array}{l}\text{Complete the square by} \\ \text{adding 1 and 9 to each side}\end{array}$$

$$(x + 1)^2 + (y - 3)^2 = 3$$

Comparing this equation with the standard equation of a circle, we see that $h = -1$, $k = 3$, and $r = \sqrt{3}$, so the given equation represents a circle with center $(-1, 3)$ and radius $\sqrt{3}$. The circle is sketched in Figure 17.

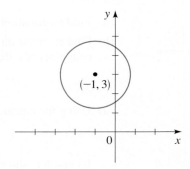

FIGURE 17
$x^2 + y^2 + 2x - 6y + 7 = 0$

■

■ Symmetry

Figure 18 shows the graph of $y = x^2$. Notice that the part of the graph to the left of the y-axis is the mirror image of the part to the right of the y-axis. The reason is that if the point (x, y) is on the graph, then so is $(-x, y)$, and these points are reflections of each other about the y-axis. In this situation we say the graph is **symmetric with respect to the y-axis**. Similarly, we say a graph is **symmetric with respect to the x-axis** if whenever the point (x, y) is on the graph, then so is $(x, -y)$. A graph is **symmetric with respect to the origin** if whenever (x, y) is on the graph, so is $(-x, -y)$.

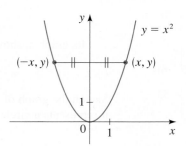

FIGURE 18

DEFINITION OF SYMMETRY

Type of symmetry	How to test for symmetry	What the graph looks like (figures in this section)	Geometric meaning
Symmetry with respect to the x-axis	The equation is unchanged when y is replaced by $-y$	(Figures 13, 20)	Graph is unchanged when reflected in the x-axis
Symmetry with respect to the y-axis	The equation is unchanged when x is replaced by $-x$	(Figures 9, 10, 11, 13, 18, 20)	Graph is unchanged when reflected in the y-axis
Symmetry with respect to the origin	The equation is unchanged when x is replaced by $-x$ and y by $-y$	(Figures 13, 19, 20)	Graph is unchanged when rotated 180° about the origin

The remaining examples in this section show how symmetry helps us sketch the graphs of equations.

EXAMPLE 11 ■ Using Symmetry to Sketch a Graph

Test the equation $y = x^3 - 9x$ for symmetry and sketch its graph.

SOLUTION

If we replace x by $-x$ and y by $-y$ in the equation, we get

$$-y = (-x)^3 - 9(-x)$$

$$-y = -x^3 + 9x$$

$$y = x^3 - 9x$$

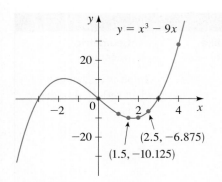

FIGURE 19

and so the equation is unchanged. This means that the graph is symmetric with respect to the origin. We sketch it by first plotting points for $x > 0$ and then using symmetry about the origin (see Figure 19).

x	$y = x^3 - 9x$	(x, y)
0	0	$(0, 0)$
1	-8	$(1, -8)$
1.5	-10.125	$(1.5, -10.125)$
2	-10	$(2, -10)$
2.5	-6.875	$(2.5 -6.875)$
3	0	$(3, 0)$
4	28	$(4, 28)$

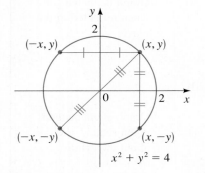

FIGURE 20

EXAMPLE 12 ■ A Circle That Has All Three Types of Symmetry

Test the equation of the circle $x^2 + y^2 = 4$ for symmetry.

SOLUTION

The equation $x^2 + y^2 = 4$ remains unchanged when x is replaced by $-x$ and y is replaced by $-y$, since $(-x)^2 = x^2$ and $(-y)^2 = y^2$, so the circle exhibits all three types of symmetry. It is symmetric with respect to the x-axis, the y-axis, and the origin, as shown in Figure 20. ■

1.1 EXERCISES

1. Plot the given points in a coordinate plane:

$(2, 3), (-2, 3), (4, 5), (4, -5), (-4, 5), (-4, -5)$

2. Find the coordinates of the points shown in the figure.

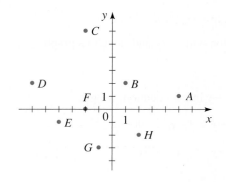

3–8 ■ A pair of points is given.
(a) Plot the points in a coordinate plane.
(b) Find the distance between them.
(c) Find the midpoint of the segment that joins them.

3. $(2, 3),   (5, 2)$

4. $(2, -1),   (4, 3)$

5. $(6, -2),   (-1, 3)$

6. $(1, -6),   (-1, -3)$

7. $(3, 4),   (-3, -4)$

8. $(5, 0),   (0, 6)$

9. Draw the rectangle with vertices $A(1, 3)$, $B(5, 3)$, $C(1, -3)$, and $D(5, -3)$ in a coordinate plane. Find the area of the rectangle.

10. Draw the parallelogram with vertices $A(1, 2)$, $B(5, 2)$, $C(3, 6)$, and $D(7, 6)$ in a coordinate plane. Find the area of the parallelogram.

11. Plot the points $A(1, 0)$, $B(5, 0)$, $C(4, 3)$, and $D(2, 3)$ in a coordinate plane. Draw the segments AB, BC, CD, and DA. What kind of quadrilateral is $ABCD$, and what is its area?

12. Plot the points $P(5, 1)$, $Q(0, 6)$, and $R(-5, 1)$ in a coordinate plane. Where must the point S be located so that the quadrilateral $PQRS$ is a square? Find the area of this square.

13–22 ■ Sketch the region given by the set.

13. $\{(x, y) \mid x \leqslant 0\}$

14. $\{(x, y) \mid y \geqslant 0\}$

15. $\{(x, y) \mid x = 3\}$

16. $\{(x, y) \mid y = -2\}$

17. $\{(x, y) \mid 1 < x < 2\}$

18. $\{(x, y) \mid 0 \leqslant y \leqslant 4\}$

19. $\{(x, y) \mid x \geqslant 1 \text{ and } y < 3\}$

20. $\{(x, y) \mid |y| > 1\}$

21. $\{(x, y) \mid |x| \leqslant 2\}$

22. $\{(x, y) \mid |x| < 3 \text{ and } |y| \leqslant 5\}$

23. Which of the points $A(6, 7)$ or $B(-5, 8)$ is closer to the origin?

24. Which of the points $C(-6, 3)$ or $D(3, 0)$ is closer to the point $E(-2, 1)$?

25. Which of the points $P(3, 1)$ or $Q(-1, 3)$ is closer to the point $R(-1, -1)$?

26. (a) Show that the points $(7, 3)$ and $(3, 7)$ are the same distance from the origin.
(b) Show that the points (a, b) and (b, a) are the same distance from the origin.

27. Show that the triangle with vertices $A(0, 2)$, $B(-3, -1)$, and $C(-4, 3)$ is isosceles.

28. Find the area of the triangle shown in the figure.

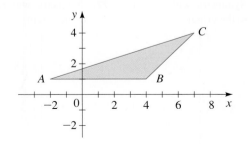

29. Refer to triangle ABC in the figure.
(a) Show that triangle ABC is a right triangle by using the converse of the Pythagorean Theorem.
(b) Find the area of triangle ABC.

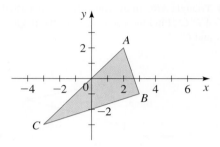

30. Show that the triangle with vertices $A(6, -7)$, $B(11, -3)$, and $C(2, -2)$ is a right triangle by using the converse of the Pythagorean Theorem. Find the area of the triangle.

31. Show that the points $A(-1, 3)$, $B(3, 11)$, and $C(5, 15)$ are collinear by showing that $d(A, B) + d(B, C) = d(A, C)$.

32. Find a point on the y-axis that is equidistant from the points $(5, -5)$ and $(1, 1)$.

33. Find the lengths of the medians of the triangle with vertices $A(1, 0)$, $B(3, 6)$, and $C(8, 2)$. (A *median* is a line segment from a vertex to the midpoint of the opposite side.)

34. Find the point that is one-fourth of the distance from the point $P(-1, 3)$ to the point $Q(7, 5)$ along the segment PQ.

35. (a) Sketch the parallelogram with vertices $A(-2, -1)$, $B(4, 2)$, $C(7, 7)$, and $D(1, 4)$.
(b) Find the midpoints of the diagonals of this parallelogram.
(c) From part (b) show that the diagonals bisect each other.

36. The point M in the figure is the midpoint of the line segment AB. Show that M is equidistant from the vertices of triangle ABC.

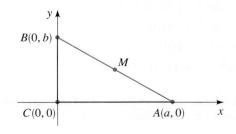

37. Suppose that each point in the coordinate plane is shifted 3 units to the right and 2 units upward.
   (a) The point $(5, 3)$ is shifted to what new point?
   (b) The point (a, b) is shifted to what new point?
   (c) What point is shifted to $(3, 4)$?
   (d) Triangle ABC in the figure has been shifted to triangle $A'B'C'$. Find the coordinates of the points A', B', and C'.

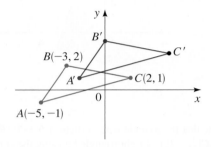

38. Suppose that the y-axis acts as a mirror that reflects each point to the right of it into a point to the left of it.
   (a) The point $(3, 7)$ is reflected to what point?
   (b) The point (a, b) is reflected to what point?
   (c) What point is reflected to $(-4, -1)$?
   (d) Triangle ABC in the figure is reflected to triangle $A'B'C'$. Find the coordinates of the points A', B', and C'.

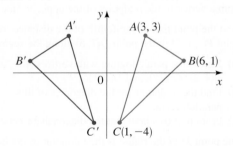

39–42 ■ Determine whether the given points are on the graph of the equation.

39. $y = 2x + 3$; $(0, 0)$, $\left(\frac{1}{2}, 4\right)$, $(1, 4)$

40. $y = \sqrt{x + 1}$; $(1, 0)$, $(0, 1)$, $(3, 2)$

41. $2y - x + 1 = 0$; $(0, 0)$, $(1, 0)$, $(-1, -1)$

42. $y(x^2 + 1) = 1$; $(1, 1)$, $\left(1, \frac{1}{2}\right)$, $\left(-1, \frac{1}{2}\right)$

43–62 ■ Make a table of values and sketch the graph of the equation. Find x- and y-intercepts and test for symmetry.

43. $y = x$

44. $y = -x$

45. $y = x - 1$

46. $y = 2x + 5$

47. $3x - y = 5$

48. $x + y = 3$

49. $y = 1 - x^2$

50. $y = x^2 + 2$

51. $4y = x^2$

52. $8y = x^3$

53. $y = x^2 - 9$

54. $y = 9 - x^2$

55. $y = \sqrt{x}$

56. $x + y^2 = 4$

57. $y = |x|$

58. $x = |y|$

59. $y = 4 - |x|$

60. $y = |4 - x|$

61. $y = x^4$

62. $y = x^3 - 1$

63–68 ■ Test the equation for symmetry.

63. $y = x^4 + x^2$

64. $x = y^4 - y^2$

65. $x^2y^2 + xy = 1$

66. $x^4y^4 + x^2y^2 = 1$

67. $y = x^3 + 10x$

68. $y = x^2 + |x|$

69–72 ■ Complete the graph using the given symmetry property.

69. Symmetric with respect to the y-axis

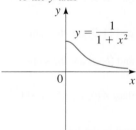

70. Symmetric with respect to the x-axis

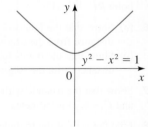

71. Symmetric with respect to the origin

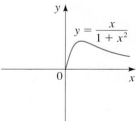

72. Symmetric with respect to the origin

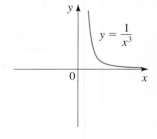

73–78 ■ Find an equation of the circle that satisfies the given conditions.

73. Center $(2, -1)$;   radius 3

74. Center at the origin;   passes through $(4, 7)$

75. Center $(-1, 5)$;   passes through $(-4, -6)$

76. Endpoints of a diameter are $P(-1, 3)$ and $Q(7, -5)$

77. Center $(7, -3)$;   tangent to the x-axis

78. Circle lies in the first quadrant, tangent to both x- and y-axes;   radius 5

79–80 ■ Find the equation of the circle shown in the figure.

79.

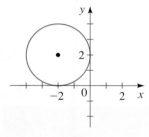

80.

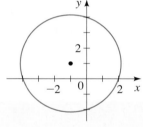

81–86 ■ Show that the equation represents a circle, and find the center and radius of the circle.

81. $x^2 + y^2 - 2x + 4y + 1 = 0$

82. $x^2 + y^2 - 4x + 10y + 13 = 0$

83. $x^2 + y^2 + 6y + 2 = 0$

84. $x^2 + y^2 + x = 0$

85. $x^2 + y^2 + 2x + y + 1 = 0$

86. $x^2 + y^2 - \frac{1}{2}x + \frac{1}{2}y = \frac{1}{8}$

87–88 ■ Sketch the region given by the set.

87. $\{(x, y) \mid x^2 + y^2 \leq 1\}$

88. $\{(x, y) \mid x^2 + y^2 > 4\}$

89. Find the area of the region that lies outside the circle $x^2 + y^2 = 4$ but inside the circle

$$x^2 + y^2 - 4y - 12 = 0$$

90. Sketch the region in the coordinate plane that satisfies both the inequalities $x^2 + y^2 \leq 9$ and $y \geq |x|$. What is the area of this region?

DISCOVERY · DISCUSSION

91. Completing a Line Segment   Plot the points $M(6, 8)$ and $A(2, 3)$ on a coordinate plane. If M is the midpoint of the line segment AB, find the coordinates of B. Write a brief description of the steps you took in finding B, and your reasons for taking them.

92. Completing a Parallelogram   Plot the points $P(-1, -4)$, $Q(1, 1)$, and $R(4, 2)$ on a coordinate plane. Where should the point S be located so that the figure $PQRS$ is a parallelogram? Write a brief description of the steps you took and your reasons for taking them.

93. Circle, Point, or Empty Set?   Complete the squares in the general equation $x^2 + ax + y^2 + by + c = 0$ and simplify the result as much as possible. Under what conditions on the coefficients a, b, and c does this equation represent a circle? a single point? the empty set? In the case that the equation does represent a circle, find its center and radius.

94. Do the Circles Intersect?
   (a) Find the radius of each circle in the pair, and the distance between their centers; then use this information to determine whether the circles intersect.
      (i) $(x - 2)^2 + (y - 1)^2 = 9$; $(x - 6)^2 + (y - 4)^2 = 16$
      (ii) $x^2 + (y - 2)^2 = 4$; $(x - 5)^2 + (y - 14)^2 = 9$
      (iii) $(x - 3)^2 + (y + 1)^2 = 1$; $(x - 2)^2 + (y - 2)^2 = 25$
   (b) How can you tell, just by knowing the radii of two circles and the distance between their centers, whether the circles intersect? Write a short paragraph describing how you would decide this and draw graphs to illustrate your answer.

95. Making a Graph Symmetric   The graph shown in the figure is not symmetric about the x-axis, the y-axis, or the origin. Add more line segments to the graph so that it exhibits the indicated symmetry. In each case, add as little as possible.
   (a) Symmetry about the x-axis.
   (b) Symmetry about the y-axis.
   (c) Symmetry about the origin.

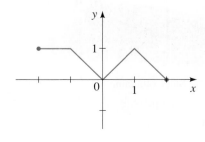

96. Geometry Versus Coordinate Geometry   What are the differences between geometry and coordinate geometry? Consider a circle drawn in a plane (geometry) and in a coordinate plane (coordinate geometry); they are described as follows.

In geometry: The circle is the set of points whose distance from P is 5.

In coordinate geometry: The circle is the set of points satisfying $x^2 + y^2 = 25$.

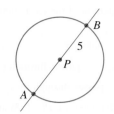

(a) The circle and line to the right are drawn first in a plane and then in a coordinate plane. Use the figures to give a description of the line and the points A and B in geometry and in coordinate geometry. Which description gives more information about the figure?

(b) Sketch the graph of the equation $y - x^3 = 0$. Explain why there is no easy geometric description (like that for the circle) for the shape of this graph.

(c) Explain why coordinate geometry allows us to easily describe many more curves than in geometry without coordinates.

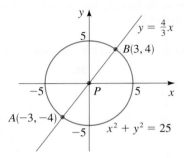

1.2 LINES

In this section we find equations for straight lines lying in a coordinate plane. We first need a way to measure the "steepness" of a line, or how quickly it rises (or falls) as we move from left to right. We define *run* to be the distance we move to the right and *rise* to be the corresponding distance that the line rises (or falls). The *slope* of a line is the ratio of rise to run:

$$\text{slope} = \frac{\text{rise}}{\text{run}}$$

Figure 1 shows situations where slope is important. Carpenters use the term *pitch* for the slope of a roof or a staircase; the term *grade* is used for the slope of a road.

Slope of a ramp

Slope $= \frac{1}{12}$

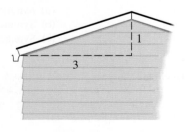

Pitch of a roof

Slope $= \frac{1}{3}$

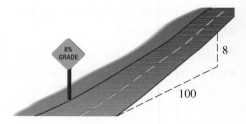

Grade of a road

Slope $= \frac{8}{100}$

FIGURE 1

If a line lies in a coordinate plane, then the **run** is the change in the x-coordinate and the **rise** is the corresponding change in the y-coordinate between any two points on the line (see Figure 2). This gives us the following definition of slope.

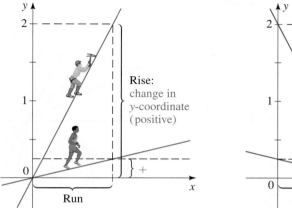

FIGURE 2

SLOPE OF A LINE

The **slope** m of a nonvertical line that passes through the points $A(x_1, y_1)$ and $B(x_2, y_2)$ is

$$m = \frac{\text{rise}}{\text{run}} = \frac{y_2 - y_1}{x_2 - x_1}$$

The slope of a vertical line is not defined.

The slope is independent of which two points are chosen on the line. We can see that this is true from the similar triangles in Figure 3:

$$\frac{y_2 - y_1}{x_2 - x_1} = \frac{y_2' - y_1'}{x_2' - x_1'}$$

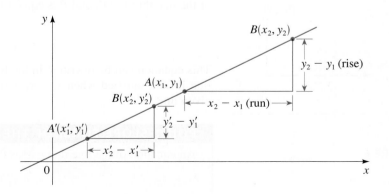

FIGURE 3

Figure 4 shows several lines labeled with their slopes. Notice that lines with positive slope slant upward to the right, whereas lines with negative slope slant downward to the right. The steepest lines are those for which the absolute value of the slope is the largest; a horizontal line has slope zero.

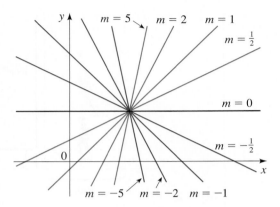

FIGURE 4

Lines with various slopes

EXAMPLE 1 ■ Finding the Slope of a Line through Two Points

Find the slope of the line that passes through the points $P(2, 1)$ and $Q(8, 5)$.

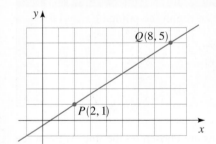

FIGURE 5

SOLUTION

Since any two different points determine a line, only one line passes through these two points. From the definition, the slope is

$$m = \frac{y_2 - y_1}{x_2 - x_1} = \frac{5 - 1}{8 - 2} = \frac{4}{6} = \frac{2}{3}$$

This says that for every 3 units we move to the right, the line rises 2 units. The line is drawn in Figure 5.   ■

Now let's find the equation of the line that passes through a given point $P(x_1, y_1)$ and has slope m. A point $P(x, y)$ with $x \neq x_1$ lies on this line if and only if the slope of the line through P_1 and P is equal to m (see Figure 6), that is,

$$\frac{y - y_1}{x - x_1} = m$$

This equation can be rewritten in the form $y - y_1 = m(x - x_1)$; note that the equation is also satisfied when $x = x_1$ and $y = y_1$. Therefore, it is an equation of the given line.

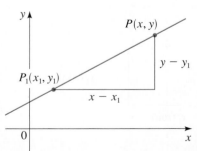

FIGURE 6

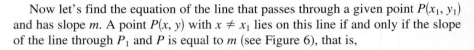

POINT-SLOPE FORM OF THE EQUATION OF A LINE

An equation of the line that passes through the point (x_1, y_1) and has slope m is

$$y - y_1 = m(x - x_1)$$

EXAMPLE 2 ■ Finding the Equation of a Line with Given Point and Slope

(a) Find an equation of the line through $(1, -3)$ with slope $-\frac{1}{2}$.

(b) Sketch the line.

SOLUTION

(a) Using the point-slope form with $m = -\frac{1}{2}$, $x_1 = 1$, and $y_1 = -3$, we obtain an equation of the line as

$$y + 3 = -\frac{1}{2}(x - 1) \qquad \text{From point-slope equation}$$

$$2y + 6 = -x + 1 \qquad \text{Multiply by 2}$$

$$x + 2y + 5 = 0 \qquad \text{Rearrange}$$

(b) The fact that the slope is $-\frac{1}{2}$ tells us that when we move to the right 2 units, the line drops 1 unit. This enables us to sketch the line in Figure 7. ■

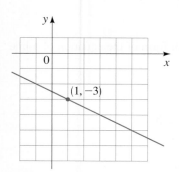

FIGURE 7

EXAMPLE 3 ■ Finding the Equation of a Line through Two Given Points

Find an equation of the line through the points $(-1, 2)$ and $(3, -4)$.

SOLUTION

The slope of the line is

$$m = \frac{-4 - 2}{3 - (-1)} = -\frac{6}{4} = -\frac{3}{2}$$

Using the point-slope form with $x_1 = -1$ and $y_1 = 2$, we obtain

$$y - 2 = -\frac{3}{2}(x + 1) \qquad \text{From point-slope equation}$$

$$2y - 4 = -3x - 3 \qquad \text{Multiply by 2}$$

$$3x + 2y - 1 = 0 \qquad \text{Rearrange}$$ ■

Suppose a nonvertical line has slope m and y-intercept b (see Figure 8). This means the line intersects the y-axis at the point $(0, b)$, so the point-slope form of the equation of the line, with $x = 0$ and $y = b$, becomes

$$y - b = m(x - 0)$$

This simplifies to $y = mx + b$, which is called the **slope-intercept form** of the equation of a line.

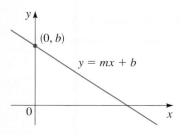

FIGURE 8

SLOPE-INTERCEPT FORM OF THE EQUATION OF A LINE

An equation of the line that has slope m and y-intercept b is

$$y = mx + b$$

EXAMPLE 4 ■ Lines in Slope-Intercept Form

(a) Find the equation of the line with slope 3 and y-intercept -2.
(b) Find the slope and y-intercept of the line $3y - 2x = 1$.

SOLUTION

(a) Since $m = 3$ and $b = 2$, from the slope-intercept form of the equation of a line we get

$$y = 3x - 2$$

(b) We first write the equation in the form $y = mx + b$:

$$3y - 2x = 1$$
$$3y = 2x + 1 \qquad \text{Add } 2x$$
$$y = \tfrac{2}{3}x + \tfrac{1}{3} \qquad \text{Divide by 3}$$

From the slope-intercept form of the equation of a line, we see that the slope is $m = \tfrac{2}{3}$ and the y-intercept is $b = \tfrac{1}{3}$. ■

If a line is horizontal, its slope is $m = 0$, so its equation is $y = b$, where b is the y-intercept (see Figure 9). A vertical line does not have a slope, but we can write its equation as $x = a$, where a is the x-intercept, because the x-coordinate of every point on the line is a.

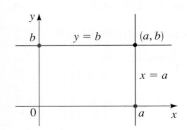

FIGURE 9

VERTICAL AND HORIZONTAL LINES

An equation of the vertical line through (a, b) is $x = a$.
An equation of the horizontal line through (a, b) is $y = b$.

EXAMPLE 5 ■ Vertical and Horizontal Lines

(a) The graph of the equation $x = 3$ is a vertical line with x-intercept 3.
(b) The graph of the equation $y = -2$ is a horizontal line with y-intercept -2.

The lines are graphed in Figure 10. ■

A **linear equation** is an equation of the form

$$Ax + By + C = 0$$

where A, B, and C are constants and A and B are not both 0. The equation of a line is a linear equation:

■ A nonvertical line has the equation $y = mx + b$ or $-mx + y - b = 0$, which is a linear equation with $A = -m$, $B = 1$, and $C = -b$.

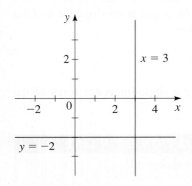

FIGURE 10

- A vertical line has the equation $x = a$ or $x - a = 0$, which is a linear equation with $A = 1$, $B = 0$, and $C = -a$.

Conversely, the graph of a linear equation is a line:

- If $B \neq 0$, the equation becomes

$$y = -\frac{A}{B}x - \frac{C}{B}$$

and this is the slope-intercept form of the equation of a line (with $m = -A/B$ and $b = -C/B$).

- If $B = 0$, the equation becomes $Ax + C = 0$, or $x = -C/A$, which represents a vertical line.

We have proved the following.

GENERAL EQUATION OF A LINE

The graph of every **linear equation**

$$Ax + By + C = 0 \qquad (A, B \text{ not both zero})$$

is a line. Conversely, every line is the graph of a linear equation.

EXAMPLE 6 ■ Graphing a Linear Equation

Sketch the graph of the equation $2x - 3y - 12 = 0$.

SOLUTION 1

Since the equation is linear, its graph is a line. To draw the graph, it is enough to find any two points on the line. The intercepts are the easiest points to find.

x-intercept: Substitute $y = 0$, to get $2x - 12 = 0$, so $x = 6$

y-intercept: Substitute $x = 0$, to get $-3y - 12 = 0$, so $y = -4$

With these points we can sketch the graph in Figure 11.

SOLUTION 2

We write the equation in slope-intercept form:

$$2x - 3y - 12 = 0$$

$$2x - 3y = 12 \qquad \text{Add 12}$$

$$-3y = -2x + 12 \qquad \text{Subtract } 2x$$

$$y = \tfrac{2}{3}x - 4 \qquad \text{Divide by } -3$$

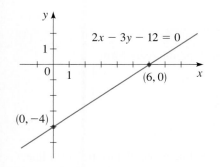

FIGURE 11

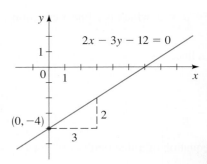

FIGURE 12

This equation is in the form $y = mx + b$, so the slope is $m = \frac{2}{3}$ and the y-intercept is $b = -4$. To sketch the graph, we plot the y-intercept, and then move 3 units to the right and 2 units up as shown in Figure 12. ∎

Parallel and Perpendicular Lines

Since slope measures the steepness of a line, it seems reasonable that parallel lines should have the same slope. In fact, we can prove this.

PARALLEL LINES

Two nonvertical lines are parallel if and only if they have the same slope.

■ **Proof**   Let the lines l_1 and l_2 in Figure 13 have slopes m_1 and m_2. If the lines are parallel, then the right triangles ABC and DEF are similar, so

$$m_1 = \frac{d(B, C)}{d(A, C)} = \frac{d(E, F)}{d(D, F)} = m_2$$

Conversely, if the slopes are equal, then the triangles will be similar, so $\angle BAC = \angle EDF$ and the lines are parallel. □

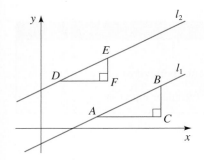

FIGURE 13

EXAMPLE 7 ■ **Finding the Equation of a Line Parallel to a Given Line**

Find an equation of the line through the point $(5, 2)$ that is parallel to the line $4x + 6y + 5 = 0$.

SOLUTION

First we write the equation of the given line in slope-intercept form.

$$4x + 6y + 5 = 0$$

$$6y = -4x - 5 \qquad \text{Subtract } 4x + 5$$

$$y = -\frac{2}{3}x - \frac{5}{6} \qquad \text{Divide by 6}$$

So the line has slope $m = -\frac{2}{3}$. Since the required line is parallel to the given line, it also has slope $m = -\frac{2}{3}$. From the point-slope form of the equation of a line, we get

$$y - 2 = -\frac{2}{3}(x - 5) \qquad \text{Slope } m = -\frac{2}{3}, \text{ point } (5, 2)$$

$$3y - 6 = -2x + 10 \qquad \text{Multiply by 3}$$

$$2x + 3y - 16 = 0 \qquad \text{Rearrange}$$

Thus, the equation of the required line is $2x + 3y - 16 = 0$. ∎

The condition for perpendicular lines is not as obvious as that for parallel lines.

PERPENDICULAR LINES

Two lines with slopes m_1 and m_2 are perpendicular if and only if $m_1 m_2 = -1$, that is, their slopes are negative reciprocals:

$$m_2 = -\frac{1}{m_1}$$

Also, a horizontal line (slope 0) is perpendicular to a vertical line (no slope).

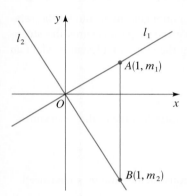

FIGURE 14

■ **Proof** In Figure 14 we show two lines intersecting at the origin. (If the lines intersect at some other point, we consider lines parallel to these that intersect at the origin. These lines have the same slopes as the original lines.)

If the lines l_1 and l_2 have slopes m_1 and m_2, then their equations are $y = m_1 x$ and $y = m_2 x$. Notice that $A(1, m_1)$ lies on l_1 and $B(1, m_2)$ lies on l_2. By the Pythagorean Theorem and its converse, $OA \perp OB$ if and only if

$$[d(O, A)]^2 + [d(O, B)]^2 = [d(A, B)]^2$$

By the Distance Formula, this becomes

$$(1^2 + m_1^2) + (1^2 + m_2^2) = (1 - 1)^2 + (m_2 - m_1)^2$$
$$2 + m_1^2 + m_2^2 = m_2^2 - 2m_1 m_2 + m_1^2$$
$$2 = -2m_1 m_2$$
$$m_1 m_2 = -1$$

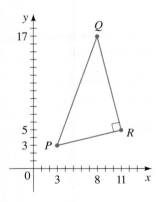

FIGURE 15

EXAMPLE 8 ■ Perpendicular Lines

Show that the points $P(3, 3)$, $Q(8, 17)$, and $R(11, 5)$ are the vertices of a right triangle.

SOLUTION

The slopes of the lines containing PR and QR are, respectively,

$$m_1 = \frac{5 - 3}{11 - 3} = \frac{1}{4} \qquad \text{and} \qquad m_2 = \frac{5 - 17}{11 - 8} = -4$$

Since $m_1 m_2 = -1$, these lines are perpendicular and so PQR is a right triangle. It is sketched in Figure 15. ■

EXAMPLE 9 ■ Finding an Equation of a Line Perpendicular to a Given Line

Find an equation of the line that is perpendicular to the line $4x + 6y + 5 = 0$ and passes through the origin.

SOLUTION

In Example 7 we found that the slope of the line $4x + 6y + 5 = 0$ is $-\frac{2}{3}$. Thus, the slope of a perpendicular line is the negative reciprocal, that is, $\frac{3}{2}$. Since the required line passes through $(0, 0)$, the point-slope form gives

$$y - 0 = \tfrac{3}{2}(x - 0)$$

$$y = \tfrac{3}{2}x \qquad \blacksquare$$

■ Applications of Linear Equations; Rates of Change

Linear equations and their graphs are often used in applications to model the relationship between two quantities. We have seen that the slope measures the steepness of a line. In the next two examples we see that the slope in a linear model can be interpreted as a **rate of change**.

EXAMPLE 10 ■ Slope as Rate of Change

A dam is built on a river to create a reservoir. The water level w in the reservoir is given by the equation

$$w = 4.5t + 28$$

where t is the number of years since the dam was constructed, and w is measured in feet.

(a) Sketch a graph of this equation.

(b) What do the slope and w-intercept of this graph represent?

SOLUTION

(a) This equation is linear, so its graph is a line. Since two points determine a line, we plot two points that lie on the graph and draw a line through them.

   When $t = 0$, then $w = 4.5(0) + 28 = 28$, so $(0, 28)$ is on the line.

   When $t = 2$, then $w = 4.5(2) + 28 = 37$, so $(2, 37)$ is on the line.

The line determined by these points is shown in Figure 16.

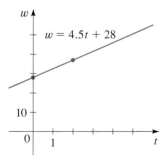

FIGURE 16

(b) The slope is $m = 4.5$; it represents the rate of change of water level with respect to time. This means that the water level *increases* 4.5 ft per year. The w-intercept is 28, and occurs when $t = 0$, so it represents the water level when the dam was constructed. ∎

EXAMPLE 11 ■ **Linear Relationship between Temperature and Elevation**

(a) As dry air moves upward, it expands and cools. If the ground temperature is 20°C and the temperature at a height of 1 km is 10°C, express the temperature T (in °C) in terms of the height h (in kilometers). (Assume that the relationship between T and h is linear.)

(b) Draw the graph of the linear equation. What does its slope represent?

(c) What is the temperature at a height of 2.5 km?

SOLUTION

(a) Because we are assuming a linear relationship between T and h, the equation must be of the form

$$T = mh + b$$

where m and b are constants. When $h = 0$, we are given that $T = 20$, so

$$20 = m(0) + b$$
$$b = 20$$

Thus, we have

$$T = mh + 20$$

When $h = 1$, we have $T = 10$ and so

$$10 = m(1) + 20$$
$$m = 10 - 20 = -10$$

The required expression is

$$T = -10h + 20$$

(b) The graph is sketched in Figure 17. The slope is $m = -10°C/km$, and this represents the rate of change of temperature with respect to distance above the ground.

(c) At a height of $h = 2.5$ km, the temperature is

$$T = -10(2.5) + 20 = -25 + 20 = 5°C$$ ∎

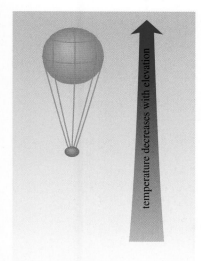

Weather balloons are used to measure temperature at high elevations.

temperature decreases with elevation

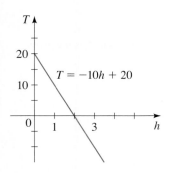

$T = -10h + 20$

FIGURE 17

most exciting of these just within the past decade.

In other *Mathematics in the Modern World*, we will describe in more detail how mathematics affects us in our everyday activities.

1.2 EXERCISES

1–8 ■ Find the slope of the line through P and Q.

1. $P(0, 0)$, $Q(2, 4)$

2. $P(0, 0)$, $Q(2, -6)$

3. $P(2, 2)$, $Q(10, 0)$

4. $P(1, 2)$, $Q(3, 3)$

5. $P(2, 4)$, $Q(4, 12)$

6. $P(2, -5)$, $Q(-4, 3)$

7. $P(1, -3)$, $Q(-1, 6)$

8. $P(-1, -4)$, $Q(6, 0)$

9. Find the slopes of the lines l_1, l_2, l_3, and l_4 in the figure below.

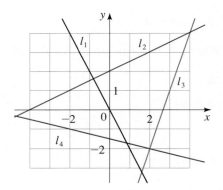

10. (a) Sketch lines through $(0, 0)$ with slopes 1, 0, $\frac{1}{2}$, 2, and -1.
  (b) Sketch lines through $(0, 0)$ with slopes $\frac{1}{3}$, $\frac{1}{2}$, $-\frac{1}{3}$, and 3.

11–14 ■ Find an equation for the line whose graph is sketched.

11.

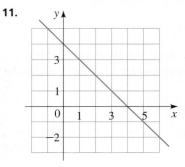

12.

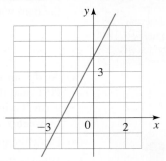

13.

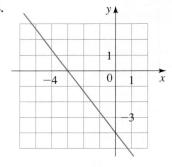

14.

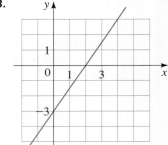

15–34 ■ Find an equation of the line that satisfies the given conditions.

15. Through $(2, 3)$;   slope 1

16. Through $(-2, 4)$;   slope -1

17. Through $(1, 7)$;   slope $\frac{2}{3}$

18. Through $(-3, -5)$;   slope $-\frac{7}{2}$

19. Through $(2, 1)$ and $(1, 6)$

20. Through $(-1, -2)$ and $(4, 3)$

21. Slope 3; y-intercept -2

22. Slope $\frac{2}{5}$; y-intercept 4

23. x-intercept 1; y-intercept -3

24. x-intercept -8; y-intercept 6

25. Through $(4, 5)$;   parallel to the x-axis

26. Through $(4, 5)$;   parallel to the y-axis

27. Through $(1, -6)$;   parallel to the line $x + 2y = 6$

28. y-intercept 6;   parallel to the line $2x + 3y + 4 = 0$

29. Through $(-1, 2)$;   parallel to the line $x = 5$

30. Through $(2, 6)$;   perpendicular to the line $y = 1$

31. Through $(-1, -2)$;   perpendicular to the line
$2x + 5y + 8 = 0$

32. Through $\left(\frac{1}{2}, -\frac{2}{3}\right)$;   perpendicular to the line
$4x - 8y = 1$

33. Through $(1, 7)$;   parallel to the line passing through $(2, 5)$
and $(-2, 1)$

34. Through $(-2, -11)$;   perpendicular to the line passing
through $(1, 1)$ and $(5, -1)$

35. (a) Sketch the line with slope $\frac{3}{2}$ that passes through the
point $(-2, 1)$.
(b) Find an equation for this line.

36. (a) Sketch the line with slope -2 that passes through the
point $(4, -1)$.
(b) Find an equation for this line.

 37–38 ■ Use a graphing device to graph the given family of
lines in the same viewing rectangle. What do the lines have in
common?

37. $y = 2 + m(x - 3)$ for $m = 0, \pm0.5, \pm1, \pm2, \pm10$

38. $y = 1.3x + b$ for $b = 0, \pm1, \pm2.8$

39–50 ■ Find the slope and y-intercept of the line and draw its
graph.

39. $x + y = 3$ **40.** $3x - 2y = 12$

41. $x + 3y = 0$ **42.** $2x - 5y = 0$

43. $\frac{1}{2}x - \frac{1}{3}y + 1 = 0$ **44.** $-3x - 5y + 30 = 0$

45. $y = 4$ **46.** $4y + 8 = 0$

47. $3x - 4y = 12$ **48.** $x = -5$

49. $3x + 4y - 1 = 0$ **50.** $4x + 5y = 10$

51. Show that $A(1, 1)$, $B(7, 4)$, $C(5, 10)$, and $D(-1, 7)$ are vertices of a parallelogram.

52. Show that $A(-3, -1)$, $B(3, 3)$, and $C(-9, 8)$ are vertices of
a right triangle.

53. Show that $A(1, 1)$, $B(11, 3)$, $C(10, 8)$, and $D(0, 6)$ are vertices of a rectangle.

54. Use slopes to determine whether the given points are
collinear (lie on a line).
(a) $(1, 1)$, $(3, 9)$, $(6, 21)$
(b) $(-1, 3)$, $(1, 7)$, $(4, 15)$

55. Find an equation of the perpendicular bisector of the line
segment joining the points $A(1, 4)$ and $B(7, -2)$.

56. Find the area of the triangle formed by the coordinate axes
and the line $2y + 3x - 6 = 0$.

57. (a) Show that if the x- and y-intercepts of a line are
nonzero numbers a and b, then the equation of the line
can be written in the form

$$\frac{x}{a} + \frac{y}{b} = 1$$

This is called the **two-intercept form** of the equation
of a line.
(b) Use part (a) to find an equation of the line whose
x-intercept is 6 and whose y-intercept is -8.

58. (a) Find an equation for the line tangent to the circle
$x^2 + y^2 = 25$ at the point $(3, -4)$. (See the figure.)
(b) At what other point on the circle will a tangent line be
parallel to the tangent line in part (a)?

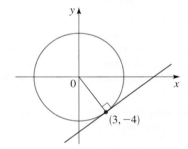

59. West of Albuquerque, New Mexico, Route 40 eastbound is
straight and makes a steep descent towards the city. The
highway has a 6% grade, which means that its slope is
$-\frac{6}{100}$. Driving on this road you notice from elevation signs
that you have descended a distance of 1000 ft. What is the
change in your horizontal distance?

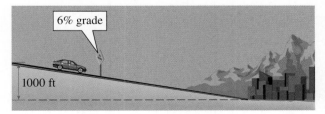

60. Some scientists believe that the average surface temperature of the world has been rising steadily. The average surface temperature is given by

$$T = 0.02t + 8.50$$

where T is temperature in °C and t is years since 1900.
(a) What do the slope and T-intercept represent?
(b) Use the equation to predict the average global surface temperature in 2100.

61. If the recommended adult dosage for a drug is D (in mg), then to determine the appropriate dosage c for a child of age a, pharmacists use the equation

$$c = 0.0417D(a + 1)$$

Suppose the dosage for an adult is 200 mg.
(a) Find the slope. What does it represent?
(b) What is the dosage for a newborn?

62. The manager of a weekend flea market knows from past experience that if she charges x dollars for a rental space at the flea market, then the number y of spaces she can rent is given by the equation $y = 200 - 4x$.
(a) Sketch a graph of this linear equation. (Remember that the rental charge per space and the number of spaces rented must both be nonnegative quantities.)
(b) What do the slope, the y-intercept, and the x-intercept of the graph represent?

63. A small-appliance manufacturer finds that if he produces x toaster ovens in a month his production cost is given by the equation $y = 6x + 3000$ (where y is measured in dollars).
(a) Sketch a graph of this linear equation.
(b) What do the slope and y-intercept of the graph represent?

64. The relationship between the Fahrenheit (F) and Celsius (C) temperature scales is given by the equation $F = \frac{9}{5}C + 32$.
(a) Complete the table to compare the two scales at the given values.
(b) Find the temperature at which the scales agree.
[*Hint:* Suppose that a is the temperature at which the scales agree. Set $F = a$ and $C = a$. Then solve for a.]

C	F
$-30°$	
$-20°$	
$-10°$	
$0°$	
	$50°$
	$68°$
	$86°$

65. Biologists have observed that the chirping rate of crickets of a certain species is related to temperature, and the relationship appears to be very nearly linear. A cricket produces 120 chirps per minute at 70°F and 168 chirps per minute at 80°F.
(a) Find the linear equation that relates the temperature t and the number of chirps per minute n.
(b) If the crickets are chirping at 150 chirps per minute, estimate the temperature.

66. A small business buys a computer for $4000. After 4 years the value of the computer is expected to be $200. For accounting purposes, the business uses *linear depreciation* to assess the value of the computer at a given time. This means that if V is the value of the computer at time t, then a linear equation is used to relate V and t.
(a) Find a linear equation that relates V and t.
(b) Find the depreciated value of the computer 3 years from the date of purchase.

67. At the surface of the ocean, the water pressure is the same as the air pressure above the water, 15 lb/in². Below the surface, the water pressure increases by 4.34 lb/in² for every 10 ft of descent.
(a) Find an equation for the relationship between pressure and depth below the ocean surface.
(b) At what depth is the pressure 100 lb/in²?

water pressure increases with depth

68. Jason and Debbie leave Detroit at 2:00 P.M. and drive at a constant speed, traveling west on I-90. They pass Ann Arbor, 40 mi from Detroit, at 2:50 P.M.
(a) Express the distance traveled in terms of the time elapsed.
(b) Draw the graph of the equation in part (a).
(c) What is the slope of this line? What does it represent?

69. The monthly cost of driving a car depends on the number of miles driven. Lynn found that in May her driving cost was $380 for 480 mi and in June her cost was $460 for 800 mi.
(a) Express the monthly cost C in terms of the distance driven d, assuming that a linear relationship gives a suitable model.
(b) Use part (a) to predict the cost of driving 1500 mi per month.
(c) Draw the graph of the linear equation. What does the slope of the line represent?
(d) What does the y-intercept of the graph represent?
(e) Why is a linear relationship a suitable model for this situation?

70. The manager of a furniture factory finds that it costs $2200 to manufacture 100 chairs in one day and $4800 to produce 300 chairs in one day.
(a) Assuming that the relationship between cost and the number of chairs produced is linear, find an equation that expresses this relationship. Then graph the equation.
(b) What is the slope of the line in part (a), and what does it represent?
(c) What is the y-intercept of this line, and what does it represent?

 DISCOVERY • DISCUSSION

71. What Does the Slope Mean?   Suppose that the graph of the outdoor temperature over a certain period of time is a line. How is the weather changing if the slope of the line is positive? If it's negative? If it's zero?

72. Collinear Points   Suppose you are given the coordinates of three points in the plane, and you want to see whether they lie on the same line. How can you do this using slopes? Using the Distance Formula? Can you think of another method?

Discovery Project

VISUALIZING DATA

When scientists analyze data, they look for a trend or pattern from which they can draw a conclusion about the process they are studying. It's often hard to look at lists of numbers and see any kind of pattern. One of the best ways to reveal a hidden pattern in data is to draw a graph. For instance, a biologist measures the levels of three different enzymes (call them A, B, and C) in 20 blood samples taken from expectant mothers, yielding the data shown in the table (enzyme levels in mg/dL).

Sample	A	B	C	Sample	A	B	C
1	1.3	1.7	49	11	2.2	0.6	25
2	2.6	6.8	22	12	1.5	4.8	32
3	0.9	0.6	53	13	3.1	1.9	20
4	3.5	2.4	15	14	4.1	3.1	10
5	2.4	3.8	25	15	1.8	7.5	31
6	1.7	3.3	30	16	2.9	5.8	18
7	4.0	6.7	12	17	2.1	5.1	30
8	3.2	4.3	17	18	2.7	2.5	20
9	1.3	8.4	45	19	1.4	2.0	39
10	1.4	5.8	47	20	0.8	2.3	56

The biologist wishes to determine whether there is a relationship between the serum levels of these enzymes, so he decides to make some **scatter plots** of the data. The scatter plot in Figure 1 shows the levels of enzymes A and B. Each point represents the results for one sample—for instance, sample 1 had 1.3 mg/dL of enzyme A and 1.7 mg/dL of enzyme B, so we plot the point $(1.3, 1.7)$ to represent this pair of data. Similarly, Figure 2 shows the levels of enzymes A and C. From Figure 1 the biologist sees that there is no obvious relationship between enzymes A and B, but from Figure 2 it appears that when the level of enzyme A goes up, the level of enzyme C goes down.

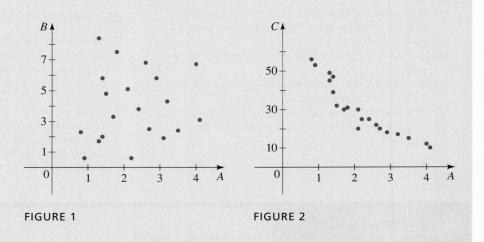

FIGURE 1   FIGURE 2

1. Make a scatter plot of enzyme B and C levels in the blood samples. Do you detect any relationship from your graph?

2. For each scatter plot, determine whether there is a relationship between the two variables in the graphs. If there is, describe the relationship; that is, explain what happens to y as x increases.

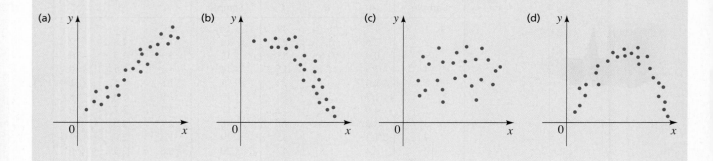

3. In each scatter plot below, the value of y increases as x increases. Explain how the relationship between x and y differs in the two cases.

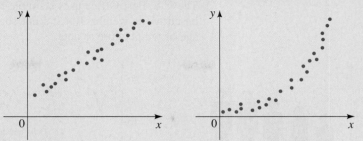

4. For the data given in the following table, make three scatter plots; one for A and B, one for B and C, and one for A and C. Determine whether any of these pairs of variables are related. If so, describe the relationship.

Sample	A	B	C
1	58	4.1	51.7
2	39	5.2	15.4
3	15	7.6	2.0
4	30	6.0	7.3
5	46	4.3	34.2
6	59	3.9	72.4
7	22	6.3	4.1
8	7	8.1	0.5
9	41	4.7	22.6
10	62	3.7	96.3
11	10	7.9	1.3
12	6	8.3	0.2

1.3 FUNCTIONS

One of the most basic and important ideas in all of mathematics is the concept of a *function*. In this section we explore the idea of a function and then give the mathematical definition of function.

Functions All Around Us

In nearly every physical phenomenon, we observe that one quantity depends on another. For example, your height depends on your age, the temperature depends on the date, the cost of mailing a package depends on its weight (see Figure 1). We use the term *function* to describe this dependence of one quantity on another. That is, we say the following:

- Height is a function of age
- Temperature is a function of date
- Cost of mailing a package is a function of weight

The U.S. Post Office uses a simple rule to determine the cost of mailing a package based on its weight. But it's not so easy to describe the rule that relates height to age or temperature to date.

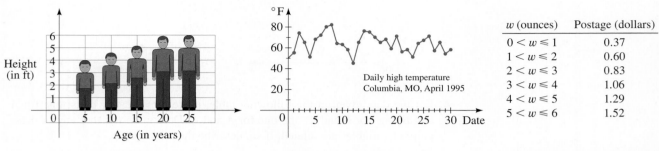

w (ounces)	Postage (dollars)
$0 < w \le 1$	0.37
$1 < w \le 2$	0.60
$2 < w \le 3$	0.83
$3 < w \le 4$	1.06
$4 < w \le 5$	1.29
$5 < w \le 6$	1.52

Height is a function of age.   Temperature is a function of date.   Postage is a function of weight.

FIGURE 1

Can you think of other functions? Here are some more examples:

- The area of a circle is a function of its radius
- The number of bacteria in a culture is a function of time
- The weight of an astronaut is a function of her elevation

The area A of a circle depends on its radius r. The rule that describes this dependence is given by the formula $A = \pi r^2$. The number N of bacteria in a culture depends on the time t (see Table 1). The rule that connects N and t in this case is given by the formula $N = 50 \cdot 2^t$. The weight w of an astronaut depends on her elevation h. Physicists use the rule $w = w_0 R^2/(R + h)^2$, where R is the radius of the earth.

t **(min)**	N **(bacteria)**
0	50
1	100
2	200
3	400
4	800
5	1600
6	3200

TABLE 1

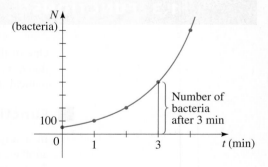

FIGURE 2

We can visualize a function by sketching its *graph*. For instance, to see how the number N of bacteria in a culture depends on the time t, we graph the data given in Table 1. The height of the graph above the horizontal axis represents the number of bacteria at a given time t—the higher the graph, the more bacteria. The shape of the graph in Figure 2 indicates how quickly the bacteria population grows.

Even when a precise rule or formula describing a function is not available, we can still describe the function by a graph. For example, when you turn on a hot water faucet, the temperature of the water depends on how long the water has been running. So we can say

■ Temperature of water from the faucet is a function of time

Figure 3 shows a rough graph of the temperature T of the water as a function of the time t that has elapsed since the faucet was turned on. The graph shows that the initial temperature of the water is close to room temperature. When the water from the hot water tank reaches the faucet, the water's temperature T increases quickly. In the next phase, T is constant at the temperature of the water in the tank. When the tank is drained, T decreases to the temperature of the cold water supply.

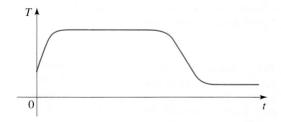

FIGURE 3

Graph of water temperature T as a function of time t

You can see why scientists routinely use functions in their work. For instance, a biologist observes that the number of bacteria in a culture increases with time. To predict the size of the bacteria culture in the future, the biologist tries to find the rule or function that relates the number of bacteria to the time. A physicist observes that the weight of an astronaut depends on her elevation. The physicist then tries to discover the rule or function that relates these quantities. The process of finding a function to describe a real-world phenomenon is called *modeling*.

In the *Focus on Modeling*, pages 102–111, we learn how to find functions that model real-life data.

Definition of Function

Before we give the formal definition of a function, let's examine one more example. In the following list the numbers on the right are related to those on the left.

$$1 \rightarrow 1$$
$$2 \rightarrow 4$$
$$3 \rightarrow 9$$
$$4 \rightarrow 16$$

Can you discover the rule that relates these numbers? The rule is "square the number." Thus, if x is any number, we have

$$x \rightarrow x^2$$

In order to talk about this rule, we need to give it a name. Let's call it f. So, in this example, f is the rule "square the number." When we apply the rule f to the number x, we get x^2. We express this mathematically as

$$f(x) = x^2$$

When we write $f(2)$, we mean "apply the rule f to the number 2." Applying the rule gives $f(2) = 2^2 = 4$. Similarly, $f(3) = 3^2 = 9$ and $f(4) = 4^2 = 16$.

The following definition concisely captures these ideas.

DEFINITION OF FUNCTION

A **function** f is a rule that assigns to each element x in a set A exactly one element, called $f(x)$, in a set B.

We have previously used letters to stand for numbers. Here we do something quite different. We use letters to represent *rules*. If the letter f represents a function, then the notation $f(x)$ means "apply the rule f to the number x."

We usually consider functions for which the sets A and B are sets of real numbers. The symbol $f(x)$ is read "f of x" or "f at x" and is called the **value of f at x**, or the **image of x under f**. The set A is called the **domain** of the function. The **range** of f is the set of all possible values of $f(x)$ as x varies throughout the domain, that is,

$$\{f(x) \mid x \in A\}$$

The symbol that represents an arbitrary number in the domain of a function f is called an **independent variable**. The symbol that represents a number in the range of f is called a **dependent variable**. For instance, in the bacteria example, t is the independent variable and N is the dependent variable.

The $\boxed{\sqrt{}}$ key on your calculator is a good example of a function as a machine. First you input x into the display. Then you press the key labeled $\boxed{\sqrt{}}$. If $x < 0$, then x is not in the domain of this function; that is, x is not an acceptable input and the calculator will indicate an error. If $x \geq 0$, then an approximation to $\sqrt{x}$ appears in the display, correct to a certain number of decimal places. [Thus, the $\boxed{\sqrt{}}$ key on your calculator is not quite the same as the exact mathematical function f defined by $f(x) = \sqrt{x}$.]

It's helpful to think of a function as a **machine** (see Figure 4). If x is in the domain of the function f, then when x enters the machine, it is accepted as an input and the machine produces an output $f(x)$ according to the rule of the function. Thus, we can think of the domain as the set of all possible inputs and the range as the set of all possible outputs.

$$x \longrightarrow \boxed{f} \longrightarrow f(x)$$
input   output

FIGURE 4   Machine diagram of f

Another way to picture a function is by an **arrow diagram** as in Figure 5. Each arrow connects an element of A to an element of B. The arrow indicates that $f(x)$ is associated with x, $f(a)$ is associated with a, and so on.

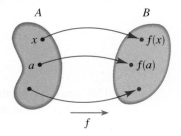

FIGURE 5
Arrow diagram of f

EXAMPLE 1 ■ The Squaring Function

The squaring function assigns to each real number x its square x^2. It is defined by

$$f(x) = x^2$$

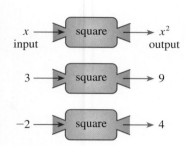

x → square → x^2
input   output

3 → square → 9

−2 → square → 4

FIGURE 6

Machine diagram

(a) Evaluate $f(3)$, $f(-2)$, and $f(\sqrt{5})$.

(b) Find the domain and range of f.

(c) Draw a machine diagram for f.

SOLUTION

(a) The values of f are found by substituting for x in $f(x) = x^2$.

$$f(3) = 3^2 = 9 \qquad f(-2) = (-2)^2 = 4 \qquad f(\sqrt{5}) = (\sqrt{5})^2 = 5$$

(b) The domain of f is the set $\mathbb{R}$ of all real numbers. The range of f consists of all values of $f(x)$, that is, all numbers of the form x^2. Since $x^2 \geq 0$ for all real numbers x, we can see that the range of f is $\{y \mid y \geq 0\} = [0, \infty)$.

(c) A machine diagram for this function is shown in Figure 6.   ∎

Evaluating a Function

In the definition of a function the independent variable x plays the role of a "placeholder." For example, the function $f(x) = 3x^2 + x - 5$ can be thought of as

$$f(\;\;) = 3 \cdot \;\;^2 + \;\; - 5$$

To evaluate f at a number, we substitute the number for the placeholder.

EXAMPLE 2 ∎ **Evaluating a Function**

Let $f(x) = 3x^2 + x - 5$. Evaluate each function value.

(a) $f(-2)$ (b) $f(0)$ (c) $f(4)$ (d) $f\left(\frac{1}{2}\right)$

SOLUTION

To evaluate f at a number, we substitute the number for x in the definition of f.

(a) $f(-2) = 3 \cdot (-2)^2 + (-2) - 5 = 5$

(b) $f(0) = 3 \cdot 0^2 + 0 - 5 = -5$

(c) $f(4) = 3 \cdot 4^2 + 4 - 5 = 47$

(d) $f\left(\frac{1}{2}\right) = 3 \cdot \left(\frac{1}{2}\right)^2 + \frac{1}{2} - 5 = -\frac{15}{4}$ ∎

EXAMPLE 3 ∎ **A Piecewise Defined Function**

Evaluate the following function at $x = -2, 1, 2$, and 3.

$$f(x) = \begin{cases} 1 - x & \text{if } x \leq 1 \\ x^2 & \text{if } x > 1 \end{cases}$$

SOLUTION

Remember that a function is a rule. Here is how we apply the rule for this particular function: First look at the value of the input x. If it happens that $x \leq 1$, then the value of $f(x)$ is $1 - x$. On the other hand, if $x > 1$, then the value of $f(x)$ is x^2.

Since $-2 \leqslant 1$, we have $f(-2) = 1 - (-2) = 3$.

Since $1 \leqslant 1$, we have $f(1) = 1 - 1 = 0$.

Since $2 > 1$, we have $f(2) = 2^2 = 4$.

Since $3 > 1$, we have $f(3) = 3^2 = 9$.   ■

EXAMPLE 4 ■ Evaluating a Function

Expressions like the one in part (d) of Example 4 occur frequently in calculus; they are called *difference quotients*, and they represent the average change in the value of f between $x = a$ and $x = a + h$.

If $f(x) = 2x^2 + 3x - 1$, evaluate the following.

(a) $f(a)$ (b) $f(-a)$

(c) $f(a + h)$ (d) $\dfrac{f(a + h) - f(a)}{h}$, $h \neq 0$

SOLUTION

(a) $f(a) = 2a^2 + 3a - 1$

(b) $f(-a) = 2(-a)^2 + 3(-a) - 1 = 2a^2 - 3a - 1$

(c) $f(a + h) = 2(a + h)^2 + 3(a + h) - 1$
$$= 2(a^2 + 2ah + h^2) + 3(a + h) - 1$$
$$= 2a^2 + 4ah + 2h^2 + 3a + 3h - 1$$

(d) Using the results from parts (c) and (a), we have

$$\frac{f(a + h) - f(a)}{h} = \frac{(2a^2 + 4ah + 2h^2 + 3a + 3h - 1) - (2a^2 + 3a - 1)}{h}$$

$$= \frac{4ah + 2h^2 + 3h}{h} = 4a + 2h + 3$$ ■

EXAMPLE 5 ■ The Weight of an Astronaut

If an astronaut weighs 130 pounds on the surface of the earth, then her weight when she is h miles above the earth is given by the function

$$w(h) = 130\left(\frac{3960}{3960 + h}\right)^2$$

(a) What is her weight when she is 100 mi above the earth?

(b) Construct a table of values for the function w that gives her weight at heights from 0 to 500 mi. What do you conclude from the table?

SOLUTION

(a) We want the value of the function w when $h = 100$; that is, we must calculate $w(100)$.

$$w(100) = 130\left(\frac{3960}{3960 + 100}\right)^2 \approx 123.67$$

So at a height of 100 mi, she weighs about 124 lb.

(b) The table gives the astronaut's weight, rounded to the nearest pound, at 100-mile increments. The values in the table are calculated as in part (a).

h	$w(h)$
0	130
100	124
200	118
300	112
400	107
500	102

The table indicates that the higher the astronaut travels, the less she weighs.   ∎

The weight of an object on or near the earth is the gravitational force that the earth exerts on it. When in orbit around the earth, an astronaut experiences the sensation of "weightlessness" because the centripetal force that keeps her in orbit is exactly the same as the gravitational pull of the earth.

■ The Domain of a Function

The domain of a function may be stated explicitly. For example, if we write

$$f(x) = x^2, \qquad 0 \leqslant x \leqslant 5$$

then the domain is the set of all real numbers x for which $0 \leqslant x \leqslant 5$. If the function is given by an algebraic expression and the domain is not stated explicitly, then by convention *the domain is the set of all real numbers for which the expression is defined as a real number.* For example, the function

$$f(x) = \frac{1}{x - 4}$$

is not defined at $x = 4$, so its domain is $\{x \mid x \neq 4\}$. The function

$$f(x) = \sqrt{x}$$

is not defined for negative x, so its domain is $\{x \mid x \geqslant 0\}$.

EXAMPLE 6   ■   Finding Domains of Functions

Find the domain of each function.

(a) $f(x) = \dfrac{1}{x^2 - x}$ (b) $g(x) = \sqrt{9 - x^2}$ (c) $h(t) = \dfrac{t}{\sqrt{t + 1}}$

SOLUTION

(a) The function is not defined when the denominator is 0. Since

$$f(x) = \frac{1}{x^2 - x} = \frac{1}{x(x - 1)}$$

we see that $f(x)$ is not defined when $x = 0$ or $x = 1$. Thus, the domain of f is

$$\{x \mid x \neq 0, x \neq 1\}$$

The domain may also be written in interval notation as

$$(\infty, 0) \cup (0, 1) \cup (1, \infty)$$

(b) We can't take the square root of a negative number, so we must have $9 - x^2 \geq 0$. So, $x^2 \leq 9$, and hence $-3 \leq x \leq 3$. Thus, the domain of g is

$$\{x \mid -3 \leq x \leq 3\} = [-3, 3]$$

(c) We can't take the square root of a negative number, and we can't divide by 0, so we must have $t + 1 > 0$, that is, $t > -1$. So the domain of h is

$$\{t \mid t > -1\} = (-1, \infty)$$ ∎

■ Four Ways to Represent a Function

To help us understand what a function is, we have used machine and arrow diagrams. To describe a specific function, we can use the following four ways:

- verbally (by a description in words)
- algebraically (by an explicit formula)
- visually (by a graph)
- numerically (by a table of values)

A single function may be represented in all four ways, and it is often useful to go from one representation to another to gain insight into the function. However, certain functions are described more naturally by one method than by the other. An example of a verbal description is

$$P(t) \qquad \text{is} \qquad \text{"the population of the world at time } t\text{"}$$

The function P can also be described numerically by giving a table of values (see Table 1 on page 34). A useful representation of the area of a circle as a function of its radius is the algebraic formula

$$A(r) = \pi r^2$$

The graph produced by a seismograph (see the box) is a visual representation of the vertical acceleration function $a(t)$ of the ground during an earthquake. As a final example, consider the function $C(w)$, which is described verbally as "the cost of mailing a first-class letter with weight w." The most convenient way of describing this function is numerically—that is, using a table of values.

We will be using all four representations of functions throughout this book. We summarize them in the following box.

FOUR WAYS TO REPRESENT A FUNCTION

Verbal

Using words:

$P(t)$ is "the population of the world at time t"

Relation of population P and time t

Algebraic

Using a formula:

$$A(r) = \pi r^2$$

Area of a circle

Visual

Using a graph:

Source: Calif. Dept. of Mines and Geology

Vertical acceleration during an earthquake

Numerical

Using a table of values:

w (ounces)	$C(w)$ (dollars)
$0 < w \le 1$	0.37
$1 < w \le 2$	0.60
$2 < w \le 3$	0.83
$3 < w \le 4$	1.06
$4 < w \le 5$	1.29
$\vdots$	$\vdots$

Cost of mailing a first-class letter

1.3   EXERCISES

1–4 ■ Express the rule in function notation. [For example, the rule "square, then subtract 5" is expressed as the function $f(x) = x^2 - 5$.]

1. Multiply by 7, then add 2

2. Add 14, then divide by 7

3. Subtract 4, then square

4. Square, add 9, then take the square root

5–8 ■ Express the function (or rule) in words.

5. $f(x) = \dfrac{x}{2} + 7$

6. $g(x) = \dfrac{x + 7}{2}$

7. $h(x) = 3x^2 - 2$

8. $k(x) = \sqrt{3x - 2}$

9–10 ■ Draw a machine diagram for the function.

9. $f(x) = \sqrt{x}$

10. $f(x) = \dfrac{2}{x}$

11–12 ■ Complete the table.

11. $f(x) = 2x^2 + 1$ **12.** $g(x) = |2x - 3|$

x	$f(x)$
-1	
0	
1	
2	
3	

x	$g(x)$
-2	
0	
1	
3	
5	

13–20 ■ Evaluate the function at the indicated values.

13. $f(x) = 2x + 1$;

$f(1), f(-2), f\left(\frac{1}{2}\right), f(a), f(-a), f(a + b)$

14. $f(x) = x^2 + 2x$;

$f(0), f(3), f(-3), f(a), f(-x), f\left(\frac{1}{a}\right)$

15. $g(x) = \dfrac{1 - x}{1 + x}$;

$g(2), g(-2), g\left(\frac{1}{2}\right), g(a), g(a - 1), g(-1)$

16. $h(t) = t + \dfrac{1}{t}$;

$h(1), h(-1), h(2), h\left(\frac{1}{2}\right), h(x), h\left(\frac{1}{x}\right)$

17. $f(x) = 2x^2 + 3x - 4$;

$f(0), f(2), f(-2), f(\sqrt{2}), f(x + 1), f(-x)$

18. $f(x) = x^3 - 4x^2$;

$f(0), f(1), f(-1), f\left(\frac{3}{2}\right), f\left(\frac{x}{2}\right), f(x^2)$

19. $f(x) = 2|x - 1|$;

$f(-2), f(0), f\left(\frac{1}{2}\right), f(2), f(x + 1), f(x^2 + 2)$

20. $f(x) = \dfrac{|x|}{x}$;

$f(-2), f(-1), f(0), f(5), f(x^2), f\left(\frac{1}{x}\right)$

21–24 ■ Evaluate the piecewise defined function at the indicated values.

21. $f(x) = \begin{cases} x^2 & \text{if } x < 0 \\ x + 1 & \text{if } x \geqslant 0 \end{cases}$

$f(-2), f(-1), f(0), f(1), f(2)$

22. $f(x) = \begin{cases} 5 & \text{if } x \leqslant 2 \\ 2x - 3 & \text{if } x > 2 \end{cases}$

$f(-3), f(0), f(2), f(3), f(5)$

23. $f(x) = \begin{cases} x^2 + 2x & \text{if } x \leqslant -1 \\ x & \text{if } x > -1 \end{cases}$

$f(-4), f\left(-\frac{3}{2}\right), f(-1), f(0), f(1)$

24. $f(x) = \begin{cases} 3x & \text{if } x < 0 \\ x + 1 & \text{if } 0 \leqslant x \leqslant 2 \\ (x - 2)^2 & \text{if } x > 2 \end{cases}$

$f(-5), f(0), f(1), f(2), f(5)$

25–28 ■ Use the function to evaluate the indicated expressions and simplify.

25. $f(x) = x^2 + 1$; $f(x + 2), f(x) + f(2)$

26. $f(x) = 3x - 1$; $f(2x), 2f(x)$

27. $f(x) = x + 4$; $f(x^2), (f(x))^2$

28. $f(x) = 6x - 18$; $f\left(\dfrac{x}{3}\right), \dfrac{f(x)}{3}$

29–34 ■ Find $f(a), f(a + h)$, and $\dfrac{f(a + h) - f(a)}{h}$, where $h \neq 0$.

29. $f(x) = 3x + 2$ **30.** $f(x) = x^2 + 1$

31. $f(x) = 5$ **32.** $f(x) = \dfrac{1}{x + 1}$

33. $f(x) = 3 - 5x + 4x^2$ **34.** $f(x) = x^3$

35. The cost C in dollars of producing x yards of a certain fabric is given by the function

$$C(x) = 1500 + 3x + 0.02x^2 + 0.0001x^3$$

(a) Find $C(10)$ and $C(100)$.
(b) What do your answers in part (a) represent?
(c) Find $C(0)$. (This number represents the *fixed costs*.)

36. The surface area S of a sphere is a function of its radius r given by

$$S(r) = 4\pi r^2$$

(a) Find $S(2)$ and $S(3)$.
(b) What do your answers in part (a) represent?

37. Due to the curvature of the earth, the maximum distance D that you can see from the top of a tall building or from an airplane at height h is given by the function

$$D(h) = \sqrt{2rh + h^2}$$

where $r = 3960$ mi is the radius of the earth and D and h are measured in miles.
(a) Find $D(0.1)$ and $D(0.2)$.
(b) How far can you see from the observation deck of Toronto's CN Tower, 1135 ft above the ground?
(c) Commercial aircraft fly at an altitude of about 7 mi. How far can the pilot see?

38. A tank holds 50 gallons of water, which drains from a leak at the bottom, causing the tank to empty in 20 minutes. The tank drains faster when it is nearly full because the pressure on the leak is greater. **Torricelli's Law** gives the volume of water remaining in the tank after t minutes as

$$V(t) = 50\left(1 - \frac{t}{20}\right)^2 \qquad 0 \leq t \leq 20$$

(a) Find $V(0)$ and $V(20)$.
(b) What do your answers to part (a) represent?
(c) Make a table of values for $V(t)$ for $t = 0, 5, 10, 15, 20$.

39. As blood moves through a vein or an artery, its velocity v is greatest along the central axis and decreases as the distance r from the central axis increases (see the figure). The formula that gives v as a function of r is called the **law of laminar flow**. For an artery with a radius 0.5 cm, we have

$$v(r) = 18{,}500(0.25 - r^2) \qquad 0 \leq r \leq 0.5$$

(a) Find $v(0.1)$ and $v(0.4)$.
(b) What do your answers to part (a) tell you about the flow of blood in this artery?

(c) Make a table of values of $v(r)$ for $r = 0, 0.1, 0.2, 0.3, 0.4, 0.5$.

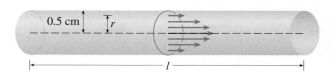

40. When the brightness x of a light source is increased, the eye reacts by decreasing the radius R of the pupil. The dependence of R on x is given by the function

$$R(x) = \sqrt{\frac{13 + 7x^{0.4}}{1 + 4x^{0.4}}}$$

(a) Find $R(1)$, $R(10)$, and $R(100)$.
(b) Make a table of values of $R(x)$.

41. In a certain country, income tax is assessed according to the following function:

$$T(x) = \begin{cases} 0 & \text{if } 0 \leq x \leq 10{,}000 \\ 0.08x & \text{if } 10{,}000 < x \leq 20{,}000 \\ 1600 + 0.15x & \text{if } 20{,}000 < x \end{cases}$$

(a) Find $T(5{,}000)$, $T(12{,}000)$, and $T(25{,}000)$.
(b) What do your answers in part (a) represent?

42. According to the theory of relativity, the length L of an object is a function of its velocity v with respect to an observer. For an object whose length at rest is 10 m, the function is given by

$$L(v) = 10\sqrt{1 - \frac{v^2}{c^2}}$$

where c is the speed of light.
(a) Find $L(0.5c)$, $L(0.75c)$, and $L(0.9c)$.
(b) How does the length of an object change as its velocity increases?

43–60 ■ Find the domain of the function.

43. $f(x) = 2x$

44. $f(x) = x^2 + 1$

45. $f(x) = 2x, \quad -1 \le x \le 5$

46. $f(x) = x^2 + 1, \quad 0 \le x \le 5$

47. $f(x) = \dfrac{1}{x - 3}$

48. $f(x) = \dfrac{1}{3x - 6}$

49. $f(x) = \dfrac{x + 2}{x^2 - 1}$

50. $f(x) = \dfrac{x^4}{x^2 + x - 6}$

51. $f(x) = \sqrt{x - 5}$

52. $f(x) = \sqrt[4]{x + 9}$

53. $f(t) = \sqrt[3]{t - 1}$

54. $g(x) = \sqrt{7 - 3x}$

55. $h(x) = \sqrt{2x - 5}$

56. $G(x) = \sqrt{x^2 - 9}$

57. $g(x) = \dfrac{\sqrt{2 + x}}{3 - x}$

58. $g(x) = \dfrac{\sqrt{x}}{2x^2 + x - 1}$

59. $g(x) = \sqrt[4]{x^2 - 6x}$

60. $g(x) = \sqrt{x^2 - 2x - 8}$

61. The graph gives the weight of a certain person as a function of age. Describe in words how this person's weight has varied over time. What do you think happened when this person was 30 years old?

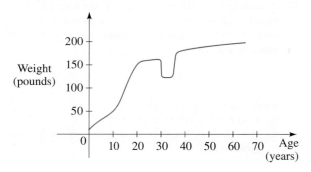

62. The graph gives a salesman's distance from his home as a function of time on a certain day. Describe in words what the graph indicates about his travels on this day.

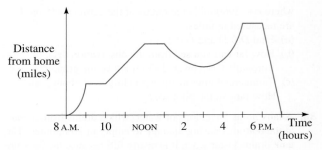

63. You put some ice cubes in a glass, fill the glass with cold water, and then let the glass sit on a table. Sketch a rough graph of the temperature of the water as a function of the elapsed time.

64. A home owner mows the lawn every Wednesday afternoon. Sketch a rough graph of the height of the grass as a function of time over the course of a four-week period beginning on a Sunday.

65. Three runners compete in a 100-meter hurdle race. The graph depicts the distance run as a function of time for each runner. Describe in words what the graph tells you about this race. Who won the race? Did each runner finish the race? What do you think happened to runner B?

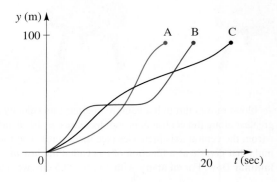

66. Sketch a rough graph of the number of hours of daylight as a function of the time of year in the Northern Hemisphere.

67. The number of Christmas cards sold by a greeting-card store depends on the time of year. Sketch a rough graph of the number of Christmas cards sold as a function of the time of year.

68. You place a frozen pie in an oven and bake it for an hour. Then you take it out and let it cool before eating it. Sketch a rough graph of the temperature of the pie as a function of time.

69. The figure shows the power consumption in San Francisco for September 19, 1996 (P is measured in megawatts; t is measured in hours starting at midnight).
   (a) What was the power consumption at 6 A.M.? At 6 P.M.?
   (b) When was the power consumption the lowest?
   (c) When was the power consumption the highest?

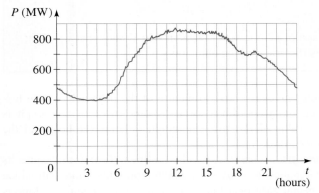

Source: Pacific Gas & Electric

70. The graph shows the vertical acceleration of the ground from the 1994 Northridge earthquake in Los Angeles, as measured by a seismograph. (Here t represents the time in seconds.)
   (a) At what time t did the earthquake first make noticeable movements of the earth?
   (b) At what time t did the earthquake seem to end?
   (c) At what time t was the maximum intensity of the earthquake reached?

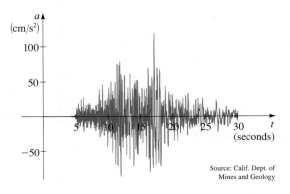

Source: Calif. Dept. of Mines and Geology

71. Temperature readings T (in °F) were recorded every 2 hours from midnight to noon in Atlanta, Georgia, on March 18, 1996. The time t was measured in hours from midnight. Sketch a rough graph of T as a function of t.

t	T
0	58
2	57
4	53
6	50
8	51
10	57
12	61

72. The population P (in thousands) of San Jose, California, from 1984 to 1994 is shown in the table. (Midyear estimates are given.) Draw a rough graph of P as a function of time t.

t	P
1984	695
1986	716
1988	733
1990	782
1992	800
1994	817

⬤ **DISCOVERY · DISCUSSION**

73. Examples of Functions   At the beginning of this section we discussed three examples of everyday, ordinary functions: Height is a function of age, temperature is a function of date, and postage cost is a function of weight. Give three other examples of functions from everyday life.

74. Four Ways to Represent a Function   In the table on page 41 we represented four different functions verbally, algebraically, visually, and numerically. Think of a function that can be represented all four ways, and write the four representations.

1.4 GRAPHS OF FUNCTIONS

The most important way to visualize a function is through its graph. In this section we investigate in more detail the concept of graphing a function.

Graphing Functions

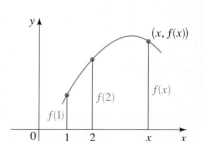

FIGURE 1
The graph of f

The height of the graph above the point x is the value of $f(x)$.

> **THE GRAPH OF A FUNCTION**
>
> If f is a function with domain A, then the **graph** of f is the set of ordered pairs
>
> $$\{(x, f(x)) \mid x \in A\}$$
>
> In other words, the graph of f is the set of all points (x, y) such that $y = f(x)$; that is, the graph of f is the graph of the equation $y = f(x)$.

The graph of a function f gives us a useful picture of the behavior or "life history" of a function. Since the y-coordinate of any point (x, y) on the graph is $y = f(x)$, we can read the value of $f(x)$ from the graph as being the height of the graph above the point x (see Figure 1).

A function f of the form $f(x) = mx + b$ is called a **linear function** because its graph is the graph of the equation $y = mx + b$, which represents a line with slope m and y-intercept b. A special case of a linear function occurs when the slope is $m = 0$. The function $f(x) = b$, where b is a given number, is called a **constant function** because all its values are the same number, namely, b. Its graph is the horizontal line $y = b$. Figure 2 shows the graphs of the constant function $f(x) = 3$ and the linear function $f(x) = 2x + 1$.

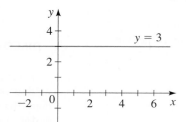

The constant function $f(x) = 3$

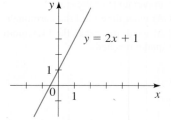

The linear function $f(x) = 2x + 1$

FIGURE 2

EXAMPLE 1 ■ Graphing Functions

Sketch the graphs of the following functions.

(a) $f(x) = x^2$ (b) $g(x) = x^3$ (c) $h(x) = \sqrt{x}$

SOLUTION

We first make a table of values. Then we plot the points given by the table and join them by a smooth curve to obtain the graph. The graphs are sketched in Figure 3.

x	$f(x) = x^2$
0	0
$\pm\frac{1}{2}$	$\frac{1}{4}$
± 1	1
± 2	4
± 3	9

x	$g(x) = x^3$
0	0
$\frac{1}{2}$	$\frac{1}{8}$
1	1
2	8
$-\frac{1}{2}$	$-\frac{1}{8}$
-1	-1
-2	-8

x	$h(x) = \sqrt{x}$
0	0
1	1
2	$\sqrt{2}$
3	$\sqrt{3}$
4	2
5	$\sqrt{5}$

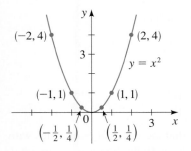

(a) $f(x) = x^2$

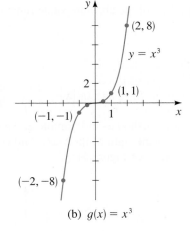

(b) $g(x) = x^3$

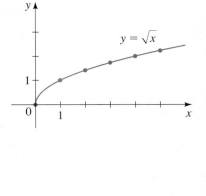

(c) $h(x) = \sqrt{x}$

FIGURE 3

EXAMPLE 2 ■ Graph of a Piecewise Defined Function

Sketch the graph of the function

$$f(x) = \begin{cases} x^2 & \text{if } x \le 1 \\ 2x + 1 & \text{if } x > 1 \end{cases}$$

SOLUTION

If $x \le 1$, then $f(x) = x^2$, so the part of the graph to the left of $x = 1$ coincides with the graph of $y = x^2$, which we sketched in Figure 3. If $x > 1$, then $f(x) = 2x + 1$,

On many graphing calculators the graph in Figure 4 can be produced by using the logical functions in the calculator. For example, on the TI-83 the following equation gives the required graph:

$$y = (x \leq 1)x\text{^}2 + (x > 1)(2x + 1)$$

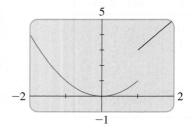

so the part of the graph to the right of $x = 1$ coincides with the line $y = 2x + 1$, which we graphed in Figure 2. This enables us to sketch the graph in Figure 4.

The solid dot at $(1, 1)$ indicates that this point is included in the graph; the open dot at $(1, 3)$ indicates that this point is excluded from the graph.

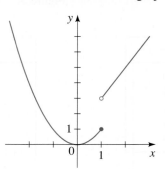

FIGURE 4

$$f(x) = \begin{cases} x^2 & \text{if } x \leq 1 \\ 2x + 1 & \text{if } x > 1 \end{cases}$$

EXAMPLE 3 ■ Graph of the Absolute Value Function

Sketch the graph of the absolute value function $f(x) = |x|$.

SOLUTION

Recall that

$$|x| = \begin{cases} x & \text{if } x \geq 0 \\ -x & \text{if } x < 0 \end{cases}$$

Using the same method as in Example 2, we note that the graph of f coincides with the line $y = x$ to the right of the y-axis and coincides with the line $y = -x$ to the left of the y-axis (see Figure 5).

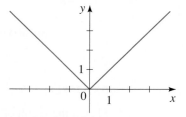

FIGURE 5

Graph of $f(x) = |x|$

To understand how the equation of a function relates to its graph, it's helpful to graph a **family of functions**, that is, a collection of functions whose equations are related. Usually, the equations differ only in a single constant called a *parameter*. In the next example, we graph a family of **power functions** $f(x) = x^n$, when n is a positive integer. In this case, n is the parameter.

EXAMPLE 4 ■ A Family of Power Functions

(a) Graph the functions $f(x) = x^n$ for $n = 2, 4$, and 6 in the viewing rectangle $[-2, 2]$ by $[-1, 3]$.

(b) Graph the functions $f(x) = x^n$ for $n = 1, 3$, and 5 in the viewing rectangle $[-2, 2]$ by $[-2, 2]$.

(c) What conclusions can you draw from these graphs?

SOLUTION

The graphs for parts (a) and (b) are shown in Figure 6.

(c) We see that the general shape of the graph of $f(x) = x^n$ depends on whether n is even or odd.

If n is even, the graph of $f(x) = x^n$ is similar to the parabola $y = x^2$.

If n is odd, the graph of $f(x) = x^n$ is similar to that of $y = x^3$.

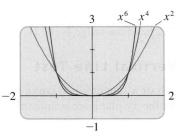

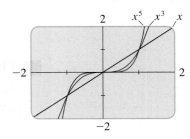

FIGURE 6
A family of power functions $f(x) = x^n$

(a) Even powers of x

(b) Odd powers of x

Notice from part (c) that as n increases the graph of $y = x^n$ becomes flatter near 0 and steeper when $x > 1$. When $0 < x < 1$, the lower powers of x are the "bigger" functions. But when $x > 1$, the higher powers of x are the dominant functions.

■ Finding Domain and Range from the Graph

The graph of a function helps us picture the domain and range of the function on the x-axis and y-axis as shown in Figure 7.

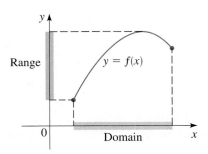

FIGURE 7
Domain and range of f

EXAMPLE 5 ■ Finding the Domain and Range from a Graph

(a) Sketch the graph of $f(x) = \sqrt{4 - x^2}$.

(b) Find the domain and range of f.

SOLUTION

(a) We must graph the equation $y = \sqrt{4 - x^2}$. Because we are taking the positive square root, we know that $y \geq 0$. Squaring each side of the equation, we get

$$y^2 = 4 - x^2 \qquad \text{Square both sides}$$

$$x^2 + y^2 = 4 \qquad \text{Add } x^2$$

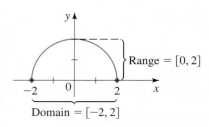

Range = $[0, 2]$

Domain = $[-2, 2]$

FIGURE 8
Graph of $f(x) = \sqrt{4 - x^2}$

which we recognize as the equation of a circle with center the origin and radius 2. But, since $y \geq 0$, the graph of f consists of just the upper half of this circle. See Figure 8.

(b) From the graph in Figure 8 we see that the domain is the closed interval $[-2, 2]$ and the range is $[0, 2]$. ∎

▋ The Vertical Line Test

The graph of a function is a curve in the xy-plane. But the question arises: Which curves in the xy-plane are graphs of functions? This is answered by the following test.

THE VERTICAL LINE TEST

A curve in the coordinate plane is the graph of a function if and only if no vertical line intersects the curve more than once.

We can see from Figure 9 why the Vertical Line Test is true. If each vertical line $x = a$ intersects a curve only once at (a, b), then exactly one functional value is defined by $f(a) = b$. But if a line $x = a$ intersects the curve twice, at (a, b) and at (a, c), then the curve can't represent a function because a function cannot assign two different values to a.

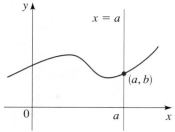

Graph of a function

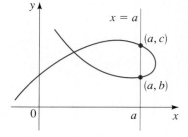

Not a graph of a function

FIGURE 9
Vertical Line Test

EXAMPLE 6 ▪ Using the Vertical Line Test

Using the Vertical Line Test, we see that the curves in parts (b) and (c) of Figure 10 represent functions, whereas those in parts (a) and (d) do not.

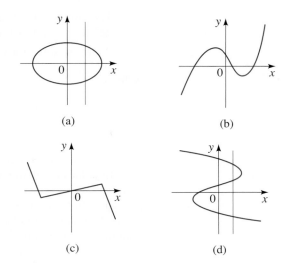

FIGURE 10   (c)   (d)

Equations That Define Functions

Any equation in the variables x and y defines a relationship between these variables. For example, the equation

$$y - x^2 = 0$$

defines a relationship between y and x. Does this equation define y as a *function* of x? To find out, we solve for y and get

$$y = x^2$$

We see that the equation defines a rule, or function, that gives one value of y for each value of x. We can express this rule in function notation as

$$f(x) = x^2$$

But not every equation defines y as a function of x, as the following example shows.

EXAMPLE 7 ■ Equations That Define Functions

Does the equation define y as a function of x?

(a) $y - x^2 = 2$ (b) $x^2 + y^2 = 4$

SOLUTION

(a) Solving for y in terms of x gives

$$y - x^2 = 2$$
$$y = x^2 + 2 \qquad \text{Add } x^2$$

Donald Knuth was born in Milwaukee in 1938 and is now Professor of Computer Science at Stanford University. While still a graduate student at Caltech, he started writing a monumental series of books entitled *The Art of Computer Programming*. President Carter awarded him the National Medal of Science in 1979. When Knuth was a high school student, he became fascinated with graphs of functions and laboriously drew many hundreds of them because he wanted to see the behavior of a great variety of functions. (Now, of course, it is far easier to use computers and graphing calculators to do this.) Knuth is also famous for his invention of T$_E$X, a system of computer-assisted typesetting. This system was used in the preparation of the manuscript for this textbook. He has also written a novel entitled *Surreal Numbers: How Two Ex-Students Turned On to Pure Mathematics and Found Total Happiness*.

The last equation is a rule that gives one value of y for each value of x, so it defines y as a function of x. We can write the function as $f(x) = x^2 + 2$.

(b) We try to solve for y in terms of x:

$$x^2 + y^2 = 4$$

$$y^2 = 4 - x^2 \qquad \text{Subtract } x^2$$

$$y = \pm \sqrt{4 - x^2} \qquad \text{Take square roots}$$

The last equation gives two values of y for a given value of x. Thus, the equation does not define y as a function of x.   ∎

The graphs of the equations in Example 7 are shown in Figure 11. The Vertical Line Test shows graphically that the equation in Example 7(a) defines a function but the equation in Example 7(b) does not.

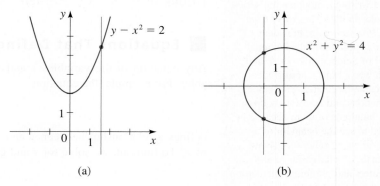

FIGURE 11

(a)   (b)

Increasing and Decreasing Functions

It is very useful to know where the graph of a function rises and where it falls. The graph shown in Figure 12 rises, falls, then rises again as we move from left to right: It rises from A to B, falls from B to C, and rises again from C to D. The function f is said to be *increasing* when its graph rises and *decreasing* when its graph falls. We have the following definition.

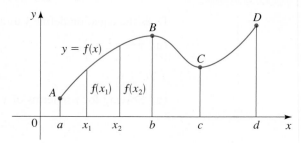

FIGURE 12

DEFINITION OF INCREASING AND DECREASING FUNCTIONS

Definition	What the graph looks like
f is **increasing** on an interval I if $f(x_1) < f(x_2)$ whenever $x_1 < x_2$ in I	
f is **decreasing** on an interval I if $f(x_1) > f(x_2)$ whenever $x_1 < x_2$ in I	

EXAMPLE 8 ■ Intervals on which a Function Increases or Decreases

State the intervals on which the function whose graph is shown in Figure 13 is increasing or decreasing.

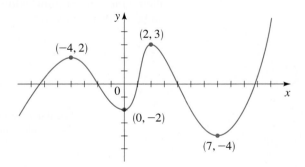

FIGURE 13

SOLUTION

The function is increasing on $(-\infty, -4]$, $[0, 2]$, and $[7, \infty)$. It is decreasing on $[-4, 0]$ and $[2, 7]$. ■

EXAMPLE 9 ■ **Using a Graph to Find Intervals where a Function Increases and Decreases**

Some graphing calculators, such as the TI-82 do not evaluate $x^{2/3}$ [entered as $x\char`^(2/3)$] for negative $x$. To graph a function like $f(x) = x^{2/3}$, we enter it as $y_1 = (x\char`^(1/3))\char`^2$ because these calculators correctly evaluate powers of the form $x\char`^(1/n)$. Newer calculators, such as the TI-83 and TI-86, do not have this problem.

(a) Sketch the graph of the function $f(x) = x^{2/3}$.

(b) Find the domain and range of the function.

(c) Find the intervals on which f increases and decreases.

SOLUTION

(a) We use a graphing calculator to sketch the graph in Figure 14.

(b) From the graph we observe that the domain of f is $\mathbb{R}$ and the range is $[0, \infty)$.

(c) From the graph we see that f is decreasing on $(-\infty, 0]$ and increasing on $[0, \infty)$.

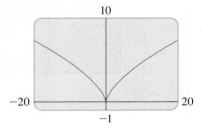

FIGURE 14

Graph of $f(x) = x^{2/3}$

■

 Local Maximum and Minimum Values of a Function

If there is a viewing rectangle such that the point $(a, f(a))$ is the highest point on the graph of f *within* the viewing rectangle (not on the edge), then the number $f(a)$ is called a **local maximum value** of f (see Figure 15). Notice that $f(a) \geqslant f(x)$ for all numbers x that are close to a.

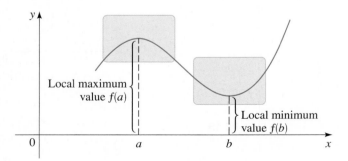

FIGURE 15

Similarly, if there is a viewing rectangle such that the point $(b, f(b))$ is the lowest point on the graph of f within the viewing rectangle, then the number $f(b)$ is called a **local minimum value** of f. In this case, $f(b) \leqslant f(x)$ for all numbers x that are close to b.

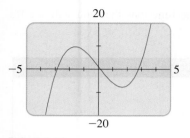

FIGURE 16
Graph of $f(x) = x^3 - 8x + 1$

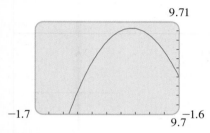

FIGURE 17

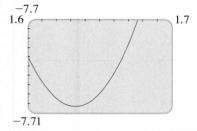

FIGURE 18

EXAMPLE 10 ■ Finding Local Maxima and Minima from a Graph

Find the local maximum and minimum values of the function $f(x) = x^3 - 8x + 1$, correct to three decimals.

SOLUTION

The graph of f is shown in Figure 16. There appears to be one local maximum between $x = -2$ and $x = -1$, and one local minimum between $x = 1$ and $x = 2$.

Let's find the coordinates of the local maximum point first. We zoom in to enlarge the area near this point, as shown in Figure 17. Using the ⟨ TRACE ⟩ feature on the graphing device, we move the cursor along the curve and observe how the y-coordinates change. The local maximum value of y is 9.709, and this value occurs when x is -1.633, correct to three decimals.

We locate the minimum value in a similar fashion. By zooming in to the viewing rectangle shown in Figure 18, we find that the local minimum value is -7.709, and this value occurs when $x \approx 1.633$. ■

The **maximum** and **minimum** commands on a TI-82 or TI-83 calculator provide another method for finding extreme values of functions. We use this method in the next example.

EXAMPLE 11 ■ A Model for the Food Price Index

A model for the food price index (the price of a representative "basket" of foods) between 1990 and 2000 is given by the function

$$I(t) = -0.0113t^3 + 0.0681t^2 + 0.198t + 99.1$$

where t is measured in years since midyear 1990, so $0 \leq t \leq 10$, and $I(t)$ is scaled so that $I(3) = 100$. Estimate the time when food was most expensive during the period 1990–2000.

SOLUTION

The graph of I as a function of t is shown in Figure 19(a). There appears to be a maximum between $t = 4$ and $t = 7$. Using the **maximum** command, as shown in Figure 19(b), we see that the maximum value of I is about 100.38, and it occurs when $t \approx 5.15$, which corresponds to August 1995.

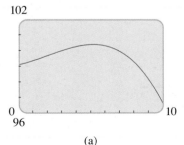

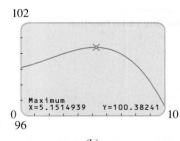

FIGURE 19   (a)   (b)   ■

The following table shows the graphs of some functions that you will see frequently in this book.

SOME FUNCTIONS AND THEIR GRAPHS

Linear functions
$f(x) = mx + b$

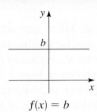

$f(x) = b$

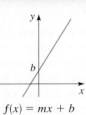

$f(x) = mx + b$

Power functions
$f(x) = x^n$

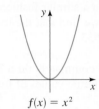

$f(x) = x^2$

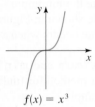

$f(x) = x^3$

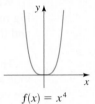

$f(x) = x^4$

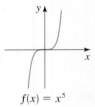

$f(x) = x^5$

Root functions
$f(x) = \sqrt[n]{x}$

$f(x) = \sqrt{x}$

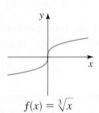

$f(x) = \sqrt[3]{x}$

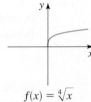

$f(x) = \sqrt[4]{x}$

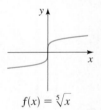

$f(x) = \sqrt[5]{x}$

Reciprocal functions
$f(x) = 1/x^n$

$f(x) = \dfrac{1}{x}$

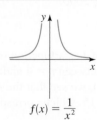

$f(x) = \dfrac{1}{x^2}$

Absolute value function
$f(x) = |x|$

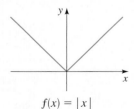

$f(x) = |x|$

1.4 EXERCISES

1. The graph of a function h is given.
   (a) State the values of $h(-2)$, $h(0)$, $h(2)$, and $h(3)$.
   (b) State the domain and range of h.

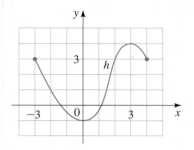

2. The graph of a function g is given.
   (a) State the values of $g(-4)$, $g(-2)$, $g(0)$, $g(2)$, and $g(4)$.
   (b) State the domain and range of g.

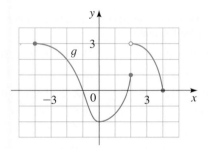

3. Graphs of the functions f and g are given.
   (a) Which is larger, $f(0)$ or $g(0)$?
   (b) Which is larger, $f(-3)$ or $g(-3)$?
   (c) For which values of x is $f(x) = g(x)$?

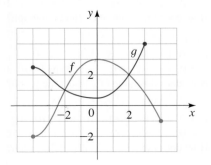

4. The graph of a function f is given.
   (a) Estimate $f(0.5)$ to the nearest tenth.
   (b) Estimate $f(3)$ to the nearest tenth.
   (c) Find all the numbers x in the domain of f so that
       $f(x) = 1$.

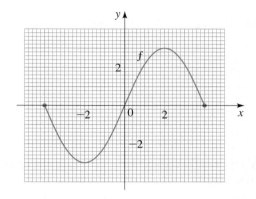

5–6 ■ Determine whether the curve is the graph of a function of x.

5. (a)

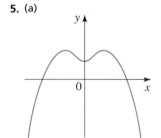

(b)

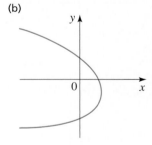

(c)

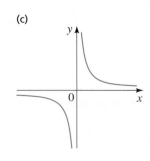

(d)

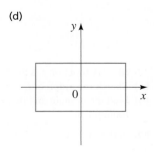

6. (a)

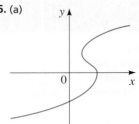

(b)

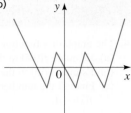

(c)

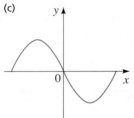

(d)

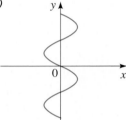

7–10 ■ Determine whether the curve is the graph of a function x. If it is, state the domain and range of the function.

7.

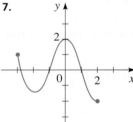

8.

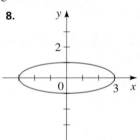

9.

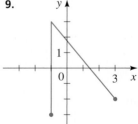

10.

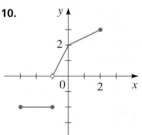

11–18 ■ A function f is given.
(a) Sketch the graph of f.
(b) Find the domain and range of f from the graph, as in Example 5.

11. $f(x) = x - 1$
12. $f(x) = 2(x + 1)$

13. $f(x) = x^2 - 4$
14. $f(x) = x^2 + 4$
15. $f(x) = \sqrt{16 - x^2}$
16. $f(x) = -\sqrt{25 - x^2}$
17. $f(x) = \sqrt{x - 2}$
18. $f(x) = \sqrt{x + 2}$

19–34 ■ Sketch the graph of the function by first making a table of values, as in Example 1.

19. $f(x) = 3$
20. $f(x) = -5$
21. $f(x) = 2x + 3$
22. $f(x) = 6 - 3x$
23. $f(x) = -x^2$
24. $g(x) = x^3 - 8$
25. $g(x) = \sqrt{-x}$
26. $g(x) = \sqrt{x + 4}$
27. $F(x) = \dfrac{1}{x}$
28. $F(x) = \dfrac{1}{x + 4}$
29. $H(x) = |2x|$
30. $H(x) = |x + 1|$
31. $G(x) = |x| + x$
32. $G(x) = |x| - x$
33. $f(x) = |2x - 2|$
34. $f(x) = \dfrac{x}{|x|}$

35–42 ■ Determine whether the equation defines y as a function of x. (See Example 7.)

35. $x^2 + 2y = 4$
36. $3x + 7y = 21$
37. $x + y^2 = 9$
38. $x^2 y + y = 1$
39. $\sqrt{x} + y = 12$
40. $2|x| + y = 0$
41. $x = y^3$
42. $x = y^4$

 43–48 ■ A family of functions is given. In parts (a) and (b) graph all the given members of the family in the viewing rectangle indicated. In part (c) state the conclusions you can make from your graphs.

43. $f(x) = x^2 + c$
   (a) $c = 0, 2, 4, 6$; $[-5, 5]$ by $[-10, 10]$
   (b) $c = 0, -2, -4, -6$; $[-5, 5]$ by $[-10, 10]$
   (c) How does the value of c affect the graph?

44. $f(x) = (x - c)^2$
   (a) $c = 0, 1, 2, 3$; $[-5, 5]$ by $[-10, 10]$
   (b) $c = 0, -1, -2, -3$; $[-5, 5]$ by $[-10, 10]$
   (c) How does the value of c affect the graph?

45. $f(x) = (x - c)^3$
   (a) $c = 0, 2, 4, 6$; $[-10, 10]$ by $[-10, 10]$
   (b) $c = 0, -2, -4, -6$; $[-10, 10]$ by $[-10, 10]$
   (c) How does the value of c affect the graph?

46. $f(x) = cx^2$
   (a) $c = 1, \frac{1}{2}, 2, 4;$ $[-5, 5]$ by $[-10, 10]$
   (b) $c = 1, -1, -\frac{1}{2}, -2;$ $[-5, 5]$ by $[-10, 10]$
   (c) How does the value of c affect the graph?

47. $f(x) = x^c$
   (a) $c = \frac{1}{2}, \frac{1}{4}, \frac{1}{6};$ $[-1, 4]$ by $[-1, 3]$
   (b) $c = 1, \frac{1}{3}, \frac{1}{5};$ $[-3, 3]$ by $[-2, 2]$
   (c) How does the value of c affect the graph?

48. $f(x) = 1/x^n$
   (a) $n = 1, 3;$ $[-3, 3]$ by $[-3, 3]$
   (b) $n = 2, 4;$ $[-3, 3]$ by $[-3, 3]$
   (c) How does the value of n affect the graph?

49–58 ■ Sketch the graph of the piecewise defined function.

49. $f(x) = \begin{cases} 0 & \text{if } x < 2 \\ 1 & \text{if } x \geq 2 \end{cases}$

50. $f(x) = \begin{cases} 1 & \text{if } x \leq 1 \\ x + 1 & \text{if } x > 1 \end{cases}$

51. $f(x) = \begin{cases} 3 & \text{if } x < 2 \\ x - 1 & \text{if } x \geq 2 \end{cases}$

52. $f(x) = \begin{cases} 1 - x & \text{if } x < -2 \\ 5 & \text{if } x \geq -2 \end{cases}$

53. $f(x) = \begin{cases} x & \text{if } x \leq 0 \\ x + 1 & \text{if } x > 0 \end{cases}$

54. $f(x) = \begin{cases} 2x + 3 & \text{if } x < -1 \\ 3 - x & \text{if } x \geq -1 \end{cases}$

55. $f(x) = \begin{cases} -1 & \text{if } x < -1 \\ 1 & \text{if } -1 \leq x \leq 1 \\ -1 & \text{if } x > 1 \end{cases}$

56. $f(x) = \begin{cases} -1 & \text{if } x < -1 \\ x & \text{if } -1 \leq x \leq 1 \\ 1 & \text{if } x > 1 \end{cases}$

57. $f(x) = \begin{cases} 2 & \text{if } x \leq -1 \\ x^2 & \text{if } x > -1 \end{cases}$

58. $f(x) = \begin{cases} 1 - x^2 & \text{if } x \leq 2 \\ x & \text{if } x > 2 \end{cases}$

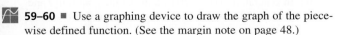 **59–60** ■ Use a graphing device to draw the graph of the piece-wise defined function. (See the margin note on page 48.)

59. $f(x) = \begin{cases} x + 2 & \text{if } x \leq -1 \\ x^2 & \text{if } x > -1 \end{cases}$

60. $f(x) = \begin{cases} 2x - x^2 & \text{if } x > 2 \\ (x - 1)^3 & \text{if } x \leq 2 \end{cases}$

61–64 ■ The graph of a function is given. Determine the intervals on which the function is increasing and on which it is decreasing.

61.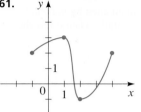

62.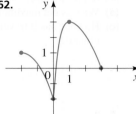

63.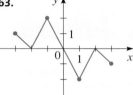

64.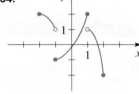

65–72 ■ A function f is given.
   (a) Use a graphing device to draw the graph of f.
   (b) State approximately the intervals on which f is increasing and on which f is decreasing.

65. $f(x) = x^{2/5}$ **66.** $f(x) = 4 - x^{2/3}$

67. $f(x) = x^2 - 5x$ **68.** $f(x) = x^3 - 4x$

69. $f(x) = 2x^3 - 3x^2 - 12x$

70. $f(x) = x^4 - 16x^2$

71. $f(x) = x^3 + 2x^2 - x - 2$

72. $f(x) = x^4 - 4x^3 + 2x^2 + 4x - 3$

73–82 ■ Find the local maximum and minimum values of the function and the value of x at which each occurs. State each answer correct to two decimal places.

73. $f(x) = x^2 + 1.79x - 3.21$

74. $f(x) = 1 + x - \sqrt{2}\,x^2$

75. $f(x) = x^3 - x$ **76.** $f(x) = 3 + x + x^2 - x^3$

77. $g(x) = x^4 - 2x^3 - 11x^2$ **78.** $g(x) = x^5 - 8x^3 + 20x$

79. $U(x) = x\sqrt{6 - x}$ **80.** $U(x) = x\sqrt{x - x^2}$

81. $V(x) = \dfrac{1 - x^2}{x^3}$ **82.** $V(x) = \dfrac{1}{x^2 + x + 1}$

83. A ball is thrown across a playing field. Its path is given by the equation $y = -0.005x^2 + x + 5$, where x is the distance the ball has traveled horizontally, and y is its height above ground level, both measured in feet.
   (a) What is the maximum height attained by the ball?
   (b) How far has it traveled horizontally when it hits the ground?

 84. When a certain drug is taken orally, the concentration of the drug in the patient's bloodstream after t minutes is given by $C(t) = 0.06t - 0.0002t^2$, where $0 \le t \le 240$ and the concentration is measured in mg/L. When is the maximum serum concentration reached, and what is that maximum concentration?

85. The number of apples produced by each tree in an apple orchard depends on how densely the trees are planted. If n trees are planted on an acre of land, then each tree produces $900 - 9n$ apples. So the number of apples produced per acre is

$$A(n) = n(900 - 9n)$$

How many trees should be planted per acre in order to obtain the maximum yield of apples?

86. A highway engineer wants to estimate the maximum number of cars that can safely travel a particular highway at a given speed. She assumes that each car is 17 ft long, travels at a speed s, and follows the car in front of it at the "safe following distance" for that speed. She finds that the num-

ber N of cars that can pass a given point per minute is modeled by the function

$$N(s) = \frac{88s}{17 + 17\left(\dfrac{s}{20}\right)^2}$$

At what speed can the greatest number of cars travel the highway safely?

 87. A fish swims at a speed v relative to the water, against a current of 5 mi/h. Using a mathematical model of energy expenditure, it can be shown that the total energy E required to swim a distance of 10 mi is given by

$$E(v) = 2.73v^3 \frac{10}{v - 5}$$

Biologists believe that migrating fish try to minimize the total energy required to swim a fixed distance. Find the value of v that minimizes energy required.

   NOTE This result has been verified; migrating fish swim against a current at a speed 50% greater than the speed of the current.

 DISCOVERY · DISCUSSION

88. When Does a Graph Represent a Function?   For every integer n, the graph of the equation $y = x^n$ is the graph of a function, namely $f(x) = x^n$. Explain why the graph of $x = y^2$ is *not* the graph of a function of x. Is the graph of $x = y^3$ the graph of a function of x? If so, of what function of x is it the graph? Determine for what integers n the graph of $x = y^n$ is the graph of a function of x.

 89. Graph of the Absolute Value of a Function
   (a) Draw the graphs of the functions $f(x) = x^2 + x - 6$ and $g(x) = |x^2 + x - 6|$. How are the graphs of f and g related?

   (b) Draw the graphs of the functions $f(x) = x^4 - 6x^2$ and $g(x) = |x^4 - 6x^2|$. How are the graphs of f and g related?

   (c) In general, if $g(x) = |f(x)|$, how are the graphs of f and g related? Draw graphs to illustrate your answer.

90. Maxima and Minima   In Example 11 we saw a real-world situation in which the maximum value of a function is important. Name several other everyday situations in which a maximum or minimum value is important.

1.5 TRANSFORMATIONS OF FUNCTIONS

In this section we study how certain transformations of a function affect its graph. This will give us a better understanding of how to graph functions. The transformations we study are shifting, reflecting, and stretching.

■ Vertical Shifting

Adding a constant to a function shifts its graph vertically: upward if the constant is positive and downward if it is negative.

EXAMPLE 1 ■ Vertical Shifts of Graphs

Sketch the graph of each function.

(a) $f(x) = x^2 + 3$ 　　　　　　　　　　 (b) $g(x) = x^2 - 2$

SOLUTION

Recall that the graph of the function f is the same as the graph of the equation $y = f(x)$. It is often convenient to express a function in equation form, particularly when discussing its graph. For instance, we may refer to the function $f(x) = x^2$ by the equation $y = x^2$, as we do in Example 1.

(a) We start with the graph of the function

$$y = x^2$$

(from Example 1(a) in Section 1.4). The equation

$$y = x^2 + 3$$

indicates that the y-coordinate of a point on the graph of f is 3 more than the y-coordinate of the corresponding point on the graph of $y = x^2$. This means that we obtain the graph of $f(x) = x^2 + 3$ simply by shifting the graph of $y = x^2$ upward 3 units, as shown in Figure 1.

(b) Similarly, we get the graph of $g(x) = x^2 - 2$ by shifting the parabola $y = x^2$ downward 2 units (see Figure 1). ■

In general, suppose we know the graph of $y = f(x)$. How do we obtain from it the graphs of

$$y = f(x) + c \qquad \text{and} \qquad y = f(x) - c \qquad (c > 0)$$

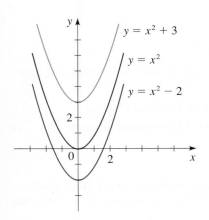

FIGURE 1

The equation $y = f(x) + c$ tells us that the y-coordinate of each point on its graph is c units above the y-coordinate of the corresponding point on the graph of $y = f(x)$. So, we obtain the graph of $y = f(x) + c$ simply by shifting the graph of $y = f(x)$ upward c units. Similarly, we obtain the graph of $y = f(x) - c$ by shifting the graph of $y = f(x)$ downward c units.

We summarize these observations in the following box.

VERTICAL SHIFTS OF GRAPHS

Equation	How to obtain the graph	What the graph looks like
$y = f(x) + c$ $(c > 0)$	Shift graph of $y = f(x)$ upward c units	
$y = f(x) - c$ $(c > 0)$	Shift graph of $y = f(x)$ downward c units	

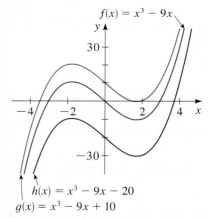

FIGURE 2

EXAMPLE 2 ■ Vertical Shifts of Graphs

Sketch the graph of each function.

(a) $f(x) = x^3 - 9x$

(b) $g(x) = x^3 - 9x + 10$

(c) $h(x) = x^3 - 9x - 20$

SOLUTION

The graphs of f, g, and h are sketched in Figure 2.

(a) The graph of f was sketched in Example 11 in Section 1.1. It is sketched again in Figure 2.

(b) To obtain the graph of g, we shift the graph of f upward 10 units.

(c) To obtain the graph of h, we shift the graph of f downward 20 units.   ■

Horizontal Shifting

Now let's consider transformations of functions that shift the graph horizontally.

Suppose we know the graph of $y = f(x)$. How do we use it to obtain the graphs of

$$y = f(x + c) \quad \text{and} \quad y = f(x - c) \quad (c > 0)$$

The value of $f(x - c)$ at x is the same as the value of $f(x)$ at $x - c$. Since $x - c$ is c units to the left of x, it follows that the graph of $y = f(x - c)$ is just the graph of

$y = f(x)$ shifted to the right c units. Similar reasoning shows that the graph of $y = f(x + c)$ is the graph of $y = f(x)$ shifted to the left c units. The following box summarizes these facts.

HORIZONTAL SHIFTS OF GRAPHS

Equation	How to obtain the graph	What the graph looks like
$y = f(x - c)$ $(c > 0)$	Shift graph of $y = f(x)$ to the right c units	
$y = f(x + c)$ $(c > 0)$	Shift graph of $y = f(x)$ to the left c units	

EXAMPLE 3 ■ Horizontal Shifts of Graphs

Sketch the graph of each function.

(a) $f(x) = (x + 4)^2$ (b) $g(x) = (x - 2)^2$

SOLUTION

We start with the graph of $y = x^2$, then move it to the left 4 units to get the graph of f and to the right 2 units to obtain the graph of g. See Figure 3.

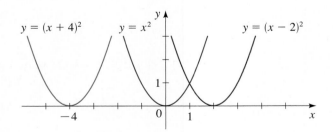

FIGURE 3

EXAMPLE 4 ■ Combining Horizontal and Vertical Shifts

Sketch the graph of the function $f(x) = \sqrt{x - 3} + 4$.

SOLUTION

We start with the graph of the square root function $y = \sqrt{x}$ (Example 1(c) in Section 1.4). We move it to the right 3 units to get the graph of $y = \sqrt{x - 3}$. Then we move the resulting graph upward 4 units to obtain the graph of $f(x) = \sqrt{x - 3} + 4$ shown in Figure 4.

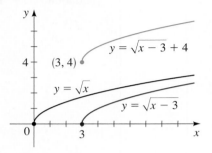

FIGURE 4

Reflecting

Suppose we know the graph of $y = f(x)$. How do we use it to obtain the graphs of $y = -f(x)$ and $y = f(-x)$? The y-coordinate of each point on the graph of $y = -f(x)$ is simply the negative of the y-coordinate of the corresponding point on the graph of $y = f(x)$. So the desired graph is the reflection of the graph of $y = f(x)$ in the x-axis. On the other hand, the value of $y = f(-x)$ at x is the same as the value of $y = f(x)$ at $-x$ and so the desired graph here is the reflection of the graph of $y = f(x)$ in the y-axis. The following box summarizes these observations.

REFLECTING GRAPHS

Equation	How to obtain the graph	What the graph looks like
$y = -f(x)$	Reflect the graph of $y = f(x)$ in the x-axis	
$y = f(-x)$	Reflect the graph of $y = f(x)$ in the y-axis	

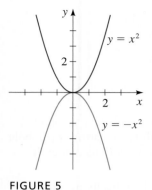

FIGURE 5

EXAMPLE 5 ■ Reflecting Graphs

Sketch the graph of each function.

(a) $f(x) = -x^2$

(b) $g(x) = \sqrt{-x}$

SOLUTION

(a) We start with the graph of $y = x^2$. The graph of $f(x) = -x^2$ is the graph of $y = x^2$ reflected in the x-axis (see Figure 5).

(b) We start with the graph of $y = \sqrt{x}$ (Example 1(c) in Section 1.4). The graph of $g(x) = \sqrt{-x}$ is the graph of $y = \sqrt{x}$ reflected in the y-axis (see Figure 6). Note that the domain of the function $g(x) = \sqrt{-x}$ is $\{x \mid x \leq 0\}$.

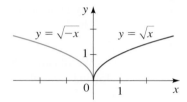

FIGURE 6

■

Vertical Stretching and Shrinking

Suppose we know the graph of $y = f(x)$. How do we use it to obtain the graph of $y = af(x)$? The y-coordinate of $y = af(x)$ at x is the same as the corresponding y-coordinate of $y = f(x)$ multiplied by a. Multiplying the y-coordinates by a has the effect of vertically stretching or shrinking the graph by a factor of a.

VERTICAL STRETCHING AND SHRINKING OF GRAPHS

Equation	How to obtain the graph	What the graph looks like
$y = af(x)$ $(a > 1)$	Stretch the graph of $y = f(x)$ vertically by a factor of a	
$y = af(x)$ $(0 < a < 1)$	Shrink the graph of $y = f(x)$ vertically by a factor of a	

EXAMPLE 6 ■ Vertical Stretching and Shrinking of Graphs

Sketch the graph of each function.

(a) $f(x) = 3x^2$ (b) $g(x) = \frac{1}{3}x^2$

SOLUTION

(a) We start with the graph of $y = x^2$. The graph of $f(x) = 3x^2$ is the graph of $y = x^2$ stretched vertically by a factor of 3. The result is the narrower parabola in Figure 7. The graph is obtained by multiplying the y-coordinate of each point on the graph of $y = x^2$ by 3.

(b) The graph of $g(x) = \frac{1}{3}x^2$ is the graph of $y = x^2$ shrunk vertically by a factor of $\frac{1}{3}$. The result is the wider parabola in Figure 7. The graph is obtained by multiplying the y-coordinate of each point on the graph of $y = x^2$ by $\frac{1}{3}$.   ■

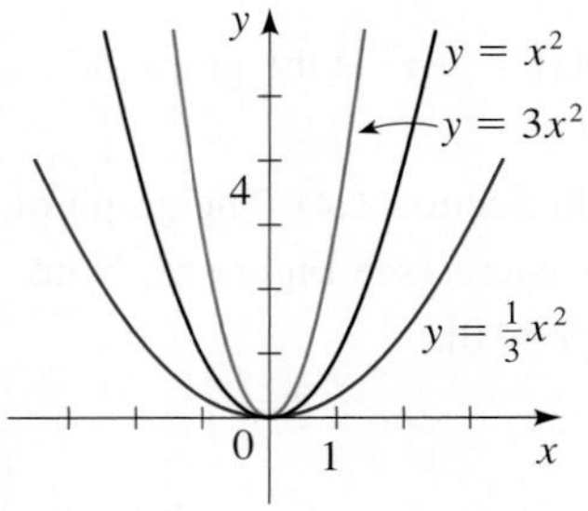

FIGURE 7

We illustrate the effect of combining shifts, reflections, and stretching in the following example.

EXAMPLE 7 ■ Combining Shifting, Stretching, and Reflecting

Sketch the graph of the function $f(x) = 1 - 2(x - 3)^2$.

SOLUTION

Starting with the graph of $y = x^2$, we first shift to the right 3 units to get the graph of $y = (x - 3)^2$. Then we reflect in the x-axis and stretch by a factor of 2 to get the graph of $y = -2(x - 3)^2$. Finally, we shift upward 1 unit to get the graph of $f(x) = 1 - 2(x - 3)^2$ shown in Figure 8.

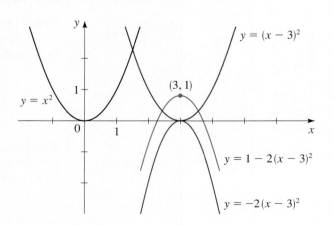

FIGURE 8   ■

■ Horizontal Stretching and Shrinking

Now we consider horizontal shrinking and stretching of graphs. If we know the graph of $y = f(x)$, then how is the graph of $y = f(ax)$ related to it? The y-coordinate of $y = f(ax)$ at x is the same as the y-coordinate of $y = f(x)$ at ax. Thus, the x-coordinates in the graph of $y = f(x)$ correspond to the x-coordinates in the graph of $y = f(ax)$ multiplied by a. Looking at this the other way around, we see that the x-coordinates in the graph of $y = f(ax)$ are the x-coordinates in the graph of $y = f(x)$ multiplied by $1/a$. In other words, to change the graph of $y = f(x)$ to the graph of $y = f(ax)$, we must shrink (or stretch) the graph horizontally by a factor of $1/a$, as summarized in the following box.

Sonya Kovalevsky (1850–1891) is considered the most important woman mathematician of the 19th century. She was born in Moscow to an aristocratic family. While a child, she was exposed to the principles of calculus in a very unusual fashion—her bedroom was temporarily wallpapered with the pages of a calculus book. She later wrote that she "spent many hours in front of that wall, trying to understand it." Since Russian law forbade women from studying in universities, she entered a marriage of convenience, which allowed her to travel to Germany and obtain a doctorate in mathematics from the University of Göttingen. She eventually was awarded a full professorship at the University of Stockholm, where she taught for eight years before dying in an influenza epidemic at the age of 41. Her research was instrumental in helping put the ideas and applications of functions and calculus on a sound and logical foundation. She received many accolades and prizes for her research work.

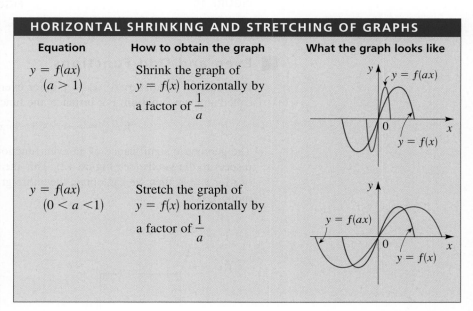

HORIZONTAL SHRINKING AND STRETCHING OF GRAPHS		
Equation	**How to obtain the graph**	**What the graph looks like**
$y = f(ax)$ $(a > 1)$	Shrink the graph of $y = f(x)$ horizontally by a factor of $\dfrac{1}{a}$	
$y = f(ax)$ $(0 < a < 1)$	Stretch the graph of $y = f(x)$ horizontally by a factor of $\dfrac{1}{a}$	

EXAMPLE 8 ■ Horizontal Stretching and Shrinking of Graphs

The graph of $y = f(x)$ is shown in Figure 9. Sketch the graph of each function.

(a) $y = f(2x)$ (b) $y = f\left(\tfrac{1}{2}x\right)$

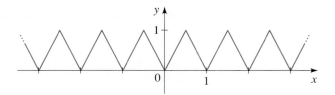

FIGURE 9
$y = f(x)$

SOLUTION

Using the principles described in the preceding box, we obtain the graphs shown in Figures 10 and 11.

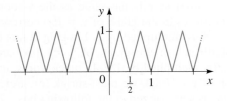

FIGURE 10
$y = f(2x)$

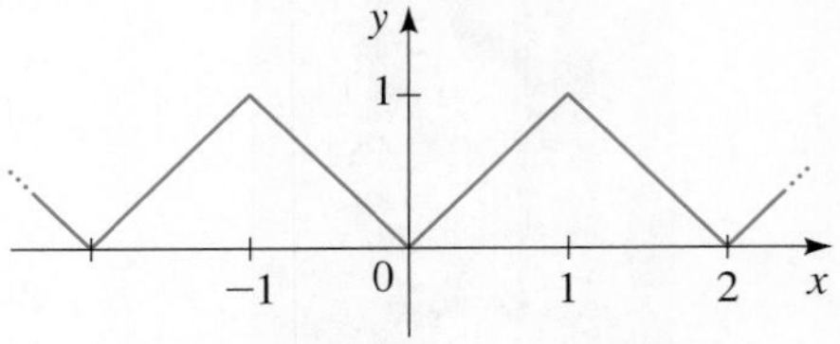

FIGURE 11
$y = f\left(\frac{1}{2}x\right)$

Even and Odd Functions

If a function f satisfies $f(-x) = f(x)$ for every number x in its domain, then f is called an **even function**. For instance, the function $f(x) = x^2$ is even because

$$f(-x) = (-x)^2 = (-1)^2 x^2 = x^2 = f(x)$$

The geometric significance of an even function is that its graph is symmetric with respect to the y-axis (see Figure 12). This means that if we have plotted the graph of f for $x \geq 0$, then we can obtain the entire graph simply by reflecting this portion in the y-axis.

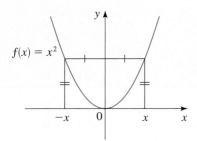

FIGURE 12
$f(x) = x^2$ is an even function.

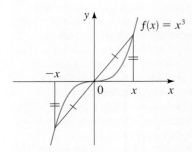

FIGURE 13
$f(x) = x^3$ is an odd function.

If f satisfies $f(-x) = -f(x)$ for every number x in its domain, then f is called an **odd function**. For example, the function $f(x) = x^3$ is odd because

$$f(-x) = (-x)^3 = (-1)^3 x^3 = -x^3 = -f(x)$$

The graph of an odd function is symmetric about the origin (see Figure 13). If we have plotted the graph of f for $x \geq 0$, then we can obtain the entire graph by rotating this portion through $180°$ about the origin. (This is equivalent to reflecting first in the x-axis and then in the y-axis.)

EVEN AND ODD FUNCTIONS

Definition	Symmetry of graph of f	What the graph looks like
f is **even** if $$f(-x) = f(x)$$ for all x in the domain of f	Graph of f is symmetric with respect to the y-axis	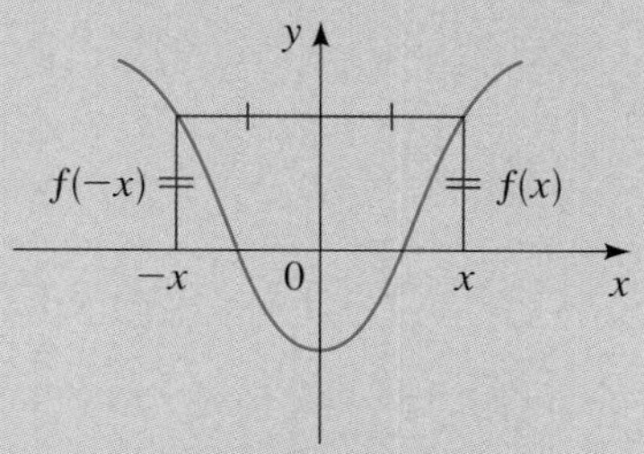
f is **odd** if $$f(-x) = -f(x)$$ for all x in the domain of f	Graph of f is symmetric with respect to the origin	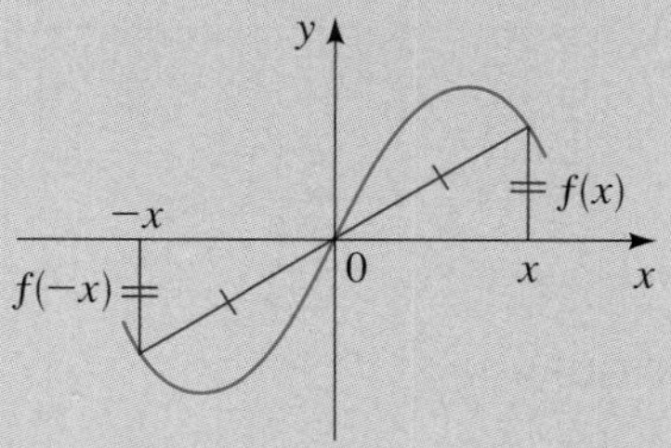

EXAMPLE 9 ■ Even and Odd Functions

Determine whether the functions are even, odd, or neither even nor odd.

(a) $f(x) = x^5 + x$

(b) $g(x) = 1 - x^4$

(c) $h(x) = 2x - x^2$

SOLUTION

(a) $f(-x) = (-x)^5 + (-x)$

$\qquad\qquad = -x^5 - x = -(x^5 + x)$

$\qquad\qquad = -f(x)$

Therefore, f is an odd function.

(b) $g(-x) = 1 - (-x)^4 = 1 - x^4 = g(x)$

So g is even.

(c) $h(-x) = 2(-x) - (-x)^2 = -2x - x^2$

Since $h(-x) \neq h(x)$ and $h(-x) \neq -h(x)$, we conclude that h is neither even nor odd.   ■

The graphs of the functions in Example 9 are shown in Figure 14. The graph of f is symmetric about the origin, and the graph of g is symmetric about the y-axis. The graph of h is not symmetric either about the y-axis or the origin.

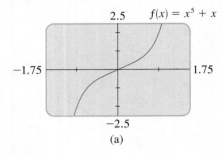

(a)

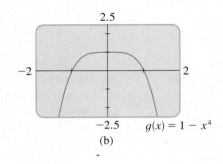

(b)

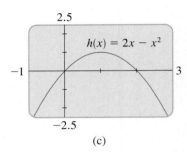

(c)

FIGURE 14

1.5 EXERCISES

1–10 ■ Suppose the graph of f is given. Describe how the graph of each function can be obtained from the graph of f.

1. (a) $y = f(x) - 3$ (b) $y = f(x - 3)$

2. (a) $y = f(x + 4)$ (b) $y = f(x) + 4$

3. (a) $y = 3f(x)$ (b) $y = \frac{1}{3}f(x)$

4. (a) $y = -f(x)$ (b) $y = f(-x)$

5. (a) $y = -2f(x)$ (b) $y = -\frac{1}{2}f(x)$

6. (a) $y = -f(x) + 5$ (b) $y = 3f(x) - 5$

7. (a) $y = f(x - 4) + \frac{3}{4}$ (b) $y = f(x + 4) - \frac{3}{4}$

8. (a) $y = 2f(x + 2) - 2$ (b) $y = 2f(x - 2) + 2$

9. (a) $y = f(4x)$ (b) $y = f(\frac{1}{4}x)$

10. (a) $y = -f(2x)$ (b) $y = f(2x) - 1$

11. The graph of f is given. Sketch the graphs of the following functions.

(a) $y = f(x - 2)$

(b) $y = f(x) - 2$

(c) $y = 2f(x)$

(d) $y = -f(x) + 3$

(e) $y = f(-x)$

(f) $y = \frac{1}{2}f(x - 1)$

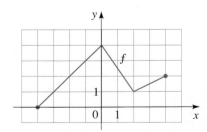

12. The graph of $y = f(x)$ is given. Match each equation with its graph.

(a) $y = f(x - 4)$
(b) $y = f(x) + 3$
(c) $y = \frac{1}{3}f(x)$
(d) $y = -f(x + 4)$
(e) $y = 2f(x + 6)$

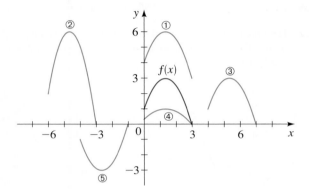

13. (a) Sketch the graph of $f(x) = \dfrac{1}{x}$ by plotting points.

(b) Use the graph of f to sketch the graphs of the following functions.

(i) $y = -\dfrac{1}{x}$ (ii) $y = \dfrac{1}{x - 1}$

(iii) $y = \dfrac{2}{x + 2}$ (iv) $y = 1 + \dfrac{1}{x - 3}$

14. (a) Sketch the graph of $g(x) = \sqrt[3]{x}$ by plotting points.

(b) Use the graph of g to sketch the graphs of the following functions.

(i) $y = \sqrt[3]{x} - 2$ (ii) $y = \sqrt[3]{x + 2} + 2$
(iii) $y = 1 - \sqrt[3]{x}$

15–18 ■ Explain how the graph of g is obtained from the graph of f.

15. (a) $f(x) = x^2$, $g(x) = (x + 2)^2$
(b) $f(x) = x^2$, $g(x) = x^2 + 2$

16. (a) $f(x) = x^3$, $g(x) = (x - 4)^3$
(b) $f(x) = x^3$, $g(x) = x^3 - 4$

17. (a) $f(x) = \sqrt{x}$, $g(x) = 2\sqrt{x}$
(b) $f(x) = \sqrt{x}$, $g(x) = \frac{1}{2}\sqrt{x - 2}$

18. (a) $f(x) = |x|$, $g(x) = 3|x| + 1$
(b) $f(x) = |x|$, $g(x) = -|x + 1|$

19–24 ■ A function f is given, and the indicated transformations are applied to its graph (in the given order). Write the equation for the final transformed graph.

19. $f(x) = x^2$; shift upward 3 units and shift 2 units to the right

20. $f(x) = x^3$; shift downward 1 unit and shift 4 units to the left

21. $f(x) = \sqrt{x}$; shift 3 units to the left, stretch vertically by a factor of 5, and reflect in the x-axis

22. $f(x) = \sqrt[3]{x}$; reflect in the y-axis, shrink vertically by a factor of $\frac{1}{2}$, and shift upward $\frac{3}{5}$ unit

23. $f(x) = |x|$; shift to the right $\frac{1}{2}$ unit, shrink vertically by a factor of 0.1, and shift downward 2 units

24. $f(x) = |x|$; shift to the left 1 unit, stretch vertically by a factor of 3, and shift upward 10 units

25–40 ■ Sketch the graph of the function, not by plotting points, but by starting with the graph of a standard function and applying transformations.

25. $f(x) = (x - 2)^2$ **26.** $f(x) = (x + 7)^2$

27. $f(x) = -(x + 1)^2$ **28.** $f(x) = 1 - x^2$

29. $f(x) = x^3 + 2$ **30.** $f(x) = -x^3$

31. $y = 1 + \sqrt{x}$ **32.** $y = 2 - \sqrt{x + 1}$

33. $y = \frac{1}{2}\sqrt{x + 4} - 3$ **34.** $y = 3 - 2(x - 1)^2$

35. $y = 5 + (x + 3)^2$ **36.** $y = \frac{1}{3}x^3 - 1$

37. $y = |x| - 1$ **38.** $y = |x - 1|$

39. $y = |x + 2| + 2$ **40.** $y = 2 - |x|$

41–44 ■ Graph the functions on the same screen using the given viewing rectangle. How is each graph related to the graph in part (a)?

41. Viewing rectangle $[-8, 8]$ by $[-2, 8]$
(a) $y = \sqrt[4]{x}$ (b) $y = \sqrt[4]{x + 5}$
(c) $y = 2\sqrt[4]{x + 5}$ (d) $y = 4 + 2\sqrt[4]{x + 5}$

42. Viewing rectangle $[-8, 8]$ by $[-6, 6]$
(a) $y = |x|$ (b) $y = -|x|$
(c) $y = -3|x|$ (d) $y = -3|x - 5|$

43. Viewing rectangle $[-4, 6]$ by $[-4, 4]$

   (a) $y = x^6$ (b) $y = \frac{1}{3}x^6$

   (c) $y = -\frac{1}{3}x^6$ (d) $y = -\frac{1}{3}(x - 4)^6$

44. Viewing rectangle $[-6, 6]$ by $[-4, 4]$

   (a) $y = \dfrac{1}{\sqrt{x}}$ (b) $y = \dfrac{1}{\sqrt{x + 3}}$

   (c) $y = \dfrac{1}{2\sqrt{x + 3}}$ (d) $y = \dfrac{1}{2\sqrt{x + 3}} - 3$

45. The graph of g is given. Use it to graph each of the following functions.

   (a) $y = g(2x)$ (b) $y = g\left(\frac{1}{2}x\right)$

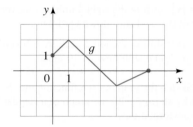

46. The graph of h is given. Use it to graph each of the following functions.

   (a) $y = h(3x)$ (b) $y = h\left(\frac{1}{3}x\right)$

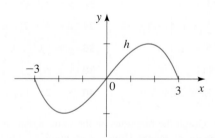

47. If $f(x) = \sqrt{2x - x^2}$, graph the following functions in the viewing rectangle $[-5, 5]$ by $[-4, 4]$. How is each graph related to the graph in part (a)?

   (a) $y = f(x)$ (b) $y = f(2x)$ (c) $y = f\left(\frac{1}{2}x\right)$

48. If $f(x) = \sqrt{2x - x^2}$, graph the following functions in the viewing rectangle $[-5, 5]$ by $[-4, 4]$. How is each graph related to the graph in part (a)?

   (a) $y = f(x)$ (b) $y = f(-x)$ (c) $y = -f(-x)$

   (d) $y = f(-2x)$ (e) $y = f\left(-\frac{1}{2}x\right)$

49–56 ■ Determine whether the function f is even, odd, or neither. If f is even or odd, use symmetry to sketch its graph.

49. $f(x) = x^{-2}$ **50.** $f(x) = x^{-3}$

51. $f(x) = x^2 + x$ **52.** $f(x) = x^4 - 4x^2$

53. $f(x) = x^3 - x$ **54.** $f(x) = 3x^3 + 2x^2 + 1$

55. $f(x) = 1 - \sqrt[3]{x}$ **56.** $f(x) = x + \dfrac{1}{x}$

57. The graphs of $f(x) = x^2 - 4$ and $g(x) = |x^2 - 4|$ are shown. Explain how the graph of g is obtained from the graph of f.

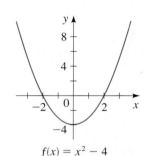

$f(x) = x^2 - 4$

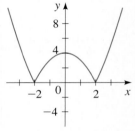

$g(x) = |x^2 - 4|$

58. The graph of $f(x) = x^4 - 4x^2$ is shown. Use this graph to sketch the graph of $g(x) = |x^4 - 4x^2|$.

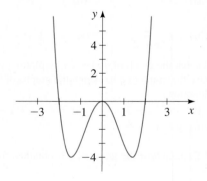

59–60 ■ Sketch the graph of each function.

59. (a) $f(x) = 4x - x^2$ (b) $g(x) = |4x - x^2|$

60. (a) $f(x) = x^3$ (b) $g(x) = |x^3|$

 DISCOVERY · DISCUSSION

61. Sums of Even and Odd Functions If f and g are both even functions, is $f + g$ necessarily even? If both are odd, is their sum necessarily odd? What can you say about the sum if one is odd and one is even? In each case, prove your answer.

62. **Products of Even and Odd Functions**   Answer the same questions as in Exercise 61, except this time consider the *product* of f and g instead of the sum.

63. **Even and Odd Power Functions**   What must be true about the integer n if the function

$$f(x) = x^n$$

is an even function? If it is an odd function? Why do you think the names "even" and "odd" were chosen for these function properties?

1.6   COMBINING FUNCTIONS

Two functions f and g can be combined to form new functions $f + g$, $f - g$, fg, and f/g in a manner similar to the way we add, subtract, multiply, and divide real numbers. For example, we define the function $f + g$ by

$$(f + g)(x) = f(x) + g(x)$$

The sum of f and g is defined by
$$(f + g)(x) = f(x) + g(x)$$
The name of the new function is "$f + g$." So this $+$ sign stands for the operation of addition of *functions*. The $+$ sign on the right side, however, stands for addition of the *numbers* $f(x)$ and $g(x)$.

The new function $f + g$ is called the **sum** of the functions f and g; its value at x is $f(x) + g(x)$. Of course, the sum on the right-hand side makes sense only if both $f(x)$ and $g(x)$ are defined, that is, if x belongs to the domain of f and also to the domain of g. So, if the domain of f is A and the domain of g is B, then the domain of $f + g$ is the intersection of these domains, that is, $A \cap B$. Similarly, we can define the **difference** $f - g$, the **product** fg, and the **quotient** f/g of the functions f and g. Their domains are $A \cap B$, but in the case of the quotient we must remember not to divide by 0.

ALGEBRA OF FUNCTIONS

Let f and g be functions with domains A and B. Then the functions $f + g$, $f - g$, fg, and f/g are defined as follows.

$$(f + g)(x) = f(x) + g(x) \qquad \text{Domain } A \cap B$$

$$(f - g)(x) = f(x) - g(x) \qquad \text{Domain } A \cap B$$

$$(fg)(x) = f(x)g(x) \qquad \text{Domain } A \cap B$$

$$\left(\frac{f}{g}\right)(x) = \frac{f(x)}{g(x)} \qquad \text{Domain } \{x \in A \cap B \mid g(x) \neq 0\}$$

EXAMPLE 1 ■ Combining Functions

Let $f(x) = x^3$ and $g(x) = \sqrt{x}$.

(a) Find the functions $f + g$, $f - g$, fg, and f/g and their domains.
(b) Find $(f + g)(4)$, $(f - g)(4)$, $(fg)(3)$, and $(f/g)(1)$.

SOLUTION

(a) The domain of f is $\mathbb{R}$ and the domain of g is $\{x \mid x \geq 0\}$. We have

$$(f + g)(x) = f(x) + g(x) = x^3 + \sqrt{x} \qquad \text{Domain } \{x \mid x \geq 0\}$$

$$(f - g)(x) = f(x) - g(x) = x^3 - \sqrt{x} \qquad \text{Domain } \{x \mid x \geq 0\}$$

$$(fg)(x) = f(x)g(x) = x^3 \sqrt{x} \qquad \text{Domain } \{x \mid x \geq 0\}$$

$$\left(\frac{f}{g}\right)(x) = \frac{f(x)}{g(x)} = \frac{x^3}{\sqrt{x}} \qquad \text{Domain } \{x \mid x > 0\}$$

Note that in the domain of f/g we exclude 0 because $g(0) = 0$.

(b) $(f + g)(4) = f(4) + g(4) = 4^3 + \sqrt{4} = 66$

$(f - g)(4) = f(4) - g(4) = 4^3 - \sqrt{4} = 62$

$(fg)(3) = f(3)g(3) = 3^3 \sqrt{3} = 27\sqrt{3}$

$\left(\dfrac{f}{g}\right)(1) = \dfrac{f(1)}{g(1)} = \dfrac{1^3}{\sqrt{1}} = 1$

■

EXAMPLE 2 ■ Finding Domains of Combinations of Functions

If $f(x) = \sqrt{x}$ and $g(x) = \sqrt{4 - x^2}$, find the functions $f + g$, $f - g$, fg, and f/g and their domains.

SOLUTION

The domain of $f(x) = \sqrt{x}$ is $[0, \infty)$. The domain of $g(x) = \sqrt{4 - x^2}$ is the interval $[-2, 2]$ (from Example 5 in Section 1.4). The intersection of the domains of f and g is

$$[0, \infty) \cap [-2, 2] = [0, 2]$$

Thus, we have

$$(f + g)(x) = \sqrt{x} + \sqrt{4 - x^2} \qquad \text{Domain } \{x \mid 0 \leq x \leq 2\}$$

$$(f - g)(x) = \sqrt{x} - \sqrt{4 - x^2} \qquad \text{Domain } \{x \mid 0 \leq x \leq 2\}$$

$$(fg)(x) = \sqrt{x}\sqrt{4 - x^2} = \sqrt{4x - x^3} \qquad \text{Domain } \{x \mid 0 \leq x \leq 2\}$$

$$\left(\frac{f}{g}\right)(x) = \frac{\sqrt{x}}{\sqrt{4 - x^2}} = \sqrt{\frac{x}{4 - x^2}} \qquad \text{Domain } \{x \mid 0 \leq x < 2\}$$

Notice that the domain of f/g is the interval $[0, 2)$ because we must exclude the points where $g(x) = 0$, that is, $x = \pm 2$.

■

The graph of the function $f + g$ can be obtained from the graphs of f and g by **graphical addition**. This means that we add corresponding y-coordinates, as illustrated in the next example.

EXAMPLE 3 ■ Using Graphical Addition

The graphs of f and g are shown in Figure 1. Use graphical addition to graph the function $f + g$.

SOLUTION

In Figure 2 we obtain the graph of $f + g$ by "graphically adding" the value of $f(x)$ to $g(x)$. This is implemented by copying the line segment PQ on top of PR to obtain the point S on the graph of $f + g$.

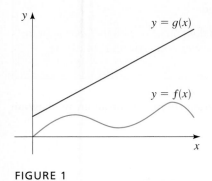

FIGURE 1

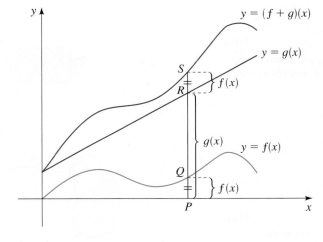

FIGURE 2
Graphical addition

Composition of Functions

Now let's consider a very important way of combining two functions to get a new function. Suppose $f(x) = \sqrt{x}$ and $g(x) = x^2 + 1$. We may define a function h as

$$h(x) = f(g(x)) = f(x^2 + 1) = \sqrt{x^2 + 1}$$

The function h is made up of the functions f and g in an interesting way: Given a number x, we first apply to it the function g, then apply f to the result. In this case, f is the rule "take the square root," g is the rule "square, then add 1," and h is the rule "square, then add 1, then take the square root." In other words, we get the rule h by applying the rule g and then the rule f.

In general, given any two functions f and g, we start with a number x in the domain of g and find its image $g(x)$. If this number $g(x)$ is in the domain of f, we can then calculate the value of $f(g(x))$. The result is a new function $h(x) = f(g(x))$ obtained by substituting g into f. It is called the *composition* (or *composite*) of f and g and is denoted by $f \circ g$ ("f composed with g").

COMPOSITION OF FUNCTIONS

Given two functions f and g, the **composite function** $f \circ g$ (also called the **composition** of f and g) is defined by

$$(f \circ g)(x) = f(g(x))$$

The domain of $f \circ g$ is the set of all x in the domain of g such that $g(x)$ is in the domain of f. Thus, $(f \circ g)(x)$ is defined whenever both $g(x)$ and $f(g(x))$ are defined.

We can picture $f \circ g$ using a machine diagram (Figure 3) or an arrow diagram (Figure 4).

FIGURE 3

The $f \circ g$ machine is composed of the g machine (first) and then the f machine.

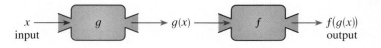

FIGURE 4

Arrow diagram for $f \circ g$

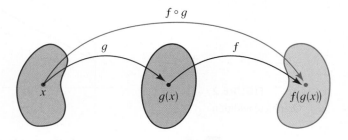

EXAMPLE 4 ■ Finding the Composition of Functions

Let $f(x) = x^2$ and $g(x) = x - 3$.

(a) Find the functions $f \circ g$ and $g \circ f$ and their domains.
(b) Find $(f \circ g)(5)$ and $(g \circ f)(7)$.

SOLUTION

In Example 4, f is the rule "square" and g is the rule "subtract 3." The function $f \circ g$ *first* subtracts 3 and *then* squares; the function $g \circ f$ *first* squares and *then* subtracts 3.

(a) We have

$$\begin{aligned}
(f \circ g)(x) &= f(g(x)) & &\text{Definition of } f \circ g \\
&= f(x - 3) & &\text{Definition of } g \\
&= (x - 3)^2 & &\text{Definition of } f
\end{aligned}$$

and

$$(g \circ f)(x) = g(f(x)) \qquad \text{Definition of } g \circ f$$

$$= g(x^2) \qquad \text{Definition of } f$$

$$= x^2 - 3 \qquad \text{Definition of } g$$

The domains of both $f \circ g$ and $g \circ f$ are $\mathbb{R}$.

(b) We have

$$(f \circ g)(5) = f(g(5)) = f(2) = 2^2 = 4$$

$$(g \circ f)(7) = g(f(7)) = g(49) = 49 - 3 = 46 \qquad \blacksquare$$

You can see from Example 4 that, in general, $f \circ g \neq g \circ f$. Remember that the notation $f \circ g$ means that the function g is applied first and then f is applied second.

The graphs of f and g of Example 5, as well as $f \circ g$, $g \circ f$, $f \circ f$, and $g \circ g$, are shown below and on page 78. These graphs indicate that the operation of composition can produce functions quite different from the original functions.

EXAMPLE 5 ■ Finding the Composition of Functions

If $f(x) = \sqrt{x}$ and $g(x) = \sqrt{2 - x}$, find the following functions and their domains.

(a) $f \circ g$ (b) $g \circ f$ (c) $f \circ f$ (d) $g \circ g$

SOLUTION

(a)
$$(f \circ g)(x) = f(g(x)) \qquad \text{Definition of } f \circ g$$

$$= f\left(\sqrt{2 - x}\right) \qquad \text{Definition of } g$$

$$= \sqrt{\sqrt{2 - x}} \qquad \text{Definition of } f$$

$$= \sqrt[4]{2 - x}$$

The domain of $f \circ g$ is $\{x \mid 2 - x \geq 0\} = \{x \mid x \leq 2\} = (-\infty, 2]$.

(b)
$$(g \circ f)(x) = g(f(x)) \qquad \text{Definition of } g \circ f$$

$$= g\left(\sqrt{x}\right) \qquad \text{Definition of } f$$

$$= \sqrt{2 - \sqrt{x}} \qquad \text{Definition of } g$$

For $\sqrt{x}$ to be defined, we must have $x \geq 0$. For $\sqrt{2 - \sqrt{x}}$ to be defined, we must have $2 - \sqrt{x} \geq 0$, that is, $\sqrt{x} \leq 2$, or $x \leq 4$. Thus, we have $0 \leq x \leq 4$, so the domain of $g \circ f$ is the closed interval $[0, 4]$.

(c)
$$(f \circ f)(x) = f(f(x)) \qquad \text{Definition of } f \circ f$$

$$= f\left(\sqrt{x}\right) \qquad \text{Definition of } f$$

$$= \sqrt{\sqrt{x}} \qquad \text{Definition of } f$$

$$= \sqrt[4]{x}$$

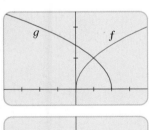

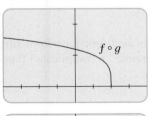

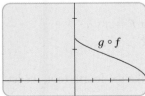

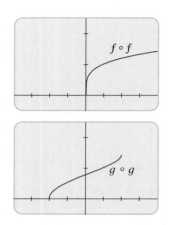

The domain of $f \circ f$ is $[0, \infty)$.

(d)
$$(g \circ g)(x) = g(g(x)) \qquad \text{Definition of } g \circ g$$

$$= g\left(\sqrt{2 - x}\right) \qquad \text{Definition of } g$$

$$= \sqrt{2 - \sqrt{2 - x}} \qquad \text{Definition of } g$$

This expression is defined when both $2 - x \geqslant 0$ and $2 - \sqrt{2 - x} \geqslant 0$. The first inequality means $x \leqslant 2$, and the second is equivalent to $\sqrt{2 - x} \leqslant 2$, or $2 - x \leqslant 4$, or $x \geqslant -2$. Thus, $-2 \leqslant x \leqslant 2$, so the domain of $g \circ g$ is $[-2, 2]$. ∎

It is possible to take the composition of three or more functions. For instance, the composite function $f \circ g \circ h$ is found by first applying h, then g, and then f as follows:

$$(f \circ g \circ h)(x) = f(g(h(x)))$$

EXAMPLE 6 ■ A Composition of Three Functions

Find $f \circ g \circ h$ if $f(x) = x/(x + 1)$, $g(x) = x^{10}$, and $h(x) = x + 3$.

SOLUTION

$$(f \circ g \circ h)(x) = f(g(h(x))) \qquad \text{Definition of } f \circ g \circ h$$

$$= f(g(x + 3)) \qquad \text{Definition of } h$$

$$= f((x + 3)^{10}) \qquad \text{Definition of } g$$

$$= \frac{(x + 3)^{10}}{(x + 3)^{10} + 1} \qquad \text{Definition of } f$$

∎

So far we have used composition to build complicated functions from simpler ones. But in calculus it is useful to be able to "decompose" a complicated function into simpler ones, as shown in the following example.

EXAMPLE 7 ■ Recognizing a Composition of Functions

Given $F(x) = \sqrt[4]{x + 9}$, find functions f and g such that $F = f \circ g$.

SOLUTION

Since the formula for F says to first add 9 and then take the fourth root, we let

$$g(x) = x + 9 \qquad \text{and} \qquad f(x) = \sqrt[4]{x}$$

Then

$$(f \circ g)(x) = f(g(x))$$

$$= f(x + 9)$$

$$= \sqrt[4]{x + 9}$$

$$= F(x) \qquad \blacksquare$$

EXAMPLE 8 ■ An Application of Composition of Functions

A ship is traveling at 20 mi/h parallel to a straight shoreline. The ship is 5 mi from shore. It passes a lighthouse at noon.

(a) Express the distance s between the lighthouse and the ship as a function of d, the distance the ship has traveled since noon; that is, find f so that $s = f(d)$.

(b) Express d as a function of t, the time elapsed since noon; that is, find g so that $d = g(t)$.

(c) Find $f \circ g$. What does this function represent?

SOLUTION

We first draw a diagram as in Figure 5.

(a) We can relate the distances s and d by the Pythagorean Theorem. Thus, s can be expressed as a function of d by

$$s = f(d) = \sqrt{25 + d^2}$$

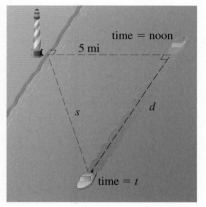

FIGURE 5

(b) Since the ship is traveling at 20 mi/h, the distance d it has traveled is a function of t as follows:

distance = rate × time

$$d = g(t) = 20t$$

(c) We have

$$(f \circ g)(t) = f(g(t)) \qquad \text{Definition of } f \circ g$$

$$= f(20t) \qquad \text{Definition of } g$$

$$= \sqrt{25 + (20t)^2} \qquad \text{Definition of } f$$

The function $f \circ g$ gives the distance of the ship from the lighthouse as a function of time. $\blacksquare$

1.6   EXERCISES

1–6 ■ Find $f + g$, $f - g$, fg, and f/g and their domains.

1. $f(x) = x^2$, $g(x) = x + 2$

2. $f(x) = x^3 + 2x^2$, $g(x) = 3x^2 - 1$

3. $f(x) = \sqrt{1 + x^2}$, $g(x) = \sqrt{1 - x}$

4. $f(x) = \sqrt{9 - x^2}$, $g(x) = \sqrt{x^2 - 1}$

5. $f(x) = \dfrac{2}{x}$, $g(x) = -\dfrac{2}{x + 4}$

6. $f(x) = \dfrac{1}{x + 1}$, $g(x) = \dfrac{x}{x + 1}$

7–10 ■ Find the domain of the function.

7. $f(x) = \sqrt{x} + \sqrt{1 - x}$

8. $g(x) = \sqrt{x + 1} - \dfrac{1}{x}$

9. $h(x) = (x + 1)^2 (2x - 8)^{1/4}$

10. $k(x) = \dfrac{\sqrt{x + 3}}{x - 1}$

11–12 ■ Use graphical addition to sketch the graph of $f + g$.

11.

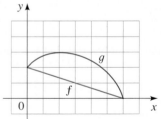

12.

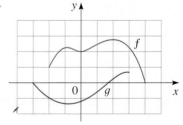

13–16 ■ Draw the graphs of f, g, and $f + g$ on a common screen to illustrate graphical addition.

13. $f(x) = \sqrt{1 + x}$, $g(x) = \sqrt{1 - x}$

14. $f(x) = x^2$, $g(x) = \sqrt{x}$

15. $f(x) = x^2$, $g(x) = x^3$

16. $f(x) = \sqrt[4]{1 - x}$, $g(x) = \sqrt{1 - \dfrac{x^2}{9}}$

17–22 ■ Use $f(x) = 3x - 5$ and $g(x) = 2 - x^2$ to evaluate the expression.

17. (a) $f(g(0))$ (b) $g(f(0))$

18. (a) $f(f(4))$ (b) $g(g(3))$

19. (a) $(f \circ g)(-2)$ (b) $(g \circ f)(-2)$

20. (a) $(f \circ f)(-1)$ (b) $(g \circ g)(2)$

21. (a) $(f \circ g)(x)$ (b) $(g \circ f)(x)$

22. (a) $(f \circ f)(x)$ (b) $(g \circ g)(x)$

23–28 ■ Use the given graphs of f and g to evaluate the expression.

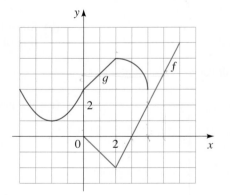

23. $f(g(2))$ **24.** $g(f(0))$

25. $(g \circ f)(4)$ **26.** $(f \circ g)(0)$

27. $(g \circ g)(-2)$

28. $(f \circ f)(4)$

29–40 ■ Find the functions $f \circ g$, $g \circ f$, $f \circ f$, and $g \circ g$ and their domains.

29. $f(x) = 2x + 3$, $\quad g(x) = 4x - 1$

30. $f(x) = 6x - 5$, $\quad g(x) = \dfrac{x}{2}$

31. $f(x) = x^2$, $\quad g(x) = x + 1$

32. $f(x) = x^3 + 2$, $\quad g(x) = \sqrt[3]{x}$

33. $f(x) = \dfrac{1}{x}$, $\quad g(x) = 2x + 4$

34. $f(x) = x^2$, $\quad g(x) = \sqrt{x - 3}$

35. $f(x) = |x|$, $\quad g(x) = 2x + 3$

36. $f(x) = x - 4$, $\quad g(x) = |x + 4|$

37. $f(x) = \dfrac{x}{x + 1}$, $\quad g(x) = 2x - 1$

38. $f(x) = \dfrac{1}{\sqrt{x}}$, $\quad g(x) = x^2 - 4x$

39. $f(x) = \sqrt[3]{x}$, $\quad g(x) = \sqrt[4]{x}$

40. $f(x) = \dfrac{2}{x}$, $\quad g(x) = \dfrac{x}{x - 2}$

41–44 ■ Find $f \circ g \circ h$.

41. $f(x) = x - 1$, $\quad g(x) = \sqrt{x}$, $\quad h(x) = x - 1$

42. $f(x) = \dfrac{1}{x}$, $\quad g(x) = x^3$, $\quad h(x) = x^2 + 2$

43. $f(x) = x^4 + 1$, $\quad g(x) = x - 5$, $\quad h(x) = \sqrt{x}$

44. $f(x) = \sqrt{x}$, $\quad g(x) = \dfrac{x}{x - 1}$, $\quad h(x) = \sqrt[3]{x}$

45–50 ■ Express the function in the form $f \circ g$.

45. $F(x) = (x - 9)^5$

46. $F(x) = \sqrt{x} + 1$

47. $G(x) = \dfrac{x^2}{x^2 + 4}$

48. $G(x) = \dfrac{1}{x + 3}$

49. $H(x) = |1 - x^3|$

50. $H(x) = \sqrt{1 + \sqrt{x}}$

51–54 ■ Express the function in the form $f \circ g \circ h$.

51. $F(x) = \dfrac{1}{x^2 + 1}$

52. $F(x) = \sqrt[3]{\sqrt{x} - 1}$

53. $G(x) = (4 + \sqrt[3]{x})^9$

54. $G(x) = \dfrac{2}{(3 + \sqrt{x})^2}$

55. A stone is dropped in a lake, creating a circular ripple that travels outward at a speed of 60 cm/s. Express the area of this circle as a function of time t (in seconds).

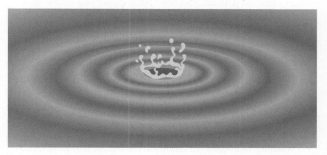

56. A spherical balloon is being inflated. The radius of the balloon is increasing at the rate of 1 cm/s.
   (a) Find a function f that models the radius as a function of time.
   (b) Find a function g that models the volume as a function of the radius.
   (c) Find $g \circ f$. What does this function represent?

57. A spherical weather balloon is being inflated. The radius of the balloon is increasing at the rate of 2 cm/s. Express the surface area of the balloon as a function of time t (in seconds).

58. You have a $50 coupon from the manufacturer good for the purchase of a cell phone. The store where you are purchasing your cell phone is offering a 20% discount on all cell phones. Let x represent the regular price of the cell phone.

(a) Suppose only the 20% discount applies. Find a function f that models the purchase price of the cell phone as a function of the regular price x.

(b) Suppose only the $50 coupon applies. Find a function g that models the purchase price of the cell phone as a function of the sticker price x.

(c) If you can use the coupon and the discount, then the purchase price is either $f \circ g(x)$ or $g \circ f(x)$, depending on the order in which they are applied to the price. Find both $f \circ g(x)$ and $g \circ f(x)$. Which composition gives the lower price?

59. An appliance dealer advertises a 10% discount on all his washing machines. In addition, the manufacturer offers a $100 rebate on the purchase of a washing machine. Let x represent the sticker price of the washing machine.

(a) Suppose only the 10% discount applies. Find a function f that models the purchase price of the washer as a function of the sticker price x.

(b) Suppose only the $100 rebate applies. Find a function g that models the purchase price of the washer as a function of the sticker price x.

(c) Find $f \circ g$ and $g \circ f$. What do these functions represent? Which is the better deal?

60. An airplane is flying at a speed of 350 mi/h at an altitude of one mile. The plane passes directly above a radar station at time $t = 0$.

(a) Express the distance s (in miles) between the plane and the radar station as a function of the horizontal distance d (in miles) that the plane has flown.

(b) Express d as a function of the time t (in hours) that the plane has flown.

(c) Use composition to express s as a function of t.

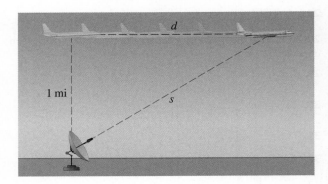

◆ DISCOVERY · DISCUSSION

61. Compound Interest   A savings account earns 5% interest compounded annually. If you invest x dollars in such an account, then the amount $A(x)$ of the investment after one year is the initial investment plus 5%; that is, $A(x) = x + 0.05x = 1.05x$. Find

$$A \circ A, \quad A \circ A \circ A \quad \text{and} \quad A \circ A \circ A \circ A$$

What do these compositions represent? Find a formula for what you get when you compose n copies of A.

62. Composing Linear Functions   The graphs of the functions

$$f(x) = m_1 x + b_1 \quad \text{and} \quad g(x) = m_2 x + b_2$$

are lines with slopes m_1 and m_2, respectively. Is the graph of $f \circ g$ a line? If so, what is its slope?

63. Solving an Equation for an Unknown Function   Suppose that

$$g(x) = 2x + 1 \quad \text{and} \quad h(x) = 4x^2 + 4x + 7$$

Find a function f such that $f \circ g = h$. (Think about what operations you would have to perform on the formula for g to end up with the formula for h.) Now suppose that

$$f(x) = 3x + 5 \quad \text{and} \quad h(x) = 3x^2 + 3x + 2$$

Use the same sort of reasoning to find a function g such that $f \circ g = h$.

64. Compositions of Odd and Even Functions   Suppose that

$$h = f \circ g$$

If g is an even function, is h necessarily even? If g is odd, is h odd? What if g is odd and f is odd? What if g is odd and f is even?

Laboratory Project

Iteration and Chaos

The **iterates** of a function f at a point x_0 are $f(x_0)$, $f(f(x_0))$, $f(f(f(x_0)))$, and so on. We write

$$x_1 = f(x_0) \qquad \text{The first iterate}$$

$$x_2 = f(f(x_0)) \qquad \text{The second iterate}$$

$$x_3 = f(f(f(x_0))) \qquad \text{The third iterate}$$

For example, if $f(x) = x^2$, then the iterates of f at 2 are $x_1 = 4$, $x_2 = 16$, $x_3 = 256$, and so on. (Check this.) Iterates can be described graphically as in Figure 1. Start with x_0 on the x-axis, move vertically to the graph of f, then horizontally to the line $y = x$, then vertically to the graph of f, and so on. The x-coordinates of the points on the graph of f are the iterates of f at x_0.

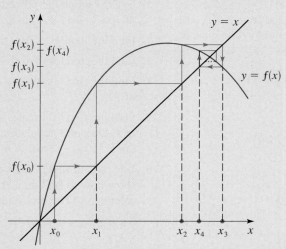

FIGURE 1

Iterates are important in studying the **logistic function**

$$f(x) = kx(1 - x)$$

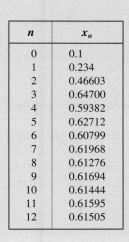

n	x_n
0	0.1
1	0.234
2	0.46603
3	0.64700
4	0.59382
5	0.62712
6	0.60799
7	0.61968
8	0.61276
9	0.61694
10	0.61444
11	0.61595
12	0.61505

which models the population of a species with limited potential for growth (such as rabbits on an island or fish in a pond). In this model the maximum population that the environment can support is 1 (that is, 100%); if we start with a fraction of that population, say 0.1 (10%), then the iterates of f at 0.1 give the population after each time interval (days, months, or years, depending on the species). The constant k depends on the rate of growth of the species being modeled; it is called the **growth constant**. For example, for $k = 2.6$ and $x_0 = 0.1$ the iterates shown in the table give the population of the species for the first 12 time intervals. The population seems to be stabilizing around 0.615 (that is, 61.5% of maximum).

In the three graphs in Figure 2 we plot the iterates of f at 0.1 for different values of the growth constant k. For $k = 2.6$ the population appears to stabilize at a value 0.615 of maximum, for $k = 3.1$ the population appears to oscillate between two values, and for $k = 3.8$ no obvious pattern emerges. This latter situation is described mathematically by the word **chaos**.

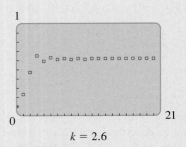

$k = 2.6$

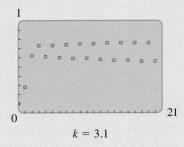

$k = 3.1$

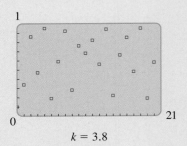

$k = 3.8$

FIGURE 2

The following TI-83 program draws the first graph in Figure 2. The other graphs are obtained by choosing the appropriate value for K in the program.

```
PROGRAM:ITERATE
: ClrDraw
: 2.6 → K
: 0.1 → X
: For(N, 1, 20)
: K*X*(1 − X) → Z
: Pt-On(N, Z, 2)
: Z → X
: End
```

1. Use the graphical procedure illustrated in Figure 1 to find the first five iterates of $f(x) = 2x(1 - x)$ at $x = 0.1$.

2. Find the iterates of $f(x) = x^2$ at $x = 1$.

3. Find the iterates of $f(x) = 1/x$ at $x = 2$.

4. Find the first six iterates of $f(x) = 1/(1 - x)$ at $x = 2$. What is 1000th iterate of f at 2?

5. Find the first 10 iterates of the logistic function at $x = 0.1$ for the given value of k. Does the population appear to stabilize, oscillate, or is it chaotic?
   (a) $k = 2.1$ (b) $k = 3.2$ (c) $k = 3.9$

6. It is easy to find iterates using a graphing calculator. The following steps show how to find the iterates of $f(x) = kx(1 - x)$ at 0.1 for $k = 3$ on a TI-85 calculator. (The procedure can be adapted for any graphing calculator.)

y1 = K * x * (1 − x)	Enter f as Y1 on the graph list
3 → K	Store 3 in the variable K
0.1 → x	Store 0.1 in the variable x
y1 → x	Evaluate f at x and store result back in x
0.27	Press ENTER and obtain first iterate
0.5913	Keep pressing ENTER to re-execute the
0.72499293	command and obtain successive iterates
0.59813454435	

You can also use the program in the margin to graph the iterates and study them visually.

Use a graphing calculator to experiment with how the value of k affects the iterates of $f(x) = kx(1 - x)$ at 0.1. Find several different values of k that make the iterates stabilize at one value, oscillate between two values, and exhibit chaos. (Use values of k between 1 and 4). Can you find a value of k that makes the iterates oscillate between *four* values?

1.7   ONE-TO-ONE FUNCTIONS AND THEIR INVERSES

Let's compare the functions f and g whose arrow diagrams are shown in Figure 1. Note that f never takes on the same value twice (any two numbers in A have different images), whereas g does take on the same value twice (both 2 and 3 have the same image, 4). In symbols, $g(2) = g(3)$ but $f(x_1) \neq f(x_2)$ whenever $x_1 \neq x_2$. Functions that have this latter property are called *one-to-one*.

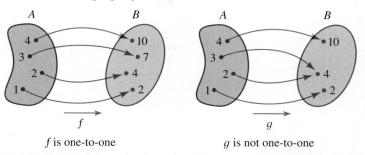

FIGURE 1

f is one-to-one g is not one-to-one

DEFINITION OF A ONE-TO-ONE FUNCTION

A function within domain A is called a **one-to-one function** if no two elements of A have the same image, that is,

$$f(x_1) \neq f(x_2) \qquad \text{whenever } x_1 \neq x_2$$

An equivalent way of writing the condition for a one-to-one function is this:

$$\text{If } f(x_1) = f(x_2), \text{ then } x_1 = x_2.$$

If a horizontal line intersects the graph of f at more than one point, then we see from Figure 2 that there are numbers $x_1 \neq x_2$ such that $f(x_1) = f(x_2)$. This means that f is not one-to-one. Therefore, we have the following geometric method for determining whether a function is one-to-one.

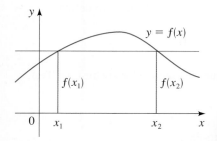

FIGURE 2
This function is not one-to-one because $f(x_1) = f(x_2)$.

HORIZONTAL LINE TEST

A function is one-to-one if and only if no horizontal line intersects its graph more than once.

EXAMPLE 1 ■ **Deciding whether a Function Is One-to-One**

Is the function $f(x) = x^3$ one-to-one?

SOLUTION 1

If $x_1 \neq x_2$, then $x_1^3 \neq x_2^3$ (two different numbers cannot have the same cube). Therefore, $f(x) = x^3$ is one-to-one.

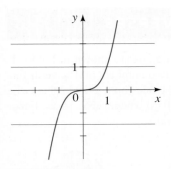

FIGURE 3
$f(x) = x^3$ is one-to-one.

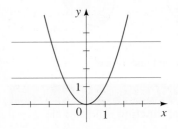

FIGURE 4
$g(x) = x^2$ is not one-to-one.

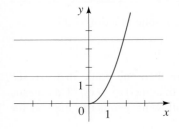

FIGURE 5
$h(x) = x^2 \ (x \geqslant 0)$ is one-to-one.

SOLUTION 2

From Figure 3 we see that no horizontal line intersects the graph of $f(x) = x^3$ more than once. Therefore, by the Horizontal Line Test, f is one-to-one. ∎

Notice that the function f of Example 1 is increasing and is also one-to-one. In fact, it can be proved that every increasing function and every decreasing function is one-to-one.

EXAMPLE 2 ■ Deciding whether a Function Is One-to-One

Is the function $g(x) = x^2$ one-to-one?

SOLUTION 1

This function is not one-to-one because, for instance,

$$g(1) = 1 = g(-1)$$

and so 1 and -1 have the same image.

SOLUTION 2

From Figure 4 we see that there are horizontal lines that intersect the graph of g more than once. Therefore, by the Horizontal Line Test, g is not one-to-one. ∎

Although the function g in Example 2 is not one-to-one, it is possible to restrict its domain so that the resulting function is one-to-one. In fact, if we define

$$h(x) = x^2, \qquad x \geqslant 0$$

then h is one-to-one, as you can see from Figure 5 and the Horizontal Line Test.

EXAMPLE 3 ■ Showing That a Function Is One-to-One

Show that the function $f(x) = 3x + 4$ is one-to-one.

SOLUTION

Suppose there are numbers x_1 and x_2 such that $f(x_1) = f(x_2)$. Then

$$3x_1 + 4 = 3x_2 + 4$$

$$3x_1 = 3x_2$$

$$x_1 = x_2$$

Therefore, f is one-to-one. ∎

■ The Inverse of a Function

One-to-one functions are important because they are precisely the functions that possess inverse functions according to the following definition.

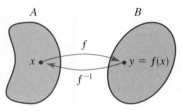

⊘ Don't mistake the -1 in f^{-1} for an exponent.

$$f^{-1} \quad does \ not \ mean \quad \frac{1}{f(x)}$$

The reciprocal $1/f(x)$ is written as $(f(x))^{-1}$.

DEFINITION OF THE INVERSE OF A FUNCTION

Let f be a one-to-one function with domain A and range B. Then its **inverse function** f^{-1} has domain B and range A and is defined by

$$f^{-1}(y) = x \quad \Leftrightarrow \quad f(x) = y$$

for any y in B.

This definition says that if f takes x into y, then f^{-1} takes y back into x. (If f were not one-to-one, then f^{-1} would not be defined uniquely.) The arrow diagram in Figure 6 indicates that f^{-1} reverses the effect of f. From the definition we have

$$\text{domain of } f^{-1} = \text{range of } f$$

$$\text{range of } f^{-1} = \text{domain of } f$$

FIGURE 6

EXAMPLE 4 ■ Finding f^{-1} for Specific Values

If $f(1) = 5$, $f(3) = 7$, and $f(8) = -10$, find $f^{-1}(5)$, $f^{-1}(7)$, and $f^{-1}(-10)$.

SOLUTION

From the definition of f^{-1} we have

$$f^{-1}(5) = 1 \qquad \text{because} \qquad f(1) = 5$$

$$f^{-1}(7) = 3 \qquad \text{because} \qquad f(3) = 7$$

$$f^{-1}(-10) = 8 \qquad \text{because} \qquad f(8) = -10$$

Figure 7 shows how f^{-1} reverses the effect of f in this case.

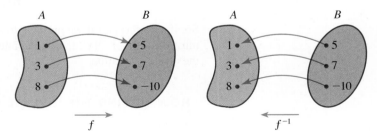

FIGURE 7

By definition the inverse function f^{-1} undoes what f does: If we start with x, apply f, and then apply f^{-1}, we arrive back at x, where we started. Similarly, f undoes what f^{-1} does. In general, any function that reverses the effect of f in this way must be the inverse of f. These observations are expressed precisely as follows.

PROPERTY OF INVERSE FUNCTIONS

Let f be a one-to-one function with domain A and range B. The inverse function f^{-1} satisfies the following cancellation properties.

$$f^{-1}(f(x)) = x \qquad \text{for every } x \text{ in } A$$

$$f(f^{-1}(x)) = x \qquad \text{for every } x \text{ in } B$$

Conversely, any function f^{-1} satisfying these equations is the inverse of f.

These properties indicate that f is the inverse function of f^{-1}, so we say that f and f^{-1} are *inverses of each other*.

EXAMPLE 5 ■ Verifying That Two Functions Are Inverses

Show that $f(x) = x^3$ and $g(x) = x^{1/3}$ are inverses of each other.

SOLUTION

Note that the domain and range of both f and g is $\mathbb{R}$. We have

$$g(f(x)) = g(x^3) = (x^3)^{1/3} = x$$

$$f(g(x)) = f(x^{1/3}) = (x^{1/3})^3 = x$$

So, by the Property of Inverse Functions, f and g are inverses of each other. These equations simply say that the cube function and the cube root function, when composed, cancel each other. ■

Now let's examine how we compute inverse functions. We first observe from the definition of f^{-1} that

$$y = f(x) \quad \Leftrightarrow \quad f^{-1}(y) = x$$

So, if $y = f(x)$ and if we are able to solve this equation for x in terms of y, then we must have $x = f^{-1}(y)$. If we then interchange x and y, we have $y = f^{-1}(x)$, which is the desired equation.

HOW TO FIND THE INVERSE OF A ONE-TO-ONE FUNCTION

1. Write $y = f(x)$.

2. Solve this equation for x in terms of y (if possible).

3. Interchange x and y. The resulting equation is $y = f^{-1}(x)$.

Note that Steps 2 and 3 can be reversed. In other words, we can interchange x and y first and then solve for y in terms of x.

In Example 6 note how f^{-1} reverses the effect of f. The function f is the rule "multiply by 3, then subtract 2," whereas f^{-1} is the rule "add 2, then divide by 3."

EXAMPLE 6 ■ Finding the Inverse of a Function

Find the inverse of the function $f(x) = 3x - 2$.

SOLUTION

First we write $y = f(x)$.

$$y = 3x - 2$$

Then we solve this equation for x:

$$3x = y + 2 \qquad \text{Add 2}$$

$$x = \frac{y + 2}{3} \qquad \text{Divide by 3}$$

Finally, we interchange x and y:

$$y = \frac{x + 2}{3}$$

Therefore, the inverse function is $f^{-1}(x) = \dfrac{x + 2}{3}$.

CHECK YOUR ANSWER
We use the Inverse Function Property.

$$f^{-1}(f(x)) = f^{-1}(3x - 2) \qquad\qquad f(f^{-1}(x)) = f\left(\frac{x + 2}{3}\right)$$

$$= \frac{(3x - 2) + 2}{3} \qquad\qquad\qquad = 3\left(\frac{x + 2}{3}\right) - 2$$

$$= \frac{3x}{3} = x \qquad\qquad\qquad\qquad = x + 2 - 2 = x \quad \checkmark$$

EXAMPLE 7 ■ Finding the Inverse of a Function

In Example 7 note how f^{-1} reverses the effect of f. The function f is the rule "take the fifth power, subtract 3, then divide by 2," whereas f^{-1} is the rule "multiply by 2, add 3, then take the fifth root."

Find the inverse of the function $f(x) = \dfrac{x^5 - 3}{2}$.

SOLUTION

We first write $y = (x^5 - 3)/2$ and solve for x.

$$y = \frac{x^5 - 3}{2} \qquad \text{Equation defining function}$$

$$2y = x^5 - 3 \qquad \text{Multiply by 2}$$

$$x^5 = 2y + 3 \qquad \text{Add 3}$$

$$x = (2y + 3)^{1/5} \qquad \text{Take fifth roots}$$

Then we interchange x and y to get $y = (2x + 3)^{1/5}$. Therefore, the inverse function is $f^{-1}(x) = (2x + 3)^{1/5}$. (We verify that this is correct in *Check Your Answer* in the margin.) ∎

The principle of interchanging x and y to find the inverse function also gives us a method for obtaining the graph of f^{-1} from the graph of f. If $f(a) = b$, then $f^{-1}(b) = a$. Thus, the point (a, b) is on the graph of f if and only if the point (b, a) is on the graph of f^{-1}. But we get the point (b, a) from the point (a, b) by reflecting in the line $y = x$ (see Figure 8).

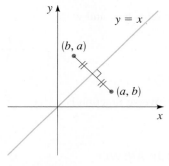

FIGURE 8

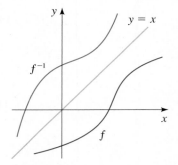

FIGURE 9

Therefore, as Figure 9 illustrates, the following is true.

> The graph of f^{-1} is obtained by reflecting the graph of f in the line $y = x$.

EXAMPLE 8 ■ Finding the Inverse of a Function

(a) Sketch the graph of $f(x) = \sqrt{x - 2}$.
(b) Use the graph of f to sketch the graph of f^{-1}.
(c) Find an equation for f^{-1}.

SOLUTION

(a) Using the transformations from Section 1.5, we sketch the graph of $y = \sqrt{x - 2}$ by plotting the graph of the function $y = \sqrt{x}$ (Example 1(c) in Section 1.4) and moving it to the right 2 units.

(b) The graph of f^{-1} is obtained from the graph of f in part (a) by reflecting it in the line $y = x$, as shown in Figure 10.

(c) Solve $y = \sqrt{x - 2}$ for x, noting that $y \geq 0$.

$$\sqrt{x - 2} = y$$

$$x - 2 = y^2 \qquad \text{Square each side}$$

$$x = y^2 + 2, \quad y \geq 0 \qquad \text{Add 2}$$

Interchange x and y:

In Example 8 note how f^{-1} reverses the effect of f. The function f is the rule "subtract 2, then take the square root"; f^{-1} is the rule "square, then add 2."

$$y = x^2 + 2, \qquad x \geq 0$$

Thus $\qquad f^{-1}(x) = x^2 + 2, \qquad x \geq 0$

This expression shows that the graph of f^{-1} is the right half of the parabola $y = x^2 + 2$ and, from the graph shown in Figure 10, this seems reasonable.

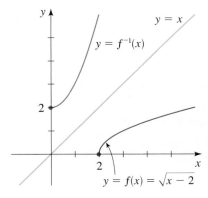

FIGURE 10

1.7 EXERCISES

1–6 ■ The graph of a function f is given. Determine whether f is one-to-one.

1.

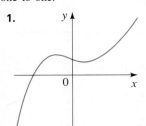

2.

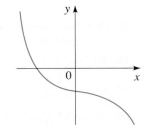

3.

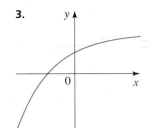

4.

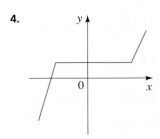

5.

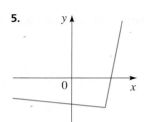

6.

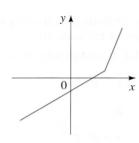

27. $f(x) = x^2 - 4, \quad x \geqslant 0;$
$g(x) = \sqrt{x + 4}, \quad x \geqslant -4$

28. $f(x) = x^3 + 1; \quad g(x) = (x - 1)^{1/3}$

29. $f(x) = \dfrac{1}{x - 1}, \quad x \neq 1;$

$g(x) = \dfrac{1}{x} + 1, \quad x \neq 0$

30. $f(x) = \sqrt{4 - x^2}, \quad 0 \leqslant x \leqslant 2;$
$g(x) = \sqrt{4 - x^2}, \quad 0 \leqslant x \leqslant 2$

7–16 ■ Determine whether the function is one-to-one.

7. $f(x) = 7x - 3$

8. $f(x) = x^2 - 2x + 5$

9. $g(x) = \sqrt{x}$

10. $g(x) = |x|$

11. $h(x) = x^3 + 1$

12. $h(x) = \sqrt[3]{x}$

13. $f(x) = x^4 + 5$

14. $f(x) = x^4 + 5, \quad 0 \leqslant x \leqslant 2$

15. $f(x) = \dfrac{1}{x^2}$

16. $f(x) = \dfrac{1}{x}$

17–20 ■ Assume f is a one-to-one function.

17. (a) If $f(2) = 7$, find $f^{-1}(7)$.
(b) If $f^{-1}(3) = -1$, find $f(-1)$.

18. (a) If $f(5) = 18$, find $f^{-1}(18)$.
(b) If $f^{-1}(4) = 2$, find $f(2)$.

19. If $f(x) = 5 - 2x$, find $f^{-1}(3)$.

20. If $g(x) = x^2 + 4x$ with $x \geqslant -2$, find $g^{-1}(5)$.

21–30 ■ Use the Property of Inverse Functions to show that f and g are inverses of each other.

21. $f(x) = x + 3, \quad g(x) = x - 3$

22. $f(x) = 2x, \quad g(x) = \dfrac{x}{2}$

23. $f(x) = 2x - 5; \quad g(x) = \dfrac{x + 5}{2}$

24. $f(x) = \dfrac{3 - x}{4}; \quad g(x) = 3 - 4x$

25. $f(x) = \dfrac{1}{x}, \quad g(x) = \dfrac{1}{x}$

26. $f(x) = x^5, \quad g(x) = \sqrt[5]{x}$

31–50 ■ Find the inverse function of f.

31. $f(x) = 2x + 1$

32. $f(x) = 6 - x$

33. $f(x) = 4x + 7$

34. $f(x) = 3 - 5x$

35. $f(x) = \dfrac{x}{2}$

36. $f(x) = \dfrac{1}{x^2} \quad (x > 0)$

37. $f(x) = \dfrac{1}{x + 2}$

38. $f(x) = \dfrac{x - 2}{x + 2}$

39. $f(x) = \dfrac{1 + 3x}{5 - 2x}$

40. $f(x) = 5 - 4x^3$

41. $f(x) = \sqrt{2 + 5x}$

42. $f(x) = x^2 + x, \quad x \geqslant -\frac{1}{2}$

43. $f(x) = 4 - x^2, \quad x \geqslant 0$

44. $f(x) = \sqrt{2x - 1}$

45. $f(x) = 4 + \sqrt[3]{x}$

46. $f(x) = (2 - x^3)^5$

47. $f(x) = 1 + \sqrt{1 + x}$

48. $f(x) = \sqrt{9 - x^2}, \quad 0 \leqslant x \leqslant 3$

49. $f(x) = x^4, \quad x \geqslant 0$

50. $f(x) = 1 - x^3$

51–54 ■ A function f is given.
(a) Sketch the graph of f.
(b) Use the graph of f to sketch the graph of f^{-1}.
(c) Find f^{-1}.

51. $f(x) = 3x - 6$

52. $f(x) = 16 - x^2, \quad x \geqslant 0$

53. $f(x) = \sqrt{x + 1}$

54. $f(x) = x^3 - 1$

55–60 ■ Draw the graph of f and use it to determine whether the function is one-to-one.

55. $f(x) = x^3 - x$

56. $f(x) = x^3 + x$

57. $f(x) = \dfrac{x + 12}{x - 6}$

58. $f(x) = \sqrt{x^3 - 4x + 1}$

59. $f(x) = |x| - |x - 6|$

60. $f(x) = x \cdot |x|$

61–64 ■ The given function is not one-to-one. Restrict its domain so that the resulting function *is* one-to-one. Find the inverse of the function with the restricted domain. (There is more than one correct answer.)

61. $f(x) = 4 - x^2$

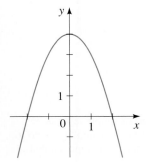

62. $g(x) = (x - 1)^2$

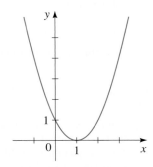

63. $h(x) = (x + 2)^2$

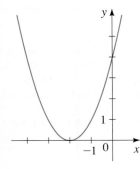

64. $k(x) = |x - 3|$

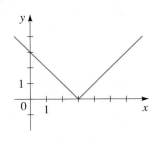

65–66 ■ Use the graph of f to sketch the graph of f^{-1}.

65.

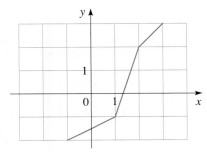

66.

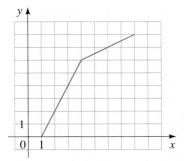

67. For his services, a private investigator requires a $500 retention fee plus $80 per hour. Let x represent the number of hours the investigator spends working on a case.
 (a) Find a function f that models the investigator's fee as a function of x.
 (b) Find f^{-1}. What does f^{-1} represent?
 (c) Find $f^{-1}(1220)$. What does your answer represent?

68. A tank holds 100 gallons of water, which drains from a leak at the bottom, causing the tank to empty in 40 minutes. Toricelli's Law gives the volume of water remaining in the tank after t minutes as

$$V(t) = 100\left(1 - \frac{t}{40}\right)^2$$

 (a) Find V^{-1}. What does V^{-1} represent?
 (b) Find $V^{-1}(15)$. What does your answer represent?

69. As blood moves through a vein or artery, its velocity v is greatest along the central axis and decreases as the distance r from the central axis increases. For an artery with radius 0.5 cm, v is given as a function of r by

$$v(r) = 18,500(0.25 - r^2)$$

 (a) Find v^{-1}. What does v^{-1} represent?
 (b) Find $v^{-1}(30)$. What does your answer represent?

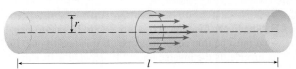

70. The relative value of currencies fluctuates every day. When this problem was written, one Canadian dollar was worth 0.6478 U.S. dollars.
 (a) Find a function f that gives the U.S. dollar value $f(x)$ of x Canadian dollars.
 (b) Find f^{-1}. What does f^{-1} represent?
 (c) How much Canadian money would $12,250 in U.S. currency be worth?

71. The relationship between the Fahrenheit (F) and Celsius (C) scales is given by

$$F(C) = \tfrac{9}{5}C + 32$$

(a) Find F^{-1}. What does F^{-1} represent?

(b) Find $F^{-1}(86)$. What does your answer represent?

72. A car dealership advertises a 15% discount on all its new cars. In addition, the manufacturer offers a $1000 rebate on the purchase of a new car. Let x represent the sticker price of the car.

(a) Suppose only the 15% discount applies. Find a function f that models the purchase price of the car as a function of the sticker price x.

(b) Suppose only the $1000 rebate applies. Find a function g that models the purchase price of the car as a function of the sticker price x.

(c) Find a formula for $H = f \circ g$.

(d) Find H^{-1}. What does H^{-1} represent?

(e) Find $H^{-1}(13,000)$. What does your answer represent?

73. In a certain country, the tax on incomes less than or equal to €20,000 is 10%. For incomes more than €20,000, the tax is €2000 plus 20% of the amount over €20,000.

(a) Find a function f that gives the income tax on an income x. Express f as a piecewise defined function.

(b) Find f^{-1}. What does f^{-1} represent?

(c) How much income would require paying a tax of €10,000?

74. Marcello's Pizza charges a base price of $7 for a large pizza, plus $2 for each topping. Thus, if you order a large pizza with x toppings, the price of your pizza is given by the function $f(x) = 7 + 2x$. Find f^{-1}. What does the function f^{-1} represent?

◼ DISCOVERY · DISCUSSION

75. Determining when a Linear Function Has an Inverse For the linear function $f(x) = mx + b$ to be one-to-one, what must be true about its slope? If it is one-to-one, find its inverse. Is the inverse linear? If so, what is its slope?

76. Finding an Inverse "In Your Head" In the margin notes in this section we pointed out that the inverse of a function can be found by simply reversing the operations that make up the function. For instance, in Example 6 we saw that the inverse of

$$f(x) = 3x - 2 \quad \text{is} \quad f^{-1}(x) = \frac{x + 2}{3}$$

because the "reverse" of "multiply by 3 and subtract 2" is "add 2 and divide by 3." Use the same procedure to find the inverse of the following functions.

(a) $f(x) = \dfrac{2x + 1}{5}$

(b) $f(x) = 3 - \dfrac{1}{x}$

(c) $f(x) = \sqrt{x^3 + 2}$

Now consider another function:

$$f(x) = \frac{3x - 2}{x + 7}$$

Is it possible to use the same sort of simple reversal of operations to find the inverse of this function? If so, do it. If not, explain what is different about this function that makes this task difficult.

77. The Identity Function The function $I(x) = x$ is called the **identity function**. Show that for any function f we have $f \circ I = f$, $I \circ f = f$, and $f \circ f^{-1} = f^{-1} \circ f = I$. (This means that the identity function I behaves for functions and composition just like the number 1 behaves for real numbers and multiplication.)

78. Solving an Equation for an Unknown Function In Exercise 63 of Section 1.6 you were asked to solve equations in which the unknowns were functions. Now that we know about inverses and the identity function (see Exercise 77), we can use algebra to solve such equations. For instance, to solve $f \circ g = h$ for the unknown function f, we perform the following steps:

$f \circ g = h$	Problem: Solve for f
$f \circ g \circ g^{-1} = h \circ g^{-1}$	Compose with g^{-1} on the right
$f \circ I = h \circ g^{-1}$	$g \circ g^{-1} = I$
$f = h \circ g^{-1}$	$f \circ I = f$

So the solution is $f = h \circ g^{-1}$. Use this technique to solve the equation $f \circ g = h$ for the indicated unknown function.

(a) Solve for f, where $g(x) = 2x + 1$ and $h(x) = 4x^2 + 4x + 7$

(b) Solve for g, where $f(x) = 3x + 5$ and $h(x) = 3x^2 + 3x + 2$

1 REVIEW

CONCEPT CHECK

1. (a) Describe the coordinate plane.
(b) How do you locate points in the coordinate plane?

2. State each formula.
(a) The Distance Formula
(b) The Midpoint Formula

3. Given an equation, what is its graph?

4. How do you find the x-intercepts and y-intercepts of a graph?

5. Write an equation of the circle with center (h, k) and radius r.

6. Explain the meaning of each type of symmetry. How do you test for it?
(a) Symmetry with respect to the x-axis
(b) Symmetry with respect to the y-axis
(c) Symmetry with respect to the origin

7. Define the slope of a line.

8. Write each form of the equation of a line.
(a) The point-slope form
(b) The slope-intercept form

9. (a) What is the equation of a vertical line?
(b) What is the equation of a horizontal line?

10. What is the general equation of a line?

11. Given lines with slopes m_1 and m_2, explain how you can tell if the lines are
(a) parallel
(b) perpendicular

12. Define each concept in your own words. (Check by referring to the definition in the text.)
(a) Function
(b) Domain and range of a function
(c) Graph of a function
(d) Independent and dependent variables

13. Sketch by hand, on the same axes, the graphs of the following functions.
(a) $f(x) = x$ (b) $g(x) = x^2$
(c) $h(x) = x^3$ (d) $j(x) = x^4$

14. (a) State the Vertical Line Test.
(b) State the Horizontal Line Test.

15. Define each concept in your own words.
(a) Increasing function
(b) Decreasing function
(c) Constant function

16. Suppose the graph of f is given. Write an equation for each graph that is obtained from the graph of f as follows.
(a) Shift 3 units upward.
(b) Shift 3 units downward.
(c) Shift 3 units to the right.
(d) Shift 3 units to the left.
(e) Reflect in the x-axis.
(f) Reflect in the y-axis.
(g) Stretch vertically by a factor of 3.
(h) Shrink vertically by a factor of $\frac{1}{3}$.

17. (a) What is an even function? What symmetry does its graph possess? Give an example of an even function.
(b) What is an odd function? What symmetry does its graph possess? Give an example of an odd function.

18. Write the standard form of a quadratic function.

19. What does it mean to say that $f(3)$ is a local maximum value of f?

20. Suppose that f has domain A and g has domain B.
(a) What is the domain of $f + g$?
(b) What is the domain of fg?
(c) What is the domain of f/g?

21. How is the composite function $f \circ g$ defined?

22. (a) What is a one-to-one function?
(b) How can you tell from the graph of a function whether it is one-to-one?
(c) Suppose f is a one-to-one function with domain A and range B. How is the inverse function f^{-1} defined? What is the domain of f^{-1}? What is the range of f^{-1}?
(d) If you are given a formula for f, how do you find a formula for f^{-1}?
(e) If you are given the graph of f, how do you find the graph of f^{-1}?

EXERCISES

1–2 ■ Two points P and Q are given.
(a) Plot P and Q on a coordinate plane.
(b) Find the distance from P to Q.
(c) Find the midpoint of the segment PQ.
(d) Sketch the line determined by P and Q, and find its equation in slope-intercept form.
(e) Sketch the circle that passes through Q and has center P, and find the equation of this circle.

1. $P(2, 0)$, $Q(-5, 12)$ **2.** $P(7, -1)$, $Q(2, -11)$

3–4 ■ Sketch the region given by the set.

3. $\{(x, y) \mid -4 < x < 4 \quad \text{and} \quad -2 < y < 2\}$

4. $\{(x, y) \mid x \geqslant 4 \quad \text{or} \quad y \geqslant 2\}$

5. Which of the points $A(4, 4)$ or $B(5, 3)$ is closer to the point $C(-1, -3)$?

6. Find an equation of the circle that has center $(2, -5)$ and radius $\sqrt{2}$.

7. Find an equation of the circle that has center $(-5, -1)$ and passes through the origin.

8. Find an equation of the circle that contains the points $P(2, 3)$ and $Q(-1, 8)$ and has the midpoint of the segment PQ as its center.

9–12 ■ Determine whether the equation represents a circle, a point, or has no graph. If the equation is that of a circle, find its center and radius.

9. $x^2 + y^2 + 2x - 6y + 9 = 0$

10. $2x^2 + 2y^2 - 2x + 8y = \frac{1}{2}$

11 $x^2 + y^2 + 72 = 12x$

12. $x^2 + y^2 - 6x - 10y + 34 = 0$

13–18 ■ Test the equation for symmetry and sketch its graph.

13. $y = 2 - 3x$

14. $2x - y + 1 = 0$

15. $y = 16 - x^2$

16. $8x + y^2 = 0$

17. $x = \sqrt{y}$

18. $y = -\sqrt{1 - x^2}$

19. Find an equation for the line that passes through the points $(-1, -6)$ and $(2, -4)$.

20. Find an equation for the line that passes through the point $(6, -3)$ and has slope $-\frac{1}{2}$.

21. Find an equation for the line that has x-intercept 4 and y-intercept 12.

22. Find an equation for the line that passes through the point $(1, 7)$ and is perpendicular to the line $x - 3y + 16 = 0$.

23. Find an equation for the line that passes through the origin and is parallel to the line $3x + 15y = 22$.

24. Find an equation for the line that passes through the point $(5, 2)$ and is parallel to the line passing through $(-1, -3)$ and $(3, 2)$.

25–26 ■ Find equations for the circle and the line in the figure.

25.

26.

27. If $f(x) = x^3 + 2x - 4$, find $f(0)$, $f(2)$, $f(-2)$, $f(a)$, $f(-a)$, $f(x + 1)$, $f(2x)$, and $2f(x) - 2$.

28. If $f(x) = 2 - \sqrt{2x - 6}$, find $f(5)$, $f(9)$, $f(a + 3)$, $f(-x)$, $f(x^2)$, and $[f(x)]^2$.

29. The graph of a function is given.
(a) Find $f(-2)$ and $f(2)$.
(b) Find the domain of f.
(c) Find the range of f.

(d) On what intervals is f increasing? On what intervals is f decreasing?

(e) Is f one-to-one?

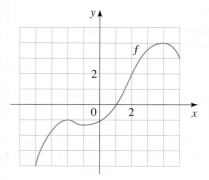

30. Which of the following figures are graphs of functions? Which of the functions are one-to-one?

(a)
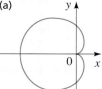

(b)
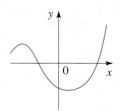

(c)
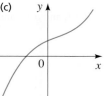

(d)
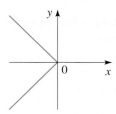

31–32 ■ Find the domain and range of the function.

31. $f(x) = \sqrt{x + 3}$

32. $F(t) = t^2 + 2t + 5$

33–38 ■ Find the domain of the function.

33. $f(x) = 7x + 15$

34. $f(x) = \dfrac{2x + 1}{2x - 1}$

35. $f(x) = \sqrt{x + 4}$

36. $f(x) = 3x - \dfrac{2}{\sqrt{x + 1}}$

37. $f(x) = \dfrac{1}{x} + \dfrac{1}{x + 1} + \dfrac{1}{x + 2}$

38. $g(x) = \dfrac{2x^2 + 5x + 3}{2x^2 - 5x - 3}$

39–54 ■ Sketch the graph of the function.

39. $f(x) = 1 - 2x$

40. $g(t) = t^2 - 2t$

41. $f(t) = 1 - \frac{1}{2}t^2$

42. $f(x) = x^2 - 6x + 6$

43. $y = 1 - \sqrt{x}$

44. $y = -|x|$

45. $y = \frac{1}{2}x^3$

46. $y = \sqrt{x + 3}$

47. $h(x) = \sqrt[3]{x}$

48. $H(x) = x^3 - 3x^2$

49. $g(x) = \dfrac{1}{x^2}$

50. $G(x) = \dfrac{1}{(x - 3)^2}$

51. $f(x) = \begin{cases} 1 - x & \text{if } x < 0 \\ 1 & \text{if } x \geqslant 0 \end{cases}$

52. $f(x) = \begin{cases} 1 - 2x & \text{if } x \leqslant 0 \\ 2x - 1 & \text{if } x > 0 \end{cases}$

53. $f(x) = \begin{cases} x + 6 & \text{if } x < -2 \\ x^2 & \text{if } x \geqslant -2 \end{cases}$

54. $f(x) = \begin{cases} -x & \text{if } x < 0 \\ x^2 & \text{if } 0 \leqslant x < 2 \\ 1 & \text{if } x \geqslant 2 \end{cases}$

 55. Determine which viewing rectangle produces the most appropriate graph of the function $f(x) = 6x^3 - 15x^2 + 4x - 1$.
   (i) $[-2, 2]$ by $[-2, 2]$
   (ii) $[-8, 8]$ by $[-8, 8]$
   (iii) $[-4, 4]$ by $[-12, 12]$
   (iv) $[-100, 100]$ by $[-100, 100]$

 56. Determine which viewing rectangle produces the most appropriate graph of the function $f(x) = \sqrt{100 - x^3}$.
   (i) $[-4, 4]$ by $[-4, 4]$
   (ii) $[-10, 10]$ by $[-10, 10]$
   (iii) $[-10, 10]$ by $[-10, 40]$
   (iv) $[-100, 100]$ by $[-100, 100]$

57–60 ■ Draw the graph of the function in an appropriate viewing rectangle.

57. $f(x) = x^2 + 25x + 173$

58. $f(x) = 1.1x^3 - 9.6x^2 - 1.4x + 3.2$

59. $y = \dfrac{x}{\sqrt{x^2 + 16}}$

60. $y = |x(x + 2)(x + 4)|$

 61–62 ■ Draw a graph of the function f, and determine the intervals on which f is increasing and on which f is decreasing.

61. $f(x) = x^3 - 4x^2$

62. $f(x) = |x^4 - 16|$

63. Suppose the graph of f is given. Describe how the graphs of the following functions can be obtained from the graph of f.

(a) $y = f(x) + 8$ (b) $y = f(x + 8)$
(c) $y = 1 + 2f(x)$ (d) $y = f(x - 2) - 2$
(e) $y = f(-x)$ (f) $y = -f(-x)$
(g) $y = -f(x)$ (h) $y = f^{-1}(x)$

64. The graph of f is given. Draw the graphs of the following functions.

(a) $y = f(x - 2)$ (b) $y = -f(x)$
(c) $y = 3 - f(x)$ (d) $y = \frac{1}{2}f(x) - 1$
(e) $y = f^{-1}(x)$ (f) $y = f(-x)$

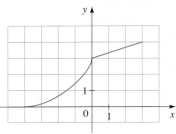

65. Determine whether f is even, odd, or neither.

(a) $f(x) = 2x^5 - 3x^2 + 2$ (b) $f(x) = x^3 - x^7$
(c) $f(x) = \dfrac{1 - x^2}{1 + x^2}$ (d) $f(x) = \dfrac{1}{x + 2}$

66. Determine whether the function in the figure is even, odd, or neither.

(a)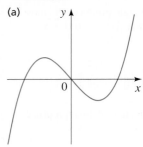

(b)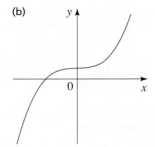

(c)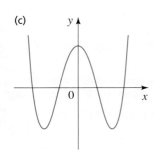

(d)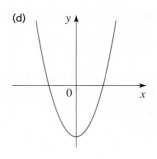

 67. A stone is thrown upward from the top of a building. Its height (in feet) above the ground after t seconds is given by $h(t) = -16t^2 + 48t + 32$. What maximum height does it reach?

 68. The profit P (in dollars) generated by selling x units of a certain commodity is given by

$$P(x) = -1500 + 12x - 0.0004x^2$$

What is the maximum profit, and how many units must be sold to generate it?

69–70 ■ Find the local maximum and minimum values of the function and the values of x at which they occur. State each answer correct to two decimal places.

69. $f(x) = 3.3 + 1.6x - 2.5x^3$

70. $f(x) = x^{2/3}(6 - x)^{1/3}$

71. If $f(x) = x^2 - 3x + 2$ and $g(x) = 4 - 3x$, find the following functions.

(a) $f + g$ (b) $f - g$ (c) fg
(d) f/g (e) $f \circ g$ (f) $g \circ f$

72. If $f(x) = 1 + x^2$ and $g(x) = \sqrt{x - 1}$, find the following functions.

(a) $f \circ g$ (b) $g \circ f$ (c) $(f \circ g)(2)$
(d) $(f \circ f)(2)$ (e) $f \circ g \circ f$ (f) $g \circ f \circ g$

73–74 ■ Find the functions $f \circ g$, $g \circ f$, $f \circ f$, and $g \circ g$ and their domains.

73. $f(x) = 3x - 1, \quad g(x) = 2x - x^2$

74. $f(x) = \sqrt{x}, \quad g(x) = \dfrac{2}{x - 4}$

75. Find $f \circ g \circ h$, where $f(x) = \sqrt{1 - x}$, $g(x) = 1 - x^2$, and $h(x) = 1 + \sqrt{x}$.

76. If $T(x) = \dfrac{1}{\sqrt{1 + \sqrt{x}}}$, find functions f, g, and h such that $f \circ g \circ h = T$.

77–82 ■ Determine whether the function is one-to-one.

77. $f(x) = 3 + x^3$ **78.** $g(x) = 2 - 2x + x^2$

79. $h(x) = \dfrac{1}{x^4}$ **80.** $r(x) = 2 + \sqrt{x + 3}$

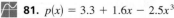 **81.** $p(x) = 3.3 + 1.6x - 2.5x^3$

82. $q(x) = 3.3 + 1.6x + 2.5x^3$

83–86 ■ Find the inverse of the function.

83. $f(x) = 3x - 2$

84. $f(x) = \dfrac{2x + 1}{3}$

85. $f(x) = (x + 1)^3$

86. $f(x) = 1 + \sqrt[5]{x - 2}$

87. (a) Sketch the graph of the function

$$f(x) = x^2 - 4, \quad x \geqslant 0$$

(b) Use part (a) to sketch the graph of f^{-1}.

(c) Find an equation for f^{-1}.

88. (a) Show that the function $f(x) = 1 + \sqrt[4]{x}$ is one-to-one.

(b) Sketch the graph of f.

(c) Use part (b) to sketch the graph of f^{-1}.

(d) Find an equation for f^{-1}.

1   TEST

1. (a) Plot the points $P(0, 3)$, $Q(3, 0)$, and $R(6, 3)$ in the coordinate plane. Where must the point S be located so that $PQRS$ is a square?
   (b) Find the area of $PQRS$.

2. (a) Sketch the graph of $y = x^2 - 4$.
   (b) Find the x- and y-intercepts of the graph.
   (c) Is the graph symmetric about the x-axis, the y-axis, or the origin?

3. Let $A(-7, 4)$ and $B(5, -12)$ be points in the plane.
   (a) Find the length of the segment AB.
   (b) Find the midpoint of the segment AB.
   (c) Find an equation of the line that passes through the points A and B.
   (d) Find an equation of the perpendicular bisector of AB.
   (e) Find an equation of the circle with center B and radius 13.
   (f) Find an equation of the circle for which AB is a diameter.

4. Find the center and radius of each circle and sketch its graph.
   (a) $x^2 + (y - 4)^2 = 9$ (b) $x^2 + y^2 - 6x + 10y + 9 = 0$

5. Write the linear equation

   $$3x - 4y + 24 = 0$$

   in slope-intercept form. What are the slope and y-intercept? Sketch the graph.

6. Find an equation for the line with the given property.
   (a) Passing through $(-2, 3)$ and parallel to the line $2x + 6y = 17$
   (b) Having x-intercept -3 and y-intercept 12

7. A manufacturer finds that the cost C of producing x blenders is

   $$C = 7x + 17,500$$

   (a) How much does it cost to produce 2500 blenders?
   (b) What do the slope and C-intercept of the cost equation represent?

8. Which of the following are graphs of functions? If the graph is that of a function, is it one-to-one?

   (a)
   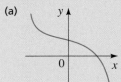

   (b)
   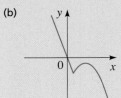

   (c)
   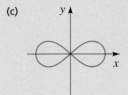

   (d)
   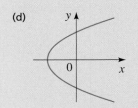

9. Let $f(x) = \dfrac{\sqrt{x}}{x-1}$.

    (a) Evaluate $f(4)$, $f(6)$, and $f(a+1)$.

    (b) Find the domain of f.

10. (a) Sketch the graph of the function $f(x) = x^3$.

    (b) Use part (a) to graph the function $g(x) = (x-1)^3 - 2$.

11. (a) How is the graph of $y = f(x-3) + 2$ obtained from the graph of f?

    (b) How is the graph of $y = f(-x)$ obtained from the graph of f?

12. Let $f(x) = \begin{cases} 1 - x^2 & \text{if } x \leqslant 0 \\ 2x + 1 & \text{if } x > 0 \end{cases}$

    (a) Evaluate $f(-2)$ and $f(1)$.

    (b) Sketch the graph of f.

13. If $f(x) = x^2 + 2x - 1$ and $g(x) = 2x - 3$, find the following functions.

    (a) $f \circ g$ **(b)** $g \circ f$

    (c) $f(g(2))$ **(d)** $g(f(2))$

    (e) $g \circ g \circ g$

14. (a) If $f(x) = \sqrt{3 - x}$, find the inverse function f^{-1}.

    (b) Sketch the graphs of f and f^{-1} on the same coordinate axes.

15. The graph of a function f is given.

    (a) Find the domain and range of f.

    (b) Sketch the graph of f^{-1}.

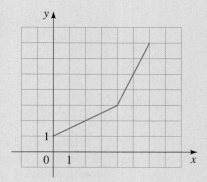

16. Let $f(x) = 3x^4 - 14x^2 + 5x - 3$.

    (a) Draw the graph of f in an appropriate viewing rectangle.

    (b) Is f one-to-one?

    (c) Find the local maximum and minimum values of f and the values of x at which they occur. State each answer correct to two decimal places.

    (d) Use the graph to determine the range of f.

    (e) Find the intervals on which f is increasing and on which f is decreasing.

Focus on Modeling
Fitting Lines to Data

A model is a representation of an object or process. For example, a toy Ferrari is a *model* of the actual car; a road map is a model of the streets and highways in a city. A model usually represents just one aspect of the original thing. The toy Ferrari is not an actual car, but it does represent what a real Ferrari looks like; a road map does not contain the actual streets in a city, but it does represent the relationship of the streets to each other.

A **mathematical model** is a mathematical representation of an object or process. Often a mathematical model is a function that describes a certain phenomenon. In Example 11 of Section 1.2 we found that the function $T = -10h + 20$ models the atmospheric temperature T at elevation h. We then used this function to predict the temperature at a certain height. Figure 1 illustrates the process of mathematical modeling.

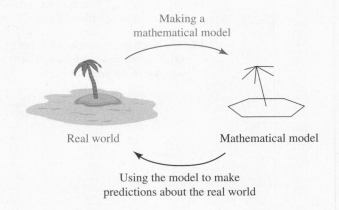

Making a
mathematical model

Real world

Mathematical model

Using the model to make
predictions about the real world

FIGURE 1

Mathematical models are useful because they enable us to isolate critical aspects of the thing we are studying and then to predict how it will behave. Models are used extensively in engineering, industry, and manufacturing. For example, engineers use computer models of skyscrapers to predict their strength and how they would behave in an earthquake. Aircraft manufacturers use elaborate mathematical models to predict the aerodynamic properties of a new design *before* the aircraft is actually built.

How are mathematical models developed? How are they used to predict the behavior of a process? In the next few pages and in subsequent *Focus on Modeling* sections, we explain how mathematical models can be constructed from real-world data, and we describe some of their applications.

Linear Functions as Models

Consider the following table, which gives the winning Olympic pole vaults in the 20th century.

Year	Gold medalist(s)	Height (ft)	Year	Gold medalist	Height (ft)
1900	Irving Baxter, USA	10.83	1956	Robert Richards, USA	14.96
1904	Charles Dvorak, USA	11.48	1960	Don Bragg, USA	15.42
1908	A. Gilbert, E. Cook, USA	12.17	1964	Fred Hansen, USA	16.73
1912	Harry Babcock, USA	12.96	1968	Bob Seagren, USA	17.71
1920	Frank Foss, USA	13.42	1972	W. Nordwig, E. Germany	18.04
1924	Lee Barnes, USA	12.96	1976	Tadeusz Slusarski, Poland	18.04
1928	Sabin Carr, USA	13.77	1980	W. Kozakiewicz, Poland	18.96
1932	William Miller, USA	14.15	1984	Pierre Quinon, France	18.85
1936	Earle Meadows, USA	14.27	1988	Sergei Bubka, USSR	19.77
1948	Guinn Smith, USA	14.10	1992	M. Tarassob, Unified Team	19.02
1952	Robert Richards, USA	14.92	1996	Jean Jalfione, France	19.42

From the table we see that athletes generally pole-vault higher as time goes on. To see this trend better we make a **scatter plot**, as shown in Figure 2. How can we model this data mathematically? Since it appears that the points lie more or less along a line, we can try to fit a line visually to approximate the points in the scatter plot. In other words, we may be able to use a linear function as our model.

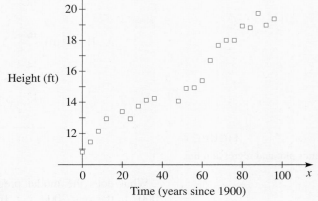

FIGURE 2

Scatter plot of
pole-vault data

What Is the Line of Best Fit?

How do we find a line that best fits the data? It seems reasonable to choose the line that is as close as possible to all the data points in the scatter plot. So, we want the line for which the sum of the distances from the data points to the line is smallest (see Figure 3).

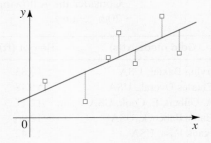

FIGURE 3

Distances from the points to the line

```
LinReg
 y=ax+b
 a=.089119747
 b=11.08719447
 r=.9755015763
```

Output of the **LinReg** function on the TI-83.

For technical reasons it is better to find the line where the sum of the squares of these distances is smallest. The resulting line is called the **regression line** or the **least squares line**. The formula for the regression line is found using calculus. Fortunately, this formula is programmed into most graphing calculators (such as the TI-83, TI-85, or TI-86). Using the pole-vault data and the **Lin Reg** command on a TI-83 calculator, we find that the regression line is

$$y = 0.0891x + 11.09 \qquad \text{Model}$$

In Figure 4 the regression line is graphed, together with the scatter plot.

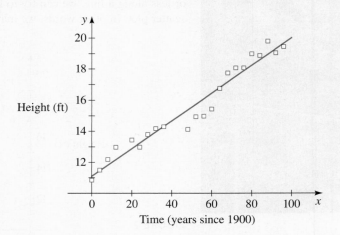

FIGURE 4

Scatter plot and regression line

What does the model predict for the Olympic pole-vault record in the year 2000? In the year 2000, $x = 100$ so the regression line gives

$$y = 0.0891(100) + 11.09 \approx 19.99 \text{ ft}$$

(Look up the actual record for 2000, and compare with this prediction.) Such predictions are reasonable for points close to our measured data, but we can't predict too far away from the measured data. Is it reasonable to use this model to predict the record 100 years from now?

Another Example

When laboratory rats are exposed to asbestos fibers, some of them develop lung tumors. The following table lists the results of several such experiments by different scientists. Using a graphing calculator we get the regression line

$$y = 0.0177x + 0.54047 \qquad \text{Model}$$

The scatter plot and the regression line are graphed in Figure 5. Is it reasonable to use a linear model for this data?

Asbestos exposure (fibers/mL)	Percent that develop lung tumors
50	2
400	6
500	5
900	10
1100	26
1600	42
1800	37
2000	28
3000	50

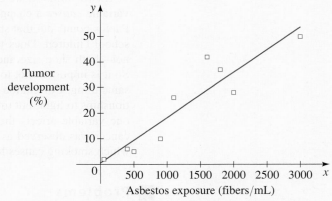

FIGURE 5 Scatter plot and regression line for asbestos-tumor data

How Good Is the Fit?

For any given data it is always possible to find the regression line, even if the data do not tend to lie along a line. Consider the three scatter plots in Figure 6.

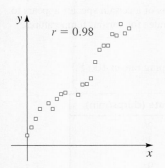

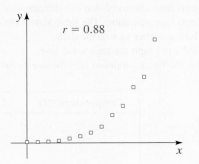

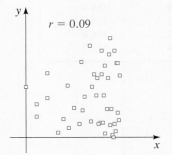

FIGURE 6

The data in the first scatter plot appear to lie along a line, in the second they appear to lie along a parabola, and in the third there appears to be no discernible trend. We can easily find the regression lines for each scatter plot using a graphing calculator. But how well do these lines represent the data? The calculator gives a correlation coefficient r, which is a statistical measure of how well the data lie along the regression line, or how well the two variables are **correlated**. The correlation coefficient is a number between -1 and 1. A correlation coefficient r close to 1 or -1 indicates strong correlation and a coefficient close to 0 indicates very little correlation; the slope of the line determines whether the correlation coefficient is positive or negative. Also, the more data points we have, the more meaningful the correlation coefficient will be. Using a calculator we find that the correlation coefficient between asbestos fibers and lung tumors in rats is $r = 0.92$. We can reasonably conclude that the presence of asbestos and the risk of lung tumors in rats are related. Can we conclude that asbestos *causes* lung tumors in rats?

If two variables are correlated, it does not necessarily mean that a change in one variable *causes* a change in the other. For example, the mathematician John Allen Paulos points out that shoe size is strongly correlated to mathematics scores among school children. Does this mean that big feet cause high math scores? Certainly not—both shoe size and math skills increase independently as children get older. So it is important not to jump to conclusions: Correlation and causation are not the same thing. Correlation is a useful tool in bringing important cause and effect relationships to light, but to prove causation, we must explain the mechanism by which one variable affects the other. For example, the link between smoking and lung cancer was observed as a correlation long before science found the mechanism by which smoking causes lung cancer.

■ Problems

Year	CO₂ level (ppm)
1980	338.5
1982	341.0
1984	344.3
1986	347.0
1988	351.3
1990	354.0
1992	356.3
1994	358.9
1996	362.7

1. The table at the left lists average carbon dioxide (CO_2) levels in the atmosphere, measured in parts per million (ppm) at Mauna Loa Observatory from 1980 to 1996.
   (a) Make a scatter plot of the data.
   (b) Find and graph the regression line.
   (c) Use the linear model in part (b) to estimate the CO_2 level in the atmosphere in 1998. Compare your answer with the actual CO_2 level of 366.7 measured in 1998.

2. Biologists have observed that the chirping rate of crickets of a certain species appears to be related to temperature. The table shows the chirping rates for various temperatures.
   (a) Make a scatter plot of the data.
   (b) Find and graph the regression line.
   (c) Use the linear model in part (b) to estimate the chirping rate at 100°F.

Temperature (°F)	Chirping rate (chirps/min)
50	20
55	46
60	79
65	91
70	113
75	140
80	173
85	198
90	211

Income	Ulcer rate
$4,000	14.1
$6,000	13.0
$8,000	13.4
$12,000	12.4
$16,000	12.0
$20,000	12.5
$30,000	10.5
$45,000	9.4
$60,000	8.2

3. The table at the left shows (lifetime) peptic ulcer rates (per 100 population) for various family incomes as reported by the 1989 National Health Interview Survey.
   (a) Make a scatter plot of the data.
   (b) Find and graph the regression line.
   (c) Estimate the peptic ulcer rate for an income level of $25,000 according to the linear model in part (b).
   (d) Estimate the peptic ulcer rate for an income level of $80,000 according to the linear model in part (b).

4. The table lists the relative abundance of mosquitoes (as measured by the mosquito positive rate) versus the flow rate (measured as a percentage of maximum flow) of canal networks in Saga City, Japan.
   (a) Make a scatter plot of the data.
   (b) Find and graph the regression line.
   (c) Use the linear model in part (b) to estimate the mosquito positive rate if the canal flow is 70% of maximum.

Flow rate (%)	Mosquito positive rate (%)
0	22
10	16
40	12
60	11
90	6
100	2

5. The tables show the results of experiments measuring the average number of mosquito bites per 15 minutes versus temperature and wind speed.
   (a) Make a scatter plot for each set of data.
   (b) Find and graph the regression line for the temperature-bites data and for the wind-bites data.
   (c) Find the correlation coefficient for each set of data. Are linear models appropriate for these data?

Temperature (°C)	Bites/15 min
10	0.03
15	7.2
20	46.2
25	65.5
30	37.8

Wind speed (km/h)	Bites/15 min
0.5	59.3
2	35.7
4	24.8
6	21.9
8	12.0
14	4.8

6. The table shows (lifetime) peptic ulcer rates (per 100 population) for various education levels as reported by the 1989 National Health Interview Survey.
   (a) Make a scatter plot of the data.
   (b) Find and graph the regression line.
   (c) Use the linear model in part (b) to estimate the ulcer rate for a person with 20 years of education.

Education level (years)	Ulcer rate
8	12
11	12.5
12	11
15	10
16	8
18	9

7. Audiologists study the intelligibility of spoken sentences under different noise levels. Intelligibility, the MRT score, is measured as the percent of a spoken sentence that the listener can decipher at a certain noise level in decibels (dB). The table shows the results of one such test.
   (a) Make a scatter plot of the data.
   (b) Find and graph the regression line.
   (c) Find the correlation coefficient. Is a linear model appropriate?
   (d) Use the linear model in part (b) to estimate the intelligibility of a sentence at a 94-dB noise level.

Noise level (dB)	MRT score (%)
80	99
84	91
88	84
92	70
96	47
100	23
104	11

Year	IQ index
1940	85
1950	89
1960	90
1970	95
1980	97
1990	100

8. Average IQ scores in the United States have risen dramatically since the tests were first introduced, as shown in the table at the left.
   (a) Make a scatter plot of the data.
   (b) Find and graph the regression line.
   (c) Use the linear model you found in part (b) to predict the IQ index in the year 2000.

9. The average life expectancy in the United States has been rising steadily over the past few decades, as shown in the table.
   (a) Make a scatter plot of the data.
   (b) Find and graph the regression line.
   (c) Use the linear model you found in part (b) to predict the life expectancy in the year 2000.
   (d) Search the Internet or your campus library to find the actual 2000 average life expectancy. Compare to your answer in part (c).

Year	Life expectancy
1920	54.1
1930	59.7
1940	62.9
1950	68.2
1960	69.7
1970	70.8
1980	73.7
1990	75.4

10. The table gives the heights and number of stories for 10 tall buildings.
    (a) Make a scatter plot of the data.
    (b) Find and graph the regression line.
    (c) What is the slope of your regression line? What does its value indicate?

Building	Height (ft)	Stories
Empire State Building, New York	1250	102
One Liberty Place, Philadelphia	945	61
Canada Trust Tower, Toronto	863	51
Bank of America Tower, Seattle	943	76
Sears Tower, Chicago	1450	110
Petronas Tower I, Malaysia	1483	88
Commerzbank Tower, Germany	850	60
Palace of Culture and Science, Poland	758	42
Republic Plaza, Singapore	919	66
Transamerica Pyramid, San Francisco	853	48

11. The tables give the gold medal times in the men's and women's 100-m freestyle Olympic swimming event. The data are graphed in the scatter plot, with the women's times in red and the men's in blue.
   (a) Find the regression lines for the men's data and the women's data.
   (b) Sketch both regression lines on the same graph. When do these lines predict that the women will overtake the men in this event? Does this conclusion seem reasonable?

MEN

Year	Gold medalist	Time (s)
1908	C. Daniels, USA	65.6
1912	D. Kahanamoku, USA	63.4
1920	D. Kahanamoku, USA	61.4
1924	J. Weissmuller, USA	59.0
1928	J. Weissmuller, USA	58.6
1932	Y. Miyazaki, Japan	58.2
1936	F. Csik, Hungary	57.6
1948	W. Ris, USA	57.3
1952	C. Scholes, USA	57.4
1956	J. Henricks, Australia	55.4
1960	J. Devitt, Australia	55.2
1964	D. Schollander, USA	53.4
1968	M. Wenden, Australia	52.2
1972	M. Spitz, USA	51.22
1976	J. Montgomery, USA	49.99
1980	J. Woithe, E. Germany	50.40
1984	R. Gaines, USA	49.80
1988	M. Biondi, USA	48.63
1992	A. Popov, Russia	49.02
1996	A. Popov, Russia	48.74

WOMEN

Year	Gold medalist(s)	Time (s)
1912	F. Durack, Australia	82.2
1920	E. Bleibtrey, USA	73.6
1924	E. Lackie, USA	72.4
1928	A. Osipowich, USA	71.0
1932	H. Madison, USA	66.8
1936	H. Mastenbroek, Holland	65.9
1948	G. Andersen, Denmark	66.3
1952	K. Szoke, Hungary	66.8
1956	D. Fraser, Australia	62.0
1960	D. Fraser, Australia	61.2
1964	D. Fraser, Australia	59.5
1968	J. Henne, USA	60.0
1972	S. Nielson, USA	58.59
1976	K. Ender, E. Germany	55.65
1980	B. Krause, E. Germany	54.79
1984	(Tie) C. Steinseifer, USA	55.92
	N. Hogshead, USA	55.92
1988	K. Otto, E. Germany	54.93
1992	Z. Yong, China	54.64
1996	L. Jingyi, China	54.50

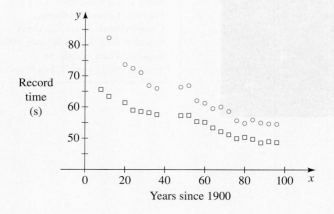

Years since 1900

12. Do you think that shoe size and height are correlated? Find out by surveying the shoe sizes and heights of people in your class. (Of course, the data for men and women should be separate.) Find the correlation coefficient.

13. In this problem you will find a linear function that describes the number of candy bars your classmates would be willing to buy at a given price. (Economists call this type of function a *demand function*.) Survey your classmates to determine what price they would be willing to pay for a candy bar. Your survey form might look like the sample below.
    (a) Make a table of the number of respondents who answered "yes" at each price level.
    (b) Make a scatter plot of your data.
    (c) Find and graph the regression line $y = mp + b$, which gives the number of respondents y who would buy a candy bar if the price were p cents. Why is the slope m negative?
    (d) What is the p-intercept? What does this intercept tell you about pricing candy bars?

Would you buy a candy bar from the vending machine in the hallway if the price is as indicated?

Price	Yes or No
30¢	
40¢	
50¢	
60¢	
70¢	
80¢	
90¢	
$1.00	
$1.10	
$1.20	

2 Trigonometric Functions of Real Numbers

Trigonometric functions are used to describe periodic phenomena such as the ebb and flow of tides, or the vibrations of a violin string.

Trigonometry contains the science of continually undulating magnitude . . .

AUGUSTUS DE MORGAN

In this chapter and the next, we introduce two different but equivalent ways of viewing the trigonometric functions. One way is to view them as *functions of real numbers* (Chapter 2), the other as *functions of angles* (Chapter 3). The two approaches to trigonometry are independent of each other, so either Chapter 2 or Chapter 3 may be studied first.

The trigonometric functions defined in these two different ways are identical—they assign the same value to a given real number. In the first case, the real number is the length of an arc along the unit circle; in the second case, it is the measure of an angle. We study both approaches because different applications require that we view these functions differently. One approach (Chapter 2) lends itself to dynamic applications such as the modeling of harmonic motion, whereas the other approach (Chapter 3) lends itself to static applications such as the measurement of distance using triangles. The power and versatility of trigonometry stems from the fact that it can be viewed in these different ways. In modern times, trigonometry has found application in such diverse fields as signal processing, coding of music on compact discs, designing guidance systems for the space shuttle, finding distances to stars, producing CAT scans for medical imaging, and many others.

2.1 THE UNIT CIRCLE

In this section we explore some properties of the circle of radius 1 centered at the origin. These properties are used in the next section to define the trigonometric functions.

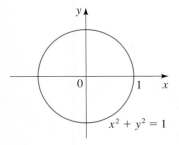

FIGURE 1
The unit circle

■ The Unit Circle

The set of points at a distance 1 from the origin is a circle of radius 1 (see Figure 1). In Section 1.1 we learned that the equation of this circle is $x^2 + y^2 = 1$.

THE UNIT CIRCLE

The **unit circle** is the circle of radius 1 centered at the origin in the xy-plane. Its equation is

$$x^2 + y^2 = 1$$

EXAMPLE 1 ■ A Point on the Unit Circle

Show that the point $P\left(\dfrac{\sqrt{3}}{3}, \dfrac{\sqrt{2}}{\sqrt{3}}\right)$ is on the unit circle.

SOLUTION

We need to show that this point satisfies the equation of the unit circle, that is, $x^2 + y^2 = 1$. Since

$$\left(\frac{\sqrt{3}}{3}\right)^2 + \left(\frac{\sqrt{2}}{\sqrt{3}}\right)^2 = \frac{3}{9} + \frac{2}{3} = \frac{1}{3} + \frac{2}{3} = 1$$

P is on the unit circle.   ∎

EXAMPLE 2   ■   Locating a Point on the Unit Circle

The point $P(\sqrt{3}/2, y)$ is on the unit circle in quadrant IV. Find its y-coordinate.

SOLUTION   Since the point is on the unit circle, we have

$$\left(\frac{\sqrt{3}}{2}\right)^2 + y^2 = 1$$

$$y^2 = 1 - \frac{3}{4} = \frac{1}{4}$$

$$y = \pm\frac{1}{2}$$

Since the point is in quadrant IV, its y-coordinate must be negative, so $y = -\frac{1}{2}$.   ∎

Terminal Points on the Unit Circle

Suppose t is a real number. Let's mark off a distance t along the unit circle, starting at the point $(1, 0)$ and moving in a counterclockwise direction if t is positive or in a clockwise direction if t is negative (Figure 2). In this way we arrive at a point $P(x, y)$ on the unit circle. The point $P(x, y)$ obtained in this way is called the **terminal point** determined by the real number t.

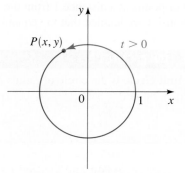

(a) Terminal point $P(x, y)$ determined by $t > 0$

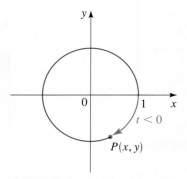

(b) Terminal point $P(x, y)$ determined by $t < 0$

FIGURE 2

The circumference of the unit circle is $C = 2\pi(1) = 2\pi$. So, if a point starts at $(1, 0)$ and moves counterclockwise all the way around the unit circle and returns to $(1, 0)$, it travels a distance of 2π. To move halfway around the circle, it travels a distance of $\frac{1}{2}(2\pi) = \pi$. To move a quarter of the distance around the circle, it travels a distance of $\frac{1}{4}(2\pi) = \pi/2$. Where does the point end up when it travels these distances along the circle? From Figure 3 we see, for example, that when it travels a distance of π starting at $(1, 0)$, its terminal point is $(-1, 0)$.

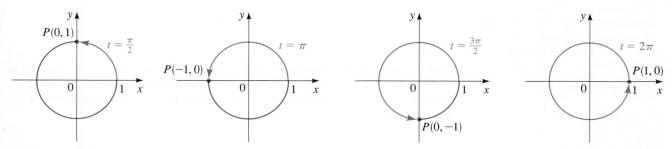

FIGURE 3
Terminal points determined by $t = \frac{\pi}{2}$, π, $\frac{3\pi}{2}$, and 2π

EXAMPLE 3 ■ Finding Terminal Points

Find the terminal point on the unit circle determined by each real number t.

(a) $t = 3\pi$ (b) $t = -\pi$ (c) $t = -\dfrac{\pi}{2}$

SOLUTION

From Figure 4 we get the following.

(a) The terminal point determined by 3π is $(-1, 0)$.

(b) The terminal point determined by $-\pi$ is $(-1, 0)$.

(c) The terminal point determined by $-\pi/2$ is $(0, -1)$.

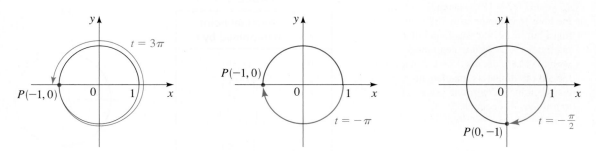

FIGURE 4

Notice that different values of t can determine the same terminal point.   ■

The Value of π

The number π is the ratio of the circumference of a circle to its diameter. It has been known since ancient times that this ratio is the same for all circles. The first systematic effort to find a numerical approximation for π was made by Archimedes (ca. 240 B.C.), who proved that $\frac{22}{7} < \pi < \frac{223}{71}$ by finding the perimeters of regular polygons inscribed in and circumscribed about a circle.

In about A.D. 480, the Chinese physicist Tsu Ch'ung-chih gave the approximation

$$\pi \approx \frac{355}{113} = 3.141592\ldots$$

which is correct to six decimals. This remained the most accurate estimation of π until the Dutch mathematician Adrianus Romanus (1593) used polygons with more than a billion sides to compute π correct to 15 decimals. In the 17th century, mathematicians began to use infinite series and trigonometric identities in the quest for π. The Englishman William Shanks spent 15 years (1858–1873) using these methods to compute π to 707 decimals, but in 1946 it was found that his figures were wrong beginning with the 528th decimal. Today, with the aid of computers, mathematicians routinely determine π correct to millions of decimals.

The terminal point $P(x, y)$ determined by $t = \pi/4$ is the same distance from $(1, 0)$ as from $(0, 1)$ along the unit circle (see Figure 5).

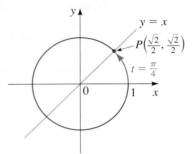

FIGURE 5

Since the unit circle is symmetric with respect to the line $y = x$, it follows that P lies on the line $y = x$. So P is the point of intersection (in the first quadrant) of the circle $x^2 + y^2 = 1$ and the line $y = x$. Substituting x for y in the equation of the circle, we get

$$x^2 + x^2 = 1$$
$$2x^2 = 1 \qquad \text{Combine like terms}$$
$$x^2 = \frac{1}{2} \qquad \text{Divide by 2}$$
$$x = \pm\frac{1}{\sqrt{2}} \qquad \text{Take square roots}$$

Since P is in the first quadrant, $x = 1/\sqrt{2}$ and since $y = x$, we have $y = 1/\sqrt{2}$ also. Thus, the terminal point determined by $\pi/4$ is

$$P\left(\frac{1}{\sqrt{2}}, \frac{1}{\sqrt{2}}\right) = P\left(\frac{\sqrt{2}}{2}, \frac{\sqrt{2}}{2}\right)$$

Similar methods can be used to find the terminal points determined by $t = \pi/6$ and $t = \pi/3$ (see Exercises 47 and 48). Table 1 and Figure 6 give the terminal points for some special values of t.

TABLE 1

t	Terminal point determined by t
0	$(1, 0)$
$\frac{\pi}{6}$	$\left(\frac{\sqrt{3}}{2}, \frac{1}{2}\right)$
$\frac{\pi}{4}$	$\left(\frac{\sqrt{2}}{2}, \frac{\sqrt{2}}{2}\right)$
$\frac{\pi}{3}$	$\left(\frac{1}{2}, \frac{\sqrt{3}}{2}\right)$
$\frac{\pi}{2}$	$(0, 1)$

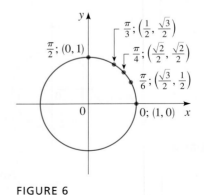

FIGURE 6

EXAMPLE 4 ■ **Finding Terminal Points**

Find the terminal point determined by each given real number t.

(a) $t = -\dfrac{\pi}{4}$ (b) $t = \dfrac{3\pi}{4}$ (c) $t = -\dfrac{5\pi}{6}$

SOLUTION

(a) Let P be the terminal point determined by $-\pi/4$, and let Q be the terminal point determined by $\pi/4$. From Figure 7(a) we see that the point P has the same coordinates as Q except for sign. Since P is in quadrant IV, its x-coordinate is positive and its y-coordinate is negative. Thus, the terminal point is $P(\sqrt{2}/2, -\sqrt{2}/2)$.

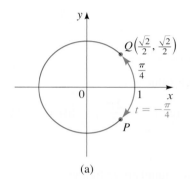

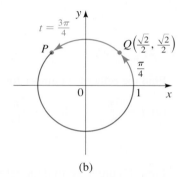

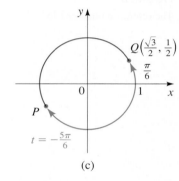

FIGURE 7   (a)   (b)   (c)

(b) Let P be the terminal point determined by $3\pi/4$, and let Q be the terminal point determined by $\pi/4$. From Figure 7(b) we see that the point P has the same coordinates as Q except for sign. Since P is in quadrant II, its x-coordinate is negative and its y-coordinate is positive. Thus, the terminal point is $P(-\sqrt{2}/2, \sqrt{2}/2)$.

(c) Let P be the terminal point determined by $-5\pi/6$, and let Q be the terminal point determined by $\pi/6$. From Figure 7(c) we see that the point P has the same coordinates as Q except for sign. Since P is in quadrant III, its coordinates are both negative. Thus, the terminal point is $P\left(-\sqrt{3}/2, -\tfrac{1}{2}\right)$. ■

■ The Reference Number

From Examples 3 and 4, we see that to find a terminal point in any quadrant we need only know the "corresponding" terminal point in the first quadrant. We give a procedure for finding such terminal points using the idea of the *reference number*.

REFERENCE NUMBER

Let t be a real number. The **reference number** $\bar{t}$ associated with t is the shortest distance along the unit circle between the terminal point determined by t and the x-axis.

Figure 8 shows that to find the reference number $\bar{t}$ it's helpful to know the quadrant in which the terminal point determined by t lies.

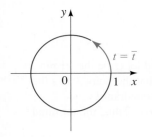   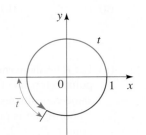   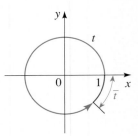

FIGURE 8

The reference number $\bar{t}$ for t

EXAMPLE 5 ■ Finding Reference Numbers

Find the reference number for each value of t.

(a) $t = \dfrac{5\pi}{6}$ (b) $t = \dfrac{7\pi}{4}$ (c) $t = -\dfrac{2\pi}{3}$ (d) $t = 5.80$

SOLUTION

From Figure 9 we find the reference numbers as follows.

(a) $\bar{t} = \pi - \dfrac{5\pi}{6} = \dfrac{\pi}{6}$

(b) $\bar{t} = 2\pi - \dfrac{7\pi}{4} = \dfrac{\pi}{4}$

(c) $\bar{t} = \pi - \dfrac{2\pi}{3} = \dfrac{\pi}{3}$

(d) $\bar{t} = 2\pi - 5.80 \approx 0.48$

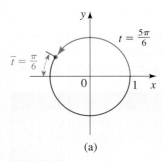   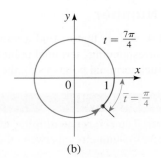   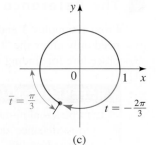   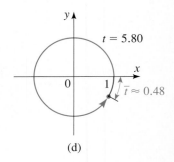

    (a)   (b)   (c)   (d)

FIGURE 9

■

> ### USING REFERENCE NUMBERS TO FIND TERMINAL POINTS
>
> To find the terminal point P determined by any value of t, we use the following steps:
>
> 1. Find the reference number $\bar{t}$.
>
> 2. Find the terminal point $Q(a, b)$ determined by $\bar{t}$.
>
> 3. The terminal point determined by t is $P(\pm a, \pm b)$, where the signs are chosen according to the quadrant in which this terminal point lies.

EXAMPLE 6 ■ Using Reference Numbers to Find Terminal Points

Find the terminal point determined by each given real number t.

(a) $t = \dfrac{5\pi}{6}$ (b) $t = \dfrac{7\pi}{4}$ (c) $t = -\dfrac{2\pi}{3}$

SOLUTION

The reference numbers associated with these values of t were found in Example 5.

(a) The reference number is $\bar{t} = \pi/6$, which determines the terminal point $\left(\sqrt{3}/2, \frac{1}{2}\right)$ from Table 1. Since the terminal point determined by t is in quadrant II, its x-coordinate is negative and its y-coordinate is positive. Thus, the desired terminal point is

$$\left(-\frac{\sqrt{3}}{2}, \frac{1}{2}\right)$$

(b) The reference number is $\bar{t} = \pi/4$, which determines the terminal point $\left(\sqrt{2}/2, \sqrt{2}/2\right)$ from Table 1. Since the terminal point is in quadrant IV, its x-coordinate is positive and its y-coordinate is negative. Thus, the desired terminal point is

$$\left(\frac{\sqrt{2}}{2}, -\frac{\sqrt{2}}{2}\right)$$

(c) The reference number is $\bar{t} = \pi/3$, which determines the terminal point $\left(\frac{1}{2}, \sqrt{3}/2\right)$ from Table 1. Since the terminal point determined by t is in quadrant III, its coordinates are both negative. Thus, the desired terminal point is

$$\left(-\frac{1}{2}, -\frac{\sqrt{3}}{2}\right)$$

■

Since the circumference of the unit circle is 2π, the terminal point determined by t is the same as that determined by $t + 2\pi$ or $t - 2\pi$. In general, we can add or subtract 2π any number of times without changing the terminal point determined by t. We use this observation in the next example to find terminal points for large t.

EXAMPLE 7 ■ **Finding the Terminal Point for Large** t

Find the terminal point determined by $t = \dfrac{29\pi}{6}$.

SOLUTION

Since

$$t = \frac{29\pi}{6} = 4\pi + \frac{5\pi}{6}$$

we see that the terminal point of t is the same as that of $5\pi/6$ (that is, we subtract 4π). So by Example 6(a) the terminal point is $\left(-\sqrt{3}/2, \tfrac{1}{2}\right)$.   ■

2.1   EXERCISES

1–4 ■ Show that the point is on the unit circle.

1. $\left(\tfrac{3}{5}, \tfrac{4}{5}\right)$

2. $\left(\tfrac{5}{13}, -\tfrac{12}{13}\right)$

3. $\left(-\tfrac{2}{3}, -\tfrac{\sqrt{5}}{3}\right)$

4. $\left(\tfrac{\sqrt{11}}{6}, \tfrac{5}{6}\right)$

5–10 ■ The point P is on the unit circle. Find $P(x, y)$ from the given information.

5. The x-coordinate of P is $\tfrac{4}{5}$ and P is in quadrant I.

6. The y-coordinate of P is $-\tfrac{1}{3}$ and P is in quadrant IV.

7. The y-coordinate of P is $\tfrac{2}{3}$ and the x-coordinate is negative.

8. The x-coordinate of P is positive and the y-coordinate of P is $-\sqrt{5}/5$.

9. The x-coordinate of P is $-\sqrt{2}/3$ and P is in quadrant III.

10. The x-coordinate of P is $-\tfrac{2}{5}$ and P is in quadrant II.

11–12 ■ Find t and the terminal point determined by t for each point in the figure. In Exercise 11, t increases in increments of $\pi/4$; in Exercise 12, t increases in increments of $\pi/6$.

11.

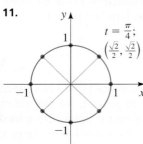

12.

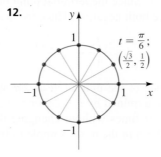

13–22 ■ Find the terminal point $P(x, y)$ on the unit circle determined by the given value of t.

13. $t = \dfrac{\pi}{2}$

14. $t = \dfrac{3\pi}{2}$

15. $t = \dfrac{5\pi}{6}$

16. $t = \dfrac{7\pi}{6}$

17. $t = -\dfrac{\pi}{3}$

18. $t = \dfrac{5\pi}{3}$

19. $t = \dfrac{2\pi}{3}$

20. $t = -\dfrac{\pi}{2}$

21. $t = -\dfrac{3\pi}{4}$

22. $t = \dfrac{11\pi}{6}$

23. Suppose that the terminal point determined by t is the point $\left(\tfrac{3}{5}, \tfrac{4}{5}\right)$ on the unit circle. Find the terminal point determined by each of the following.
(a) $\pi - t$ (b) $-t$ (c) $\pi + t$ (d) $2\pi + t$

24. Suppose that the terminal point determined by t is the point $\left(\tfrac{3}{4}, \sqrt{7}/4\right)$ on the unit circle. Find the terminal point determined by each of the following.
(a) $-t$ (b) $4\pi + t$ (c) $\pi - t$ (d) $t - \pi$

25–28 ■ Find the reference number for each value of t.

25. (a) $t = \dfrac{5\pi}{4}$ (b) $t = \dfrac{7\pi}{3}$

(c) $t = -\dfrac{4\pi}{3}$ (d) $t = \dfrac{\pi}{6}$

26. (a) $t = \dfrac{5\pi}{7}$ (b) $t = -\dfrac{9\pi}{8}$

    (c) $t = 3.55$ (d) $t = -2.9$

27. (a) $t = -\dfrac{11\pi}{5}$ (b) $t = \dfrac{13\pi}{6}$

    (c) $t = \dfrac{7\pi}{3}$ (d) $t = -\dfrac{5\pi}{6}$

28. (a) $t = 3$ (b) $t = 6$
    (c) $t = -3$ (d) $t = -6$

29–42 ■ Find (a) the reference number for each value of t, and (b) the terminal point determined by t.

29. $t = \dfrac{2\pi}{3}$ **30.** $t = \dfrac{4\pi}{3}$

31. $t = \dfrac{3\pi}{4}$ **32.** $t = \dfrac{7\pi}{3}$

33. $t = -\dfrac{2\pi}{3}$ **34.** $t = -\dfrac{7\pi}{6}$

35. $t = \dfrac{13\pi}{4}$ **36.** $t = \dfrac{13\pi}{6}$

37. $t = \dfrac{7\pi}{6}$ **38.** $t = \dfrac{17\pi}{4}$

39. $t = -\dfrac{11\pi}{3}$ **40.** $t = \dfrac{31\pi}{6}$

41. $t = \dfrac{16\pi}{3}$ **42.** $t = -\dfrac{41\pi}{4}$

43–46 ■ Use the figure to find the terminal point determined by the real number t, with coordinates correct to one decimal place.

43. $t = 1$

44. $t = 2.5$

45. $t = -1.1$

46. $t = 4.2$

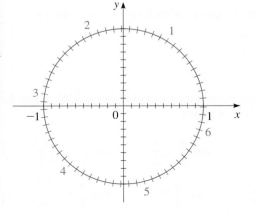

 DISCOVERY · DISCUSSION

47. Finding the Terminal Point for $\pi/6$ Suppose the terminal point determined by $t = \pi/6$ is $P(x, y)$ and the points Q and R are as shown in the figure. Why are the distances PQ and PR the same? Use this fact, together with the Distance Formula, to show that the coordinates of P satisfy the equation $2y = \sqrt{x^2 + (y - 1)^2}$. Simplify this equation using the fact that $x^2 + y^2 = 1$. Solve the simplified equation to find $P(x, y)$.

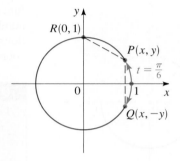

48. Finding the Terminal Point for $\pi/3$ Now that you know the terminal point determined by $t = \pi/6$, use symmetry to find the terminal point determined by $t = \pi/3$ (see the figure). Explain your reasoning.

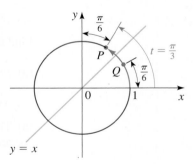

2.2   TRIGONOMETRIC FUNCTIONS OF REAL NUMBERS

A function is a rule that assigns to each real number another real number. In this section we use properties of the unit circle from the preceding section to define certain functions of real numbers, the trigonometric functions.

The Trigonometric Functions

Recall that to find the terminal point $P(x, y)$ for a given real number t, we move a distance t along the unit circle, starting at the point $(1, 0)$. We move in a counterclockwise direction if t is positive and in a clockwise direction if t is negative (see Figure 1). We now use the x- and y-coordinates of the point $P(x, y)$ to define several functions. For instance, we define the function called *sine* by assigning to each real number t the y-coordinate of the terminal point $P(x, y)$ determined by t. The functions *cosine, tangent, cosecant, secant,* and *cotangent* are also defined using the coordinates of $P(x, y)$.

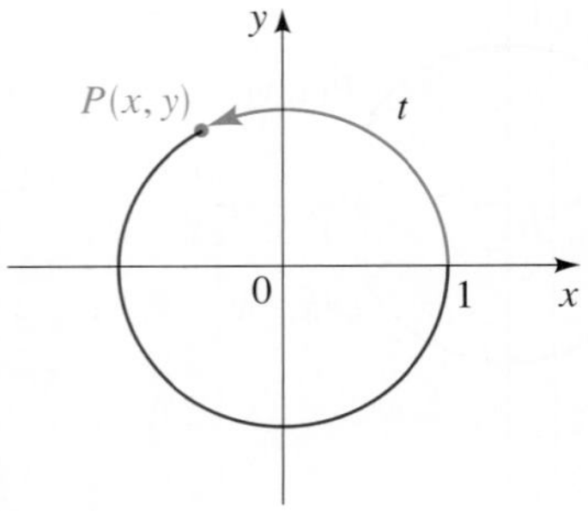

FIGURE 1

DEFINITION OF THE TRIGONOMETRIC FUNCTIONS

Let t be any real number and let $P(x, y)$ be the terminal point on the unit circle determined by t. We define

$$\sin t = y \qquad\qquad \cos t = x \qquad\qquad \tan t = \frac{y}{x} \quad (x \neq 0)$$

$$\csc t = \frac{1}{y} \quad (y \neq 0) \qquad \sec t = \frac{1}{x} \quad (x \neq 0) \qquad \cot t = \frac{x}{y} \quad (y \neq 0)$$

Because the trigonometric functions can be defined in terms of the unit circle, they are sometimes called the **circular functions**.

EXAMPLE 1   ■   Evaluating Trigonometric Functions

Find the six trigonometric functions of each given real number t.

(a) $t = \dfrac{\pi}{3}$ (b) $t = \dfrac{\pi}{2}$

SOLUTION

(a) The terminal point determined by $t = \pi/3$ is $P\left(\frac{1}{2}, \sqrt{3}/2\right)$. Since the coordinates are $x = \frac{1}{2}$ and $y = \sqrt{3}/2$, we have

$$\sin \frac{\pi}{3} = \frac{\sqrt{3}}{2} \qquad \cos \frac{\pi}{3} = \frac{1}{2} \qquad \tan \frac{\pi}{3} = \frac{\sqrt{3}/2}{1/2} = \sqrt{3}$$

$$\csc \frac{\pi}{3} = \frac{2\sqrt{3}}{3} \qquad \sec \frac{\pi}{3} = 2 \qquad \cot \frac{\pi}{4} = \frac{1/2}{\sqrt{3}/2} = \frac{\sqrt{3}}{3}$$

Relationship to the Trigonometric Functions of Angles

If you have previously studied trigonometry of right triangles (Chapter 3), you are probably wondering how the sine and cosine of an *angle* relate to those of this section. To see how, let's start with a right triangle, $\triangle OPQ$.

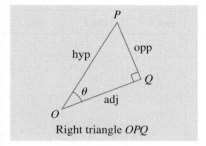
Right triangle OPQ

Place the triangle in the coordinate plane as shown, with angle θ in standard position.

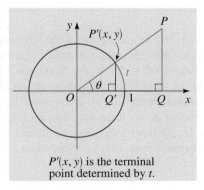
$P'(x, y)$ is the terminal point determined by t.

The point $P'(x, y)$ in the figure is the terminal point determined by the arc t. Note that triangle OPQ is similar to the small triangle $OP'Q'$ whose legs have lengths x and y.

Now, by the definition of the trigonometric functions of the *angle* θ we have

$$\sin \theta = \frac{\text{opp}}{\text{hyp}} = \frac{PQ}{OP} = \frac{P'Q'}{OP'}$$
$$= \frac{y}{1} = y$$
$$\cos \theta = \frac{\text{adj}}{\text{hyp}} = \frac{OQ}{OP} = \frac{OQ'}{OP'}$$
$$= \frac{x}{1} = x$$

By the definition of the trigonometric functions of the *real number t*, we have

$$\sin t = y$$
$$\cos t = x$$

Now, if θ is measured in radians, then $\theta = t$ (see the figure). So the trigonometric functions of the angle with radian measure θ are exactly the same as the trigonometric functions defined in terms of the terminal point determined by the real number t.

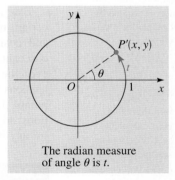
The radian measure of angle θ is t.

Why then study trigonometry in two different ways? Because different applications require that we view the trigonometric functions differently. (Compare Section 2.5 with Sections 3.2, 3.4, and 3.5.)

**Evaluating Functions
on a Calculator**

How does your calculator evaluate $\sin t$, $\cos t$, e^t, $\ln t$, $\sqrt{t}$, and other such functions? The calculator uses *numerical methods*, which are mathematical techniques for approximating the values of functions. One such method is to approximate these functions by polynomials, exploiting the fact that polynomial functions are easy to evaluate. For example,

$$\sin t = t - \frac{t^3}{3!} + \frac{t^5}{5!} - \frac{t^7}{7!} + \cdots$$

$$\cos t = 1 - \frac{t^2}{2!} + \frac{t^4}{4!} - \frac{t^6}{6!} + \cdots$$

where $n! = 1 \cdot 2 \cdot 3 \cdots n$ (for example, $4! = 1 \cdot 2 \cdot 3 \cdot 4 = 24$). These remarkable formulas were proved by the British mathematician Brook Taylor (1685–1731). The more terms we use from the series on the right-hand side of these formulas, the more accurate the values obtained for $\sin t$ and $\cos t$. For instance, if we use the first three terms of Taylor's series to find $\sin 0.9$, we get

$$\sin 0.9 \approx 0.9 - \frac{(0.9)^3}{3!} + \frac{(0.9)^5}{5!}$$

$$\approx 0.78342075$$

(Compare this with the value obtained using your calculator.) Formulas like these are programmed into your calculator, which uses them to compute functions like $\sin t$, $\cos t$, e^t, and $\log t$. The calculator uses enough terms to ensure that all displayed digits are accurate.

(b) The terminal point determined by $\pi/2$ is $P(0, 1)$. So

$$\sin \frac{\pi}{2} = 1 \qquad \cos \frac{\pi}{2} = 0 \qquad \csc \frac{\pi}{2} = \frac{1}{1} = 1 \qquad \cot \frac{\pi}{2} = \frac{0}{1} = 0$$

But $\tan \pi/2$ and $\sec \pi/2$ are undefined because $x = 0$ appears in the denominator in each of their definitions. ∎

Some special values of the trigonometric functions are listed in Table 1. This table is easily obtained from Table 1 of Section 2.1, together with the definitions of the trigonometric functions.

TABLE 1 Special values of the trigonometric functions

t	$\sin t$	$\cos t$	$\tan t$	$\csc t$	$\sec t$	$\cot t$
0	0	1	0	—	1	—
$\dfrac{\pi}{6}$	$\dfrac{1}{2}$	$\dfrac{\sqrt{3}}{2}$	$\dfrac{\sqrt{3}}{3}$	2	$\dfrac{2\sqrt{3}}{3}$	$\sqrt{3}$
$\dfrac{\pi}{4}$	$\dfrac{\sqrt{2}}{2}$	$\dfrac{\sqrt{2}}{2}$	1	$\sqrt{2}$	$\sqrt{2}$	1
$\dfrac{\pi}{3}$	$\dfrac{\sqrt{3}}{2}$	$\dfrac{1}{2}$	$\sqrt{3}$	$\dfrac{2\sqrt{3}}{3}$	2	$\dfrac{\sqrt{3}}{3}$
$\dfrac{\pi}{2}$	1	0	—	1	—	0

Example 1 shows that some of the trigonometric functions fail to be defined for certain real numbers. So we need to determine their domains. The functions sine and cosine are defined for all values of t. Since the functions cotangent and cosecant have y in the denominator of their definitions, they are not defined whenever the y-coordinate of the terminal point $P(x, y)$ determined by t is 0. This happens when $t = n\pi$ for any integer n, so their domains do not include these points. The functions tangent and secant have x in the denominator in their definitions, so they are not defined whenever $x = 0$. This happens when $t = (\pi/2) + n\pi$ for any integer n.

DOMAINS OF THE TRIGONOMETRIC FUNCTIONS

Function	Domain
sin, cos	All real numbers
tan, sec	All real numbers other than $\dfrac{\pi}{2} + n\pi$ for any integer n
cot, csc	All real numbers other than $n\pi$ for any integer n

Values of the Trigonometric Functions

To compute other values of the trigonometric functions, we first determine their signs. The signs of the trigonometric functions depend on the quadrant in which the terminal point of t lies. For example, if the terminal point $P(x, y)$ determined by t lies in quadrant III, then its coordinates are both negative. So $\sin t$, $\cos t$, $\csc t$, and $\sec t$ are all negative, while $\tan t$ and $\cot t$ are positive. You can check the other entries in the following box.

The following mnemonic device can be used to remember which trigonometric functions are positive in each quadrant: **A**ll of them, **S**ine, **T**angent, or **C**osine.

Sine	All
Tangent	Cosine

You can remember this as "All Students Take Calculus."

SIGNS OF THE TRIGONOMETRIC FUNCTIONS

Quadrant	Positive Functions	Negative functions
I	all	none
II	sin, csc	cos, sec, tan, cot
III	tan, cot	sin, csc, cos, sec
IV	cos, sec	sin, csc, tan, cot

EXAMPLE 2 ■ Determining the Sign of a Trigonometric Function

(a) $\cos \dfrac{\pi}{3} > 0$, since the terminal point of $t = \dfrac{\pi}{3}$ is in quadrant I.

(b) $\tan 4 > 0$, since the terminal point of $t = 4$ is in quadrant III.

(c) If $\cos t < 0$ and $\sin t > 0$, then the terminal point of t must be in quadrant II. ■

In Section 2.1 we used the reference number to find the terminal point determined by a real number t. Since the trigonometric functions are defined in terms of the coordinates of terminal points, we can use the reference number to find values of the trigonometric functions. Suppose that $\bar{t}$ is the reference number for t. Then the terminal point of $\bar{t}$ has the same coordinates, except possibly for sign, as the terminal point of t. So the values of the trigonometric functions at t are the same, except possibly for sign, as their values at $\bar{t}$. We illustrate the procedure in the next example.

EXAMPLE 3 ■ Evaluating Trigonometric Functions

Find each value.

(a) $\cos \dfrac{2\pi}{3}$ (b) $\tan\left(-\dfrac{\pi}{3}\right)$ (c) $\sin \dfrac{19\pi}{4}$

SOLUTION

(a) The reference number for $2\pi/3$ is $\pi/3$. Since the terminal point of $2\pi/3$ is in quadrant II, $\cos(2\pi/3)$ is negative. Thus

$$\cos \frac{2\pi}{3} = -\cos \frac{\pi}{3} = -\frac{1}{2}$$

        ↑   ↑   ↑
     sign reference from
         number Table 1

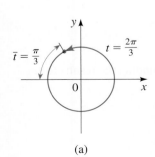

(a)

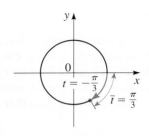

(b)

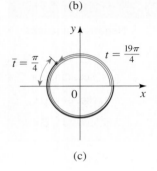

(c)

(b) The reference number for $-\pi/3$ is $\pi/3$. Since the terminal point of $-\pi/3$ is in quadrant IV, $\tan(-\pi/3)$ is negative. Thus

$$\tan\left(-\frac{\pi}{3}\right) = -\tan\frac{\pi}{3} = -\sqrt{3}$$

$$\begin{array}{ccc} \uparrow & \uparrow & \uparrow \\ \text{sign} & \text{reference} & \text{from} \\ & \text{number} & \text{Table 1} \end{array}$$

(c) Since $(19\pi/4) - 4\pi = 3\pi/4$, the terminal points determined by $19\pi/4$ and $3\pi/4$ are the same. The reference number for $3\pi/4$ is $\pi/4$. Since the terminal point of $3\pi/4$ is in quadrant II, $\sin(3\pi/4)$ is positive. Thus

$$\sin\frac{19\pi}{4} = \sin\frac{3\pi}{4} = +\sin\frac{\pi}{4} = \frac{\sqrt{2}}{2}$$

$$\begin{array}{cccc} \uparrow & & \uparrow & \uparrow \\ \text{subtract } 4\pi & & \text{sign} & \text{reference} \quad \text{from} \\ & & & \text{number} \quad \text{Table 1} \end{array}$$ ■

So far we have been able to compute the values of the trigonometric functions only for certain values of t. In fact, we can compute the values of the trigonometric functions whenever t is a multiple of $\pi/6$, $\pi/4$, $\pi/3$, and $\pi/2$. How can we compute the trigonometric functions for other values of t? For example, how can we find $\sin 1.5$? One way is to carefully sketch a diagram and read the value (see Exercises 35–42); however, this method is not very accurate. Fortunately, programmed directly into scientific calculators are mathematical procedures (see the margin note on page 124) that find the values of *sine, cosine,* and *tangent* correct to the number of digits in the display. The calculator must be put in *radian mode* to evaluate these functions. To find values of cosecant, secant, and cotangent using a calculator, we need to use the following *reciprocal relations:*

$$\csc t = \frac{1}{\sin t} \qquad \sec t = \frac{1}{\cos t} \qquad \cot t = \frac{1}{\tan t}$$

These identities follow from the definitions of the trigonometric functions. For instance, since $\sin t = y$ and $\csc t = 1/y$, we have $\csc t = 1/y = 1/(\sin t)$. The others follow similarly.

EXAMPLE 4 ■ Using a Calculator to Evaluate Trigonometric Functions

Making sure our calculator is set to radian mode and rounding the results to six decimal places, we get

(a) $\sin 2.2 \approx 0.808496$

(b) $\cos 1.1 \approx 0.453596$

(c) $\cot 28 = \dfrac{1}{\tan 28} \approx -3.553286$

(d) $\csc 0.98 = \dfrac{1}{\sin 0.98} \approx 1.204098$ ∎

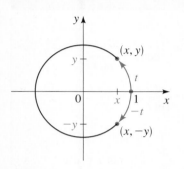

FIGURE 2

Let's consider the relationship between the trigonometric functions of t and those of $-t$. From Figure 2 we see that

$$\sin(-t) = -y = -\sin t$$

$$\cos(-t) = x = \cos t$$

$$\tan(-t) = \dfrac{-y}{x} = -\dfrac{y}{x} = -\tan t$$

These equations show that sine and tangent are odd functions, whereas cosine is an even function. It's easy to see that the reciprocal of an even function is even and the reciprocal of an odd function is odd (see Section 1.5). This fact, together with the reciprocal relations, completes our knowledge of the even-odd properties for all the trigonometric functions.

EVEN-ODD PROPERTIES

Sine, cosecant, tangent, and cotangent are odd functions; cosine and secant are even functions.

$$\sin(-t) = -\sin t \qquad \cos(-t) = \cos t \qquad \tan(-t) = -\tan t$$
$$\csc(-t) = -\csc t \qquad \sec(-t) = \sec t \qquad \cot(-t) = -\cot t$$

EXAMPLE 5 ■ Even and Odd Trigonometric Functions

Use the even-odd properties of the trigonometric functions to determine each value.

(a) $\sin\left(-\dfrac{\pi}{6}\right)$ (b) $\cos\left(-\dfrac{\pi}{4}\right)$

SOLUTION

By the even-odd properties and Table 1, we have

(a) $\sin\left(-\dfrac{\pi}{6}\right) = -\sin\dfrac{\pi}{6} = -\dfrac{1}{2}$ Sine is odd

(b) $\cos\left(-\dfrac{\pi}{4}\right) = \cos\dfrac{\pi}{4} = \dfrac{\sqrt{2}}{2}$ Cosine is even ∎

■ Fundamental Identities

The trigonometric functions are related to each other through equations called **trigonometric identities**. We give the most important ones in the following box.*

FUNDAMENTAL IDENTITIES

Reciprocal Identities

$$\csc t = \frac{1}{\sin t} \qquad \sec t = \frac{1}{\cos t} \qquad \cot t = \frac{1}{\tan t}$$

$$\tan t = \frac{\sin t}{\cos t} \qquad \cot t = \frac{\cos t}{\sin t}$$

Pythagorean Identities

$$\sin^2 t + \cos^2 t = 1 \qquad \tan^2 t + 1 = \sec^2 t \qquad 1 + \cot^2 t = \csc^2 t$$

■ **Proof**   The reciprocal identities follow immediately from the definition on page 122. We now prove the Pythagorean identities. By definition, $\cos t = x$ and $\sin t = y$, where x and y are the coordinates of a point $P(x, y)$ on the unit circle. Since $P(x, y)$ is on the unit circle, we have $x^2 + y^2 = 1$. Thus

$$\sin^2 t + \cos^2 t = 1$$

Dividing both sides by $\cos^2 t$ (provided $\cos t \neq 0$), we get

$$\frac{\sin^2 t}{\cos^2 t} + \frac{\cos^2 t}{\cos^2 t} = \frac{1}{\cos^2 t}$$

$$\left(\frac{\sin t}{\cos t}\right)^2 + 1 = \left(\frac{1}{\cos t}\right)^2$$

$$\tan^2 t + 1 = \sec^2 t$$

We have used the reciprocal identities $\sin t / \cos t = \tan t$ and $1/\cos t = \sec t$. Similarly, dividing both sides of the first Pythagorean identity by $\sin^2 t$ (provided $\sin t \neq 0$) gives us $1 + \cot^2 t = \csc^2 t$. □

As their name indicates, the fundamental identities play a central role in trigonometry because we can use them to relate any trigonometric function to any

---

*We follow the usual convention of writing $\sin^2 t$ for $(\sin t)^2$. In general, we write $\sin^n t$ for $(\sin t)^n$ for all integers n except $n = -1$. The exponent $n = -1$ will be assigned another meaning in Section 4.4. Of course, the same convention applies to the other five trigonometric functions.

other. So, if we know the value of any one of the trigonometric functions at t, then we can find the values of all the others at t.

EXAMPLE 6 ■ Finding All Trigonometric Functions from the Value of One

If $\cos t = \frac{3}{5}$ and t is in quadrant IV, find the values of all the trigonometric functions at t.

SOLUTION

From the Pythagorean identities we have

$$\sin^2 t + \cos^2 t = 1$$

$$\sin^2 t + \left(\tfrac{3}{5}\right)^2 = 1 \qquad \text{Substitute } \cos t = \tfrac{3}{5}$$

$$\sin^2 t = 1 - \tfrac{9}{25} = \tfrac{16}{25} \qquad \text{Solve for } \sin^2 t$$

$$\sin t = \pm \tfrac{4}{5} \qquad \text{Take square roots}$$

Since this point is in quadrant IV, $\sin t$ is negative, so $\sin t = -\frac{4}{5}$. Now that we know both $\sin t$ and $\cos t$, we can find the values of the other trigonometric functions using the reciprocal identities:

$$\sin t = -\frac{4}{5} \qquad \cos t = \frac{3}{5} \qquad \tan t = \frac{\sin t}{\cos t} = \frac{-\tfrac{4}{5}}{\tfrac{3}{5}} = -\frac{4}{3}$$

$$\csc t = \frac{1}{\sin t} = -\frac{5}{4} \qquad \sec t = \frac{1}{\cos t} = \frac{5}{3} \qquad \cot t = \frac{1}{\tan t} = -\frac{3}{4} \qquad ■$$

EXAMPLE 7 ■ Writing One Trigonometric Function in Terms of Another

Write $\tan t$ in terms of $\cos t$, where t is in quadrant III.

SOLUTION

Since $\tan t = \sin t / \cos t$, we need to write $\sin t$ in terms of $\cos t$. By the Pythagorean identities we have

$$\sin^2 t + \cos^2 t = 1$$

$$\sin^2 t = 1 - \cos^2 t \qquad \text{Solve for } \sin^2 t$$

$$\sin t = \pm\sqrt{1 - \cos^2 t} \qquad \text{Take square roots}$$

Since $\sin t$ is negative in quadrant III, the negative sign applies here. Thus

$$\tan t = \frac{\sin t}{\cos t} = \frac{-\sqrt{1 - \cos^2 t}}{\cos t} \qquad ■$$

2.2 EXERCISES

1–2 ■ Find sin t and cos t for the values of t whose terminal points are shown on the unit circle in the figure. In Exercise 1, t increases in increments of $\pi/4$; in Exercise 2, t increases in increments of $\pi/6$. (See Exercises 11 and 12 in Section 2.1.)

1.
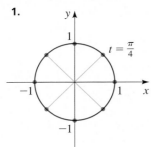

2.
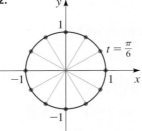

3–22 ■ Find the exact value of the trigonometric function at the given real number.

3. (a) $\sin\left(-\dfrac{\pi}{3}\right)$

(b) $\cos\left(-\dfrac{\pi}{3}\right)$

4. (a) $\sin \pi$

(b) $\sin(-\pi)$

5. (a) $\cos \pi$

(b) $\cos(-\pi)$

6. (a) $\cos \dfrac{\pi}{6}$

(b) $\cos \dfrac{5\pi}{6}$

7. (a) $\sin \dfrac{\pi}{2}$

(b) $\sin \dfrac{3\pi}{2}$

8. (a) $\sin \dfrac{7\pi}{6}$

(b) $\cos \dfrac{7\pi}{6}$

9. (a) $\cos \dfrac{\pi}{2}$

(b) $\cos \dfrac{5\pi}{2}$

10. (a) $\sin \dfrac{5\pi}{6}$

(b) $\csc \dfrac{5\pi}{6}$

11. (a) $\cos \dfrac{7\pi}{3}$

(b) $\sec \dfrac{7\pi}{3}$

12. (a) $\sin \dfrac{3\pi}{4}$

(b) $\cos \dfrac{3\pi}{4}$

13. (a) $\cos \dfrac{\pi}{3}$

(b) $\cos\left(-\dfrac{\pi}{3}\right)$

14. (a) $\sin \dfrac{\pi}{6}$

(b) $\sin\left(-\dfrac{\pi}{6}\right)$

15. (a) $\tan \dfrac{\pi}{6}$

(b) $\tan\left(-\dfrac{\pi}{6}\right)$

16. (a) $\tan \dfrac{\pi}{3}$

(b) $\cot \dfrac{\pi}{3}$

17. (a) $\sec \dfrac{11\pi}{3}$

(b) $\csc \dfrac{11\pi}{3}$

18. (a) $\sec \dfrac{13\pi}{6}$

(b) $\sec\left(-\dfrac{13\pi}{6}\right)$

19. (a) $\sin \dfrac{9\pi}{4}$

(b) $\csc \dfrac{9\pi}{4}$

20. (a) $\sec \pi$

(b) $\csc \dfrac{\pi}{2}$

21. (a) $\tan\left(-\dfrac{\pi}{4}\right)$

(b) $\cot\left(-\dfrac{\pi}{4}\right)$

22. (a) $\tan \dfrac{3\pi}{4}$

(b) $\tan \dfrac{11\pi}{4}$

23–26 ■ Find the value of each of the six trigonometric functions (if it is defined) at the given real number t. Use your answers to complete the table.

23. $t = 0$ **24.** $t = \dfrac{\pi}{2}$ **25.** $t = \pi$ **26.** $t = \dfrac{3\pi}{2}$

t	sin t	cos t	tan t	csc t	sec t	cot t
0	0	1		undefined		
$\dfrac{\pi}{2}$						
π		0				undefined
$\dfrac{3\pi}{2}$						

27–34 ■ The terminal point $P(x, y)$ determined by t is given. Find sin t, cos t, and tan t.

27. $\left(\dfrac{3}{5}, \dfrac{4}{5}\right)$

28. $\left(-\dfrac{3}{5}, \dfrac{4}{5}\right)$

29. $\left(\dfrac{\sqrt{5}}{4}, -\dfrac{\sqrt{11}}{4}\right)$

30. $\left(-\dfrac{1}{3}, -\dfrac{2\sqrt{2}}{3}\right)$

31. $\left(\dfrac{40}{41}, \dfrac{9}{41}\right)$

32. $\left(-\dfrac{6}{7}, \dfrac{\sqrt{13}}{7}\right)$

33. $\left(-\dfrac{5}{13}, -\dfrac{12}{13}\right)$

34. $\left(\dfrac{\sqrt{5}}{5}, \dfrac{2\sqrt{5}}{5}\right)$

35–42 ■ Find the approximate value of the given trigonometric function by using (a) the figure and (b) a calculator. Compare the two values.

35. sin 1

36. cos 0.8

37. sin 1.2

38. cos 5

39. tan 0.8

40. tan(−1.3)

41. cos 4.1

42. sin(−5.2)

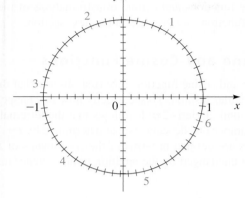

43–46 ■ Find the sign of the expression if the terminal point determined by t is in the given quadrant.

43. sin t cos t,   quadrant II   **44.** tan t sec t,   quadrant IV

45. $\dfrac{\tan t \sin t}{\cot t}$,   quadrant III   **46.** cos t sec t,   any quadrant

47–50 ■ From the information given, find the quadrant in which the terminal point determined by t lies.

47. sin $t > 0$ and cos $t < 0$ **48.** tan $t > 0$ and sin $t < 0$

49. csc $t > 0$ and sec $t < 0$ **50.** cos $t < 0$ and cot $t < 0$

51–60 ■ Write the first expression in terms of the second if the terminal point determined by t is in the given quadrant.

51. sin t, cos t;   quadrant II   **52.** cos t, sin t;   quadrant IV

53. tan t, sin t;   quadrant IV   **54.** tan t, cos t;   quadrant III

55. sec t, tan t;   quadrant II   **56.** csc t, cot t;   quadrant III

57. tan t, sec t;   quadrant III   **58.** sin t, sec t;   quadrant IV

59. $\tan^2 t$, sin t;   any quadrant

60. $\sec^2 t \sin^2 t$, cos t;   any quadrant

61–68 ■ Find the values of the trigonometric functions of t from the given information.

61. sin $t = \frac{3}{5}$,   terminal point of t is in quadrant II

62. cos $t = -\frac{4}{5}$,   terminal point of t is in quadrant III

63. sec $t = 3$,   terminal point of t is in quadrant IV

64. tan $t = \frac{1}{4}$,   terminal point of t is in quadrant III

65. tan $t = -\frac{3}{4}$,   cos $t > 0$ **66.** sec $t = 2$,   sin $t < 0$

67. sin $t = -\frac{1}{4}$,   sec $t < 0$ **68.** tan $t = -4$,   csc $t > 0$

69–76 ■ Determine whether the function is even, odd, or neither.

69. $f(x) = x^2 \sin x$ **70.** $f(x) = x^2 \cos 2x$

71. $f(x) = \sin x \cos x$ **72.** $f(x) = \sin x + \cos x$

73. $f(x) = |x| \cos x$ **74.** $f(x) = x \sin^3 x$

75. $f(x) = x^3 + \cos x$ **76.** $f(x) = \cos(\sin x)$

DISCOVERY · DISCUSSION

77. Reduction Formulas   Explain how the figure shows that the following "reduction formulas" are valid:

$$\sin(t + \pi) = -\sin t \qquad \cos(t + \pi) = -\cos t$$
$$\tan(t + \pi) = \tan t$$

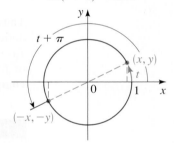

78. More Reduction Formulas   By the "Angle-Side-Angle" theorem from elementary geometry, triangles CDO and AOB in the figure are congruent. Explain how this proves that if B has coordinates (x, y), then D has coordinates $(-y, x)$. Then explain how the figure shows that the following "reduction formulas" are valid:

$$\sin\left(t + \frac{\pi}{2}\right) = \cos t$$

$$\cos\left(t + \frac{\pi}{2}\right) = -\sin t$$

$$\tan\left(t + \frac{\pi}{2}\right) = -\cot t$$

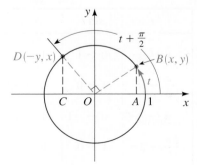

2.3 TRIGONOMETRIC GRAPHS

The graph of a function gives us a better idea of its behavior. So, in this section we graph the sine and cosine functions and certain transformations of these functions. The other trigonometric functions are graphed in the next section.

◼ Graphs of the Sine and Cosine Functions

To help us graph the sine and cosine functions, we first observe that these functions repeat their values in a regular fashion. To see exactly how this happens, recall that the circumference of the unit circle is 2π. It follows that the terminal point $P(x, y)$ determined by the real number t is the same as that determined by $t + 2\pi$. Since the sine and cosine functions are defined in terms of the coordinates of $P(x, y)$, it follows that their values are unchanged by the addition of any integer multiple of 2π. In other words,

$$\sin(t + 2n\pi) = \sin t \qquad \text{for any integer } n$$

$$\cos(t + 2n\pi) = \cos t \qquad \text{for any integer } n$$

Thus, the sine and cosine functions are *periodic* according to the following definition: A function f is **periodic** if there is a positive number p such that $f(t + p) = f(t)$ for every t. The least such positive number (if it exists) is the **period** of f. If f has period p, then the graph of f on any interval of length p is called **one complete period** of f.

PERIODIC PROPERTIES OF SINE AND COSINE

The function sine has period 2π: $\sin(t + 2\pi) = \sin t$

The function cosine has period 2π: $\cos(t + 2\pi) = \cos t$

So the sine and cosine functions repeat their values in any interval of length 2π. To sketch their graphs, we first graph one period. To sketch the graphs on the interval $0 \le t \le 2\pi$, we could try to make a table of values and use those points to draw the graph. Since no such table can be complete, let's look more closely at the definitions of these functions.

Recall that $\sin t$ is the y-coordinate of the terminal point $P(x, y)$ on the unit circle determined by the real number t. How does the y-coordinate of this point vary as t increases? It's easy to see that the y-coordinate of $P(x, y)$ increases to 1, then decreases to -1 repeatedly as the point $P(x, y)$ travels around the unit circle. (See Figure 1.) In fact, as t increases from 0 to $\pi/2$, $y = \sin t$ increases from 0 to 1. As t increases from $\pi/2$ to π, the value of $y = \sin t$ decreases from 1 to 0. Table 1 shows the variation of the sine and cosine functions for t between 0 and 2π.

TABLE 1

t	$\sin t$	$\cos t$
$0 \rightarrow \dfrac{\pi}{2}$	$0 \rightarrow 1$	$1 \rightarrow 0$
$\dfrac{\pi}{2} \rightarrow \pi$	$1 \rightarrow 0$	$0 \rightarrow -1$
$\pi \rightarrow \dfrac{3\pi}{2}$	$0 \rightarrow -1$	$-1 \rightarrow 0$
$\dfrac{3\pi}{2} \rightarrow 2\pi$	$-1 \rightarrow 0$	$0 \rightarrow 1$

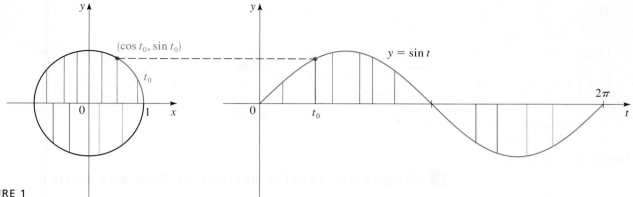

FIGURE 1

To draw the graphs more accurately, we find a few other values of $\sin t$ and $\cos t$ in Table 2. We could find still other values with the aid of a calculator.

TABLE 2

t	0	$\dfrac{\pi}{6}$	$\dfrac{\pi}{3}$	$\dfrac{\pi}{2}$	$\dfrac{2\pi}{3}$	$\dfrac{5\pi}{6}$	π	$\dfrac{7\pi}{6}$	$\dfrac{4\pi}{3}$	$\dfrac{3\pi}{2}$	$\dfrac{5\pi}{3}$	$\dfrac{11\pi}{6}$	2π
$\sin t$	0	$\dfrac{1}{2}$	$\dfrac{\sqrt{3}}{2}$	1	$\dfrac{\sqrt{3}}{2}$	$\dfrac{1}{2}$	0	$-\dfrac{1}{2}$	$-\dfrac{\sqrt{3}}{2}$	-1	$-\dfrac{\sqrt{3}}{2}$	$-\dfrac{1}{2}$	0
$\cos t$	1	$\dfrac{\sqrt{3}}{2}$	$\dfrac{1}{2}$	0	$-\dfrac{1}{2}$	$-\dfrac{\sqrt{3}}{2}$	-1	$-\dfrac{\sqrt{3}}{2}$	$-\dfrac{1}{2}$	0	$\dfrac{1}{2}$	$\dfrac{\sqrt{3}}{2}$	1

Now we use this information to graph the functions $\sin t$ and $\cos t$ for t between 0 and 2π in Figures 2 and 3. These are the graphs of one period. Using the fact that these functions are periodic with period 2π, we get their complete graphs by continuing the same pattern to the left and to the right in every successive interval of length 2π.

The graph of the sine function is symmetric with respect to the origin. This is as expected, since sine is an odd function. Since the cosine function is an even function, its graph is symmetric with respect to the y-axis.

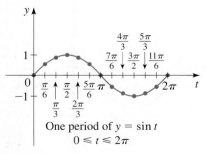

One period of $y = \sin t$
$0 \leq t \leq 2\pi$

FIGURE 2 Graph of $\sin t$

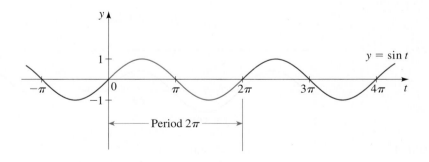

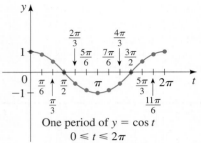

One period of $y = \cos t$
$0 \leq t \leq 2\pi$

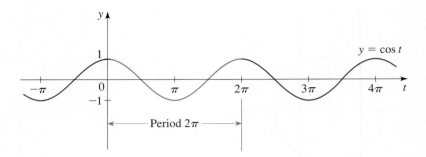

FIGURE 3 Graph of $\cos t$

Graphs of Transformations of Sine and Cosine

We now consider graphs of functions that are transformations of the sine and cosine functions. Thus, the graphing techniques of Section 1.5 are very useful here. The graphs we obtain are important for understanding applications to physical situations such as harmonic motion (see Section 2.5), but some of them are beautiful graphs that are interesting in their own right.

It's traditional to use the letter x to denote the variable in the domain of a function. So, from here on we use the letter x and write $y = \sin x$, $y = \cos x$, $y = \tan x$, and so on to denote these functions.

EXAMPLE 1 ■ Cosine Curves

Sketch the graph of each function.

(a) $f(x) = 2 + \cos x$ (b) $g(x) = -\cos x$

SOLUTION

(a) The graph of $y = 2 + \cos x$ is the same as the graph of $y = \cos x$, but shifted up 2 units [see Figure 4(a)].

(b) The graph of $y = -\cos x$ in Figure 4(b) is the reflection of the graph of $y = \cos x$ in the x-axis.

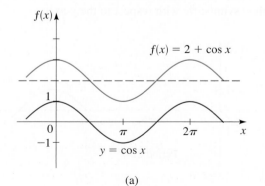

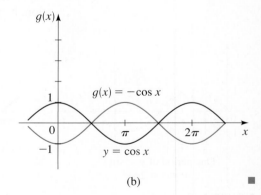

FIGURE 4   (a)   (b)   ■

Vertical stretching and shrinking of graphs is discussed in Section 1.5.

Let's graph $y = 2 \sin x$. We start with the graph of $y = \sin x$ and multiply the y-coordinate of each point by 2. This has the effect of stretching the graph vertically by a factor of 2. To graph $y = \frac{1}{2} \sin x$, we start with the graph of $y = \sin x$ and multiply the y-coordinate of each point by $\frac{1}{2}$. This has the effect of shrinking the graph vertically by a factor of $\frac{1}{2}$ (see Figure 5).

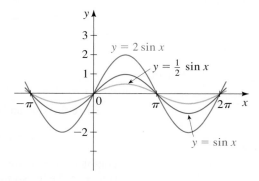

FIGURE 5

In general, for the functions

$$y = a \sin x \qquad \text{and} \qquad y = a \cos x$$

the number $|a|$ is called the **amplitude** and is the largest value these functions attain. Graphs of $y = a \sin x$ for several values of a are shown in Figure 6.

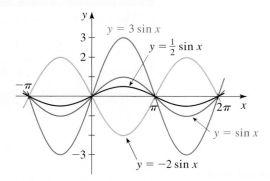

FIGURE 6

EXAMPLE 2 ■ Stretching a Cosine Curve

Find the amplitude of $y = -3 \cos x$ and sketch its graph.

SOLUTION

The amplitude is $|-3| = 3$, so the largest value the graph attains is 3 and the smallest value is -3. To sketch the graph, we begin with the graph of $y = \cos x$, stretch the graph vertically by a factor of 3, and reflect in the x-axis, arriving at the graph in Figure 7.

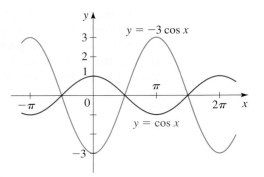

FIGURE 7

Since the sine and cosine functions have period 2π, the functions

$$y = a \sin kx \qquad \text{and} \qquad y = a \cos kx \qquad (k > 0)$$

complete one period as kx varies from 0 to 2π, that is, for $0 \leqslant kx \leqslant 2\pi$ or for $0 \leqslant x \leqslant 2\pi/k$. So these functions complete one period as x varies between 0 and $2\pi/k$ and thus have period $2\pi/k$. The graphs of these functions are called **sine curves** and **cosine curves**, respectively. (Collectively, sine and cosine curves are often referred to as **sinusoidal** curves.)

SINE AND COSINE CURVES

The sine and cosine curves

$$y = a \sin kx \qquad \text{and} \qquad y = a \cos kx \qquad (k > 0)$$

have amplitude $|a|$ and period $2\pi/k$.

An appropriate interval on which to graph one complete period is $[0, 2\pi/k]$.

Horizontal stretching and shrinking of graphs is discussed in Section 1.5.

To see how the value of k affects the graph of $y = \sin kx$, let's graph the sine curve $y = \sin 2x$. Since the period is $2\pi/2 = \pi$, the graph completes one period in the interval $0 \leqslant x \leqslant \pi$ [see Figure 8(a)]. For the sine curve $y = \sin \frac{1}{2}x$, the period is $2\pi \div \frac{1}{2} = 4\pi$, and so the graph completes one period in the interval $0 \leqslant x \leqslant 4\pi$ [see Figure 8(b)]. We see that the effect is to shrink the graph if $k > 1$ or to stretch the graph if $k < 1$.

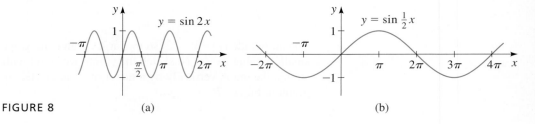

FIGURE 8   (a)   (b)

For comparison, in Figure 9 we show the graphs of one period of the sine curve $y = a \sin kx$ for several values of k.

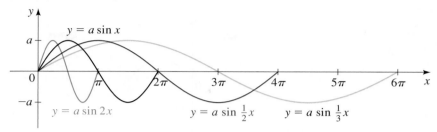

FIGURE 9

EXAMPLE 3 ■ Amplitude and Period

Find the amplitude and period of each function, and sketch its graph.

(a) $y = 4 \cos 3x$ (b) $y = -2 \sin \frac{1}{2} x$

SOLUTION

(a) For $y = 4 \cos 3x$,

$$\text{amplitude} = |a| = 4$$

$$\text{period} = \frac{2\pi}{3}$$

The graph is shown in Figure 10.

(b) For $y = -2 \sin \frac{1}{2} x$,

$$\text{amplitude} = |a| = |-2| = 2$$

$$\text{period} = \frac{2\pi}{\frac{1}{2}} = 4\pi$$

The graph is shown in Figure 11.   ∎

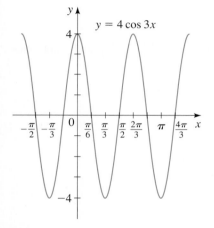

FIGURE 10

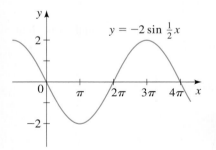

FIGURE 11

The graphs of functions of the form $y = a \sin k(x - b)$ and $y = a \cos k(x - b)$ are simply sine and cosine curves shifted horizontally by an amount $|b|$. They are shifted to the right if $b > 0$ or to the left if $b < 0$. The number b is the **phase shift**. We summarize the properties of these functions in the following box.

SHIFTED SINE AND COSINE CURVES

The sine and cosine curves

$$y = a \sin k(x - b) \qquad \text{and} \qquad y = a \cos k(x - b) \qquad (k > 0)$$

have amplitude $|a|$, period $2\pi/k$, and phase shift b.

An appropriate interval on which to graph one complete period is $[b, b + (2\pi/k)]$.

The graphs of $y = \sin\left(x - \dfrac{\pi}{3}\right)$ and $y = \sin\left(x + \dfrac{\pi}{6}\right)$ are shown in Figure 12.

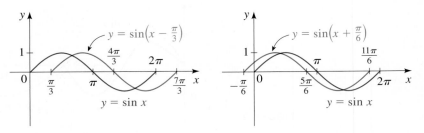

FIGURE 12

EXAMPLE 4 ■ A Shifted Sine Curve

Find the amplitude, period, and phase shift of $y = 3 \sin 2\left(x - \dfrac{\pi}{4}\right)$, and graph one complete period.

SOLUTION

We have

$$\text{amplitude} = |a| = 3$$

$$\text{period} = \frac{2\pi}{2} = \pi$$

$$\text{phase shift} = \frac{\pi}{4} \qquad \text{Shift } \tfrac{\pi}{4} \text{ to the } right$$

Since the phase shift is $\pi/4$ and the period is π, one complete period occurs on the interval

$$\left[\frac{\pi}{4}, \frac{\pi}{4} + \pi\right] = \left[\frac{\pi}{4}, \frac{5\pi}{4}\right]$$

As an aid in sketching the graph, we divide this interval into four equal parts, then graph a sine curve with amplitude 3 as in Figure 13.

Here is another way to find an appropriate interval on which to graph one complete period. Since the period of $y = \sin x$ is 2π, the function $y = 3 \sin 2(x - \tfrac{\pi}{4})$ will go through one complete period as $2(x - \tfrac{\pi}{4})$ varies from 0 to 2π.

Start of period: End of period:

$2\left(x - \tfrac{\pi}{4}\right) = 0 \qquad 2\left(x - \tfrac{\pi}{4}\right) = 2\pi$

$x - \tfrac{\pi}{4} = 0 \qquad\quad x - \tfrac{\pi}{4} = \pi$

$x = \tfrac{\pi}{4} \qquad\qquad x = \tfrac{5\pi}{4}$

So we graph one period on the interval $\left[\tfrac{\pi}{4}, \tfrac{5\pi}{4}\right]$.

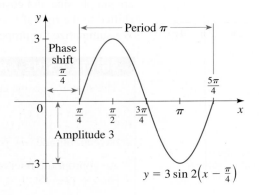

FIGURE 13

EXAMPLE 5 ■ A Shifted Cosine Curve

Find the amplitude, period, and phase shift of

$$y = \frac{3}{4} \cos\left(2x + \frac{2\pi}{3}\right)$$

and graph one complete period.

SOLUTION

We first write this function in the form $y = a \cos k(x - b)$. To do this, we factor 2 from the expression $2x + \frac{2\pi}{3}$ to get

$$y = \frac{3}{4} \cos 2\left[x - \left(-\frac{\pi}{3}\right)\right]$$

We can also find one complete period as follows:

Start of period:

$2x + \frac{2\pi}{3} = 0$

$2x = -\frac{2\pi}{3}$

$x = -\frac{\pi}{3}$

End of period:

$2x + \frac{2\pi}{3} = 2\pi$

$2x = \frac{4\pi}{3}$

$x = \frac{2\pi}{3}$

So we graph one period on the interval $\left[-\frac{\pi}{3}, \frac{2\pi}{3}\right]$.

Thus, we have

$$\text{amplitude} = |a| = \frac{3}{4}$$

$$\text{period} = \frac{2\pi}{k} = \frac{2\pi}{2} = \pi$$

$$\text{phase shift} = b = -\frac{\pi}{3} \qquad \text{Shift } \tfrac{\pi}{3} \text{ to the } \textit{left}$$

From this information it follows that one period of this cosine curve begins at $-\pi/3$ and ends at $(-\pi/3) + \pi = 2\pi/3$. To sketch the graph over the interval $[-\pi/3, 2\pi/3]$, we divide this interval into four equal parts and graph a cosine curve with amplitude $\frac{3}{4}$ as shown in Figure 14.

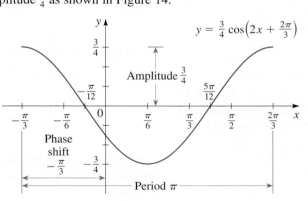

FIGURE 14

Using Graphing Devices to Graph Trigonometric Functions

See Appendix C.1 for guidelines on choosing an appropriate viewing rectangle.

When using a graphing calculator or a computer to graph a function, it is important to choose the viewing rectangle carefully in order to produce a reasonable graph of the function. This is especially true for trigonometric functions; Example 6 shows that, if care is not taken, it's easy to produce a very misleading graph of a trigonometric function.

EXAMPLE 6 ■ Choosing the Viewing Rectangle

Graph the function $f(x) = \sin 50x$ in an appropriate viewing rectangle.

SOLUTION

Figure 15(a) shows the graph of f produced by a graphing calculator using the viewing rectangle $[-12, 12]$ by $[-1.5, 1.5]$. At first glance the graph appears to be reasonable. But if we change the viewing rectangle to the ones shown in Figure 15, the graphs look very different. Something strange is happening.

The appearance of the graphs in Figure 15 depends on the machine used. The graphs you get with your own graphing device might not look like these figures, but they will also be quite inaccurate.

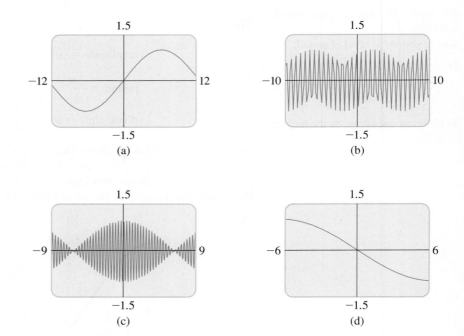

FIGURE 15

Graphs of $f(x) = \sin 50x$ in different viewing rectangles

To explain the big differences in appearance of these graphs and to find an appropriate viewing rectangle, we need to find the period of the function $y = \sin 50x$:

$$\text{period} = \frac{2\pi}{50} = \frac{\pi}{25} \approx 0.126$$

This suggests that we should deal only with small values of x in order to show just a few oscillations of the graph. If we choose the viewing rectangle $[-0.25, 0.25]$ by $[-1.5, 1.5]$, we get the graph shown in Figure 16.

The function h in Example 7 is **periodic** with period 2π. In general, functions that are sums of functions from the following list

$1, \cos kx, \cos 2kx, \cos 3kx, \ldots$

$\sin kx, \sin 2kx, \sin 3kx, \ldots$

are periodic. Although these functions appear to be special, they are actually fundamental to describing all periodic functions that arise in practice. The French mathematician J. B. J. Fourier (see page 253) discovered that nearly every periodic function can be written as a sum (usually an infinite sum) of these functions. This is remarkable because it means that any situation in which periodic variation occurs can be described mathematically using the functions sine and cosine. A modern application of Fourier's discovery is the digital encoding of sound on compact discs.

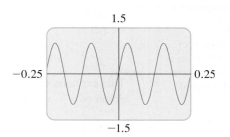

FIGURE 16

$f(x) = \sin 50x$

Now we see what went wrong in Figure 15. The oscillations of $y = \sin 50x$ are so rapid that when the calculator plots points and joins them, it misses most of the maximum and minimum points and therefore gives a very misleading impression of the graph.   ∎

EXAMPLE 7 ■ A Sum of Sine and Cosine Curves

Graph $f(x) = 2 \cos x$, $g(x) = \sin 2x$, and $h(x) = 2 \cos x + \sin 2x$ on a common screen to illustrate the method of graphical addition.

SOLUTION

Notice that $h = f + g$, so its graph is obtained by adding the corresponding y-coordinates of the graphs of f and g. The graphs of f, g, and h are shown in Figure 17.

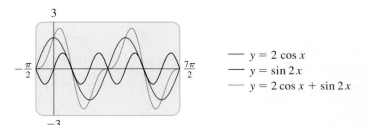

FIGURE 17

EXAMPLE 8 ■ A Cosine Curve with Variable Amplitude

Graph the functions $y = x^2$, $y = -x^2$, and $y = x^2 \cos 6\pi x$ on a common screen. Comment on and explain the relationship among the graphs.

SOLUTION

Figure 18 shows all three graphs in the viewing rectangle $[-1.5, 1.5]$ by $[-2, 2]$. It appears that the graph of $y = x^2 \cos 6\pi x$ lies between the graphs of the functions $y = x^2$ and $y = -x^2$.

To understand this, recall that the values of $\cos 6\pi x$ lie between -1 and 1, that is,

$$-1 \leqslant \cos 6\pi x \leqslant 1$$

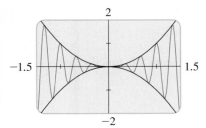

FIGURE 18

$y = x^2 \cos 6\pi x$

AM and FM Radio

Radio transmissions consist of sound waves superimposed on a harmonic electromagnetic wave form called the **carrier signal**.

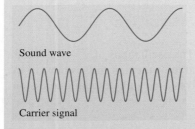

Sound wave

Carrier signal

There are two types of radio transmission, called **amplitude modulation (AM)** and **frequency modulation (FM)**. In AM broadcasting the sound wave changes, or **modulates**, the amplitude of the carrier, but the frequency remains unchanged.

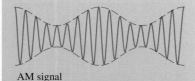

AM signal

In FM broadcasting the sound wave modulates the frequency, but the amplitude remains the same.

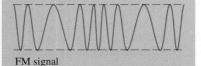

FM signal

for all values of x. Multiplying the inequalities by x^2, and noting that $x^2 \geq 0$, we get

$$-x^2 \leq x^2 \cos 6\pi x \leq x^2$$

This explains why the functions $y = x^2$ and $y = -x^2$ form a boundary for the graph of $y = x^2 \cos 6\pi x$. (Note that the graphs touch when $\cos 6\pi x = \pm 1$.)   ■

Example 8 shows that the function $y = x^2$ controls the amplitude of the graph of $y = x^2 \cos 6\pi x$. In general, if $f(x) = a(x) \sin kx$ or $f(x) = a(x) \cos kx$, the function a determines how the amplitude of f varies, and the graph of f lies between the graphs of $y = -a(x)$ and $y = a(x)$. Here is another example.

EXAMPLE 9 ■ A Cosine Curve with Variable Amplitude

Graph the function $f(x) = \cos 2\pi x \cos 16\pi x$.

SOLUTION

The graph is shown in Figure 19. Although it was drawn by a computer, we could have drawn it by hand, by first sketching the boundary curves $y = \cos 2\pi x$ and $y = -\cos 2\pi x$. The graph of f is a cosine curve that lies between the graphs of these two functions.

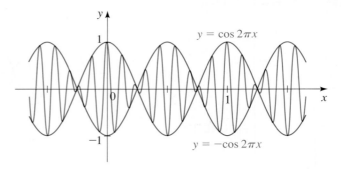

FIGURE 19 $f(x) = \cos 2\pi x \cos 16\pi x$ ■

EXAMPLE 10 ■ A Sine Curve with Decaying Amplitude

The function $f(x) = \dfrac{\sin x}{x}$ is important in calculus. Graph this function and comment on its behavior when x is close to 0.

SOLUTION

The viewing rectangle $[-15, 15]$ by $[-0.5, 1.5]$ shown in Figure 20(a) gives a good global view of the graph of f. The viewing rectangle $[-1, 1]$ by $[-0.5, 1.5]$ in Figure 20(b) focuses on the behavior of f when $x \approx 0$. Notice that although $f(x)$

is not defined when $x = 0$ (in other words, 0 is not in the domain of f), the values of f seem to approach 1 when x gets close to 0. This fact is crucial in calculus.

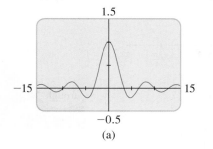

(a)

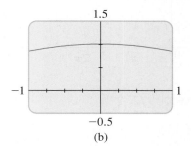

(b)

FIGURE 20

$$f(x) = \frac{\sin x}{x}$$

The function in Example 10 can be written as

$$f(x) = \left(\frac{1}{x}\right) \cdot \sin x$$

and may thus be viewed as a sine function whose amplitude is controlled by the function $a(x) = 1/x$.

2.3 EXERCISES

1–10 ■ Graph the function.

1. $y = 1 + \sin x$

2. $y = -\sin x$

3. $y = 1 - \cos x$

4. $y = -2 + \cos x$

5. $y = -2 \sin x$

6. $y = 3 \cos x$

7. $y = 4 - 2 \cos x$

8. $y = 3 + 3 \sin x$

9. $y = |\cos x|$

10. $y = |\sin x|$

11–20 ■ Find the amplitude and period of the function, and sketch its graph.

11. $y = \cos 4x$

12. $y = -\sin 2x$

13. $y = 3 \sin 3x$

14. $y = -2 \sin 2\pi x$

15. $y = 10 \sin \frac{1}{2}x$

16. $y = \cos 10\pi x$

17. $y = -\cos \frac{1}{3}x$

18. $y = \sin(-2x)$

19. $y = 3 \cos 3\pi x$

20. $y = 5 - 2 \sin 2x$

21–34 ■ Find the amplitude, period, and phase shift of the function, and graph one complete period.

21. $y = \cos\left(x - \frac{\pi}{2}\right)$

22. $y = 2 \sin\left(x - \frac{\pi}{3}\right)$

23. $y = -2 \sin\left(x - \frac{\pi}{6}\right)$

24. $y = 3 \cos\left(x + \frac{\pi}{4}\right)$

25. $y = 5 \cos\left(3x - \frac{\pi}{4}\right)$

26. $y = -4 \sin 2\left(x + \frac{\pi}{2}\right)$

27. $y = 2 \sin\left(\frac{2}{3}x - \frac{\pi}{6}\right)$

28. $y = \sin \frac{1}{2}\left(x + \frac{\pi}{4}\right)$

29. $y = 3 \cos \pi\left(x + \frac{1}{2}\right)$

30. $y = 1 + \cos\left(3x + \frac{\pi}{2}\right)$

31. $y = -\frac{1}{2} \cos\left(2x - \frac{\pi}{3}\right)$

32. $y = 3 + 2 \sin 3(x + 1)$

33. $y = \sin(3x + \pi)$

34. $y = \cos\left(\frac{\pi}{2} - x\right)$

35–40 ■ The graph of one complete period of a sine or cosine curve is given.

(a) Find the amplitude, period, and phase shift.

(b) Write an equation that represents the curve in the form

$$y = a \sin k(x - b) \qquad \text{or} \qquad y = a \cos k(x - b)$$

35.

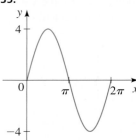

36.

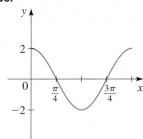

37.

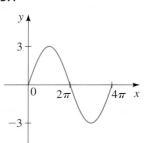

38.

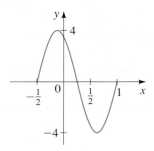

39.

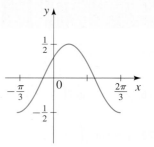

40.

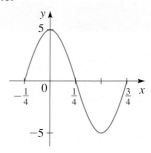

41–48 ■ Determine an appropriate viewing rectangle for each function, and use it to draw the graph.

41. $f(x) = \cos 100x$

42. $f(x) = 3 \sin 120x$

43. $f(x) = \sin(x/40)$

44. $f(x) = \cos(x/80)$

45. $y = \tan 25x$

46. $y = \csc 40x$

47. $y = \sin^2 20x$

48. $y = \sqrt{\tan 10\pi x}$

49. As a wave passes by an offshore piling, the height of the water is modeled by the function

$$h(t) = 3 \cos\left(\frac{\pi}{10}t\right)$$

where $h(t)$ is the height in feet above mean sea level at time t seconds.

(a) Find the period of the wave.
(b) Find the wave height, that is, the vertical distance between the trough and the crest of the wave.

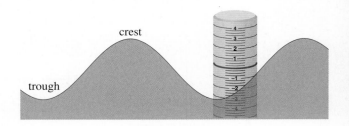

50. A tuning fork is struck, producing a pure tone as its tines vibrate. The vibrations are modeled by the function

$$v(t) = 0.7 \sin(880\pi t)$$

where $v(t)$ is the displacement of the tines in millimeters at time t seconds.

(a) Find the period of the vibration.
(b) Find the frequency of the vibration, that is, the number of times the fork vibrates per second.
(c) Graph the function v.

51. Each time your heart beats, your blood pressure first increases and then decreases as the heart rests between beats. The maximum and minimum blood pressures are called the *systolic* and *diastolic* pressures, respectively. Your *blood pressure reading* is written as systolic/diastolic. A reading of 120/80 is considered normal.

A certain person's blood pressure is modeled by the function

$$p(t) = 115 + 25 \sin(160\pi t)$$

where $p(t)$ is the pressure in mmHg, at time t measured in minutes.

(a) Find the period of p.
(b) Find the number of heartbeats per minute.
(c) Graph the function p.
(d) Find the blood pressure reading. How does this compare to normal blood pressure?

52. Variable stars are ones whose brightness varies periodically. One of the most visible is R Leonis; its brightness is modeled by the function

$$b(t) = 7.9 - 2.1 \cos\left(\frac{\pi}{156}t\right)$$

where t is measured in days.

(a) Find the period of R Leonis.

(b) Find the maximum and minimum brightness.
(c) Graph the function b.

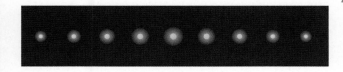

 53–54 ■ Graph f, g, and $f + g$ on a common screen to illustrate graphical addition.

53. $f(x) = x$, $\quad g(x) = \sin x$

54. $f(x) = \sin x$, $\quad g(x) = \sin 2x$

 55–60 ■ Graph the three functions on a common screen. How are the graphs related?

55. $y = x^2$, $\quad y = -x^2$, $\quad y = x^2 \sin x$

56. $y = x$, $\quad y = -x$, $\quad y = x \cos x$

57. $y = \sqrt{x}$, $\quad y = -\sqrt{x}$, $\quad y = \sqrt{x} \sin 5\pi x$

58. $y = \dfrac{1}{1 + x^2}$, $\quad y = -\dfrac{1}{1 + x^2}$, $\quad y = \dfrac{\cos 2\pi x}{1 + x^2}$

59. $y = \cos 3\pi x$, $\quad y = -\cos 3\pi x$, $\quad y = \cos 3\pi x \cos 21\pi x$

60. $y = \sin 2\pi x$, $\quad y = -\sin 2\pi x$, $\quad y = \sin 2\pi x \sin 10\pi x$

 61–64 ■ Find the maximum and minimum values of the function.

61. $y = \sin x + \sin 2x$

62. $y = x - 2 \sin x$, $\quad 0 \leq x \leq 2\pi$

63. $y = 2 \sin x + \sin^2 x$ $\qquad$ **64.** $y = \dfrac{\cos x}{2 + \sin x}$

 65–68 ■ Find all solutions of the equation that lie in the interval $[0, \pi]$. State each answer correct to two decimal places.

65. $\cos x = 0.4$ $\qquad\qquad$ **66.** $\tan x = 2$

67. $\csc x = 3$ $\qquad\qquad$ **68.** $\cos x = x$

 69. Let $f(x) = \dfrac{1 - \cos x}{x}$.

(a) Is the function f even, odd, or neither?
(b) Find the x-intercepts of the graph of f.
(c) Graph f in an appropriate viewing rectangle.
(d) Describe the behavior of the function as x becomes large.
(e) Notice that $f(x)$ is not defined when $x = 0$. What happens as x approaches 0?

 DISCOVERY · DISCUSSION

 70. Compositions Involving Trigonometric Functions This exercise explores the effect of the inner function g on a composite function $y = f(g(x))$.
(a) Graph the function $y = \sin(\sqrt{x})$ using the viewing rectangle $[0, 400]$ by $[-1.5, 1.5]$. In what ways does this graph differ from the graph of the sine function?
(b) Graph the function $y = \sin(x^2)$ using the viewing rectangle $[-5, 5]$ by $[-1.5, 1.5]$. In what ways does this graph differ from the graph of the sine function?

71. Periodic Functions I Recall that a function f is *periodic* if there is a positive number p such that $f(t + p) = f(t)$ for every t, and the least such p (if it exists) is the *period* of f. The graph of a function of period p looks the same on each interval of length p, so we can easily determine the period from the graph. Determine whether the function whose graph is shown is periodic; if it is periodic, find the period.

(a)

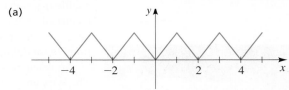

(b)

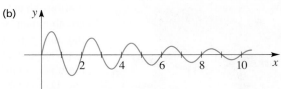

(c)

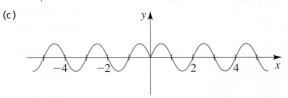

(d)

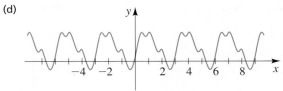

 72. Periodic Functions II Use a graphing device to graph the following functions. From the graph, determine whether the function is periodic; if it is periodic find the period.
(a) $y = |\sin x|$ $\qquad\qquad$ (b) $y = \sin|x|$
(c) $y = \cos(\sin x)$ $\qquad$ (d) $y = \cos(x^2)$

73. Sinusoidal Curves   The graph of $y = \sin x$ is the same as the graph of $y = \cos x$ shifted to the right $\pi/2$ units. So the sine curve $y = \sin x$ is also at the same time a cosine curve: $y = \cos(x - \pi/2)$. In fact, any sine curve is also a cosine curve with a different phase shift, and any cosine curve is also a sine curve. Sine and cosine curves are collectively referred to as *sinusoidal*. For the curve whose graph is shown, find all possible ways of expressing it as a sine curve $y = a \sin(x - b)$ or as a cosine curve $y = a \cos(x - b)$. Explain why you think you have found all possible choices for a and b in each case.

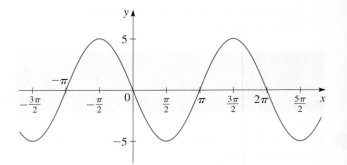

Discovery Project

Predator/Prey Models

Sine and cosine functions are used primarily in physics and engineering to model oscillatory behavior, such as the motion of a pendulum or the current in an AC electrical circuit. (See Section 2.5.) But these functions also arise in the other sciences. In this project, we consider an application to biology—we use sine functions to model the population of a predator and its prey.

An isolated island is inhabited by two species of mammals: lynx and hares. The lynx are *predators* who feed on the hares, their *prey*. The lynx and hare populations change cyclically, as graphed in Figure 1. In part A of the graph, hares are abundant, so the lynx have plenty to eat and their population increases. By the time portrayed in part B, so many lynx are feeding on the hares that the hare population declines. In part C, the hare population has declined so much that there is not enough food for the lynx, so the lynx population starts to decrease. In part D, so many lynx have died that the hares have few enemies and their population increases again. This takes us back to where we started, and the cycle repeats over and over again.

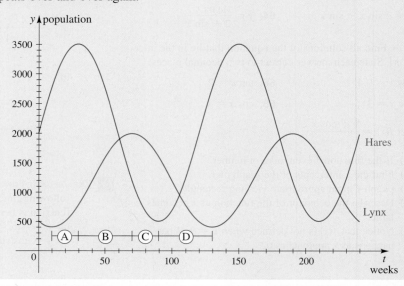

FIGURE 1

The graphs in Figure 1 are sine curves that have been shifted upward, so they are graphs of functions of the form

$$y = a \sin k(t - b) + c$$

Here c is the amount by which the sine curve has been shifted vertically (see Section 1.5). Note that c is the average value of the function, halfway between the highest and lowest values on the graph. The amplitude $|a|$ is the amount by which the graph varies above and below the average value (see Figure 2).

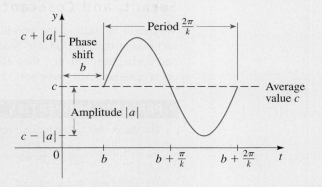

1. Find functions of the form $y = a \sin k(t - b) + c$ that model the lynx and hare populations graphed in Figure 1. Graph both functions on your calculator and compare to Figure 1 to verify that your functions are the right ones.

2. Add the lynx and hare population functions to get a new function that models the total *mammal* population on this island. Graph this function on your calculator, and find its average value, amplitude, period, and phase shift. How are the average value and period of the mammal population function related to the average value and period of the lynx and hare population functions?

3. A small lake on the island contains two species of fish: hake and redfish. The hake are predators that eat the redfish. The fish population in the lake varies periodically with period 180 days. The number of hake varies between 500 and 1500, and the number of redfish varies between 1000 and 3000. The hake reach their maximum population 30 days after the redfish have reached *their* maximum population in the cycle.

   (a) Sketch a graph (like the one in Figure 1) that shows two complete periods of the population cycle for these species of fish. Assume that $t = 0$ corresponds to a time when the redfish population is at a maximum.

   (b) Find cosine functions of the form $y = a \cos k(t - b) + c$ that model the hake and redfish populations in the lake.

4. In real life, most predator/prey populations do not behave as simply as the examples we have described here. In most cases, the populations of predator and prey oscillate, but the amplitude of the oscillations gets smaller and smaller, so that eventually both populations stabilize near a constant value. Sketch a rough graph that illustrates how the populations of predator and prey might behave in this case.

2.4 MORE TRIGONOMETRIC GRAPHS

In this section we graph the tangent, cotangent, secant, and cosecant functions, and transformations of these functions.

■ Graphs of the Tangent, Cotangent, Secant, and Cosecant Function

We begin by stating the periodic properties of these functions. Recall that sine and cosine have period 2π. Since cosecant and secant are the reciprocals of sine and cosine, respectively, they also have period 2π (see Exercise 47). Tangent and cotangent, however, have period π (see Exercise 77 of Section 2.2).

PERIODIC PROPERTIES

The functions tangent and cotangent have period π:

$$\tan(x + \pi) = \tan x \qquad \cot(x + \pi) = \cot x$$

The functions cosecant and secant have period 2π:

$$\csc(x + 2\pi) = \csc x \qquad \sec(x + 2\pi) = \sec x$$

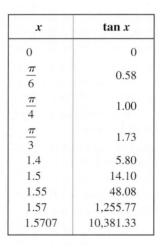

x	$\tan x$
0	0
$\dfrac{\pi}{6}$	0.58
$\dfrac{\pi}{4}$	1.00
$\dfrac{\pi}{3}$	1.73
1.4	5.80
1.5	14.10
1.55	48.08
1.57	1,255.77
1.5707	10,381.33

We first sketch the graph of tangent. Since it has period π, we need only sketch the graph on any interval of length π and then repeat the pattern to the left and to the right. We sketch the graph on the interval $(-\pi/2, \pi/2)$. Since $\tan \pi/2$ and $\tan(-\pi/2)$ aren't defined, we need to be careful in sketching the graph at points near $\pi/2$ and $-\pi/2$. As x gets near $\pi/2$ through values less than $\pi/2$, the value of $\tan x$ becomes large. To see this, notice that as x gets close to $\pi/2$, $\cos x$ approaches 0 and $\sin x$ approaches 1 and so $\tan x = \sin x/\cos x$ is large. A table of values of $\tan x$ for x close to $\pi/2$ (≈ 1.570796) is shown in the margin.

Thus, by choosing x close enough to $\pi/2$ through values less than $\pi/2$, we can make the value of $\tan x$ larger than any given positive number. We express this by writing

$$\tan x \to \infty \qquad \text{as} \qquad x \to \frac{\pi}{2}^-$$

This is read "$\tan x$ approaches infinity as x approaches $\pi/2$ from the left."

In a similar way, by choosing x close to $-\pi/2$ through values greater than $-\pi/2$, we can make $\tan x$ smaller than any given negative number. We write this as

$$\tan x \to -\infty \qquad \text{as} \qquad x \to -\frac{\pi}{2}^+$$

This is read "$\tan x$ approaches negative infinity as x approaches $-\pi/2$ from the right."

Thus, the graph of $y = \tan x$ will approach the vertical lines $x = \pi/2$ and $x = -\pi/2$. These lines are called **vertical asymptotes**. With the information we have so far, we sketch the graph of $y = \tan x$ for $-\pi/2 < x < \pi/2$ in Figure 1. The complete graph of tangent [see Figure 5(a) on page 150] is now obtained using the fact that tangent is periodic with period π.

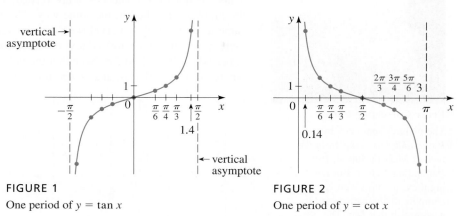

FIGURE 1

One period of $y = \tan x$

FIGURE 2

One period of $y = \cot x$

The function $y = \cot x$ is graphed on the interval $(0, \pi)$ by a similar analysis (see Figure 2). Since $\cot x$ is undefined for $x = n\pi$ with n an integer, its complete graph [in Figure 5(b)] has vertical asymptotes at these values.

To graph the cosecant and secant functions, we use the reciprocal identities

$$\csc x = \frac{1}{\sin x} \quad \text{and} \quad \sec x = \frac{1}{\cos x}$$

So, to graph $y = \csc x$, we take the reciprocals of the y-coordinates of the points of the graph of $y = \sin x$. (See Figure 3.) Similarly, to graph $y = \sec x$, we take the reciprocals of the y-coordinates of the points of the graph of $y = \cos x$. (See Figure 4.)

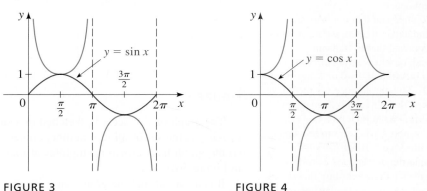

FIGURE 3

One period of $y = \csc x$

FIGURE 4

One period of $y = \sec x$

Let's consider more closely the graph of the function $y = \csc x$ on the interval $0 < x < \pi$. We need to examine the values of the function near 0 and π since at

these values $\sin x = 0$, and $\csc x$ is thus undefined. We see that

$$\csc x \to \infty \qquad \text{as} \qquad x \to 0^+$$

$$\csc x \to \infty \qquad \text{as} \qquad x \to \pi^-$$

Thus, the lines $x = 0$ and $x = \pi$ are vertical asymptotes. In the interval $\pi < x < 2\pi$ the graph is sketched in the same way. The values of $\csc x$ in that interval are the same as those in the interval $0 < x < \pi$ except for sign (see Figure 3). The complete graph in Figure 5(c) is now obtained from the fact that the function cosecant is periodic with period 2π. Note that the graph has vertical asymptotes at the points where $\sin x = 0$, that is, at $x = n\pi$, for n an integer.

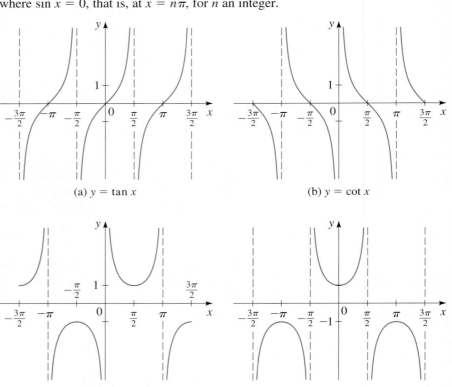

(a) $y = \tan x$

(b) $y = \cot x$

(c) $y = \csc x$

(d) $y = \sec x$

FIGURE 5

The graph of $y = \sec x$ is sketched in a similar manner. Observe that the domain of $\sec x$ is the set of all real numbers other than $x = (\pi/2) + n\pi$, for n an integer, so the graph has vertical asymptotes at those points. The complete graph is shown in Figure 5(d).

It is apparent that the graphs of $y = \tan x$, $y = \cot x$, and $y = \csc x$ are symmetric about the origin, whereas that of $y = \sec x$ is symmetric about the y-axis. This is because tangent, cotangent, and cosecant are odd functions, whereas secant is an even function.

it in blocks of a million digits. If the first block is mostly 1's, he concludes that you are probably trying to transmit a 1, and so on. To say that this code is not efficient is a bit of an understatement; it requires sending a million times more data than the original message. Another method inserts "check digits." For example, for each block of eight digits insert a ninth digit; the inserted digit is 0 if there is an even number of 1's in the block and 1 if there is an odd number. So, if a single digit is wrong (a 0 changed to a 1, or vice versa), the check digits allow us to recognize that an error has occurred. This method does not tell us where the error is, so we can't correct it. Modern error-correcting codes use interesting mathematical algorithms that require inserting relatively few digits but which allow the receiver to not only recognize, but also correct, errors. The first error-correcting code was developed in the 1940s by Richard Hamming at MIT. It is interesting to note that the English language has a built-in error-correcting mechanism; to test it, try reading this error-laden sentence: Gve mo libty ox giv ne deth.

◼ Graphs Involving Tangent and Cotangent Functions

We now consider graphs of transformations of the tangent and cotangent functions.

EXAMPLE 1 ◼ Graphing Tangent Curves

Graph each function.

(a) $y = 2 \tan x$ (b) $y = -\tan x$

SOLUTION

We first graph $y = \tan x$ and then transform it as required.

(a) To graph $y = 2 \tan x$, we multiply the y -coordinate of each point on the graph of $y = \tan x$ by 2. The resulting graph is shown in Figure 6(a).

(b) The graph of $y = -\tan x$ in Figure 6(b) is obtained from that of $y = \tan x$ by reflecting in the x -axis.

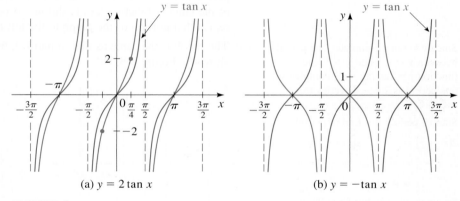

(a) $y = 2 \tan x$ (b) $y = -\tan x$

FIGURE 6 ◼

Since the tangent and cotangent functions have period π , the functions

$$y = a \tan kx \qquad \text{and} \qquad y = a \cot kx \qquad (k > 0)$$

complete one period as kx varies from 0 to π , that is, for $0 \le kx \le \pi$. Solving this inequality, we get $0 \le x \le \pi/k$. So they each have period π/k .

TANGENT AND COTANGENT CURVES

The functions

$$y = a \tan kx \qquad \text{and} \qquad y = a \cot kx \qquad (k > 0)$$

have period π/k .

Thus, one complete period of the graphs of these functions occurs on any interval of length π/k. To sketch a complete period of these graphs, it's convenient to select an interval between vertical asymptotes:

To graph one period of $y = a \tan kx$, an appropriate interval is $\left(-\dfrac{\pi}{2k}, \dfrac{\pi}{2k}\right)$.

To graph one period of $y = a \cot kx$, an appropriate interval is $\left(0, \dfrac{\pi}{k}\right)$.

EXAMPLE 2 ■ Graphing Tangent Curves

Graph each function.

(a) $y = \tan 2x$

(b) $y = \tan 2\left(x - \dfrac{\pi}{4}\right)$

SOLUTION

(a) The period is $\pi/2$ and an appropriate interval is $(-\pi/4, \pi/4)$. The endpoints $x = -\pi/4$ and $x = \pi/4$ are vertical asymptotes. Thus, we graph one complete period of the function on $(-\pi/4, \pi/4)$. The graph has the same shape as that of the tangent function, but is shrunk horizontally by a factor of $\frac{1}{2}$. We then repeat that portion of the graph to the left and to the right. See Figure 7(a).

(b) The graph is the same as that in part (a), but it is shifted to the right $\pi/4$, as shown in Figure 7(b).

Since $y = \tan x$ completes one period between $x = -\frac{\pi}{2}$ and $x = \frac{\pi}{2}$, the function $y = \tan 2\left(x - \frac{\pi}{4}\right)$ completes one period as $2\left(x - \frac{\pi}{4}\right)$ varies from $-\frac{\pi}{2}$ to $\frac{\pi}{2}$.

Start of period: End of period:

$2\left(x - \frac{\pi}{4}\right) = -\frac{\pi}{2}$ $2\left(x - \frac{\pi}{4}\right) = \frac{\pi}{2}$

$x - \frac{\pi}{4} = -\frac{\pi}{4}$ $x - \frac{\pi}{4} = \frac{\pi}{4}$

$x = 0$ $x = \frac{\pi}{2}$

So we graph one period on the interval $\left(0, \frac{\pi}{2}\right)$.

FIGURE 7

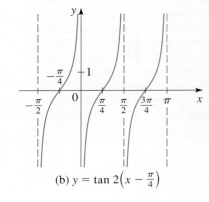

(a) $y = \tan 2x$ (b) $y = \tan 2\left(x - \frac{\pi}{4}\right)$ ■

EXAMPLE 3 ■ A Shifted Cotangent Curve

Graph $y = 2 \cot\left(3x - \dfrac{\pi}{2}\right)$.

SOLUTION

We first put this in the form $y = a \cot k(x - b)$ by factoring 3 from the expression $3x - \dfrac{\pi}{2}$:

$$y = 2 \cot\left(3x - \frac{\pi}{2}\right) = 2 \cot 3\left(x - \frac{\pi}{6}\right)$$

Since $y = \cot x$ completes one period between $x = 0$ and $x = \pi$, the function $y = 2 \cot\left(3x - \frac{\pi}{2}\right)$ completes one period as $3x - \frac{\pi}{2}$ varies from 0 to π.

Start of period: End of period:

$3x - \frac{\pi}{2} = 0$ $3x - \frac{\pi}{2} = \pi$

$3x = \frac{\pi}{2}$ $3x = \frac{3\pi}{2}$

$x = \frac{\pi}{6}$ $x = \frac{\pi}{2}$

So we graph one period on the interval $\left(\frac{\pi}{6}, \frac{\pi}{2}\right)$.

Thus, the graph is the same as that of $y = 2 \cot 3x$, but is shifted to the right $\pi/6$. The period of $y = 2 \cot 3x$ is $\pi/3$, and an appropriate interval is $(0, \pi/3)$. To get the corresponding interval for the desired graph, we shift this interval to the right $\pi/6$. This gives

$$\left(0 + \frac{\pi}{6}, \frac{\pi}{3} + \frac{\pi}{6}\right) = \left(\frac{\pi}{6}, \frac{\pi}{2}\right)$$

Finally, we graph one period in the shape of cotangent on the interval $(\pi/6, \pi/2)$ and repeat that portion of the graph to the left and to the right. See Figure 8.

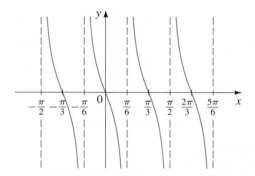

FIGURE 8
$y = 2 \cot\left(3x - \frac{\pi}{2}\right)$

■

Graphs Involving the Cosecant and Secant Functions

We have already observed that the cosecant and secant functions are the reciprocals of the sine and cosine functions. Thus, the following result is the counterpart of the result for sine and cosine curves in Section 2.3.

> **COSECANT AND SECANT CURVES**
>
> The functions
>
> $$y = a \csc kx \qquad \text{and} \qquad y = a \sec kx \qquad (k > 0)$$
>
> have period $2\pi/k$.

An appropriate interval on which to graph one complete period is $[0, 2\pi/k]$.

EXAMPLE 4 ■ Graphing Cosecant Curves

Graph each function.

(a) $y = \frac{1}{2} \csc 2x$

(b) $y = \frac{1}{2} \csc\left(2x + \frac{\pi}{2}\right)$

SOLUTION

(a) The period is $2\pi/2 = \pi$. An appropriate interval is $[0, \pi]$, and the asymptotes occur in this interval whenever $\sin 2x = 0$. So the asymptotes in this interval are $x = 0$, $x = \pi/2$, and $x = \pi$. With this information we sketch on the interval $[0, \pi]$ a graph with the same general shape as that of one period of the cosecant function. The complete graph in Figure 9(a) is obtained by repeating this portion of the graph to the left and to the right.

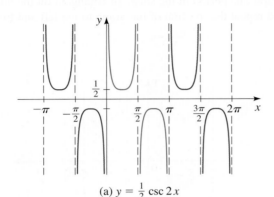

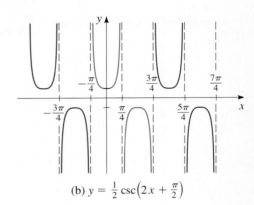

FIGURE 9

(a) $y = \frac{1}{2}\csc 2x$

(b) $y = \frac{1}{2}\csc\left(2x + \frac{\pi}{2}\right)$

Since $y = \csc x$ completes one period between $x = 0$ and $x = 2\pi$, the function $y = \frac{1}{2}\csc\left(2x + \frac{\pi}{2}\right)$ completes one period as $2x + \frac{\pi}{2}$ varies from 0 to 2π.

Start of period: End of period:

$2x + \frac{\pi}{2} = 0$ $2x + \frac{\pi}{2} = 2\pi$

$\quad 2x = -\frac{\pi}{2}$ $\quad 2x = \frac{3\pi}{2}$

$\quad\ x = -\frac{\pi}{4}$ $\quad\ x = \frac{3\pi}{4}$

So we graph one period on the interval $\left(-\frac{\pi}{4}, \frac{3\pi}{4}\right)$.

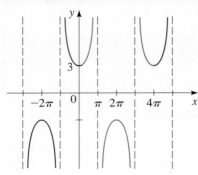

FIGURE 10

$y = 3\sec\frac{1}{2}x$

(b) We first write

$$y = \frac{1}{2}\csc\left(2x + \frac{\pi}{2}\right) = \frac{1}{2}\csc 2\left(x + \frac{\pi}{4}\right)$$

From this we see that the graph is the same as that in part (a), but shifted to the left $\pi/4$. The graph is shown in Figure 9(b). ∎

EXAMPLE 5 ■ Graphing a Secant Curve

Graph $y = 3\sec\frac{1}{2}x$.

SOLUTION

The period is $2\pi \div \frac{1}{2} = 4\pi$. An appropriate interval is $[0, 4\pi]$, and the asymptotes occur in this interval wherever $\cos\frac{1}{2}x = 0$. Thus, the asymptotes in this interval are $x = \pi$, $x = 3\pi$. With this information we sketch on the interval $[0, 4\pi]$ a graph with the same general shape as that of one period of the secant function. The complete graph in Figure 10 is obtained by repeating this portion of the graph to the left and to the right. ∎

2.4   EXERCISES

1–46 ■ Find the period and graph the function.

1. $y = 4 \tan x$

2. $y = -4 \tan x$

3. $y = -\frac{1}{2} \tan x$

4. $y = \frac{1}{2} \tan x$

5. $y = -\cot x$

6. $y = 2 \cot x$

7. $y = 2 \csc x$

8. $y = \frac{1}{2} \csc x$

9. $y = 3 \sec x$

10. $y = -3 \sec x$

11. $y = \tan\left(x + \frac{\pi}{2}\right)$

12. $y = \tan\left(x - \frac{\pi}{4}\right)$

13. $y = \csc\left(x - \frac{\pi}{2}\right)$

14. $y = \sec\left(x + \frac{\pi}{4}\right)$

15. $y = \cot\left(x + \frac{\pi}{4}\right)$

16. $y = 2 \csc\left(x - \frac{\pi}{3}\right)$

17. $y = \frac{1}{2} \sec\left(x - \frac{\pi}{6}\right)$

18. $y = 3 \csc\left(x + \frac{\pi}{2}\right)$

19. $y = \tan 2x$

20. $y = \tan \frac{1}{2}x$

21. $y = \tan \pi x$

22. $y = \cot \frac{\pi}{2}x$

23. $y = \sec 2x$

24. $y = 5 \csc 3x$

25. $y = \csc 2x$

26. $y = \csc \frac{1}{2}x$

27. $y = 2 \tan 3x$

28. $y = 2 \tan \frac{\pi}{2}x$

29. $y = 5 \csc 3x$

30. $y = 5 \sec 2\pi x$

31. $y = \tan 2\left(x + \frac{\pi}{2}\right)$

32. $y = \csc 2\left(x + \frac{\pi}{2}\right)$

33. $y = \tan 2(x - \pi)$

34. $y = \sec 2\left(x - \frac{\pi}{2}\right)$

35. $y = \cot\left(2x - \frac{\pi}{2}\right)$

36. $y = \frac{1}{2} \tan(\pi x - \pi)$

37. $y = 2 \csc\left(\pi x - \frac{\pi}{3}\right)$

38. $y = 2 \sec\left(\frac{1}{2}x - \frac{\pi}{3}\right)$

39. $y = 5 \sec\left(3x - \frac{\pi}{2}\right)$

40. $y = \frac{1}{2} \sec(2\pi x - \pi)$

41. $y = \tan\left(\frac{2}{3}x - \frac{\pi}{6}\right)$

42. $y = \tan \frac{1}{2}\left(x + \frac{\pi}{4}\right)$

43. $y = 3 \sec \pi\left(x + \frac{1}{2}\right)$

44. $y = \sec\left(3x + \frac{\pi}{2}\right)$

45. $y = -2 \tan\left(2x - \frac{\pi}{3}\right)$

46. $y = 2 \csc(3x + 3)$

47. (a) Prove that if f is periodic with period p, then $1/f$ is also periodic with period p.

(b) Prove that cosecant and secant each have period 2π.

 DISCOVERY · DISCUSSION

48. Reduction Formulas   Use the graphs in Figure 5 to explain why the following formulas are true.

$$\tan\left(x - \frac{\pi}{2}\right) = -\cot x$$

$$\sec\left(x - \frac{\pi}{2}\right) = \csc x$$

2.5   MODELING HARMONIC MOTION

Periodic behavior—behavior that repeats over and over again—is common in nature. Perhaps the most familiar example is the daily rising and setting of the sun, which results in the repetitive pattern of day, night, day, night, ... Another example is the daily variation of tide levels at the beach, which results in the repetitive pattern of high tide, low tide, high tide, low tide, ... Certain animal populations increase and decrease in a predictable periodic pattern: A large population exhausts the food supply, which causes the population to dwindle; this in turn results in a more plentiful food supply, which makes it possible for the population to increase; and the pattern then repeats over and over (see pages 146–147).

Other common examples of periodic behavior involve motion that is caused by vibration or oscillation. A mass suspended from a spring that has been compressed and then allowed to vibrate vertically is a simple example. This same "back and forth" motion also occurs in such diverse phenomena as sound waves, light waves, alternating electrical current, and pulsating stars, to name a few. In this section we consider the problem of modeling periodic behavior.

■ Modeling Periodic Behavior

The trigonometric functions are ideally suited for modeling periodic behavior. A glance at the graphs of the sine and cosine functions, for instance, tells us that these functions themselves exhibit periodic behavior. Figure 1 shows the graph of $y = \sin t$. If we think of t as time, we see that as time goes on, $y = \sin t$ increases and decreases over and over again. Figure 2 shows that the motion of a vibrating mass on a spring is modeled very accurately by $y = \sin t$.

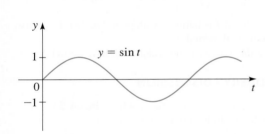

FIGURE 1
$y = \sin t$

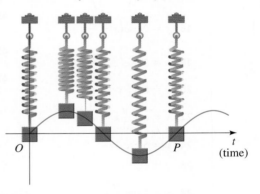

FIGURE 2
Motion of a vibrating spring is modeled by $y = \sin t$.

Notice that the mass returns to its original position over and over again. A **cycle** is one complete vibration of an object, so the mass in Figure 2 completes one cycle of its motion between O and P. Our observations about how the sine and cosine functions model periodic behavior are summarized in the following box.

The main difference between the two equations describing simple harmonic motion is the starting point. At $t = 0$, we get

$$y = a \sin \omega \cdot 0 = 0$$

or

$$y = a \cos \omega \cdot 0 = a$$

In other words, in the first case the motion "starts" with zero displacement, while in the second case the motion "starts" with the displacement at maximum (at the amplitude a).

SIMPLE HARMONIC MOTION

If the equation describing the displacement y of an object at time t is

$$y = a \sin \omega t \qquad \text{or} \qquad y = a \cos \omega t$$

then the object is in **simple harmonic motion**. In this case,

amplitude $= |a|$ Maximum displacement of the object

period $= \dfrac{2\pi}{\omega}$ Time required to complete one cycle

frequency $= \dfrac{\omega}{2\pi}$ Number of cycles per unit of time

Notice that the functions

$$y = a \sin 2\pi \nu t \quad \text{and} \quad y = a \cos 2\pi \nu t$$

have frequency ν, because $2\pi\nu/(2\pi) = \nu$. Since we can immediately read the frequency from these equations, we often write equations of simple harmonic motion in this form.

EXAMPLE 1 ■ A Vibrating Spring

The displacement of a mass suspended by a spring is modeled by the function

$$y = 10 \sin 4\pi t$$

where y is measured in inches and t in seconds (see Figure 3).

(a) Find the amplitude, period, and frequency of the motion of the mass.
(b) Sketch the graph of the displacement of the mass.

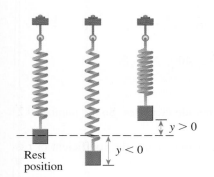

Rest position

FIGURE 3

SOLUTION

(a) From the formulas for amplitude, period, and frequency, we get

$$\text{amplitude} = |a| = 10 \text{ in.}$$

$$\text{period} = \frac{2\pi}{\omega} = \frac{2\pi}{4\pi} = \frac{1}{2} \text{ s}$$

$$\text{frequency} = \frac{\omega}{2\pi} = \frac{4\pi}{2\pi} = 2 \text{ Hz}$$

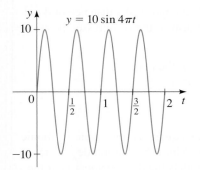

FIGURE 4

(b) The graph of the displacement of the mass at time t is shown in Figure 4. ■

An important situation where simple harmonic motion occurs is in the production of sound. Sound is produced by a regular variation in air pressure from the normal pressure. If the pressure varies in simple harmonic motion, then a pure sound is produced. The tone of the sound depends on the frequency and the loudness depends on the amplitude.

EXAMPLE 2 ■ Vibrations of a Musical Note

A tuba player plays the note E and sustains the sound for some time. For a pure E the variation in pressure from normal air pressure is given by

$$V(t) = 0.2 \sin 80\pi t$$

where V is measured in pounds per square inch and t in seconds.

(a) Find the amplitude, period, and frequency of V.
(b) Sketch a graph of V.
(c) If the tuba player increases the loudness of the note, how does the equation for V change?
(d) If the player is playing the note incorrectly and it is a little flat, how does the equation for V change?

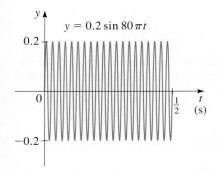

FIGURE 5

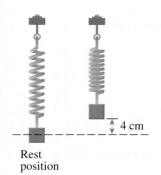

Rest position

4 cm

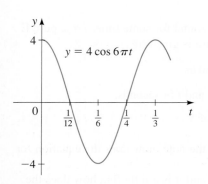

$y = 4 \cos 6\pi t$

FIGURE 6

SOLUTION

(a) From the formulas for amplitude, period, and frequency, we get

$$\text{amplitude} = |0.2| = 0.2$$

$$\text{period} = \frac{2\pi}{80\pi} = \frac{1}{40}$$

$$\text{frequency} = \frac{80\pi}{2\pi} = 40$$

(b) The graph of V is shown in Figure 5.

(c) If the player increases the loudness the amplitude increases. So the number 0.2 is replaced by a larger number.

(d) If the note is flat, then the frequency is decreased. Thus, the coefficient of t is less than 80π. ■

EXAMPLE 3 ■ Modeling a Vibrating Spring

A mass is suspended from a spring. The spring is compressed a distance of 4 cm and then released. It is observed that the mass returns to the compressed position after $\frac{1}{3}$ s.

(a) Find a function that models the displacement of the mass.
(b) Sketch the graph of the displacement of the mass.

SOLUTION

(a) The motion of the mass is given by one of the equations for simple harmonic motion. The amplitude of the motion is 4 cm. Since this amplitude is reached at time $t = 0$, an appropriate function that models the displacement is of the form

$$y = a \cos \omega t$$

Since the period is $p = \frac{1}{3}$, we can find ω from the following equation:

$$\text{period} = \frac{2\pi}{\omega}$$

$$\frac{1}{3} = \frac{2\pi}{\omega} \qquad \text{Period} = \frac{1}{3}$$

$$\omega = 6\pi \qquad \text{Solve for } \omega$$

So, the motion of the mass is modeled by the function

$$y = 4 \cos 6\pi t$$

where y is the displacement from the rest position at time t. Notice that when $t = 0$, the displacement is $y = 4$, as we expect.

(b) The graph of the displacement of the mass at time t is shown in Figure 6. ■

In general, the sine or cosine functions representing harmonic motion may be shifted horizontally or vertically. In this case, the equations take the form

$$y = a\sin(\omega(t - c)) + b \qquad \text{or} \qquad y = a\cos(\omega(t - c)) + b$$

The vertical shift b indicates that the variation occurs around an average value b. The horizontal shift c indicates the position of the object at $t = 0$. (See Figure 7.)

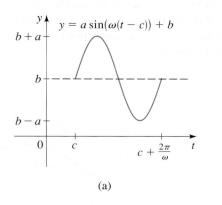

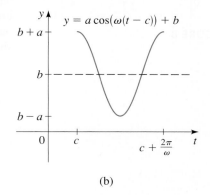

FIGURE 7   (a)   (b)

EXAMPLE 4 ■ Modeling the Brightness of a Variable Star

A variable star is one whose brightness alternately increases and decreases. For the variable star Delta Cephei, the time between periods of maximum brightness is 5.4 days. The average brightness (or magnitude) of the star is 4.0, and its brightness varies by ± 0.35 magnitude.

(a) Find a function that models the brightness of Delta Cephei as a function of time.
(b) Sketch a graph of the brightness of Delta Cephei as a function of time.

SOLUTION

(a) Let's find a function in the form

$$y = a\cos(\omega(t - c)) + b$$

The amplitude is the maximum variation from average brightness, so the amplitude is $a = 0.35$ magnitude. We are given that the period is 5.4 days, so

$$\omega = \frac{2\pi}{5.4} \approx 1.164$$

Since the brightness varies from an average value of 4.0 magnitudes, the graph is shifted upward by $b = 4.0$. If we take $t = 0$ to be a time when the star is at maximum brightness, there is no horizontal shift, so $c = 0$ (this is because a cosine curve achieves its maximum at $t = 0$). Thus, the function we want is

$$y = 0.35\cos(1.16t) + 4.0$$

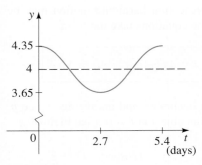

FIGURE 8

where t is the number of days from a time when the star is at maximum brightness.

(b) The graph is sketched in Figure 8. ■

The number of hours of daylight varies throughout the course of a year. In the Northern Hemisphere, the longest day is June 21, and the shortest is December 21. The average length of daylight is 12 h, and the variation from this average depends on the latitude. (For example, Fairbanks, Alaska, experiences more than 20 h of daylight on the longest day and less than 4 h on the shortest day!) The graph in Figure 9 shows the number of hours of daylight at different times of the year for various latitudes. It's apparent from the graph that the variation in hours of daylight is simple harmonic.

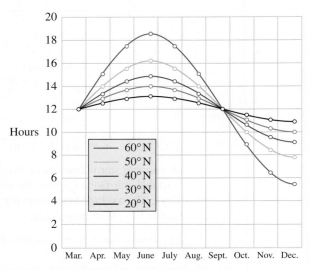

FIGURE 9

Graph of the length of daylight from March 21 through December 21 at various latitudes

Source: Lucia C. Harrison, *Daylight, Twilight, Darkness and Time*
(New York: Silver, Burdett, 1935) page 40.

EXAMPLE 5 ■ **Modeling the Number of Hours of Daylight**

In Philadelphia (40° N latitude), the longest day of the year has 14 h 50 min of daylight and the shortest day has 9 h 10 min of daylight.

(a) Find a function L that models the length of daylight as a function of t, the number of days from January 1.

(b) An astronomer needs at least 11 hours of darkness for a long exposure astronomical photograph. During which days of the year can he do this?

SOLUTION

(a) We need to find a function in the form

$$y = a \sin(\omega(t - c)) + b$$

whose graph is the 40° N latitude curve in Figure 9. From the information given, we see that the amplitude is

$$a = \tfrac{1}{2}\left(14\tfrac{5}{6} - 9\tfrac{1}{6}\right) \approx 2.83 \text{ h}$$

Since there are 365 days in a year, the period is 365, so

$$\omega = \frac{2\pi}{365} \approx 0.0172$$

Since the average length of daylight is 12 h, the graph is shifted upward by 12, so $b = 12$. Since the curve attains the average value (12) on March 21, the 80th day of the year, the curve is shifted 80 units to the right. Thus, $c = 80$. So a function that models the number of hours of daylight is

$$y = 2.83 \sin(0.0172(t - 80)) + 12$$

where t is the number of days from January 1.

(b) Since a day has 24 h, 11 h of night correspond to 13 h of daylight. So we need to solve the inequality $y \leq 13$. To solve this inequality graphically, we graph $y = 2.83 \sin 0.0172(t - 80) + 12$ and $y = 13$ on the same graph. From the graph in Figure 10 we see that there are fewer than 13 h of daylight between day 1 (January 1) and day 101 (April 11) and from day 241 (August 29) to day 365 (December 31).   ■

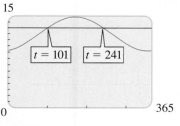

15

$t = 101$ $t = 241$

0   365

FIGURE 10

Another situation where simple harmonic motion occurs is in alternating current (AC) generators. Alternating current is produced when an armature rotates about its axis in a magnetic field.

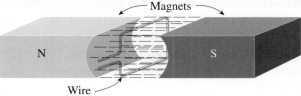

Magnets

N   S

Wire

FIGURE 11

Figure 11 represents a simple version of such a generator. As the wire passes through the magnetic field, a voltage E is generated in the wire. It can be shown that the voltage generated is given by

$$E(t) = E_0 \cos \omega t$$

where E_0 is the maximum voltage produced (which depends on the strength of the magnetic field) and $\omega/(2\pi)$ is the number of revolutions per second of the armature (the frequency).

EXAMPLE 6 ■ Modeling Alternating Current

Ordinary 110-V household alternating current varies from $+155$ V to -155 V with a frequency of 60 Hz (cycles per second). Find an equation that describes this variation in voltage.

SOLUTION

The variation in voltage is simple harmonic. Since the frequency is 60 cycles per second, we have

$$\frac{\omega}{2\pi} = 60 \qquad \text{or} \qquad \omega = 120\pi$$

Let us take $t = 0$ to be a time when the voltage is $+155$ V. Then

$$E(t) = a \cos \omega t = 155 \cos 120\pi t \qquad \blacksquare$$

If we hang a weight on the end of a spring and set the system in motion, resistance forces from the air and inside the spring will cause the amplitude of the oscillations to decline, as shown in Figure 12(b). This kind of motion is called **damped harmonic motion**, as opposed to the simple harmonic motion illustrated in Figure 12(a). Damped harmonic motion is studied in Section 7.6.

Why do we say that household current is 110 V when the maximum voltage produced is 155 V? From the symmetry of the cosine function, we see that the average voltage produced is zero. This average value would be the same for all AC generators and so gives no information about the voltage generated. To obtain a more informative measure of voltage, engineers use the **root-mean-square** (rms) method. It can be shown that the rms voltage is $1/\sqrt{2}$ times the maximum voltage. So, for household current the rms voltage is

$$155 \times \frac{1}{\sqrt{2}} \approx 110 \text{ V}$$

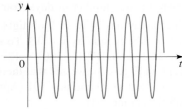

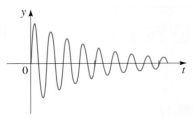

FIGURE 12   (a) Simple harmonic motion   (b) Damped harmonic motion

2.5 EXERCISES

1–8 ■ The given function models the displacement of an object moving in simple harmonic motion.

(a) Find the amplitude, period, and frequency of the motion.

(b) Sketch a graph of the displacement of the object over one complete period.

1. $y = 2 \sin 3t$

2. $y = 3 \cos \frac{1}{2}t$

3. $y = -\cos 0.3t$

4. $y = 2.4 \sin 3.6t$

5. $y = -0.25 \cos\left(1.5t - \frac{\pi}{3}\right)$

6. $y = -\frac{3}{2} \sin(0.2t + 1.4)$

7. $y = 5 \cos\left(\frac{2}{3}t + \frac{3}{4}\right)$

8. $y = 1.6 \sin(t - 1.8)$

9–12 ■ Find a function that models the simple harmonic motion having the given properties. Assume that the displacement is zero at time $t = 0$.

9. amplitude 10 cm,   period 3 s

10. amplitude 24 ft,   period 2 min

11. amplitude 6 in,   frequency $5/\pi$ Hz

12. amplitude 1.2 m,   frequency 0.5 Hz

13–16 ■ Find a function that models the simple harmonic motion having the given properties. Assume that the displacement is at its maximum at time $t = 0$.

13. amplitude 60 ft,   period 0.5 min

14. amplitude 35 cm,   period 8 s

15. amplitude 2.4 m,   frequency 750 Hz

16. amplitude 6.25 in,   frequency 60 Hz

17. A cork floating in a lake is bobbing in simple harmonic motion. Its displacement above the bottom of the lake is modeled by

$$y = 0.2 \cos 20\pi t + 8$$

where y is measured in meters and t is measured in minutes.

(a) Find the frequency of the motion of the cork.

(b) Sketch a graph of y.

(c) Find the maximum displacement of the cork above the lake bottom.

18. The carrier wave for an FM radio signal is modeled by the function

$$y = a \sin(2\pi(9.15 \times 10^7)t)$$

where t is measured in seconds. Find the period and frequency of the carrier wave.

19. In a predator/prey model (see page 146), the predator population is modeled by the function

$$y = 900 \cos 2t + 8000$$

where t is measured in years.
(a) What is the maximum population?
(b) Find the length of time between successive periods of maximum population.

20. Each time your heart beats, your blood pressure increases, then decreases as the heart rests between beats. A certain person's blood pressure is modeled by the function

$$p(t) = 115 + 25 \sin(160\pi t)$$

where $p(t)$ is the pressure in mmHg, at time t measured in minutes.
(a) Find the amplitude, period, and frequency of p.
(b) Sketch a graph of p.
(c) If a person is exercising, his heart beats faster. How does this affect the period and frequency of p?

21–34 ■ These problems require you to find a function that models a real-life case of simple harmonic motion.

21. A mass attached to a spring is moving up and down in simple harmonic motion. The graph gives its displacement $d(t)$ from equilibrium at time t. Express the function d in the form $d(t) = a \sin \omega t$.

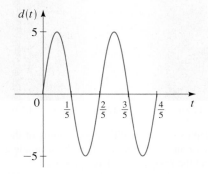

22. The graph shows the variation of the water level relative to mean sea level in Commencement Bay at Tacoma, Washington, for a particular 24-hour period. Assuming that this variation is modeled by simple harmonic motion, find an equation of the form $y = a \sin \omega t$ that describes the variation in water level as a function of the number of hours after midnight.

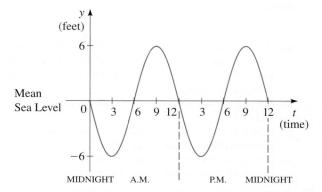

23. The Bay of Fundy in Nova Scotia has the highest tides in the world. In one 12-hour period, the water starts at mean sea level, rises to 21 ft above, drops to 21 ft below, then returns to mean sea level. Assuming that the motion of the tides is simple harmonic, find an equation that describes the height of the tide in the Bay of Fundy above mean sea level. Sketch a graph that shows the level of the tides over a 12-hour period.

24. A mass suspended from a spring is pulled down a distance of 2 ft from its rest position, as shown in the figure. The mass is released at time $t = 0$ and allowed to oscillate. If the mass returns to this position after 1 s, find an equation that describes its motion.

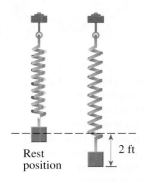

25. A mass is suspended on a spring. The spring is compressed so that the mass is located 5 cm above its rest position. The mass is released at time $t = 0$ and allowed to oscillate. It is observed that the mass reaches its lowest point $\frac{1}{2}$ s after it is released. Find an equation that describes the motion of the mass.

26. The frequency of oscillation of an object suspended on a spring depends on the stiffness k of the spring (called the *spring constant*) and the mass m of the object. If the spring is compressed a distance a and then allowed to oscillate, its displacement is given by

$$f(t) = a \cos \sqrt{k/m}\; t$$

(a) A 10-g mass is suspended from a spring with stiffness $k = 3$. If the spring is compressed a distance 5 cm and then released, find the equation that describes the oscillation of the spring.
(b) Find a general formula for the frequency (in terms of k and m).
(c) How is the frequency affected if the mass is increased? Is the oscillation faster or slower?
(d) How is the frequency affected if a stiffer spring is used (larger k)? Is the oscillation faster or slower?

27. A ferris wheel has a radius of 10 m, and the bottom of the wheel passes 1 m above the ground. If the ferris wheel makes one complete revolution every 20 s, find an equation that gives the height above the ground of a person on the ferris wheel as a function of time.

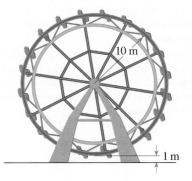

10 m

1 m

28. The pendulum in a grandfather clock makes one complete swing every 2 s. The maximum angle that the pendulum makes with respect to its rest position is 10°. We know from physical principles that the angle θ between the pendulum and its rest position changes in simple harmonic fashion. Find an equation that describes the size of the angle θ as a function of time. (Take $t = 0$ to be a time when the pendulum is vertical.)

θ

29. The variable star Zeta Gemini has a period of 10 days. The average brightness of the star is 3.8 magnitudes, and the maximum variation from the average is 0.2 magnitude. Assuming that the variation in brightness is simple harmonic, find an equation that gives the brightness of the star as a function of time.

30. Astronomers believe that the radius of a variable star increases and decreases with the brightness of the star. The variable star Delta Cephei (Example 4) has an average radius of 20 million miles and changes by a maximum of 1.5 million miles from this average during a single pulsation. Find an equation that describes the radius of this star as a function of time.

31. The armature in an electric generator is rotating at the rate of 100 revolutions per second (rps). If the maximum voltage produced is 310 V, find an equation that describes this variation in voltage. What is the rms voltage? (See Example 6 and the margin note adjacent to it.)

32. *Circadian rhythms* are biological processes that oscillate with a period of approximately 24 hours. That is, a circadian rhythm is an internal daily biological clock. Blood pressure appears to follow such a rhythm. For a certain individual the average resting blood pressure varies from a maximum of 100 mmHg at 2:00 P.M. to a minimum of 80 mmHg at 2:00 A.M. Find a sine function of the form

$$f(t) = a \sin(\omega(t - c)) + b$$

that models the blood pressure at time t, measured in hours from midnight.

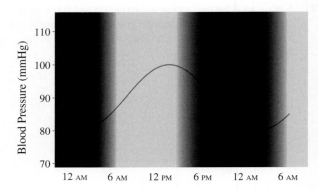

33. The graph shows an oscilloscope reading of the variation in voltage of an AC current produced by a simple generator.
(a) Find the maximum voltage produced.
(b) Find the frequency (cycles per second) of the generator.
(c) How many revolutions per second does the armature in the generator make?

(d) Find a formula that describes the variation in voltage as a function of time.

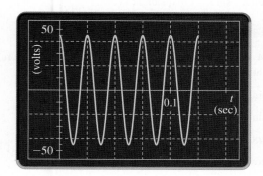

34. When a car with its horn blowing drives by an observer, the pitch of the horn seems higher as it approaches and lower as it recedes (see the figure). This phenomenon is called the **Doppler effect**. If the sound source is moving at speed v relative to the observer and if the speed of sound is v_0, then the perceived frequency f is related to the actual frequency f_0 as follows:

$$f = f_0 \left(\frac{v_0}{v_0 \pm v} \right)$$

We choose the minus sign if the source is moving toward the observer and the plus sign if it is moving away.

Suppose that a car drives at 110 ft/s past a woman standing on the shoulder of a highway, blowing its horn, which has a frequency of 500 Hz. Assume that the speed of sound is 1130 ft/s. (This is the speed in dry air at 70°F.)

(a) What are the frequencies of the sounds that the woman hears as the car approaches her and as it moves away from her?

(b) Let A be the amplitude of the sound. Find functions of the form

$$y = A \sin \omega t$$

that model the perceived sound as the car approaches the woman and as it recedes.

2   REVIEW

CONCEPT CHECK

1. (a) What is the unit circle?

    (b) Use a diagram to explain what is meant by the terminal point determined by a real number t.

    (c) What is the reference number $\bar{t}$ associated with t?

    (d) If t is a real number and $P(x, y)$ is the terminal point determined by t, write equations that define $\sin t$, $\cos t$, $\tan t$, $\cot t$, $\sec t$, and $\csc t$.

    (e) What are the domains of the six functions that you defined in part (d)?

    (f) Which trigonometric functions are positive in quadrants I, II, III, and IV?

2. (a) What is an even function?

    (b) Which trigonometric functions are even?

    (c) What is an odd function?

    (d) Which trigonometric functions are odd?

3. (a) State the reciprocal identities.

    (b) State the Pythagorean identities.

4. (a) What is a periodic function?

    (b) What are the periods of the six trigonometric functions?

5. Graph the sine and cosine functions. How is the graph of cosine related to the graph of sine?

6. Write expressions for the amplitude, period, and phase shift of the sine curve $y = a \sin k(x - b)$ and the cosine curve $y = a \cos k(x - b)$.

7. (a) Graph the tangent and cotangent functions.

    (b) State the periods of the tangent curve $y = a \tan kx$ and the cotangent curve $y = a \cot kx$.

8. (a) Graph the secant and cosecant functions.

    (b) State the periods of the secant curve $y = a \sec kx$ and the cosecant curve $y = a \csc kx$.

9. (a) What is simple harmonic motion?

    (b) Give three real-life examples of simple harmonic motion.

EXERCISES

1–2 ■ A point $P(x, y)$ is given.
(a) Show that P is on the unit circle.
(b) Suppose that P is the terminal point determined by t. Find $\sin t$, $\cos t$, and $\tan t$.

1. $P\left(-\dfrac{\sqrt{3}}{2}, \dfrac{1}{2}\right)$ **2.** $P\left(\dfrac{3}{5}, -\dfrac{4}{5}\right)$

3–6 ■ A real number t is given.
(a) Find the reference number for t.
(b) Find the terminal point $P(x, y)$ on the unit circle determined by t.
(c) Find the six trigonometric functions of t.

3. $t = \dfrac{2\pi}{3}$ **4.** $t = \dfrac{5\pi}{3}$

5. $t = -\dfrac{11\pi}{4}$ **6.** $t = -\dfrac{7\pi}{6}$

7–16 ■ Find the value of the trigonometric function. If possible, give the exact value; otherwise, use a calculator to find an approximate value correct to five decimal places.

7. (a) $\sin \dfrac{3\pi}{4}$ (b) $\cos \dfrac{3\pi}{4}$

8. (a) $\tan \dfrac{\pi}{3}$ (b) $\tan\left(-\dfrac{\pi}{3}\right)$

9. (a) $\sin 1.1$ (b) $\cos 1.1$

10. (a) $\cos \dfrac{\pi}{5}$ (b) $\cos\left(-\dfrac{\pi}{5}\right)$

11. (a) $\cos \dfrac{9\pi}{2}$ (b) $\sec \dfrac{9\pi}{2}$

12. (a) $\sin \dfrac{\pi}{7}$ (b) $\csc \dfrac{\pi}{7}$

13. (a) $\tan \dfrac{5\pi}{2}$ (b) $\cot \dfrac{5\pi}{2}$

14. (a) $\sin 2\pi$ (b) $\csc 2\pi$

15. (a) $\tan \dfrac{5\pi}{6}$ (b) $\cot \dfrac{5\pi}{6}$

16. (a) $\cos \dfrac{\pi}{3}$ (b) $\sin \dfrac{\pi}{6}$

17–20 ■ Use the fundamental identities to write the first expression in terms of the second.

17. $\dfrac{\tan t}{\cos t}$, $\sin t$ **18.** $\tan^2 t \sec t$, $\cos t$

19. $\tan t$, $\sin t$; t in quadrant IV

20. $\sec t$, $\sin t$; t in quadrant II

21–24 ■ Find the values of the remaining trigonometric functions at t from the given information.

21. $\sin t = \dfrac{5}{13}$, $\cos t = -\dfrac{12}{13}$

22. $\sin t = -\dfrac{1}{2}$, $\cos t > 0$

23. $\cot t = -\dfrac{1}{2}$, $\csc t = \sqrt{5}/2$

24. $\cos t = -\dfrac{3}{5}$, $\tan t < 0$

25. If $\tan t = \dfrac{1}{4}$ and the terminal point for t is in quadrant III, find $\sec t + \cot t$.

26. If $\sin t = -\dfrac{8}{17}$ and the terminal point for t is in quadrant IV, find $\csc t + \sec t$.

27. If $\cos t = \dfrac{3}{5}$ and the terminal point for t is in quadrant I, find $\tan t + \sec t$.

28. If $\sec t = -5$ and the terminal point for t is in quadrant II, find $\sin^2 t + \cos^2 t$.

29–36 ■ A trigonometric function is given.
(a) Find the amplitude, period, and phase shift of the function.
(b) Sketch the graph.

29. $y = 10 \cos \frac{1}{2} x$ **30.** $y = 4 \sin 2\pi x$

31. $y = -\sin \frac{1}{2} x$ **32.** $y = 2 \sin\left(x - \dfrac{\pi}{4}\right)$

33. $y = 3 \sin(2x - 2)$ **34.** $y = \cos 2\left(x - \dfrac{\pi}{2}\right)$

35. $y = -\cos\left(\dfrac{\pi}{2} x + \dfrac{\pi}{6}\right)$ **36.** $y = 10 \sin\left(2x - \dfrac{\pi}{2}\right)$

37–40 ■ The graph of one period of a function of the form $y = a \sin k(x - b)$ or $y = a \cos k(x - b)$ is shown. Determine the function.

37.

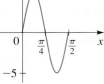

38.

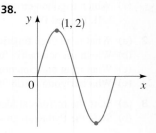

39.

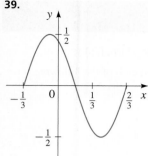

40.

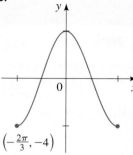

$\left(-\frac{2\pi}{3}, -4\right)$

41–48 ■ Find the period, and sketch the graph.

41. $y = 3 \tan x$

42. $y = \tan \pi x$

43. $y = 2 \cot\left(x - \frac{\pi}{2}\right)$

44. $y = \sec\left(\frac{1}{2}x - \frac{\pi}{2}\right)$

45. $y = 4 \csc(2x + \pi)$

46. $y = \tan\left(x + \frac{\pi}{6}\right)$

47. $y = \tan\left(\frac{1}{2}x - \frac{\pi}{8}\right)$

48. $y = -4 \sec 4\pi x$

49–54 ■ A function is given.
(a) Use a graphing device to graph the function.
(b) Determine from the graph whether the function is periodic and, if so, determine the period.
(c) Determine from the graph whether the function is odd, even, or neither.

49. $y = |\cos x|$

50. $y = \sin(\cos x)$

51. $y = \cos(2^{0.1x})$

52. $y = 1 + 2^{\cos x}$

53. $y = |x| \cos 3x$

54. $y = \sqrt{x} \sin 3x \quad (x > 0)$

55–58 ■ Graph the three functions on a common screen. How are the graphs related?

55. $y = x, \quad y = -x, \quad y = x \sin x$

56. $y = 2^{-x}, \quad y = -2^{-x}, \quad y = 2^{-x} \cos 4\pi x$

57. $y = x, \quad y = \sin 4x, \quad y = x + \sin 4x$

58. $y = \sin^2 x, \quad y = \cos^2 x, \quad y = \sin^2 x + \cos^2 x$

59–60 ■ Find the maximum and minimum values of the function.

59. $y = \cos x + \sin 2x$

60. $y = \cos x + \sin^2 x$

61. Find the solutions of $\sin x = 0.3$ in the interval $[0, 2\pi]$.

62. Find the solutions of $\cos 3x = x$ in the interval $[0, \pi]$.

63. Let $f(x) = \dfrac{\sin^2 x}{x}$.
(a) Is the function f even, odd, or neither?
(b) Find the x-intercepts of the graph of f.
(c) Graph f in an appropriate viewing rectangle.
(d) Describe the behavior of the function as x becomes large.
(e) Notice that $f(x)$ is not defined when $x = 0$. What happens as x approaches 0?

64. Let $y_1 = \cos(\sin x)$ and $y_2 = \sin(\cos x)$.
(a) Graph y_1 and y_2 in the same viewing rectangle.
(b) Determine the period of each of these functions from its graph.
(c) Find an inequality between $\sin(\cos x)$ and $\cos(\sin x)$ that is valid for all x.

65. A point P moving in simple harmonic motion completes 8 cycles every second. If the amplitude of the motion is 50 cm, find an equation that describes the motion of P as a function of time. Assume the point P is at its maximum displacement when $t = 0$.

66. A mass suspended from a spring oscillates in simple harmonic motion at a frequency of 4 cycles per second. The distance from the highest point to the lowest point of the oscillation is 100 cm. Find an equation that describes the distance of the mass from its rest position as a function of time. Assume the mass is at its lowest point when $t = 0$.

67. The graph shows the variation of the water level relative to mean sea level in the Long Beach harbor for a particular 24-hour period. Assuming that this variation is simple harmonic, find an equation of the form $y = a \cos \omega t$ that describes the variation in water level as a function of the number of hours after midnight.

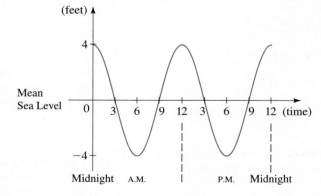

2 TEST

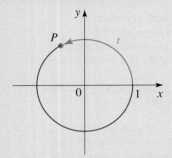

1. The point $P(x, y)$ is on the unit circle in quadrant IV. If $x = \sqrt{11}/6$, find y.

2. The point P in the figure at the left has y-coordinate $\frac{4}{5}$. Find each of the following.
   (a) $\sin t$ (b) $\cos t$
   (c) $\tan t$ (d) $\sec t$

3. Find the exact value of each of the following.
   (a) $\sin \dfrac{7\pi}{6}$ (b) $\cos \dfrac{13\pi}{4}$
   (c) $\tan \left(-\dfrac{5\pi}{3} \right)$ (d) $\csc \dfrac{3\pi}{2}$

4. Express $\tan t$ in terms of $\sin t$, if the terminal point determined by t is in quadrant II.

5. If $\cos t = -\frac{8}{17}$ and if the terminal point determined by t is in quadrant III, find $\tan t \cot t + \csc t$.

6–7 ■ A trigonometric function is given.
(a) Find the amplitude, period, and phase shift of the function.
(b) Sketch the graph.

6. $y = -5 \cos 4x$ 7. $y = 2 \sin \left(\dfrac{1}{2}x - \dfrac{\pi}{6} \right)$

8–9 ■ Find the period, and graph the function.

8. $y = -\csc 2x$ 9. $y = \tan \left(2x - \dfrac{\pi}{2} \right)$

10. The graph shown is one period of a function of the form $y = a \sin k(x - b)$. Determine the function.

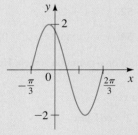

11. (a) Use a graphing device to graph the function in an appropriate viewing rectangle.
    (b) Determine from the graph if the function is even, odd, or neither.
    (c) Find the minimum and maximum values of the function.

    $$y = \frac{\cos x}{1 + x^2}$$

12. A mass suspended from a spring oscillates in simple harmonic motion. The mass completes 2 cycles every second and the distance between the highest point and the lowest point of the oscillation is 10 cm. Find an equation of the form $y = a \sin \omega t$ that gives the distance of the mass from its rest position as a function of time.

Focus on Modeling

Modeling Periodic Behavior from Data

In the *Focus on Modeling* that follows Chapter 1 (pages 102–111), we learned how to construct linear models from data. Figure 1 shows some scatter plots of data; the first plot appears to be linear but the others are not. What do we do when the data we are studying are not linear? In this case, our model would be some other type of function that best fits the data. If the scatter plot indicates simple harmonic motion, then we might try to model the data with a sine or cosine function. The next example illustrates the process.

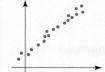   

FIGURE 1

TABLE 1

Time	Depth (ft)
12:00 A.M.	9.8
1:00 A.M.	11.4
2:00 A.M.	11.6
3:00 A.M.	11.2
4:00 A.M.	9.6
5:00 A.M.	8.5
6:00 A.M.	6.5
7:00 A.M.	5.7
8:00 A.M.	5.4
9:00 A.M.	6.0
10:00 A.M.	7.0
11:00 A.M.	8.6
12:00 P.M.	10.0

EXAMPLE 1 ■ Modeling the Height of a Tide

The water depth in a narrow channel varies with the tides. Table 1 shows the water depth over a 12-hour period.

(a) Make a scatter plot of the water depth data.
(b) Find a function that models the water depth with respect to time.
(c) If a boat needs at least 11 ft of water to cross the channel, during which times can it safely do so?

SOLUTION

(a) A scatter plot of the data is shown in Figure 2.

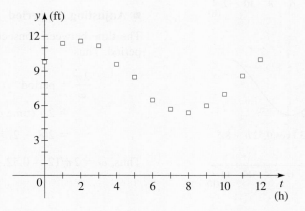

FIGURE 2

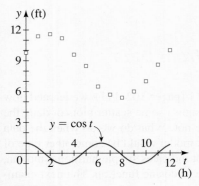

FIGURE 3

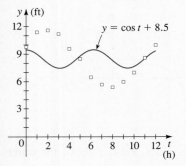

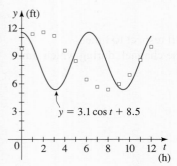

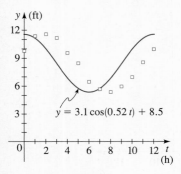

(b) The data appear to lie on a cosine (or sine) curve. But if we graph $y = \cos t$ on the same graph as the scatter plot, the result in Figure 3 is not even close to the data—to fit the data we need to adjust the vertical shift, amplitude, period, and phase shift of the cosine curve. In other words, we need to find a function of the form.

$$y = a \cos(\omega(t - c)) + b$$

We use the following steps, which are illustrated by the graphs in the margin.

■ **Adjusting the vertical shift**

The vertical shift b is the average of the maximum and minimum values:

$$b = \text{vertical shift}$$

$$= \tfrac{1}{2} \cdot (\text{maximum value} + \text{minimum value})$$

$$= \tfrac{1}{2}(11.6 + 5.4) = 8.5$$

■ **Adjusting the amplitude**

The amplitude a is half of the difference between the maximum and minimum values:

$$a = \text{amplitude}$$

$$= \tfrac{1}{2} \cdot (\text{maximum value} - \text{minimum value})$$

$$= \tfrac{1}{2}(11.6 - 5.4) = 3.1$$

■ **Adjusting the period**

The time between consecutive maximum and minimum values is half of one period. Thus

$$\frac{2\pi}{\omega} = \text{period}$$

$$= 2 \cdot (\text{time of maximum value} - \text{time of minimum value})$$

$$= 2(8 - 2) = 12$$

Thus, $\omega = 2\pi/12 = 0.52$.

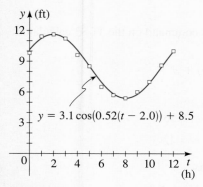

$$y = 3.1 \cos(0.52(t - 2.0)) + 8.5$$

FIGURE 4

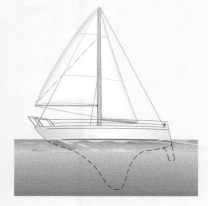

■ **Adjusting the horizontal shift**

Since the maximum value of the data occurs at approximately $t = 2.0$, it represents a cosine curve shifted 2 h to the right. So

$$c = \text{phase shift}$$

$$= \text{time of maximum value}$$

$$= 2.0$$

■ **The model**

We have shown that a function that models the tides over the given time period is given by

$$y = 3.1 \cos(0.52(t - 2.0)) + 8.5$$

A graph of the function and the scatter plot are shown in Figure 4. It appears that the model we found is a good approximation to the data.

(c) We need to solve the inequality $y \geq 11$. We solve this inequality graphically by graphing $y = 3.1 \cos 0.52(t - 2.0) + 8.5$ and $y = 11$ on the same graph. From the graph in Figure 5 we see the water depth is higher than 11 ft between $t \approx 0.8$ and $t \approx 3.2$. This corresponds to the times 12:48 A.M. to 3:12 A.M.

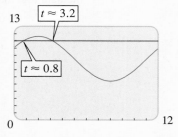

FIGURE 5

In Example 1 we used the scatter plot to guide us in finding a cosine curve that gives an approximate model of the data. Some graphing calculators are capable of finding a sine or cosine curve that best fits a given set of data points. The method the calculator uses is similar to the method of finding a line of best fit, as explained on pages 103–104.

For the TI-83 and TI-86 the command **SinReg** (for sine regression) finds the sine curve that best fits the given data.

EXAMPLE 2 ■ Fitting a Sine Curve to Data

(a) Use a graphing device to find the sine curve that best fits the depth of water data in Table 1 on page 169.

(b) Compare the result to the model found in Example 1.

SOLUTION

(a) Using the data in Table 1 and the **SinReg** command on the TI-83 calculator, we get a function of the form

$$y = a \sin(bt + c) + d$$

where

$$a = 3.1 \qquad b = 0.53$$
$$c = 0.55 \qquad d = 8.42$$

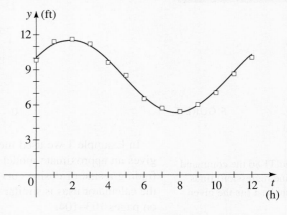

```
SinReg
 y=a*sin(bx+c)+d
 a=3.097877596
 b=.5268322697
 c=.5493035195
 d=8.424021899
```

Output of the **SinReg** function on the TI-83.

So, the sine function that best fits the data is

$$y = 3.1 \sin(0.53t + 0.55) + 8.42$$

(b) To compare this with the function in Example 1, we change the sine function to a cosine function by using the reduction formula $\sin u = \cos\left(u - \frac{\pi}{2}\right)$.

$$\begin{aligned}
y &= 3.1 \sin(0.53t + 0.55) + 8.42 \\
&= 3.1 \cos\left(0.53t + 0.55 - \frac{\pi}{2}\right) + 8.42 \qquad \text{Reduction formula} \\
&= 3.1 \cos(0.53t - 1.02) + 8.42 \\
&= 3.1 \cos(0.53(t - 1.92)) + 8.42 \qquad \text{Factor 0.53}
\end{aligned}$$

Comparing this with the function we obtained in Example 1, we see that there are small differences in the coefficients. In Figure 6 we graph a scatter plot of the data together with the sine function of best fit.

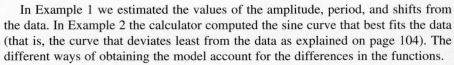

FIGURE 6

In Example 1 we estimated the values of the amplitude, period, and shifts from the data. In Example 2 the calculator computed the sine curve that best fits the data (that is, the curve that deviates least from the data as explained on page 104). The different ways of obtaining the model account for the differences in the functions.

Problems

1–4 ■ A set of data is given.

(a) Make a scatter plot of the data.

(b) Find a cosine function of the form $y = a \cos(\omega(t - c)) + b$ that models the data, as in Example 1.

(c) Graph the function you found in part (b) together with the scatter plot. How well does the curve fit the data?

(d) Use a graphing calculator to find the sine function that best fits the data, as in Example 2.

(e) Compare the functions you found in parts (b) and (d). [Use the reduction formula $\sin u = \cos(u - \pi/2)$.]

1.

t	y
0	2.1
2	1.1
4	−0.8
6	−2.1
8	−1.3
10	0.6
12	1.9
14	1.5

2.

t	y
0	190
25	175
50	155
75	125
100	110
125	95
150	105
175	120
200	140
225	165
250	185
275	200
300	195
325	185
350	165

3.

t	y
0.1	21.1
0.2	23.6
0.3	24.5
0.4	21.7
0.5	17.5
0.6	12.0
0.7	5.6
0.8	2.2
0.9	1.0
1.0	3.5
1.1	7.6
1.2	13.2
1.3	18.4
1.4	23.0
1.5	25.1

4.

t	y
0.0	0.56
0.5	0.45
1.0	0.29
1.5	0.13
2.0	0.05
2.5	−0.10
3.0	0.02
3.5	0.12
4.0	0.26
4.5	0.43
5.0	0.54
5.5	0.63
6.0	0.59

5. The table gives the average monthly temperature in Montgomery County, Maryland.

(a) Make a scatter plot of the data.

(b) Find a cosine curve that models the data (as in Example 1).

(c) Graph the function you found in part (b) together with the scatter plot.

(d) Use a graphing calculator to find the sine curve that best fits the data (as in Example 2).

Month	Average temperature (°F)
January	40.0
February	43.1
March	54.6
April	64.2
May	73.8
June	81.8
July	85.8
August	83.9
September	76.9
October	66.8
November	55.5
December	44.5

Time	Body temperature (°C)
0	36.8
2	36.7
4	36.6
6	36.7
8	36.8
10	37.0
12	37.2
14	37.3
16	37.4
18	37.3
20	37.2
22	37.0
24	36.8

6. Circadian rhythm (from the Latin *circa*—about, and *diem*—day) is the daily biological pattern by which body temperature, blood pressure, and other physiological variables change. The data show typical changes in human body temperature over a 24-hour period ($t = 0$ corresponds to midnight).
   (a) Make a scatter plot of the data.
   (b) Find a cosine curve that models the data (as in Example 1).
   (c) Graph the function you found in part (b) together with the scatter plot.
    (d) Use a graphing calculator to find the sine curve that best fits the data (as in Example 2).

7. When two species interact in a predator/prey relationship (see page 146), the populations of both species tend to vary in a sinusoidal fashion. In a certain midwestern county, the main food source for barn owls consists of field mice and other small mammals. The table gives the population of barn owls in this county every July 1 over a 12-year period.
   (a) Make a scatter plot of the data.
   (b) Find a sine curve that models the data (as in Example 1).
   (c) Graph the function you found in part (b) together with the scatter plot.
   (d) Use a graphing calculator to find the sine curve that best fits the data (as in Example 2). Compare to your answer from part (b).

Year	Owl population
0	50
1	62
2	73
3	80
4	71
5	60
6	51
7	43
8	29
9	20
10	28
11	41
12	49

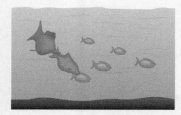

8. For reasons not yet fully understood, the number of fingerling salmon that survive the trip from their riverbed spawning grounds to the open ocean varies approximately sinusoidally from year to year. The table shows the number of salmon that hatch in a certain British Columbia creek and then make their way to the Strait of Georgia. The data is given in thousands of fingerlings, over a period of 16 years.

(a) Make a scatter plot of the data.
(b) Find a sine curve that models the data (as in Example 1).
(c) Graph the function you found in part (b) together with the scatter plot.
(d) Use a graphing calculator to find the sine curve that best fits the data (as in Example 2). Compare to your answer from part (b).

Year	Salmon (× 1000)	Year	Salmon (× 1000)
1985	43	1993	56
1986	36	1994	63
1987	27	1995	57
1988	23	1996	50
1989	26	1997	44
1990	33	1998	38
1991	43	1999	30
1992	50	2000	22

3 Trigonometric Functions of Angles

Trigonometric functions are important in surveying, navigation, and astronomy. They are used, for instance, to find heights of mountains or distances to nearby stars.

No one can bypass the science of triangles [trigonometry]
and hope to reach a satisfying knowledge of the stars.

REGIOMONTANUS

The trigonometric functions can be viewed in two different but equivalent ways. One way is to view them as *functions of angles* (Chapter 3), the other as *functions of real numbers* (Chapter 2). The two approaches to trigonometry are independent of each other, so either Chapter 2 or Chapter 3 may be studied first.

The trigonometric functions defined in these two different ways are identical—they assign the same value to a given real number. In the first case, the real number is the measure of an angle; in the second, it is the length of an arc along the unit circle. We study both approaches because different applications require that we view these functions differently. One approach (Chapter 3) lends itself to static applications such as the measurement of distance using triangles. The other approach (Chapter 2) lends itself to dynamic applications such as modeling harmonic motion. The power and versatility of trigonometry stem from the fact that it can be viewed in these different ways. Today, trigonometry is an indispensable tool in physics, engineering, computer science, biology, and in practically all the sciences.

3.1 ANGLE MEASURE

An **angle** AOB consists of two rays R_1 and R_2 with a common vertex O (see Figure 1). We often interpret an angle as a rotation of the ray R_1 onto R_2. In this case, R_1 is called the **initial side**, and R_2 is called the **terminal side** of the angle. If the rotation is counterclockwise, the angle is considered **positive**, and if the rotation is clockwise, the angle is considered **negative**.

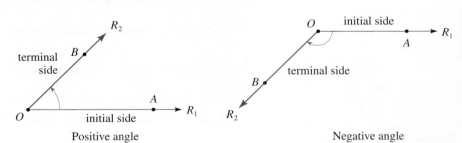

FIGURE 1   Positive angle   Negative angle

■ Angle Measure

The **measure** of an angle is the amount of rotation about the vertex required to move R_1 onto R_2. Intuitively, this is how much the angle "opens." One unit of measurement for angles is the **degree**. An angle of measure 1 degree is formed by rotating the initial side $\frac{1}{360}$ of a complete revolution. In calculus and other branches of mathematics, a more natural method of measuring angles is used—*radian measure*. The amount an angle opens is measured along the arc of a circle of radius 1 with its center at the vertex of the angle.

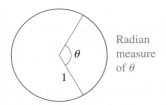

FIGURE 2

DEFINITION OF RADIAN MEASURE

If a circle of radius 1 is drawn with the vertex of an angle at its center, then the measure of this angle in **radians** (abbreviated **rad**) is the length of the arc that subtends the angle (see Figure 2).

The circumference of the circle of radius 1 is 2π and so a complete revolution has measure 2π rad, a straight angle has measure π rad, and a right angle has measure $\pi/2$ rad. An angle that is subtended by an arc of length 2 along the unit circle has radian measure 2 (see Figure 3).

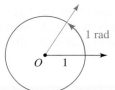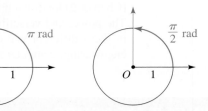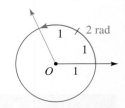

FIGURE 3
Radian measure

Since a complete revolution measured in degrees is 360° and measured in radians is 2π rad, we get the following simple relationship between these two methods of angle measurement.

RELATIONSHIP BETWEEN DEGREES AND RADIANS

$$180° = \pi \text{ rad} \qquad 1 \text{ rad} = \left(\frac{180}{\pi}\right)° \qquad 1° = \frac{\pi}{180} \text{ rad}$$

1. To convert degrees to radians, multiply by $\dfrac{\pi}{180}$.

2. To convert radians to degrees, multiply by $\dfrac{180}{\pi}$.

Measure of $\theta = 1$ rad
Measure of $\theta \approx 57.296°$

FIGURE 4

To get some idea of the size of a radian, notice that

$$1 \text{ rad} \approx 57.296° \qquad \text{and} \qquad 1° \approx 0.01745 \text{ rad}$$

An angle θ of measure 1 rad is shown in Figure 4.

EXAMPLE 1 ■ **Converting between Radians and Degrees**

(a) Express 60° in radians.

(b) Express $\dfrac{\pi}{6}$ rad in degrees.

SOLUTION

The relationship between degrees and radians gives

(a) $60° = 60\left(\dfrac{\pi}{180}\right)$ rad $= \dfrac{\pi}{3}$ rad

(b) $\dfrac{\pi}{6}$ rad $= \left(\dfrac{\pi}{6}\right)\left(\dfrac{180}{\pi}\right) = 30°$

■

A note on terminology: We often use a phrase such as "a 30° angle" to mean *an angle whose measure is* 30°. Also, for an angle θ, we write $\theta = 30°$ or $\theta = \pi/6$ to mean *the measure of θ is* 30° *or* $\pi/6$ *rad.* When no unit is given, the angle is assumed to be measured in radians.

■ **Angles in Standard Position**

An angle is in **standard position** if it is drawn in the xy-plane with its vertex at the origin and its initial side on the positive x-axis. Figure 5 gives examples of angles in standard position.

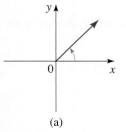

(a)

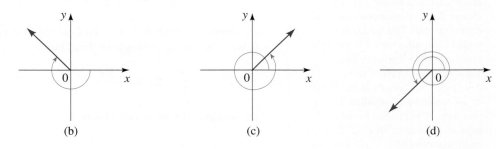

(b)   (c)   (d)

FIGURE 5
Angles in standard position

Two angles in standard position are **coterminal** if their sides coincide. In Figure 5 the angles in (a) and (c) are coterminal.

EXAMPLE 2 ■ Coterminal Angles

(a) Find angles that are coterminal with the angle $\theta = 30°$ in standard position.

(b) Find angles that are coterminal with the angle $\theta = \dfrac{\pi}{3}$ in standard position.

SOLUTION

(a) To find positive angles that are coterminal with θ, we add any multiple of 360°. Thus

$$30° + 360° = 390° \quad \text{and} \quad 30° + 720° = 750°$$

are coterminal with $\theta = 30°$. To find negative angles that are coterminal with θ, we subtract any multiple of $360°$. Thus

$$30° - 360° = -330° \quad \text{and} \quad 30° - 720° = -690°$$

are coterminal with θ. See Figure 6.

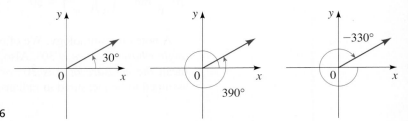

FIGURE 6

(b) To find positive angles that are coterminal with θ, we add any multiple of 2π. Thus

$$\frac{\pi}{3} + 2\pi = \frac{7\pi}{3} \quad \text{and} \quad \frac{\pi}{3} + 4\pi = \frac{13\pi}{3}$$

are coterminal with $\theta = \pi/3$. To find negative angles that are coterminal with θ, we subtract any multiple of 2π. Thus

$$\frac{\pi}{3} - 2\pi = -\frac{5\pi}{3} \quad \text{and} \quad \frac{\pi}{3} - 4\pi = -\frac{11\pi}{3}$$

are coterminal with θ. See Figure 7.

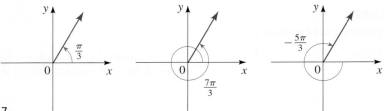

FIGURE 7

EXAMPLE 3 ■ Coterminal Angles

Find an angle with measure between $0°$ and $360°$ that is coterminal with the angle of measure $1290°$ in standard position.

SOLUTION

We can subtract $360°$ as many times as we wish from $1290°$, and the resulting angle will be coterminal with $1290°$. Thus, $1290° - 360° = 930°$ is coterminal with $1290°$, and so is the angle $1290° - 2(360)° = 570°$.

To find the angle we want between $0°$ and $360°$, we subtract $360°$ from $1290°$ as many times as necessary. An efficient way to do this is to determine how many times 360° goes into 1290°, that is, divide 1290 by 360, and the remainder will be the angle we are looking for. We see that 360 goes into 1290 three times with a remainder of 210. Thus, 210° is the desired angle (see Figure 8).

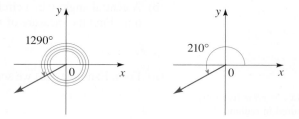

FIGURE 8

Length of a Circular Arc

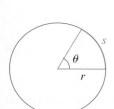

FIGURE 9
$s = \theta r$

An angle whose radian measure is θ is subtended by an arc that is the fraction $\theta/(2\pi)$ of the circumference of a circle. Thus, in a circle of radius r, the length s of an arc that subtends the angle θ (see Figure 9) is

$$s = \frac{\theta}{2\pi} \times \text{circumference of circle}$$

$$= \frac{\theta}{2\pi}(2\pi r) = \theta r$$

> **LENGTH OF A CIRCULAR ARC**
>
> In a circle of radius r, the length s of an arc that subtends a central angle of θ radians is
>
> $$s = r\theta$$

Solving for θ, we get the important formula

$$\theta = \frac{s}{r}$$

This formula allows us to define radian measure using a circle of any radius r: The radian measure of an angle θ is s/r, where s is the length of the circular arc that subtends θ in a circle of radius r (see Figure 10).

FIGURE 10

The radian measure of θ is the number of "radiuses" that can fit in the arc that subtends θ; hence the term *radian*.

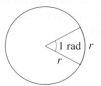

EXAMPLE 4 ■ Arc Length and Angle Measure

(a) Find the length of an arc of a circle with radius 10 m that subtends a central angle of 30°.

(b) A central angle θ in a circle of radius 4 m is subtended by an arc of length 6 m. Find the measure of θ in radians.

SOLUTION

(a) From Example 1(b) we see that $30° = \pi/6$ rad. So the length of the arc is

$$s = r\theta = (10)\frac{\pi}{6} = \frac{5\pi}{3} \text{ m}$$

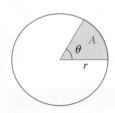 The formula $s = r\theta$ is true only when θ is measured in radians.

(b) By the formula $\theta = s/r$, we have

$$\theta = \frac{s}{r} = \frac{6}{4} = \frac{3}{2} \text{ rad}$$

■ Area of a Circular Sector

The area of a circle of radius r is $A = \pi r^2$. A sector of this circle with central angle θ has an area that is the fraction $\theta/(2\pi)$ of the area of the entire circle (see Figure 11). So the area of this sector is

$$A = \frac{\theta}{2\pi} \times \text{area of circle}$$

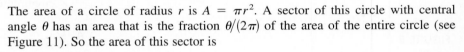

FIGURE 11
$A = \frac{1}{2}r^2\theta$

$$= \frac{\theta}{2\pi}(\pi r^2) = \frac{1}{2}r^2\theta$$

AREA OF A CIRCULAR SECTOR

In a circle of radius r, the area A of a sector with a central angle of θ radians is

$$A = \frac{1}{2}r^2\theta$$

EXAMPLE 5 ■ Area of a Sector

Find the area of a sector of a circle with central angle 60° if the radius of the circle is 3 m.

SOLUTION

To use the formula for the area of a circular sector, we must find the central angle of the sector in radians: $60° = 60(\pi/180)$ rad $= \pi/3$ rad. Thus, the area of the sector is

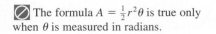 The formula $A = \frac{1}{2}r^2\theta$ is true only when θ is measured in radians.

$$A = \frac{1}{2}r^2\theta = \frac{1}{2}(3)^2\left(\frac{\pi}{3}\right) = \frac{3\pi}{2} \text{ m}^2$$

Circular Motion

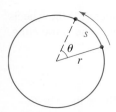

FIGURE 12

Suppose a point moves along a circle as shown in Figure 12. There are two ways to describe the motion of the point—linear speed and angular speed. **Linear speed** is the rate at which the distance traveled is changing, so linear speed is the distance traveled divided by the time elapsed. **Angular speed** is the rate at which the central angle θ is changing, so angular speed is the number of radians this angle changes divided by the time elapsed.

LINEAR SPEED AND ANGULAR SPEED

Suppose a point moves along a circle of radius r and the ray from the center of the circle to the point traverses θ radians in time t. Let $s = r\theta$ be the distance the point travels in time t. Then the speed of the object is given by

$$\textbf{Angular speed} \qquad \omega = \frac{\theta}{t}$$

$$\textbf{Linear speed} \qquad v = \frac{s}{t}$$

EXAMPLE 6 ■ Finding Linear and Angular Speed

A boy rotates a stone in a 3-ft-long sling at the rate of 15 revolutions every 10 seconds. Find the angular and linear velocities of the stone.

SOLUTION

In 10 s, the angle θ changes by $15 \cdot 2\pi = 30\pi$ radians. So the *angular speed* of the stone is

$$\omega = \frac{\theta}{t} = \frac{30\pi \text{ rad}}{10 \text{ s}} = 3\pi \text{ rad/s}$$

The distance traveled by the stone in 10 s is $s = 15 \cdot 2\pi r = 15 \cdot 2\pi \cdot 3 = 90\pi$ ft. So the *linear speed* of the stone is

$$v = \frac{s}{t} = \frac{90\pi \text{ ft}}{10 \text{ s}} = 9\pi \text{ ft/s} \qquad ■$$

Notice that angular speed does *not* depend on the radius of the circle, but only on the angle θ. However, if we know the angular speed ω and the radius r, we can find linear speed as follows: $v = s/t = r\theta/t = r(\theta/t) = r\omega$.

RELATIONSHIP BETWEEN LINEAR AND ANGULAR SPEED

If a point moves along a circle of radius r with angular speed ω, then its linear speed v is given by

$$v = r\omega$$

EXAMPLE 7 ■ Finding Linear Speed from Angular Speed

A woman is riding a bicycle whose wheels are 26 inches in diameter. If the wheels rotate at 125 revolutions per minute (rpm), find the speed at which she is traveling, in mi/h.

SOLUTION

The angular speed of the wheels is $2\pi \cdot 125 = 250\pi$ rad/min. Since the wheels have radius 13 in. (half the diameter), the linear speed is

$$v = r\omega = 13 \cdot 250\pi \approx 10{,}210.2 \text{ in./min}$$

Since there are 12 inches per foot, 5280 feet per mile, and 60 minutes per hour, her speed in miles per hour is

$$\frac{10{,}210.2 \text{ in./min} \times 60 \text{ min/h}}{12 \text{ in./ft} \times 5280 \text{ ft/mi}} \approx 9.7 \text{ mi/h} \qquad ■$$

3.1 EXERCISES

1–8 ■ Find the radian measure of the angle with the given degree measure.

1. $36°$ 　　　　**2.** $200°$ 　　　　**3.** $-480°$

4. $-72°$ 　　　**5.** $60°$ 　　　　**6.** $45°$

7. $-135°$ 　　**8.** $150°$

9–16 ■ Find the degree measure of the angle with the given radian measure.

9. $\dfrac{3\pi}{4}$ 　　**10.** $-\dfrac{7\pi}{2}$ 　　**11.** $\dfrac{5\pi}{6}$

12. 2 　　**13.** -1.5 　　**14.** $\dfrac{2\pi}{9}$

15. $-\dfrac{\pi}{12}$ 　　**16.** $\dfrac{\pi}{18}$

17–22 ■ The measure of an angle in standard position is given. Find two positive angles and two negative angles that are coterminal with the given angle.

17. $50°$ 　　**18.** $135°$ 　　**19.** $\dfrac{3\pi}{4}$

20. $\dfrac{11\pi}{6}$ 　　**21.** $-\dfrac{\pi}{4}$ 　　**22.** $-45°$

23–28 ■ The measures of two angles in standard position are given. Determine whether the angles are coterminal.

23. $70°$, 　$430°$ 　　　　**24.** $-30°$, 　$330°$

25. $\dfrac{5\pi}{6}$, 　$\dfrac{17\pi}{6}$ 　　**26.** $\dfrac{32\pi}{3}$, 　$\dfrac{11\pi}{3}$

27. $155°$, 　$875°$ 　　**28.** $50°$, 　$340°$

29–34 ■ Find an angle between $0°$ and $360°$ that is coterminal with the given angle.

29. $733°$ 　　　　　　**30.** $361°$

31. $1110°$ 　　　　　**32.** $-100°$

33. $-800°$ 　　　　　**34.** $1270°$

35–40 ■ Find an angle between 0 and 2π that is coterminal with the given angle.

35. $\dfrac{17\pi}{6}$ 　　**36.** $-\dfrac{7\pi}{3}$ 　　**37.** 87π

38. 10 　　**39.** $\dfrac{17\pi}{4}$ 　　**40.** $\dfrac{51\pi}{2}$

41. Find the length of the arc s in the figure.

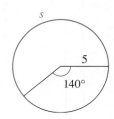

42. Find the angle θ in the figure.

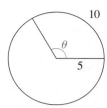

43. Find the radius r of the circle in the figure.

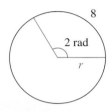

44. Find the length of an arc that subtends a central angle of 45° in a circle of radius 10 m.

45. Find the length of an arc that subtends a central angle of 2 rad in a circle of radius 2 mi.

46. A central angle θ in a circle of radius 5 m is subtended by an arc of length 6 m. Find the measure of θ in degrees and in radians.

47. An arc of length 100 m subtends a central angle θ in a circle of radius 50 m. Find the measure of θ in degrees and in radians.

48. A circular arc of length 3 ft subtends a central angle of 25°. Find the radius of the circle.

49. Find the radius of the circle if an arc of length 6 m on the circle subtends a central angle of $\pi/6$ rad.

50. How many revolutions will a car wheel of diameter 30 in. make as the car travels a distance of one mile?

51. Pittsburgh, Pennsylvania, and Miami, Florida, lie approximately on the same meridian. Pittsburgh has a latitude of 40.5° N and Miami, 25.5° N. Find the distance between these two cities. (The radius of the earth is 3960 mi.)

52. Memphis, Tennessee, and New Orleans, Louisiana, lie approximately on the same meridian. Memphis has latitude 35° N and New Orleans, 30° N. Find the distance between these two cities. (The radius of the earth is 3960 mi.)

53. Find the distance that the earth travels in one day in its path around the sun. Assume that a year has 365 days and that the path of the earth around the sun is a circle of radius 93 million miles. [The path of the earth around the sun is actually an *ellipse* with the sun at one focus (see Section 6.2). This ellipse, however, has very small eccentricity, so it is nearly circular.]

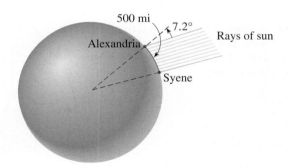

54. The Greek mathematician Eratosthenes (ca. 276–195 B.C.) measured the circumference of the earth from the following observations. He noticed that on a certain day the sun shone directly down a deep well in Syene (modern Aswan). At the same time in Alexandria, 500 miles north (on the same meridian), the rays of the sun shone at an angle of 7.2° to the zenith. Use this information and the figure to find the radius and circumference of the earth. (The data used in this problem are more accurate than those available to Eratosthenes.)

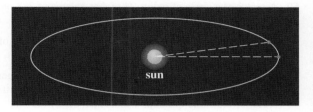

55. Find the distance along an arc on the surface of the earth that subtends a central angle of 1 minute (1 minute = $\frac{1}{60}$ degree). This distance is called a *nautical mile*. (The radius of the earth is 3960 mi.)

56. Find the area of the sector shown in each figure.

(a)   (b)

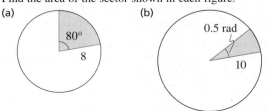

57. Find the area of a sector with central angle 1 rad in a circle of radius 10 m.

58. A sector of a circle has a central angle of 60°. Find the area of the sector if the radius of the circle is 3 mi.

59. The area of a sector of a circle with a central angle of 2 rad is 16 m^2. Find the radius of the circle.

60. A sector of a circle of radius 24 mi has an area of 288 mi^2. Find the central angle of the sector.

61. The area of a circle is 72 cm^2. Find the area of a sector of this circle that subtends a central angle of $\pi/6$ rad.

62. Three circles with radii 1, 2, and 3 ft are externally tangent to one another, as shown in the figure. Find the area of the sector of the circle of radius 1 that is cut off by the line segments joining the center of that circle to the centers of the other two circles.

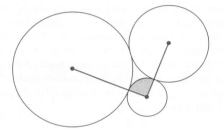

63. A winch of radius 2 ft is used to lift heavy loads. If the winch makes 8 revolutions every 15 s, find the speed at which the load is rising.

64. A ceiling fan with 16-in. blades rotates at 45 rpm.
 (a) Find the angular speed of the fan in rad/min.
 (b) Find the linear speed of the tips of the blades in in/min.

65. A radial saw has a blade with a 6-in. radius. Suppose that the blade spins at 1000 rpm.
 (a) Find the angular speed of the blade in rad/min.
 (b) Find the linear speed of the sawteeth in ft/s.

66. The earth rotates about its axis once every 23 h 56 min 4 s, and the radius of the earth is 3960 mi. Find the linear speed of a point on the equator in mi/h.

67. The wheels of a car have radius 11 in. and are rotating at 600 rpm. Find the speed of the car in mi/h.

68. A truck with 48-in. diameter wheels is traveling at 50 mi/h.
 (a) Find the angular speed of the wheels in rad/min.
 (b) How many revolutions per minute do the wheels make?

69. To measure the speed of a current, scientists place a paddle wheel in the stream and observe the rate at which it rotates. If the paddle wheel has radius 0.20 m and rotates at 100 rpm, find the speed of the current in m/s.

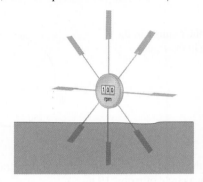

70. The sprockets and chain of a bicycle are shown in the figure. The pedal sprocket has a radius of 4 in, the wheel sprocket a radius of 2 in, and the wheel a radius of 13 in. The cyclist pedals at 40 rpm.
 (a) Find the angular speed of the wheel sprocket.
 (b) Find the speed of the bicycle. (Assume that the wheel turns at the same rate as the wheel sprocket.)

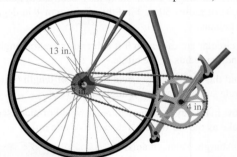

 DISCOVERY · DISCUSSION

71. Different Ways of Measuring Angles   The custom of measuring angles using degrees, with 360° in a circle, dates back to the ancient Babylonians, who used a number system based on groups of 60. Another system of measuring angles divides the circle into 400 units, called *grads*. In this system a right angle is 100 grad, so this fits in with our base 10 number system.

   Write a short essay comparing the advantages and disadvantages of these two systems and the radian system of measuring angles. Which system do you prefer?

72. Clocks and Angles   In one hour, the minute hand on a clock moves through a complete circle, and the hour hand moves through $\frac{1}{12}$ of a circle. Through how many radians do the minute and the hour hand move between 1:00 P.M. and 6:45 P.M. (on the same day)?

3.2   TRIGONOMETRY OF RIGHT TRIANGLES

In this section we study certain ratios of the sides of right triangles, called trigonometric ratios, and give several applications.

■ Trigonometric Ratios

Consider a right triangle with θ as one of its acute angles. The trigonometric ratios are defined as follows (see Figure 1).

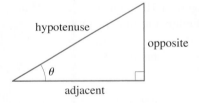

FIGURE 1

THE TRIGONOMETRIC RATIOS		
$\sin\theta = \dfrac{\text{opposite}}{\text{hypotenuse}}$	$\cos\theta = \dfrac{\text{adjacent}}{\text{hypotenuse}}$	$\tan\theta = \dfrac{\text{opposite}}{\text{adjacent}}$
$\csc\theta = \dfrac{\text{hypotenuse}}{\text{opposite}}$	$\sec\theta = \dfrac{\text{hypotenuse}}{\text{adjacent}}$	$\cot\theta = \dfrac{\text{adjacent}}{\text{opposite}}$

The symbols we use for these ratios are abbreviations for their full names: **sine**, **cosine**, **tangent**, **cosecant**, **secant**, **cotangent**. Since any two right triangles with angle θ are similar, these ratios are the same, regardless of the size of the triangle; they depend only on the angle θ (see Figure 2).

Hipparchus (circa 140 B.C.) is considered the founder of trigonometry. He constructed tables for a function closely related to the modern sine function and evaluated for angles at half-degree intervals. These are considered the first trigonometric tables. He used his tables mainly to calculate the paths of the planets through the heavens.

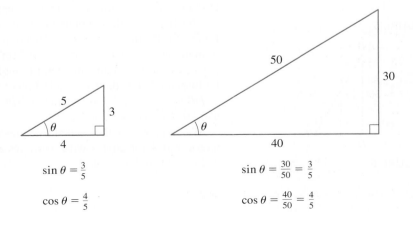

FIGURE 2

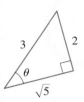

FIGURE 3

EXAMPLE 1 ■ Finding Trigonometric Ratios

Find the six trigonometric ratios of the angle θ in Figure 3.

SOLUTION

$$\sin \theta = \frac{2}{3} \qquad \cos \theta = \frac{\sqrt{5}}{3} \qquad \tan \theta = \frac{2}{\sqrt{5}}$$

$$\csc \theta = \frac{3}{2} \qquad \sec \theta = \frac{3}{\sqrt{5}} \qquad \cot \theta = \frac{\sqrt{5}}{2}$$

■

EXAMPLE 2 ■ Finding Trigonometric Ratios

If $\cos \alpha = \frac{3}{4}$, sketch a right triangle with acute angle α, and find the other five trigonometric ratios of α.

SOLUTION

Since $\cos \alpha$ is defined as the ratio of the adjacent side to the hypotenuse, we sketch a triangle with hypotenuse of length 4 and a side of length 3 adjacent to α. If the opposite side is x, then by the Pythagorean Theorem, $3^2 + x^2 = 4^2$ or $x^2 = 7$, so $x = \sqrt{7}$. We then use the triangle in Figure 4 to find the ratios.

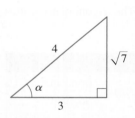

FIGURE 4

$$\sin \alpha = \frac{\sqrt{7}}{4} \qquad \cos \alpha = \frac{3}{4} \qquad \tan \alpha = \frac{\sqrt{7}}{3}$$

$$\csc \alpha = \frac{4}{\sqrt{7}} \qquad \sec \alpha = \frac{4}{3} \qquad \cot \alpha = \frac{3}{\sqrt{7}}$$

■

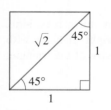

FIGURE 5

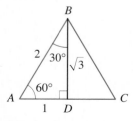

FIGURE 6

■ Special Triangles

Certain right triangles have ratios that can be calculated easily from the Pythagorean Theorem. Since they are used frequently, we mention them here.

The first triangle is obtained by drawing a diagonal in a square of side 1 (see Figure 5). By the Pythagorean Theorem this diagonal has length $\sqrt{2}$. The resulting triangle has angles 45°, 45°, and 90° (or $\pi/4$, $\pi/4$, and $\pi/2$). To get the second triangle, we start with an equilateral triangle ABC of side 2 and draw the perpendicular bisector DB of the base, as in Figure 6. By the Pythagorean Theorem the length of DB is $\sqrt{3}$. Since DB bisects angle ABC, we obtain a triangle with angles 30°, 60°, and 90° (or $\pi/6$, $\pi/3$, and $\pi/2$).

We can now use the special triangles in Figures 5 and 6 to calculate the trigonometric ratios for angles with measures 30°, 45°, and 60° (or $\pi/6$, $\pi/4$, and $\pi/3$). These are listed in Table 1.

TABLE 1 Values of the trigonometric ratios for special angles

θ in degrees	θ in radians	$\sin\theta$	$\cos\theta$	$\tan\theta$	$\csc\theta$	$\sec\theta$	$\cot\theta$
30°	$\dfrac{\pi}{6}$	$\dfrac{1}{2}$	$\dfrac{\sqrt{3}}{2}$	$\dfrac{\sqrt{3}}{3}$	2	$\dfrac{2\sqrt{3}}{3}$	$\sqrt{3}$
45°	$\dfrac{\pi}{4}$	$\dfrac{\sqrt{2}}{2}$	$\dfrac{\sqrt{2}}{2}$	1	$\sqrt{2}$	$\sqrt{2}$	1
60°	$\dfrac{\pi}{3}$	$\dfrac{\sqrt{3}}{2}$	$\dfrac{1}{2}$	$\sqrt{3}$	$\dfrac{2\sqrt{3}}{3}$	2	$\dfrac{\sqrt{3}}{3}$

It's useful to remember these special trigonometric ratios because they occur often. Of course, they can be recalled easily if we remember the triangles from which they are obtained.

To find the values of the trigonometric ratios for other angles, we use a calculator. Mathematical methods (called *numerical methods*) used in finding the trigonometric ratios are programmed directly into scientific calculators. For instance, when the $\boxed{\text{SIN}}$ key is pressed, the calculator computes an approximation to the value of the sine of the given angle. Calculators give the values of sine, cosine, and tangent; the other ratios can be easily calculated from these using the following *reciprocal relations:*

$$\csc t = \frac{1}{\sin t} \qquad \sec t = \frac{1}{\cos t} \qquad \cot t = \frac{1}{\tan t}$$

For an explanation of numerical methods, see the marginal note on page 124.

You should check that these relations follow immediately from the definitions of the trigonometric ratios.

We follow the convention that when we write $\sin t$*, we mean the sine of the angle whose radian measure is t.* For instance, $\sin 1$ means the sine of the angle whose radian measure is 1. When using a calculator to find an approximate value for this number, set your calculator to radian mode; you will find that

$$\sin 1 \approx 0.841471$$

If you want to find the sine of the angle whose measure is 1°, set your calculator to degree mode; you will find that

$$\sin 1° \approx 0.0174524$$

EXAMPLE 3 ■ **Using a Calculator to Find Trigonometric Ratios**

With our calculator in degree mode, and writing the results correct to five decimal places, we find

$$\sin 17° \approx 0.29237 \qquad \sec 88° = \frac{1}{\cos 88°} \approx 28.65371$$

Aristarchus of Samos (310–230 B.C.) was a famous Greek scientist, musician, astronomer, and geometer. In his book *On the Sizes and Distances of the Sun and the Moon,* he estimated the distance to the sun by observing that when the moon is exactly half full, the triangle formed by the sun, moon, and the earth has a right angle at the moon. His method was similar to the one described in Exercise 51 in this section. Aristarchus was the first to advance the theory that the earth and planets move around the sun, an idea that did not gain full acceptance until after the time of Copernicus, 1800 years later. For this reason he is often called the "Copernicus of antiquity."

With our calculator in radian mode, and writing the results correct to five decimal places, we find

$$\cos 1.2 \approx 0.36236 \qquad \cot 1.54 = \frac{1}{\tan 1.54} \approx 0.03081 \qquad \blacksquare$$

■ Applications of Trigonometry of Right Triangles

A triangle has six parts: three angles and three sides. To **solve a triangle** means to determine all of its parts from the information known about the triangle, that is, to determine the lengths of the three sides and the measures of the three angles.

EXAMPLE 4 ■ Solving a Right Triangle

Solve triangle ABC, shown in Figure 7.

SOLUTION

It's clear that $\angle B = 60°$. To find a, we look for an equation that relates a to the lengths and angles we already know. In this case, we have $\sin 30° = a/12$, so

$$a = 12 \sin 30° = 12\left(\tfrac{1}{2}\right) = 6$$

Similarly, $\cos 30° = b/12$, so

$$b = 12 \cos 30° = 12\left(\frac{\sqrt{3}}{2}\right) = 6\sqrt{3} \qquad \blacksquare$$

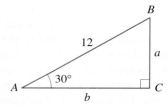

FIGURE 7

It's very useful to know that, using the information given in Figure 8, the lengths of the legs of a right triangle are

$$a = r \sin \theta \qquad \text{and} \qquad b = r \cos \theta$$

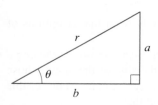

FIGURE 8

$a = r \sin \theta$

$b = r \cos \theta$

The ability to solve right triangles using the trigonometric ratios is fundamental to many problems in navigation, surveying, astronomy, and the measurement of distances. The applications we consider in this section always involve right triangles but, as we will see in the next three sections, trigonometry is also useful in solving triangles that are not right triangles.

To discuss the next examples, we need some terminology. If an observer is looking at an object, then the line from the observer's eye to the object is called the **line of sight** (Figure 9). If the object being observed is above the horizontal, then the angle between the line of sight and the horizontal is called the **angle of elevation**. If the object is below the horizontal, then the angle between the line of sight and the horizontal is called the **angle of depression**. In many of the examples and exercises in this chapter, angles of elevation and depression will be given for a hypothetical observer at ground level. If the line of sight follows a physical object, such as an inclined plane or a hillside, we use the term **angle of inclination**.

Thales of Miletus (circa 625–547 B.C.) is the legendary founder of Greek geometry. It is said that he calculated the height of a Greek column by comparing the length of the shadow of his staff with that of the column. Using properties of similar triangles, he argued that the ratio of the height h of the column to the height h' of his staff was equal to the ratio of the length s of the column's shadow to the length s' of the staff's shadow:

$$\frac{h}{h'} = \frac{s}{s'}$$

Since three of these quantities are known, Thales was able to calculate the height of the column.

According to legend, Thales used a similar method to find the height of the Great Pyramid in Egypt, a feat that impressed Egypt's king. Plutarch wrote that "although he [the king of Egypt] admired you [Thales] for other things, yet he particularly liked the manner by which you measured the height of the pyramid without any trouble or instrument." The principle Thales used, the fact that ratios of corresponding sides of similar triangles are equal, is the foundation of the subject of trigonometry.

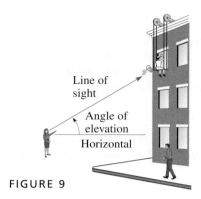

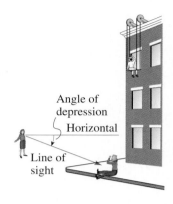

FIGURE 9

The next example gives an important application of trigonometry to the problem of measurement: We measure the height of a tall tree without having to climb it! Although the example is simple, the result is fundamental to the method of applying the trigonometric ratios to such problems.

EXAMPLE 5 ■ Finding the Height of a Tree

A giant redwood tree casts a shadow 532 ft long. Find the height of the tree if the angle of elevation of the sun is 25.7°.

SOLUTION

Let the height of the tree be h. From Figure 10 we see that

$$\frac{h}{532} = \tan 25.7° \qquad \text{Definition of tan}$$

$$h = 532 \tan 25.7° \qquad \text{Multiply by 532}$$

$$\approx 532(0.48127) \approx 256 \qquad \text{Use a calculator}$$

Therefore, the height of the tree is about 256 ft.

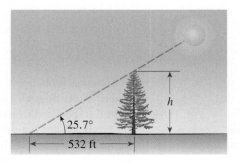

FIGURE 10

■

EXAMPLE 6 ■ **A Problem Involving Right Triangles**

From a point on the ground 500 ft from the base of a building, it is observed that the angle of elevation to the top of the building is 24° and the angle of elevation to the top of a flagpole atop the building is 27°. Find the height of the building and the length of the flagpole.

SOLUTION

Figure 11 illustrates the situation. The height of the building is found in the same way that we found the height of the tree in Example 5.

$$\frac{h}{500} = \tan 24° \qquad \text{Definition of tan}$$

$$h = 500 \tan 24° \qquad \text{Multiply by 500}$$

$$\approx 500(0.4452) \approx 223 \qquad \text{Use a calculator}$$

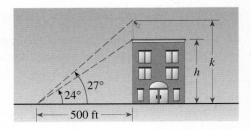

FIGURE 11

The height of the building is approximately 223 ft. To find the length of the flagpole, let's first find the height from the ground to the top of the pole:

$$\frac{k}{500} = \tan 27°$$

$$k = 500 \tan 27° \approx 500(0.5095) \approx 255$$

To find the length of the flagpole, we subtract h from k. So the length of the pole is approximately $255 - 223 = 32$ ft.   ■

In some problems we need to find an angle in a right triangle whose sides are given. To do this, we use Table 1 (page 189) "backward"; that is, we find the *angle* with the specified trigonometric ratio. For example, if $\sin \theta = \frac{1}{2}$, what is the angle θ? From Table 1 we can tell that $\theta = 30°$. To find an angle whose sine is not given in the table, we use the $\boxed{\text{SIN}^{-1}}$ or $\boxed{\text{INV}}$ $\boxed{\text{SIN}}$ or $\boxed{\text{ARCSIN}}$ keys on a calculator. For example, if $\sin \theta = 0.8$, we apply the $\boxed{\text{SIN}^{-1}}$ key to get $\theta = 53.13°$ or 0.927 rad. The calculator also gives angles whose cosine or tangent are known, using the $\boxed{\text{COS}^{-1}}$ or $\boxed{\text{TAN}^{-1}}$ key.

The key labels $\boxed{\text{SIN}^{-1}}$ or $\boxed{\text{INV}}$ $\boxed{\text{SIN}}$ stand for "inverse sine." The inverse trigonometric functions are studied in Section 4.4.

EXAMPLE 7 ■ Solving for an Angle in a Right Triangle

A 40-ft ladder leans against a building. If the base of the ladder is 6 ft from the base of the building, what is the angle formed by the ladder and the building?

SOLUTION

First we sketch a diagram as in Figure 12. If θ is the angle between the ladder and the building, then

$$\sin \theta = \tfrac{6}{40} = 0.15$$

So θ is the angle whose sine is 0.15. To find the angle θ, we use a calculator and use the $\boxed{\text{SIN}^{-1}}$ key. With our calculator in degree mode, we get

$$\theta \approx 8.6°$$

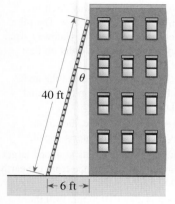

FIGURE 12

3.2 EXERCISES

1–6 ■ Find the exact values of the six trigonometric ratios of the angle θ in the triangle.

1.
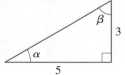

2.
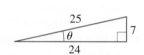

3.

4.

5.
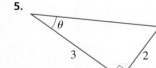

6.
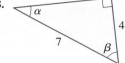

7–8 ■ Find (a) sin α and cos β, (b) tan α and cot β, and (c) sec α and csc β.

7.
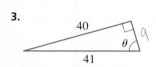

8.
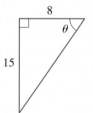

9–14 ■ Find the side labeled x. In Exercises 13 and 14 state your answer correct to five decimal places.

9.
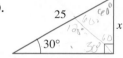

10.

11.
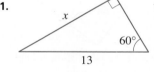

12.
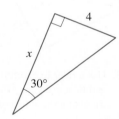

13.
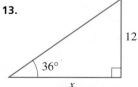

14.
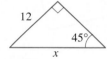

15–16 ■ Express x and y in terms of trigonometric ratios of θ.

15.
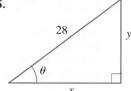

16.
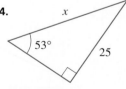
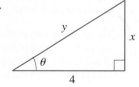
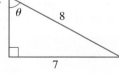

17–22 ■ Sketch a triangle that has acute angle θ, and find the other five trigonometric ratios of θ.

17. $\sin \theta = \frac{3}{5}$

18. $\cos \theta = \frac{9}{40}$

19. $\cot \theta = 1$

20. $\tan \theta = \sqrt{3}$

21. $\sec \theta = \frac{7}{2}$

22. $\csc \theta = \frac{13}{12}$

23–28 ■ Evaluate the expression without using a calculator.

23. $\sin \dfrac{\pi}{6} + \cos \dfrac{\pi}{6}$

24. $\sin 30° \csc 30°$

25. $\sin 30° \cos 60° + \sin 60° \cos 30°$

26. $(\sin 60°)^2 + (\cos 60°)^2$

27. $(\cos 30°)^2 - (\sin 30°)^2$

28. $\left(\sin \dfrac{\pi}{3} \cos \dfrac{\pi}{4} - \sin \dfrac{\pi}{4} \cos \dfrac{\pi}{3} \right)^2$

29–32 ■ Solve the right triangle.

29.

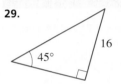

30.

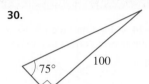

31.

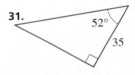

32.

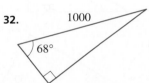

33. Use a ruler to carefully measure the sides of the triangle, and then use your measurements to estimate the six trigonometric ratios of θ.

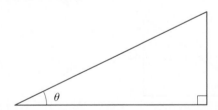

34. Using a protractor, sketch a right triangle that has the acute angle 40°. Measure the sides carefully and use your results to estimate the six trigonometric ratios of 40°.

35. The angle of elevation to the top of the Empire State Building in New York is found to be 11° from the ground at a distance of 1 mi from the base of the building. Using this information, find the height of the Empire State Building.

36. A plane is flying within sight of the Gateway Arch in St. Louis, Missouri, at an elevation of 35,000 ft. The pilot would like to estimate her distance from the Gateway Arch. She finds that the angle of depression to a point on the ground below the arch is 22°.
   (a) What is the distance between the plane and the arch?
   (b) What is the distance between a point on the ground directly below the plane and the arch?

37. A laser beam is to be directed toward the center of the moon, but the beam strays 0.5° from its intended path.
   (a) How far has the beam diverged from its assigned target when it reaches the moon? (The distance from the earth to the moon is 240,000 mi.)
   (b) The radius of the moon is about 1000 mi. Will the beam strike the moon?

38. From the top of a 200-ft lighthouse, the angle of depression to a ship in the ocean is 23°. How far is the ship from the base of the lighthouse?

39. A 20-ft ladder leans against a building so that the angle between the ground and the ladder is 72°. How high does the ladder reach on the building?

40. A 20-ft ladder is leaning against a building. If the base of the ladder is 6 ft from the base of the building, what is the angle of elevation of the ladder? How high does the ladder reach on the building?

41. A 96-ft tree casts a shadow that is 120 ft long. What is the angle of elevation of the sun?

42. A 600-ft guy wire is attached to the top of a communication tower. If the wire makes an angle of 65° with the ground, how tall is the communication tower?

43. A man is lying on the beach, flying a kite. He holds the end of the kite string at ground level, and estimates the angle of elevation of the kite to be 50°. If the string is 450 ft long, how high is the kite above the ground?

44. A woman standing on a hill sees a flagpole that she knows is 60 ft tall. The angle of depression to the bottom of the pole is 14°, and the angle of elevation to the top of the pole is 18°. Find her distance x from the pole.

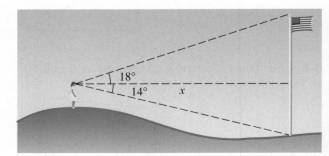

45. A water tower is located 325 ft from a building (see the figure). From a window in the building it is observed that the angle of elevation to the top of the tower is 39° and the angle of depression to the bottom of the tower is 25°. How tall is the tower? How high is the window?

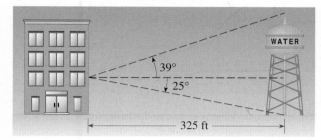

46. An airplane is flying at an elevation of 5150 ft, directly above a straight highway. Two motorists are driving cars on the highway on opposite sides of the plane, and the angle of depression to one car is 35° and to the other is 52°. How far apart are the cars?

47. If both cars in Exercise 46 are on one side of the plane and if the angle of depression to one car is 38° and to the other car is 52°, how far apart are the cars?

48. A hot-air balloon is floating above a straight road. To estimate their height above the ground, the balloonists simultaneously measure the angle of depression to two consecutive mileposts on the road on the same side of the balloon. The angles of depression are found to be 20° and 22°. How high is the balloon?

49. To estimate the height of a mountain above a level plain, the angle of elevation to the top of the mountain is measured to be 32°. One thousand feet closer to the mountain along the plain, it is found that the angle of elevation is 35°. Estimate the height of the mountain.

50. To measure the height of the cloud cover at an airport, a worker shines a spotlight upward at an angle 75° from the horizontal. An observer 600 m away measures the angle of elevation to the spot of light to be 45°. Find the height h of the cloud cover.

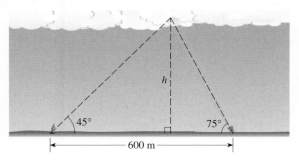

51. When the moon is exactly half full, the earth, moon, and sun form a right angle (see the figure). At that time the angle formed by the sun, earth, and moon is measured to be 89.85°. If the distance from the earth to the moon is 240,000 mi, estimate the distance from the earth to the sun.

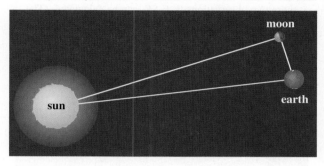

52. To find the distance to the sun as in Exercise 51, we needed to know the distance to the moon. Here is a way to estimate that distance: When the moon is seen at its zenith at a point A on the earth, it is observed to be at the horizon from point B (see the figure). Points A and B are 6155 mi apart, and the radius of the earth is 3960 mi.
(a) Find the angle θ in degrees.
(b) Estimate the distance from point A to the moon.

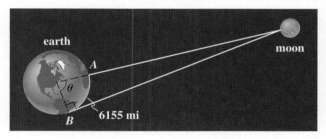

53. In Exercise 54 of Section 3.1 a method was given for finding the radius of the earth. Here is a more modern method: From a satellite 600 mi above the earth, it is observed that the angle formed by the vertical and the line of sight to the horizon is 60.276°. Use this information to find the radius of the earth.

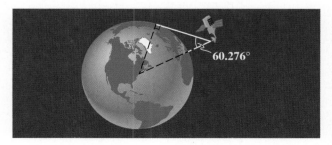

54. To find the distance to nearby stars, the method of parallax is used. The idea is to find a triangle with the star at one vertex and with a base as large as possible. To do this, the star is observed at two different times exactly 6 months apart, and its apparent change in position is recorded. From these two observations, $\angle E_1SE_2$ can be calculated. (The times are chosen so that $\angle E_1SE_2$ is as large as possible, which guarantees that $\angle E_1OS$ is $90°$.) The angle E_1SO is called the *parallax* of the star. Alpha Centauri, the star nearest the earth, has a parallax of $0.000211°$. Estimate the distance to this star. (Take the distance from the earth to the sun to be 9.3×10^7 mi.)

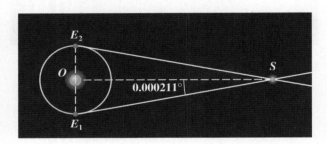

55–58 ■ Find x correct to one decimal place.

55.

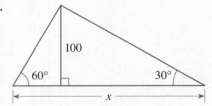

56.

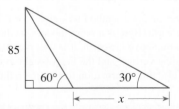

57.

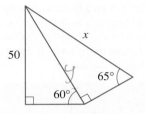

58.

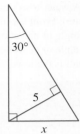

59. Express the lengths a, b, c, and d in the figure in terms of the trigonometric ratios of θ.

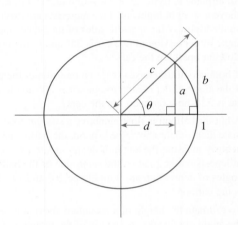

60. Similar Triangles   If two triangles are similar, what properties do they share? Explain how these properties make it possible to define the trigonometric ratios without regard to the size of the triangle.

3.3 TRIGONOMETRIC FUNCTIONS OF ANGLES

In the preceding section we defined the trigonometric ratios for acute angles. Here we extend the trigonometric ratios to all angles by defining the trigonometric functions of angles. With these functions we can solve practical problems that involve angles which are not necessarily acute.

■ Trigonometric Functions of Angles

Let POQ be a right triangle with acute angle θ as shown in Figure 1(a). Place θ in standard position as shown in Figure 1(b).

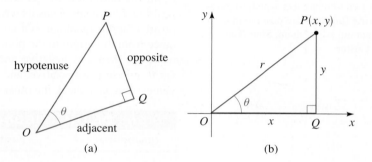

FIGURE 1

(a)   (b)

Then $P = P(x, y)$ is a point on the terminal side of θ. In triangle POQ, the opposite side has length y and the adjacent side has length x. Using the Pythagorean Theorem, we see that the hypotenuse has length $r = \sqrt{x^2 + y^2}$. So

$$\sin \theta = \frac{y}{r}, \qquad \cos \theta = \frac{x}{r}, \qquad \tan \theta = \frac{y}{x}$$

The other trigonometric ratios can be found in the same way.

These observations allow us to extend the trigonometric ratios to any angle. We define the trigonometric functions of angles as follows (see Figure 2).

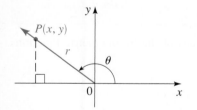

FIGURE 2

DEFINITION OF THE TRIGONOMETRIC FUNCTIONS

Let θ be an angle in standard position and let $P(x, y)$ be a point on the terminal side. If $r = \sqrt{x^2 + y^2}$ is the distance from the origin to the point $P(x, y)$, then

$$\sin \theta = \frac{y}{r} \qquad\qquad \cos \theta = \frac{x}{r} \qquad\qquad \tan \theta = \frac{y}{x} \quad (x \neq 0)$$

$$\csc \theta = \frac{r}{y} \quad (y \neq 0) \qquad \sec \theta = \frac{r}{x} \quad (x \neq 0) \qquad \cot \theta = \frac{x}{y} \quad (y \neq 0)$$

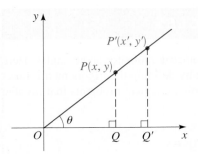

FIGURE 3

The following mnemonic device can be used to remember which trigonometric functions are positive in each quadrant: **A**ll of them, **S**ine, **T**angent, or **C**osine.

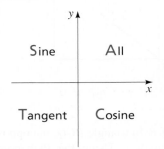

You can remember this as "All Students Take Calculus."

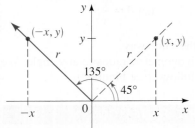

FIGURE 4

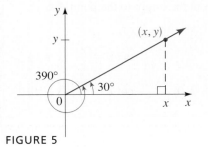

FIGURE 5

Since division by 0 is an undefined operation, certain trigonometric functions are not defined for certain angles. For example, $\tan 90° = y/x$ is undefined because $x = 0$. The angles for which the trigonometric functions may be undefined are the angles for which either the x- or y-coordinate of a point on the terminal side of the angle is 0. These are **quadrantal angles**—angles that are coterminal with the coordinate axes.

It is a crucial fact that the values of the trigonometric functions do *not* depend on the choice of the point $P(x, y)$. This is because if $P'(x', y')$ is any other point on the terminal side, as in Figure 3, then triangles POQ and $P'OQ'$ are similar.

Evaluating Trigonometric Functions at Any Angle

From the definition we see that the values of the trigonometric functions are all positive if the angle θ has its terminal side in quadrant I. This is because x and y are positive in this quadrant. [Of course, r is always positive, since it is simply the distance from the origin to the point $P(x, y)$.] If the terminal side of θ is in quadrant II, however, then x is negative and y is positive. Thus, in quadrant II the functions $\sin \theta$ and $\csc \theta$ are positive, and all the other trigonometric functions have negative values. You can check the other entries in the following table.

SIGNS OF THE TRIGONOMETRIC FUNCTIONS		
Quadrant	Positive functions	Negative functions
I	all	none
II	sin, csc	cos, sec, tan, cot
III	tan, cot	sin, csc, cos, sec
IV	cos, sec	sin, csc, tan, cot

We now turn our attention to finding the values of the trigonometric functions for angles that are not acute.

EXAMPLE 1 ■ Finding Trigonometric Functions of Angles

Find (a) $\cos 135°$ and (b) $\tan 390°$.

SOLUTION

(a) From Figure 4 we see that $\cos 135° = -x/r$. But $\cos 45° = x/r$, and since $\cos 45° = \sqrt{2}/2$, we have

$$\cos 135° = -\frac{\sqrt{2}}{2}$$

(b) The angles 390° and 30° are coterminal. From Figure 5 it's clear that $\tan 390° = \tan 30°$ and, since $\tan 30° = \sqrt{3}/3$, we have

$$\tan 390° = \frac{\sqrt{3}}{3}$$

Relationship to the Trigonometric Functions of Real Numbers

You may have already studied the trigonometric functions defined using the unit circle (Chapter 2). To see how they relate to the trigonometric functions of an *angle*, let's start with the unit circle in the coordinate plan.

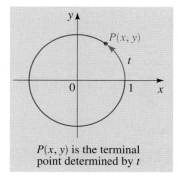

$P(x, y)$ is the terminal point determined by t

Let $P(x, y)$ be the terminal point determined by an arc of length t on the unit circle. Then t subtends an angle θ at the center of the circle. If we drop a perpendicular from P onto the point Q on the *x*-axis, then triangle $\triangle OPQ$ is a right triangle with legs of length x and y, as shown in the figure.

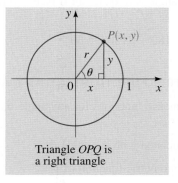

Triangle OPQ is a right triangle

Now, by the definition of the trigonometric functions of the *real number t*, we have

$$\sin t = y$$

$$\cos t = x$$

By the definition of the trigonometric functions of the *angle θ*, we have

$$\sin \theta = \frac{\text{opp}}{\text{hyp}} = \frac{y}{1} = y$$

$$\cos \theta = \frac{\text{adj}}{\text{hyp}} = \frac{x}{1} = x$$

If θ is measured in radians, then $\theta = t$. (See the figure below.) Comparing the two ways of defining the trigonometric functions, we see that they are identical. In other words, as functions, they assign identical values to a given real number (the real number is the radian measure of θ in one case or the length t of an arc in the other).

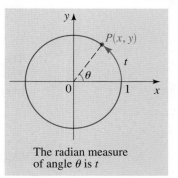

The radian measure of angle θ is t

Why then do we study trigonometry in two different ways? Because different applications require that we view the trigonometric functions differently. (See *Focus on Modeling*, pages 169, 232, and 287, and Sections 3.2, 3.4, and 3.5.)

From Example 1 we see that the trigonometric functions for angles that aren't acute have the same value, except possibly for sign, as the corresponding trigonometric functions of an acute angle. That acute angle will be called the *reference angle*.

REFERENCE ANGLE

Let θ be an angle in standard position. The **reference angle** $\bar{\theta}$ associated with θ is the acute angle formed by the terminal side of θ and the x-axis.

Figure 6 shows that to find a reference angle it's useful to know the quadrant in which the terminal side of the angle lies.

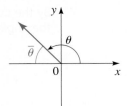 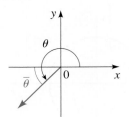 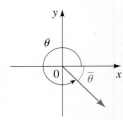

FIGURE 6
The reference angle $\bar{\theta}$ for an angle θ

EXAMPLE 2 ■ Finding Reference Angles

Find the reference angle for (a) $\theta = \dfrac{5\pi}{3}$ and (b) $\theta = 870°$.

SOLUTION

(a) The reference angle is the acute angle formed by the terminal side of the angle $5\pi/3$ and the x-axis (see Figure 7). Since the terminal side of this angle is in quadrant IV, the reference angle is

$$\bar{\theta} = 2\pi - \frac{5\pi}{3} = \frac{\pi}{3}$$

(b) The angles 870° and 150° are coterminal [because $870 - 2(360) = 150$]. Thus, the terminal side of this angle is in quadrant II (see Figure 8). So the reference angle is

$$\bar{\theta} = 180° - 150° = 30° \qquad\blacksquare$$

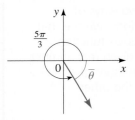

FIGURE 7

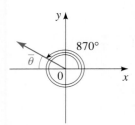

FIGURE 8

EVALUATING TRIGONOMETRIC FUNCTIONS AT ANY ANGLE

To find the values of the trigonometric functions for any angle θ, we carry out the following steps.

1. Find the reference angle $\bar{\theta}$ associated with the angle θ.

2. Determine the sign of the trigonometric function of θ.

3. The value of the trigonometric function of θ is the same, except possibly for sign, as the value of the trigonometric function of $\bar{\theta}$.

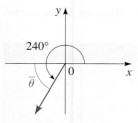

240°

FIGURE 9

$\frac{S|A}{T|C}$ sin 240° *is negative.*

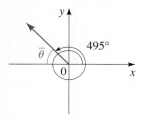

495°

FIGURE 10

$\frac{S|A}{T|C}$ tan 495° *is negative,*
so cot 495° *is negative.*

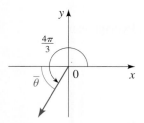

$\frac{4\pi}{3}$

FIGURE 11

$\frac{S|A}{T|C}$ sin $\frac{16\pi}{3}$ *is negative.*

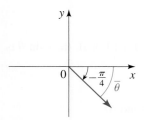

$-\frac{\pi}{4}$

FIGURE 12

$\frac{S|A}{T|C}$ cos$\left(-\frac{\pi}{4}\right)$ *is positive,*

so sec$\left(-\frac{\pi}{4}\right)$ *is positive.*

EXAMPLE 3 ■ **Using the Reference Angle to Evaluate Trigonometric Functions**

Find (a) sin 240° and (b) cot 495°.

SOLUTION

(a) This angle has its terminal side in quadrant III, as shown in Figure 9. The reference angle is therefore 240° − 180° = 60°, and the value of sin 240° is negative. Thus

$$\sin 240° = \underset{\underset{\text{sign}}{\uparrow}}{-}\underset{\underset{\text{reference angle}}{\uparrow}}{\sin 60°} = -\frac{\sqrt{3}}{2}$$

(b) The angle 495° is coterminal with the angle 135°, and the terminal side of this angle is in quadrant II, as shown in Figure 10. So the reference angle is 180° − 135° = 45°, and the value of cot 495° is negative. We have

$$\cot 495° = \underset{\underset{\text{coterminal angles}}{\uparrow}}{\cot 135°} = \underset{\underset{\text{sign}}{\uparrow}}{-}\underset{\underset{\text{reference angle}}{\uparrow}}{\cot 45°} = -1$$

■

EXAMPLE 4 ■ **Using the Reference Angle to Evaluate Trigonometric Functions**

Find (a) sin $\frac{16\pi}{3}$ and (b) sec$\left(-\frac{\pi}{4}\right)$.

SOLUTION

(a) The angle $16\pi/3$ is coterminal with $4\pi/3$, and these angles are in quadrant III (see Figure 11). Thus, the reference angle is $(4\pi/3) - \pi = \pi/3$. Since the value of sine is negative in quadrant III, we have

$$\sin \frac{16\pi}{3} = \underset{\underset{\text{coterminal angles}}{\uparrow}}{\sin \frac{4\pi}{3}} = \underset{\underset{\text{sign}}{\uparrow}}{-}\underset{\underset{\text{reference angle}}{\uparrow}}{\sin \frac{\pi}{3}} = -\frac{\sqrt{3}}{2}$$

(b) The angle $-\pi/4$ is in quadrant IV, and its reference angle is $\pi/4$ (see Figure 12). Since secant is positive in this quadrant, we get

$$\sec\left(-\frac{\pi}{4}\right) = \underset{\underset{\text{sign}}{\uparrow}}{+}\underset{\underset{\text{reference angle}}{\uparrow}}{\sec \frac{\pi}{4}} = \frac{\sqrt{2}}{2}$$

■

■ **Trigonometric Identities**

The trigonometric functions of angles are related to each other through several important equations called **trigonometric identities**. We've already encountered the reciprocal identities. These identities continue to hold for any angle θ, provided both sides of the equation are defined. The Pythagorean identities are a consequence of the Pythagorean Theorem.*

FUNDAMENTAL IDENTITIES

Reciprocal Identities

$$\csc\theta = \frac{1}{\sin\theta} \qquad \sec\theta = \frac{1}{\cos\theta} \qquad \cot\theta = \frac{1}{\tan\theta}$$

$$\tan\theta = \frac{\sin\theta}{\cos\theta} \qquad \cot\theta = \frac{\cos\theta}{\sin\theta}$$

Pythagorean Identities

$$\sin^2\theta + \cos^2\theta = 1 \qquad \tan^2\theta + 1 = \sec^2\theta \qquad 1 + \cot^2\theta = \csc^2\theta$$

■ **Proof**   Let's prove the first Pythagorean identity. Using $x^2 + y^2 = r$ (the Pythagorean Theorem) in Figure 13, we have

$$\sin^2\theta + \cos^2\theta = \left(\frac{y}{r}\right)^2 + \left(\frac{x}{r}\right)^2 = \frac{x^2 + y^2}{r^2} = \frac{r^2}{r^2} = 1$$

Thus, $\sin^2\theta + \cos^2\theta = 1$. (Although the figure indicates an acute angle, you should check that the proof holds for all angles θ.)   □

See Exercises 59 and 60 for the proofs of the other two Pythagorean identities.

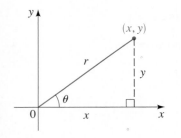

FIGURE 13

EXAMPLE 5 ■ Expressing One Trigonometric Function in Terms of Another

(a) Express $\sin\theta$ in terms of $\cos\theta$.
(b) Express $\tan\theta$ in terms of $\sin\theta$, where θ is in quadrant II.

SOLUTION

(a) From the first Pythagorean identity we get

$$\sin\theta = \pm\sqrt{1 - \cos^2\theta}$$

where the sign depends on the quadrant. If θ is in quadrant I or II, then $\sin\theta$ is positive, and hence

$$\sin\theta = \sqrt{1 - \cos^2\theta}$$

whereas if θ is in quadrant III or IV, $\sin\theta$ is negative and so

$$\sin\theta = -\sqrt{1 - \cos^2\theta}$$

---

*We follow the usual convention of writing $\sin^2\theta$ for $(\sin\theta)^2$. In general, we write $\sin^n\theta$ for $(\sin\theta)^n$ for all integers n except $n = -1$. The exponent $n = -1$ will be assigned another meaning in Section 4.4. Of course, the same convention applies to the other five trigonometric functions.

(b) Since $\tan \theta = \sin \theta / \cos \theta$, we need to write $\cos \theta$ in terms of $\sin \theta$. By part (a)

$$\cos \theta = \pm\sqrt{1 - \sin^2\theta}$$

and since $\cos \theta$ is negative in quadrant II, the negative sign applies here. Thus

$$\tan \theta = \frac{\sin \theta}{\cos \theta} = \frac{\sin \theta}{-\sqrt{1 - \sin^2\theta}}$$ ■

EXAMPLE 6 ■ Evaluating a Trigonometric Function

If $\tan \theta = \frac{2}{3}$ and θ is in quadrant III, find $\cos \theta$.

SOLUTION 1

We need to write $\cos \theta$ in terms of $\tan \theta$. From the identity $\tan^2\theta + 1 = \sec^2\theta$, we get $\sec \theta = \pm\sqrt{\tan^2\theta + 1}$. In quadrant III, $\sec \theta$ is negative, so

$$\sec \theta = -\sqrt{\tan^2\theta + 1}$$

Thus

$$\cos \theta = \frac{1}{\sec \theta} = \frac{1}{-\sqrt{\tan^2\theta + 1}}$$

$$= \frac{1}{-\sqrt{\left(\frac{2}{3}\right)^2 + 1}} = \frac{1}{-\sqrt{\frac{13}{9}}} = -\frac{3}{\sqrt{13}}$$

SOLUTION 2

This problem can be solved more easily using the method of Example 2 of Section 3.2. Recall that, except for sign, the values of the trigonometric functions of any angle are the same as those of an acute angle (the reference angle). So, ignoring the sign for the moment, let's sketch a right triangle with an acute angle $\bar{\theta}$ satisfying $\tan \bar{\theta} = \frac{2}{3}$ (see Figure 14). By the Pythagorean Theorem the hypotenuse of this triangle has length $\sqrt{13}$. From the triangle in Figure 14 we immediately see that $\cos \bar{\theta} = 3/\sqrt{13}$. Since θ is in quadrant III, $\cos \theta$ is negative and so

$$\cos \theta = -\frac{3}{\sqrt{13}}$$ ■

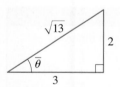

FIGURE 14

EXAMPLE 7 ■ Evaluating Trigonometric Functions

If $\sec \theta = 2$ and θ is in quadrant IV, find the other five trigonometric functions of θ.

SOLUTION

We sketch a triangle as in Figure 15 so that $\sec \bar{\theta} = 2$. Taking into account the fact

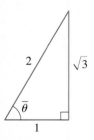

FIGURE 15

that θ is in quadrant IV, we get

$$\sin \theta = -\frac{\sqrt{3}}{2} \qquad \cos \theta = \frac{1}{2} \qquad \tan \theta = -\sqrt{3}$$

$$\csc \theta = -\frac{2}{\sqrt{3}} \qquad \sec \theta = 2 \qquad \cot \theta = -\frac{1}{\sqrt{3}}$$ ∎

▪ Areas of Triangles

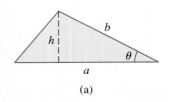

(a)

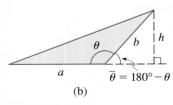

(b)

FIGURE 16

We end this section by giving an application of the trigonometric functions that involves angles that are not necessarily acute. More extensive applications appear in the next two sections.

The area of a triangle is $\mathscr{A} = \frac{1}{2} \times$ base $\times$ height. If we know two sides and the included angle of a triangle, then we can find the height using the trigonometric functions, and from this we can find the area.

If θ is an acute angle, then the height of the triangle in Figure 16(a) is given by $h = b \sin \theta$. Thus, the area is

$$\mathscr{A} = \tfrac{1}{2} \times \text{base} \times \text{height} = \tfrac{1}{2} ab \sin \theta$$

If the angle θ is not acute, then from Figure 16(b) we see that the height of the triangle is

$$h = b \sin(180° - \theta) = b \sin \theta$$

This is so because the reference angle of θ is the angle $180° - \theta$. Thus, in this case also, the area of the triangle is

$$\mathscr{A} = \tfrac{1}{2} \times \text{base} \times \text{height} = \tfrac{1}{2} ab \sin \theta$$

AREA OF A TRIANGLE

The area $\mathscr{A}$ of a triangle with sides of lengths a and b and with included angle θ is

$$\mathscr{A} = \tfrac{1}{2} ab \sin \theta$$

EXAMPLE 8 ▪ Finding the Area of a Triangle

Find the area of triangle ABC shown in Figure 17.

SOLUTION

The triangle has sides of length 10 cm and 3 cm, with included angle 120°. Therefore

$$\mathscr{A} = \tfrac{1}{2} ab \sin \theta$$

$$= \tfrac{1}{2} (10)(3) \sin 120°$$

$$= 15 \sin 60° \qquad \text{Reference angle}$$

$$= 15 \frac{\sqrt{3}}{2} \approx 13 \text{ cm}^2$$ ∎

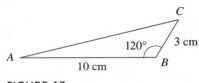

FIGURE 17

3.3 EXERCISES

1–6 ■ Find the reference angle for the given angle.

1. (a) $210°$ (b) $300°$ (c) $-120°$

2. (a) $225°$ (b) $450°$ (c) $-200°$

3. (a) $\dfrac{9\pi}{4}$ (b) $\dfrac{23\pi}{6}$ (c) $-\dfrac{\pi}{3}$

4. (a) $\dfrac{17\pi}{6}$ (b) $\dfrac{31\pi}{4}$ (c) $-\dfrac{4\pi}{3}$

5. (a) $\dfrac{11\pi}{5}$ (b) $\dfrac{11}{5}$ (c) $-\dfrac{4\pi}{7}$

6. (a) 2.3 (b) 2.3π (c) $-\pi$

7–30 ■ Find the exact value of the trigonometric function.

7. $\sin 150°$

8. $\sin 225°$

9. $\cos 135°$

10. $\cos(-60°)$

11. $\tan(-60°)$

12. $\sec 300°$

13. $\csc(-630°)$

14. $\cot 210°$

15. $\cos 570°$

16. $\sec 120°$

17. $\tan 750°$

18. $\cos 660°$

19. $\sin \dfrac{2\pi}{3}$

20. $\sin \dfrac{5\pi}{3}$

21. $\sin \dfrac{3\pi}{2}$

22. $\cos \dfrac{7\pi}{3}$

23. $\cos\left(-\dfrac{7\pi}{3}\right)$

24. $\tan \dfrac{5\pi}{6}$

25. $\sec \dfrac{17\pi}{3}$

26. $\csc \dfrac{5\pi}{4}$

27. $\cot\left(-\dfrac{\pi}{4}\right)$

28. $\cos \dfrac{7\pi}{4}$

29. $\tan \dfrac{5\pi}{2}$

30. $\sin \dfrac{11\pi}{6}$

31–34 ■ Find the quadrant in which θ lies from the information given.

31. $\sin \theta < 0$ and $\cos \theta < 0$

32. $\tan \theta < 0$ and $\sin \theta < 0$

33. $\sec \theta > 0$ and $\tan \theta < 0$

34. $\csc \theta > 0$ and $\cos \theta < 0$

35–40 ■ Write the first trigonometric function in terms of the second for θ in the given quadrant.

35. $\tan \theta$, $\cos \theta$; θ in quadrant III

36. $\cot \theta$, $\sin \theta$; θ in quadrant II

37. $\cos \theta$, $\sin \theta$; θ in quadrant IV

38. $\sec \theta$, $\sin \theta$; θ in quadrant I

39. $\sec \theta$, $\tan \theta$; θ in quadrant II

40. $\csc \theta$, $\cot \theta$; θ in quadrant III

41–48 ■ Find the values of the trigonometric functions of θ from the information given.

41. $\sin \theta = \frac{3}{5}$, θ in quadrant II

42. $\cos \theta = -\frac{7}{12}$, θ in quadrant III

43. $\tan \theta = -\frac{3}{4}$, $\cos \theta > 0$

44. $\sec \theta = 5$, $\sin \theta < 0$

45. $\csc \theta = 2$, θ in quadrant I

46. $\cot \theta = \frac{1}{4}$, $\sin \theta < 0$

47. $\cos \theta = -\frac{2}{7}$, $\tan \theta < 0$

48. $\tan \theta = -4$, $\sin \theta > 0$

49. If $\theta = \pi/3$, find the value of each expression.

   (a) $\sin 2\theta$, $2 \sin \theta$ (b) $\sin \frac{1}{2}\theta$, $\dfrac{\sin \theta}{2}$

   (c) $\sin^2\theta$, $\sin(\theta^2)$

50. Find the area of a triangle with sides of length 7 and 9 and included angle $72°$.

51. Find the area of a triangle with sides of length 10 and 22 and included angle $10°$.

52. Find the area of an equilateral triangle with side of length 10.

53. A triangle has an area of 16 in², and two of the sides of the triangle have lengths 5 in. and 7 in. Find the angle included by these two sides.

54. Find the area of the shaded region in the figure.

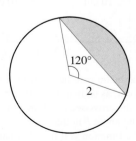

55–58 ■ In the following exercises you are asked to use the trigonometric functions to model real-life situations.

55. A steel pipe is being carried down a hallway 9 ft wide. At the end of the hall there is a right-angled turn into a narrower hallway 6 ft wide.
  (a) Show that the length of the pipe in the figure is modeled by the function

$$L(\theta) = 9 \csc \theta + 6 \sec \theta$$

  (b) Graph the function L for $0 < \theta < \pi/2$.
  (c) Find the minimum value of the function L.
  (d) Explain why the value of L you found in part (c) is the length of the longest pipe that can be carried around the corner.

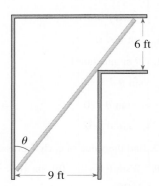

6 ft

θ

9 ft

56. A rain gutter is to be constructed from a metal sheet of width 30 cm by bending up one-third of the sheet on each side through an angle θ.
  (a) Show that the cross-sectional area of the gutter is modeled by the function

$$A(\theta) = 100 \sin \theta + 100 \sin \theta \cos \theta$$

  (b) Graph the function A for $0 \le \theta \le \pi/2$.
  (c) For what angle θ is the largest cross-sectional area achieved?

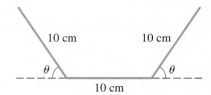

10 cm   10 cm

θ θ

10 cm

57. A rectangular beam is to be cut from a cylindrical log of diameter 20 cm, as shown in the figure.
  (a) Express the cross-sectional area of the beam as a function of the angle θ in the figures.
  (b) Graph the function you found in part (a).
  (c) Find the dimensions of the beam with largest cross-sectional area.

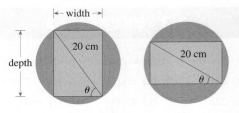

width

20 cm

depth

θ

20 cm

θ

58. The strength of a beam is proportional to the width and the square of the depth. A beam is cut from a log as in Exercise 57. Express the strength of the beam as a function of the angle θ in the figures.

59. Use the first Pythagorean identity to prove the second. [*Hint:* Divide by $\cos^2\theta$.]

60. Use the first Pythagorean identity to prove the third.

▲ **DISCOVERY · DISCUSSION**

61. Using a Calculator   To solve a certain problem, you need to find the sine of 4 rad. Your study partner uses his calculator and tells you that sin 4 is 0.0697564737. On your calculator you get -0.7568024953. What is wrong? What mistake did your partner make?

62. Viète's Trigonometric Diagram   In the 16th century, the French mathematician François Viète (see page 540) published the following remarkable diagram. Each of the six trigonometric functions of θ is equal to the length of a line segment in the figure. For instance, $\sin \theta = |PR|$, since from $\triangle OPR$ we see that

$$\sin \theta = \frac{\text{opp}}{\text{hyp}} = \frac{|PR|}{|OR|} = \frac{|PR|}{1}$$

For each of the five other trigonometric functions, find a line segment in the figure whose length equals the value of the function at θ. (Note that the radius of the circle is 1, the center is O, segment QS is tangent to the circle at R, and $\angle SOQ$ is a right angle.)

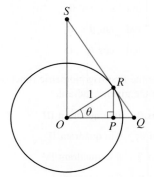

S

R

1

O θ P Q

Discovery Project

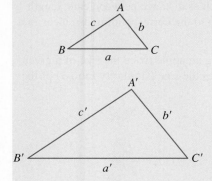

Thales used similar triangles to find the height of a tall column. See page 191.

Similarity

In geometry you learned that two triangles are similar if they have the same angles. (See Appendix B.1.) In this case, the ratios of corresponding sides are equal. Triangles ABC and $A'B'C'$ in the margin are similar, so

$$\frac{a'}{a} = \frac{b'}{b} = \frac{c'}{c}$$

Similarity is the crucial idea underlying trigonometry. We can define $\sin\theta$ as the ratio of the opposite side to the hypotenuse in *any* right triangle with an angle θ, because all such right triangles are similar. So the ratio represented by $\sin\theta$ does not depend on the size of the right triangle but only on the angle θ. This is a powerful idea because angles are often easier to measure than distances. For example, the angle formed by the sun, earth, and moon can be measured from the earth. The secret to finding the distance to the sun is that the trigonometric ratios are the same for the huge triangle formed by the sun, earth, and moon as for any other similar triangle (see Exercise 51 in Section 3.2).

In general, two objects are **similar** if they have the same shape even though they may not be the same size.* For example, we recognize the following as representations of the letter A because they are all similar.

If two figures are similar, then the distances between corresponding points in the figures are proportional. The blue and red A's above are similar—the ratio of distances between corresponding points is $\frac{3}{2}$. We say that the **similarity ratio** is $s = \frac{3}{2}$. To obtain the distance d' between any two points in the blue A, we multiply the corresponding distance d in the red A by $\frac{3}{2}$. So

$$d' = sd \qquad \text{or} \qquad d' = \tfrac{3}{2}d$$

Likewise, the similarity ratio between the first and last letters is $s = 5$, so $x' = 5x$.

1. Write a short paragraph explaining how the concept of similarity is used to define the trigonometric ratios.

---

*If they have the same shape *and* size, they are congruent, which is a special case of similarity. (See Appendix B.1.)

2. How is similarity used in map making? How are distances on a city road map related to actual distances?

3. How is your yearbook photograph similar to you? Compare distances between different points on your face (such as distance between ears, length of nose, distance between eyes, and so on) to the corresponding distances in a photograph. What is the similarity ratio?

4. The figure illustrates a method for drawing an apple twice the size of a given apple. Use the method to draw a tie 3 times the size (similarity ratio 3) of the blue tie.

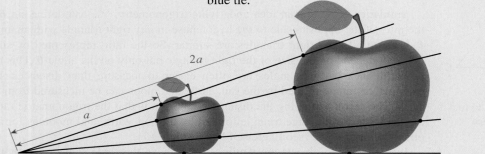

5. Give conditions under which two rectangles are similar to each other. Do the same for two isosceles triangles.

6. Suppose that two similar triangles have similarity ratio s.
   (a) How are the perimeters of the triangles related?
   (b) How are the areas of the triangles related?

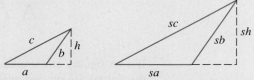

7. (a) If two squares have similarity ratio s, show that their areas A_1 and A_2 have the property that $A_2 = s^2 A_1$.
   (b) If the side of a square is tripled, its area is multiplied by what factor?
   (c) A plane figure can be approximated by squares (as shown). Explain how we can conclude that for any two plane figures with similarity ratio s, their areas satisfy $A_2 = s^2 A_1$. [Use part (a).]

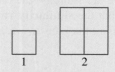

1   2

If the side of a square is doubled, its area is multiplied by 2^2.

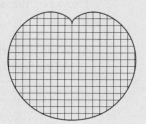

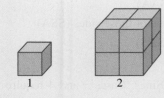

If the side of a cube is doubled, its volume is multiplied by 2^3.

8. (a) If two cubes have similarity ratio s, show that their volumes V_1 and V_2 have the property that $V_2 = s^3 V_1$.

(b) If the side of a cube is multiplied by 10, by what factor is the volume multiplied?

(c) How can we use the fact that a solid object can be "filled" by little cubes to show that for any two solids with similarity ratio s, the volumes satisfy $V_2 = s^3 V_1$?

9. King Kong is 10 times as tall as Joe, a normal-sized 300-lb gorilla. Assuming that King Kong and Joe are similar, use the results from Problems 7 and 8 to answer the following questions.

(a) How much does King Kong weigh?

(b) If Joe's hand is 13 in. long, how long is King Kong's hand?

(c) If it takes 2 square yards of material to make a shirt for Joe, how much material would a shirt for King Kong require?

3.4 THE LAW OF SINES

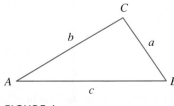

FIGURE 1

In Section 3.2 we used the trigonometric ratios to solve right triangles. The trigonometric functions can also be used to solve *oblique triangles*, that is, triangles with no right angles. To do this, we first study the Law of Sines here and then the Law of Cosines in the next section. To state these laws (or formulas) more easily, we follow the convention of labeling the angles of a triangle as A, B, C, and the lengths of the corresponding opposite sides as a, b, c, as in Figure 1.

To solve a triangle, we need to know certain information about its sides and angles. To decide whether we have enough information, it's often helpful to make a sketch. For instance, if we are given two angles and the included side, then it's clear that one and only one triangle can be formed [see Figure 2(a)]. Similarly, if two sides and the included angle are known, then a unique triangle is determined [Figure 2(c)]. But if we know all three angles and no sides, we cannot uniquely determine the triangle because many triangles can have the same three angles. (All these triangles would be similar, of course.) So we won't consider this last case.

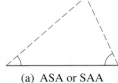
(a) ASA or SAA

(b) SSA

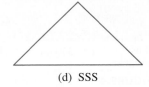
(c) SAS

(d) SSS

FIGURE 2

In general, a triangle is determined by three of its six parts (angles and sides) as long as at least one of these three parts is a side. (See Appendix B.1.) So, the possibilities, illustrated in Figure 2, are as shown on page 210.

Case 1 One side and two angles (ASA or SAA)

Case 2 Two sides and the angle opposite one of those sides (SSA)

Case 3 Two sides and the included angle (SAS)

Case 4 Three sides (SSS)

The first two cases are solved using the Law of Sines; Cases 3 and 4 require the Law of Cosines.

■ The Law of Sines

The **Law of Sines** says that in any triangle the lengths of the sides are proportional to the sines of the corresponding opposite angles.

THE LAW OF SINES

In triangle ABC we have

$$\frac{\sin A}{a} = \frac{\sin B}{b} = \frac{\sin C}{c}$$

■ **Proof** To see why the Law of Sines is true, refer to Figure 3. By the formula in Section 3.3 the area of triangle ABC is $\frac{1}{2}\,ab \sin C$. By the same formula the area of this triangle is also $\frac{1}{2}\,ac \sin B$ and $\frac{1}{2}\,bc \sin A$. Thus

$$\tfrac{1}{2}\,bc \sin A = \tfrac{1}{2}\,ac \sin B = \tfrac{1}{2}\,ab \sin C$$

Multiplying by $2/(abc)$ gives the Law of Sines. □

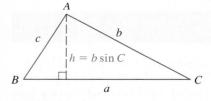

FIGURE 3

EXAMPLE 1 ■ Tracking a Satellite (ASA)

A satellite orbiting the earth passes directly overhead at observation stations in Phoenix and Los Angeles, 340 mi apart. At an instant when the satellite is between these two stations, its angle of elevation is simultaneously observed to be 60° at Phoenix and 75° at Los Angeles. How far is the satellite from Los Angeles? In other words, find the distance AC in Figure 4.

SOLUTION

Whenever two angles in a triangle are known, the third angle can be determined immediately because the sum of the angles of a triangle is 180°. In this case, $\angle C = 180° - (75° + 60°) = 45°$ (see Figure 4), so we have

$$\frac{\sin B}{b} = \frac{\sin C}{c} \qquad \text{Law of Sines}$$

$$\frac{\sin 60°}{b} = \frac{\sin 45°}{340} \qquad \text{Substitute}$$

$$b = \frac{340 \sin 60°}{\sin 45°} \approx 416 \qquad \text{Solve for } b$$

The distance of the satellite from Los Angeles is approximately 416 mi. ■

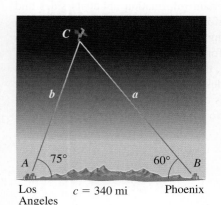

FIGURE 4

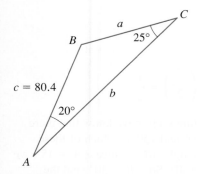

FIGURE 5

EXAMPLE 2 ■ Solving a Triangle (SAA)

Solve the triangle in Figure 5.

SOLUTION

First, $\angle B = 180° - (20° + 25°) = 135°$. Since side c is known, to find side a we use the relation

$$\frac{\sin A}{a} = \frac{\sin C}{c} \qquad \text{Law of Sines}$$

$$a = \frac{c \sin A}{\sin C} = \frac{80.4 \sin 20°}{\sin 25°} \approx 65.1 \qquad \text{Solve for } a$$

Similarly, to find b we use

$$\frac{\sin B}{b} = \frac{\sin C}{c} \qquad \text{Law of Sines}$$

$$b = \frac{c \sin B}{\sin C} = \frac{80.4 \sin 135°}{\sin 25°} \approx 134.5 \qquad \text{Solve for } b \qquad ■$$

The Ambiguous Case

In Examples 1 and 2 a unique triangle was determined by the information given. This is always true of Case 1 (ASA or SAA). But in Case 2 (SSA) there may be two triangles, one triangle, or no triangle with the given properties. For this reason, Case 2 is sometimes called the **ambiguous case**. To see why this is so, we show in Figure 6 the possibilities when angle A and sides a and b are given. In part (a) no solution is possible, since side a is too short to complete the triangle. In part (b) the solution is a right triangle. In part (c) two solutions are possible, and in part (d) there is a unique triangle with the given properties. We illustrate the possibilities of Case 2 in the following examples.

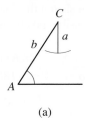 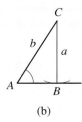 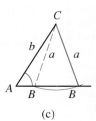 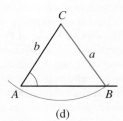

FIGURE 6

The ambiguous case

(a)   (b)   (c)   (d)

EXAMPLE 3 ■ SSA, the One-Solution Case

Solve triangle ABC, where $\angle A = 45°$, $a = 7\sqrt{2}$, and $b = 7$.

SOLUTION

We first sketch the triangle with the information we have (see Figure 7). Our sketch is necessarily tentative, since we don't yet know the other angles. Nevertheless, we can now see the possibilities.

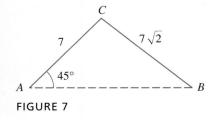

FIGURE 7

We first find $\angle B$.

$$\frac{\sin A}{a} = \frac{\sin B}{b} \qquad \text{Law of Sines}$$

$$\sin B = \frac{b \sin A}{a} = \frac{7}{7\sqrt{2}} \sin 45° = \left(\frac{1}{\sqrt{2}}\right)\left(\frac{\sqrt{2}}{2}\right) = \frac{1}{2} \qquad \text{Solve for } \sin B$$

We consider only angles smaller than 180°, since no triangle can contain an angle of 180° or larger.

Which angles B have $\sin B = \frac{1}{2}$? From the preceding section we know that there are two such angles smaller than 180° (they are 30° and 150°). Which of these angles is compatible with what we know about triangle ABC? Since $\angle A = 45°$, we cannot have $\angle B = 150°$, because $45° + 150° > 180°$. So $\angle B = 30°$, and the remaining angle is $\angle C = 180° - (30° + 45°) = 105°$.

Now we can find side c.

$$\frac{\sin B}{b} = \frac{\sin C}{c} \qquad \text{Law of Sines}$$

$$c = \frac{b \sin C}{\sin B} = \frac{7 \sin 105°}{\sin 30°} = \frac{7 \sin 105°}{\frac{1}{2}} \approx 13.5 \qquad \text{Solve for } c$$ ∎

 In Example 3 there were two possibilities for angle B, and one of these was not compatible with the rest of the information. In general, if $\sin A < 1$, we must check the angle and its supplement as possibilities, because any angle smaller than 180° can be in the triangle. To decide whether either possibility works, we check to see whether the resulting sum of the angles exceeds 180°. It can happen, as in Figure 6(c), that both possibilities are compatible with the given information. In that case, two different triangles are solutions to the problem.

EXAMPLE 4 ■ SSA, the Two-Solution Case

Solve triangle ABC if $\angle A = 43.1°$, $a = 186.2$, and $b = 248.6$.

SOLUTION

From the given information we sketch the triangle shown in Figure 8. Note that side a may be drawn in two possible positions to complete the triangle. From the Law of Sines

$$\sin B = \frac{b \sin A}{a} = \frac{248.6 \sin 43.1°}{186.2} \approx 0.91225$$

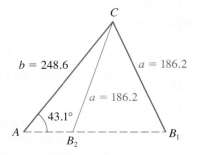

FIGURE 8

Surveying is a method of land measurement used for mapmaking. Surveyors use a process called *triangulation* in which a network of thousands of interlocking triangles is created on the area to be mapped. The process is started by measuring the length of a *baseline* between two surveying stations. Then, using an instrument called a *theodolite*, the angles between these two stations and a third station are measured. The Law of Sines is then used to calculate the two other sides of the triangle formed by the three stations. The calculated sides are used as baselines, and the process is repeated over and over to create a network of triangles. In this

(continued)

There are two possible angles B between $0°$ and $180°$ such that $\sin B = 0.91225$. Using the $\boxed{\text{SIN}^{-1}}$ key on a calculator (or $\boxed{\text{INV}}$ $\boxed{\text{SIN}}$ or $\boxed{\text{ARCSIN}}$), we find that one of these angles is approximately $65.8°$. The other is approximately $180° - 65.8° = 114.2°$. We denote these two angles by B_1 and B_2 so that

$$\angle B_1 \approx 65.8° \qquad \text{and} \qquad \angle B_2 \approx 114.2°$$

Thus, two triangles satisfy the given conditions: triangle $A_1B_1C_1$ and triangle $A_2B_2C_2$.

Solve triangle $A_1B_1C_1$:

$$\angle C_1 \approx 180° - (43.1° + 65.8°) = 71.1° \qquad \text{Find } \angle C_1$$

Thus $$c_1 = \frac{a_1 \sin C_1}{\sin A_1} \approx \frac{186.2 \sin 71.1°}{\sin 43.1°} \approx 257.8 \qquad \text{Law of Sines}$$

Solve triangle $A_2B_2C_2$:

$$\angle C_2 \approx 180° - (43.1° + 114.2°) = 22.7° \qquad \text{Find } \angle C_2$$

Thus $$c_2 = \frac{a_2 \sin C_2}{\sin A_2} \approx \frac{186.2 \sin 22.7°}{\sin 43.1°} \approx 105.2 \qquad \text{Law of Sines}$$

Triangles $A_1B_1C_1$ and $A_2B_2C_2$ are shown in Figure 9.

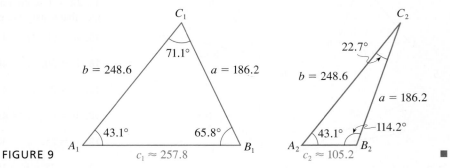

FIGURE 9

The next example presents a situation for which no triangle is compatible with the given data.

EXAMPLE 5 ■ SSA, the No-Solution Case

Solve triangle ABC, where $\angle A = 42°$, $a = 70$, and $b = 122$.

---

method, the only distance measured is the initial baseline; all other distances are calculated from the Law of Sines. This method is practical because it is much easier to measure angles than distances.

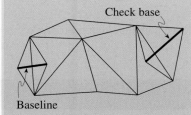

Check base

Baseline

One of the most ambitious map-making efforts of all time was the Great Trigonometric Survey of India (see Problem 8, page 235) which required several expeditions and took over a century to complete. The famous expedition of 1823, led by **Sir George Everest**, lasted 20 years. Ranging over treacherous terrain and encountering the dreaded malaria-carrying mosquitoes, this expedition reached the foothills of the Himalayas. A later expedition, using triangulation, calculated the height of the highest peak of the Himalayas to be 29,002 ft. The peak was named in honor of Sir George Everest.

Today, using satellites, the height of Mt. Everest is estimated to be 29,028 ft. The very close agreement of these two estimates shows the great accuracy of the trigonometric method.

SOLUTION

First, let's try to find $\angle B$. We have

$$\frac{\sin A}{a} = \frac{\sin B}{b} \qquad \text{Law of Sines}$$

$$\sin B = \frac{b \sin A}{a} = \frac{122 \sin 42°}{70} \approx 1.17 \qquad \text{Solve for } \sin B$$

Since the sine of an angle is never greater than 1, we conclude that no triangle satisfies the conditions given in this problem. ∎

3.4 EXERCISES

1–6 ■ Use the Law of Sines to find the indicated side x or angle θ.

1.

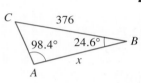

2.

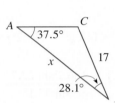

3.

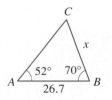

4.

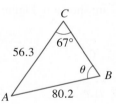

5.

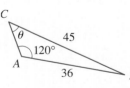

6.

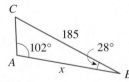

7–8 ■ Solve the triangle using the Law of Sines.

7.

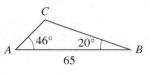

8.

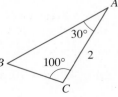

9–14 ■ Sketch each triangle and then solve the triangle using the Law of Sines.

9. $\angle A = 50°$, $\angle B = 68°$, $c = 230$

10. $\angle A = 23°$, $\angle B = 110°$, $c = 50$

11. $\angle A = 30°$, $\angle C = 65°$, $b = 10$

12. $\angle A = 22°$, $\angle B = 95°$, $a = 420$

13. $\angle B = 29°$, $\angle C = 51°$, $b = 44$

14. $\angle B = 10°$, $\angle C = 100°$, $c = 115$

15–22 ■ Use the Law of Sines to solve for all possible triangles that satisfy the given conditions.

15. $a = 28$, $b = 15$, $\angle A = 110°$

16. $a = 30$, $c = 40$, $\angle A = 37°$

17. $a = 20$, $c = 45$, $\angle A = 125°$

18. $b = 45$, $c = 42$, $\angle C = 38°$

19. $b = 25$, $c = 30$, $\angle B = 25°$

20. $a = 75$, $b = 100$, $\angle A = 30°$

21. $a = 50$, $b = 100$, $\angle A = 50°$

22. $a = 100$, $b = 80$, $\angle A = 135°$

23. To find the distance across a river, a surveyor chooses points A and B, which are 200 ft apart on one side of the river (see the figure). She then chooses a reference point C on the opposite side of the river and finds that

$\angle BAC \approx 82°$ and $\angle ABC \approx 52°$. Approximate the distance from A to C.

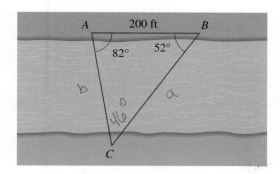

24. A pilot is flying over a straight highway. He determines the angles of depression to two mileposts, 5 mi apart, to be $32°$ and $48°$, as shown in the figure.
(a) Find the distance of the plane from point A.
(b) Find the elevation of the plane.

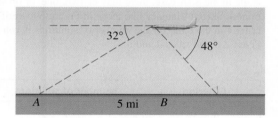

25. The path of a satellite orbiting the earth causes it to pass directly over two tracking stations A and B, which are 50 mi apart. When the satellite is on one side of the two stations, the angles of elevation at A and B are measured to be $87.0°$ and $84.2°$, respectively.
(a) How far is the satellite from station A?
(b) How high is the satellite above the ground?

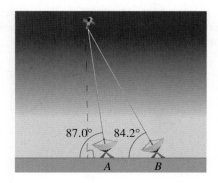

26. A tree on a hillside casts a shadow 215 ft down the hill. If the angle of inclination of the hillside is $22°$ to the horizontal and the angle of elevation of the sun is $52°$, find the height of the tree.

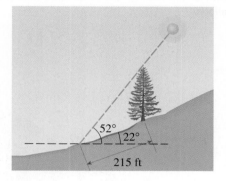

27. A communication tower is located at the top of a steep hill, as shown. The angle of inclination of the hill is $58°$. A guy wire is to be attached to the top of the tower and to the ground, 100 m downhill from the base of the tower. The angle α in the figure is determined to be $12°$. Find the length of cable required for the guy wire.

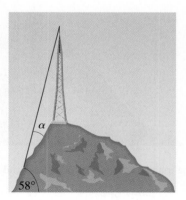

28. Points A and B are separated by a lake. To find the distance between them, a surveyor locates a point C on land such that $\angle CAB = 48.6°$. He also measures CA as 312 ft and CB as 527 ft. Find the distance between A and B.

29. Observers at P and Q are located on the side of a hill that is inclined 32° to the horizontal, as shown. The observer at P determines the angle of elevation to a hot-air balloon to be 62°. At the same instant, the observer at Q measures the angle of elevation to the balloon to be 71°. If P is 60 m down the hill from Q, find the distance from Q to the balloon.

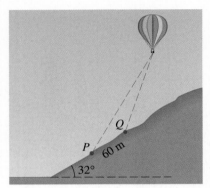

30. A water tower 30 m tall is located at the top of a hill. From a distance of 120 m down the hill, it is observed that the angle formed between the top and base of the tower is 8°. Find the angle of inclination of the hill.

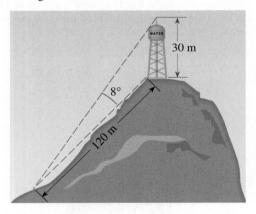

31. For the triangle shown, find **(a)** $\angle BCD$ and **(b)** $\angle DCA$.

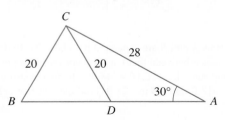

32. In triangle ABC, $\angle A = 40°$, $a = 15$, and $b = 20$.
   (a) Show that there are two triangles, ABC and $A'B'C'$, that satisfy these conditions.
   (b) Show that the areas of the triangles in part (a) are proportional to the sines of the angles C and C', that is,

$$\frac{\text{area of } \triangle ABC}{\text{area of } \triangle A'B'C'} = \frac{\sin C}{\sin C'}$$

33. Show that, given the three angles A, B, C of a triangle and one side, say a, the area of the triangle is

$$\text{area} = \frac{a^2 \sin B \sin C}{2 \sin A}$$

◆ **DISCOVERY • DISCUSSION**

34. Number of Solutions in the Ambiguous Case We have seen that when using the Law of Sines to solve a triangle in the SSA case, there may be two, one, or no solution(s). Sketch triangles like those in Figure 6 to verify the criteria in the table for the number of solutions if you are given $\angle A$ and sides a and b.

Criterion	Number of solutions
$a \geq b$	1
$b > a > b \sin A$	2
$a = b \sin A$	1
$a < b \sin A$	0

If $\angle A = 30°$ and $b = 100$, use these crieteria to find the range of values of a for which the triangle ABC has two solutions, one solution, or no solution.

3.5 THE LAW OF COSINES

The Law of Sines cannot be used directly to solve triangles if we know two sides and the angle between them or if we know all three sides (these are Cases 3 and 4 of the preceding section). In these two cases, the **Law of Cosines** applies.

THE LAW OF COSINES

In any triangle ABC, we have

$$a^2 = b^2 + c^2 - 2bc \cos A$$

$$b^2 = a^2 + c^2 - 2ac \cos B$$

$$c^2 = a^2 + b^2 - 2ab \cos C$$

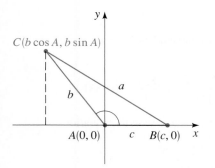

FIGURE 1

■ **Proof**   To prove the Law of Cosines, place triangle ABC so that $\angle A$ is at the origin, as shown in Figure 1. The coordinates of the vertices B and C are $(c, 0)$ and $(b \cos A, b \sin A)$, respectively. (You should check that the coordinates of these points will be the same if we draw angle A as an acute angle.) Using the Distance Formula, we get

$$a^2 = (b \cos A - c)^2 + (b \sin A - 0)^2$$

$$= b^2 \cos^2 A - 2bc \cos A + c^2 + b^2 \sin^2 A$$

$$= b^2(\cos^2 A + \sin^2 A) - 2bc \cos A + c^2$$

$$= b^2 + c^2 - 2bc \cos A \qquad \text{Because } \sin^2 A + \cos^2 A = 1$$

This proves the first formula. The other two formulas are obtained in the same way by placing each of the other vertices of the triangle at the origin and repeating the preceding argument.   □

In words, the Law of Cosines says that the square of any side of a triangle is equal to the sum of the squares of the other two sides, minus twice the product of those two sides times the cosine of the included angle.

If one of the angles of a triangle, say $\angle C$, is a right angle, then $\cos C = 0$ and the Law of Cosines reduces to the Pythagorean Theorem, $c^2 = a^2 + b^2$. Thus, the Pythagorean Theorem is a special case of the Law of Cosines.

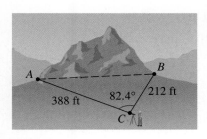

FIGURE 2

EXAMPLE 1 ■ Length of a Tunnel

A tunnel is to be built through a mountain. To estimate the length of the tunnel, a surveyor makes the measurements shown in Figure 2. Use the surveyor's data to approximate the length of the tunnel.

SOLUTION

To approximate the length c of the tunnel, we use the Law of Cosines:

$$c^2 = a^2 + b^2 - 2ab \cos C \qquad \text{Law of Cosines}$$

$$= 388^2 + 212^2 - 2(388)(212) \cos 82.4° \qquad \text{Substitute}$$

$$\approx 173730.2367 \qquad \text{Use a calculator}$$

$$c \approx \sqrt{173730.2367} \approx 416.8 \qquad \text{Take square roots}$$

Thus, the tunnel will be approximately 417 ft long. ∎

EXAMPLE 2 ■ SSS, the Law of Cosines

The sides of a triangle are $a = 5$, $b = 8$, and $c = 12$ (see Figure 3). Find the angles of the triangle.

SOLUTION

We first find $\angle A$. From the Law of Cosines, we have $a^2 = b^2 + c^2 - 2bc \cos A$. Solving for $\cos A$, we get

$$\cos A = \frac{b^2 + c^2 - a^2}{2bc} = \frac{8^2 + 12^2 - 5^2}{2(8)(12)} = \frac{183}{192} = 0.953125$$

Using a calculator, we find that $\angle A \approx 18°$. In the same way the equations

$$\cos B = \frac{a^2 + c^2 - b^2}{2ac} = \frac{5^2 + 12^2 - 8^2}{2(5)(12)} = 0.875$$

$$\cos C = \frac{a^2 + b^2 - c^2}{2ab} = \frac{5^2 + 8^2 - 12^2}{2(5)(8)} = -0.6875$$

give $\angle B \approx 29°$ and $\angle C \approx 133°$. Of course, once two angles are calculated, the third can more easily be found from the fact that the sum of the angles of a triangle is 180°. However, it's a good idea to calculate all three angles using the Law of Cosines and add the three angles as a check on your computations. ∎

EXAMPLE 3 ■ SAS, the Law of Cosines and the Law of Sines

Solve triangle ABC, where $\angle A = 46.5°$, $b = 10.5$, and $c = 18.0$.

SOLUTION

We can find a using the Law of Cosines.

$$a^2 = b^2 + c^2 - 2bc \cos A$$

$$= (10.5)^2 + (18.0)^2 - 2(10.5)(18.0)(\cos 46.5°) \approx 174.05$$

Thus, $a \approx \sqrt{174.05} \approx 13.2$. The two remaining angles can now be found using the

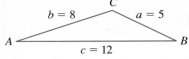

FIGURE 3

$\boxed{\text{C O S}^{-1}}$

or

$\boxed{\text{I N V}}\ \boxed{\text{C O S}}$

or

$\boxed{\text{A R C}}\ \boxed{\text{C O S}}$

Law of Sines. We have

$$\sin B = \frac{b \sin A}{a} \approx \frac{10.5 \sin 46.5°}{13.2} \approx 0.577$$

So B is the angle whose sine is 0.577. For this, we use our calculator to get $\angle B \approx 35.2°$. Since angle B can have measure between 0° and 180°, another possibility for angle B is $\angle B = 180° - 35.2° = 144.8°$. It's a simple matter to choose between these two possibilities, since the largest angle in a triangle must be opposite the longest side. So the correct choice is $\angle B \approx 35.2°$. In this case, $\angle C \approx 180° - (46.5° + 35.2°) = 98.3°$, and indeed the largest angle, $\angle C$, is opposite the longest side, $c = 18.0$.

To summarize: $\angle B \approx 35.2°$, $\angle C \approx 98.3°$, and $a \approx 13.2$. (See Figure 4.) ∎

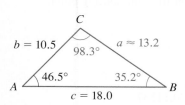

FIGURE 4

 We see from Example 3 that, when using both the Law of Cosines and the Law of Sines to solve a triangle in the SAS case, we must be careful to choose the correct measure for the remaining angle. In any triangle, the longest side is opposite the largest angle, and the shortest side is opposite the smallest angle. Thus, when using the Law of Sines, we must choose the angle so that this condition is satisfied. That's why it's a good idea to sketch the triangle so you can check your final answer.

■ Navigation: Heading and Bearing

In navigation a direction is often given as a **bearing**, that is, as an acute angle measured from due north or due south. The bearing N 30° E, for example, indicates a direction that points 30° to the east of due north (see Figure 5).

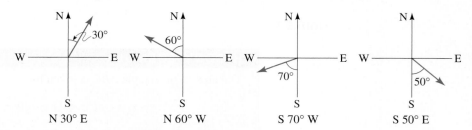

FIGURE 5   N 30° E   N 60° W   S 70° W   S 50° E

EXAMPLE 4 ■ Navigation

A pilot sets out from an airport and heads in the direction N 20° E, flying at 200 mi/h. After one hour, he makes a course correction and heads in the direction N 40° E. Half an hour after that, engine trouble forces him to make an emergency landing.

(a) Find the distance between the airport and his final landing point.
(b) Find the bearing from the airport to his final landing point.

SOLUTION

(a) In one hour the plane travels 200 mi, and in half an hour it travels 100 mi, so we can plot the pilot's course as in Figure 6. When he makes his course correction, he turns 20° to the right, so the angle between the two legs of his trip

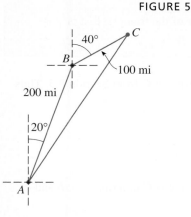

FIGURE 6

is $180° - 20° = 160°$. So by the Law of Cosines we have

$$b^2 = 200^2 + 100^2 - 2 \cdot 200 \cdot 100 \cos 160°$$

$$\approx 87{,}587.70$$

Thus, $b \approx 295.95$. The pilot lands about 296 mi from his starting point.

(b) We first use the Law of Sines to find $\angle A$.

$$\frac{\sin A}{100} = \frac{\sin 160°}{295.95}$$

$$\sin A = 100 \cdot \frac{\sin 160°}{295.95} \approx 0.11557$$

Another angle with sine 0.11557 is $180° - 6.636° = 173.364°$. But this is clearly too large to be $\angle A$ in $\angle ABC$.

Using the $\boxed{\text{SIN}^{-1}}$ key on a calculator, we find that $\angle A \approx 6.636°$. From Figure 6 we see that the line from the airport to the final landing site points in the direction $20° + 6.636° = 26.636°$ east of due north. Thus, the bearing is about N 26.6° E.   ■

■ The Area of a Triangle

An interesting application of the Law of Cosines involves a formula for finding the area of a triangle from the lengths of its three sides (see Figure 7).

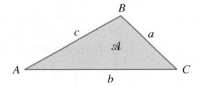

FIGURE 7

HERON'S FORMULA

The area $\mathcal{A}$ of triangle ABC is given by

$$\mathcal{A} = \sqrt{s(s-a)(s-b)(s-c)}$$

where $s = \frac{1}{2}(a + b + c)$ is the **semiperimeter** of the triangle; that is, s is half the perimeter.

■ **Proof**   We start with the formula $\mathcal{A} = \frac{1}{2}ab \sin C$ from Section 3.3. Thus

$$\mathcal{A}^2 = \tfrac{1}{4} a^2 b^2 \sin^2 C$$

$$= \tfrac{1}{4} a^2 b^2 (1 - \cos^2 C) \qquad \text{Pythagorean identity}$$

$$= \tfrac{1}{4} a^2 b^2 (1 - \cos C)(1 + \cos C) \qquad \text{Factor}$$

Next, we write the expressions $1 - \cos C$ and $1 + \cos C$ in terms of a, b and c.

By the Law of Cosines we have

$$\cos C = \frac{a^2 + b^2 - c^2}{2ab} \qquad \text{Law of Cosines}$$

$$1 + \cos C = 1 + \frac{a^2 + b^2 - c^2}{2ab} \qquad \text{Add 1}$$

$$= \frac{2ab + a^2 + b^2 - c^2}{2ab} \qquad \text{Common denominator}$$

$$= \frac{(a + b)^2 - c^2}{2ab} \qquad \text{Factor}$$

$$= \frac{(a + b + c)(a + b - c)}{2ab} \qquad \text{Difference of squares}$$

Similarly

$$1 - \cos C = \frac{(c + a - b)(c - a + b)}{2ab}$$

Substituting these expressions in the formula we obtained for $\mathcal{A}^2$ gives

$$\mathcal{A}^2 = \tfrac{1}{4} a^2 b^2 \, \frac{(a + b + c)(a + b - c)}{2ab} \, \frac{(c + a - b)(c - a + b)}{2ab}$$

$$= \frac{(a + b + c)}{2} \, \frac{(a + b - c)}{2} \, \frac{(c + a - b)}{2} \, \frac{(c - a + b)}{2}$$

$$= s(s - c)(s - b)(s - a)$$

Showing that each factor in the last expression equals the corresponding factor in the preceding expression is left as an exercise. Heron's Formula now follows by taking the square root of each side.   ☐

EXAMPLE 5 ■ Area of a Lot

A businessman wishes to buy a triangular lot in a busy downtown location (see Figure 8). The lot frontages on the three adjacent streets are 125, 280, and 315 ft. Find the area of the lot.

SOLUTION

The semiperimeter of the lot is

$$s = \frac{125 + 280 + 315}{2} = 360$$

By Heron's Formula the area is

$$\mathcal{A} = \sqrt{360(360 - 125)(360 - 280)(360 - 315)} \approx 17{,}451.6$$

Thus, the area is approximately 17,452 ft^2.   ■

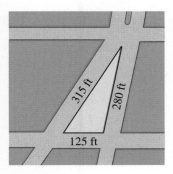

315 ft

280 ft

125 ft

FIGURE 8

3.5 EXERCISES

1–8 ■ Use the Law of Cosines to determine the indicated side *x* or angle *θ*.

1.

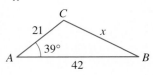

2.

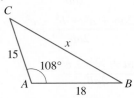

3.

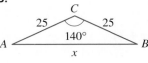

4.

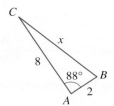

5.

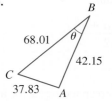

6.

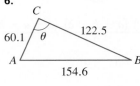

7.

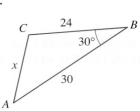

8.

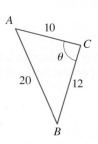

9–18 ■ Solve triangle *ABC*.

9.

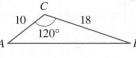

10.

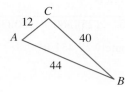

11. $a = 3.0$, $b = 4.0$, $\angle C = 53°$

12. $b = 60$, $c = 30$, $\angle A = 70°$

13. $a = 20$, $b = 25$, $c = 22$

14. $a = 10$, $b = 12$, $c = 16$

15. $b = 125$, $c = 162$, $\angle B = 40°$

16. $a = 65$, $c = 50$, $\angle C = 52°$

17. $a = 50$, $b = 65$, $\angle A = 55°$

18. $a = 73.5$, $\angle B = 61°$, $\angle C = 83°$

19–26 ■ Find the indicated side *x* or angle *θ*. (Use either the Law of Sines or the Law of Cosines, as appropriate.)

19.

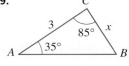

20.

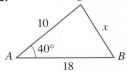

21.

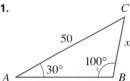

22.

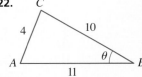

23.

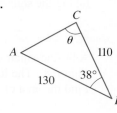

24.

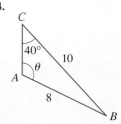

25.

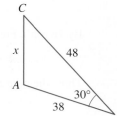

26.

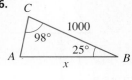

27. To find the distance across a small lake, a surveyor has taken the measurements shown. Find the distance across the lake using this information.

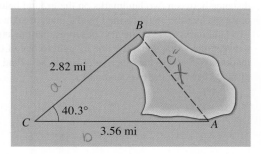

28. A parallelogram has sides of lengths 3 and 5, and one angle is 50°. Find the lengths of the diagonals.

29. Two straight roads diverge at an angle of 65°. Two cars leave the intersection at 2:00 P.M., one traveling at 50 mi/h and the other at 30 mi/h. How far apart are the cars at 2:30 P.M.?

30. A car travels along a straight road, heading east for 1 h, then traveling for 30 min on another road that leads northeast. If the car has maintained a constant speed of 40 mi/h, how far is it from its starting position?

31. A pilot flies in a straight path for 1 h 30 min. She then makes a course correction, heading 10° to the right of her original course, and flies 2 h in the new direction. If she maintains a constant speed of 625 mi/h, how far is she from her starting position?

32. Two boats leave the same port at the same time. One travels at a speed of 30 mi/h in the direction N 50° E and the other travels at a speed of 26 mi/h in a direction S 70° E (see the figure). How far apart are the two boats after one hour?

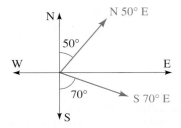

33. A fisherman leaves his home port and heads in the direction N 70° W. He travels 30 mi and reaches Egg Island. The next day he sails N 10° E for 50 mi, reaching Forrest Island.
   (a) Find the distance between the fisherman's home part and Forrest Island.

(b) Find the bearing from Forrest Island back to his home port.

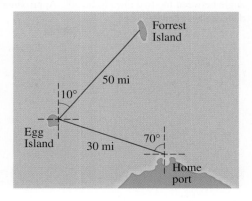

34. Airport B is 300 mi from airport A at a bearing N 50° E (see the figure). A pilot wishing to fly from A to B mistakenly flies due east at 200 mi/h for 30 minutes, when he notices his error.
   (a) How far is the pilot from his destination at the time he notices the error?
   (b) What bearing should he head his plane in order to arrive at airport B?

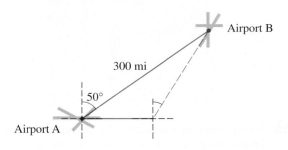

35. A triangular field has sides of lengths 22, 36, and 44 yd. Find the largest angle.

36. Two tugboats that are 120 ft apart pull a barge, as shown. If the length of one cable is 212 ft and the length of the other is 230 ft, find the angle formed by the two cables.

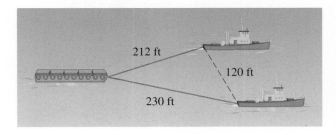

37. A boy is flying two kites at the same time. He has 380 ft of line out to one kite and 420 ft to the other. He estimates the angle between the two lines to be 30°. Approximate the distance between the kites.

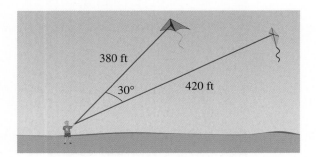

38. A 125-ft tower is located on the side of a mountain that is inclined 32° to the horizontal. A guy wire is to be attached to the top of the tower and anchored at a point 55 ft downhill from the base of the tower. Find the shortest length of wire needed.

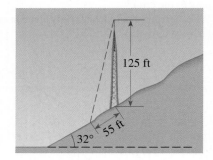

39. A steep mountain is inclined 74° to the horizontal and rises 3400 ft above the surrounding plain. A cable car is to be installed from a point 800 ft from the base to the top of the mountain, as shown. Find the shortest length of cable needed.

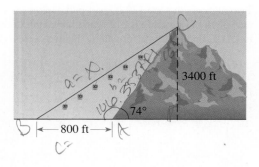

40. The CN Tower in Toronto, Canada, is the tallest free-standing structure in the world. A woman on the observation deck, 1150 ft above the ground, wants to determine the distance between two landmarks on the ground below. She observes that the angle formed by the lines of sight to these two landmarks is 43°. She also observes that the angle between the vertical and the line of sight to one of the landmarks is 62° and to the other landmark is 54°. Find the distance between the two landmarks.

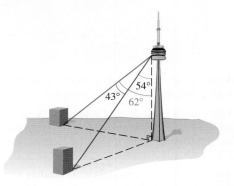

41. Three circles of radii 4, 5, and 6 cm are mutually tangent. Find the shaded area enclosed between the circles.

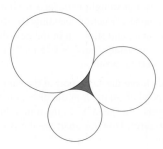

42. Prove that in triangle ABC

$$a = b \cos C + c \cos B$$

$$b = c \cos A + a \cos C$$

$$c = a \cos B + b \cos A$$

These are called the *Projection Laws*. [*Hint:* To get the first equation, add together the second and third equations in the Law of Cosines and solve for a.]

43. Find the area of a triangle with sides of lengths 12, 18, and 24 m.

44. Land in downtown Columbia is valued at $20 a square foot. What is the value of a triangular lot with sides of lengths 112, 148, and 190 ft?

45. Find the area of the quadrilateral in the figure, correct to two decimal places.

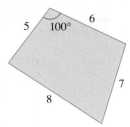

46. Solving for the Angles in a Triangle When we solved for $\angle B$ in Example 3 using the Law of Sines, we had to be careful because there were two possibilities, 35.2° and 144.8°. That is because these are the *two* angles between 0° and 180° whose sine is 0.577. What if we use the Law of Cosines to find $\angle B$? Would the problem of two possible measures for $\angle B$ still arise? Which method do you prefer here: the Law of Sines or the Law of Cosines?

---

3 REVIEW

CONCEPT CHECK

1. (a) Explain the difference between a positive angle and a negative angle.
  (b) How is an angle of measure 1 degree formed?
  (c) How is an angle of measure 1 radian formed?
  (d) How is the radian measure of an angle θ defined?
  (e) How do you convert from degrees to radians?
  (f) How do you convert from radians to degrees?

2. (a) When is an angle in standard position?
  (b) When are two angles coterminal?

3. (a) What is the length s of an arc of a circle with radius r that subtends a central angle of θ radians?
  (b) What is the area A of a sector of a circle with radius r and central angle θ radians?

4. If θ is an acute angle in a right triangle, define the six trigonometric ratios in terms of the adjacent and opposite sides and the hypotenuse.

5. What does it mean to solve a triangle?

6. If θ is an angle in standard position, $P(x, y)$ is a point on the terminal side, and r is the distance from the origin to P, write expressions for the six trigonometric functions of θ.

7. Which trigonometric functions are positive in quadrants I, II, III, and IV?

8. If θ is an angle in standard position, what is its reference angle $\overline{\theta}$?

9. (a) State the reciprocal identities.
  (b) State the Pythagorean identities.

10. (a) What is the area of a triangle with sides of length a and b and with included angle θ?
  (b) What is the area of a triangle with sides of length a, b and c?

11. (a) State the Law of Sines.
  (b) State the Law of Cosines.

12. Explain the ambiguous case in the Law of Sines.

EXERCISES

1–2 ■ Find the radian measure that corresponds to the given degree measure.

1. (a) 60°   (b) 330°   (c) −135°   (d) −90°

2. (a) 24°   (b) −330°   (c) 750°   (d) 5°

3–4 ■ Find the degree measure that corresponds to the given radian measure.

3. (a) $\dfrac{5\pi}{2}$ (b) $-\dfrac{\pi}{6}$ (c) $\dfrac{9\pi}{4}$ (d) 3.1

4. (a) 8   (b) $-\dfrac{5}{2}$ (c) $\dfrac{11\pi}{6}$ (d) $\dfrac{3\pi}{5}$

5. Find the length of an arc of a circle of radius 8 m if the arc subtends a central angle of 1 rad.

6. Find the measure of a central angle θ in a circle of radius 5 ft if the angle is subtended by an arc of length 7 ft.

7. A circular arc of length 100 ft subtends a central angle of 70°. Find the radius of the circle.

8. How many revolutions will a car wheel of diameter 28 in. make over a period of half an hour if the car is traveling at 60 mi/h?

9. New York and Los Angeles are 2450 mi apart. Find the angle that the arc between these two cities subtends at the center of the earth. (The radius of the earth is 3960 mi.)

10. Find the area of a sector with central angle 2 rad in a circle of radius 5 m.

11. Find the area of a sector with central angle 52° in a circle of radius 200 ft.

12. A sector in a circle of radius 25 ft has an area of 125 ft². Find the central angle of the sector.

13. A potter's wheel with radius 8 in. spins at 150 rpm. Find the angular and linear speeds of a point on the rim of the wheel.

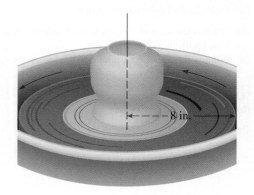

14. In an automobile transmission a *gear ratio g* is the ratio

$$g = \frac{\text{angular speed of engine}}{\text{angular speed of wheels}}$$

The angular speed of the engine is shown on the tachometer (in rpm).

A certain sports car has wheels with radius 11 in. Its gear ratios are shown in the table. Suppose the car is in fourth gear and the tachometer reads 3500 rpm.
(a) Find the angular speed of the engine.
(b) Find the angular speed of the wheels.
(c) How fast (in mi/h) is the car traveling?

Gear	Ratio
1st	4.1
2nd	3.0
3rd	1.6
4th	0.9
5th	0.7

15–16 ■ Find the values of the six trigonometric ratios of θ.

15.

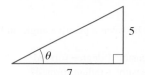

16.

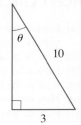

17–20 ■ Find the sides labeled x and y, correct to two decimal places.

17.

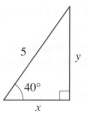

18.

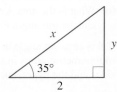

19.

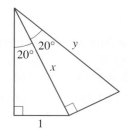

20.

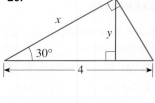

21–22 ■ Solve the triangle.

21.

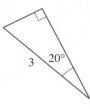

22.

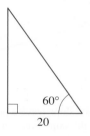

23. Express the lengths a and b in the figure in terms of the trigonometric ratios of θ.

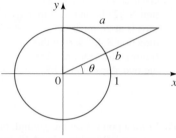

24. The highest tower in the world is the CN Tower in Toronto, Canada. From a distance of 1 km from its base, the angle of elevation to the top of the tower is 28.81°. Find the height of the tower.

25. Find the perimeter of a regular hexagon that is inscribed in a circle of radius 8 m.

26. The pistons in a car engine move up and down repeatedly to turn the crankshaft, as shown. Find the height of the point P above the center O of the crankshaft in terms of the angle θ.

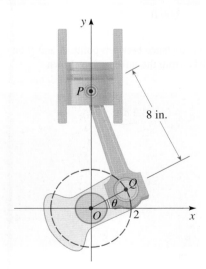

27. As viewed from the earth, the angle subtended by the full moon is 0.518°. Use this information and the fact that the distance AB from the earth to the moon is 236,900 mi to find the radius of the moon.

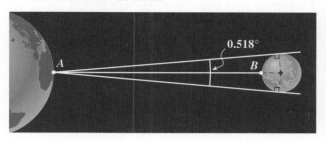

28. A pilot measures the angles of depression to two ships to be 40° and 52° (see the figure). If the pilot is flying at an elevation of 35,000 ft, find the distance between the two ships.

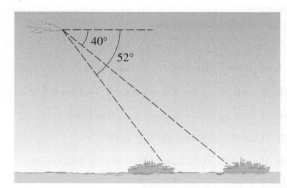

29–40 ■ Find the exact value.

29. $\sin 315°$

30. $\csc \dfrac{9\pi}{4}$

31. $\tan(-135°)$

32. $\cos \dfrac{5\pi}{6}$

33. $\cot\left(-\dfrac{22\pi}{3}\right)$

34. $\sin 405°$

35. $\cos 585°$

36. $\sec \dfrac{22\pi}{3}$

37. $\csc \dfrac{8\pi}{3}$

38. $\sec \dfrac{13\pi}{6}$

39. $\cot(-390°)$

40. $\tan \dfrac{23\pi}{4}$

41. Find the values of the six trigonometric ratios of the angle θ in standard position if the point $(-5, 12)$ is on the terminal side of θ.

42. Find $\sin \theta$ if θ is in standard position and its terminal side intersects the circle of radius 1 centered at the origin at the point $\left(-\sqrt{3}/2, \frac{1}{2}\right)$.

43. Find the acute angle that is formed by the line $y - \sqrt{3}\, x + 1 = 0$ and the x-axis.

44. Find the six trigonometric ratios of the angle θ in standard position if its terminal side is in quadrant III and is parallel to the line $4y - 2x - 1 = 0$.

45–48 ■ Write the first expression in terms of the second, for θ in the given quadrant.

45. $\tan \theta$, $\cos \theta$; θ in quadrant II

46. $\sec \theta$, $\sin \theta$; θ in quadrant III

47. $\tan^2\theta$, $\sin \theta$; θ in any quadrant

48. $\csc^2\theta \cos^2\theta$, $\sin \theta$; θ in any quadrant

49–52 ■ Find the values of the six trigonometric functions of θ from the information given.

49. $\tan \theta = \sqrt{7}/3$, $\sec \theta = \frac{4}{3}$

50. $\sec \theta = \frac{41}{40}$, $\csc \theta = -\frac{41}{9}$

51. $\sin \theta = \frac{3}{5}$, $\cos \theta < 0$

52. $\sec \theta = -\frac{13}{5}$, $\tan \theta > 0$

53. If $\tan \theta = -\frac{1}{2}$ for θ in quadrant II, find $\sin \theta + \cos \theta$.

54. If $\sin \theta = \frac{1}{2}$ for θ in quadrant I, find $\tan \theta + \sec \theta$.

55. If $\tan \theta = -1$, find $\sin^2\theta + \cos^2\theta$.

56. If $\cos \theta = -\sqrt{3}/2$ and $\pi/2 < \theta < \pi$, find $\sin 2\theta$.

57–62 ■ Find the side labeled x.

57.

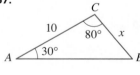

58.

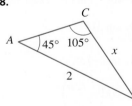

59.

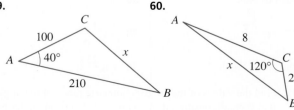

60.

61.

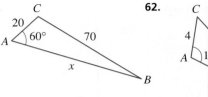

62.

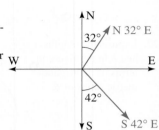

63. Two ships leave a port at the same time. One travels at 20 mi/h in a direction N 32° E, and the other travels at 28 mi/h in a direction S 42° E (see the figure). How far apart are the two ships after 2 h?

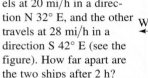

64. From a point A on the ground, the angle of elevation to the top of a tall building is 24.1°. From a point B, which is 600 ft closer to the building, the angle of elevation is measured to be 30.2°. Find the height of the building.

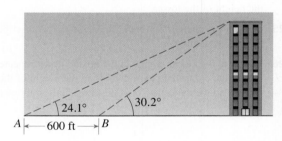

65. Find the distance between points A and B on opposite sides of a lake from the information shown.

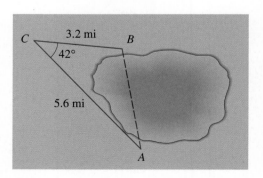

66. A boat is cruising the ocean off a straight shoreline. Points A and B are 120 mi apart on the shore, as shown. It is found that $\angle A = 42.3°$ and $\angle B = 68.9°$. Find the shortest distance from the boat to the shore.

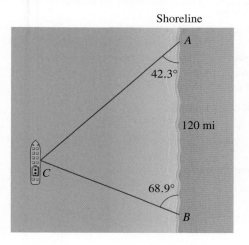

Shoreline

42.3°

120 mi

C

68.9°

A

B

67. Find the area of a triangle with sides of length 8 and 14 and included angle 35°.

68. Find the area of a triangle with sides of length 5, 6, and 8.

3 TEST

1. Find the radian measures that correspond to the degree measures $300°$ and $-18°$.

2. Find the degree measures that correspond to the radian measures $\dfrac{5\pi}{6}$ and 2.4.

3. The rotor blades of a helicopter are 25 ft long and are rotating at 200 rpm.
   (a) Find the angular speed of the rotor.
   (b) Find the linear speed of a point on the tip of a blade.

4. Find the exact value of each of the following.
   (a) $\sin 405°$ (b) $\tan(-150°)$
   (c) $\sec \dfrac{5\pi}{3}$ (d) $\csc \dfrac{5\pi}{2}$

5. Find $\tan \theta + \sin \theta$ for the angle θ shown.

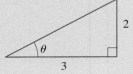

6. Find the lengths a and b shown in the figure in terms of θ.

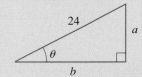

7. If $\cos \theta = -\frac{1}{3}$ and θ is in quadrant III, find $\tan \theta \cot \theta + \csc \theta$.

8. If $\sin \theta = \frac{5}{13}$ and $\tan \theta = -\frac{5}{12}$, find $\sec \theta$.

9. Express $\tan \theta$ in terms of $\sec \theta$ for θ in quadrant II.

10. The base of the ladder in the figure is 6 ft from the building, and the angle formed by the ladder and the ground is $73°$. How high up the building does the ladder touch?

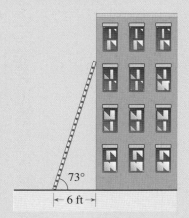

11–14 ■ Find the side labeled x.

11.

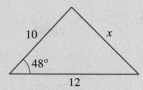

12.

13.

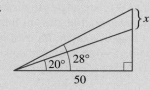

14.

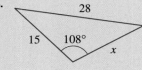

15. Refer to the figure at the left.
   (a) Find the area of the shaded region.
   (b) Find the perimeter of the shaded region.

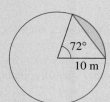

16. Refer to the figure at the right.
   (a) Find the angle opposite the longest side.
   (b) Find the area of the triangle.

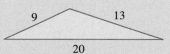

17. Two wires tether a balloon to the ground, as shown. How high is the balloon above the ground?

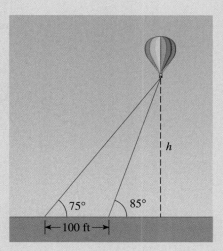

Focus on Modeling
Surveying

How can we measure the height of a mountain, or the distance across a lake? Obviously it may be difficult, inconvenient, or impossible to measure these distances directly (that is, using a tape measure or a yard stick). On the other hand, it is easy to measure *angles* to distant objects. That's where trigonometry comes in—the trigonometric ratios relate angles to distances, so they can be used to *calculate* distances from the *measured* angles. In this *Focus* we examine how trigonometry is used to make a map of a town. Modern map making methods use satellites and the Global Positioning System, but mathematics remains at the core of the process.

■ Mapping a Town

A student wants to draw a map of his hometown. To construct an accurate map (or scale model), he needs to find distances between various landmarks in the town. The student makes the measurements shown in Figure 1. Note that only one distance is measured, between City Hall and the first bridge. All other measurements are angles.

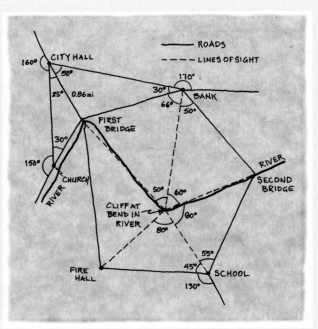

FIGURE 1

The distances between other landmarks can now be found using the Law of Sines. For example, the distance x from the bank to the first bridge is calculated by applying the Law of Sines to the triangle with vertices at City Hall, the bank, and the first bridge:

$$\frac{x}{\sin 50°} = \frac{0.86}{\sin 30°} \qquad \text{Law of Sines}$$

$$x = \frac{0.86 \sin 50°}{\sin 30°} \qquad \text{Solve for } x$$

$$\approx 1.32 \text{ mi} \qquad \text{Calculator}$$

So the distance between the bank and the first bridge is 1.32 mi.

The distance we just found can now be used to find other distances. For instance, we find the distance y between the bank and the cliff as follows:

$$\frac{y}{\sin 64°} = \frac{1.32}{\sin 50°} \qquad \text{Law of Sines}$$

$$y = \frac{1.32 \sin 64°}{\sin 50°} \qquad \text{Solve for } y$$

$$\approx 1.55 \text{ mi} \qquad \text{Calculator}$$

Continuing in this fashion, we can calculate all the distances between the landmarks shown in the rough sketch in Figure 1. We can use this information to draw the map shown in Figure 2.

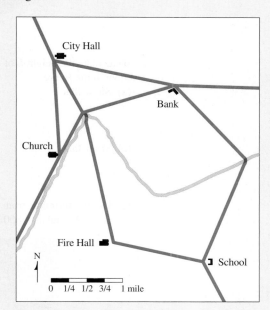

FIGURE 2

234   Focus on Modeling

To make a topographic map, we need to measure elevation. This concept is explored in Problems 4–6.

Problems

1. Find the distance between the church and City Hall.

2. Find the distance between the fire hall and the school. (You will need to find other distances first.)

3. A surveyor on one side of a river wishes to find the distance between points *A* and *B* on the opposite side of the river. On her side, she chooses points *C* and *D*, which are 20 m apart, and measures the angles shown in the figure at the left. Find the distance between *A* and *B*.

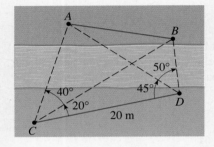

4. To measure the height of an inaccessible cliff on the opposite side of a river, a surveyor makes the measurements shown. Find the height of the cliff.

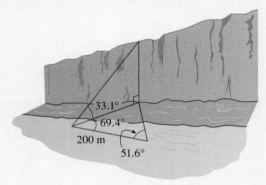

5. To calculate the height *h* of a mountain, angle α, β, and distance *d* are measured, as shown in the figure.
   (a) Show that

   $$h = \frac{d}{\cot \alpha - \cot \beta}$$

   (b) Show that

   $$h = d\,\frac{\sin \alpha \sin \beta}{\sin(\beta - \alpha)}$$

   (c) Use the formulas from parts (a) and (b) to find the height of a mountain if $\alpha = 25°$, $\beta = 29°$, and $d = 800$ ft. Do you get the same answer from each formula?

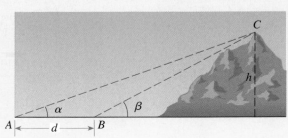

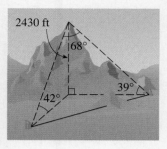

6. A surveyor has determined that a mountain is 2430 ft high. From the top of the mountain he measures the angles of depression to two landmarks at the base of the mountain, and finds them to be 42° and 39°. (Observe that these are the same as the angles of elevation from the landmarks as shown in the figure.) The angle between the lines of sight to the landmarks is 68°. Calculate the distance between the two landmarks.

7. A surveyor surveys two adjacent lots and makes the following rough sketch showing his measurements. Calculate all the distances shown in the figure and use your result to draw an accurate map of the two lots.

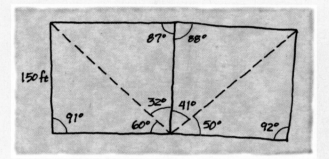

8. The Great Trigonometric Survey of India was one of the most massive mapping projects ever undertaken (see the margin note on page 213). Do some research at your library or on the Internet to learn more about the Survey, and write a report on your findings.

4 Analytic Trigonometry

Trigonometric equations and inverse trigonometric functions are used when designing software to track the lift-off of the space shuttle or to plot the path of an orbiting satellite.

A mathematician must often use a rule, and, naturally, he begins by proving the rule.

HENRI POINCARÉ

In Chapters 2 and 3 we studied the graphical and geometric properties of trigonometric functions. In this chapter we study the algebraic aspects of trigonometry, that is, simplifying and factoring expressions and solving equations that involve trigonometric functions. The basic tools in the algebra of trigonometry are trigonometric identities. We will find identities for trigonometric functions of sums and differences of real numbers, multiple-angle formulas, and other related identities. These identities are used in the study of complex numbers, vectors, and analytic geometry.

4.1 TRIGONOMETRIC IDENTITIES

We begin this section by reviewing some of the basic trigonometric identities that we studied in Chapters 2 and 3.

FUNDAMENTAL TRIGONOMETRIC IDENTITIES

Reciprocal Identities

$$\csc x = \frac{1}{\sin x} \qquad \sec x = \frac{1}{\cos x} \qquad \cot x = \frac{1}{\tan x}$$

$$\tan x = \frac{\sin x}{\cos x} \qquad \cot x = \frac{\cos x}{\sin x}$$

Pythagorean Identities

$$\sin^2 x + \cos^2 x = 1 \qquad \tan^2 x + 1 = \sec^2 x \qquad 1 + \cot^2 x = \csc^2 x$$

Even-Odd Identities

$$\sin(-x) = -\sin x \qquad \cos(-x) = \cos x \qquad \tan(-x) = -\tan x$$

Cofunction Identities

$$\sin\left(\frac{\pi}{2} - u\right) = \cos u \qquad \tan\left(\frac{\pi}{2} - u\right) = \cot u \qquad \sec\left(\frac{\pi}{2} - u\right) = \csc u$$

$$\cos\left(\frac{\pi}{2} - u\right) = \sin u \qquad \cot\left(\frac{\pi}{2} - u\right) = \tan u \qquad \csc\left(\frac{\pi}{2} - u\right) = \sec u$$

▪ Simplifying Trigonometric Expressions

Identities enable us to write the same expression in different ways. It is often possible to rewrite a complicated looking expression as a much simpler one. To simplify algebraic expressions, we used factoring, common denominators, and the Special Product Formulas. To simplify trigonometric expressions, we use these same techniques together with the fundamental trigonometric identities.

EXAMPLE 1 ▪ Simplifying a Trigonometric Expression

Simplify the expression $\cos t + \tan t \sin t$.

SOLUTION

We start by rewriting the expression in terms of sine and cosine.

$$\cos t + \tan t \sin t = \cos t + \left(\frac{\sin t}{\cos t}\right) \sin t \qquad \text{Reciprocal identity}$$

$$= \frac{\cos^2 t + \sin^2 t}{\cos t} \qquad \text{Common denominator}$$

$$= \frac{1}{\cos t} \qquad \text{Pythagorean identity}$$

$$= \sec t \qquad \text{Reciprocal identity} \qquad ▪$$

EXAMPLE 2 ▪ Simplifying by Combining Fractions

Simplify the expression $\dfrac{\sin \theta}{\cos \theta} + \dfrac{\cos \theta}{1 + \sin \theta}$.

SOLUTION

We combine the fractions by using a common denominator.

$$\frac{\sin \theta}{\cos \theta} + \frac{\cos \theta}{1 + \sin \theta} = \frac{\sin \theta \,(1 + \sin \theta) + \cos^2\theta}{\cos \theta \,(1 + \sin \theta)} \qquad \text{Common denominator}$$

$$= \frac{\sin \theta + \sin^2\theta + \cos^2\theta}{\cos \theta \,(1 + \sin \theta)} \qquad \text{Expand}$$

$$= \frac{\sin \theta + 1}{\cos \theta \,(1 + \sin \theta)} \qquad \text{Pythagorean identity}$$

$$= \frac{1}{\cos \theta} = \sec \theta \qquad \text{Cancel and use reciprocal identity} \qquad ▪$$

■ Proving Trigonometric Identities

Many identities follow from the fundamental identities. In the examples that follow, we learn how to prove that a given trigonometric equation is an identity, and in the process we will see how to discover new identities.

First, it's easy to decide when a given equation is *not* an identity. All we need to do is show that the equation does not hold for some value of the variable (or variables). Thus, the equation

$$\sin x + \cos x = 1$$

is not an identity, because when $x = \pi/4$, we have

$$\sin \frac{\pi}{4} + \cos \frac{\pi}{4} = \frac{\sqrt{2}}{2} + \frac{\sqrt{2}}{2} = \sqrt{2} \neq 1$$

To verify that a trigonometric equation is an identity, we transform one side of the equation into the other side by a series of steps, each of which is itself an identity.

GUIDELINES FOR PROVING TRIGONOMETRIC IDENTITIES

1. START WITH ONE SIDE.   Pick one side of the equation and write it down. Your goal is to transform it into the other side. It's usually easier to start with the more complicated side.

2. USE KNOWN IDENTITIES.   Use algebra and the identities you know to change the side you started with. Bring fractional expressions to a common denominator, factor, and use the fundamental identities to simplify expressions.

3. CONVERT TO SINES AND COSINES.   If you are stuck, you may find it helpful to rewrite all functions in terms of sines and cosines.

EXAMPLE 3 ■ Proving an Identity by Rewriting in Terms of Sine and Cosine

Verify the identity $\cos \theta \, (\sec \theta - \cos \theta) = \sin^2\theta$.

SOLUTION

The left-hand side looks more complicated, so we start with it and try to transform it into the right-hand side.

$$\begin{aligned}
\text{LHS} &= \cos \theta \, (\sec \theta - \cos \theta) \\[2mm]
&= \cos \theta \left(\frac{1}{\cos \theta} - \cos \theta \right) && \text{Reciprocal identity} \\[2mm]
&= 1 - \cos^2\theta && \text{Expand} \\[2mm]
&= \sin^2\theta = \text{RHS} && \text{Pythagorean identity}
\end{aligned}$$

■

In Example 3 it isn't easy to see how to change the right-hand side into the left-hand side, but it's definitely possible. Simply notice that each step is reversible. In other words, if we start with the last expression in the proof and work backward through the steps, the right side is transformed into the left side. You will probably agree, however, that it's more difficult to prove the identity this way. That's why it's often better to change the more complicated side of the identity into the simpler side.

EXAMPLE 4 ■ Proving an Identity by Combining Fractions

Verify the identity

$$2 \tan x \sec x = \frac{1}{1 - \sin x} - \frac{1}{1 + \sin x}$$

SOLUTION

Finding a common denominator and combining the fractions on the right-hand side of this equation, we get

$$
\begin{aligned}
\text{RHS} &= \frac{1}{1 - \sin x} - \frac{1}{1 + \sin x} \\[2mm]
&= \frac{(1 + \sin x) - (1 - \sin x)}{(1 - \sin x)(1 + \sin x)} && \text{Common denominator} \\[2mm]
&= \frac{2 \sin x}{1 - \sin^2 x} && \text{Simplify} \\[2mm]
&= \frac{2 \sin x}{\cos^2 x} && \text{Pythagorean identity} \\[2mm]
&= 2\, \frac{\sin x}{\cos x} \left(\frac{1}{\cos x} \right) && \text{Factor} \\[2mm]
&= 2 \tan x \sec x = \text{LHS} && \text{Reciprocal identities} \qquad ■
\end{aligned}
$$

In Example 5 we introduce "something extra" to the problem by multiplying the numerator and the denominator by a trigonometric expression, chosen so that we can simplify the result.

EXAMPLE 5 ■ Proving an Identity by Introducing Something Extra

Verify the identity $\dfrac{\cos u}{1 - \sin u} = \sec u + \tan u.$

SOLUTION

We start with the left-hand side and multiply numerator and denominator by $1 + \sin u$.

$$\text{LHS} = \frac{\cos u}{1 - \sin u}$$

We multiply by $1 + \sin u$ because we know by the difference of squares formula that $(1 - \sin u)(1 + \sin u) = 1 - \sin^2 u$, and this is just $\cos^2 u$, a simpler expression.

$$= \frac{\cos u}{1 - \sin u} \cdot \frac{1 + \sin u}{1 + \sin u} \qquad \text{Multiply numerator and denominator by } 1 + \sin u$$

$$= \frac{\cos u (1 + \sin u)}{1 - \sin^2 u} \qquad \text{Expand denominator}$$

$$= \frac{\cos u (1 + \sin u)}{\cos^2 u} \qquad \text{Pythagorean identity}$$

$$= \frac{1 + \sin u}{\cos u} \qquad \text{Cancel common factor}$$

$$= \frac{1}{\cos u} + \frac{\sin u}{\cos u} \qquad \text{Separate into two fractions}$$

$$= \sec u + \tan u \qquad \text{Reciprocal identities} \qquad\blacksquare$$

Here is another method for proving that an equation is an identity. If we can transform each side of the equation separately, by way of identities, to arrive at the same result, then the equation is an identity. Example 6 illustrates this procedure.

EXAMPLE 6 ■ Proving an Identity by Working with Both Sides

Verify the identity $\dfrac{1 + \cos \theta}{\cos \theta} = \dfrac{\tan^2\theta}{\sec \theta - 1}$.

SOLUTION

We prove the identity by changing each side separately into the same expression. Supply the reasons for each step.

$$\text{LHS} = \frac{1 + \cos \theta}{\cos \theta} = \frac{1}{\cos \theta} + \frac{\cos \theta}{\cos \theta} = \sec \theta + 1$$

$$\text{RHS} = \frac{\tan^2\theta}{\sec \theta - 1} = \frac{\sec^2\theta - 1}{\sec \theta - 1} = \frac{(\sec \theta - 1)(\sec \theta + 1)}{\sec \theta - 1} = \sec \theta + 1$$

It follows that LHS = RHS, so the equation is an identity. $\blacksquare$

 Warning: To prove an identity, we do *not* just perform the same operations on both sides of the equation. For example, if we start with an equation that is not an identity, such as

(1) $$\sin x = -\sin x$$

and square both sides, we get the equation

(2) $$\sin^2 x = \sin^2 x$$

which is clearly an identity. Does this mean that the original equation is an identity? Of course not. The problem here is that the operation of squaring is not **reversible** in the sense that we cannot arrive back at (1) from (2) by taking square roots (reversing the procedure). Only operations that are reversible will necessarily transform an identity into an identity.

We end this section by describing the technique of *trigonometric substitution*, which we use to convert algebraic expressions to trigonometric ones. This is often useful in calculus, for instance, in finding the area of a circle or an ellipse.

EXAMPLE 7　■　Trigonometric Substitution

Substitute $\sin \theta$ for x in the expression $\sqrt{1 - x^2}$ and simplify. Assume that $0 \leqslant \theta \leqslant \pi/2$.

SOLUTION

Setting $x = \sin \theta$, we have

$$\sqrt{1 - x^2} = \sqrt{1 - \sin^2\theta} \qquad \text{Substitute } x = \sin \theta$$

$$= \sqrt{\cos^2\theta} \qquad \text{Pythagorean identity}$$

$$= \cos \theta \qquad \text{Take square root}$$

The last equality is true because $\cos \theta \geqslant 0$ for the values of θ in question.　■

4.1　EXERCISES

1–8 ■ Write the trigonometric expression in terms of sine and cosine, and then simplify.

1. $\sin t \cot t$

2. $\sin t \sec t$

3. $\tan x \csc x$

4. $\sin x \cos x \sec x$

5. $\tan^2 x - \sec^2 x$

6. $\dfrac{\sec x}{\csc x}$

7. $\sin u + \cot u \cos u$

8. $\cos^2\theta(1 + \tan^2\theta)$

9–22 ■ Simplify the trigonometric expression.

9. $\dfrac{\sin x \sec x}{\tan x}$

10. $\cos^3 x + \sin^2 x \cos x$

11. $\dfrac{1 + \cos y}{1 + \sec y}$

12. $\dfrac{\tan x}{\sec(-x)}$

13. $\dfrac{\sec^2 x - 1}{\sec^2 x}$

14. $\dfrac{\sec x - \cos x}{\tan x}$

15. $\dfrac{1 + \csc x}{\cos x + \cot x}$

16. $\dfrac{\sin x}{\csc x} + \dfrac{\cos x}{\sec x}$

17. $\dfrac{1 + \sin u}{\cos u} + \dfrac{\cos u}{1 + \sin u}$

18. $\tan x \cos x \csc x$

19. $\dfrac{2 + \tan^2 x}{\sec^2 x} - 1$

20. $\dfrac{1 + \cot A}{\csc A}$

21. $\tan \theta + \cos(-\theta) + \tan(-\theta)$

22. $\dfrac{\cos x}{\sec x + \tan x}$

23–84 ■ Verify the identity.

23. $\dfrac{\sin \theta}{\tan \theta} = \cos \theta$

24. $\dfrac{\tan x}{\sec x} = \sin x$

25. $\dfrac{\cos u \sec u}{\tan u} = \cot u$

26. $\dfrac{\cot x \sec x}{\csc x} = 1$

27. $\dfrac{\tan y}{\csc y} = \sec y - \cos y$

28. $\dfrac{\cos v}{\sec v \sin v} = \csc v - \sin v$

29. $\sin B + \cos B \cot B = \csc B$

30. $\cos(-x) - \sin(-x) = \cos x + \sin x$

31. $\cot(-\alpha) \cos(-\alpha) + \sin(-\alpha) = -\csc \alpha$

32. $\csc x \left[\csc x + \sin(-x)\right] = \cot^2 x$

33. $\tan \theta + \cot \theta = \sec \theta \csc \theta$

34. $(\sin x + \cos x)^2 = 1 + 2 \sin x \cos x$

35. $(1 - \cos \beta)(1 + \cos \beta) = \dfrac{1}{\csc^2 \beta}$

36. $\dfrac{\cos x}{\sec x} + \dfrac{\sin x}{\csc x} = 1$

37. $\dfrac{(\sin x + \cos x)^2}{\sin^2 x - \cos^2 x} = \dfrac{\sin^2 x - \cos^2 x}{(\sin x - \cos x)^2}$

38. $(\sin x + \cos x)^4 = (1 + 2 \sin x \cos x)^2$

39. $\dfrac{\sec t - \cos t}{\sec t} = \sin^2 t$

40. $\dfrac{1 - \sin x}{1 + \sin x} = (\sec x - \tan x)^2$

41. $\dfrac{1}{1 - \sin^2 y} = 1 + \tan^2 y$

42. $\csc x - \sin x = \cos x \cot x$

43. $(\cot x - \csc x)(\cos x + 1) = -\sin x$

44. $\sin^4 \theta - \cos^4 \theta = \sin^2 \theta - \cos^2 \theta$

45. $(1 - \cos^2 x)(1 + \cot^2 x) = 1$

46. $\cos^2 x - \sin^2 x = 2 \cos^2 x - 1$

47. $2 \cos^2 x - 1 = 1 - 2 \sin^2 x$

48. $(\tan y + \cot y) \sin y \cos y = 1$

49. $\dfrac{1 - \cos \alpha}{\sin \alpha} = \dfrac{\sin \alpha}{1 + \cos \alpha}$

50. $\sin^2 \alpha + \cos^2 \alpha + \tan^2 \alpha = \sec^2 \alpha$

51. $\dfrac{\sin x - 1}{\sin x + 1} = \dfrac{-\cos^2 x}{(\sin x + 1)^2}$

52. $\dfrac{\sin w}{\sin w + \cos w} = \dfrac{\tan w}{1 + \tan w}$

53. $\dfrac{(\sin t + \cos t)^2}{\sin t \cos t} = 2 + \sec t \csc t$

54. $\sec t \csc t (\tan t + \cot t) = \sec^2 t + \csc^2 t$

55. $\dfrac{1 + \tan^2 u}{1 - \tan^2 u} = \dfrac{1}{\cos^2 u - \sin^2 u}$

56. $\dfrac{1 + \sec^2 x}{1 + \tan^2 x} = 1 + \cos^2 x$

57. $\dfrac{\sec x}{\sec x - \tan x} = \sec x (\sec x + \tan x)$

58. $\dfrac{\sec x + \csc x}{\tan x + \cot x} = \sin x + \cos x$

59. $\sec v - \tan v = \dfrac{1}{\sec v + \tan v}$

60. $\dfrac{\sin A}{1 - \cos A} - \cot A = \csc A$

61. $\dfrac{\sin x + \cos x}{\sec x + \csc x} = \sin x \cos x$

62. $\dfrac{1 - \cos x}{\sin x} + \dfrac{\sin x}{1 - \cos x} = 2 \csc x$

63. $\dfrac{\csc x - \cot x}{\sec x - 1} = \cot x$

64. $\dfrac{\csc^2 x - \cot^2 x}{\sec^2 x} = \cos^2 x$

65. $\tan^2 u - \sin^2 u = \tan^2 u \sin^2 u$

66. $\dfrac{\tan v \sin v}{\tan v + \sin v} = \dfrac{\tan v - \sin v}{\tan v \sin v}$

67. $\sec^4 x - \tan^4 x = \sec^2 x + \tan^2 x$

68. $\dfrac{\cos \theta}{1 - \sin \theta} = \sec \theta + \tan \theta$

69. $\dfrac{\cos \theta}{1 - \sin \theta} = \dfrac{\sin \theta - \csc \theta}{\cos \theta - \cot \theta}$

70. $\dfrac{1 + \tan x}{1 - \tan x} = \dfrac{\cos x + \sin x}{\cos x - \sin x}$

71. $\dfrac{\cos^2 t + \tan^2 t - 1}{\sin^2 t} = \tan^2 t$

72. $\dfrac{1}{1 - \sin x} - \dfrac{1}{1 + \sin x} = 2 \sec x \tan x$

73. $\dfrac{1}{\sec x + \tan x} + \dfrac{1}{\sec x - \tan x} = 2 \sec x$

74. $\dfrac{1 + \sin x}{1 - \sin x} - \dfrac{1 - \sin x}{1 + \sin x} = 4 \tan x \sec x$

75. $(\tan x + \cot x)^2 = \sec^2 x + \csc^2 x$

76. $\tan^2 x - \cot^2 x = \sec^2 x - \csc^2 x$

77. $\dfrac{\sec u - 1}{\sec u + 1} = \dfrac{1 - \cos u}{1 + \cos u}$ **78.** $\dfrac{\cot x + 1}{\cot x - 1} = \dfrac{1 + \tan x}{1 - \tan x}$

79. $\dfrac{\sin^3 x + \cos^3 x}{\sin x + \cos x} = 1 - \sin x \cos x$

80. $\dfrac{\tan v - \cot v}{\tan^2 v - \cot^2 v} = \sin v \cos v$

81. $\dfrac{1 + \sin x}{1 - \sin x} = (\tan x + \sec x)^2$

82. $\dfrac{\tan x + \tan y}{\cot x + \cot y} = \tan x \tan y$

83. $(\tan x + \cot x)^4 = \csc^4 x \sec^4 x$

84. $(\sin \alpha - \tan \alpha)(\cos \alpha - \cot \alpha) = (\cos \alpha - 1)(\sin \alpha - 1)$

85–90 ■ Make the indicated trigonometric substitution in the given algebraic expression and simplify (see Example 7). Assume $0 \leqslant \theta < \pi/2$.

85. $\dfrac{x}{\sqrt{1 - x^2}}, \quad x = \sin \theta$

86. $\sqrt{1 + x^2}, \quad x = \tan \theta$

87. $\sqrt{x^2 - 1}, \quad x = \sec \theta$

88. $\dfrac{1}{x^2 \sqrt{4 + x^2}}, \quad x = 2 \tan \theta$

89. $\sqrt{9 - x^2}, \quad x = 3 \sin \theta$

90. $\dfrac{\sqrt{x^2 - 25}}{x}, \quad x = 5 \sec \theta$

 91–94 ■ Graph f and g in the same viewing rectangle. Do the graphs suggest that the equation $f(x) = g(x)$ is an identity? Prove your answer.

91. $f(x) = \cos^2 x - \sin^2 x, \quad g(x) = 1 - 2 \sin^2 x$

92. $f(x) = \tan x \,(1 + \sin x), \quad g(x) = \dfrac{\sin x \cos x}{1 + \sin x}$

93. $f(x) = (\sin x + \cos x)^2, \quad g(x) = 1$

94. $f(x) = \cos^4 x - \sin^4 x, \quad g(x) = 2 \cos^2 x - 1$

95. Show that the equation is not an identity.

(a) $\sin 2x = 2 \sin x$

(b) $\sin(x + y) = \sin x + \sin y$

(c) $\sec^2 x + \csc^2 x = 1$

(d) $\dfrac{1}{\sin x + \cos x} = \csc x + \sec x$

● DISCOVERY · DISCUSSION

96. Cofunction Identities   In the right triangle shown, explain why

$$v = \dfrac{\pi}{2} - u$$

Explain how you can obtain all six cofunction identities from this triangle, for $0 < u < \pi/2$.

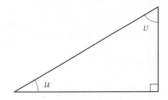

97. Graphs and Identities   Suppose you graph two functions, f and g, on a graphing device, and their graphs appear identical in the viewing rectangle. Does this prove that the equation $f(x) = g(x)$ is an identity? Explain.

98. Making Up Your Own Identity   If you start with a trigonometric expression and rewrite it or simplify it, then setting the original expression equal to the rewritten expression yields a trigonometric identity. For instance, from Example 1, we get the identity

$$\cos t + \tan t \sin t = \sec t$$

Use this technique to make up your own identity, then give it to a classmate to verify.

4.2   ADDITION AND SUBTRACTION FORMULAS

We now derive identities for trigonometric functions of sums and differences.

ADDITION AND SUBTRACTION FORMULAS

Formulas for sine

$$\sin(s + t) = \sin s \cos t + \cos s \sin t$$

$$\sin(s - t) = \sin s \cos t - \cos s \sin t$$

Formulas for cosine

$$\cos(s + t) = \cos s \cos t - \sin s \sin t$$

$$\cos(s - t) = \cos s \cos t + \sin s \sin t$$

Formulas for tangent

$$\tan(s + t) = \frac{\tan s + \tan t}{1 - \tan s \tan t}$$

$$\tan(s - t) = \frac{\tan s - \tan t}{1 + \tan s \tan t}$$

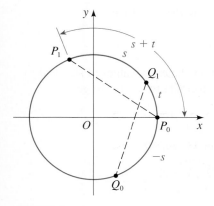

FIGURE 1

■ **Proof of Addition Formula for Cosine**   To prove the formula $\cos(s + t) = \cos s \cos t - \sin s \sin t$, we use Figure 1. In the figure, the distances t, $s + t$, and $-s$ have been marked on the unit circle, starting at $P_0(1, 0)$ and terminating at Q_1, P_1, and Q_0, respectively. The coordinates of these points are

$$P_0(1, 0) \qquad\qquad Q_0(\cos(-s), \sin(-s))$$
$$P_1(\cos(s + t), \sin(s + t)) \qquad Q_1(\cos t, \sin t)$$

Since $\cos(-s) = \cos s$ and $\sin(-s) = -\sin s$, it follows that the point Q_0 has the coordinates $Q_0(\cos s, -\sin s)$. Notice that the distances between P_0 and P_1 and between Q_0 and Q_1 measured along the arc of the circle are equal. Since equal arcs are subtended by equal chords, it follows that $d(P_0, P_1) = d(Q_0, Q_1)$. Using the Distance Formula, we get

$$\sqrt{[\cos(s + t) - 1]^2 + [\sin(s + t) - 0]^2} = \sqrt{(\cos t - \cos s)^2 + (\sin t + \sin s)^2}$$

Squaring both sides and expanding, we have

these add to 1

$$\cos^2(s + t) - 2\cos(s + t) + 1 + \sin^2(s + t)$$
$$= \cos^2 t - 2\cos s \cos t + \cos^2 s + \sin^2 t + 2\sin s \sin t + \sin^2 s$$

these add to 1   these add to 1

Using the Pythagorean identity $\sin^2 z + \cos^2 z = 1$ three times gives

$$2 - 2\cos(s + t) = 2 - 2\cos s \cos t + 2 \sin s \sin t$$

Finally, subtracting 2 from each side and dividing both sides by -2, we get

$$\cos(s + t) = \cos s \cos t - \sin s \sin t$$

which proves the addition formula for cosine.

■ **Proof of Subtraction Formula for Cosine** Replacing t with $-t$ in the addition formula for cosine, we get

$$\cos(s - t) = \cos(s + (-t))$$

$$= \cos s \cos(-t) - \sin s \sin(-t) \qquad \text{Addition formula for cosine}$$

$$= \cos s \cos t + \sin s \sin t \qquad \text{Even-odd identities}$$

This proves the subtraction formula for cosine.   □

See Exercises 52 and 53 for proofs of the other addition formulas.

EXAMPLE 1 ■ Using the Addition and Subtraction Formulas

Find the exact value of each expression: (a) $\cos 75°$ (b) $\cos \dfrac{\pi}{12}$

SOLUTION

(a) Notice that $75° = 45° + 30°$. Since we know the exact values of sine and cosine at $45°$ and $30°$, we use the addition formula for cosine to get

$$\cos 75° = \cos(45° + 30°)$$

$$= \cos 45° \cos 30° - \sin 45° \sin 30°$$

$$= \frac{\sqrt{2}}{2} \frac{\sqrt{3}}{2} - \frac{\sqrt{2}}{2} \frac{1}{2} = \frac{\sqrt{2}\sqrt{3} - \sqrt{2}}{4} = \frac{\sqrt{6} - \sqrt{2}}{4}$$

(b) Since $\dfrac{\pi}{12} = \dfrac{\pi}{4} - \dfrac{\pi}{6}$, the subtraction formula for cosine gives

$$\cos \frac{\pi}{12} = \cos\left(\frac{\pi}{4} - \frac{\pi}{6}\right)$$

$$= \cos \frac{\pi}{4} \cos \frac{\pi}{6} + \sin \frac{\pi}{4} \sin \frac{\pi}{6}$$

$$= \frac{\sqrt{2}}{2} \frac{\sqrt{3}}{2} + \frac{\sqrt{2}}{2} \frac{1}{2} = \frac{\sqrt{6} + \sqrt{2}}{4}$$

■

message they must know p and q, the factors of N. When the RSA code was developed, it was thought that a carefully selected 80-digit number would provide an unbreakable code. But interestingly, recent advances in the study of factoring have made much larger numbers necessary.

EXAMPLE 2 ■ Using the Addition Formula for Sine

Find the exact value of the expression: $\sin 20° \cos 40° + \cos 20° \sin 40°$

SOLUTION

We recognize the expression as the right-hand side of the addition formula for sine with $s = 20°$ and $t = 40°$. So we have

$$\sin 20° \cos 40° + \cos 20° \sin 40° = \sin(20° + 40°) = \sin 60° = \frac{\sqrt{3}}{2} \quad \blacksquare$$

EXAMPLE 3 ■ Proving an Identity

Prove the cofunction identity: $\cos\left(\dfrac{\pi}{2} - u\right) = \sin u$

SOLUTION

By the subtraction formula for cosine,

$$\cos\left(\frac{\pi}{2} - u\right) = \cos \frac{\pi}{2} \cos u + \sin \frac{\pi}{2} \sin u$$

$$= 0 \cdot \cos u + 1 \cdot \sin u = \sin u \quad \blacksquare$$

EXAMPLE 4 ■ Proving an Identity

Verify the identity: $\dfrac{1 + \tan x}{1 - \tan x} = \tan\left(\dfrac{\pi}{4} + x\right)$

SOLUTION

Starting with the right-hand side and using the addition formula for tangent, we get

$$\text{RHS} = \tan\left(\frac{\pi}{4} + x\right) = \frac{\tan \dfrac{\pi}{4} + \tan x}{1 - \tan \dfrac{\pi}{4} \tan x}$$

$$= \frac{1 + \tan x}{1 - \tan x} = \text{LHS} \quad \blacksquare$$

The next example is a typical use of the addition and subtraction formulas in calculus.

EXAMPLE 5 ■ An Identity from Calculus

If $f(x) = \sin x$, show that

$$\frac{f(x + h) - f(x)}{h} = \sin x \left(\frac{\cos h - 1}{h}\right) + \cos x \left(\frac{\sin h}{h}\right)$$

SOLUTION

$$\frac{f(x+h) - f(x)}{h} = \frac{\sin(x+h) - \sin x}{h} \qquad \text{Definition of } f$$

$$= \frac{\sin x \cos h + \cos x \sin h - \sin x}{h} \qquad \text{Addition formula for sine}$$

$$= \frac{\sin x \,(\cos h - 1) + \cos x \sin h}{h} \qquad \text{Factor}$$

$$= \sin x \left(\frac{\cos h - 1}{h}\right) + \cos x \left(\frac{\sin h}{h}\right) \qquad \text{Separate the fraction} \qquad ■$$

■ Expressions of the Form $A \sin x + B \cos x$

We can write expressions of the form $A \sin x + B \cos x$ in terms of a single trigonometric function using the addition formula for sine. For example, consider the expression

$$\frac{1}{2} \sin x + \frac{\sqrt{3}}{2} \cos x$$

If we set $\phi = \pi/3$, then $\cos \phi = \frac{1}{2}$ and $\sin \phi = \sqrt{3}/2$, and we can write

$$\frac{1}{2} \sin x + \frac{\sqrt{3}}{2} \cos x = \cos \phi \sin x + \sin \phi \cos x$$

$$= \sin(x + \phi) = \sin\left(x + \frac{\pi}{3}\right)$$

We are able to do this because the coefficients $\frac{1}{2}$ and $\sqrt{3}/2$ are precisely the cosine and sine of a particular number, in this case, $\pi/3$. We can use this same idea in general to write $A \sin x + B \cos x$ in the form $k \sin(x + \phi)$. We start by multiplying the numerator and denominator by $\sqrt{A^2 + B^2}$ to get

$$A \sin x + B \cos x = \sqrt{A^2 + B^2}\left(\frac{A}{\sqrt{A^2 + B^2}} \sin x + \frac{B}{\sqrt{A^2 + B^2}} \cos x\right)$$

We need a number ϕ with the property that

$$\cos \phi = \frac{A}{\sqrt{A^2 + B^2}} \qquad \text{and} \qquad \sin \phi = \frac{B}{\sqrt{A^2 + B^2}}$$

Figure 2 shows that the point (A, B) in the plane determines a number ϕ with precisely this property. With this ϕ, we have

$$A \sin x + B \cos x = \sqrt{A^2 + B^2}\,(\cos \phi \sin x + \sin \phi \cos x)$$

$$= \sqrt{A^2 + B^2}\,\sin(x + \phi)$$

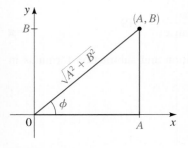

FIGURE 2

We have proved the following theorem.

SUMS OF SINES AND COSINES

If A and B are real numbers, then

$$A \sin x + B \cos x = k \sin(x + \phi)$$

where $k = \sqrt{A^2 + B^2}$ and ϕ satisfies

$$\cos \phi = \frac{A}{\sqrt{A^2 + B^2}} \quad \text{and} \quad \sin \phi = \frac{B}{\sqrt{A^2 + B^2}}$$

EXAMPLE 6 ■ A Sum of Sine and Cosine Terms

Express $3 \sin x + 4 \cos x$ in the form $k \sin(x + \phi)$.

SOLUTION

By the preceding theorem, $k = \sqrt{A^2 + B^2} = \sqrt{3^2 + 4^2} = 5$. The angle ϕ has the property that $\sin \phi = \frac{4}{5}$ and $\cos \phi = \frac{3}{5}$. Using a calculator, we find $\phi \approx 53.1°$. Thus

$$3 \sin x + 4 \cos x \approx 5 \sin(x + 53.1°) \qquad ■$$

EXAMPLE 7 ■ Graphing a Trigonometric Function

Write the function $f(x) = -\sin 2x + \sqrt{3} \cos 2x$ in the form $k \sin(2x + \phi)$ and use the new form to graph the function.

SOLUTION

Since $A = -1$ and $B = \sqrt{3}$, we have $k = \sqrt{A^2 + B^2} = \sqrt{1 + 3} = 2$. The angle ϕ satisfies $\cos \phi = -\frac{1}{2}$ and $\sin \phi = \sqrt{3}/2$. From the signs of these quantities we conclude that ϕ is in quadrant II. Thus, $\phi = 2\pi/3$. By the preceding theorem we can write

$$f(x) = -\sin 2x + \sqrt{3} \cos 2x = 2 \sin\left(2x + \frac{2\pi}{3}\right)$$

Using the form

$$f(x) = 2 \sin 2\left(x + \frac{\pi}{3}\right)$$

we see that the graph is a sine curve with amplitude 2, period $2\pi/2 = \pi$, and phase shift $-\pi/3$. The graph is shown in Figure 3. ■

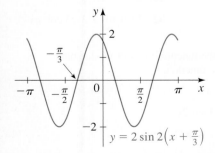

$y = 2 \sin 2\left(x + \frac{\pi}{3}\right)$

FIGURE 3

4.2 EXERCISES

1–10 ■ Use an addition or subtraction formula to find the exact value of the expression, as demonstrated in Example 1.

1. $\cos 15°$

2. $\sin 105°$

3. $\sin 165°$

4. $\tan 195°$

5. $\tan 75°$

6. $\cos \dfrac{11\pi}{12}$

7. $\sin \dfrac{19\pi}{12}$

8. $\tan \dfrac{17\pi}{12}$

9. $\cos\left(-\dfrac{\pi}{12}\right)$

10. $\sin\left(-\dfrac{5\pi}{12}\right)$

11–16 ■ Use an addition or subtraction formula to write the expression as a trigonometric function of one number, and find its exact value.

11. $\sin 18° \cos 27° + \cos 18° \sin 27°$

12. $\cos 10° \cos 80° - \sin 10° \sin 80°$

13. $\cos \dfrac{3\pi}{7} \cos \dfrac{2\pi}{21} + \sin \dfrac{3\pi}{7} \sin \dfrac{2\pi}{21}$

14. $\dfrac{\tan \dfrac{\pi}{18} + \tan \dfrac{\pi}{9}}{1 - \tan \dfrac{\pi}{18} \tan \dfrac{\pi}{9}}$

15. $\dfrac{\tan 73° - \tan 13°}{1 + \tan 73° \tan 13°}$

16. $\cos \dfrac{13\pi}{15} \cos\left(-\dfrac{\pi}{5}\right) - \sin \dfrac{13\pi}{15} \sin\left(-\dfrac{\pi}{5}\right)$

17–20 ■ Prove the cofunction identity using the addition and subtraction formulas.

17. $\tan\left(\dfrac{\pi}{2} - u\right) = \cot u$

18. $\cot\left(\dfrac{\pi}{2} - u\right) = \tan u$

19. $\sec\left(\dfrac{\pi}{2} - u\right) = \csc u$

20. $\csc\left(\dfrac{\pi}{2} - u\right) = \sec u$

21–38 ■ Prove the identity.

21. $\sin\left(x - \dfrac{\pi}{2}\right) = -\cos x$

22. $\cos\left(x - \dfrac{\pi}{2}\right) = \sin x$

23. $\sin(x - \pi) = -\sin x$

24. $\cos(x - \pi) = -\cos x$

25. $\tan(x - \pi) = \tan x$

26. $\sin\left(\dfrac{\pi}{2} - x\right) = \sin\left(\dfrac{\pi}{2} + x\right)$

27. $\cos\left(x + \dfrac{\pi}{6}\right) + \sin\left(x - \dfrac{\pi}{3}\right) = 0$

28. $\tan\left(x - \dfrac{\pi}{4}\right) = \dfrac{\tan x - 1}{\tan x + 1}$

29. $\sin(x + y) - \sin(x - y) = 2 \cos x \sin y$

30. $\cos(x + y) + \cos(x - y) = 2 \cos x \cos y$

31. $\cot(x - y) = \dfrac{\cot x \cot y + 1}{\cot y - \cot x}$

32. $\cot(x + y) = \dfrac{\cot x \cot y - 1}{\cot x + \cot y}$

33. $\tan x - \tan y = \dfrac{\sin(x - y)}{\cos x \cos y}$

34. $1 - \tan x \tan y = \dfrac{\cos(x + y)}{\cos x \cos y}$

35. $\dfrac{\sin(x + y) - \sin(x - y)}{\cos(x + y) + \cos(x - y)} = \tan y$

36. $\cos(x + y) \cos(x - y) = \cos^2 x - \sin^2 y$

37. $\sin(x + y + z) = \sin x \cos y \cos z + \cos x \sin y \cos z + \cos x \cos y \sin z - \sin x \sin y \sin z$

38. $\tan(x - y) + \tan(y - z) + \tan(z - x) = \tan(x - y) \tan(y - z) \tan(z - x)$

39–42 ■ Write the expression in terms of sine only.

39. $-\sqrt{3} \sin x + \cos x$

40. $\sin x + \cos x$

41. $5(\sin 2x - \cos 2x)$

42. $3 \sin \pi x + 3 \sqrt{3} \cos \pi x$

43–44 ■ (a) Express the function in terms of sine only.
(b) Graph the function.

43. $f(x) = \sin x + \cos x$

44. $g(x) = \cos 2x + \sqrt{3} \sin 2x$

45. Show that if $\beta - \alpha = \pi/2$, then

$$\sin(x + \alpha) + \cos(x + \beta) = 0$$

46. Let $g(x) = \cos x$. Show that

$$\frac{g(x + h) - g(x)}{h} = -\cos x \left(\frac{1 - \cos h}{h}\right) - \sin x \left(\frac{\sin h}{h}\right)$$

47. Refer to the figure. Show that $\alpha + \beta = \gamma$, and find $\tan \gamma$.

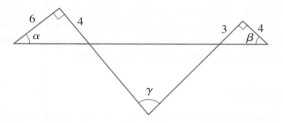

48. (a) If L is a line in the plane and θ is the angle formed by the line and the x-axis as shown in the figure, show that the slope m of the line is given by

$$m = \tan \theta$$

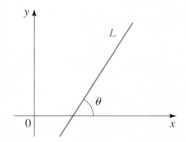

(b) Let L_1 and L_2 be two nonparallel lines in the plane with slopes m_1 and m_2, respectively. Let ψ be the acute angle formed by the two lines (see the figure). Show that

$$\tan \psi = \frac{m_2 - m_1}{1 + m_1 m_2}$$

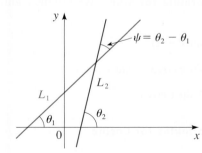

(c) Find the acute angle formed by the two lines

$$y = \tfrac{1}{3}x + 1 \qquad \text{and} \qquad y = -\tfrac{1}{2}x - 3$$

(d) Show that if two lines are perpendicular, then the slope of one is the negative reciprocal of the slope of the other. [*Hint:* First find an expression for $\cot \psi$.]

49–50 ■ (a) Graph the function and make a conjecture, then (b) prove that your conjecture is true.

49. $y = \sin^2\left(x + \dfrac{\pi}{4}\right) + \sin^2\left(x - \dfrac{\pi}{4}\right)$

50. $y = -\tfrac{1}{2}[\cos(x + \pi) + \cos(x - \pi)]$

51. A digital delay-device echoes an input signal by repeating it a fixed length of time after it is received. If such a device receives the pure note $f_1(t) = 5 \sin t$ and echoes the pure note $f_2(t) = 5 \cos t$, then the combined sound is $f(t) = f_1(t) + f_2(t)$.

(a) Graph $y = f(t)$ and observe that the graph has the form of a sine curve $y = k \sin(t + \phi)$.

(b) Find k and ϕ.

■ DISCOVERY · DISCUSSION

52. Addition Formula for Sine   In the text we proved only the addition and subtraction formulas for cosine. Use these formulas and the cofunction identities

$$\sin x = \cos\left(\frac{\pi}{2} - x\right)$$

$$\cos x = \sin\left(\frac{\pi}{2} - x\right)$$

to prove the addition formula for sine. [*Hint:* To get started, use the first cofunction identity to write

$$\sin(s + t) = \cos\left(\frac{\pi}{2} - (s + t)\right)$$

$$= \cos\left(\left(\frac{\pi}{2} - s\right) - t\right)$$

and use the subtraction formula for cosine.]

53. Addition Formula for Tangent   Use the addition formulas for cosine and sine to prove the addition formula for tangent. [*Hint:* Use

$$\tan(s + t) = \frac{\sin(s + t)}{\cos(s + t)}$$

and divide the numerator and denominator by $\cos s \cos t$.]

4.3 DOUBLE-ANGLE, HALF-ANGLE, AND PRODUCT-SUM FORMULAS

The identities we consider in this section are consequences of the addition formulas. The **double-angle formulas** allow us to find the values of the trigonometric functions at $2x$ from their values at x. The **half-angle formulas** relate the values of the trigonometric functions at $\frac{1}{2}x$ to their values at x. The **product-sum formulas** relate products of sines and cosines to sums of sines and cosines.

Double-Angle Formulas

The formulas in the following box are consequences of the addition formulas, which we proved in the preceding section.

DOUBLE-ANGLE FORMULAS

Formula for sine

$$\sin 2x = 2 \sin x \cos x$$

Formulas for cosine

$$\cos 2x = \cos^2 x - \sin^2 x$$
$$= 1 - 2 \sin^2 x$$
$$= 2 \cos^2 x - 1$$

Formula for tangent

$$\tan 2x = \frac{2 \tan x}{1 - \tan^2 x}$$

■ **Proof of Double-Angle Formula for Sine**   We use the addition formula for sine.

$$\sin 2x = \sin(x + x)$$
$$= \sin x \cos x + \sin x \cos x$$
$$= 2 \sin x \cos x$$

■ **Proof of Double-Angle Formulas for Cosine**

$$\cos 2x = \cos(x + x)$$
$$= \cos x \cos x - \sin x \sin x$$
$$= \cos^2 x - \sin^2 x$$

The second and third formulas for $\cos 2x$ are obtained from the formula we just proved and the Pythagorean identity. Substituting $\cos^2 x = 1 - \sin^2 x$ gives

$$\cos 2x = \cos^2 x - \sin^2 x$$
$$= (1 - \sin^2 x) - \sin^2 x$$
$$= 1 - 2\sin^2 x$$

The third formula is obtained in the same way, by substituting $\sin^2 x = 1 - \cos^2 x$.

■ **Proof of Double-Angle Formula for Tangent**   We use the addition formula for tangent.

$$\tan 2x = \tan(x + x)$$
$$= \frac{\tan x + \tan x}{1 - \tan x \tan x}$$
$$= \frac{2\tan x}{1 - \tan^2 x}$$

☐

EXAMPLE 1 ■ **Using the Double-Angle Formulas**

If $\cos x = -\frac{2}{3}$ and x is in quadrant II, find $\cos 2x$ and $\sin 2x$.

SOLUTION

Using one of the double-angle formulas for cosine, we get

$$\cos 2x = 2\cos^2 x - 1$$
$$= 2\left(-\frac{2}{3}\right)^2 - 1 = \frac{8}{9} - 1 = -\frac{1}{9}$$

To use the formula $\sin 2x = 2\sin x \cos x$, we need to find $\sin x$ first. We have

$$\sin x = \sqrt{1 - \cos^2 x} = \sqrt{1 - \left(-\frac{2}{3}\right)^2} = \frac{\sqrt{5}}{3}$$

where we have used the positive square root because $\sin x$ is positive in quadrant II. Thus

$$\sin 2x = 2\sin x \cos x$$
$$= 2\left(\frac{\sqrt{5}}{3}\right)\left(-\frac{2}{3}\right) = -\frac{4\sqrt{5}}{9}$$

■

EXAMPLE 2 ■ **A Triple-Angle Formula**

Write $\cos 3x$ in terms of $\cos x$.

SOLUTION

$$\cos 3x = \cos(2x + x)$$

$$= \cos 2x \cos x - \sin 2x \sin x \qquad \text{Addition formula}$$

$$= (2 \cos^2 x - 1) \cos x - (2 \sin x \cos x) \sin x \qquad \text{Double-angle formulas}$$

$$= 2 \cos^3 x - \cos x - 2 \sin^2 x \cos x \qquad \text{Expand}$$

$$= 2 \cos^3 x - \cos x - 2 \cos x \, (1 - \cos^2 x) \qquad \text{Pythagorean identity}$$

$$= 2 \cos^3 x - \cos x - 2 \cos x + 2 \cos^3 x \qquad \text{Expand}$$

$$= 4 \cos^3 x - 3 \cos x \qquad \text{Simplify} \qquad \blacksquare$$

Example 2 shows that $\cos 3x$ can be written as a polynomial of degree 3 in $\cos x$. The identity $\cos 2x = 2 \cos^2 x - 1$ shows that $\cos 2x$ is a polynomial of degree 2 in $\cos x$. In fact, for any natural number n, we can write $\cos nx$ as a polynomial in $\cos x$ of degree n (see Exercise 83). The analogous result for $\sin nx$ is not true in general.

EXAMPLE 3 ■ Proving an Identity

Prove the identity: $\dfrac{\sin 3x}{\sin x \cos x} = 4 \cos x - \sec x$

SOLUTION

We start with the left-hand side.

$$\frac{\sin 3x}{\sin x \cos x} = \frac{\sin(x + 2x)}{\sin x \cos x}$$

$$= \frac{\sin x \cos 2x + \cos x \sin 2x}{\sin x \cos x} \qquad \text{Addition formula}$$

$$= \frac{\sin x \, (2 \cos^2 x - 1) + \cos x \, (2 \sin x \cos x)}{\sin x \cos x} \qquad \text{Double-angle formulas}$$

$$= \frac{\sin x \, (2 \cos^2 x - 1)}{\sin x \cos x} + \frac{\cos x \, (2 \sin x \cos x)}{\sin x \cos x} \qquad \text{Separate fraction}$$

$$= \frac{2 \cos^2 x - 1}{\cos x} + 2 \cos x \qquad \text{Cancel}$$

$$= 2 \cos x - \frac{1}{\cos x} + 2 \cos x \qquad \text{Separate fraction}$$

$$= 4 \cos x - \sec x \qquad \text{Reciprocal identity} \qquad \blacksquare$$

■ Half-Angle Formulas

The following formulas allow us to write any trigonometric expression involving even powers of sine and cosine in terms of the first power of cosine only. This

Pierre de Fermat (1601–1665) was a French lawyer who became interested in mathematics at the age of 30. Because of his job as a magistrate, Fermat had little time to write complete proofs of his discoveries and often wrote them in the margin of whatever book he was reading at the time. After his death, his copy of Diophantus' *Arithmetica* (see page 530) was found to contain a particularly tantalizing comment. Where Diophantus discusses the solutions of $x^2 + y^2 = z^2$ (for example, $x = 3$, $y = 4$, $z = 5$), Fermat states in the margin that for $n \geq 3$ there are no natural number solutions to the equation $x^n + y^n = z^n$. In other words, it's impossible for a cube to equal the sum of two cubes, a fourth power to equal the sum of two fourth powers, and so on. Fermat writes "I have discovered a truly wonderful proof for this but the margin is too small to contain it." All the other margin comments in Fermat's copy of *Arithmetica* have been proved. This one, however, remained unproved, and it came to be known as "Fermat's Last Theorem."

In 1994, Andrew Wiles of Princeton University announced a proof of Fermat's Last Theorem, an astounding 350 years after it was conjectured. His proof is one of the most widely reported mathematical results in the popular press.

technique is important in calculus. The half-angle formulas are immediate consequences of these formulas.

FORMULAS FOR LOWERING POWERS

$$\sin^2 x = \frac{1 - \cos 2x}{2} \qquad \cos^2 x = \frac{1 + \cos 2x}{2}$$

$$\tan^2 x = \frac{1 - \cos 2x}{1 + \cos 2x}$$

■ **Proof**   The first formula is obtained by solving for $\sin^2 x$ in the double-angle formula $\cos 2x = 1 - 2\sin^2 x$. Similarly, the second formula is obtained by solving for $\cos^2 x$ in the double-angle formula $\cos 2x = 2\cos^2 x - 1$.

The last formula follows from the first two and the reciprocal identities as follows:

$$\tan^2 x = \frac{\sin^2 x}{\cos^2 x} = \frac{\dfrac{1 - \cos 2x}{2}}{\dfrac{1 + \cos 2x}{2}} = \frac{1 - \cos 2x}{1 + \cos 2x}$$

□

EXAMPLE 4 ■ **Lowering Powers in a Trigonometric Expression**

Express $\sin^2 x \cos^2 x$ in terms of the first power of cosine.

SOLUTION

We use the formulas for lowering powers repeatedly.

$$\sin^2 x \cos^2 x = \left(\frac{1 - \cos 2x}{2}\right)\left(\frac{1 + \cos 2x}{2}\right)$$

$$= \frac{1 - \cos^2 2x}{4} = \frac{1}{4} - \frac{1}{4}\cos^2 2x$$

$$= \frac{1}{4} - \frac{1}{4}\left(\frac{1 + \cos 4x}{2}\right) = \frac{1}{4} - \frac{1}{8} - \frac{\cos 4x}{8}$$

$$= \tfrac{1}{8} - \tfrac{1}{8}\cos 4x = \tfrac{1}{8}(1 - \cos 4x)$$

Another way to obtain this identity is to use the double-angle formula for sine in the form $\sin x \cos x = \frac{1}{2}\sin 2x$. Thus

$$\sin^2 x \cos^2 x = \frac{1}{4}\sin^2 2x = \frac{1}{4}\left(\frac{1 - \cos 4x}{2}\right) = \frac{1}{8}(1 - \cos 4x)$$

■

HALF-ANGLE FORMULAS

$$\sin \frac{u}{2} = \pm \sqrt{\frac{1 - \cos u}{2}} \qquad \cos \frac{u}{2} = \pm \sqrt{\frac{1 + \cos u}{2}}$$

$$\tan \frac{u}{2} = \frac{1 - \cos u}{\sin u} = \frac{\sin u}{1 + \cos u}$$

The choice of the $+$ or $-$ sign depends on the quadrant in which $u/2$ lies.

■ **Proof** We substitute $x = u/2$ in the formulas for lowering powers and take the square root of each side. This yields the first two half-angle formulas. In the case of the half-angle formula for tangent, we get

$$\tan \frac{u}{2} = \pm \sqrt{\frac{1 - \cos u}{1 + \cos u}}$$

$$= \pm \sqrt{\left(\frac{1 - \cos u}{1 + \cos u}\right)\left(\frac{1 - \cos u}{1 - \cos u}\right)} \qquad \text{Multiply numerator and denominator by } 1 - \cos u$$

$$= \pm \sqrt{\frac{(1 - \cos u)^2}{1 - \cos^2 u}} \qquad \text{Simplify}$$

$$= \pm \frac{|1 - \cos u|}{|\sin u|} \qquad \sqrt{A^2} = |A|$$

Now, $1 - \cos u$ is nonnegative for all values of u. It is also true that $\sin u$ and $\tan(u/2)$ always have the same sign. (Verify this.) It follows that

$$\tan \frac{u}{2} = \frac{1 - \cos u}{\sin u}$$

The other half-angle formula for tangent is derived from this by multiplying the numerator and denominator by $1 + \cos u$. ◻

EXAMPLE 5 ■ **Using a Half-Angle Formula**

Find the exact value of $\sin 22.5°$.

SOLUTION

Since $22.5°$ is half of $45°$, we use the half-angle formula for sine with $u = 45°$. We choose the $+$ sign because $22.5°$ is in the first quadrant.

$$\sin \frac{45°}{2} = \sqrt{\frac{1 - \cos 45°}{2}} \qquad \text{Half-angle formula}$$

$$= \sqrt{\frac{1 - \sqrt{2}/2}{2}} \qquad \cos 45° = \sqrt{2}/2$$

$$= \sqrt{\frac{2 - \sqrt{2}}{4}} \qquad \text{Common denominator}$$

$$= \tfrac{1}{2}\sqrt{2 - \sqrt{2}} \qquad \text{Simplify} \qquad ■$$

EXAMPLE 6 ■ Using a Half-Angle Formula

Find $\tan(u/2)$ if $\sin u = \frac{2}{5}$ and u is in quadrant II.

SOLUTION

To use the half-angle formulas for tangent, we first need to find $\cos u$. Since cosine is negative in quadrant II, we have

$$\cos u = -\sqrt{1 - \sin^2 u}$$

$$= -\sqrt{1 - \left(\tfrac{2}{5}\right)^2} = -\frac{\sqrt{21}}{5}$$

Thus
$$\tan \frac{u}{2} = \frac{1 - \cos u}{\sin u}$$

$$= \frac{1 + \sqrt{21}/5}{\frac{2}{5}} = \frac{5 + \sqrt{21}}{2} \qquad ■$$

Product-Sum Formulas

It is possible to write the product $\sin u \cos v$ as a sum of trigonometric functions. To see this, consider the addition and subtraction formulas for the sine function:

$$\sin(u + v) = \sin u \cos v + \cos u \sin v$$

$$\sin(u - v) = \sin u \cos v - \cos u \sin v$$

Adding the left- and right-hand sides of these formulas gives

$$\sin(u + v) + \sin(u - v) = 2 \sin u \cos v$$

Dividing by 2 yields the formula

$$\sin u \cos v = \tfrac{1}{2}\left[\sin(u + v) + \sin(u - v)\right]$$

The other three **product-to-sum formulas** follow from the addition formulas in a similar way.

PRODUCT-TO-SUM FORMULAS
$\sin u \cos v = \tfrac{1}{2}\left[\sin(u + v) + \sin(u - v)\right]$
$\cos u \sin v = \tfrac{1}{2}\left[\sin(u + v) - \sin(u - v)\right]$
$\cos u \cos v = \tfrac{1}{2}\left[\cos(u + v) + \cos(u - v)\right]$
$\sin u \sin v = \tfrac{1}{2}\left[\cos(u - v) - \cos(u + v)\right]$

EXAMPLE 7 ■ Expressing a Trigonometric Product as a Sum

Express $\sin 3x \sin 5x$ as a sum of trigonometric functions.

SOLUTION

Using the fourth product-to-sum formula with $u = 3x$ and $v = 5x$ and the fact that cosine is an even function, we get

$$\sin 3x \sin 5x = \tfrac{1}{2}\left[\cos(3x - 5x) - \cos(3x + 5x)\right]$$

$$= \tfrac{1}{2}\cos(-2x) - \tfrac{1}{2}\cos 8x$$

$$= \tfrac{1}{2}\cos 2x - \tfrac{1}{2}\cos 8x \qquad\blacksquare$$

The product-to-sum formulas can also be used as sum-to-product formulas. This is possible because the right-hand side of each product-to-sum formula is a sum and the left side is a product. For example, if we let

$$u = \frac{x + y}{2} \qquad \text{and} \qquad v = \frac{x - y}{2}$$

in the first product-to-sum formula, we get

$$\sin \frac{x + y}{2} \cos \frac{x - y}{2} = \tfrac{1}{2}[\sin x + \sin y]$$

so $$\sin x + \sin y = 2 \sin \frac{x + y}{2} \cos \frac{x - y}{2}$$

The remaining three of the following **sum-to-product formulas** are obtained in a similar manner.

SUM-TO-PRODUCT FORMULAS

$$\sin x + \sin y = 2 \sin \frac{x + y}{2} \cos \frac{x - y}{2}$$

$$\sin x - \sin y = 2 \cos \frac{x + y}{2} \sin \frac{x - y}{2}$$

$$\cos x + \cos y = 2 \cos \frac{x + y}{2} \cos \frac{x - y}{2}$$

$$\cos x - \cos y = -2 \sin \frac{x + y}{2} \sin \frac{x - y}{2}$$

EXAMPLE 8 ■ Expressing a Trigonometric Sum as a Product

Write $\sin 7x + \sin 3x$ as a product.

SOLUTION

The first sum-to-product formula gives

$$\sin 7x + \sin 3x = 2 \sin \frac{7x + 3x}{2} \cos \frac{7x - 3x}{2}$$

$$= 2 \sin 5x \cos 2x$$

EXAMPLE 9 ■ Proving an Identity

Verify the identity: $\dfrac{\sin 3x - \sin x}{\cos 3x + \cos x} = \tan x$

SOLUTION

We apply the second sum-to-product formula to the numerator and the third formula to the denominator.

$$\text{LHS} = \frac{\sin 3x - \sin x}{\cos 3x + \cos x} = \frac{2 \cos \dfrac{3x + x}{2} \sin \dfrac{3x - x}{2}}{2 \cos \dfrac{3x + x}{2} \cos \dfrac{3x - x}{2}} \qquad \text{Sum-to-product formulas}$$

$$= \frac{2 \cos 2x \sin x}{2 \cos 2x \cos x} \qquad \text{Simplify}$$

$$= \frac{\sin x}{\cos x} = \tan x = \text{RHS} \qquad \text{Cancel}$$

4.3 EXERCISES

1–8 ■ Find $\sin 2x$, $\cos 2x$, and $\tan 2x$ from the given information.

1. $\sin x = \frac{5}{13}$, x in quadrant I

2. $\tan x = -\frac{4}{3}$, x in quadrant II

3. $\cos x = \frac{4}{5}$, $\csc x < 0$ **4.** $\csc x = 4$, $\tan x < 0$

5. $\sin x = -\frac{3}{5}$, x in quadrant III

6. $\sec x = 2$, x in quadrant IV

7. $\tan x = -\frac{1}{3}$, $\cos x > 0$

8. $\cot x = \frac{2}{3}$, $\sin x > 0$

9–14 ■ Use the formulas for lowering powers to rewrite the expression in terms of the first power of cosine, as in Example 4.

9. $\sin^4 x$ **10.** $\cos^4 x$

11. $\cos^4 x \sin^4 x$ **12.** $\cos^4 x \sin^2 x$

13. $\cos^2 x \sin^4 x$ **14.** $\cos^6 x$

15–22 ■ Use an appropriate half-angle formula to find the exact value of the expression.

15. $\sin 15°$ **16.** $\tan 15°$

17. $\cos 22.5°$ **18.** $\sin 75°$

19. $\tan \dfrac{\pi}{8}$

20. $\cos \dfrac{3\pi}{8}$

21. $\sin \dfrac{\pi}{12}$

22. $\cos \dfrac{5\pi}{12}$

23–28 ■ Simplify the expression by using a double-angle formula or a half-angle formula.

23. (a) $2 \sin 18° \cos 18°$ (b) $2 \sin 3\theta \cos 3\theta$

24. (a) $\dfrac{2 \tan 7°}{1 - \tan^2 7°}$ (b) $\dfrac{2 \tan 7\theta}{1 - \tan^2 7\theta}$

25. (a) $\cos^2 34° - \sin^2 34°$ (b) $\cos^2 5\theta - \sin^2 5\theta$

26. (a) $\cos^2 \dfrac{\theta}{2} - \sin^2 \dfrac{\theta}{2}$ (b) $2 \sin \dfrac{\theta}{2} \cos \dfrac{\theta}{2}$

27. (a) $\dfrac{\sin 8°}{1 + \cos 8°}$ (b) $\dfrac{1 - \cos 4\theta}{\sin 4\theta}$

28. (a) $\sqrt{\dfrac{1 - \cos 30°}{2}}$ (b) $\sqrt{\dfrac{1 - \cos 8\theta}{2}}$

29–34 ■ Find $\sin \dfrac{x}{2}$, $\cos \dfrac{x}{2}$, and $\tan \dfrac{x}{2}$ from the given information.

29. $\sin x = \frac{3}{5}$, $0° < x < 90°$

30. $\cos x = -\frac{4}{5}$, $180° < x < 270°$

31. $\csc x = 3$, $90° < x < 180°$

32. $\tan x = 1$, $0° < x < 90°$

33. $\sec x = \frac{3}{2}$, $270° < x < 360°$

34. $\cot x = 5$, $180° < x < 270°$

35–40 ■ Write the product as a sum.

35. $\sin 2x \cos 3x$

36. $\sin x \sin 5x$

37. $\cos x \sin 4x$

38. $\cos 5x \cos 3x$

39. $3 \cos 4x \cos 7x$

40. $11 \sin \dfrac{x}{2} \cos \dfrac{x}{4}$

41–46 ■ Write the sum as a product.

41. $\sin 5x + \sin 3x$

42. $\sin x - \sin 4x$

43. $\cos 4x - \cos 6x$

44. $\cos 9x + \cos 2x$

45. $\sin 2x - \sin 7x$

46. $\sin 3x + \sin 4x$

47–52 ■ Find the value of the product or sum.

47. $2 \sin 52.5° \sin 97.5°$

48. $3 \cos 37.5° \cos 7.5°$

49. $\cos 37.5° \sin 7.5°$

50. $\sin 75° + \sin 15°$

51. $\cos 255° - \cos 195°$

52. $\cos \dfrac{\pi}{12} + \cos \dfrac{5\pi}{12}$

53–70 ■ Prove the identity.

53. $\cos^2 5x - \sin^2 5x = \cos 10x$

54. $\sin 8x = 2 \sin 4x \cos 4x$

55. $(\sin x + \cos x)^2 = 1 + \sin 2x$

56. $\dfrac{2 \tan x}{1 + \tan^2 x} = \sin 2x$ **57.** $\dfrac{\sin 4x}{\sin x} = 4 \cos x \cos 2x$

58. $\dfrac{1 + \sin 2x}{\sin 2x} = 1 + \frac{1}{2} \sec x \csc x$

59. $\dfrac{2(\tan x - \cot x)}{\tan^2 x - \cot^2 x} = \sin 2x$ **60.** $\cot 2x = \dfrac{1 - \tan^2 x}{2 \tan x}$

61. $\tan 3x = \dfrac{3 \tan x - \tan^3 x}{1 - 3 \tan^2 x}$

62. $4(\sin^6 x + \cos^6 x) = 4 - 3 \sin^2 2x$

63. $\cos^4 x - \sin^4 x = \cos 2x$ **64.** $\tan^2 \left(\dfrac{x}{2} + \dfrac{\pi}{4} \right) = \dfrac{1 + \sin x}{1 - \sin x}$

65. $\dfrac{\sin x + \sin 5x}{\cos x + \cos 5x} = \tan 3x$ **66.** $\dfrac{\sin 3x + \sin 7x}{\cos 3x - \cos 7x} = \cot 2x$

67. $\dfrac{\sin 10x}{\sin 9x + \sin x} = \dfrac{\cos 5x}{\cos 4x}$

68. $\dfrac{\sin x + \sin 3x + \sin 5x}{\cos x + \cos 3x + \cos 5x} = \tan 3x$

69. $\dfrac{\sin x + \sin y}{\cos x + \cos y} = \tan \left(\dfrac{x + y}{2} \right)$

70. $\tan y = \dfrac{\sin(x + y) - \sin(x - y)}{\cos(x + y) + \cos (x - y)}$

71. Show that $\sin 45° + \sin 15° = \sin 75°$.

72. Show that $\cos 87° + \cos 33° = \sin 63°$.

73. Prove the identity

$$\dfrac{\sin x + \sin 2x + \sin 3x + \sin 4x + \sin 5x}{\cos x + \cos 2x + \cos 3x + \cos 4x + \cos 5x} = \tan 3x$$

74. Use the identity

$$\sin 2x = 2 \sin x \cos x$$

n times to show that

$$\sin(2^n x) = 2^n \sin x \cos x \cos 2x \cos 4x \cdots \cos 2^{n-1} x$$

75. (a) Graph $f(x) = \dfrac{\sin 3x}{\sin x} - \dfrac{\cos 3x}{\cos x}$ and make a conjecture.

(b) Prove the conjecture you made in part (a).

76. (a) Graph $f(x) = \cos 2x + 2 \sin^2 x$ and make a conjecture.
   (b) Prove the conjecture you made in part (a).

77. Let $f(x) = \sin 6x + \sin 7x$.
   (a) Graph $y = f(x)$.
   (b) Verify that $f(x) = 2 \cos \frac{1}{2}x \sin \frac{13}{2}x$.
   (c) Graph $y = 2 \cos \frac{1}{2}x$ and $y = -2 \cos \frac{1}{2}x$, together with the graph in part (a), in the same viewing rectangle. How are these graphs related to the graph of f?

78. When two pure notes that are close in frequency are played together, their sounds interfere to produce *beats*; that is, the loudness (or amplitude) of the sound alternately increases and decreases. If the two notes are given by

$$f_1(t) = \cos 11t \qquad \text{and} \qquad f_2(t) = \cos 13t$$

the resulting sound is $f(t) = f_1(t) + f_2(t)$.
   (a) Graph the function $y = f(t)$.
   (b) Verify that $f(t) = 2 \cos t \cos 12t$.
   (c) Graph $y = 2 \cos t$ and $y = -2 \cos t$, together with the graph in part (a), in the same viewing rectangle. How do these graphs describe the variation in the loudness of the sound?

79–81 ■ In these exercises you are asked to use the trigonometric functions to model real-life situations.

79. A rectangular beam is to be cut from a cylindrical log of diameter 20 in.
   (a) Show that the cross-sectional area of the beam is modeled by the function

$$A(\theta) = 200 \sin 2\theta$$

   where θ is as shown in the figure.
   (b) Show that the maximum cross-sectional area of such a beam is 200 in². [*Hint*: Use the fact that $\sin u$ achieves its maximum value at $u = \pi/2$.]

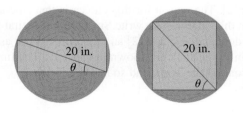

80. A rectangle is to be inscribed in a semicircle of radius 5 cm as shown in the figure.
   (a) Show that the area of the rectangle is modeled by the function

$$A(\theta) = 25 \sin 2\theta$$

   (b) Find the largest possible area for such an inscribed rectangle.
   (c) Find the dimensions of the inscribed rectangle with the largest possible area.

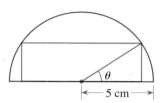

81. The lower right-hand corner of a long piece of paper 6 in. wide is folded over to the left-hand edge as shown. The length L of the fold depends on the angle θ. Show that

$$L = \frac{3}{\sin \theta \cos^2 \theta}$$

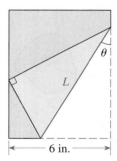

82. Let $3x = \pi/3$ and let $y = \cos x$. Use the result of Example 2 to show that y satisfies the equation

$$8y^3 - 6y - 1 = 0$$

   N O T E This equation has roots of a certain kind that are used to show that the angle $\pi/3$ cannot be trisected using a ruler and compass only.

83. (a) Show that there is a polynomial $P(t)$ of degree 4 such that $\cos 4x = P(\cos x)$ (see Example 2).
   (b) Show that there is a polynomial $Q(t)$ of degree 5 such that $\cos 5x = Q(\cos x)$.

   N O T E In general, there is a polynomial $P_n(t)$ of degree n such that $\cos nx = P_n(\cos x)$. These polynomials are called *Tchebycheff polynomials*, after the Russian mathematician P. L. Tchebycheff (1821–1894).

84. In triangle *ABC* (see the figure) the line segment *s* bisects angle *C*. Show that the length of *s* is given by

$$s = \frac{2ab \cos x}{a + b}$$

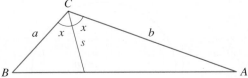

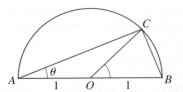

Hint: Find the area of triangle *ABC* in two different ways. You will need the following facts from geometry:

An angle inscribed in a semicircle is a right angle, so ∠*ACB* is a right angle.

 DISCOVERY · DISCUSSION

85. Geometric Proof of a Double-Angle Formula   Use the figure to prove that sin 2θ = 2 sin θ cos θ.

The central angle subtended by the chord of a circle is twice the angle subtended by the chord on the circle, so ∠*BOC* is 2θ.

4.4 INVERSE TRIGONOMETRIC FUNCTIONS

If *f* is a one-to-one function with domain *A* and range *B*, then its inverse *f*⁻¹ is the function with domain *B* and range *A* defined by

$$f^{-1}(x) = y \iff f(y) = x$$

(See Section 1.7.) In other words, *f*⁻¹ is the rule that reverses the action of *f*. Figure 1 represents the actions of *f* and *f*⁻¹ graphically.

For a function to have an inverse, it must be one-to-one. Since the trigonometric functions are not one-to-one, they do not have inverses. It is possible, however, to restrict the domains of the trigonometric functions in such a way that the resulting functions are one-to-one.

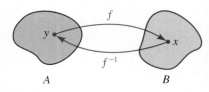

FIGURE 1
$f^{-1}(x) = y \Leftrightarrow f(y) = x$

The Inverse Sine Function

Let's first consider the sine function. There are many ways to restrict the domain of sine so that the new function is one-to-one. A natural way to do this is to restrict the domain to the interval $[-\pi/2, \pi/2]$. The reason for this choice is that sine attains each of its values exactly once on this interval. We write Sin *x* (with a capital S) for the new function, which has the domain $[-\pi/2, \pi/2]$ and the same values as sin *x* on this interval. The graphs of sin *x* and Sin *x* are shown in Figure 2. The function Sin *x* is one-to-one (by the Horizontal Line Test), and so has an inverse.

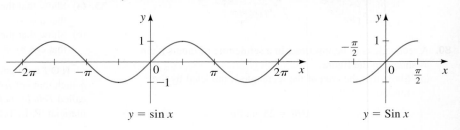

FIGURE 2 $y = \sin x$ $y = \text{Sin } x$

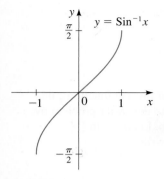

FIGURE 3

The inverse of the function Sin is the function Sin^{-1} defined by

$$\text{Sin}^{-1}x = y \iff \text{Sin } y = x$$

for $-1 \leqslant x \leqslant 1$ and $-\pi/2 \leqslant y \leqslant \pi/2$. The graph of $y = \text{Sin}^{-1}x$ is shown in Figure 3; it is obtained by reflecting the graph of $y = \text{Sin } x$ in the line $y = x$. It is customary to write $\text{Sin}^{-1}x$ simply as $\sin^{-1}x$.

DEFINITION OF THE INVERSE SINE FUNCTION

The **inverse sine function** is the function $\sin^{-1}$ with domain $[-1, 1]$ and range $[-\pi/2, \pi/2]$ defined by

$$\sin^{-1}x = y \iff \sin y = x$$

The inverse sine function is also called **arcsine** and is denoted by **arcsin**.

Thus, $\sin^{-1}x$ *is the number in the interval* $[-\pi/2, \pi/2]$ *whose sine is* x. In other words, $\sin(\sin^{-1}x) = x$. In fact, from the general properties of inverse functions studied in Section 1.7, we have the following relations.

$$\sin(\sin^{-1}x) = x \qquad \text{for } -1 \leqslant x \leqslant 1$$

$$\sin^{-1}(\sin x) = x \qquad \text{for } -\frac{\pi}{2} \leqslant x \leqslant \frac{\pi}{2}$$

EXAMPLE 1 ■ Evaluating the Inverse Sine Function

Find (a) $\sin^{-1}\frac{1}{2}$, (b) $\sin^{-1}\left(-\frac{1}{2}\right)$, and (c) $\sin^{-1}\frac{3}{2}$.

SOLUTION

(a) The number in the interval $[-\pi/2, \pi/2]$ whose sine is $\frac{1}{2}$ is $\pi/6$. Thus, $\sin^{-1}\frac{1}{2} = \pi/6$.

(b) The number in the interval $[-\pi/2, \pi/2]$ whose sine is $-\frac{1}{2}$ is $-\pi/6$. Thus, $\sin^{-1}\left(-\frac{1}{2}\right) = -\pi/6$.

(c) Since $\frac{3}{2} > 1$, it is not in the domain of $\sin^{-1}x$, so $\sin^{-1}\frac{3}{2}$ is not defined. ∎

EXAMPLE 2 ■ Using a Calculator to Evaluate Inverse Sine

Find approximate values for (a) $\sin^{-1}(0.82)$ and (b) $\sin^{-1}\frac{1}{3}$.

SOLUTION

Since no rational multiple of π has a sine of 0.82 or $\frac{1}{3}$, we use a calculator to approximate these values. Using the ⟨INV⟩ ⟨SIN⟩, or ⟨SIN⁻¹⟩, or ⟨ARCSIN⟩ key(s) on the calculator (with the calculator in radian mode), we get

(a) $\sin^{-1}(0.82) \approx 0.96141$ 　　　　　　(b) $\sin^{-1}\frac{1}{3} \approx 0.33984$ ∎

EXAMPLE 3 ■ **Composing Trigonometric Functions and Their Inverses**

Find $\cos\left(\sin^{-1}\frac{3}{5}\right)$.

SOLUTION 1

It's easy to find $\sin\left(\sin^{-1}\frac{3}{5}\right)$. In fact, by the properties of inverse functions, this value is exactly $\frac{3}{5}$. To find $\cos\left(\sin^{-1}\frac{3}{5}\right)$, we reduce this to the easier problem by writing the cosine function in terms of the sine function. Let $u = \sin^{-1}\frac{3}{5}$. Since $-\pi/2 \leq u \leq \pi/2$, $\cos u$ is positive and we can write

$$\cos u = +\sqrt{1 - \sin^2 u}$$

Thus

$$\cos\left(\sin^{-1}\tfrac{3}{5}\right) = \sqrt{1 - \sin^2\left(\sin^{-1}\tfrac{3}{5}\right)}$$

$$= \sqrt{1 - \left(\tfrac{3}{5}\right)^2} = \sqrt{1 - \tfrac{9}{25}} = \sqrt{\tfrac{16}{25}} = \tfrac{4}{5}$$

SOLUTION 2

Let $\theta = \sin^{-1}\frac{3}{5}$. Then θ is the number in the interval $[-\pi/2, \pi/2]$ whose sine is $\frac{3}{5}$. Let's interpret θ as an angle and draw a right triangle with θ as one of its acute angles, with opposite side 3 and hypotenuse 5 (see Figure 4). The remaining leg of the triangle is found by the Pythagorean Theorem to be 4. From the figure we get

$$\cos\left(\sin^{-1}\tfrac{3}{5}\right) = \cos\theta = \tfrac{4}{5}$$ ■

FIGURE 4

From Solution 2 of Example 3 we can immediately find the values of the other trigonometric functions of $\theta = \sin^{-1}\frac{3}{5}$ from the triangle. Thus

$$\tan\left(\sin^{-1}\tfrac{3}{5}\right) = \tfrac{3}{4} \qquad \sec\left(\sin^{-1}\tfrac{3}{5}\right) = \tfrac{5}{4} \qquad \csc\left(\sin^{-1}\tfrac{3}{5}\right) = \tfrac{5}{3}$$

■ The Inverse Cosine Function

If the domain of the cosine function is restricted to the interval $[0, \pi]$, the resulting function is one-to-one and so has an inverse. We choose this interval because on it, cosine attains each of its values exactly once (see Figure 5).

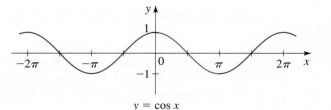

FIGURE 5 $y = \cos x$ $y = \cos x,\ 0 \leq x \leq \pi$

DEFINITION OF THE INVERSE COSINE FUNCTION

The **inverse cosine function** is the function $\cos^{-1}$ with domain $[-1, 1]$ and range $[0, \pi]$ defined by

$$\cos^{-1}x = y \iff \cos y = x$$

The inverse cosine function is also called **arccosine** and is denoted by **arccos**.

Thus, $y = \cos^{-1}x$ *is the number in the interval* $[0, \pi]$ *whose cosine is* x. The following relations follow from the inverse function properties.

$$
\begin{array}{ll}
\cos(\cos^{-1}x) = x & \text{for } -1 \leqslant x \leqslant 1 \\[1ex]
\cos^{-1}(\cos x) = x & \text{for } 0 \leqslant x \leqslant \pi
\end{array}
$$

The graph of $y = \cos^{-1}x$ is shown in Figure 6; it is obtained by reflecting the graph of $y = \cos x$, $0 \leqslant x \leqslant \pi$, in the line $y = x$.

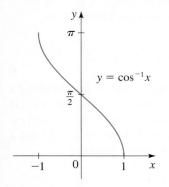

FIGURE 6

EXAMPLE 4 ■ Evaluating the Inverse Cosine Function

Find (a) $\cos^{-1}(\sqrt{3}/2)$, (b) $\cos^{-1}0$, and (c) $\cos^{-1}\frac{5}{7}$.

SOLUTION

(a) The number in the interval $[0, \pi]$ whose cosine is $\sqrt{3}/2$ is $\pi/6$. Thus, $\cos^{-1}(\sqrt{3}/2) = \pi/6$.

(b) The number in the interval $[0, \pi]$ whose cosine is 0 is $\pi/2$. Thus, $\cos^{-1}0 = \pi/2$.

(c) Since no rational multiple of π has cosine $\frac{5}{7}$, we use a calculator to find this value approximately: $\cos^{-1}\frac{5}{7} \approx 0.77519$. ■

EXAMPLE 5 ■ Composing Trigonometric Functions and Their Inverses

Write $\sin(\cos^{-1}x)$ and $\tan(\cos^{-1}x)$ as algebraic expressions in x for $-1 \leqslant x \leqslant 1$.

SOLUTION 1

Let $u = \cos^{-1}x$. We need to find $\sin u$ and $\tan u$ in terms of x. As in Example 3 the idea here is to write sine and tangent in terms of cosine. We have

$$\sin u = \pm\sqrt{1 - \cos^2 u} \qquad \text{and} \qquad \tan u = \frac{\sin u}{\cos u} = \frac{\pm\sqrt{1 - \cos^2 u}}{\cos u}$$

To choose the proper signs, note that u lies in the interval $[0, \pi]$ because $u = \cos^{-1}x$. Since $\sin u$ is positive on this interval, the $+$ sign is the correct choice. Substituting $u = \cos^{-1}x$ in the displayed equations and using the relation $\cos(\cos^{-1}x) = x$ gives

$$\sin(\cos^{-1}x) = \sqrt{1 - x^2} \qquad \text{and} \qquad \tan(\cos^{-1}x) = \frac{\sqrt{1 - x^2}}{x}$$

SOLUTION 2

Let $\theta = \cos^{-1}x$, so $\cos \theta = x$. In Figure 7 we draw a right triangle with an acute angle θ, adjacent side x, and hypotenuse 1. By the Pythagorean Theorem, the remaining leg is $\sqrt{1 - x^2}$. From the figure,

$$\sin(\cos^{-1}x) = \sin \theta = \sqrt{1 - x^2} \qquad \text{and} \qquad \tan(\cos^{-1}x) = \tan \theta = \frac{\sqrt{1 - x^2}}{x} \qquad \blacksquare$$

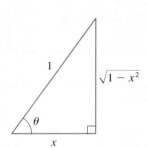

FIGURE 7

$$\cos \theta = \frac{x}{1} = x$$

NOTE In Solution 2 of Example 5 it may seem that because we are sketching a triangle, the angle $\theta = \cos^{-1}x$ must be acute. But it turns out that the triangle method works for any θ and for any x. The domains and ranges of all six inverse trigonometric functions have been chosen in such a way that we can always use a triangle to find $S(T^{-1}(x))$, where S and T are any trigonometric functions.

EXAMPLE 6 ■ Composing a Trigonometric Function and an Inverse

Write $\sin(2 \cos^{-1}x)$ as an algebraic expression in x for $-1 \leq x \leq 1$.

SOLUTION

Let $\theta = \cos^{-1}x$ and sketch a triangle as shown in Figure 8. We need to find $\sin 2\theta$, but from the triangle we can find trigonometric functions only of θ, not of 2θ. The double-angle identity for sine is useful here. We have

$$\sin(2 \cos^{-1}x) = \sin 2\theta$$

$$= 2 \sin \theta \cos \theta \qquad \text{Double-angle formula}$$

$$= 2 \sqrt{1 - x^2}\, x \qquad \text{From triangle}$$

$$= 2x \sqrt{1 - x^2} \qquad \blacksquare$$

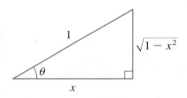

FIGURE 8

$$\cos \theta = \frac{x}{1} = x$$

■ The Inverse Tangent Function

We restrict the domain of the tangent function to the interval $(-\pi/2, \pi/2)$ in order to obtain a one-to-one function.

DEFINITION OF THE INVERSE TANGENT FUNCTION

The **inverse tangent function** is the function $\tan^{-1}$ with domain $\mathbb{R}$ and range $(-\pi/2, \pi/2)$ defined by

$$\tan^{-1}x = y \iff \tan y = x$$

The inverse tangent function is also called **arctangent** and is denoted by **arctan**.

Thus, $\tan^{-1}x$ *is the number in the interval* $(-\pi/2, \pi/2)$ *whose tangent is* x. The following relations follow from the inverse function properties.

$$\tan(\tan^{-1}x) = x \qquad \text{for } x \in \mathbb{R}$$

$$\tan^{-1}(\tan x) = x \qquad \text{for } -\frac{\pi}{2} < x < \frac{\pi}{2}$$

Figure 9 shows the graph of $y = \tan x$ on the interval $(-\pi/2, \pi/2)$ and the graph of its inverse function, $y = \tan^{-1}x$.

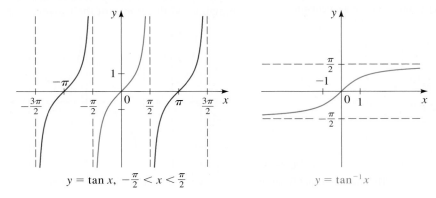

FIGURE 9

$y = \tan x, \ -\frac{\pi}{2} < x < \frac{\pi}{2}$ $y = \tan^{-1}x$

EXAMPLE 7 ■ Evaluating the Inverse Tangent Function

Find (a) $\tan^{-1}1$, (b) $\tan^{-1}\sqrt{3}$, and (c) $\tan^{-1}(-20)$.

SOLUTION

(a) The number in the interval $(-\pi/2, \pi/2)$ with tangent 1 is $\pi/4$. Thus, $\tan^{-1}1 = \pi/4$.

(b) The number in the interval $(-\pi/2, \pi/2)$ with tangent $\sqrt{3}$ is $\pi/3$. Thus, $\tan^{-1}\sqrt{3} = \pi/3$.

(c) We use a calculator to find that $\tan^{-1}(-20) \approx -1.52084$. ■

EXAMPLE 8 ■ The Angle of a Beam of Light

A lighthouse is located on an island that is 2 mi off a straight shoreline (see Figure 10). Express the angle formed by the beam of light and the shoreline in terms of the distance d in the figure.

SOLUTION

From the figure we see that $\tan \theta = 2/d$. Taking the inverse tangent of both sides, we get

$$\tan^{-1}(\tan \theta) = \tan^{-1}\left(\frac{2}{d}\right)$$

$$\theta = \tan^{-1}\left(\frac{2}{d}\right) \qquad \text{Cancellation property}$$

■

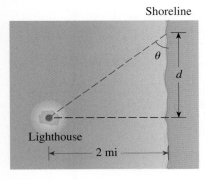

Shoreline

θ

d

Lighthouse

2 mi

FIGURE 10

The Inverse Secant, Cosecant, and Cotangent Functions

To define the inverse functions of the secant, cosecant, and cotangent functions, we restrict the domain of each function to a set on which it is one-to-one and on which it attains all its values. Although any interval satisfying these criteria is appropriate, we choose to restrict the domains in a way that simplifies the choice of sign in computations involving inverse trigonometric functions. The choices we make are also appropriate for calculus. This explains the seemingly strange restriction for the domains of the secant and cosecant functions. We end this section by displaying the graphs of the secant, cosecant, and cotangent functions with their restricted domains and the graphs of their inverse functions (Figures 11–13).

See Exercise 58 for a way of finding the values of these inverse trigonometric functions on a calculator.

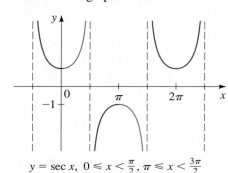

FIGURE 11
The inverse secant function

$y = \sec x, \ 0 \leq x < \frac{\pi}{2}, \ \pi \leq x < \frac{3\pi}{2}$

$y = \sec^{-1} x$

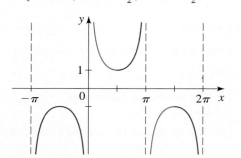

FIGURE 12
The inverse cosecant function

$y = \csc x, \ 0 < x \leq \frac{\pi}{2}, \ \pi < x \leq \frac{3\pi}{2}$

$y = \csc^{-1} x$

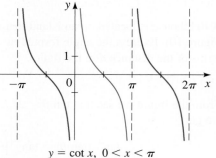
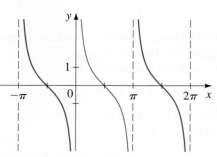
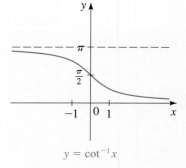

FIGURE 13
The inverse cotangent function

$y = \cot x, \ 0 < x < \pi$

$y = \cot^{-1} x$

4.4 EXERCISES

1–8 ■ Find the exact value of each expression, if it is defined.

1. (a) $\sin^{-1}\frac{1}{2}$ (b) $\cos^{-1}\frac{1}{2}$ (c) $\cos^{-1}2$

2. (a) $\sin^{-1}\frac{\sqrt{3}}{2}$ (b) $\cos^{-1}\frac{\sqrt{3}}{2}$ (c) $\cos^{-1}\left(-\frac{\sqrt{3}}{2}\right)$

3. (a) $\sin^{-1}\frac{\sqrt{2}}{2}$ (b) $\cos^{-1}\frac{\sqrt{2}}{2}$ (c) $\sin^{-1}\left(-\frac{\sqrt{2}}{2}\right)$

4. (a) $\tan^{-1}\sqrt{3}$ (b) $\tan^{-1}\left(-\sqrt{3}\right)$ (c) $\sin^{-1}\sqrt{3}$

5. (a) $\sin^{-1}1$ (b) $\cos^{-1}1$ (c) $\cos^{-1}(-1)$

6. (a) $\tan^{-1}1$ (b) $\tan^{-1}(-1)$ (c) $\tan^{-1}0$

7. (a) $\tan^{-1}\frac{\sqrt{3}}{3}$ (b) $\tan^{-1}\left(-\frac{\sqrt{3}}{3}\right)$ (c) $\sin^{-1}(-2)$

8. (a) $\sin^{-1}0$ (b) $\cos^{-1}0$ (c) $\cos^{-1}\left(-\frac{1}{2}\right)$

9–12 ■ Use a calculator to find an approximate value of each expression correct to five decimal places, if it is defined.

9. (a) $\sin^{-1}(0.13844)$ (b) $\cos^{-1}(-0.92761)$

10. (a) $\cos^{-1}(0.31187)$ (b) $\tan^{-1}(26.23110)$

11. (a) $\tan^{-1}(1.23456)$ (b) $\sin^{-1}(1.23456)$

12. (a) $\cos^{-1}(-0.25713)$ (b) $\tan^{-1}(-0.25713)$

13–28 ■ Find the exact value of the expression, if it is defined.

13. $\sin\left(\sin^{-1}\frac{1}{4}\right)$ **14.** $\cos\left(\cos^{-1}\frac{2}{3}\right)$

15. $\tan(\tan^{-1}5)$ **16.** $\sin(\sin^{-1}5)$

17. $\cos^{-1}\left(\cos\frac{\pi}{3}\right)$ **18.** $\tan^{-1}\left(\tan\frac{\pi}{6}\right)$

19. $\sin^{-1}\left[\sin\left(-\frac{\pi}{6}\right)\right]$ **20.** $\sin^{-1}\left(\sin\frac{5\pi}{6}\right)$

21. $\tan^{-1}\left(\tan\frac{2\pi}{3}\right)$ **22.** $\cos^{-1}\left[\cos\left(-\frac{\pi}{4}\right)\right]$

23. $\tan\left(\sin^{-1}\frac{1}{2}\right)$ **24.** $\sin(\sin^{-1}0)$

25. $\cos\left(\sin^{-1}\frac{\sqrt{3}}{2}\right)$ **26.** $\tan\left(\sin^{-1}\frac{\sqrt{2}}{2}\right)$

27. $\tan^{-1}\left(2\sin\frac{\pi}{3}\right)$ **28.** $\cos^{-1}\left(\sqrt{3}\sin\frac{\pi}{6}\right)$

29–40 ■ Evaluate the expression by sketching a triangle, as in Solution 2 of Example 3.

29. $\sin\left(\cos^{-1}\frac{3}{5}\right)$ **30.** $\tan\left(\sin^{-1}\frac{4}{5}\right)$

31. $\sin\left(\tan^{-1}\frac{12}{5}\right)$ **32.** $\cos(\tan^{-1}5)$

33. $\sec\left(\sin^{-1}\frac{12}{13}\right)$ **34.** $\csc\left(\cos^{-1}\frac{7}{25}\right)$

35. $\cos(\tan^{-1}2)$ **36.** $\cot\left(\sin^{-1}\frac{2}{3}\right)$

37. $\sin\left(2\cos^{-1}\frac{3}{5}\right)$ **38.** $\tan\left(2\tan^{-1}\frac{5}{13}\right)$

39. $\sin\left(\sin^{-1}\frac{1}{2}+\cos^{-1}\frac{1}{2}\right)$ **40.** $\cos\left(\sin^{-1}\frac{3}{5}-\cos^{-1}\frac{3}{5}\right)$

41–48 ■ Rewrite the expression as an algebraic expression in x.

41. $\cos(\sin^{-1}x)$ **42.** $\sin(\tan^{-1}x)$

43. $\tan(\sin^{-1}x)$ **44.** $\cos(\tan^{-1}x)$

45. $\cos(2\tan^{-1}x)$ **46.** $\sin(2\sin^{-1}x)$

47. $\cos(\cos^{-1}x+\sin^{-1}x)$ **48.** $\sin(\tan^{-1}x-\sin^{-1}x)$

49–52 ■ In these exercises you are asked to use the inverse trigonometric functions to model real-life situations.

49. An observer views the space shuttle from a distance of 2 miles from the launch pad.
(a) Express the height of the space shuttle as a function of the angle of elevation θ.
(b) Express the angle of elevation θ as a function of the height h of the space shuttle.

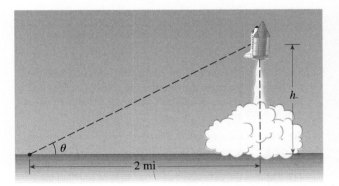

50. A 50-ft pole casts a shadow as shown in the figure.
(a) Express the angle of elevation θ of the sun as a function of the length s of the shadow.

(b) Find the angle θ of elevation of the sun when the shadow is 20 ft long.

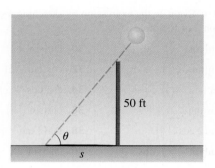

51. A 680-ft rope anchors a hot-air balloon as shown in the figure.

(a) Express the angle θ as a function of the height h of the balloon.

(b) Find the angle θ if the balloon is 500 ft high.

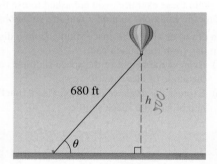

52. The figures indicate that the higher the orbit of a satellite, the more of the earth the satellite can "see." Let θ, s, and h be as in the figure, and assume the earth is a sphere of radius 3960 mi.

(a) Express the angle θ as a function of h.

(b) Express the distance s as a function of θ.

(c) Express the distance s as a function of h. [Find the composition of the functions in parts (a) and (b).]

(d) If the satellite is 100 mi above the earth, what is the distance s that it can see?

(e) How high does the satellite have to be in order to see both Los Angeles and New York, 2450 mi apart?

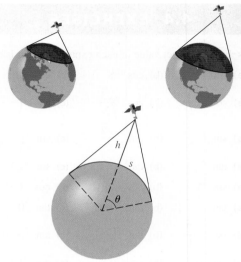

53–54 ■ (a) Graph the function and make a conjecture, and (b) prove that your conjecture is true.

53. $y = \sin^{-1}x + \cos^{-1}x$

54. $y = \tan^{-1}x + \tan^{-1}\dfrac{1}{x}$

55–56 ■ (a) Use a graphing device to find all solutions of the equation, correct to two decimal places, and (b) find the exact solution.

55. $\tan^{-1}x + \tan^{-1}2x = \dfrac{\pi}{4}$

56. $\sin^{-1}x - \cos^{-1}x = 0$

● DISCOVERY · DISCUSSION

57. Two Different Compositions The functions

$$f(x) = \sin(\sin^{-1}x) \quad \text{and} \quad g(x) = \sin^{-1}(\sin x)$$

both simplify to just x for suitable values of x. But these functions are not the same for all x. Graph both f and g to show how the functions differ. (Think carefully about the domain and range of $\sin^{-1}$.)

58. Inverse Trigonometric Functions on a Calculator Most calculators do not have keys for $\sec^{-1}$, $\csc^{-1}$, or $\cot^{-1}$. Prove the following identities, then use these identities and a calculator to find $\sec^{-1}2$, $\csc^{-1}3$, and $\cot^{-1}4$.

$$\sec^{-1}x = \cos^{-1}\left(\frac{1}{x}\right), \quad x \geqslant 1$$

$$\csc^{-1}x = \sin^{-1}\left(\frac{1}{x}\right), \quad x \geqslant 1$$

$$\cot^{-1}x = \tan^{-1}\left(\frac{1}{x}\right), \quad x > 0$$

Where to Sit at the Movies

Everyone knows that the apparent size of an object depends on its distance from the viewer. The farther away an object, the smaller its apparent size. The apparent size is determined by the angle the object subtends at the eye of the viewer.

If you are looking at a painting hanging on a wall, how far away should you stand to get the maximum view? If the painting is hung above eye level, then the following figures show that the angle subtended at the eye is small if you are too close or too far away. The same situation occurs when choosing where to sit in a movie theatre.

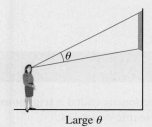
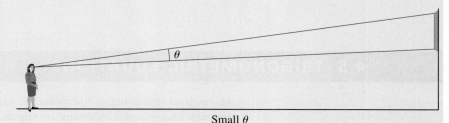

Small θ Large θ Small θ

1. The screen in a theatre is 22 ft high and is positioned 10 ft above the floor, which is flat. The first row of seats is 7 ft from the screen and the rows are 3 ft apart. You decide to sit in the row where you get the maximum view, that is, where the angle θ subtended by the screen at your eyes is a maximum. Suppose your eyes are 4 ft above the floor, as in the figure, and you sit at a distance x from the screen.

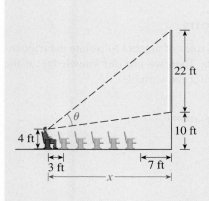

(a) Show that $\theta = \tan^{-1}\left(\dfrac{28}{x}\right) - \tan^{-1}\left(\dfrac{6}{x}\right)$.

(b) Use the subtraction formula for tangent to show that

$$\theta = \tan^{-1}\left(\frac{22x}{x^2 + 168}\right)$$

(c) Use a graphing device to graph θ as a function of x. What value of x maximizes θ? In which row should you sit? What is the viewing angle in this row?

2. Now suppose that, starting with the first row of seats, the floor of the seating area is inclined at an angle of $\alpha = 25°$ above the horizontal, and the distance that you sit up the incline is x, as shown in the figure on page 272.

(a) Use the Law of Cosines to show that

$$\theta = \cos^{-1}\left(\frac{a^2 + b^2 - 484}{2ab}\right)$$

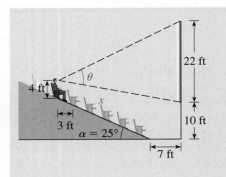

where

$$a^2 = (7 + x \cos \alpha)^2 + (28 - x \sin \alpha)^2$$

and

$$b^2 = (7 + x \cos \alpha)^2 + (x \sin \alpha - 6)^2$$

(b) Use a graphing device to graph θ as a function of x, and estimate the value of x that maximizes θ. In which row should you sit? What is the viewing angle θ in this row?

4.5   TRIGONOMETRIC EQUATIONS

An equation that contains trigonometric functions is called a **trigonometric equation**. For example, the following are trigonometric equations:

$$\sin^2 x + \cos^2 x = 1 \qquad 2 \sin x - 1 = 0 \qquad \tan^2 2x - 1 = 0$$

The first equation is an *identity*—that is, it is true for every value of the variable x. The other two equations are true only for certain values of x. To solve a trigonometric equation, we find all the values of the variable that make the equation true.

▮ Solving Trigonometric Equations

To solve a trigonometric equation, we use the rules of algebra to isolate the trigonometric function on one side of the equal sign. Then we use our knowledge of the values of the trigonometric functions to solve for the variable.

EXAMPLE 1 ■ Solving a Trigonometric Equation

Solve the equation $2 \sin x - 1 = 0$.

SOLUTION

We start by isolating $\sin x$.

$$2 \sin x - 1 = 0 \qquad \text{Given equation}$$

$$2 \sin x = 1 \qquad \text{Add 1}$$

$$\sin x = \frac{1}{2} \qquad \text{Divide by 2}$$

Because sine has period 2π, we first find the solutions in the interval $[0, 2\pi)$. These are $x = \pi/6$ and $x = 5\pi/6$. To get all other solutions, we add any integer multiple of 2π to these solutions. Thus, the solutions are

$$x = \frac{\pi}{6} + 2k\pi, \qquad x = \frac{5\pi}{6} + 2k\pi$$

where k is any integer. Figure 1 gives a graphical representation of the solutions.

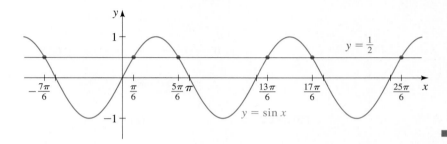

FIGURE 1

EXAMPLE 2 ■ Solving a Trigonometric Equation

Solve the equation $\tan^2 x - 3 = 0$.

SOLUTION

We start by isolating $\tan x$.

$$\tan^2 x - 3 = 0 \qquad \text{Given equation}$$

$$\tan^2 x = 3 \qquad \text{Add 3}$$

$$\tan x = \pm\sqrt{3} \qquad \text{Take square roots}$$

Because tangent has period π, we first find the solutions in the interval $(-\pi/2, \pi/2)$. These are $x = -\pi/3$ and $x = \pi/3$. To get all other solutions, we add any integer multiple of π to these solutions. Thus, the solutions are

$$x = -\frac{\pi}{3} + k\pi, \qquad x = \frac{\pi}{3} + k\pi$$

where k is any integer.   ■

EXAMPLE 3 ■ Finding Intersection Points

Find the values of x for which the graphs of $f(x) = \sin x$ and $g(x) = \cos x$ intersect.

SOLUTION 1: GRAPHICAL

The graphs intersect where $f(x) = g(x)$. In Figure 2 we graph $y_1 = \sin x$ and $y_2 = \cos x$ on the same screen, for x between 0 and 2π. Using $\boxed{\text{TRACE}}$ or the

Intersect command on the graphing calculator, we see that the two points of intersection in this interval occur where $x \approx 0.785$ and $x \approx 3.927$. Since sin and cos are periodic with period 2π, the intersection points occur where

$$x \approx 0.785 + 2k\pi \qquad \text{and} \qquad x \approx 3.927 + 2k\pi$$

where k is any integer.

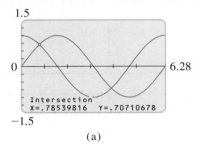

FIGURE 2   (a)   (b)

SOLUTION 2: ALGEBRAIC

To find the exact solution, we set $f(x) = g(x)$ and solve the resulting equation algebraically.

$$\sin x = \cos x \qquad \text{Equate functions}$$

Since the numbers x for which $\cos x = 0$ are not solutions of the equation, we can divide both sides by $\cos x$.

$$\frac{\sin x}{\cos x} = 1 \qquad \text{Divide by } \cos x$$

$$\tan x = 1 \qquad \text{Reciprocal identity}$$

Because tangent has period π, we first find the solutions in the interval $(-\pi/2, \pi/2)$. The only solution in this interval is $x = \pi/4$. To get all solutions, we add any integer multiple of π to this solution. Thus, the solutions are

$$x = \frac{\pi}{4} + k\pi$$

where k is any integer. The graphs intersect for these values of x. You should use your calculator to check that, correct to three decimals, these are the same values as we obtained in Solution 1.   ∎

■ Solving Trigonometric Equations by Factoring

Zero-Product Property

If $AB = 0$, then $A = 0$ or $B = 0$.

Factoring is one of the most useful techniques for solving equations, including trigonometric equations. The idea is to move all terms to one side of the equation, factor, then use the Zero-Product Property (Appendix A.4).

EXAMPLE 4 ■ **An Equation of Quadratic Type**

Solve the equation $2\cos^2 x - 7\cos x + 3 = 0$.

SOLUTION

We factor the left-hand side of the equation.

Equation of Quadratic Type

$2C^2 - 7C + 3 = 0$

$(2C - 1)(C - 3) = 0$

$2\cos^2 x - 7\cos x + 3 = 0$	Given equation
$(2\cos x - 1)(\cos x - 3) = 0$	Factor
$2\cos x - 1 = 0 \quad \text{or} \quad \cos x - 3 = 0$	Set each factor equal to 0
$\cos x = \tfrac{1}{2} \quad \text{or} \quad \cos x = 3$	Solve for $\cos x$

Because cosine has period 2π, we first find the solutions in the interval $[0, 2\pi)$. For the first equation these are $x = \pi/3$ and $x = 5\pi/3$. The second equation has no solutions because $\cos x$ is never greater than 1. Thus, the solutions are

$$x = \frac{\pi}{3} + 2k\pi, \qquad x = \frac{5\pi}{3} + 2k\pi$$

where k is any integer. ■

EXAMPLE 5 ■ **Using a Trigonometric Identity**

Solve the equation $1 + \sin x = 2\cos^2 x$.

SOLUTION

We use a trigonometric identity to rewrite the equation in terms of a single trigonometric function.

Equation of Quadratic Type

$2S^2 + S - 1 = 0$

$(2S - 1)(S + 1) = 0$

$1 + \sin x = 2\cos^2 x$	Given equation
$1 + \sin x = 2(1 - \sin^2 x)$	Pythagorean identity
$2\sin^2 x + \sin x - 1 = 0$	Put all terms on one side of the equation
$(2\sin x - 1)(\sin x + 1) = 0$	Factor
$2\sin x - 1 = 0 \quad \text{or} \quad \sin x + 1 = 0$	Set each factor equal to 0
$\sin x = \dfrac{1}{2} \quad \text{or} \quad \sin x = -1$	Solve for $\sin x$
$x = \dfrac{\pi}{6}, \dfrac{5\pi}{6} \quad \text{or} \quad x = \dfrac{3\pi}{2}$	Solve for x in the interval $[0, 2\pi)$

Because sine has period 2π, we get all the solutions of the equation by adding any integer multiple of 2π to these solutions. Thus, the solutions are

$$x = \frac{\pi}{6} + 2k\pi, \qquad x = \frac{5\pi}{6} + 2k\pi, \qquad x = \frac{3\pi}{2} + 2k\pi$$

where k is any integer.   ∎

EXAMPLE 6 ■ Using a Trigonometric Identity

Solve the equation $\sin 2x - \cos x = 0$.

SOLUTION

The first term is a function of $2x$ and the second is a function of x, so we begin by using a trigonometric identity to rewrite the first term as a function of x only.

$\sin 2x - \cos x = 0$	Given equation
$2 \sin x \cos x - \cos x = 0$	Double-angle formula
$\cos x\,(2 \sin x - 1) = 0$	Factor
$\cos x = 0 \qquad$ or $\qquad 2 \sin x - 1 = 0$	Set each factor equal to 0
$\sin x = \dfrac{1}{2}$	Solve for $\sin x$
$x = \dfrac{\pi}{2}, \dfrac{3\pi}{2} \qquad$ or $\qquad x = \dfrac{\pi}{6}, \dfrac{5\pi}{6}$	Solve for x in the interval $[0, 2\pi)$

Both sine and cosine have period 2π, so we get all the solutions of the equation by adding any integer multiple of 2π to these solutions. Thus, the solutions are

$$x = \frac{\pi}{2} + 2k\pi, \qquad x = \frac{3\pi}{2} + 2k\pi, \qquad x = \frac{\pi}{6} + 2k\pi, \qquad x = \frac{5\pi}{6} + 2k\pi$$

where k is any integer.   ∎

EXAMPLE 7 ■ Squaring and Using an Identify

Solve the equation $\cos x + 1 = \sin x$ in the interval $[0, 2\pi)$.

SOLUTION

To get an equation that involves either sine only or cosine only, we square both sides and use a Pythagorean identity.

$\cos x + 1 = \sin x$	Given equation
$\cos^2 x + 2 \cos x + 1 = \sin^2 x$	Square both sides
$\cos^2 x + 2 \cos x + 1 = 1 - \cos^2 x$	Pythagorean identity
$2 \cos^2 x + 2 \cos x = 0$	Simplify
$2 \cos x \, (\cos x + 1) = 0$	Factor

$$2 \cos x = 0 \quad \text{or} \quad \cos x + 1 = 0 \qquad \text{Set each factor equal to 0}$$

$$\cos x = 0 \quad \text{or} \quad \cos x = -1 \qquad \text{Solve for } \cos x$$

$$x = \frac{\pi}{2}, \frac{3\pi}{2} \quad \text{or} \quad x = \pi \qquad \begin{array}{l}\text{Solve for } x \text{ in the}\\ \text{interval } [0, 2\pi)\end{array}$$

Because we squared both sides, we need to check for extraneous solutions. From *Check Your Answers*, we see that the solutions of the given equation are $\pi/2$ and π.

CHECK YOUR ANSWERS

$x = \dfrac{\pi}{2}$:

$\cos \dfrac{\pi}{2} + 1 \overset{?}{=} \sin \dfrac{\pi}{2}$

$0 + 1 = 1$ ✓

$x = \dfrac{3\pi}{2}$:

$\cos \dfrac{3\pi}{2} + 1 \overset{?}{=} \sin \dfrac{3\pi}{2}$

$0 + 1 \overset{?}{=} -1$ ✗

$x = \pi$:

$\cos \pi + 1 \overset{?}{=} \sin \pi$

$-1 + 1 = 0$ ✓

■

   If we perform an operation on an equation that may introduce new roots, such as squaring both sides, then we must check that the solutions obtained are not extraneous; that is, we must verify that they satisfy the original equation, as in Example 7.

Equations with Trigonometric Functions of Multiple Angles

When solving trigonometric equations that involve functions of multiples of angles, we first solve for the multiple of the angle, then divide to solve for the angle.

EXAMPLE 8 ■ Trigonometric Functions of Multiple Angles

Consider the equation $2 \sin 3x - 1 = 0$.

(a) Find all solutions of the equation.
(b) Find the solutions in the interval $[0, 2\pi)$.

SOLUTION

(a) We start by isolating $\sin 3x$, and then solve for the multiple angle $3x$.

$$2 \sin 3x - 1 = 0 \qquad \text{Given equation}$$

$$2 \sin 3x = 1 \qquad \text{Add 1}$$

$$\sin 3x = \frac{1}{2} \qquad \text{Divide by 2}$$

$$3x = \frac{\pi}{6}, \frac{5\pi}{6} \qquad \text{Solve for } 3x \text{ in the interval } [0, 2\pi)$$

To get all solutions, we add any integer multiple of 2π to these solutions. Thus, the solutions are of the form

$$3x = \frac{\pi}{6} + 2k\pi, \qquad 3x = \frac{5\pi}{6} + 2k\pi$$

To solve for x, we divide by 3 to get the solutions

$$x = \frac{\pi}{18} + \frac{2k\pi}{3}, \qquad x = \frac{5\pi}{18} + \frac{2k\pi}{3}$$

where k is any integer.

(b) The solutions from part (a) that are in the interval $[0, 2\pi)$ correspond to $k = 0$, 1, and 2. For all other values of k, the corresponding values of x lie outside this interval. Thus, the solutions in the interval $[0, 2\pi)$ are

$$x = \frac{\pi}{18}, \frac{5\pi}{18}, \frac{13\pi}{18}, \frac{17\pi}{18}, \frac{25\pi}{18}, \frac{29\pi}{18} \qquad \blacksquare$$

EXAMPLE 9 ■ Trigonometric Functions of Multiple Angles

Consider the equation $\sqrt{3} \tan \dfrac{x}{2} - 1 = 0$.

(a) Find all solutions of the equation.

(b) Find the solutions in the interval $[0, 4\pi)$.

SOLUTION

(a) We start by isolating $\tan(x/2)$.

$$\sqrt{3} \tan \frac{x}{2} - 1 = 0 \qquad \text{Given equation}$$

$$\sqrt{3} \tan \frac{x}{2} = 1 \qquad \text{Add 1}$$

$$\tan \frac{x}{2} = \frac{1}{\sqrt{3}} \qquad \text{Divide by } \sqrt{3}$$

$$\frac{x}{2} = \frac{\pi}{3} \qquad \text{Solve for } \frac{x}{2} \text{ in the interval } \left(-\frac{\pi}{2}, \frac{\pi}{2}\right)$$

Since tan has period π, to get all solutions we add any integer multiple of π to these solutions. Thus, the solutions are of the form

$$\frac{x}{2} = \frac{\pi}{3} + k\pi$$

Multiplying by 2, we get the solutions

$$x = \frac{2\pi}{3} + 2k\pi$$

where k is any integer.

(b) The solutions from part (a) that are in the interval $[0, 4\pi)$ correspond to $k = 0$ and $k = 1$. For all other values of k, the corresponding values of x lie outside this interval. Thus, the solutions in the interval $[0, 4\pi)$ are

$$x = \frac{2\pi}{3}, \frac{8\pi}{3}$$

◼

◼ Using Inverse Trigonometric Functions to Solve Trigonometric Equations

So far, all the equations we've solved have had solutions like $\pi/4$, $\pi/3$, $5\pi/6$, and so on. We were able to find these solutions from the special values of the trigonometric functions that we've memorized. We now consider equations whose solution requires us to use the inverse trigonometric functions.

EXAMPLE 10 ◼ **Using Inverse Trigonometric Functions**

Solve the equation $\tan^2 x - \tan x - 2 = 0$.

SOLUTION

We start by factoring the left-hand side.

Equation of Quadratic Type

$T^2 - T - 2 = 0$

$(T - 2)(T + 1) = 0$

$\tan^2 x - \tan x - 2 = 0$	Given equation
$(\tan x - 2)(\tan x + 1) = 0$	Factor
$\tan x - 2 = 0 \quad\text{or}\quad \tan x + 1 = 0$	Set each factor equal to 0
$\tan x = 2 \qquad\text{or}\qquad \tan x = -1$	Solve for $\tan x$
$x = \tan^{-1} 2 \text{ or} \qquad x = -\dfrac{\pi}{4}$	Solve for x in the interval $(-\pi/2, \pi/2)$

Because tangent has period π, we get all solutions by adding integer multiples of π to these solutions. Thus, all the solutions are

$$x = \tan^{-1} 2 + k\pi, \qquad x = -\frac{\pi}{4} + k\pi$$

where k is any integer.   ∎

If we are using inverse trigonometric functions to solve an equation, we must keep in mind that $\sin^{-1}$ and $\tan^{-1}$ give values in quadrants I and IV, and $\cos^{-1}$ gives values in quadrants I and II. To find other solutions, we must look at the quadrant where the trigonometric function in the equation can take on the value we need.

EXAMPLE 11 ■ Using Inverse Trigonometric Functions

(a) Solve the equation $3 \sin \theta - 2 = 0$.

(b) Use a calculator to approximate the solutions in the interval $[0, 2\pi)$, correct to 5 decimals.

SOLUTION

(a) We start by isolating $\sin \theta$.

$$3 \sin \theta - 2 = 0 \qquad \text{Given equation}$$

$$3 \sin \theta = 2 \qquad \text{Add 2}$$

$$\sin \theta = \frac{2}{3} \qquad \text{Divide by 3}$$

From Figure 3 we see that $\sin \theta$ equals $\frac{2}{3}$ in quadrants I and II. The solution in quadrant I is $\theta = \sin^{-1} \frac{2}{3}$. The solution in quadrant II is $\theta = \pi - \sin^{-1} \frac{2}{3}$. Since these are the solutions in the interval $[0, 2\pi)$, we get all other solutions by adding integer multiples of 2π to these. Thus, all the solutions of the equation are

$$\theta = \left(\sin^{-1} \tfrac{2}{3}\right) + 2k\pi, \qquad \theta = \left(\pi - \sin^{-1} \tfrac{2}{3}\right) + 2k\pi$$

where k is any integer.

(b) Using a calculator set in radian mode, we see that $\sin^{-1} \frac{2}{3} \approx 0.72973$ and $\pi - \sin^{-1} \frac{2}{3} \approx 2.41186$, so the solutions in the interval $[0, 2\pi)$ are

$$\theta \approx 0.72973, \qquad \theta \approx 2.41186 \qquad ∎$$

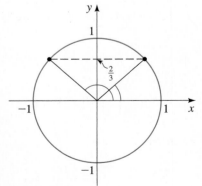

FIGURE 3

4.5 EXERCISES

1–38 ■ Find all solutions of the equation.

1. $\sin x - 1 = 0$

2. $\cos x + 1 = 0$

3. $2 \cos x - 1 = 0$

4. $\sqrt{2} \sin x - 1 = 0$

5. $2 \sin x + \sqrt{3} = 0$

6. $\tan x + 1 = 0$

7. $4 \cos^2 x - 1 = 0$

8. $2 \cos^2 x - 1 = 0$

9. $\sec^2 x - 2 = 0$

10. $\csc^2 x - 4 = 0$

11. $\cos x\,(2 \sin x + 1) = 0$

12. $\sec x\,(2 \cos x - \sqrt{2}) = 0$

13. $(\tan x + \sqrt{3})(\cos x + 2) = 0$

14. $(2 \cos x + \sqrt{3})(2 \sin x - 1) = 0$

15. $\cos x \sin x - 2 \cos x = 0$

16. $\tan x \sin x + \sin x = 0$

17. $4 \cos^2 x - 4 \cos x + 1 = 0$

18. $2 \sin^2 x - \sin x - 1 = 0$

19. $\sin^2 x = 2 \sin x + 3$

20. $3 \tan^3 x = \tan x$

21. $\sin^2 x = 4 - 2 \cos^2 x$

22. $2 \cos^2 x + \sin x = 1$

23. $2 \sin 3x + 1 = 0$

24. $2 \cos 2x + 1 = 0$

25. $\sec 4x - 2 = 0$

26. $\sqrt{3} \tan 3x + 1 = 0$

27. $\sqrt{3} \sin 2x = \cos 2x$

28. $\cos 3x = \sin 3x$

29. $\cos \dfrac{x}{2} - 1 = 0$

30. $2 \sin \dfrac{x}{3} + \sqrt{3} = 0$

31. $\tan \dfrac{x}{4} + \sqrt{3} = 0$

32. $\sec \dfrac{x}{2} = \cos \dfrac{x}{2}$

33. $\tan^5 x - 9 \tan x = 0$

34. $3 \tan^3 x - 3 \tan^2 x - \tan x + 1 = 0$

35. $4 \sin x \cos x + 2 \sin x - 2 \cos x - 1 = 0$

36. $\sin 2x = 2 \tan 2x$

37. $\cos^2 2x - \sin^2 2x = 0$

38. $\sec x - \tan x = \cos x$

39–46 ■ Find all solutions of the equation in the interval $[0, 2\pi)$.

39. $2 \cos 3x = 1$

40. $3 \csc^2 x = 4$

41. $2 \sin x \tan x - \tan x = 1 - 2 \sin x$

42. $\sec x \tan x - \cos x \cot x = \sin x$

43. $\tan x - 3 \cot x = 0$

44. $2 \sin^2 x - \cos x = 1$

45. $\tan 3x + 1 = \sec 3x$

46. $3 \sec^2 x + 4 \cos^2 x = 7$

47–54 ■ (a) Find all solutions of the equation. (b) Use a calculator to solve the equation in the interval $[0, 2\pi)$, correct to five decimal places.

47. $\cos x = 0.4$

48. $2 \tan x = 13$

49. $\sec x - 5 = 0$

50. $3 \sin x = 7 \cos x$

51. $5 \sin^2 x - 1 = 0$

52. $2 \sin 2x - \cos x = 0$

53. $3 \sin^2 x - 7 \sin x + 2 = 0$

54. $\tan^4 x - 13 \tan^2 x + 36 = 0$

55–58 ■ Graph f and g on the same axes, and find their points of intersection.

55. $f(x) = 3 \cos x + 1$, $g(x) = \cos x - 1$

56. $f(x) = \sin 2x$, $g(x) = 2 \sin 2x + 1$

57. $f(x) = \tan x$, $g(x) = \sqrt{3}$

58. $f(x) = \sin x - 1$, $g(x) = \cos x$

59. If a projectile is fired with velocity v_0 at an angle θ, then its *range*, the horizontal distance it travels (in feet), is modeled by the function

$$R(\theta) = \frac{v_0^2 \sin 2\theta}{32}$$

(See page 428.) If $v_0 = 2200$ ft/s, what angle should be chosen in order for the projectile to hit a target on the ground 5000 ft away?

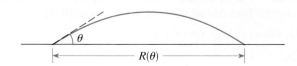

60. In Philadelphia the number of hours of daylight on day t (where t is the number of days after January 1) is modeled by the function

$$L(t) = 12 + 2.83 \sin\left(\frac{2\pi}{365}(t - 80)\right)$$

(a) Which days of the year have about 10 hours of daylight?

(b) How many days of the year have more than 10 hours of daylight?

61. It has been observed since ancient times that light refracts or "bends" as it travels from one medium to another (from air to water, for example). If v_1 is the speed of light in one medium and v_2 its speed in another medium, then according to **Snell's Law**,

$$\frac{\sin \theta_1}{\sin \theta_2} = \frac{v_1}{v_2}$$

where θ_1 is the *angle of incidence* and θ_2 is the *angle of refraction* (see the figure). The number v_1/v_2 is called the *index of refraction*. The index of refraction from air to water is 1.33. If a ray of light passes through the surface of a lake at an angle of incidence of 70°, find the angle of refraction.

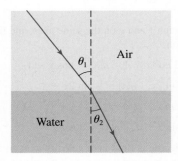

62. The displacement of a spring vibrating in damped harmonic motion is given by

$$y = 4e^{3t} \sin 2\pi t$$

Find the times when the spring is at its equilibrium position ($y = 0$).

63–66 ■ Use an addition or subtraction formula to simplify the equation. Then find all solutions in the interval $[0, 2\pi)$.

63. $\cos x \cos 3x - \sin x \sin 3x = 0$

64. $\cos x \cos 2x + \sin x \sin 2x = \frac{1}{2}$

65. $\sin 2x \cos x + \cos 2x \sin x = \sqrt{3}/2$

66. $\sin 3x \cos x - \cos 3x \sin x = 0$

67–70 ■ Use a double- or half-angle formula to solve the equation in the interval $[0, 2\pi)$.

67. $\sin 2x + \cos x = 0$

68. $\tan \frac{x}{2} - \sin x = 0$

69. $\cos 2x + \cos x = 2$

70. $\tan x + \cot x = 4 \sin 2x$

71–74 ■ Solve the equation by first using a sum-to-product formula.

71. $\sin x + \sin 3x = 0$

72. $\cos 5x - \cos 7x = 0$

73. $\cos 4x + \cos 2x = \cos x$

74. $\sin 5x - \sin 3x = \cos 4x$

75–80 ■ Use a graphing device to find the solutions of the equation, correct to two decimal places.

75. $\sin 2x = x$

76. $\cos x = \dfrac{x}{3}$

77. $2^{\sin x} = x$

78. $\sin x = x^3$

79. $\dfrac{\cos x}{1 + x^2} = x^2$

80. $\cos x = \frac{1}{2}(e^x + e^{-x})$

 DISCOVERY · DISCUSSION

81. Equations and Identities   Which of the following statements is true?

    A. Every identity is an equation.

    B. Every equation is an identity.

Give examples to illustrate your answer. Write a short paragraph to explain the difference between an equation and an identity.

82. A Special Trigonometric Equation   What makes the equation $\sin(\cos x) = 0$ different from all the other equations we've looked at in this section? Find all solutions of this equation.

4 REVIEW

CONCEPT CHECK

1. (a) State the reciprocal identities.
   (b) State the Pythagorean identities.
   (c) State the even-odd identities.
   (d) State the cofunction identities.

2. Explain the difference between an equation and an identity.

3. How do you prove a trigonometric identity?

4. (a) State the addition formulas for sine, cosine, and tangent.
   (b) State the subtraction formulas for sine, cosine, and tangent.

5. (a) State the double-angle formulas for sine, cosine, and tangent.
   (b) State the formulas for lowering powers.
   (c) State the half-angle formulas.

6. (a) State the product-to-sum formulas.
   (b) State the sum-to-product formulas.

7. (a) Define the inverse sine function $\sin^{-1}$. What are its domain and range?
   (b) For what values of x is the equation $\sin(\sin^{-1}x) = x$ true?
   (c) For what values of x is the equation $\sin^{-1}(\sin x) = x$ true?

8. (a) Define the inverse cosine function $\cos^{-1}$. What are its domain and range?
   (b) For what values of x is the equation $\cos(\cos^{-1}x) = x$ true?
   (c) For what values of x is the equation $\cos^{-1}(\cos x) = x$ true?

9. (a) Define the inverse tangent function $\tan^{-1}$. What are its domain and range?
   (b) For what values of x is the equation $\tan(\tan^{-1}x) = x$ true?
   (c) For what values of x is the equation $\tan^{-1}(\tan x) = x$ true?

EXERCISES

1–24 ■ Verify the identity.

1. $\sin\theta(\cot\theta + \tan\theta) = \sec\theta$

2. $(\sec\theta - 1)(\sec\theta + 1) = \tan^2\theta$

3. $\cos^2x \csc x - \csc x = -\sin x$

4. $\dfrac{1}{1 - \sin^2x} = 1 + \tan^2x$

5. $\dfrac{\cos^2x - \tan^2x}{\sin^2x} = \cot^2x - \sec^2x$

6. $\dfrac{1 + \sec x}{\sec x} = \dfrac{\sin^2x}{1 - \cos x}$ **7.** $\dfrac{\cos^2x}{1 - \sin x} = \dfrac{\cos x}{\sec x - \tan x}$

8. $(1 - \tan x)(1 - \cot x) = 2 - \sec x \csc x$

9. $\sin^2x \cot^2x + \cos^2x \tan^2x = 1$

10. $(\tan x + \cot x)^2 = \csc^2x \sec^2x$

11. $\dfrac{\sin 2x}{1 + \cos 2x} = \tan x$

12. $\dfrac{\cos(x + y)}{\cos x \sin y} = \cot y - \tan x$ **13.** $\tan\dfrac{x}{2} = \csc x - \cot x$

14. $\dfrac{\sin(x + y) + \sin(x - y)}{\cos(x + y) + \cos(x - y)} = \tan x$

15. $\sin(x + y)\sin(x - y) = \sin^2x - \sin^2y$

16. $\csc x - \tan\dfrac{x}{2} = \cot x$ **17.** $1 + \tan x \tan\dfrac{x}{2} = \sec x$

18. $\dfrac{\sin 3x + \cos 3x}{\cos x - \sin x} = 1 + 2\sin 2x$

19. $\left(\cos\dfrac{x}{2} - \sin\dfrac{x}{2}\right)^2 = 1 - \sin x$

20. $\dfrac{\cos 3x - \cos 7x}{\sin 3x + \sin 7x} = \tan 2x$ **21.** $\dfrac{\sin 2x}{\sin x} - \dfrac{\cos 2x}{\cos x} = \sec x$

22. $(\cos x + \cos y)^2 + (\sin x - \sin y)^2 = 2 + 2\cos(x + y)$

23. $\tan\left(x + \dfrac{\pi}{4}\right) = \dfrac{1 + \tan x}{1 - \tan x}$ **24.** $\dfrac{\sec x - 1}{\sin x \sec x} = \tan\dfrac{x}{2}$

25–28 ■ (a) Graph f and g. (b) Do the graphs suggest that the equation $f(x) = g(x)$ is an identity? Prove your answer.

25. $f(x) = 1 - \left(\cos\dfrac{x}{2} - \sin\dfrac{x}{2}\right)^2$, $g(x) = \sin x$

26. $f(x) = \sin x + \cos x$, $g(x) = \sqrt{\sin^2 x + \cos^2 x}$

27. $f(x) = \tan x \tan\dfrac{x}{2}$, $g(x) = \dfrac{1}{\cos x}$

28. $f(x) = 1 - 8\sin^2 x + 8\sin^4 x$, $g(x) = \cos 4x$

 29–30 ■ (a) Graph the function(s) and make a conjecture, and (b) prove your conjecture.

29. $f(x) = 2\sin^2 3x + \cos 6x$

30. $f(x) = \sin x \cot\dfrac{x}{2}$, $g(x) = \cos x$

31–46 ■ Solve the equation in the interval $[0, 2\pi)$.

31. $\cos x \sin x - \sin x = 0$ **32.** $\sin x - 2\sin^2 x = 0$

33. $2\sin^2 x - 5\sin x + 2 = 0$

34. $\sin x - \cos x - \tan x = -1$

35. $2\cos^2 x - 7\cos x + 3 = 0$ **36.** $4\sin^2 x + 2\cos^2 x = 3$

37. $\dfrac{1 - \cos x}{1 + \cos x} = 3$ **38.** $\sin x = \cos 2x$

39. $\tan^3 x + \tan^2 x - 3\tan x - 3 = 0$

40. $\cos 2x \csc^2 x = 2\cos 2x$ **41.** $\tan\frac{1}{2}x + 2\sin 2x = \csc x$

42. $\cos 3x + \cos 2x + \cos x = 0$

43. $\tan x + \sec x = \sqrt{3}$ **44.** $2\cos x - 3\tan x = 0$

 45. $\cos x = x^2 - 1$ **46.** $e^{\sin x} = x$

47. If a projectile is fired with velocity v_0 at an angle θ, then the maximum height it reaches (in feet) is modeled by the function

$$M(\theta) = \dfrac{v_0^2 \sin^2\theta}{64}$$

Suppose $v_0 = 400$ ft/s.
(a) At what angle θ should the projectile be fired so that the maximum height it reaches is 2000 ft?
(b) Is it possible for the projectile to reach a height of 3000 ft?
(c) Find the angle θ for which the projectile will travel highest.

48. The displacement of an automobile shock absorber is modeled by the function

$$f(t) = 2^{-0.2t}\sin 4\pi t$$

Find the times when the shock absorber is at its equilibrium position (that is, when $f(t) = 0$). [*Hint:* $2^x > 0$ for all real x.]

49–58 ■ Find the exact value of the expression.

49. $\cos 15°$

50. $\sin\dfrac{5\pi}{12}$

51. $\tan\dfrac{\pi}{8}$

52. $2\sin\dfrac{\pi}{12}\cos\dfrac{\pi}{12}$

53. $\sin 5° \cos 40° + \cos 5° \sin 40°$

54. $\dfrac{\tan 66° - \tan 6°}{1 + \tan 66° \tan 6°}$

55. $\cos^2\dfrac{\pi}{8} - \sin^2\dfrac{\pi}{8}$ **56.** $\dfrac{1}{2}\cos\dfrac{\pi}{12} + \dfrac{\sqrt{3}}{2}\sin\dfrac{\pi}{12}$

57. $\cos 37.5° \cos 7.5°$ **58.** $\cos 67.5° + \cos 22.5°$

59–64 ■ Find the exact value of the expression given that $\sec x = \frac{3}{2}$, $\csc y = 3$, and x and y are in quadrant I.

59. $\sin(x + y)$ **60.** $\cos(x - y)$

61. $\tan(x + y)$ **62.** $\sin 2x$

63. $\cos\dfrac{y}{2}$ **64.** $\tan\dfrac{y}{2}$

65–72 ■ Find the exact value of the expression.

65. $\sin^{-1}(\sqrt{3}/2)$ **66.** $\tan^{-1}(\sqrt{3}/3)$

67. $\cos(\tan^{-1}\sqrt{3})$ **68.** $\sin(\cos^{-1}(\sqrt{3}/2))$

69. $\tan(\sin^{-1}\frac{2}{5})$ **70.** $\sin(\cos^{-1}\frac{3}{8})$

71. $\cos(2\sin^{-1}\frac{1}{3})$ **72.** $\cos(\sin^{-1}\frac{5}{13} - \cos^{-1}\frac{4}{5})$

73–74 ■ Rewrite the expression as an algebraic function of x.

73. $\sin(\tan^{-1}x)$ **74.** $\sec(\sin^{-1}x)$

75–76 ■ Express θ in terms of x.

75.   **76.**

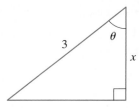

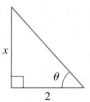

77. A 10-ft-wide highway sign is adjacent to a roadway, as shown in the figure. As a driver approaches the sign, the viewing angle θ changes.
 (a) Express viewing angle θ as a function of the distance x between the driver and the sign.
 (b) The sign is legible when the viewing angle is 2° or greater. At what distance x does the sign first become legible?

78. A 380-ft-tall building supports a 40-ft communications tower (see the figure). As a driver approaches the building, the viewing angle θ of the tower changes.
 (a) Express the viewing angle θ as a function of the distance x between the driver and the building.
 (b) At what distance from the building is the viewing angle θ as large as possible?

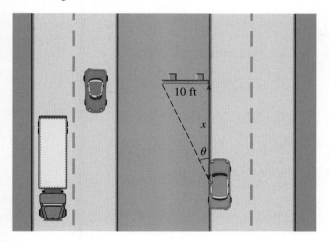

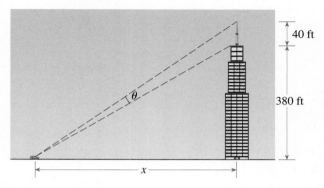

4 TEST

1. Verify each identity.

   (a) $\tan\theta\sin\theta + \cos\theta = \sec\theta$

   (b) $\dfrac{\tan x}{1 - \cos x} = \csc x(1 + \sec x)$

   (c) $\dfrac{2\tan x}{1 + \tan^2 x} = \sin 2x$

2. Let $x = 2\sin\theta$, $-\pi/2 < \theta < \pi/2$. Simplify the expression

$$\frac{x}{\sqrt{4 - x^2}}$$

3. Find the exact value of each expression.

   (a) $\sin 8°\cos 22° + \cos 8°\sin 22°$ (b) $\sin 75°$ (c) $\sin\dfrac{\pi}{12}$

4. For the angles α and β in the figures, find $\cos(\alpha + \beta)$.

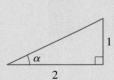
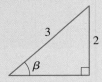

5. (a) Write $\sin 3x\cos 5x$ as a sum of trigonometric functions.
   (b) Write $\sin 2x - \sin 5x$ as a product of trigonometric functions.

6. If $\sin\theta = -\frac{4}{5}$ and θ is in quadrant III, find $\tan(\theta/2)$.

7. Graph $y = \sin x$ and $y = \sin^{-1}x$, and specify the domain of each function.

8. Express θ in each figure in terms of x.

   (a)

   (b)
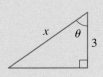

9. Solve each trigonometric equation in the interval $[0, 2\pi)$.
   (a) $2\cos^2 x + 5\cos x + 2 = 0$ (b) $\sin 2x - \cos x = 0$

10. Find all solutions in the interval $[0, 2\pi)$, correct to five decimal places:

$$5\cos 2x = 2$$

11. Find the exact value of $\cos\left(\tan^{-1}\frac{9}{40}\right)$.

Focus on Modeling
Traveling and Standing Waves

We've learned that the position of a particle in simple harmonic motion is described by a function of the form $y = A \sin \omega t$ (see Section 2.5). For example, if a string is moved up and down as in Figure 1, then the red dot on the string moves up and down in simple harmonic motion. Of course, the same holds true for each point on the string.

FIGURE 1

What function describes the shape of the whole string? If we fix an instant in time ($t = 0$) and snap a photograph of the string, we get the shape in Figure 2, which is modeled by

$$y = A \sin kx$$

where y is the height of the string above the x-axis at the point x.

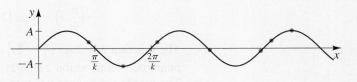

FIGURE 2
$y = A \sin kx$

Traveling Waves

If we snap photographs of the string at other instants, as in Figure 3, it appears that the waves in the string "travel" or shift to the right.

FIGURE 3

The **velocity** of the wave is the rate at which it moves to the right. If the wave has velocity v, then it moves to the right a distance vt in time t. So the graph of the shifted wave at time t is

$$y(x, t) = A \sin k(x - vt)$$

This function models the position of any point x on the string at any time t. We use the notation $y(x, t)$ to indicate that the function depends on the *two* variables x and t. Here is how this function models the motion of the string.

- **If we fix x**, then $y(x, t)$ is a function of t only, which gives the position of the fixed point x at time t.

- **If we fix t**, then $y(x, t)$ is a function of x only, whose graph is the shape of the string at the fixed time t.

EXAMPLE 1 ■ A Traveling Wave

A traveling wave is described by the function

$$y(x, t) = 3 \sin\left(2x - \frac{\pi}{2} t\right), \qquad x \geq 0$$

(a) Find the function that models the position of the point $x = \pi/6$ at any time t. Observe that the point moves in simple harmonic motion.

(b) Sketch the shape of the wave when $t = 0, 0.5, 1.0, 1.5,$ and 2.0. Does the wave appear to be traveling to the right?

(c) Find the velocity of the wave.

SOLUTION

(a) Substituting $x = \pi/6$ we get

$$y\left(\frac{\pi}{6}, t\right) = 3 \sin\left(2 \cdot \frac{\pi}{6} - \frac{\pi}{2} t\right) = 3 \sin\left(\frac{\pi}{3} - \frac{\pi}{2} t\right)$$

The function $y = 3 \sin\left(\frac{\pi}{3} - \frac{\pi}{2} t\right)$ describes simple harmonic motion with amplitude 3 and period $2\pi/(\pi/2) = 4$.

(b) The graphs are shown in Figure 4. As t increases, the wave moves to the right.

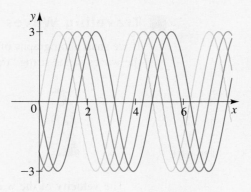

FIGURE 4
Traveling wave

(c) We express the given function in the standard form $y(x, t) = A \sin k(x - vt)$:

$$y(x, t) = 3 \sin\left(2x - \frac{\pi}{2}t\right) \quad \text{Given}$$

$$= 3 \sin 2\left(x - \frac{\pi}{4}t\right) \quad \text{Factor 2}$$

Comparing this to the standard form, we see that the wave is moving with velocity $v = \pi/4$. ∎

Standing Waves

If two waves are traveling along the same string, then the movement of the string is determined by the sum of the two waves. For example, if the string is attached to a wall, then the waves bounce back with the same amplitude and speed but in the opposite direction. In this case, one wave is described by $y = A \sin k(x - vt)$ and the reflected wave by $y = A \sin k(x + vt)$. The resulting wave is

$$y(x, t) = A \sin k(x - vt) + A \sin k(x + vt) \quad \text{Add the two waves}$$

$$= 2A \sin kx \cos kvt \quad \text{Sum-to-product formula}$$

The points where kx is a multiple of 2π are special, because at these points $y = 0$ for any time t. In other words, these points never move. Such points are called **nodes**. Figure 5 shows the graph of the wave for several values of t. We see that the wave does not travel, but simply vibrates up and down. Such a wave is called a **standing wave**.

FIGURE 5

A standing wave

EXAMPLE 2 ■ A Standing Wave

Traveling waves are generated at each end of a wave tank 30 ft long, with equations

$$y = 1.5 \sin\left(\frac{\pi}{5}x - 3t\right) \quad \text{and} \quad y = 1.5 \sin\left(\frac{\pi}{5}x + 3t\right)$$

(a) Find the equation of the combined wave, and find the nodes.
(b) Sketch the graph for $t = 0, 0.17, 0.34, 0.51, 0.68, 0.85,$ and 1.02. Is this a standing wave?

SOLUTION

(a) The combined wave is obtained by adding the two equations:

$$y = 1.5 \sin\left(\frac{\pi}{5}x - 3t\right) + 1.5 \sin\left(\frac{\pi}{5}x + 3t\right) \qquad \text{Add the two waves}$$

$$= 3 \sin \frac{\pi}{5}x \cos 3t \qquad \text{Sum-to-product formula}$$

The nodes occur at the values of x for which $\sin \frac{\pi}{5}x = 0$, that is, where $\frac{\pi}{5}x = k\pi$ (k an integer). Solving for x we get $x = 5k$. So the nodes occur at

$$x = 0, 5, 10, 15, 20, 25, 30$$

(b) The graphs are shown in Figure 6. From the graphs we see that this is a standing wave.

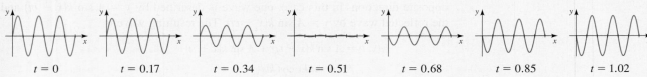

$t = 0$	$t = 0.17$	$t = 0.34$	$t = 0.51$	$t = 0.68$	$t = 0.85$	$t = 1.02$

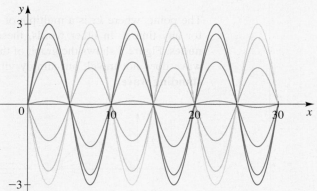

FIGURE 6

$y(x, t) = 3 \sin \dfrac{\pi}{5}x \cos 3t$

Problems

1. A wave on the surface of a long canal is described by the function

$$y(x, t) = 5 \sin\left(2x - \frac{\pi}{2}t\right), \qquad x \geqslant 0$$

(a) Find the function that models the position of the point $x = 0$ at any time t.

(b) Sketch the shape of the wave when $t = 0, 0.4, 0.8, 1.2,$ and 1.6. Is this a traveling wave?

(c) Find the velocity of the wave.

2. Traveling waves are generated at each end of a tightly stretched rope 24 ft long, with equations

$$y = 0.2 \sin(1.047x - 0.524t) \qquad \text{and} \qquad y = 0.2 \sin(1.047x + 0.524t)$$

(a) Find the equation of the combined wave, and find the nodes.
(b) Sketch the graph for $t = 0, 1, 2, 3, 4, 5,$ and 6. Is this a standing wave?

3. A traveling wave is graphed at the instant $t = 0$. If it is moving to the right with velocity 6, find an equation of the form $y(x, t) = A \sin(kx - kvt)$ for this wave.

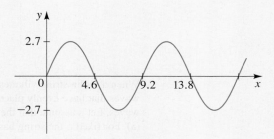

4. A traveling wave has period $2\pi/3$, amplitude 5, and velocity 0.5.
(a) Find the equation of the wave.
(b) Sketch the graph for $t = 0, 0.5, 1, 1.5,$ and 2.

5. A standing wave with amplitude 0.6 is graphed at several times t as shown in the figure. If the vibration has a frequency of 20 Hz, find an equation of the form $y(x, t) = A \sin \alpha x \cos \beta t$ that models this wave.

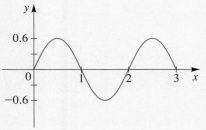

$t = 0$ s

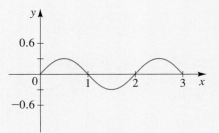

$t = 0.010$ s

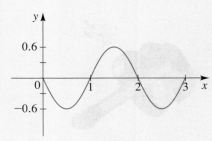

$t = 0.025$ s

6. A standing wave has maximum amplitude 7 and nodes at 0, $\pi/2$, π, $3\pi/2$, 2π, as shown in the figure. Each point that is not a node moves up and down with period 4π. Find a function of the form $y(x, t) = A \sin \alpha x \cos \beta t$ that models this wave.

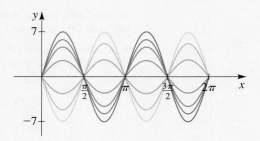

7. When a violin string vibrates, the sound produced results from a combination of standing waves that have evenly placed nodes. The figure illustrates some of the possible standing waves. Let's assume that the string has length π.

(a) For fixed t, the string has the shape of a sine curve $y = A \sin \alpha x$. Find the appropriate value of α for each of the illustrated standing waves.

(b) Do you notice a pattern in the values of α that you found in part (a)? What would the next two values of α be? Sketch rough graphs of the standing waves associated with these new values of α.

(c) Suppose that for fixed t, each point on the string that is not a node vibrates with frequency 440 Hz. Find the value of β for which an equation of the form $y = A \cos \beta t$ would model this motion.

(d) Combine your answers for parts (a) and (c) to find functions of the form $y(x, t) = A \sin \alpha x \cos \beta t$ that model each of the standing waves in the figure. (Assume $A = 1$.)

8. Standing waves in a violin string must have nodes at the ends of the string because the string is fixed at its endpoints. But this need not be the case with sound waves in a tube (such as a flute or an organ pipe). The figure shows some possible standing waves in a tube.

Suppose that a standing wave in a tube 37.7 ft long is modeled by the function

$$y(x, t) = 0.3 \cos \tfrac{1}{2} x \cos 50\pi t$$

Here $y(x, t)$ represents the variation from normal air pressure at the point x feet from the end of the tube, at time t seconds.

(a) At what points x are the nodes located? Are the endpoints of the tube nodes?

(b) At what frequency does the air vibrate at points that are not nodes?

5

Polar Coordinates, Complex Numbers, and Vectors

Trigonometry is used to analyze directed quantities, or vectors. The path of a jet aircraft is determined by resolving the vector forces of thrust, wind, and shear that act on the plane; the heading of a sailboat is determined by resolving the forces of the wind on the sails and the water currents on the hull of the boat.

A mathematician, like a painter or poet, is a maker of patterns.

G. H. HARDY

In this chapter we introduce a new coordinate system that uses angles and distance to locate points in the plane. We then use this idea of polar coordinates to work with complex numbers. Finally, we introduce vectors, which are quantities that have both magnitude and direction. The concepts explored in this chapter have many applications in engineering and the sciences.

5.1 POLAR COORDINATES

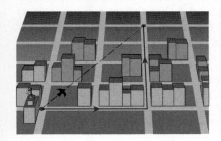

A coordinate system is a method for specifying the location of a point in the plane. Thus far we have been dealing with the rectangular (or Cartesian) coordinate system, which describes locations using a rectangular grid. Using rectangular coordinates is like describing a location in a city by saying that, for example, it's at the corner of 2nd Street and 4th Avenue. But we might also describe this same location by saying that it's 3 miles northeast of City Hall. Instead of specifying the location with respect to a grid of streets and avenues, we can describe it by giving its distance and direction from a fixed reference point.

■ Definition of Polar Coordinates

The **polar coordinate system** uses distances and directions to specify the location of a point in the plane. To set up this system, we choose a fixed point O in the plane called the **pole** (or **origin**) and draw from O a ray (half-line) called the **polar axis** as in Figure 1. Then each point P can be assigned polar coordinates $P(r, \theta)$ where

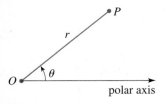

FIGURE 1

r is the *distance* from O to P

θ is the *angle* between the polar axis and the segment $\overline{OP}$

We use the convention that θ is positive if measured in a counterclockwise direction from the polar axis or negative if measured in a clockwise direction. If r is negative, then $P(r, \theta)$ is defined to be the point that lies $|r|$ units from the pole in the direction opposite to that given by θ (see Figure 2).

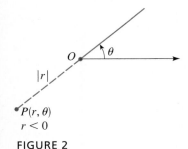

FIGURE 2

EXAMPLE 1 ■ Plotting Points in Polar Coordinates

Plot the points whose polar coordinates are given.

(a) $(1, 3\pi/4)$　　(b) $(3, -\pi/6)$　　(c) $(3, 3\pi)$　　(d) $(-4, \pi/4)$

SOLUTION

The points are plotted in Figure 3. Note that the point in part (d) lies 4 units from the origin along the angle $5\pi/4$, because the given value of r is negative.

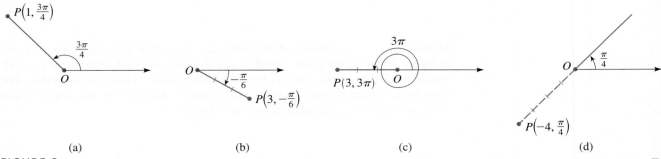

(a)   (b)   (c)   (d)

FIGURE 3

Note that the coordinates (r, θ) and $(-r, \theta + \pi)$ represent the same point, as shown in Figure 4. Moreover, because the angles $\theta + 2n\pi$ (where n is any integer) all have the same terminal side as the angle θ, each point in the plane has infinitely many representations in polar coordinates. In fact, any point $P(r, \theta)$ can also be represented by

$$P(r, \theta + 2n\pi) \qquad \text{and} \qquad P(-r, \theta + (2n + 1)\pi)$$

for any integer n.

FIGURE 4

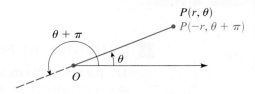

EXAMPLE 2 ■ Different Polar Coordinates for the Same Point

(a) Graph the point with polar coordinates $P(2, \pi/3)$.
(b) Find two other polar coordinate representations of P with $r > 0$, and two with $r < 0$.

SOLUTION

(a) The graph is shown in Figure 5(a).
(b) Other representations with $r > 0$ are

$$\left(2, \frac{\pi}{3} + 2\pi\right) = \left(2, \frac{7\pi}{3}\right) \qquad \text{Add } 2\pi \text{ to } \theta$$

$$\left(2, \frac{\pi}{3} - 2\pi\right) = \left(2, -\frac{5\pi}{3}\right) \qquad \text{Add } -2\pi \text{ to } \theta$$

Other representations with $r < 0$ are

$$\left(-2, \frac{\pi}{3} + \pi\right) = \left(-2, \frac{4\pi}{3}\right) \qquad \text{Replace } r \text{ by } -r, \text{ and add } \pi \text{ to } \theta$$

$$\left(-2, \frac{\pi}{3} - \pi\right) = \left(-2, -\frac{2\pi}{3}\right) \qquad \text{Replace } r \text{ by } -r, \text{ and add } -\pi \text{ to } \theta$$

The graphs in Figure 5 explain why these coordinates represent the same point.

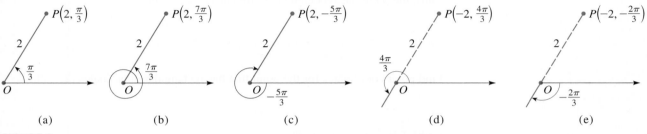

(a)   (b)   (c)   (d)   (e)

FIGURE 5   ■

Relationship between Polar and Rectangular Coordinates

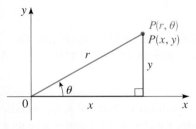

FIGURE 6

Situations often arise in which we need to consider polar and rectangular coordinates simultaneously. The connection between the two systems is illustrated in Figure 6, where the polar axis coincides with the positive x-axis. The formulas in the following box are obtained from the figure using the definitions of the trigonometric functions and the Pythagorean Theorem. (Although we have pictured the case where $r > 0$ and θ is acute, the formulas hold for any angle θ and for any value of r.)

RELATIONSHIP BETWEEN POLAR AND RECTANGULAR COORDINATES

1. To change from polar to rectangular coordinates, use the formulas

$$x = r \cos \theta \qquad \text{and} \qquad y = r \sin \theta$$

2. To change from rectangular to polar coordinates, use the formulas

$$r^2 = x^2 + y^2 \qquad \text{and} \qquad \tan \theta = \frac{y}{x} \quad (x \neq 0)$$

EXAMPLE 3 ■ Converting Polar Coordinates to Rectangular Coordinates

Find rectangular coordinates for the point that has polar coordinates $(4, 2\pi/3)$.

SOLUTION

Since $r = 4$ and $\theta = 2\pi/3$, we have

$$x = r \cos \theta = 4 \cos \frac{2\pi}{3} = 4 \cdot \left(-\frac{1}{2}\right) = -2$$

$$y = r \sin \theta = 4 \sin \frac{2\pi}{3} = 4 \cdot \frac{\sqrt{3}}{2} = 2\sqrt{3}$$

Thus, the point has rectangular coordinates $(-2, 2\sqrt{3})$.   ∎

EXAMPLE 4 ■ Converting Rectangular Coordinates
to Polar Coordinates

Find polar coordinates for the point that has rectangular coordinates $(2, -2)$.

SOLUTION

Using $x = 2$, $y = -2$, we get

$$r^2 = x^2 + y^2 = 2^2 + (-2)^2 = 8$$

so $r = 2\sqrt{2}$ or $-2\sqrt{2}$. Also

$$\tan \theta = \frac{y}{x} = \frac{-2}{2} = -1$$

so $\theta = 3\pi/4$ or $-\pi/4$. Since the point $(2, -2)$ lies in quadrant IV (see Figure 7), we can represent it in polar coordinates as $(2\sqrt{2}, -\pi/4)$ or $(-2\sqrt{2}, 3\pi/4)$.   ∎

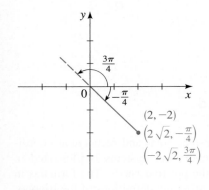

FIGURE 7

 Note that the equations relating polar and rectangular coordinates do not uniquely determine r or θ. When we use these equations to find the polar coordinates of a point, we must be careful that the values we choose for r and θ give us a point in the correct quadrant, as we saw in Example 4.

Polar Equations

In Examples 3 and 4 we converted points from one coordinate system to the other. Now we consider the same problem for equations.

EXAMPLE 5 ■ Converting an Equation from Rectangular
to Polar Coordinates

Express the equation $x^2 = 4y$ in polar coordinates.

SOLUTION

We use the formulas $x = r \cos \theta$ and $y = r \sin \theta$.

$$x^2 = 4y \qquad \text{Rectangular equation}$$

$$(r \cos \theta)^2 = 4(r \sin \theta) \qquad \text{Substitute } x = r \cos \theta,\, y = r \sin \theta$$

$$r^2 \cos^2 \theta = 4r \sin \theta \qquad \text{Expand}$$

$$r = 4\,\frac{\sin \theta}{\cos^2 \theta} \qquad \text{Divide by } r \cos^2 \theta$$

$$r = 4 \sec \theta \tan \theta \qquad \text{Simplify} \qquad\blacksquare$$

As Example 5 shows, converting from rectangular to polar coordinates is simple—just replace x by $r \cos \theta$ and y by $r \sin \theta$, and then simplify. But converting polar equations to rectangular form often requires more thought.

EXAMPLE 6 ■ Converting Equations from Polar to Rectangular Coordinates

Express the polar equation in rectangular coordinates. If possible, determine the graph of the equation from its rectangular form.
(a) $r = 5 \sec \theta$ (b) $r = 2 \sin \theta$ (c) $r = 2 + 2 \cos \theta$

SOLUTION

(a) Since $\sec \theta = 1/\cos \theta$, we multiply both sides by $\cos \theta$.

$$r = 5 \sec \theta$$

$$r \cos \theta = 5 \qquad \text{Multiply by } \cos \theta$$

$$x = 5 \qquad \text{Substitute } x = r \cos \theta$$

The graph of $x = 5$ is the vertical line in Figure 8.

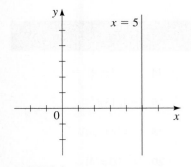

FIGURE 8

(b) We multiply both sides of the equation by r, because then we can use the formulas $r^2 = x^2 + y^2$ and $r \sin \theta = y$.

$$r^2 = 2r \sin \theta \qquad \text{Multiply by } r$$

$$x^2 + y^2 = 2y \qquad r^2 = x^2 + y^2 \text{ and } r \sin \theta = y$$

$$x^2 + y^2 - 2y = 0 \qquad \text{Subtract } 2y$$

$$x^2 + (y - 1)^2 = 1 \qquad \text{Complete the square in } y$$

This is the equation of a circle of radius 1 centered at the point $(0, 1)$. It is graphed in Figure 9.

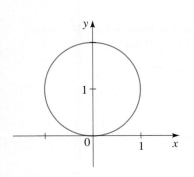

FIGURE 9

(c) We first multiply both sides of the equation by r:

$$r^2 = 2r + 2r \cos \theta$$

Using $r^2 = x^2 + y^2$ and $y = r \cos \theta$, we can convert two of the three terms in the equation into rectangular coordinates, but eliminating the remaining r requires more work:

$$x^2 + y^2 = 2r + 2x \qquad \text{\scriptsize $r^2 = x^2 + y^2$ and $r \cos \theta = x$}$$
$$x^2 + y^2 - 2x = 2r \qquad \text{\scriptsize Subtract $2y$}$$
$$(x^2 + y^2 - 2x)^2 = 4r^2 \qquad \text{\scriptsize Square both sides}$$
$$(x^2 + y^2 - 2x)^2 = 4(x^2 + y^2) \qquad \text{\scriptsize $r^2 = x^2 + y^2$}$$

In this case, the rectangular equation looks more complicated than the polar equation. Although we cannot easily determine the graph of the equation from its rectangular form, we will see in the next section how to graph it using the polar equation. ∎

5.1 EXERCISES

1–6 ■ Plot the point that has the given polar coordinates.

1. $(4, \pi/4)$ **2.** $(1, 0)$ **3.** $(6, -7\pi/6)$

4. $(3, -2\pi/3)$ **5.** $(-2, 4\pi/3)$ **6.** $(-5, -17\pi/6)$

7–12 ■ Plot the point that has the given polar coordinates. Then give two other polar coordinate representations of the point, one with $r < 0$ and the other with $r > 0$.

7. $(3, \pi/2)$ **8.** $(2, 3\pi/4)$ **9.** $(-1, 7\pi/6)$

10. $(-2, -\pi/3)$ **11.** $(-5, 0)$ **12.** $(3, 1)$

13–20 ■ Determine which point in the figure, P, Q, R, or S, has the given polar coordinates.

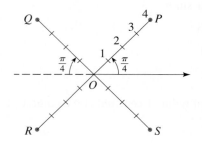

13. $(4, 3\pi/4)$ **14.** $(4, -3\pi/4)$

15. $(-4, -\pi/4)$ **16.** $(-4, 13\pi/4)$

17. $(4, -23\pi/4)$ **18.** $(-4, 23\pi/4)$

19. $(-4, 101\pi/4)$ **20.** $(4, 103\pi/4)$

21–22 ■ A point is graphed in rectangular form. Find polar coordinates for the point, with $r > 0$ and $0 < \theta < 2\pi$.

21.

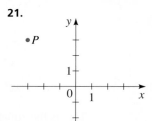

22.

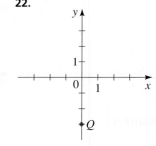

23–24 ■ A point is graphed in polar form. Find its rectangular coordinates.

23.   **24.**

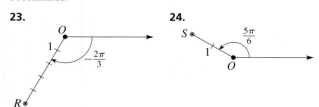

25–32 ■ Find the rectangular coordinates for the point whose polar coordinates are given.

25. $(4, \pi/6)$ **26.** $(6, 2\pi/3)$

27. $(\sqrt{2}, -\pi/4)$ **28.** $(-1, 5\pi/2)$

29. $(5, 5\pi)$ **30.** $(0, 13\pi)$

31. $(6\sqrt{2}, 11\pi/6)$ **32.** $(\sqrt{3}, -5\pi/3)$

33–40 ■ Convert the rectangular coordinates to polar coordinates with $r > 0$ and $0 \le \theta < 2\pi$.

33. $(-1, 1)$ **34.** $(3\sqrt{3}, -3)$

35. $(\sqrt{8}, \sqrt{8})$ **36.** $(-\sqrt{6}, -\sqrt{2})$

37. $(3, 4)$ **38.** $(1, -2)$

39. $(-6, 0)$ **40.** $(0, -\sqrt{3})$

41–46 ■ Convert the equation to polar form.

41. $x = y$ **42.** $x^2 + y^2 = 9$

43. $y = x^2$ **44.** $y = 5$

45. $x = 4$ **46.** $x^2 - y^2 = 1$

47–60 ■ Convert the polar equation to rectangular coordinates.

47. $r = 7$ **48.** $\theta = \pi$

49. $r \cos \theta = 6$ **50.** $r = 6 \cos \theta$

51. $r^2 = \tan \theta$ **52.** $r^2 = \sin 2\theta$

53. $r = \dfrac{1}{\sin \theta - \cos \theta}$ **54.** $r = \dfrac{1}{1 + \sin \theta}$

55. $r = 1 + \cos \theta$ **56.** $r = \dfrac{4}{1 + 2 \sin \theta}$

57. $r = 2 \sec \theta$ **58.** $r = 2 - \cos \theta$

59. $\sec \theta = 2$ **60.** $\cos 2\theta = 1$

▦ DISCOVERY · DISCUSSION

61. The Distance Formula in Polar Coordinates

(a) Use the Law of Cosines to prove that the distance between the polar points (r_1, θ_1) and (r_2, θ_2) is

$$d = \sqrt{r_1^2 + r_2^2 - 2r_1r_2 \cos(\theta_2 - \theta_1)}$$

(b) Find the distance between the points whose polar coordinates are $(3, 3\pi/4)$ and $(1, 7\pi/6)$, using the formula from part (a).

(c) Now convert the points in part (b) to rectangular coordinates. Find the distance between them using the usual distance formula. Do you get the same answer?

5.2 GRAPHS OF POLAR EQUATIONS

The **graph of a polar equation** $r = f(\theta)$ consists of all points P that have at least one polar representation (r, θ) whose coordinates satisfy the equation. Many curves that arise in mathematics and its applications are more easily and naturally represented by polar equations rather than rectangular equations.

A rectangular grid is helpful for plotting points in rectangular coordinates [see Figure 1(a)]. To plot points in polar coordinates it is convenient to use a grid consisting of circles centered at the pole and rays emanating from the pole, as in Figure 1(b). We will use such grids to help us sketch polar graphs.

In Examples 1 and 2 we see that circles centered at the origin and lines that pass through the origin have particularly simple equations in polar coordinates.

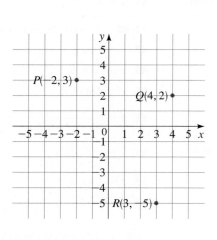

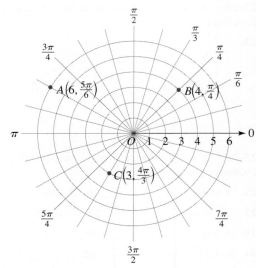

FIGURE 1   (a) Grid for rectangular coordinates   (b) Grid for polar coordinates

EXAMPLE 1 ■ Sketching the Graph of a Polar Equation

Sketch the graph of the equation $r = 3$ and express the equation in rectangular coordinates.

SOLUTION

The graph consists of all points whose r-coordinate is 3, that is, all points that are 3 units away from the origin. So the graph is a circle of radius 3 centered at the origin, as shown in Figure 2.

Squaring both sides of the equation, we get

$$r^2 = 3^2 \qquad \text{Square both sides}$$

$$x^2 + y^2 = 9 \qquad \text{Substitute } r^2 = x^2 + y^2$$

So the equivalent equation in rectangular coordinates is $x^2 + y^2 = 9$.   ■

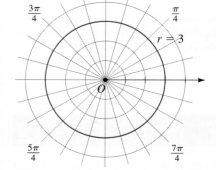

FIGURE 2

In general, the graph of the equation $r = a$ is a circle of radius $|a|$ centered at the origin. Squaring both sides of this equation, we see that the equivalent equation in rectangular coordinates is $x^2 + y^2 = a^2$.

EXAMPLE 2 ■ Sketching the Graph of a Polar Equation

Sketch the graph of the equation $\theta = \pi/3$ and express the equation in rectangular coordinates.

SOLUTION

The graph consists of all points whose θ-coordinate is $\pi/3$. This is the straight line that passes through the origin and makes an angle of $\pi/3$ with the polar axis (see

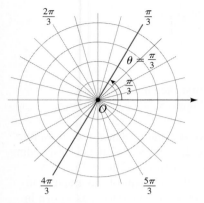

FIGURE 3

Figure 3). Note that the points $(r, \pi/3)$ on the line with $r > 0$ lie in quadrant I, whereas those with $r < 0$ lie in quadrant III. If the point (x, y) lies on this line, then

$$\frac{y}{x} = \tan \theta = \tan \frac{\pi}{3} = \sqrt{3}$$

Thus, the rectangular equation of this line is $y = \sqrt{3}\, x$. ∎

To sketch a polar curve whose graph isn't as obvious as the ones in the preceding examples, we plot points calculated for sufficiently many values of θ and then join them in a continuous curve. (This is what we did when we first learned to graph functions in rectangular coordinates.)

EXAMPLE 3 ■ Sketching the Graph of a Polar Equation

Sketch the graph of the polar equation $r = 2 \sin \theta$.

SOLUTION

We first use the equation to determine the polar coordinates of several points on the curve. The results are shown in the following table.

The polar equation $r = 2 \sin \theta$ in rectangular coordinates is

$$x^2 + (y - 1)^2 = 2$$

[See Section 5.1, Example 6(b)]. From the rectangular form of the equation we see that the graph is a circle of radius 1 centered at $(0, 1)$.

θ	0	$\pi/6$	$\pi/4$	$\pi/3$	$\pi/2$	$2\pi/3$	$3\pi/4$	$5\pi/6$	π
$r = 2 \sin \theta$	0	1	$\sqrt{2}$	$\sqrt{3}$	2	$\sqrt{3}$	$\sqrt{2}$	1	0

We plot these points in Figure 4 and then join them to sketch the curve. The graph appears to be a circle. We have used values of θ only between 0 and π, since the same points (this time expressed with negative r-coordinates) would be obtained if we allowed θ to range from π to 2π.

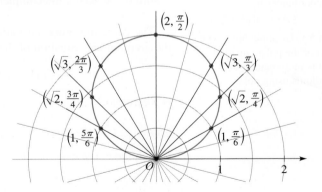

FIGURE 4
$r = 2 \sin \theta$

In general, the graphs of equations of the form

$$r = 2a \sin \theta \qquad \text{and} \qquad r = 2a \cos \theta$$

are circles with radius $|a|$ centered at the points with polar coordinates $(a, \pi/2)$ and $(a, 0)$, respectively.

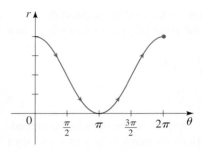

FIGURE 5
$r = 2 + 2 \cos \theta$

EXAMPLE 4 ■ Sketching the Graph of a Polar Equation

Sketch the graph of $r = 2 + 2 \cos \theta$.

SOLUTION

Instead of plotting points as in Example 3, we first sketch the graph of $r = 2 + 2 \cos \theta$ in *rectangular* coordinates in Figure 5. We can think of this graph as a table of values that enables us to read at a glance the values of r that correspond to increasing values of θ. For instance, we see that as θ increases from 0 to $\pi/2$, r (the distance from O) decreases from 4 to 2, so we sketch the corresponding part of the polar graph in Figure 6(a). As θ increases from $\pi/2$ to π, Figure 5 shows that r decreases from 2 to 0, so we sketch the next part of the graph as in Figure 6(b). As θ increases from π to $3\pi/2$, r increases from 0 to 2, as shown in

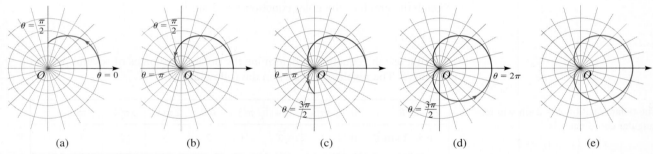

(a)   (b)   (c)   (d)   (e)

FIGURE 6   Steps in sketching $r = 2 + 2 \cos \theta$

The polar equation $r = 2 + 2 \cos \theta$ in rectangular coordinates is

$$(x^2 + y^2 - 2y)^2 = 4(x^2 + y^2)$$

[See Section 5.1, Example 6(c)]. The simpler form of the polar equation shows that it is more natural to describe cardioids using polar coordinates.

part (c). Finally, as θ increases from $3\pi/2$ to 2π, r increases from 2 to 4, as shown in part (d). If we let θ increase beyond 2π or decrease beyond 0, we would simply retrace our path. Combining the portions of the graph from parts (a) through (d) of Figure 6, we sketch the complete graph in part (e).   ■

The curve in Figure 6 is called a **cardioid** because it is heart-shaped. In general, the graph of any equation of the form

$$r = a(1 \pm \cos \theta) \qquad \text{or} \qquad r = a(1 \pm \sin \theta)$$

is a cardioid.

EXAMPLE 5 ■ Sketching the Graph of a Polar Equation

Sketch the curve $r = \cos 2\theta$.

SOLUTION

As in Example 4, we first sketch the graph of $r = \cos 2\theta$ in *rectangular* coordinates, as shown in Figure 7. As θ increases from 0 to $\pi/4$, Figure 7 shows that r decreases from 1 to 0, and so we draw the corresponding portion of the polar curve in Figure 8 (indicated by ①). As θ increases from $\pi/4$ to $\pi/2$, the value of r goes from 0 to -1. This means that the distance from the origin increases from 0 to 1, but instead of being in quadrant I, this portion of the polar curve (indicated by ②) lies on the opposite side of the origin in quadrant III. The remainder of the curve is drawn in a similar fashion, with the arrows and numbers indicating the order in which the portions are traced out. The resulting curve has four petals and is called a **four-leaved rose**.

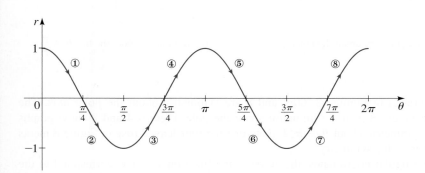

FIGURE 7

Graph of $r = \cos 2\theta$ sketched in rectangular coordinates

FIGURE 8

Four-leaved rose $r = \cos 2\theta$ sketched in polar coordinates   ■

In general, the graph of an equation of the form

$$r = a \cos n\theta \qquad \text{or} \qquad r = a \sin n\theta$$

is an **n-leaved rose** if n is odd or a $2n$-leaved rose if n is even (as in Example 5).

■ Symmetry

When graphing a polar equation, it's often helpful to take advantage of symmetry. We list three tests for symmetry; Figure 9 on page 306 shows why these tests work.

TESTS FOR SYMMETRY

1. If a polar equation is unchanged when we replace θ by $-\theta$, then the graph is symmetric about the polar axis [Figure 9(a)].

2. If the equation is unchanged when we replace r by $-r$, then the graph is symmetric about the pole [Figure 9(b)].

3. If the equation is unchanged when we replace θ by $\pi - \theta$, the graph is symmetric about the vertical line $\theta = \pi/2$ (the y-axis) [Figure 9(c)].

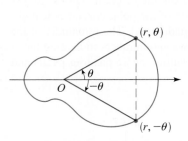

(a) Symmetry about the polar axis

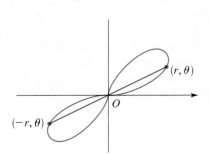

(b) Symmetry about the pole

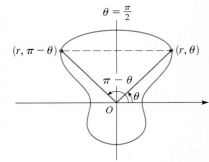

(c) Symmetry about the line $\theta = \frac{\pi}{2}$

FIGURE 9

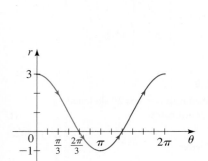

FIGURE 10

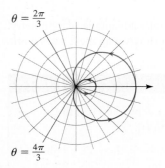

FIGURE 11

$r = 1 + 2\cos\theta$

The graphs in Figures 2, 6(e), and 8 are symmetric about the polar axis. The graph in Figure 8 is also symmetric about the pole. Figures 4 and 8 show graphs that are symmetric about $\theta = \pi/2$. Note that the four-leaved rose in Figure 8 meets all three tests for symmetry.

In rectangular coordinates, the zeros of the function $y = f(x)$ correspond to the x-intercepts of the graph. In polar coordinates, the zeros of the function $r = f(\theta)$ are the angles θ at which the curve crosses the pole. The zeros help us sketch the graph, as illustrated in the next example.

EXAMPLE 6 ■ Using Symmetry to Sketch a Polar Graph

Sketch the graph of the equation $r = 1 + 2\cos\theta$.

SOLUTION

As aids in sketching the graph, we find the following.

■ **Symmetry**   Since the equation is unchanged when θ is replaced by $-\theta$, the graph is symmetric about the polar axis.

■ **Zeros**   To find the zeros, we solve

$$0 = 1 + 2\cos\theta$$

$$\cos\theta = -\frac{1}{2}$$

$$\theta = \frac{2\pi}{3}, \frac{4\pi}{3}$$

■ **Table of values**   As in Example 4, we sketch the graph of $r = 1 + 2\cos\theta$ in *rectangular* coordinates to serve as a table of values (Figure 10).

Now we sketch the polar graph of $r = 1 + 2 \cos \theta$ from $\theta = 0$ to $\theta = \pi$, and then use symmetry to complete the graph in Figure 11. ∎

The curve in Figure 11 is called a **limaçon**, after the Middle French word for snail. In general, the graph of an equation of the form

$$r = a \pm b \cos \theta \qquad \text{or} \qquad r = a \pm b \sin \theta$$

is a limaçon. The shape of the limaçon depends on the relative size of a and b (see the table on page 308).

▦ Graphing Polar Equations with Graphing Devices

Although it's useful to be able to sketch simple polar graphs by hand, we need a graphing calculator or computer when we are faced with a graph as complicated as the one in Figure 12. Fortunately, most graphing calculators are capable of graphing polar equations directly.

EXAMPLE 7 ■ Drawing the Graph of a Polar Equation

Graph the equation $r = \cos(2\theta/3)$.

SOLUTION

We need to determine the domain for θ. So we ask ourselves: How many complete rotations are required before the graph starts to repeat itself? The graph repeats itself when the same value of r is obtained at θ and $\theta + 2n\pi$. Thus, we need to find an integer n, so that

$$\cos \frac{2(\theta + 2n\pi)}{3} = \cos \frac{2\theta}{3}$$

For this equality to hold, $4n\pi/3$ must be a multiple of 2π, and this first happens when $n = 3$. Therefore, we obtain the entire graph if we choose values of θ between $\theta = 0$ and $\theta = 0 + 2(3)\pi = 6\pi$. The graph is shown in Figure 13. ∎

EXAMPLE 8 ■ A Family of Polar Equations

Graph the family of polar equations $r = 1 + c \sin \theta$ for $c = 3, 2.5, 2, 1.5, 1$. How does the shape of the graph change as c changes?

SOLUTION

Figure 14 on page 308 shows computer-drawn graphs for the given values of c. For $c > 1$, the graph has an inner loop; the loop decreases in size as c decreases. When $c = 1$, the loop disappears and the graph becomes a cardioid (see Example 4).

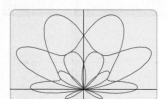

FIGURE 12
$r = \sin \theta + \sin^3(5\theta/2)$

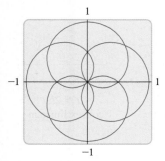

FIGURE 13
$r = \cos(2\theta/3)$

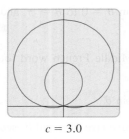 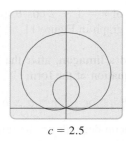 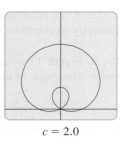 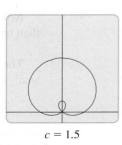 

| $c = 3.0$ | $c = 2.5$ | $c = 2.0$ | $c = 1.5$ | $c = 1.0$ |

FIGURE 14 A family of limaçons $r = 1 + c \sin \theta$ in the viewing rectangle $[-2.5, 2.5]$ by $[-0.5, 4.5]$ ∎

The following box gives a summary of some of the basic polar graphs used in calculus.

SOME COMMON POLAR CURVES

Circles and Spiral

| $r = a$ circle | $r = a \sin \theta$ circle | $r = a \cos \theta$ circle | $r = a\theta$ spiral |

Limaçons

$r = a \pm b \sin \theta$

$r = a \pm b \cos \theta$

$(a > 0, b > 0)$

Orientation depends on the trigonometric function (sine or cosine) and the sign of b.

   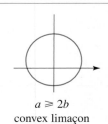

| $a < b$ limaçon with inner loop | $a = b$ cardioid | $a > b$ dimpled limaçon | $a \geqslant 2b$ convex limaçon |

Roses

$r = a \sin n\theta$

$r = a \cos n\theta$

n-leaved if n is odd
$2n$-leaved if n is even

 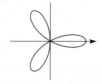 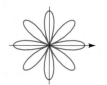 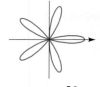

| $r = a \cos 2\theta$ 4-leaved rose | $r = a \cos 3\theta$ 3-leaved rose | $r = a \cos 4\theta$ 8-leaved rose | $r = a \cos 5\theta$ 5-leaved rose |

Lemniscates

Figure-eight-shaped curves

| $r^2 = a^2 \sin 2\theta$ lemniscate | $r^2 = a^2 \cos 2\theta$ lemniscate |

5.2   EXERCISES

1–6 ■ Match the polar equation with the graphs labeled I–VI. Use the table on page 308 to help you.

1. $r = 3 \cos \theta$

2. $r = 3$

3. $r = 2 + 2 \sin \theta$

4. $r = 1 + 2 \cos \theta$

5. $r = \sin 3\theta$

6. $r = \sin 4\theta$

I
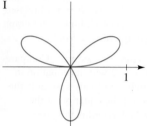

II
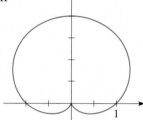

III
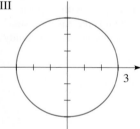

IV
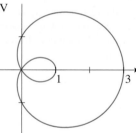

V
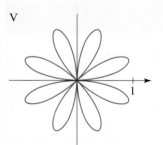

VI
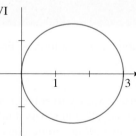

7–14 ■ Test the polar equation for symmetry with respect to the polar axis, the pole, and the line $\theta = \pi/2$.

7. $r = 2 - \sin \theta$

8. $r = 4 + 8 \cos \theta$

9. $r = 3 \sec \theta$

10. $r = 5 \cos \theta \csc \theta$

11. $r = \dfrac{4}{3 - 2 \sin \theta}$

12. $r = \dfrac{5}{1 + 3 \cos \theta}$

13. $r^2 = 4 \cos 2\theta$

14. $r^2 = 9 \sin \theta$

15–36 ■ Sketch the graph of the polar equation.

15. $r = 2$

16. $r = -1$

17. $\theta = -\pi/2$

18. $\theta = 5\pi/6$

19. $r = 6 \sin \theta$

20. $r = \cos \theta$

21. $r = -2 \cos \theta$

22. $r = 2 \sin \theta + 2 \cos \theta$

23. $r = 2 - 2 \cos \theta$

24. $r = 1 + \sin \theta$

25. $r = -3(1 + \sin \theta)$

26. $r = \cos \theta - 1$

27. $r = \theta, \quad \theta \geq 0$ (spiral)

28. $r\theta = 1, \quad \theta > 0$ (reciprocal spiral)

29. $r = \sin 2\theta$ (four-leaved rose)

30. $r = 2 \cos 3\theta$ (three-leaved rose)

31. $r^2 = \cos 2\theta$ (lemniscate)

32. $r^2 = 4 \sin 2\theta$ (lemniscate)

33. $r = 2 + \sin \theta$ (limaçon)

34. $r = 1 - 2 \cos \theta$ (limaçon)

35. $r = 2 + \sec \theta$ (conchoid)

36. $r = \sin \theta \tan \theta$ (cissoid)

 37–40 ■ Use a graphing device to graph the polar equation. Choose the domain of θ to make sure you produce the entire graph.

37. $r = \cos(\theta/2)$

38. $r = \sin(8\theta/5)$

39. $r = 1 + 2 \sin(\theta/2)$ (nephroid)

40. $r = \sqrt{1 - 0.8 \sin^2\theta}$ (hippopede)

41. Graph the family of polar equations $r = 1 + \sin n\theta$ for $n = 1, 2, 3, 4,$ and 5. How is the number of loops related to n?

42. Graph the family of polar equations $r = 1 + c \sin 2\theta$ for $c = 0.3, 0.6, 1, 1.5,$ and 2. How does the graph change as c increases?

43–46 ■ Match the polar equation with the graphs labeled I–IV. Give reasons for your answers.

43. $r = \sin(\theta/2)$

44. $r = 1/\sqrt{\theta}$

45. $r = \theta \sin \theta$

46. $r = 1 + 3\cos(3\theta)$

I

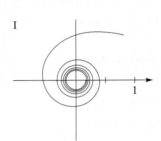

II

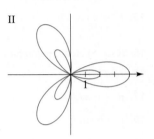

III

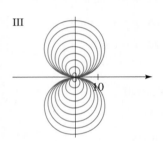

IV

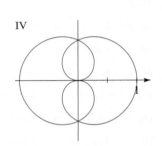

47–50 ■ Sketch a graph of the rectangular equation. [*Hint*: First convert the equation to polar coordinates.]

47. $(x^2 + y^2)^3 = 4x^2y^2$

48. $(x^2 + y^2)^3 = (x^2 - y^2)^2$

49. $(x^2 + y^2)^2 = x^2 - y^2$

50. $x^2 + y^2 = (x^2 + y^2 - x)^2$

51. Show that the graph of $r = a\cos\theta + b\sin\theta$ is a circle, and find its center and radius.

DISCOVERY • DISCUSSION

52. A Transformation of Polar Graphs   How are the graphs of $r = 1 + \sin(\theta - \pi/6)$ and $r = 1 + \sin(\theta - \pi/3)$ related to the graph of $r = 1 + \sin\theta$? In general, how is the graph of $r = f(\theta - \alpha)$ related to the graph of $r = f(\theta)$?

53. Choosing a Convenient Coordinate System   Compare the polar equation of the circle $r = 2$ with its equation in rectangular coordinates. In which coordinate system is the equation simpler? Do the same for the equation of the four-leaved rose $r = \sin 2\theta$. Which coordinate system would you choose to study these curves?

54. Choosing a Convenient Coordinate System   Compare the rectangular equation of the line $y = 2$ with its polar equation. In which coordinate system is the equation simpler? Which coordinate system would you choose to study lines?

5.3   COMPLEX NUMBERS

Not every quadratic equation has real solutions. For example, the equation

$$x^2 + 4 = 0$$

has no real solution, because if we try to solve it, we get $x^2 = -4$, so $x = \pm\sqrt{-4}$. But this is impossible, since negative numbers don't have real square roots.

To make it possible to solve *all* quadratic equations, mathematicians define the new number

$$i = \sqrt{-1}$$

This means $i^2 = -1$. A complex number is then a number of the form $a + bi$, where a and b are real numbers.

Gerolamo Cardano (1501–1576) is certainly one of the most colorful figures in the history of mathematics. He was the most renowned physician in Europe in his day, yet throughout his life he was plagued by numerous maladies, including ruptures, hemorrhoids, and an irrational fear of encountering rabid dogs. A doting father, his beloved sons broke his heart—his favorite was eventually beheaded for murdering his wife. Cardano was also a compulsive gambler; indeed, this vice may have driven him to write the *Book on Games of Chance*, the first study of probability from a mathematical point of view.

In Cardano's major mathematical work, the *Ars Magna*, he detailed the solution of the general third- and fourth-degree polynomial equations. At the time of its publication, mathematicians were uncomfortable even with negative numbers, but Cardano's formulas paved the way for the acceptance not just of negative numbers, but also of imaginary numbers, because they occurred naturally in solving polynomial equations. For example, for the cubic equation

$$x^3 - 15x - 4 = 0$$

one of his formulas gives the solution

$$x = \sqrt[3]{2 + \sqrt{-121}} + \sqrt[3]{2 - \sqrt{-121}}$$

This value for *x* actually turns out to be the *integer* 4, yet to find it Cardano had to use the imaginary number $\sqrt{-121} = 11i$.

DEFINITION OF COMPLEX NUMBERS

A **complex number** is an expression of the form

$$a + bi$$

where *a* and *b* are real numbers and $i^2 = -1$. The **real part** of this complex number is *a* and the **imaginary part** is *b*. Two complex numbers are **equal** if and only if their real parts are equal and their imaginary parts are equal.

Note that both the real and imaginary parts of a complex number are real numbers.

EXAMPLE 1 ■ Complex Numbers

The following are examples of complex numbers.

$3 + 4i$	Real part 3, imaginary part 4
$\frac{1}{2} - \frac{2}{3}i$	Real part $\frac{1}{2}$, imaginary part $-\frac{2}{3}$
$6i$	Real part 0, imaginary part 6
-7	Real part -7, imaginary part 0

A number such as $6i$, which has real part 0, is called a **pure imaginary number**. A real number like -7 can be thought of as a complex number with imaginary part 0.

In the complex number system every quadratic equation has solutions. The numbers $2i$ and $-2i$ are solutions of $x^2 = -4$ because

$$(2i)^2 = 2^2 i^2 = 4(-1) = -4 \qquad \text{and} \qquad (-2i)^2 = (-2)^2 i^2 = 4(-1) = -4$$

■ Arithmetic Operations on Complex Numbers

Complex numbers are added, subtracted, multiplied, and divided just as we would any number of the form $a + b\sqrt{c}$. The only difference we must keep in mind is that $i^2 = -1$. Thus, the following calculations are valid.

$$(a + bi)(c + di) = ac + (ad + bc)i + bdi^2 \qquad \text{Multiply and collect like terms}$$

$$= ac + (ad + bc)i + bd(-1) \qquad i^2 = -1$$

$$= (ac - bd) + (ad + bc)i \qquad \text{Combine real and imaginary parts}$$

We therefore define the sum, difference, and product of complex numbers as follows.

ADDING, SUBTRACTING, AND MULTIPLYING COMPLEX NUMBERS

Definition	Description
Addition	
$(a + bi) + (c + di) = (a + c) + (b + d)i$	To add complex numbers, add the real parts and the imaginary parts.
Subtraction	
$(a + bi) - (c + di) = (a - c) + (b - d)i$	To subtract complex numbers, subtract the real parts and the imaginary parts.
Multiplication	
$(a + bi) \cdot (c + di) = (ac - bd) + (ad + bc)i$	Multiply complex numbers like binomials, using $i^2 = -1$.

EXAMPLE 2 ■ **Adding, Subtracting, and Multiplying Complex Numbers**

Express the following in the form $a + bi$.

(a) $(3 + 5i) + (4 - 2i)$ (b) $(3 + 5i) - (4 - 2i)$

(c) $(3 + 5i)(4 - 2i)$ (d) i^{23}

Graphing calculators can perform arithmetic operations on complex numbers.

```
(3+5i)+(4-2i)
                7+3i
(3+5i)*(4-2i)
               22+14i
```

SOLUTION

We use the definitions in the preceding box.

(a) $(3 + 5i) + (4 - 2i) = (3 + 4) + (5 - 2)i = 7 + 3i$

(b) $(3 + 5i) - (4 - 2i) = (3 - 4) + [5 - (-2)]i = -1 + 7i$

(c) $(3 + 5i)(4 - 2i) = [3 \cdot 4 - 5(-2)] + [3(-2) + 5 \cdot 4]i = 22 + 14i$

(d) $i^{23} = i^{20+3} = (i^2)^{10}i^3 = (-1)^{10}i^2 i = (1)(-1)i = -i$ ■

Complex Conjugates

Number	Conjugate
$3 + 2i$	$3 - 2i$
$1 - i$	$1 + i$
$4i$	$-4i$
5	5

Division of complex numbers is much like rationalizing the denominator of a radical expression. For the complex number $z = a + bi$ we define its **complex conjugate** to be $\bar{z} = a - bi$. Note that

$$z \cdot \bar{z} = (a + bi)(a - bi) = a^2 + b^2$$

So the product of a complex number and its conjugate is always a nonnegative real number. We use this property to divide complex numbers.

DIVIDING COMPLEX NUMBERS

To simplify the quotient $\dfrac{a + bi}{c + di}$, multiply the numerator and the denominator by the complex conjugate of the denominator:

$$\frac{a + bi}{c + di} = \left(\frac{a + bi}{c + di}\right)\left(\frac{c - di}{c - di}\right) = \frac{(ac + bd) + (bc - ad)i}{c^2 + d^2}$$

Rather than memorize this entire formula, it's best just to remember the first step and then mutiply out the numerator and the denominator as usual.

EXAMPLE 3 ■ Dividing Complex Numbers

Express the following in the form $a + bi$.

(a) $\dfrac{3 + 5i}{1 - 2i}$ (b) $\dfrac{7 + 3i}{4i}$

SOLUTION

We multiply both numerator and denominator by the complex conjugate of the denominator to make the new denominator a real number.

(a) The complex conjugate of $1 - 2i$ is $\overline{1 - 2i} = 1 + 2i$.

$$\frac{3 + 5i}{1 - 2i} = \left(\frac{3 + 5i}{1 - 2i}\right)\left(\frac{1 + 2i}{1 + 2i}\right) = \frac{-7 + 11i}{5} = -\frac{7}{5} + \frac{11}{5}i$$

(b) The complex conjugate of $4i$ is $-4i$. Therefore

$$\frac{7 + 3i}{4i} = \left(\frac{7 + 3i}{4i}\right)\left(\frac{-4i}{-4i}\right) = \frac{12 - 28i}{16} = \frac{3}{4} - \frac{7}{4}i$$

■

■ Square Roots of Negative Numbers

Just as every positive real number r has two square roots ($\sqrt{r}$ and $-\sqrt{r}$), every negative number has two square roots as well. If $-r$ is a negative number, then its square roots are $\pm i \sqrt{r}$, because $(i \sqrt{r})^2 = i^2 r = -r$ and $(-i \sqrt{r})^2 = i^2 r = -r$.

SQUARE ROOTS OF NEGATIVE NUMBERS

If $-r$ is negative, then the **principal square root** of $-r$ is

$$\sqrt{-r} = i \sqrt{r}$$

The two square roots of $-r$ are $i \sqrt{r}$ and $-i \sqrt{r}$.

We usually write $i \sqrt{b}$ instead of $\sqrt{b}\, i$ to avoid confusion with $\sqrt{bi}$.

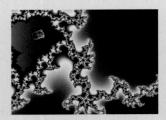

Fractals

Many of the things we model in this book have regular predictable shapes. But recent advances in mathematics have made it possible to mathematically model such seemingly random or even chaotic shapes as those of a cloud, a flickering flame, a mountain, or a jagged coastline. The basic tools in this type of modeling are the fractals invented by the mathematician Benoit Mandelbrot. A *fractal* is a geometric shape built up from a simple basic shape by scaling and repeating the shape indefinitely according to a given rule. Fractals have infinite detail; this means the closer you look, the more you see. They are also *self-similar*; that is, zooming in on a portion of the fractal yields the same detail as the original shape. Because of their beautiful shapes, fractals are used by movie makers to create fictional landscapes or exotic backgrounds.

Although a fractal is a complex shape, it is produced according to very simple rules (see page 317). This property of fractals is exploited in a process of storing pictures on a computer called *fractal image compression*. In this process a picture is stored as a simple basic shape and a rule; repeating

(continued)

EXAMPLE 4 ■ Square Roots of Negative Numbers

(a) $\sqrt{-1} = i\sqrt{1} = i$ (b) $\sqrt{-16} = i\sqrt{16} = 4i$ (c) $\sqrt{-3} = i\sqrt{3}$ ■

Special care must be taken when performing calculations involving square roots of negative numbers. Although $\sqrt{a} \cdot \sqrt{b} = \sqrt{ab}$ when a and b are positive, this is *not* true when both are negative. For example,

$$\sqrt{-2} \cdot \sqrt{-3} = i\sqrt{2} \cdot i\sqrt{3} = i^2\sqrt{6} = -\sqrt{6}$$

but

$$\sqrt{(-2)(-3)} = \sqrt{6}$$

so

$$\sqrt{-2} \cdot \sqrt{-3} \ne \sqrt{(-2)(-3)}$$

When multiplying radicals of negative numbers, express them first in the form $i\sqrt{r}$ (where $r > 0$) to avoid possible errors of this type.

EXAMPLE 5 ■ Using Square Roots of Negative Numbers

Evaluate $(\sqrt{12} - \sqrt{-3})(3 + \sqrt{-4})$ and express in the form $a + bi$.

SOLUTION

$$\begin{aligned}
(\sqrt{12} - \sqrt{-3})(3 + \sqrt{-4}) &= (\sqrt{12} - i\sqrt{3})(3 + i\sqrt{4}) \\
&= (2\sqrt{3} - i\sqrt{3})(3 + 2i) \\
&= (6\sqrt{3} + 2\sqrt{3}) + i(2 \cdot 2\sqrt{3} - 3\sqrt{3}) \\
&= 8\sqrt{3} + i\sqrt{3}
\end{aligned}$$

■

■ Complex Roots of Quadratic Equations

The solutions of the quadratic equation $ax^2 + bx + c = 0$ are given by the quadratic formula:

$$x = \frac{-b \pm \sqrt{b^2 - 4ac}}{2a}$$

(See Appendix A.4.)

If $b^2 - 4ac < 0$, then the equation has no real solution. But in the complex number system, this equation will always have solutions, because negative numbers have square roots in this expanded setting.

EXAMPLE 6 ■ Quadratic Equations with Complex Solutions

Solve each equation: (a) $x^2 + 9 = 0$ (b) $x^2 + 4x + 5 = 0$

the shape according to the rule produces the original picture. This is an extremely efficient method of storage; that's how thousands of color pictures can be put on a single compact disc.

SOLUTION

(a) The equation $x^2 + 9 = 0$ means $x^2 = -9$, so

$$x = \pm\sqrt{-9} = \pm i\,\sqrt{9} = \pm 3i$$

The solutions are therefore $3i$ and $-3i$.

(b) By the quadratic formula we have

$$x = \frac{-4 \pm \sqrt{4^2 - 4 \cdot 5}}{2}$$

$$= \frac{-4 \pm \sqrt{-4}}{2}$$

$$= \frac{-4 \pm 2i}{2} = \frac{2(-2 \pm i)}{2} = -2 \pm i$$

So, the solutions are $-2 + i$ and $-2 - i$. ∎

The solutions of each equation in Example 6 are complex conjugates. This is always true for complex solutions of polynomial equations with real coefficients (see Exercise 75).

COMPLEX CONJUGATE SOLUTIONS

If $a + bi$ is a solution of a polynomial equation with real coefficients, then so is its complex conjugate $a - bi$.

EXAMPLE 7 ■ Complex Conjugates as Solutions of a Quadratic

Show that the solutions of the equation

$$4x^2 - 24x + 37 = 0$$

are complex conjugates of each other.

SOLUTION

We use the quadratic formula to get

$$x = \frac{24 \pm \sqrt{(24)^2 - 4(4)(37)}}{2(4)}$$

$$= \frac{24 \pm \sqrt{-16}}{8} = \frac{24 \pm 4i}{8} = 3 \pm \frac{1}{2}i$$

So, the solutions are $3 + \frac{1}{2}i$ and $3 - \frac{1}{2}i$, and these are complex conjugates. ∎

5.3 EXERCISES

1–10 ■ Find the real and imaginary parts of the complex number.

1. $5 - 7i$

2. $-6 + 4i$

3. $\dfrac{-2 - 5i}{3}$

4. $\dfrac{4 + 7i}{2}$

5. 3

6. $-\frac{1}{2}$

7. $-\frac{2}{3}i$

8. $i\sqrt{3}$

9. $\sqrt{3} + \sqrt{-4}$

10. $2 - \sqrt{-5}$

11–52 ■ Evaluate the expression and write the result in the form $a + bi$.

11. $(2 - 5i) + (3 + 4i)$

12. $(2 + 5i) + (4 - 6i)$

13. $(-6 + 6i) + (9 - i)$

14. $(3 - 2i) + \left(-5 - \frac{1}{3}i\right)$

15. $\left(7 - \frac{1}{2}i\right) - \left(5 + \frac{3}{2}i\right)$

16. $(-4 + i) - (2 - 5i)$

17. $(-12 + 8i) - (7 + 4i)$

18. $6i - (4 - i)$

19. $4(-1 + 2i)$

20. $2i\left(\frac{1}{2} - i\right)$

21. $(7 - i)(4 + 2i)$

22. $(5 - 3i)(1 + i)$

23. $(3 - 4i)(5 - 12i)$

24. $\left(\frac{2}{3} + 12i\right)\left(\frac{1}{6} + 24i\right)$

25. $(6 + 5i)(2 - 3i)$

26. $(-2 + i)(3 - 7i)$

27. $\dfrac{1}{i}$

28. $\dfrac{1}{1 + i}$

29. $\dfrac{2 - 3i}{1 - 2i}$

30. $\dfrac{5 - i}{3 + 4i}$

31. $\dfrac{26 + 39i}{2 - 3i}$

32. $\dfrac{25}{4 - 3i}$

33. $\dfrac{10i}{1 - 2i}$

34. $(2 - 3i)^{-1}$

35. $\dfrac{4 + 6i}{3i}$

36. $\dfrac{-3 + 5i}{15i}$

37. $\dfrac{1}{1 + i} - \dfrac{1}{1 - i}$

38. $\dfrac{(1 + 2i)(3 - i)}{2 + i}$

39. i^3

40. $(2i)^4$

41. i^{100}

42. i^{1002}

43. $\sqrt{-25}$

44. $\sqrt{\dfrac{-9}{4}}$

45. $\sqrt{-3}\sqrt{-12}$

46. $\sqrt{\frac{1}{3}}\sqrt{-27}$

47. $(3 - \sqrt{-5})(1 + \sqrt{-1})$

48. $\dfrac{1 - \sqrt{-1}}{1 + \sqrt{-1}}$

49. $\dfrac{2 + \sqrt{-8}}{1 + \sqrt{-2}}$

50. $(\sqrt{3} - \sqrt{-4})(\sqrt{6} - \sqrt{-8})$

51. $\dfrac{\sqrt{-36}}{\sqrt{-2}\sqrt{-9}}$

52. $\dfrac{\sqrt{-7}\sqrt{-49}}{\sqrt{28}}$

53–66 ■ Find all solutions of the equation and express them in the form $a + bi$.

53. $x^2 + 9 = 0$

54. $9x^2 + 4 = 0$

55. $x^2 - 4x + 5 = 0$

56. $x^2 + 2x + 2 = 0$

57. $x^2 + x + 1 = 0$

58. $x^2 - 3x + 3 = 0$

59. $2x^2 - 2x + 1 = 0$

60. $2x^2 + 3 = 2x$

61. $t + 3 + \dfrac{3}{t} = 0$

62. $z + 4 + \dfrac{12}{z} = 0$

63. $6x^2 + 12x + 7 = 0$

64. $4x^2 - 16x + 19 = 0$

65. $\frac{1}{2}x^2 - x + 5 = 0$

66. $x^2 + \frac{1}{2}x + 1 = 0$

67–74 ■ Recall that the symbol $\bar{z}$ represents the complex conjugate of z. If $z = a + bi$ and $w = c + di$, prove each statement.

67. $\bar{z} + \bar{w} = \overline{z + w}$

68. $\overline{zw} = \bar{z} \cdot \bar{w}$

69. $(\bar{z})^2 = \overline{z^2}$

70. $\bar{\bar{z}} = z$

71. $z + \bar{z}$ is a real number

72. $z - \bar{z}$ is a pure imaginary number

73. $z \cdot \bar{z}$ is a real number

74. $z = \bar{z}$ if and only if z is real

▲ DISCOVERY · DISCUSSION

75. Complex Conjugate Roots Suppose that the equation $ax^2 + bx + c = 0$ has real coefficients and complex roots. Why must the roots be complex conjugates of each other? (Think about how you would find the roots using the quadratic formula.)

76. Powers of i Calculate the first 12 powers of i, that is, $i, i^2, i^3, \ldots, i^{12}$. Do you notice a pattern? Explain how you would calculate any whole number power of i, using the pattern you have discovered. Use this procedure to calculate i^{4446}.

Discovery
Project

Fractals

Fractals are geometric objects that exhibit more and more detail the more we magnify them (see *Mathematics in the Modern World* on page 314). Many fractals can be described by iterating functions of complex numbers. The most famous such fractal is illustrated in Figure 1. It is called the *Mandelbrot set*, named after Benoit Mandelbrot, the mathematician who discovered it in the 1950s.

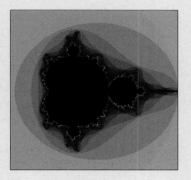

FIGURE 1

The Mandelbrot Set

Here is how the Mandelbrot set is defined. Choose a complex number c, and define the complex quadratic function

$$f(z) = z^2 + c$$

Starting with $z_0 = 0$, we form the iterates of f as follows:

$$z_1 = f(0) = c$$
$$z_2 = f(f(0)) = f(c) = c^2 + c$$
$$z_3 = f(f(f(0))) = f(c^2 + c) = (c^2 + c)^2 + c$$
$$\vdots \qquad \vdots \qquad \vdots \qquad \vdots$$

See page 320 for the definition of *modulus* (plural *moduli*).

As we continue calculating the iterates, one of two things will happen, depending on the value of c. Either the iterates $z_0, z_1, z_2, z_3, \ldots$ form a bounded set (that is, the moduli of the iterates are all less than some fixed number K), or else they eventually grow larger and larger without bound. The calculations in the table on page 318 show that for $c = 0.1 + 0.2i$, the iterates eventually stabilize at about $0.05 + 0.22i$, whereas for $c = 1 - i$, the iterates quickly become so large that a calculator can't handle them.

You can use your calculator to find the iterates, just like in the Discovery Project on page 83. With the TI-83, first put the calculator into **a+b i** mode. Then press the ⌈Y=⌉ key and enter the function $Y_1 = X^2 + C$. Now if $c = 1 + i$, for instance, enter the following commands:

$$1 + i \rightarrow C$$

$$0 \rightarrow X$$

$$Y_1 \rightarrow X$$

Press the ⌈ENTER⌉ key repeatedly to get the list of iterates. (With this value of c, you should end up with the values in the right-hand column of the table.)

$f(z) = z^2 + 0.1 + 0.2i$	$f(z) = z^2 + 1 - i$
$z_1 = f(z_0) = .1 + .2i$	$z_1 = f(z_0) = 1 - i$
$z_2 = f(z_1) = .07 + .24i$	$z_2 = f(z_1) = 1 - 3i$
$z_3 = f(z_2) = .047 + .234i$	$z_3 = f(z_2) = -7 - 7i$
$z_4 = f(z_3) = .048 + .222i$	$z_4 = f(z_3) = 1 + 97i$
$z_5 = f(z_4) = .053 + .221i$	$z_5 = f(z_4) = -9407 + 193i$
$z_6 = f(z_5) = .054 + .223i$	$z_6 = f(z_5) = 88454401 - 3631103i$
$z_7 = f(z_6) = .053 + .224i$	$z_7 = f(z_6) = 7.8 \times 10^{15} - 6.4 \times 10^{14}i$

The **Mandelbrot set** consists of those complex numbers c for which the iterates of $f(z) = z^2 + c$ are bounded. (In fact, for this function it turns out that if the iterates are bounded, the moduli of the all the iterates will be less than $K = 2$.) The numbers c that belong to the Mandelbrot set can be graphed in the complex plane. The result is the black part in Figure 1. The points not in the Mandelbrot set are assigned colors depending on how quickly the iterates become unbounded.

The TI-83 program below draws a rough graph of the Mandelbrot set. The program takes a long time to finish, even though it performs only 10 iterations for each c. For some values of c, you actually have to do many more iterations to tell whether the iterates are unbounded. [See, for instance, Problem 1(f) below.] That's why the program produces only a rough graph. But the calculator output in Figure 2 is actually a good approximation.

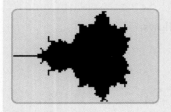

FIGURE 2

```
PROGRAM:MANDLBRT
:ClrDraw
:AxesOff
:(Xmax-Xmin)/94→H
:(Ymax-Ymin)/62→V
:For(I,0,93)
:For(J,0,61)
:Xmin+I*H→X
:Ymin+J*V→Y
:X+Yi→C
:0→Z
:For(N,1,10)
:If abs(Z)≤2
:Z²+C→Z
:End
:If abs(Z)≤2
:Pt-On(real(C),imag(C))
:DispGraph
:End
:End
:StorePic 1
```

Use the viewing rectangle $[-2, 1]$ by $[-1, 1]$ and make sure the calculator is in "**a+b i**" mode

H is the horizontal width of one pixel
V is the vertical height of one pixel
These two "**For**" loops find the complex number associated with each pixel on the screen

This "**For**" loop calculates 10 iterates, but stops iterating if **Z** has modulus larger than 2

If the iterates have modulus less than or equal to 2, the point **C** is plotted

This stores the final image under "**1**"

1. Use your calculator as described in the margin on page 318 to decide whether the complex number c is in the Mandelbrot set. [For part (f), calculate at least 60 iterates.]

    (a) $c = 1$ (b) $c = -1$

    (c) $c = -0.7 + 0.15i$ (d) $c = 0.5 + 0.5i$

    (e) $c = i$ (f) $c = -1.0404 + 0.2509i$

2. Use the **MANDLBRT** program with a smaller viewing rectangle to zoom in on a portion of the Mandelbrot set near its edge. (Store the final image in a different location if you want to keep the complete Mandelbrot picture in "1.") Do you see more detail?

3. (a) Write a calculator program that takes as input a complex number c, iterates the function $f(z) = z^2 + c$ a hundred times, and then gives the following output:

    ■ **"UNBOUNDED AT** N **"**, if z_N is the first iterate whose modulus is greater than 2

    ■ **"BOUNDED"** if each iterate from z_1 to z_{100} has modulus less than or equal to 2

    In the first case, the number c is not in the Mandelbrot set, and the index N tells us how "quickly" the iterates become unbounded. In the second case, it is likely that c is in the Mandelbrot set.

    (b) Use your program to test each of the numbers in Problem 1.

    (c) Choose other complex numbers and use your program to test them.

5.4   POLAR FORM OF COMPLEX NUMBERS; DeMOIVRE'S THEOREM

In this section we represent complex numbers in polar (or trigonometric) form. This will enable us to find the nth roots of complex numbers. To describe the polar form of complex numbers, we must first learn to work with complex numbers graphically.

Graphing Complex Numbers

To graph real numbers or sets of real numbers, we have been using the number line, which has just one dimension. Complex numbers, however have two components: the real part and the imaginary part. This suggests that we need two axes to graph complex numbers: one for the real part and one for the imaginary part. We call these the **real axis** and the **imaginary axis**, respectively. The plane determined by these two axes is called the **complex plane**. To graph the complex number $a + bi$, we plot the ordered pair of numbers (a, b) in this plane, as indicated in Figure 1.

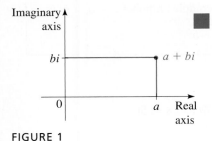

FIGURE 1

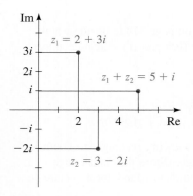

FIGURE 2

EXAMPLE 1 ■ Graphing Complex Numbers

Graph the complex numbers $z_1 = 2 + 3i$, $z_2 = 3 - 2i$, and $z_1 + z_2$.

SOLUTION

We have $z_1 + z_2 = (2 + 3i) + (3 - 2i) = 5 + i$. The graph is shown in Figure 2. ■

EXAMPLE 2 ■ Graphing Sets of Complex Numbers

Graph each of the following sets of complex numbers.
(a) $S = \{a + bi \mid a \geq 0\}$ (b) $T = \{a + bi \mid a < 1, b \geq 0\}$

SOLUTION

(a) S is the set of complex numbers whose real part is nonnegative. The graph is shown in Figure 3(a).

(b) T is the set of complex numbers for which the real part is less than 1 and the imaginary part is nonnegative. The graph is shown in Figure 3(b).

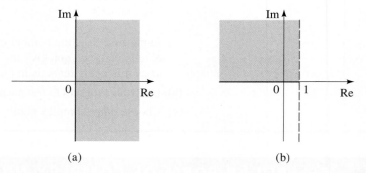

FIGURE 3   (a)   (b)   ■

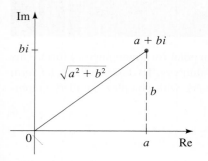

FIGURE 4

Recall that the absolute value of a real number can be thought of as its distance from the origin on the real number line (see Appendix A.1). We define absolute value for complex numbers in a similar fashion. From Figure 4 we can see, using the Pythagorean Theorem, that the distance between $a + bi$ and the origin in the complex plane is $\sqrt{a^2 + b^2}$. This leads to the following definition.

> The **modulus** (or **absolute value**) of the complex number $z = a + bi$ is
> $$|z| = \sqrt{a^2 + b^2}$$

The plural of *modulus* is *moduli*.

EXAMPLE 3 ■ Calculating the Modulus

Find the moduli of the complex numbers $3 + 4i$ and $8 - 5i$.

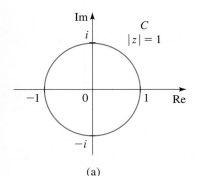

(a)

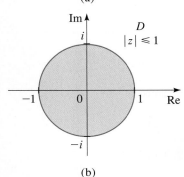

(b)

FIGURE 5

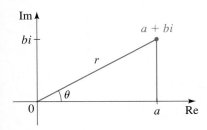

FIGURE 6

SOLUTION

$$|3 + 4i| = \sqrt{3^2 + 4^2} = \sqrt{25} = 5$$
$$|8 - 5i| = \sqrt{8^2 + (-5)^2} = \sqrt{89}$$ ∎

EXAMPLE 4 ■ Absolute Value of Complex Numbers

Graph each of the following sets of complex numbers.

(a) $C = \{z \mid |z| = 1\}$ (b) $D = \{z \mid |z| \le 1\}$

SOLUTION

(a) C is the set of complex numbers whose distance from the origin is 1. Thus, C is a circle of radius 1 with center at the origin.

(b) D is the set of complex numbers whose distance from the origin is less than or equal to 1. Thus, D is the disk that consists of all complex numbers on and inside the circle C of part (a).

The graphs of C and D are shown in Figure 5. ∎

■ Polar Form of Complex Numbers

Let $z = a + bi$ be a complex number, and in the complex plane let's draw the line segment joining the origin to the point $a + bi$ (see Figure 6). The length of this line segment is denoted by $r = |z| = \sqrt{a^2 + b^2}$. If θ is an angle in standard position whose terminal side coincides with this line segment, then by the definitions of sine and cosine (see Section 3.2)

$$a = r \cos \theta \qquad \text{and} \qquad b = r \sin \theta$$

so $z = r \cos \theta + ir \sin \theta = r(\cos \theta + i \sin \theta)$. We have shown the following.

> **POLAR FORM OF COMPLEX NUMBERS**
>
> A complex number $z = a + bi$ has the **polar form** (or **trigonometric form**)
>
> $$z = r(\cos \theta + i \sin \theta)$$
>
> where $r = |z| = \sqrt{a^2 + b^2}$ and $\tan \theta = b/a$. The number r is the **modulus** of z, and θ is an **argument** of z.

The argument of z is not unique, but any two arguments of z differ by a multiple of 2π.

EXAMPLE 5 ■ Writing Complex Numbers in Polar Form

Write each of the following complex numbers in trigonometric form.

(a) $1 + i$ (b) $-1 + \sqrt{3}\, i$ (c) $-4\sqrt{3} - 4i$ (d) $3 + 4i$

SOLUTION

These complex numbers are graphed in Figure 7, which helps us find their arguments.

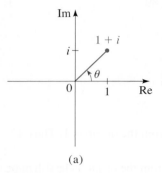

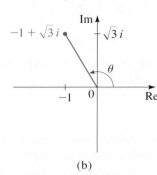

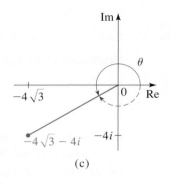

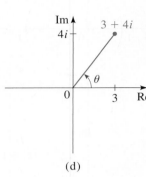

(a)　　　　　　　　　(b)　　　　　　　　　(c)　　　　　　　　　(d)

FIGURE 7

$\tan \theta = \frac{1}{1} = 1$

$\theta = \frac{\pi}{4}$

(a) An argument is $\theta = \pi/4$ and $r = \sqrt{1 + 1} = \sqrt{2}$. Thus

$$1 + i = \sqrt{2}\left(\cos \frac{\pi}{4} + i \sin \frac{\pi}{4}\right)$$

$\tan \theta = \frac{\sqrt{3}}{-1} = -\sqrt{3}$

$\theta = \frac{2\pi}{3}$

(b) An argument is $\theta = 2\pi/3$ and $r = \sqrt{1 + 3} = 2$. Thus

$$-1 + \sqrt{3}\, i = 2\left(\cos \frac{2\pi}{3} + i \sin \frac{2\pi}{3}\right)$$

$\tan \theta = \frac{-4}{-4\sqrt{3}} = \frac{1}{\sqrt{3}}$

$\theta = \frac{7\pi}{6}$

(c) An argument is $\theta = 7\pi/6$ (or we could use $\theta = -5\pi/6$), and $r = \sqrt{48 + 16} = 8$. Thus

$$-4\sqrt{3} - 4i = 8\left(\cos \frac{7\pi}{6} + i \sin \frac{7\pi}{6}\right)$$

$\tan \theta = \frac{4}{3}$

$\theta = \tan^{-1} \frac{4}{3}$

(d) An argument is $\theta = \tan^{-1} \frac{4}{3}$ and $r = \sqrt{3^2 + 4^2} = 5$. So

$$3 + 4i = 5\left[\cos\left(\tan^{-1} \tfrac{4}{3}\right) + i \sin\left(\tan^{-1} \tfrac{4}{3}\right)\right]$$

∎

The addition formulas for sine and cosine discussed in Section 4.2 greatly simplify the multiplication and division of complex numbers in polar form. The following theorem shows how.

MULTIPLICATION AND DIVISION OF COMPLEX NUMBERS

If the two complex numbers z_1 and z_2 have the polar forms

$$z_1 = r_1(\cos \theta_1 + i \sin \theta_1) \qquad \text{and} \qquad z_2 = r_2(\cos \theta_2 + i \sin \theta_2)$$

then

$$z_1 z_2 = r_1 r_2 [\cos(\theta_1 + \theta_2) + i \sin(\theta_1 + \theta_2)] \qquad\qquad \text{Multiplication}$$

$$\frac{z_1}{z_2} = \frac{r_1}{r_2}[\cos(\theta_1 - \theta_2) + i \sin(\theta_1 - \theta_2)] \qquad (z_2 \ne 0) \qquad \text{Division}$$

This theorem says:

> *To multiply two complex numbers, multiply the moduli and add the arguments.*

> *To divide two complex numbers, divide the moduli and subtract the arguments.*

■ **Proof**   To prove the multiplication formula, we simply multiply the two complex numbers.

$$z_1 z_2 = r_1 r_2 (\cos \theta_1 + i \sin \theta_1)(\cos \theta_2 + i \sin \theta_2)$$

$$= r_1 r_2 [\cos \theta_1 \cos \theta_2 - \sin \theta_1 \sin \theta_2 + i(\sin \theta_1 \cos \theta_2 + \cos \theta_1 \sin \theta_2)]$$

$$= r_1 r_2 [\cos(\theta_1 + \theta_2) + i \sin(\theta_1 + \theta_2)]$$

In the last step we used the addition formulas for sine and cosine.   ☐

The proof of the division formula is left as an exercise.

EXAMPLE 6 ■ Multiplying and Dividing Complex Numbers

Let

$$z_1 = 2\left(\cos \frac{\pi}{4} + i \sin \frac{\pi}{4}\right) \qquad \text{and} \qquad z_2 = 5\left(\cos \frac{\pi}{3} + i \sin \frac{\pi}{3}\right)$$

Find (a) $z_1 z_2$ and (b) z_1/z_2.

SOLUTION

(a) By the multiplication formula

$$z_1 z_2 = (2)(5)\left[\cos\left(\frac{\pi}{4} + \frac{\pi}{3}\right) + i \sin\left(\frac{\pi}{4} + \frac{\pi}{3}\right)\right]$$

$$= 10\left(\cos \frac{7\pi}{12} + i \sin \frac{7\pi}{12}\right)$$

To approximate the answer, we use a calculator in radian mode and get

$$z_1 z_2 \approx 10(-0.2588 + 0.9659i) = -2.588 + 9.659i$$

(b) By the division formula

$$\frac{z_1}{z_2} = \frac{2}{5}\left[\cos\left(\frac{\pi}{4} - \frac{\pi}{3}\right) + i \sin\left(\frac{\pi}{4} - \frac{\pi}{3}\right)\right]$$

$$= \frac{2}{5}\left[\cos\left(-\frac{\pi}{12}\right) + i \sin\left(-\frac{\pi}{12}\right)\right]$$

$$= \frac{2}{5}\left(\cos \frac{\pi}{12} - i \sin \frac{\pi}{12}\right)$$

Leonhard Euler (1707–1783) was born in Basel, Switzerland, the son of a pastor. At age 13 his father sent him to the University at Basel to study theology, but Euler soon decided to devote himself to the sciences. Besides theology he studied mathematics, medicine, astronomy, physics, and oriental languages. It is said that Euler could calculate as effortlessly as "men breathe or as eagles fly." One hundred years before Euler, Fermat (see page 255) had conjectured that $2^{2^n} + 1$ is a prime number for all n. The first five of these numbers are 5, 17, 257, 65537, and 4,294,967,297. It's easy to show that the first four are prime. The fifth was also thought to be prime until Euler, with his phenomenal calculating ability, showed that it is the product $641 \times 6,700,417$ and so is not prime. Euler published more than any other mathematician in history. His collected works comprise 75 large volumes. Although he was blind for the last 17 years of his life, he continued to work and publish. In his writings he popularized the use of the symbols π, e, and i, which you will find in this textbook. One of Euler's most lasting contributions is the development of complex numbers.

Using a calculator in radian mode, we get the approximate answer:

$$\frac{z_1}{z_2} \approx \frac{2}{5}(0.9659 - 0.2588i) = 0.3864 - 0.1035i$$ ∎

DeMoivre's Theorem

Repeated use of the multiplication formula gives the following useful formula for raising a complex number to a power n for any positive integer n.

DeMOIVRE'S THEOREM

If $z = r(\cos\theta + i\sin\theta)$, then for any integer n

$$z^n = r^n(\cos n\theta + i\sin n\theta)$$

This theorem says: *To take the nth power of a complex number, we take the nth power of the modulus and multiply the argument by n.*

■ **Proof** By the multiplication formula

$$z^2 = zz = r^2[\cos(\theta + \theta) + i\sin(\theta + \theta)]$$

$$= r^2(\cos 2\theta + i\sin 2\theta)$$

Now we multiply z^2 by z to get

$$z^3 = z^2z = r^3[\cos(2\theta + \theta) + i\sin(2\theta + \theta)]$$

$$= r^3(\cos 3\theta + i\sin 3\theta)$$

Repeating this argument, we see that for any positive integer n

$$z^n = r^n(\cos n\theta + i\sin n\theta)$$

A similar argument using the division formula shows that this also holds for negative integers. ☐

EXAMPLE 7 ■ Finding a Power Using DeMoivre's Theorem

Find $\left(\frac{1}{2} + \frac{1}{2}i\right)^{10}$.

SOLUTION

Since $\frac{1}{2} + \frac{1}{2}i = \frac{1}{2}(1 + i)$, it follows from Example 5(a) that

$$\frac{1}{2} + \frac{1}{2}i = \frac{\sqrt{2}}{2}\left(\cos\frac{\pi}{4} + i\sin\frac{\pi}{4}\right)$$

So by DeMoivre's Theorem,

$$\left(\frac{1}{2} + \frac{1}{2}i\right)^{10} = \left(\frac{\sqrt{2}}{2}\right)^{10}\left(\cos\frac{10\pi}{4} + i\sin\frac{10\pi}{4}\right)$$

$$= \frac{2^5}{2^{10}}\left(\cos\frac{5\pi}{2} + i\sin\frac{5\pi}{2}\right) = \frac{1}{32}i$$ ■

■ nth Roots of Complex Numbers

An **nth root** of a complex number z is any complex number w such that $w^n = z$. DeMoivre's Theorem gives us a method for calculating the nth roots of any complex number.

---

nTH ROOTS OF COMPLEX NUMBERS

If $z = r(\cos\theta + i\sin\theta)$ and n is a positive integer, then z has the n distinct nth roots

$$w_k = r^{1/n}\left[\cos\left(\frac{\theta + 2k\pi}{n}\right) + i\sin\left(\frac{\theta + 2k\pi}{n}\right)\right]$$

for $k = 0, 1, 2, \ldots, n - 1$.

■ **Proof**   To find the nth roots of z, we need to find a complex number w such that

$$w^n = z$$

Let's write z in polar form:

$$z = r(\cos\theta + i\sin\theta)$$

One nth root of z is

$$w = r^{1/n}\left(\cos\frac{\theta}{n} + i\sin\frac{\theta}{n}\right)$$

since by DeMoivre's Theorem, $w^n = z$. But the argument θ of z can be replaced by $\theta + 2k\pi$ for any integer k. Since this expression gives a different value of w for $k = 0, 1, 2, \ldots, n - 1$, we have proved the formula in the theorem.   □

The following observations help us use the preceding formula.

---

1. The modulus of each nth root is $r^{1/n}$.

2. The argument of the first root is θ/n.

3. We repeatedly add $2\pi/n$ to get the argument of each successive root.

These observations show that, when graphed, the nth roots of z are spaced equally on the circle of radius $r^{1/n}$.

EXAMPLE 8 ■ Finding Roots of a Complex Number

Find the six sixth roots of $z = -64$, and graph these roots in the complex plane.

SOLUTION

In polar form, $z = 64(\cos \pi + i \sin \pi)$. Applying the formula for nth roots with $n = 6$, we get

$$w_k = 64^{1/6}\left[\cos\left(\frac{\pi + 2k\pi}{6}\right) + i \sin\left(\frac{\pi + 2k\pi}{6}\right)\right]$$

for $k = 0, 1, 2, 3, 4, 5$. Thus, the six sixth roots of -64 are

We add $2\pi/6 = \pi/3$ to each argument to get the argument of the next root.

$$w_0 = 64^{1/6}\left(\cos\frac{\pi}{6} + i \sin\frac{\pi}{6}\right) = \sqrt{3} + i$$

$$w_1 = 64^{1/6}\left(\cos\frac{\pi}{2} + i \sin\frac{\pi}{2}\right) = 2i$$

$$w_2 = 64^{1/6}\left(\cos\frac{5\pi}{6} + i \sin\frac{5\pi}{6}\right) = -\sqrt{3} + i$$

$$w_3 = 64^{1/6}\left(\cos\frac{7\pi}{6} + i \sin\frac{7\pi}{6}\right) = -\sqrt{3} - i$$

$$w_4 = 64^{1/6}\left(\cos\frac{3\pi}{2} + i \sin\frac{3\pi}{2}\right) = -2i$$

$$w_5 = 64^{1/6}\left(\cos\frac{11\pi}{6} + i \sin\frac{11\pi}{6}\right) = \sqrt{3} - i$$

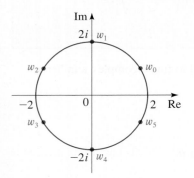

FIGURE 8
The six sixth roots of $z = -64$

All these points lie on a circle of radius 2, as shown in Figure 8. ■

When finding roots of complex numbers, we sometimes write the argument θ of the complex number in degrees. In this case, the nth roots are obtained from the formula

$$w_k = r^{1/n}\left[\cos\left(\frac{\theta + 360°k}{n}\right) + i \sin\left(\frac{\theta + 360°k}{n}\right)\right]$$

for $k = 0, 1, 2, \ldots, n - 1$.

EXAMPLE 9 ■ Finding Cube Roots of a Complex Number

Find the three cube roots of $z = 2 + 2i$, and graph these roots in the complex plane.

SOLUTION

First we write z in polar form using degrees. We have $r = \sqrt{2^2 + 2^2} = 2\sqrt{2}$ and $\theta = 45°$. Thus

$$z = 2\sqrt{2}(\cos 45° + i \sin 45°)$$

Applying the formula for nth roots (in degrees) with $n = 3$, we find the cube roots of z are of the form

$$(2\sqrt{2})^{1/3} = (2^{3/2})^{1/3} = 2^{1/2} = \sqrt{2}$$

$$w_k = (2\sqrt{2})^{1/3}\left[\cos\left(\frac{45° + 360°k}{3}\right) + i \sin\left(\frac{45° + 360°k}{3}\right)\right]$$

We add $360°/3 = 120°$ to each argument to get the argument of the next root.

where $k = 0, 1, 2$. Thus, the three cube roots are

$$w_0 = \sqrt{2}(\cos 15° + i \sin 15°) \approx 1.366 + 0.366i$$

$$w_1 = \sqrt{2}(\cos 135° + i \sin 135°) = -1 + i$$

$$w_2 = \sqrt{2}(\cos 255° + i \sin 255°) \approx -0.366 + 1.366i$$

The three cube roots of z are graphed in Figure 9. These roots are spaced equally on a circle of radius $\sqrt{2}$. ■

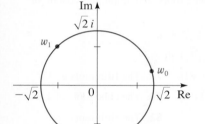

EXAMPLE 10 ■ **Solving an Equation Using the nth Roots Formula**

Solve the equation $z^6 + 64 = 0$.

SOLUTION

FIGURE 9
The three cube roots of $z = 2 + 2i$

This equation can be written as $z^6 = -64$. Thus, the solutions are the sixth roots of -64, which we found in Example 8. ■

5.4 EXERCISES

1–8 ■ Graph the complex number and find its modulus.

1. $4i$

2. -2

3. $5 + 2i$

4. $7 - 3i$

5. $\sqrt{3} + i$

6. $-1 - \dfrac{\sqrt{3}}{3}i$

7. $\dfrac{3 + 4i}{5}$

8. $\dfrac{-\sqrt{2} + i\sqrt{2}}{2}$

9–10 ■ Sketch the complex number z, and also sketch $2z$, $-z$, and $\frac{1}{2}z$ on the same complex plane.

9. $z = 1 + i$

10. $z = -1 + i\sqrt{3}$

11–12 ■ Sketch the complex number z and its complex conjugate $\bar{z}$ on the same complex plane.

11. $z = 8 + 2i$

12. $z = -5 + 6i$

13–14 ■ Sketch z_1, z_2, $z_1 + z_2$, and $z_1 z_2$ on the same complex plane.

13. $z_1 = 2 - i,\quad z_2 = 2 + i$

14. $z_1 = -1 + i,\quad z_2 = 2 - 3i$

15–22 ■ Sketch the set in the complex plane.

15. $\{z = a + bi \mid a \leqslant 0, b \geqslant 0\}$

16. $\{z = a + bi \mid a > 1, b > 1\}$

17. $\{z \mid |z| = 3\}$

18. $\{z \mid |z| \geq 1\}$

19. $\{z \mid |z| < 2\}$

20. $\{z \mid 2 \leq |z| \leq 5\}$

21. $\{z = a + bi \mid a + b < 2\}$

22. $\{z = a + bi \mid a \geq b\}$

23–46 ■ Write the complex number in polar form with argument θ between 0 and 2π.

23. $1 + i$

24. $1 + \sqrt{3}\, i$

25. $\sqrt{2} - \sqrt{2}\, i$

26. $1 - i$

27. $2\sqrt{3} - 2i$

28. $-1 + i$

29. $-3i$

30. $-3 - 3\sqrt{3}\, i$

31. $5 + 5i$

32. 4

33. $4\sqrt{3} - 4i$

34. $8i$

35. -20

36. $\sqrt{3} + i$

37. $3 + 4i$

38. $i(2 - 2i)$

39. $3i(1 + i)$

40. $2(1 - i)$

41. $4(\sqrt{3} + i)$

42. $-3 - 3i$

43. $2 + i$

44. $3 + \sqrt{3}\, i$

45. $\sqrt{2} + \sqrt{2}\, i$

46. $-\pi i$

47–54 ■ Find the product $z_1 z_2$ and the quotient z_1/z_2. Express your answer in polar form.

47. $z_1 = \cos \pi + i \sin \pi, \quad z_2 = \cos \dfrac{\pi}{3} + i \sin \dfrac{\pi}{3}$

48. $z_1 = \cos \dfrac{\pi}{4} + i \sin \dfrac{\pi}{4}, \quad z_2 = \cos \dfrac{3\pi}{4} + i \sin \dfrac{3\pi}{4}$

49. $z_1 = 3\left(\cos \dfrac{\pi}{6} + i \sin \dfrac{\pi}{6}\right), \quad z_2 = 5\left(\cos \dfrac{4\pi}{3} + i \sin \dfrac{4\pi}{3}\right)$

50. $z_1 = 7\left(\cos \dfrac{9\pi}{8} + i \sin \dfrac{9\pi}{8}\right), \quad z_2 = 2\left(\cos \dfrac{\pi}{8} + i \sin \dfrac{\pi}{8}\right)$

51. $z_1 = 4(\cos 120° + i \sin 120°)$,
$z_2 = 2(\cos 30° + i \sin 30°)$

52. $z_1 = \sqrt{2}\,(\cos 75° + i \sin 75°)$,
$z_2 = 3\sqrt{2}\,(\cos 60° + i \sin 60°)$

53. $z_1 = 4(\cos 200° + i \sin 200°)$,
$z_2 = 25(\cos 150° + i \sin 150°)$

54. $z_1 = \frac{4}{5}(\cos 25° + i \sin 25°)$,
$z_2 = \frac{1}{5}(\cos 155° + i \sin 155°)$

55–62 ■ Write z_1 and z_2 in polar form, and then find the product $z_1 z_2$ and the quotients z_1/z_2 and $1/z_1$.

55. $z_1 = \sqrt{3} + i, \quad z_2 = 1 + \sqrt{3}\, i$

56. $z_1 = \sqrt{2} - \sqrt{2}\, i, \quad z_2 = 1 - i$

57. $z_1 = 2\sqrt{3} - 2i, \quad z_2 = -1 + i$

58. $z_1 = -\sqrt{2}\, i, \quad z_2 = -3 - 3\sqrt{3}\, i$

59. $z_1 = 5 + 5i, \quad z_2 = 4$

60. $z_1 = 4\sqrt{3} - 4i, \quad z_2 = 8i$

61. $z_1 = -20, \quad z_2 = \sqrt{3} + i$

62. $z_1 = 3 + 4i, \quad z_2 = 2 - 2i$

63–74 ■ Find the indicated power using DeMoivre's Theorem.

63. $(1 + i)^{20}$

64. $(1 - \sqrt{3}\, i)^5$

65. $(2\sqrt{3} + 2i)^5$

66. $(1 - i)^8$

67. $\left(\dfrac{\sqrt{2}}{2} + \dfrac{\sqrt{2}}{2} i\right)^{12}$

68. $(\sqrt{3} - i)^{-10}$

69. $(2 - 2i)^8$

70. $\left(-\dfrac{1}{2} - \dfrac{\sqrt{3}}{2} i\right)^{15}$

71. $(-1 - i)^7$

72. $(3 + \sqrt{3}\, i)^4$

73. $(2\sqrt{3} + 2i)^{-5}$

74. $(1 - i)^{-8}$

75–84 ■ Find the indicated roots, and graph the roots in the complex plane.

75. The square roots of $4\sqrt{3} + 4i$

76. The cube roots of $4\sqrt{3} + 4i$

77. The fourth roots of $-81i$ **78.** The fifth roots of 32

79. The eighth roots of 1 **80.** The cube roots of $1 + i$

81. The cube roots of i **82.** The fifth roots of i

83. The fourth roots of -1

84. The fifth roots of $-16 - 16\sqrt{3}\, i$

85–90 ■ Solve the equation.

85. $z^4 + 1 = 0$

86. $z^8 - i = 0$

87. $z^3 - 4\sqrt{3} - 4i = 0$

88. $z^6 - 1 = 0$

89. $z^3 + 1 = -i$

90. $z^3 - 1 = 0$

91. (a) Let $w = \cos \dfrac{2\pi}{n} + i \sin \dfrac{2\pi}{n}$ where n is a positive integer. Show that $1, w, w^2, w^3, \ldots, w^{n-1}$ are the n distinct nth roots of 1.

(b) If $z \neq 0$ is any complex number and $s^n = z$, show that the n distinct nth roots of z are

$$s, sw, sw^2, sw^3, \ldots, sw^{n-1}$$

■ **DISCOVERY · DISCUSSION**

92. Sums of Roots of Unity   Find the exact values of all three cube roots of 1 (see Exercise 91) and then add them.

Do the same for the fourth, fifth, sixth, and eighth roots of 1. What do you think is the sum of the nth roots of 1, for any n?

93. Products of Roots of Unity   Find the product of the three cube roots of 1 (see Exercise 91). Do the same for the fourth, fifth, sixth, and eighth roots of 1. What do you think is the product of the nth roots of 1, for any n?

94. Complex Coefficients and the Quadratic Formula
The quadratic formula works whether the coefficients of the equation are real or complex. Solve these equations using the quadratic formula, and, if necessary, DeMoivre's Theorem.

(a) $z^2 + (1 + i)z + i = 0$

(b) $z^2 - iz + 1 = 0$

(c) $z^2 - (2 - i)z - \frac{1}{4}i = 0$

5.5 VECTORS

In applications of mathematics, certain quantities are determined completely by their magnitude—for example, length, mass, area, temperature, and energy. We speak of a length of 5 m or a mass of 3 kg; only one number is needed to describe each of these quantities. Such a quantity is called a **scalar**.

On the other hand, to describe the displacement of an object, two numbers are required: the *magnitude* and the *direction* of the displacement. To describe the velocity of a moving object, we must specify both the *speed* and the *direction* of travel. Quantities such as displacement, velocity, acceleration, and force that involve magnitude as well as direction are called *directed quantities*. One way to represent such quantities mathematically is through the use of *vectors*.

$\mathbf{u} = \overrightarrow{AB}$

FIGURE 1

Geometric Description of Vectors

A **vector** in the plane is a line segment with an assigned direction. We sketch a vector as shown in Figure 1 with an arrow to specify the direction. We denote this vector by $\overrightarrow{AB}$. Point A is the **initial point**, and B is the **terminal point** of the vector $\overrightarrow{AB}$. The length of the line segment AB is called the **magnitude** or **length** of the vector and is denoted by $|\overrightarrow{AB}|$. We use boldface letters to denote vectors. Thus, we write $\mathbf{u} = \overrightarrow{AB}$.

FIGURE 2

Two vectors are considered **equal** if they have equal magnitude and the same direction. Thus, all the vectors in Figure 2 are equal. This definition of equality makes sense if we think of a vector as representing a displacement. Two such displacements are the same if they have equal magnitudes and the same direction. So the vectors in Figure 2 can be thought of as the *same* displacement applied to objects in different locations in the plane.

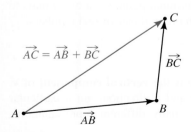

$\overrightarrow{AC} = \overrightarrow{AB} + \overrightarrow{BC}$

FIGURE 3

If the displacement $\mathbf{u} = \overrightarrow{AB}$ is followed by the displacement $\mathbf{v} = \overrightarrow{BC}$, then the resulting displacement is $\overrightarrow{AC}$ as shown in Figure 3. In other words, the single displacement represented by the vector $\overrightarrow{AC}$ has the same effect as the other two displacements together. We call the vector $\overrightarrow{AC}$ the **sum** of the vectors $\overrightarrow{AB}$ and $\overrightarrow{BC}$ and we write $\overrightarrow{AC} = \overrightarrow{AB} + \overrightarrow{BC}$. (The **zero vector**, denoted by $\mathbf{0}$, represents no displacement). Thus, to find the sum of any two vectors $\mathbf{u}$ and $\mathbf{v}$, we sketch vectors equal to $\mathbf{u}$ and $\mathbf{v}$ with the initial point of one at the terminal point of the other [see Figure 4(a)]. If we draw **u** and **v** starting at the same point, then **u** + **v** is the vector that is the diagonal of the parallelogram formed by **u** and **v**, as shown in Figure 4(b).

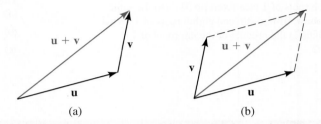

FIGURE 4
Addition of vectors

(a)   (b)

If a is a real number and **v** is a vector, we define a new vector a**v** as follows: The vector a**v** has magnitude $|a||\mathbf{v}|$ and has the same direction as **v** if $a > 0$, or the opposite direction if $a < 0$. If $a = 0$, then $a\mathbf{v} = \mathbf{0}$, the zero vector. This process is called **multiplication of a vector by a scalar**. Multiplying a vector by a scalar has the effect of stretching or shrinking the vector. Figure 5 shows graphs of the vector a**v** for different values of a. We write the vector $(-1)\mathbf{v}$ as $-\mathbf{v}$. Thus, $-\mathbf{v}$ is the vector with the same length as **v** but with the opposite direction.

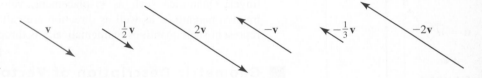

FIGURE 5
Multiplication of a vector by a scalar

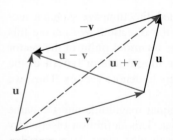

FIGURE 6
Subtraction of vectors

Note the distinction between the *vector* $\langle a, b \rangle$ and the *point* (a, b).

The **difference** of two vectors **u** and **v** is defined by $\mathbf{u} - \mathbf{v} = \mathbf{u} + (-\mathbf{v})$. Figure 6 shows that the vector $\mathbf{u} - \mathbf{v}$ is the other diagonal of the parallelogram formed by **u** and **v**.

■ Vectors in the Coordinate Plane

So far we've discussed vectors geometrically. By placing a vector in a coordinate plane, we can describe it analytically (that is, by using components). In Figure 7(a), to go from the initial point of the vector **v** to the terminal point, we move a units to the right and b units upward. We represent **v** as an ordered pair of real numbers.

$$\mathbf{v} = \langle a, b \rangle$$

where a is the **horizontal component** of **v** and b is the **vertical component** of **v**. Remember that a vector represents a magnitude and a direction, not a particular arrow in the plane. Thus, the vector $\langle a, b \rangle$ has many different representations, depending on its initial point [see Figure 7(b)].

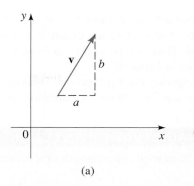

FIGURE 7

(a)

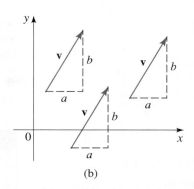

(b)

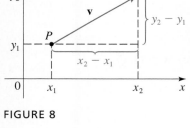

FIGURE 8

Using Figure 8, the relationship between a geometric representation of a vector and the analytic one can be stated as follows.

COMPONENT FORM OF A VECTOR

If a vector $\mathbf{v}$ is represented in the plane with initial point $P(x_1, y_1)$ and terminal point $Q(x_2, y_2)$, then

$$\mathbf{v} = \langle x_2 - x_1, y_2 - y_1 \rangle$$

EXAMPLE 1 ■ Describing Vectors in Component Form

(a) Find the component form of the vector $\mathbf{u}$ with initial point $(-2, 5)$ and terminal point $(3, 7)$.

(b) If the vector $\mathbf{v} = \langle 3, 7 \rangle$ is sketched with initial point $(2, 4)$, what is its terminal point?

(c) Sketch representations of the vector $\mathbf{w} = \langle 2, 3 \rangle$ with initial points at $(0, 0)$, $(2, 2)$, $(-2, -1)$, and $(1, 4)$.

SOLUTION

(a) The desired vector is

$$\mathbf{u} = \langle 3 - (-2), 7 - 5 \rangle = \langle 5, 2 \rangle$$

(b) Let the terminal point of $\mathbf{v}$ be (x, y). Then

$$\langle x - 2, y - 4 \rangle = \langle 3, 7 \rangle$$

So $x - 2 = 3$ and $y - 4 = 7$, or $x = 5$ and $y = 11$. The terminal point is $(5, 11)$.

(c) Representations of the vector $\mathbf{w}$ are sketched in Figure 9. ■

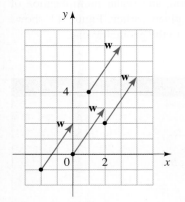

FIGURE 9

We now give analytic definitions of the various operations on vectors that we have described geometrically. Let's start with equality of vectors. We've said that two vectors are equal if they have equal magnitude and the same direction. For the

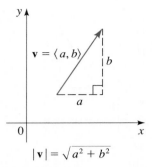

$$|\mathbf{v}| = \sqrt{a^2 + b^2}$$

FIGURE 10

vectors $\mathbf{u} = \langle a_1, b_1 \rangle$ and $\mathbf{v} = \langle a_2, b_2 \rangle$, this means that $a_1 = a_2$ and $b_1 = b_2$. In other words, two vectors are **equal** if and only if their corresponding components are equal. Thus, all the arrows in Figure 7(b) represent the same vector, as do all the arrows in Figure 9.

Applying the Pythagorean Theorem to the triangle in Figure 10, we obtain the following formula for the magnitude of a vector.

MAGNITUDE OF A VECTOR

The **magnitude** or **length** of a vector $\mathbf{v} = \langle a, b \rangle$ is

$$|\mathbf{v}| = \sqrt{a^2 + b^2}$$

EXAMPLE 2 ■ Magnitudes of Vectors

Find the magnitude of each vector.

(a) $\mathbf{u} = \langle 2, -3 \rangle$　　　(b) $\mathbf{v} = \langle 5, 0 \rangle$　　　(c) $\mathbf{w} = \left\langle \frac{3}{5}, \frac{4}{5} \right\rangle$

SOLUTION

(a) $|\mathbf{u}| = \sqrt{2^2 + (-3)^2} = \sqrt{13}$

(b) $|\mathbf{v}| = \sqrt{5^2 + 0^2} = \sqrt{25} = 5$

(c) $|\mathbf{w}| = \sqrt{\left(\frac{3}{5}\right)^2 + \left(\frac{4}{5}\right)^2} = \sqrt{\frac{9}{25} + \frac{16}{25}} = 1$　　■

The following definitions of addition, subtraction, and scalar multiplication of vectors correspond to the geometric descriptions given earlier. Figure 11 shows how the analytic definition of addition corresponds to the geometric one.

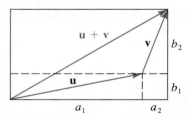

FIGURE 11

ALGEBRAIC OPERATIONS ON VECTORS

If $\mathbf{u} = \langle a_1, b_1 \rangle$ and $\mathbf{v} = \langle a_2, b_2 \rangle$, then

$$\mathbf{u} + \mathbf{v} = \langle a_1 + a_2, b_1 + b_2 \rangle$$

$$\mathbf{u} - \mathbf{v} = \langle a_1 - a_2, b_1 - b_2 \rangle$$

$$c\mathbf{u} = \langle ca_1, cb_1 \rangle, \qquad c \in \mathbb{R}$$

EXAMPLE 3 ■ Operations with Vectors

If $\mathbf{u} = \langle 2, -3 \rangle$ and $\mathbf{v} = \langle -1, 2 \rangle$, find $\mathbf{u} + \mathbf{v}$, $\mathbf{u} - \mathbf{v}$, $2\mathbf{u}$, $-3\mathbf{v}$, and $2\mathbf{u} + 3\mathbf{v}$.

SOLUTION

By the definitions of the vector operations, we have

$$\mathbf{u} + \mathbf{v} = \langle 2, -3 \rangle + \langle -1, 2 \rangle = \langle 1, -1 \rangle$$

$$\mathbf{u} - \mathbf{v} = \langle 2, -3 \rangle - \langle -1, 2 \rangle = \langle 3, -5 \rangle$$

$$2\mathbf{u} = 2\langle 2, -3 \rangle = \langle 4, -6 \rangle$$

$$-3\mathbf{v} = -3\langle -1, 2 \rangle = \langle 3, -6 \rangle$$

$$2\mathbf{u} + 3\mathbf{v} = 2\langle 2, -3 \rangle + 3\langle -1, 2 \rangle = \langle 4, -6 \rangle + \langle -3, 6 \rangle = \langle 1, 0 \rangle \qquad ■$$

The following properties for vector operations can be easily proved from the definitions. The **zero vector** is the vector $\mathbf{0} = \langle 0, 0 \rangle$. It plays the same role for addition of vectors as the number 0 does for addition of real numbers.

PROPERTIES OF VECTORS

Vector addition	Multiplication by a scalar
$\mathbf{u} + \mathbf{v} = \mathbf{v} + \mathbf{u}$	$c(\mathbf{u} + \mathbf{v}) = c\mathbf{u} + c\mathbf{v}$
$\mathbf{u} + (\mathbf{v} + \mathbf{w}) = (\mathbf{u} + \mathbf{v}) + \mathbf{w}$	$(c + d)\mathbf{u} = c\mathbf{u} + d\mathbf{u}$
$\mathbf{u} + \mathbf{0} = \mathbf{u}$	$(cd)\mathbf{u} = c(d\mathbf{u}) = d(c\mathbf{u})$
$\mathbf{u} + (-\mathbf{u}) = \mathbf{0}$	$1\mathbf{u} = \mathbf{u}$
Length of a vector	$0\mathbf{u} = \mathbf{0}$
$|c\mathbf{u}| = |c|\,|\mathbf{u}|$	$c\mathbf{0} = \mathbf{0}$

A vector of length 1 is called a **unit vector**. For instance, in Example 2(c), the vector $\mathbf{w} = \langle \frac{3}{5}, \frac{4}{5} \rangle$ is a unit vector. Two useful unit vectors are $\mathbf{i}$ and $\mathbf{j}$, defined by

$$\mathbf{i} = \langle 1, 0 \rangle \qquad \mathbf{j} = \langle 0, 1 \rangle$$

These vectors are special because any vector can be expressed in terms of them.

VECTORS IN TERMS OF i AND j

The vector $\mathbf{v} = \langle a, b \rangle$ can be expressed in terms of $\mathbf{i}$ and $\mathbf{j}$ by

$$\mathbf{v} = \langle a, b \rangle = a\mathbf{i} + b\mathbf{j}$$

EXAMPLE 4 ■ Vectors in Terms of i and j

(a) Write the vector $\mathbf{u} = \langle 5, -8 \rangle$ in terms of $\mathbf{i}$ and $\mathbf{j}$.
(b) If $\mathbf{u} = 3\mathbf{i} + 2\mathbf{j}$ and $\mathbf{v} = -\mathbf{i} + 6\mathbf{j}$, write $2\mathbf{u} + 5\mathbf{v}$ in terms of $\mathbf{i}$ and $\mathbf{j}$.

SOLUTION

(a) $\mathbf{u} = 5\mathbf{i} + (-8)\mathbf{j} = 5\mathbf{i} - 8\mathbf{j}$

(b) The properties of addition and scalar multiplication of vectors show that we can manipulate vectors in the same way as algebraic expressions. Thus

$$2\mathbf{u} + 5\mathbf{v} = 2(3\mathbf{i} + 2\mathbf{j}) + 5(-\mathbf{i} + 6\mathbf{j})$$
$$= (6\mathbf{i} + 4\mathbf{j}) + (-5\mathbf{i} + 30\mathbf{j})$$
$$= \mathbf{i} + 34\mathbf{j} \qquad \blacksquare$$

Let $\mathbf{v}$ be a vector in the plane with its initial point at the origin. The **direction** of $\mathbf{v}$ is θ, the smallest positive angle in standard position formed by the positive x-axis and $\mathbf{v}$ (see Figure 12). If we know the magnitude and direction of a vector, then Figure 12 shows that we can find the horizontal and vertical components of the vector.

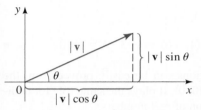

FIGURE 12

HORIZONTAL AND VERTICAL COMPONENTS OF A VECTOR

Let $\mathbf{v}$ be a vector with magnitude $|\mathbf{v}|$ and direction θ.
Then $\mathbf{v} = \langle a, b \rangle = a\mathbf{i} + b\mathbf{j}$, where

$$a = |\mathbf{v}| \cos \theta \qquad \text{and} \qquad b = |\mathbf{v}| \sin \theta$$

EXAMPLE 5 ■ Components and Direction of a Vector

(a) A vector $\mathbf{v}$ has length 8 and direction $\pi/3$. Find the horizontal and vertical components, and write $\mathbf{v}$ in terms of $\mathbf{i}$ and $\mathbf{j}$.
(b) Find the direction of the vector $\mathbf{u} = -\sqrt{3}\,\mathbf{i} + \mathbf{j}$.

SOLUTION

(a) We have $\mathbf{v} = \langle a, b \rangle$, where the components are given by

$$a = 8 \cos \frac{\pi}{3} = 4 \qquad \text{and} \qquad b = 8 \sin \frac{\pi}{3} = 4\sqrt{3}$$

Thus, $\mathbf{v} = \langle 4, 4\sqrt{3} \rangle = 4\mathbf{i} + 4\sqrt{3}\,\mathbf{j}$.

(b) From Figure 13 we see that the direction θ has the property that

$$\tan \theta = \frac{1}{-\sqrt{3}} = -\frac{\sqrt{3}}{3}$$

Thus, the reference angle for θ is $\pi/6$. Since the terminal point of the vector $\mathbf{u}$ is in quadrant II, it follows that $\theta = 5\pi/6$. $\qquad \blacksquare$

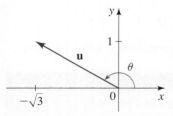

FIGURE 13

Using Vectors to Model Velocity and Force

The use of bearings (such as N 30° E) to describe directions is explained on page 219 in Section 3.5.

The **velocity** of a moving object is modeled by a vector whose direction is the direction of motion and whose magnitude is the speed. Figure 14 shows some vectors **u**, representing the velocity of wind flowing in the direction N 30° E, and a vector **v**, representing the velocity of an airplane flying through this wind at the point P. It's obvious from our experience that wind affects both the speed and the direction of an airplane. Figure 15 indicates that the true velocity of the plane (relative to the ground) is given by the vector **w** = **u** + **v**.

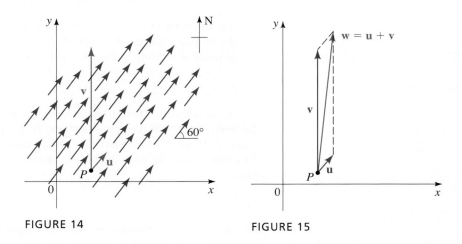

FIGURE 14   FIGURE 15

EXAMPLE 6 ■ The True Speed and Direction of an Airplane

An airplane heads due north at 300 mi/h. It experiences a 40 mi/h crosswind flowing in the direction N 30° E, as shown in Figure 14.
(a) Express the velocity **v** of the airplane relative to the air, and the velocity **u** of the wind, in component form.
(b) Find the true velocity of the airplane as a vector.
(c) Find the true speed and direction of the airplane.

SOLUTION

(a) The velocity of the airplane relative to the air is **v** = 0**i** + 300**j** = 300 **j**.
    By the formulas for the components of a vector, we find that the velocity of the wind is

$$\mathbf{u} = (40 \cos 60°)\mathbf{i} + (40 \sin 60°)\mathbf{j}$$

$$= 20\,\mathbf{i} + 20\sqrt{3}\,\mathbf{j}$$

$$\approx 20\,\mathbf{i} + 34.64\,\mathbf{j}$$

(b) The true velocity of the airplane is given by the vector $\mathbf{w} = \mathbf{u} + \mathbf{v}$.

$$\mathbf{w} = \mathbf{u} + \mathbf{v} = (20\mathbf{i} + 20\sqrt{3}\,\mathbf{j}) + (300\mathbf{j})$$

$$= 20\mathbf{i} + (20\sqrt{3} + 300)\mathbf{j}$$

$$\approx 20\mathbf{i} + 334.64\,\mathbf{j}$$

(c) The true speed of the airplane is given by the magnitude of $\mathbf{w}$.

$$|\mathbf{w}| \approx \sqrt{(20)^2 + (334.64)^2} \approx 335.2 \text{ mi/h}$$

The direction of the airplane is the direction θ of the vector $\mathbf{w}$. The angle θ has the property that $\tan \theta \approx 334.64/20 = 16.732$ and so $\theta \approx 86.6°$. Thus, the airplane is heading in the direction N 3.4° E. ∎

EXAMPLE 7 ■ Calculating a Heading

A woman launches a boat from one shore of a straight river and wants to land at the point directly on the opposite shore. If the speed of the boat (relative to the water) is 10 mi/h and the river is flowing east at the rate of 5 mi/h, in what direction should she head the boat in order to arrive at the desired landing point?

SOLUTION

We choose a coordinate system with the origin at the initial position of the boat as shown in Figure 16. Let $\mathbf{u}$ and $\mathbf{v}$ represent the velocities of the river and the boat, respectively. Clearly, $\mathbf{u} = 5\mathbf{i}$ and, since the speed of the boat is 10 mi/h, we have $|\mathbf{v}| = 10$, so

$$\mathbf{v} = (10 \cos \theta)\mathbf{i} + (10 \sin \theta)\mathbf{j}$$

where the angle θ is as shown in Figure 16. The true course of the boat is given by the vector $\mathbf{w} = \mathbf{u} + \mathbf{v}$. We have

$$\mathbf{w} = \mathbf{u} + \mathbf{v} = 5\mathbf{i} + (10 \cos \theta)\mathbf{i} + (10 \sin \theta)\mathbf{j}$$

$$= (5 + 10 \cos \theta)\mathbf{i} + (10 \sin \theta)\mathbf{j}$$

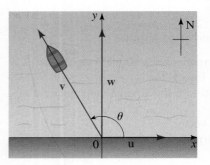

FIGURE 16

Since the woman wants to land at a point directly across the river, her direction should have horizontal component 0. In other words, she should choose θ in such a way that

$$5 + 10 \cos \theta = 0$$

$$\cos \theta = -\tfrac{1}{2}$$

$$\theta = 120°$$

Thus, she should head the boat in the direction $\theta = 120°$ (or N 30° W). ∎

Force is also represented by a vector. Intuitively, we can think of force as describing a push or a pull on an object, for example, a horizontal push of a book across a table or the downward pull of the earth's gravity on a ball. Force is measured in pounds (or in newtons, in the metric system). For instance, a man weighing 200 lb exerts a force of 200 lb downward on the ground. If several forces are acting on an object, the **resultant force** experienced by the object is the vector sum of these forces.

EXAMPLE 8 ■ Resultant Force

Two forces $\mathbf{F}_1$ and $\mathbf{F}_2$ with magnitudes 10 and 20 lb, respectively, act on an object at a point P as shown in Figure 17. Find the resultant force acting at P.

SOLUTION

We write $\mathbf{F}_1$ and $\mathbf{F}_2$ in component form:

$$\mathbf{F}_1 = (10 \cos 45°)\mathbf{i} + (10 \sin 45°)\mathbf{j} = 10\frac{\sqrt{2}}{2}\mathbf{i} + 10\frac{\sqrt{2}}{2}\mathbf{j} = 5\sqrt{2}\,\mathbf{i} + 5\sqrt{2}\,\mathbf{j}$$

$$\mathbf{F}_2 = (20 \cos 150°)\mathbf{i} + (20 \sin 150°)\mathbf{j} = -20\frac{\sqrt{3}}{2}\mathbf{i} + 20\left(\frac{1}{2}\right)\mathbf{j}$$

$$= -10\sqrt{3}\,\mathbf{i} + 10\mathbf{j}$$

So the resultant force $\mathbf{F}$ is

$$\begin{aligned}
\mathbf{F} &= \mathbf{F}_1 + \mathbf{F}_2 \\
&= \left(5\sqrt{2}\,\mathbf{i} + 5\sqrt{2}\,\mathbf{j}\right) + \left(-10\sqrt{3}\,\mathbf{i} + 10\mathbf{j}\right) \\
&= \left(5\sqrt{2} - 10\sqrt{3}\right)\mathbf{i} + \left(5\sqrt{2} + 10\right)\mathbf{j} \\
&\approx -10\mathbf{i} + 17\mathbf{j}
\end{aligned}$$

The resultant force $\mathbf{F}$ is shown in Figure 18. ■

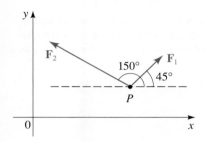

FIGURE 17

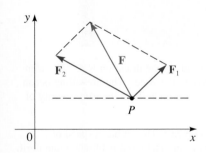

FIGURE 18

5.5 EXERCISES

1–6 ■ Sketch the vector indicated. (The vectors **u** and **v** are shown in the figure.)

1. $2\mathbf{u}$

2. $-\mathbf{v}$

3. $\mathbf{u} + \mathbf{v}$

4. $\mathbf{u} - \mathbf{v}$

5. $\mathbf{v} - 2\mathbf{u}$

6. $2\mathbf{u} + \mathbf{v}$

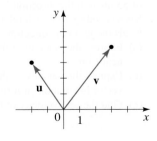

7–16 ■ Express the vector with initial point P and terminal point Q in component form.

7.

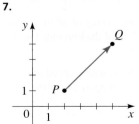

8.

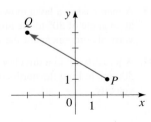

9.

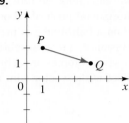

10.

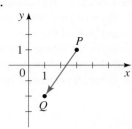

11. $P(3, 2)$, $Q(8, 9)$ **12.** $P(1, 1)$, $Q(9, 9)$

13. $P(5, 3)$, $Q(1, 0)$ **14.** $P(-1, 3)$, $Q(-6, -1)$

15. $P(-1, -1)$, $Q(-1, 1)$ **16.** $P(-8, -6)$, $Q(-1, -1)$

17–22 ■ Find $2\mathbf{u}$, $-3\mathbf{v}$, $\mathbf{u} + \mathbf{v}$, and $3\mathbf{u} - 4\mathbf{v}$ for the given vectors $\mathbf{u}$ and $\mathbf{v}$.

17. $\mathbf{u} = \langle 2, 7 \rangle$, $\mathbf{v} = \langle 3, 1 \rangle$ **18.** $\mathbf{u} = \langle -2, 5 \rangle$, $\mathbf{v} = \langle 2, -8 \rangle$

19. $\mathbf{u} = \langle 0, -1 \rangle$, $\mathbf{v} = \langle -2, 0 \rangle$

20. $\mathbf{u} = \mathbf{i}$, $\mathbf{v} = -2\mathbf{j}$

21. $\mathbf{u} = 2\mathbf{i}$, $\mathbf{v} = 3\mathbf{i} - 2\mathbf{j}$ **22.** $\mathbf{u} = \mathbf{i} + \mathbf{j}$, $\mathbf{v} = \mathbf{i} - \mathbf{j}$

23–26 ■ Find $|\mathbf{u}|$, $|\mathbf{v}|$, $|2\mathbf{u}|$, $\left|\frac{1}{2}\mathbf{v}\right|$, $|\mathbf{u} + \mathbf{v}|$, $|\mathbf{u} - \mathbf{v}|$, and $|\mathbf{u}| - |\mathbf{v}|$.

23. $\mathbf{u} = 2\mathbf{i} + \mathbf{j}$, $\mathbf{v} = 3\mathbf{i} - 2\mathbf{j}$

24. $\mathbf{u} = -2\mathbf{i} + 3\mathbf{j}$, $\mathbf{v} = \mathbf{i} - 2\mathbf{j}$

25. $\mathbf{u} = \langle 10, -1 \rangle$, $\mathbf{v} = \langle -2, -2 \rangle$

26. $\mathbf{u} = \langle -6, 6 \rangle$, $\mathbf{v} = \langle -2, -1 \rangle$

27–32 ■ Find the horizontal and vertical components of the vector with given length and direction, and write the vector in terms of the vectors $\mathbf{i}$ and $\mathbf{j}$.

27. $|\mathbf{v}| = 40$, $\theta = 30°$ **28.** $|\mathbf{v}| = 50$, $\theta = 120°$

29. $|\mathbf{v}| = 1$, $\theta = 225°$ **30.** $|\mathbf{v}| = 800$, $\theta = 125°$

31. $|\mathbf{v}| = 4$, $\theta = 10°$ **32.** $|\mathbf{v}| = \sqrt{3}$, $\theta = 300°$

33. A man pushes a lawn mower with a force of 30 lb exerted at an angle of 30° to the ground. Find the horizontal and vertical components of the force.

34. A jet is flying in a direction N 20° E with a speed of 500 mi/h. Find the north and east components of the velocity.

35–40 ■ Find the magnitude and direction (in degrees) of the vector.

35. $\mathbf{v} = \langle 3, 4 \rangle$ **36.** $\mathbf{v} = \left\langle -\dfrac{\sqrt{2}}{2}, -\dfrac{\sqrt{2}}{2} \right\rangle$

37. $\mathbf{v} = \langle -12, 5 \rangle$ **38.** $\mathbf{v} = \langle 40, 9 \rangle$

39. $\mathbf{v} = \mathbf{i} + \sqrt{3}\,\mathbf{j}$ **40.** $\mathbf{v} = \mathbf{i} + \mathbf{j}$

41. A river flows due south at 3 mi/h. A swimmer attempting to cross the river heads due east swimming at 2 mi/h relative to the water. Find the true velocity of the swimmer as a vector.

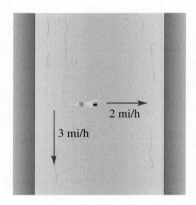

42. A migrating salmon heads in the direction N 45° E, swimming at 5 mi/h relative to the water. The prevailing ocean currents flow due east at 3 mi/h. Find the true velocity of the fish as a vector.

43. A pilot heads his jet due east. The jet has a speed of 425 mi/h relative to the air. The wind is blowing due north with a speed of 40 mi/h.
(a) Express the velocity of the wind as a vector in component form.
(b) Express the velocity of the jet relative to the air as a vector in component form.
(c) Find the true velocity of the jet as a vector.
(d) Find the true speed and direction of the jet.

44. A jet is flying through a wind that is blowing with a speed of 55 mi/h in the direction N 30° E (see the figure). The jet has a speed of 765 mi/h relative to the air, and the pilot heads the jet in the direction N 45° E.
(a) Express the velocity of the wind as a vector in component form.
(b) Express the velocity of the jet relative to the air as a vector in component form.
(c) Find the true velocity of the jet as a vector.

(d) Find the true speed and direction of the jet.

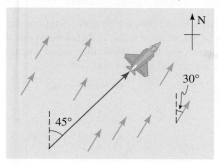

45. Find the true speed and direction of the jet in Exercise 44 if the pilot heads the plane in the direction N 30° W.

46. In what direction should the pilot in Exercise 44 head the plane for the true course to be due north?

47. A straight river flows east at a speed of 10 mi/h. A boater starts at the south shore of the river and heads in a direction 60° from the shore (see the figure). The motorboat has a speed of 20 mi/h relative to the water.
   (a) Express the velocity of the river as a vector in component form.
   (b) Express the velocity of the motorboat relative to the water as a vector in component form.
   (c) Find the true velocity of the motorboat.
   (d) Find the true speed and direction of the motorboat.

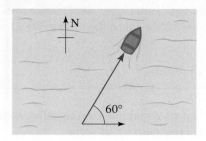

48. The boater in Exercise 47 wants to arrive at a point on the north shore of the river directly opposite the starting point. In what direction should the boat be headed?

49. A boat heads in the direction N 72° E. The speed of the boat relative to the water is 24 mi/h. The water is flowing directly south. It is observed that the true direction of the boat is directly east.
   (a) Express the velocity of the boat relative to the water as a vector in component form.
   (b) Find the speed of the water and the true speed of the boat.

50. A woman walks due west on the deck of an ocean liner at 2 mi/h. The ocean liner is moving due north at a speed of 25 mi/h. Find the speed and direction of the woman relative to the surface of the water.

51–56 ■ The forces $\mathbf{F}_1, \mathbf{F}_2, \ldots, \mathbf{F}_n$ acting at the same point P are said to be in equilibrium if the resultant force is zero, that is, if $\mathbf{F}_1 + \mathbf{F}_2 + \cdots + \mathbf{F}_n = \mathbf{0}$. Find (a) the resultant forces acting at P, and (b) the additional force required (if any) for the forces to be in equilibrium.

51. $\mathbf{F}_1 = \langle 2, 5 \rangle$, $\mathbf{F}_2 = \langle 3, -8 \rangle$

52. $\mathbf{F}_1 = \langle 3, -7 \rangle$, $\mathbf{F}_2 = \langle 4, -2 \rangle$, $\mathbf{F}_3 = \langle -7, 9 \rangle$

53. $\mathbf{F}_1 = 4\mathbf{i} - \mathbf{j}$, $\mathbf{F}_2 = 3\mathbf{i} - 7\mathbf{j}$,
$\mathbf{F}_3 = -8\mathbf{i} + 3\mathbf{j}$, $\mathbf{F}_4 = \mathbf{i} + \mathbf{j}$

54. $\mathbf{F}_1 = \mathbf{i} - \mathbf{j}$, $\mathbf{F}_2 = \mathbf{i} + \mathbf{j}$, $\mathbf{F}_3 = -2\mathbf{i} + \mathbf{j}$

55.

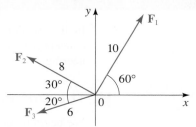

56.

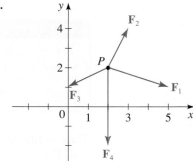

57. A 100-lb weight hangs from a string as shown in the figure. Find the tensions $\mathbf{T}_1$ and $\mathbf{T}_2$ in the string.

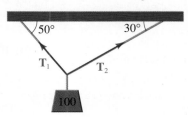

58. The cranes in the figure are lifting an object that weighs 18,278 lb. Find the tensions $\mathbf{T}_1$ and $\mathbf{T}_2$.

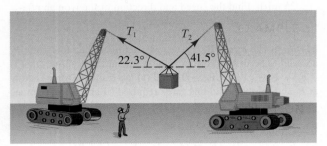

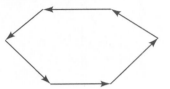

DISCOVERY · DISCUSSION

59. Vectors That Form a Polygon   Suppose that n vectors can be placed head to tail in the plane so that they form a polygon. (The figure shows the case of a hexagon.) Explain why the sum of these vectors is **0**.

5.6 THE DOT PRODUCT

In this section we define an operation on vectors called the dot product. This concept is very useful in calculus and in applications of vectors to physics and engineering.

▪ The Dot Product of Vectors

We begin by defining the dot product of two vectors.

> **DEFINITION OF THE DOT PRODUCT**
>
> If $\mathbf{u} = \langle a_1, b_1 \rangle$ and $\mathbf{v} = \langle a_2, b_2 \rangle$ are vectors, then their **dot product**, denoted by $\mathbf{u} \cdot \mathbf{v}$, is defined by
>
> $$\mathbf{u} \cdot \mathbf{v} = a_1 a_2 + b_1 b_2$$

Thus, to find the dot product of $\mathbf{u}$ and $\mathbf{v}$ we multiply corresponding components and add. The result is *not* a vector; it is a real number, or scalar.

EXAMPLE 1 ▪ Calculating Dot Products

(a) If $\mathbf{u} = \langle 3, -2 \rangle$ and $\mathbf{v} = \langle 4, 5 \rangle$, then

$$\mathbf{u} \cdot \mathbf{v} = (3)(4) + (-2)(5) = 2$$

(b) If $\mathbf{u} = 2\mathbf{i} + \mathbf{j}$ and $\mathbf{v} = 5\mathbf{i} - 6\mathbf{j}$, then

$$\mathbf{u} \cdot \mathbf{v} = (2)(5) + (1)(-6) = 4$$ ▪

The proofs of the following properties of the dot product follow easily from the definition.

PROPERTIES OF THE DOT PRODUCT

$$\mathbf{u} \cdot \mathbf{v} = \mathbf{v} \cdot \mathbf{u}$$

$$(a\mathbf{u}) \cdot \mathbf{v} = a(\mathbf{u} \cdot \mathbf{v}) = \mathbf{u} \cdot (a\mathbf{v})$$

$$(\mathbf{u} + \mathbf{v}) \cdot \mathbf{w} = \mathbf{u} \cdot \mathbf{w} + \mathbf{v} \cdot \mathbf{w}$$

$$|\mathbf{u}|^2 = \mathbf{u} \cdot \mathbf{u}$$

■ **Proof**   We prove only the last property. The proofs of the others are left as exercises. Let $\mathbf{u} = \langle a\ b \rangle$. Then

$$\mathbf{u} \cdot \mathbf{u} = \langle a, b \rangle \cdot \langle a, b \rangle = a^2 + b^2 = |\mathbf{u}|^2 \qquad \square$$

Let $\mathbf{u}$ and $\mathbf{v}$ be vectors and sketch them with initial points at the origin. We define the **angle θ between $\mathbf{u}$ and $\mathbf{v}$** to be the smaller of the angles formed by these representations of $\mathbf{u}$ and $\mathbf{v}$ (see Figure 1). Thus, $0 \leq \theta \leq \pi$. The next theorem relates the angle between two vectors to their dot product.

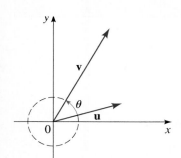

FIGURE 1

THE DOT PRODUCT THEOREM

If θ is the angle between two nonzero vectors $\mathbf{u}$ and $\mathbf{v}$, then

$$\mathbf{u} \cdot \mathbf{v} = |\mathbf{u}|\,|\mathbf{v}|\cos\theta$$

■ **Proof**   The proof is a nice application of the Law of Cosines. Applying the Law of Cosines to triangle AOB in Figure 2 gives

$$|\mathbf{u} - \mathbf{v}|^2 = |\mathbf{u}|^2 + |\mathbf{v}|^2 - 2|\mathbf{u}|\,|\mathbf{v}|\cos\theta$$

Using the properties of the dot product, we write the left-hand side as follows:

$$|\mathbf{u} - \mathbf{v}|^2 = (\mathbf{u} - \mathbf{v}) \cdot (\mathbf{u} - \mathbf{v})$$

$$= \mathbf{u} \cdot \mathbf{u} - \mathbf{u} \cdot \mathbf{v} - \mathbf{v} \cdot \mathbf{u} + \mathbf{v} \cdot \mathbf{v}$$

$$= |\mathbf{u}|^2 - 2(\mathbf{u} \cdot \mathbf{v}) + |\mathbf{v}|^2$$

Equating the right-hand sides of the displayed equations, we get

$$|\mathbf{u}|^2 - 2(\mathbf{u} \cdot \mathbf{v}) + |\mathbf{v}|^2 = |\mathbf{u}|^2 + |\mathbf{v}|^2 - 2|\mathbf{u}|\,|\mathbf{v}|\cos\theta$$

$$-2(\mathbf{u} \cdot \mathbf{v}) = -2|\mathbf{u}|\,|\mathbf{v}|\cos\theta$$

$$\mathbf{u} \cdot \mathbf{v} = |\mathbf{u}|\,|\mathbf{v}|\cos\theta$$

This proves the theorem. $\square$

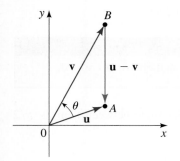

FIGURE 2

The Dot Product Theorem is useful because it allows us to find the angle between two vectors if we know the components of the vectors. The angle is obtained simply by solving the equation in the Dot Product Theorem for $\cos\theta$. We state this important result explicitly.

ANGLE BETWEEN TWO VECTORS

If θ is the angle between two nonzero vectors $\mathbf{u}$ and $\mathbf{v}$, then

$$\cos \theta = \frac{\mathbf{u} \cdot \mathbf{v}}{|\mathbf{u}||\mathbf{v}|}$$

EXAMPLE 2 ■ Finding the Angle between Two Vectors

Find the angle between the vectors $\mathbf{u} = \langle 2, 5 \rangle$ and $\mathbf{v} = \langle 4, -3 \rangle$.

SOLUTION

By the formula for the angle between two vectors, we have

$$\cos \theta = \frac{\mathbf{u} \cdot \mathbf{v}}{|\mathbf{u}||\mathbf{v}|} = \frac{(2)(4) + (5)(-3)}{\sqrt{4 + 25}\sqrt{16 + 9}} = \frac{-7}{5\sqrt{29}}$$

Thus, the angle between $\mathbf{u}$ and $\mathbf{v}$ is

$$\theta = \cos^{-1}\left(\frac{-7}{5\sqrt{29}}\right) \approx 105.1°$$

∎

Two nonzero vectors $\mathbf{u}$ and $\mathbf{v}$ are called **perpendicular**, or **orthogonal**, if the angle between them is $\pi/2$. The following theorem shows that we can determine if two vectors are perpendicular by finding their dot product.

ORTHOGONAL VECTORS

Two nonzero vectors $\mathbf{u}$ and $\mathbf{v}$ are perpendicular if and only if $\mathbf{u} \cdot \mathbf{v} = 0$.

■ **Proof** If $\mathbf{u}$ and $\mathbf{v}$ are perpendicular, then the angle between them is $\pi/2$ and so

$$\mathbf{u} \cdot \mathbf{v} = |\mathbf{u}||\mathbf{v}| \cos \frac{\pi}{2} = 0$$

Conversely, if $\mathbf{u} \cdot \mathbf{v} = 0$, then

$$|\mathbf{u}||\mathbf{v}| \cos \theta = 0$$

Since $\mathbf{u}$ and $\mathbf{v}$ are nonzero vectors, we conclude that $\cos \theta = 0$, and so $\theta = \pi/2$. Thus, $\mathbf{u}$ and $\mathbf{v}$ are orthogonal. ☐

EXAMPLE 3 ■ Checking Vectors for Perpendicularity

Determine whether the vectors in each pair are perpendicular.

(a) $\mathbf{u} = \langle 3, 5 \rangle$ and $\mathbf{v} = \langle 2, -8 \rangle$ (b) $\mathbf{u} = \langle 2, 1 \rangle$ and $\mathbf{v} = \langle -1, 2 \rangle$

SOLUTION

(a) $\mathbf{u} \cdot \mathbf{v} = (3)(2) + (5)(-8) = -34 \neq 0$, so $\mathbf{u}$ and $\mathbf{v}$ are not perpendicular.

(b) $\mathbf{u} \cdot \mathbf{v} = (2)(-1) + (1)(2) = 0$, so $\mathbf{u}$ and $\mathbf{v}$ are perpendicular. ∎

The Component of u Along v

The **component of u along v** (or the **component of u in the direction of v**) is defined to be

Note that the component of $\mathbf{u}$ along $\mathbf{v}$ is a scalar, not a vector.

$$|\mathbf{u}| \cos \theta$$

where θ is the angle between $\mathbf{u}$ and $\mathbf{v}$. Figure 3 gives a geometric interpretation of this concept. Intuitively, the component of $\mathbf{u}$ along $\mathbf{v}$ is the magnitude of the portion of $\mathbf{u}$ that points in the direction of $\mathbf{v}$. Notice that the component of $\mathbf{u}$ along $\mathbf{v}$ is negative if $\pi/2 < \theta \leq \pi$.

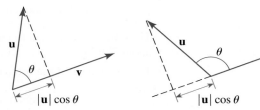

FIGURE 3

When analyzing forces in physics and engineering, it's often helpful to express a vector as a sum of two vectors lying in perpendicular directions. For example, suppose a car is parked on an inclined driveway as in Figure 4. The weight of the car is a vector $\mathbf{w}$ that points directly downward. We can write

$$\mathbf{w} = \mathbf{u} + \mathbf{v}$$

where $\mathbf{u}$ is parallel to the driveway and $\mathbf{v}$ is perpendicular to the driveway. The vector $\mathbf{u}$ is the force that tends to roll the car down the driveway, and $\mathbf{v}$ is the force experienced by the surface of the driveway. The magnitudes of these forces are the components of $\mathbf{w}$ along $\mathbf{u}$ and $\mathbf{v}$, respectively.

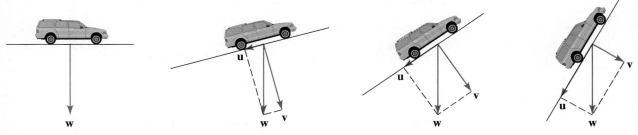

FIGURE 4

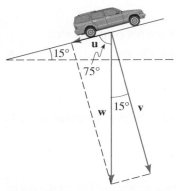

FIGURE 5

EXAMPLE 4 ■ Resolving a Force into Components

A car weighing 3000 lb is parked on a driveway that is inclined 15° to the horizontal, as shown in Figure 5.

(a) Find the magnitude of the force required to prevent the car from rolling down the driveway.
(b) Find the magnitude of the force experienced by the driveway due to the weight of the car.

SOLUTION

The car exerts a force **w** of 3000 lb directly downward. We resolve **w** into the sum of two vectors **u** and **v**, one parallel to the surface of the driveway and the other perpendicular to it, as shown in Figure 5.

(a) The magnitude of the part of the force **w** that causes the car to roll down the driveway is

$$|\mathbf{u}| = \text{component of } \mathbf{w} \text{ along } \mathbf{u} = 3000 \cos 75° \approx 776$$

Thus, the force needed to prevent the car from rolling down the driveway is about 776 lb.

(b) The magnitude of the force exerted by the car on the driveway is

$$|\mathbf{v}| = \text{component of } \mathbf{w} \text{ along } \mathbf{v} = 3000 \cos 15° \approx 2898$$

The force experienced by the driveway is about 2898 lb.   ■

The component of **u** along **v** can be computed using dot products:

$$|\mathbf{u}| \cos \theta = \frac{|\mathbf{v}| |\mathbf{u}| \cos \theta}{|\mathbf{v}|} = \frac{\mathbf{u} \cdot \mathbf{v}}{|\mathbf{v}|}$$

We have shown the following.

CALCULATING COMPONENTS

The component of **u** along **v** is $\dfrac{\mathbf{u} \cdot \mathbf{v}}{|\mathbf{v}|}$

EXAMPLE 5 ■ Finding Components

Let $\mathbf{u} = \langle 1, 4 \rangle$ and $\mathbf{v} = \langle -2, 1 \rangle$. Find the component of **u** along **v**.

SOLUTION

We have

$$\text{component of } \mathbf{u} \text{ along } \mathbf{v} = \frac{\mathbf{u} \cdot \mathbf{v}}{|\mathbf{v}|} = \frac{(1)(-2) + (4)(1)}{\sqrt{4 + 1}} = \frac{2}{\sqrt{5}}$$ ■

The Projection of u onto v

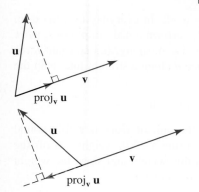

proj$_\mathbf{v}$ u

proj$_\mathbf{v}$ u

FIGURE 6

Figure 6 shows representations of the vectors **u** and **v**. The projection of **u** onto **v**, denoted by proj$_\mathbf{v}$ **u**, is the vector whose *direction* is the same as **v** and whose *length* is the component of **u** along **v**. To find an expression for proj$_\mathbf{v}$ **u**, we first find a unit vector in the direction of **v** and then multiply it by the component of **u** along **v**.

$$\text{proj}_\mathbf{v}\ \mathbf{u} = (\text{component of } \mathbf{u} \text{ along } \mathbf{v})(\text{unit vector in direction of } \mathbf{v})$$

$$= \left(\frac{\mathbf{u} \cdot \mathbf{v}}{|\mathbf{v}|}\right)\frac{\mathbf{v}}{|\mathbf{v}|} = \left(\frac{\mathbf{u} \cdot \mathbf{v}}{|\mathbf{v}|^2}\right)\mathbf{v}$$

We often need to **resolve** a vector **u** into the sum of two vectors, one parallel to **v** and one orthogonal to **v**. That is, we want to write $\mathbf{u} = \mathbf{u}_1 + \mathbf{u}_2$ where $\mathbf{u}_1$ is parallel to **v** and $\mathbf{u}_2$ is orthogonal to **v**. In this case, $\mathbf{u}_1 = \text{proj}_\mathbf{v}\ \mathbf{u}$ and $\mathbf{u}_2 = \mathbf{u} - \text{proj}_\mathbf{v}\ \mathbf{u}$ (see Exercise 45).

CALCULATING PROJECTIONS

The **projection of u onto v** is the vector proj$_\mathbf{v}$ **u** given by

$$\text{proj}_\mathbf{v}\ \mathbf{u} = \left(\frac{\mathbf{u} \cdot \mathbf{v}}{|\mathbf{v}|^2}\right)\mathbf{v}$$

If the vector **u** is **resolved** into $\mathbf{u}_1$ and $\mathbf{u}_2$, where $\mathbf{u}_1$ is parallel to **v** and $\mathbf{u}_2$ is orthogonal to **v**, then

$$\mathbf{u}_1 = \text{proj}_\mathbf{v}\ \mathbf{u} \qquad \text{and} \qquad \mathbf{u}_2 = \mathbf{u} - \text{proj}_\mathbf{v}\ \mathbf{u}$$

EXAMPLE 6 ■ Resolving a Vector into Orthogonal Vectors

Let $\mathbf{u} = \langle -2, 9 \rangle$ and $\mathbf{v} = \langle -1, 2 \rangle$.
(a) Find proj$_\mathbf{v}$ **u**.
(b) Resolve **u** into $\mathbf{u}_1$ and $\mathbf{u}_2$, where $\mathbf{u}_1$ is parallel to **v** and $\mathbf{u}_2$ is orthogonal to **v**.

SOLUTION

(a) By the formula for the projection of one vector onto another we have

$$\text{proj}_\mathbf{v}\ \mathbf{u} = \left(\frac{\mathbf{u} \cdot \mathbf{v}}{|\mathbf{v}|^2}\right)\mathbf{v} \qquad \text{Formula for projection}$$

$$= \left(\frac{\langle -2, 9 \rangle \cdot \langle -1, 2 \rangle}{(-1)^2 + 2^2}\right)\langle -1, 2 \rangle \qquad \text{Definition of } \mathbf{u} \text{ and } \mathbf{v}$$

$$= 4\langle -1, 2 \rangle = \langle -4, 8 \rangle$$

(b) By the formula in the preceding box we have $\mathbf{u} = \mathbf{u}_1 + \mathbf{u}_2$, where

$$\mathbf{u}_1 = \text{proj}_\mathbf{v}\ \mathbf{u} = \langle -4, 8 \rangle \qquad \text{From part (a)}$$

$$\mathbf{u}_2 = \mathbf{u} - \text{proj}_\mathbf{v}\ \mathbf{u} = \langle -2, 9 \rangle - \langle -4, 8 \rangle = \langle 2, 1 \rangle$$

■

■ Work

One use of the dot product occurs in calculating work. In everyday use, the term *work* means the total amount of effort required to perform a task. In physics, *work* has a technical meaning that conforms to this intuitive meaning. If a constant force of magnitude F moves an object through a distance d along a straight line, then the **work** done is

$$W = Fd \qquad \text{or} \qquad \text{work} = \text{force} \times \text{distance}$$

If F is measured in pounds and d in feet, then the unit of work is a foot-pound (ft-lb). For example, how much work is done in lifting a 20-lb weight 6 ft off the ground? Since a force of 20 lb is required to lift this weight and since the weight moves through a distance of 6 ft, the amount of work done is

$$W = Fd = (20)(6) = 120 \text{ ft-lb}$$

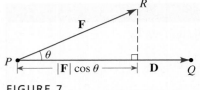

FIGURE 7

This formula applies only when the force is directed along the direction of motion. In the general case, if the force $\mathbf{F}$ moves an object from P to Q, as in Figure 7, then only the component of the force in the direction of $\mathbf{D} = \overrightarrow{PQ}$ affects the object. Thus, the effective magnitude of the force on the object is

$$\text{component of } \mathbf{F} \text{ along } \mathbf{D} = |\mathbf{F}| \cos \theta$$

So, the work done is

$$W = \text{force} \times \text{distance} = (|\mathbf{F}| \cos \theta) |\mathbf{D}| = |\mathbf{F}| |\mathbf{D}| \cos \theta = \mathbf{F} \cdot \mathbf{D}$$

We have derived the following simple formula for calculating work.

WORK

The **work** W done by a force $\mathbf{F}$ in moving along a vector $\mathbf{D}$ is

$$W = \mathbf{F} \cdot \mathbf{D}$$

EXAMPLE 7 ■ Calculating Work

A force is given by the vector $\mathbf{F} = \langle 2, 3 \rangle$ and moves an object from the point $(1, 3)$ to the point $(5, 9)$. Find the work done.

SOLUTION

The displacement vector is

$$\mathbf{D} = \langle 5 - 1, 9 - 3 \rangle = \langle 4, 6 \rangle$$

So the work done is

$$W = \mathbf{F} \cdot \mathbf{D} = \langle 2, 3 \rangle \cdot \langle 4, 6 \rangle = 26$$

If the unit of force is pounds and the distance is measured in feet, then the work done is 26 ft-lb. ∎

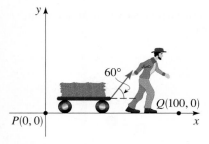

FIGURE 8

EXAMPLE 8 ■ Calculating Work

A man pulls a wagon horizontally by exerting a force of 20 lb on the handle. If the handle makes an angle of 60° with the horizontal, find the work done in moving the wagon 100 ft.

SOLUTION

We choose a coordinate system with the origin at the initial position of the wagon (see Figure 8). That is, the wagon moves from the point $P(0, 0)$ to the point $Q(100, 0)$. The vector that represents this displacement is

$$\mathbf{D} = 100\,\mathbf{i}$$

The force on the handle can be written in terms of components (see Section 5.4) as

$$\mathbf{F} = (20 \cos 60°)\mathbf{i} + (20 \sin 60°)\mathbf{j} = 10\mathbf{i} + 10\sqrt{3}\,\mathbf{j}$$

Thus, the work done is

$$W = \mathbf{F} \cdot \mathbf{D} = (10\mathbf{i} + 10\sqrt{3}\,\mathbf{j}) \cdot (100\mathbf{i}) = 1000 \text{ ft-lb} \qquad ■$$

5.6 EXERCISES

1–8 ■ Find (a) $\mathbf{u} \cdot \mathbf{v}$ and (b) the angle between $\mathbf{u}$ and $\mathbf{v}$ to the nearest degree.

1. $\mathbf{u} = \langle 2, 0 \rangle$, $\mathbf{v} = \langle 1, 1 \rangle$

2. $\mathbf{u} = \mathbf{i} + \sqrt{3}\,\mathbf{j}$, $\mathbf{v} = -\sqrt{3}\,\mathbf{i} + \mathbf{j}$

3. $\mathbf{u} = \langle 2, 7 \rangle$, $\mathbf{v} = \langle 3, 1 \rangle$

4. $\mathbf{u} = \langle -6, 6 \rangle$, $\mathbf{v} = \langle 1, -1 \rangle$

5. $\mathbf{u} = \langle 3, -2 \rangle$, $\mathbf{v} = \langle 1, 2 \rangle$

6. $\mathbf{u} = 2\mathbf{i} + \mathbf{j}$, $\mathbf{v} = 3\mathbf{i} - 2\mathbf{j}$

7. $\mathbf{u} = -5\mathbf{j}$, $\mathbf{v} = -\mathbf{i} - \sqrt{3}\,\mathbf{j}$

8. $\mathbf{u} = \mathbf{i} + \mathbf{j}$, $\mathbf{v} = \mathbf{i} - \mathbf{j}$

9–14 ■ Determine whether the given vectors are orthogonal.

9. $\mathbf{u} = \langle 6, 4 \rangle$, $\mathbf{v} = \langle -2, 3 \rangle$ **10.** $\mathbf{u} = \langle 0, -5 \rangle$, $\mathbf{v} = \langle 4, 0 \rangle$

11. $\mathbf{u} = \langle -2, 6 \rangle$, $\mathbf{v} = \langle 4, 2 \rangle$ **12.** $\mathbf{u} = 2\mathbf{i}$, $\mathbf{v} = -7\mathbf{j}$

13. $\mathbf{u} = 2\mathbf{i} - 8\mathbf{j}$, $\mathbf{v} = -12\mathbf{i} - 3\mathbf{j}$

14. $\mathbf{u} = 4\mathbf{i}$, $\mathbf{v} = -\mathbf{i} + 3\mathbf{j}$

15–18 ■ Find the indicated quantity, assuming $\mathbf{u} = 2\mathbf{i} + \mathbf{j}$, $\mathbf{v} = \mathbf{i} - 3\mathbf{j}$, and $\mathbf{w} = 3\mathbf{i} + 4\mathbf{j}$.

15. $\mathbf{u} \cdot \mathbf{v} + \mathbf{u} \cdot \mathbf{w}$ **16.** $\mathbf{u} \cdot (\mathbf{v} + \mathbf{w})$

17. $(\mathbf{u} + \mathbf{v}) \cdot (\mathbf{u} - \mathbf{v})$ **18.** $(\mathbf{u} \cdot \mathbf{v})(\mathbf{u} \cdot \mathbf{w})$

19–22 ■ Find the component of $\mathbf{u}$ along $\mathbf{v}$.

19. $\mathbf{u} = \langle 4, 6 \rangle$, $\mathbf{v} = \langle 3, -4 \rangle$

20. $\mathbf{u} = \langle -3, 5 \rangle$, $\mathbf{v} = \langle 1/\sqrt{2}, 1/\sqrt{2} \rangle$

21. $\mathbf{u} = 7\mathbf{i} - 24\mathbf{j}$, $\mathbf{v} = \mathbf{j}$

22. $\mathbf{u} = 7\mathbf{i}$, $\mathbf{v} = 8\mathbf{i} + 6\mathbf{j}$

23–28 ■ (a) Calculate $\text{proj}_{\mathbf{v}}\,\mathbf{u}$. (b) Resolve $\mathbf{u}$ into $\mathbf{u}_1$ and $\mathbf{u}_2$, where $\mathbf{u}_1$ is parallel to $\mathbf{v}$ and $\mathbf{u}_2$ is orthogonal to $\mathbf{v}$.

23. $\mathbf{u} = \langle -2, 4 \rangle$, $\mathbf{v} = \langle 1, 1 \rangle$

24. $\mathbf{u} = \langle 7, -4 \rangle$, $\mathbf{v} = \langle 2, 1 \rangle$

25. $\mathbf{u} = \langle 1, 2 \rangle$, $\mathbf{v} = \langle 1, -3 \rangle$

26. $\mathbf{u} = \langle 11, 3 \rangle$, $\mathbf{v} = \langle -3, -2 \rangle$

27. $\mathbf{u} = \langle 2, 9 \rangle$, $\mathbf{v} = \langle -3, 4 \rangle$

28. $\mathbf{u} = \langle 1, 1 \rangle$, $\mathbf{v} = \langle 2, -1 \rangle$

29–32 ■ Find the work done by the force $\mathbf{F}$ in moving an object from P to Q.

29. $\mathbf{F} = 4\mathbf{i} - 5\mathbf{j}$; $P(0, 0)$, $Q(3, 8)$

30. $\mathbf{F} = 400\mathbf{i} + 50\mathbf{j}$; $P(-1, 1)$, $Q(200, 1)$

31. $\mathbf{F} = 10\mathbf{i} + 3\mathbf{j}$; $P(2, 3)$, $Q(6, -2)$

32. $\mathbf{F} = -4\mathbf{i} + 20\mathbf{j}$; $P(0, 10)$, $Q(5, 25)$

33. The force $\mathbf{F} = 4\mathbf{i} - 7\mathbf{j}$ moves an object 4 ft along the x-axis in the positive direction. Find the work done if the unit of force is the pound.

34. A constant force $\mathbf{F} = \langle 2, 8 \rangle$ moves an object along a straight line from the point $(2, 5)$ to the point $(11, 13)$. Find the work done if the distance is measured in feet and the force is measured in pounds.

35. A lawn mower is pushed a distance of 200 ft along a horizontal path by a constant force of 50 lb. The handle of the lawn mower is held at an angle of 30° from the horizontal (see the figure). Find the work done.

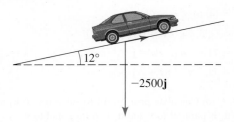

36. A car drives 500 ft on a road that is inclined 12° to the horizontal, as shown in the figure. The car weighs 2500 lb. Thus, gravity acts straight down on the car with a constant force $\mathbf{F} = -2500\mathbf{j}$. Find the work done by the car in overcoming gravity.

37. A car is on a driveway that is inclined 25° to the horizontal. If the car weighs 2755 lb, find the force required to keep it from rolling down the driveway.

38. A car is on a driveway that is inclined 10° to the horizontal. A force of 490 lb is required to keep the car from rolling down the driveway.
(a) Find the weight of the car.
(b) Find the force the car exerts against the driveway.

39. A package that weighs 200 lb is placed on an inclined plane. If a force of 80 lb is just sufficient to keep the package from sliding, find the angle of inclination of the plane. (Ignore the effects of friction.)

40. A cart weighing 40 lb is placed on a ramp inclined at 15° to the horizontal. The cart is held in place by a rope inclined at 60° to the horizontal, as shown in the figure. Find the

force that the rope must exert on the cart to keep it from rolling down the ramp.

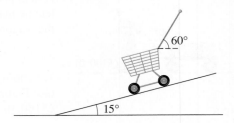

41–44 ■ Let $\mathbf{u}$, $\mathbf{v}$, and $\mathbf{w}$ be vectors and let a be a scalar. Prove the given property.

41. $\mathbf{u} \cdot \mathbf{v} = \mathbf{v} \cdot \mathbf{u}$

42. $(a\mathbf{u}) \cdot \mathbf{v} = a(\mathbf{u} \cdot \mathbf{v}) = \mathbf{u} \cdot (a\mathbf{v})$

43. $(\mathbf{u} + \mathbf{v}) \cdot \mathbf{w} = \mathbf{u} \cdot \mathbf{w} + \mathbf{v} \cdot \mathbf{w}$

44. $(\mathbf{u} - \mathbf{v}) \cdot (\mathbf{u} + \mathbf{v}) = |\mathbf{u}|^2 - |\mathbf{v}|^2$

45. Show that the vectors $\text{proj}_\mathbf{v}\, \mathbf{u}$ and $\mathbf{u} - \text{proj}_\mathbf{v}\, \mathbf{u}$ are orthogonal.

DISCOVERY · DISCUSSION

46. **Distance from a Point to a Line**   Let L be the line $2x + 4y = 8$ and let P be the point $(3, 4)$.
(a) Show that the points $Q(0, 2)$ and $R(2, 1)$ lie on L.
(b) Let $\mathbf{u} = \overrightarrow{QP}$ and $\mathbf{v} = \overrightarrow{QR}$, as shown in the figure. Find $\mathbf{w} = \text{proj}_\mathbf{v}\, \mathbf{u}$.
(c) Sketch a graph that explains why $|\mathbf{u} - \mathbf{w}|$ is the distance from P to L. Find this distance.
(d) Write a short paragraph describing the steps you would take to find the distance from a given point to a given line.

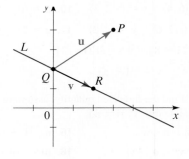

Discovery Project

Sailing against the Wind

Sailors depend on the wind to propel their boats. But what if the wind is blowing in a direction opposite to that in which they want to travel? Although it is obviously impossible to sail directly against the wind, it *is* possible to sail at an angle *into* the wind. Then by *tacking*, that is, zig-zagging on alternate sides of the wind direction, a sailor can make headway against the wind (see Figure 1).

FIGURE 1
Tacking

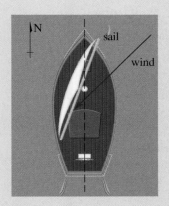

FIGURE 2

How should the sail be aligned to propel the boat in the desired direction into the wind? This question can be answered by modeling the wind as a vector and studying its components along the keel and the sail.

For example, suppose a sailboat headed due north has its sail inclined in the direction N 20° E. The wind is blowing into the sail in the direction S 45° W with a force of magnitude F (see Figure 2).

1. Show that the effective force of the wind on the sail is $F \sin 25°$. You can do this by finding the components of the wind parallel to the sail and perpendicular to the sail. The component parallel to the sail slips by and does not propel the boat. Only the perpendicular component pushes against the sail.

2. If the keel of the boat is aligned due north, what fraction of the force F actually drives the boat forward? Only the component of the force found in Problem 1 that is parallel to the keel drives the boat forward.

    (In real life, other factors, including the aerodynamic properties of the sail, influence the speed of the sailboat.)

3. If a boat heading due north has its sail inclined in the direction N $\alpha°$ E, and the wind is blowing with force F in the direction S $\beta°$ W (where $0 < \alpha < \beta < 180$), find a formula for the magnitude of the force that actually drives the boat forward.

5 REVIEW

CONCEPT CHECK

1. Describe how polar coordinates represent the position of a point in the plane.

2. (a) What equations do you use to change from polar to rectangular coordinates?
(b) What equations do you use to change from rectangular to polar coordinates?

3. How do you sketch the graph of a polar equation $r = f(\theta)$?

4. What type of curve has a polar equation of the given form?
(a) $r = a \cos \theta$ or $r = a \sin \theta$
(b) $r = a(1 \pm \cos \theta)$ or $r = a(1 \pm \sin \theta)$
(c) $r = a \pm b \cos \theta$ or $r = a \pm b \sin \theta$
(d) $r = a \cos n\theta$ or $r = a \sin n\theta$

5. (a) What is a complex number?
(b) What are the real and imaginary parts of a complex number?
(c) What is the complex conjugate of a complex number?
(d) What is the principal square root of a negative number?

6. (a) How do you add or subtract complex numbers?
(b) How do you multiply complex numbers?
(c) How do you divide complex numbers?

7. How do you graph a complex number z? What is the polar form of a complex number z? What is the modulus of z? What is the argument of z?

8. (a) How do you multiply two complex numbers if they are given in polar form?
(b) How do you divide two such numbers?

9. (a) State DeMoivre's Theorem.
(b) How do you find the nth roots of a complex number?

10. (a) What is the difference between a scalar and a vector?
(b) Draw a diagram to show how to add two vectors.
(c) Draw a diagram to show how to subtract two vectors.
(d) Draw a diagram to show how to multiply a vector by the scalars 2, $\frac{1}{2}$, -2, and $-\frac{1}{2}$.

11. If $\mathbf{u} = \langle a_1, b_1 \rangle$, $\mathbf{v} = \langle a_2, b_2 \rangle$ and c is a scalar, write expressions for $\mathbf{u} + \mathbf{v}$, $\mathbf{u} - \mathbf{v}$, $c\mathbf{u}$, and $|\mathbf{u}|$.

12. (a) If $\mathbf{v} = \langle a, b \rangle$, write $\mathbf{v}$ in terms of $\mathbf{i}$ and $\mathbf{j}$.
(b) Write the components of $\mathbf{v}$ in terms of the magnitude and direction of $\mathbf{v}$.

13. If $\mathbf{u} = \langle a_1, b_1 \rangle$ and $\mathbf{v} = \langle a_2, b_2 \rangle$, what is the dot product $\mathbf{u} \cdot \mathbf{v}$?

14. (a) How do you use the dot product to find the angle between two vectors?
(b) How do you use the dot product to determine whether two vectors are perpendicular?

15. What is the component of $\mathbf{u}$ along $\mathbf{v}$, and how do you calculate it?

16. What is the projection of $\mathbf{u}$ onto $\mathbf{v}$, and how do you calculate it?

17. How much work is done by the force $\mathbf{F}$ in moving an object along a displacement $\mathbf{D}$?

EXERCISES

1–4 ■ A point $P(r, \theta)$ is given in polar coordinates. (a) Plot the point P. (b) Find rectangular coordinates for P.

1. $\left(12, \frac{\pi}{6}\right)$

2. $\left(8, -\frac{3\pi}{4}\right)$

3. $\left(-3, -\frac{7\pi}{4}\right)$

4. $\left(-\sqrt{3}, \frac{2\pi}{3}\right)$

5–8 ■ A point $P(x, y)$ is given in rectangular coordinates.
(a) Plot the point P.
(b) Find polar coordinates for P with $r \geqslant 0$.
(c) Find polar coordinates for P with $r \leqslant 0$.

5. $(8, 8)$

6. $(-\sqrt{2}, \sqrt{6})$

7. $(-3, \sqrt{3})$

8. $(4, -4)$

9–12 ■ (a) Convert the equation to polar coordinates and simplify. (b) Graph the equation. [*Hint*: Use the form of the equation that you find easier to graph.]

9. $x + y = 4$

10. $xy = 1$

11. $x^2 + y^2 = 4x + 4y$

12. $(x^2 + y^2)^2 = 2xy$

13–20 ■ (a) Sketch the graph of the polar equation. (b) Express the equation in rectangular coordinates.

13. $r = 3 + 3 \cos \theta$

14. $r = 3 \sin \theta$

15. $r = 2 \sin 2\theta$

16. $r = 4 \cos 3\theta$

17. $r^2 = \sec 2\theta$

18. $r^2 = 4 \sin 2\theta$

19. $r = \sin \theta + \cos \theta$

20. $r = \dfrac{4}{2 + \cos \theta}$

21–24 ■ Use a graphing device to graph the polar equation. Choose the domain of θ to make sure you produce the entire graph.

21. $r = \cos(\theta/3)$

22. $r = \sin(9\theta/4)$

23. $r = 1 + 4 \cos(\theta/3)$

24. $r = \theta \sin \theta$

25–34 ■ Evaluate the expression and write in the form $a + bi$.

25. $(2 - 3i) + (1 + 4i)$

26. $(3 - 6i) - (6 - 4i)$

27. $(2 + i)(3 - 2i)$

28. $4i\left(2 - \frac{1}{2}i\right)$

29. $\dfrac{4 + 2i}{2 - i}$

30. $\dfrac{8 + 3i}{4 + 3i}$

31. i^{25}

32. $(1 + i)^3$

33. $(1 - \sqrt{-1})(1 + \sqrt{-1})$

34. $\sqrt{-10} \cdot \sqrt{-40}$

35–40 ■ A complex number is given.
(a) Graph the complex number in the complex plane.
(b) Find the modulus and argument.
(c) Write the number in polar form.

35. $4 + 4i$

36. $-10i$

37. $5 + 3i$

38. $1 + \sqrt{3} i$

39. $-1 + i$

40. -20

41–44 ■ Find the indicated power.

41. $(1 - \sqrt{3} i)^4$

42. $(1 + i)^8$

43. $(\sqrt{3} + i)^{-4}$

44. $\left(\dfrac{1}{2} + \dfrac{\sqrt{3}}{2}i\right)^{20}$

45–48 ■ Find the indicated roots.

45. The square roots of $-16i$

46. The cube roots of $4 + 4\sqrt{3} i$

47. The sixth roots of 1

48. The eighth roots of i

49–50 ■ Find $|\mathbf{u}|$, $\mathbf{u} + \mathbf{v}$, $\mathbf{u} - \mathbf{v}$, $2\mathbf{u}$, and $3\mathbf{u} - 2\mathbf{v}$.

49. $\mathbf{u} = \langle -2, 3 \rangle$, $\mathbf{v} = \langle 8, 1 \rangle$

50. $\mathbf{u} = 2\mathbf{i} + \mathbf{j}$, $\mathbf{v} = \mathbf{i} - 2\mathbf{j}$

51. Find the vector $\mathbf{u}$ with initial point $P(0, 3)$ and terminal point $Q(3, -1)$.

52. Find the vector $\mathbf{u}$ having length $|\mathbf{u}| = 20$ and direction $\theta = 60°$.

53. If the vector $5\mathbf{i} - 8\mathbf{j}$ is placed in the plane with its initial point at $P(5, 6)$, find its terminal point.

54. Find the direction of the vector $2\mathbf{i} - 5\mathbf{j}$.

55. Two tugboats are pulling a barge, as shown. One pulls with a force of 2.0×10^4 lb in the direction N 50° E and the other with a force of 3.4×10^4 lb in the direction S 75° E.
(a) Find the resultant force on the barge as a vector.
(b) Find the magnitude and direction of the resultant force.

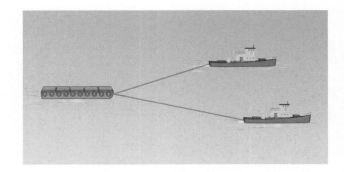

56. An airplane heads N 60° E at a speed of 600 mi/h relative to the air. A wind begins to blow in the direction N 30° W at 50 mi/h.
(a) Find the velocity of the airplane as a vector.
(b) Find the true speed and direction of the airplane.

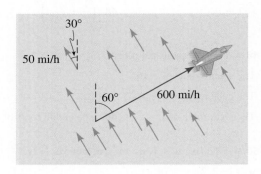

57–60 ■ Find $|\mathbf{u}|$, $\mathbf{u} \cdot \mathbf{u}$, and $\mathbf{u} \cdot \mathbf{v}$.

57. $\mathbf{u} = \langle 4, -3 \rangle$, $\mathbf{v} = \langle 9, -8 \rangle$

58. $\mathbf{u} = \langle 5, 12 \rangle$, $\mathbf{v} = \langle 10, -4 \rangle$

59. $\mathbf{u} = -2\mathbf{i} + 2\mathbf{j}$, $\mathbf{v} = \mathbf{i} + \mathbf{j}$

60. $\mathbf{u} = 10\mathbf{j}$, $\mathbf{v} = 5\mathbf{i} - 3\mathbf{j}$

61–64 ■ Are $\mathbf{u}$ and $\mathbf{v}$ orthogonal? If not, find the angle between them.

61. $\mathbf{u} = \langle -4, 2 \rangle$, $\mathbf{v} = \langle 3, 6 \rangle$

62. $\mathbf{u} = \langle 5, 3 \rangle$, $\mathbf{v} = \langle -2, 6 \rangle$

63. $\mathbf{u} = 2\mathbf{i} + \mathbf{j}$, $\mathbf{v} = \mathbf{i} + 3\mathbf{j}$

64. $\mathbf{u} = \mathbf{i} - \mathbf{j}$, $\mathbf{v} = \mathbf{i} + \mathbf{j}$

65–66 ■ The vectors $\mathbf{u}$ and $\mathbf{v}$ are given.
(a) Find the component of $\mathbf{u}$ along $\mathbf{v}$.
(b) Find $\text{proj}_{\mathbf{v}}\,\mathbf{u}$.
(c) Resolve $\mathbf{u}$ into the vectors $\mathbf{u}_1$ and $\mathbf{u}_2$, where $\mathbf{u}_1$ is parallel to $\mathbf{v}$ and $\mathbf{u}_2$ is perpendicular to $\mathbf{v}$.

65. $\mathbf{u} = \langle 3, 1 \rangle$, $\mathbf{v} = \langle 6, -1 \rangle$

66. $\mathbf{u} = \langle -8, 6 \rangle$, $\mathbf{v} = \langle 20, 20 \rangle$

67. Find the work done by the force $\mathbf{F} = 2\mathbf{i} + 9\mathbf{j}$ in moving an object from the point $(1, 1)$ to the point $(7, -1)$.

68. A force $\mathbf{F}$ with magnitude 250 lb moves an object in the direction of the vector $\mathbf{D}$ a distance of 20 ft. If the work done is 3800 ft-lb, find the angle between $\mathbf{F}$ and $\mathbf{D}$.

5 TEST

1. (a) Convert the point whose polar coordinates are $(8, 5\pi/4)$ to rectangular coordinates.
   (b) Find two polar coordinate representations for the rectangular coordinate point $(-6, 2\sqrt{3})$, one with $r > 0$ and one with $r < 0$, and both with $0 \le \theta < 2\pi$.

2. (a) Graph the polar equation $r = 8 \cos \theta$. What type of curve is this?
   (b) Convert the equation to rectangular coordinates.

3. Calculate and write the result in the form $a + bi$.
   (a) $(6 - 2i) - \left(7 - \frac{1}{2}i\right)$ (b) $(1 + i)(3 - 2i)$
   (c) $\dfrac{5 + 10i}{3 - 4i}$ (d) i^{50}
   (e) $(2 - \sqrt{-2})(8 - \sqrt{-4})$

4. Let $z = 1 + \sqrt{3}\, i$
   (a) Graph z in the complex plane.
   (b) Write z in polar form.
   (c) Find the complex number z^9.

5. Let $z_1 = 4\left(\cos \dfrac{7\pi}{12} + i \sin \dfrac{7\pi}{12}\right)$ and $z_2 = 2\left(\cos \dfrac{5\pi}{12} + i \sin \dfrac{5\pi}{12}\right)$.
   Find $z_1 z_2$ and $\dfrac{z_1}{z_2}$.

6. Find the cube roots of $27i$, and sketch these roots in the complex plane.

7. Let $\mathbf{u}$ be the vector with initial point $P(3, -1)$ and terminal point $Q(-3, 9)$.
   (a) Express $\mathbf{u}$ in terms of $\mathbf{i}$ and $\mathbf{j}$.
   (b) Find the length of $\mathbf{u}$.

8. Let $\mathbf{u} = \langle 1, 3 \rangle$ and $\mathbf{v} = \langle -6, 2 \rangle$.
   (a) Find $\mathbf{u} - 3\mathbf{v}$.   (b) Find $|\mathbf{u} + \mathbf{v}|$.
   (c) Find $\mathbf{u} \cdot \mathbf{v}$.   (d) Are $\mathbf{u}$ and $\mathbf{v}$ perpendicular?

9. A river is flowing due east at 8 mi/h. A man heads his motorboat in a direction N 30° E in the river. The speed of the motorboat relative to the water is 12 mi/h.
   (a) Express the true velocity of the motorboat as a vector.
   (b) Find the true speed and direction of the motorboat.

10. Let $\mathbf{u} = 3\mathbf{i} + 2\mathbf{j}$ and $\mathbf{v} = 5\mathbf{i} - \mathbf{j}$.
    (a) Find the angle between $\mathbf{u}$ and $\mathbf{v}$.
    (b) Find the component of $\mathbf{u}$ along $\mathbf{v}$.
    (c) Find $\text{proj}_{\mathbf{v}}\, \mathbf{u}$.

11. Find the work done by the force $\mathbf{F} = 3\mathbf{i} - 5\mathbf{j}$ in moving an object from the point $(2, 2)$ to the point $(7, -13)$.

Focus on Modeling

Mapping the World

The method used to survey and map a town (pages 232–235) works well for small areas. But there is a new difficulty in mapping the whole world: How do we represent the *spherical* world by a *flat* map? Several ingenious methods have been developed.

■ Cylindrical Projection

One method is the **cylindrical projection**. In this method we imagine a cylinder "wrapped" around the earth at the equator as in Figure 1. Each point on the earth is projected onto the cylinder by a ray emanating from the center of the earth. The "unwrapped" cylinder is the desired flat map of the world. The process is illustrated in Figure 2.

FIGURE 1

Point *P* on the earth is projected onto point *P'* on the cylinder by a ray from the center of the earth *C*.

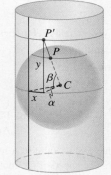

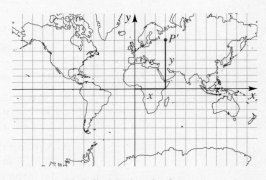

FIGURE 2   (a) Cylindrical projection

(b) Cylindrical projection map

Of course, we cannot actually wrap a large piece of paper around the world, so this whole process must be done mathematically, and the tool we need is trigonometry. On the unwrapped cylinder we take the *x*-axis to correspond to the equator and the *y*-axis to the meridian through Greenwich, England (0° longitude). Let *R* be the radius of the earth and let *P* be the point on the earth at $\alpha°$ E longitude and $\beta°$ N latitude. The point *P* is projected to the point $P'(x, y)$ on the cylinder (viewed as part of the coordinate plane) where

$$x = \left(\frac{\pi}{180}\right)\alpha R \qquad \text{Formula for length of a circular arc}$$

$$y = R \tan \beta \qquad \text{Definition of tan}$$

See Figure 2(a). These formulas can then be used to draw the map. (Note that West longitude and South latitude correspond to negative values of α and β, respectively.) Of course, using R as the radius of the earth would produce a huge map, so we replace R by a smaller value to get a map at an appropriate scale as in Figure 2(b).

Stereographic Projection

In the **stereographic projection** we imagine the earth placed on the coordinate plane with the south pole at the origin. Points on the earth are projected onto the plane by rays emanating from the north pole [see Figure 3]. The earth is placed so that the prime meridian (0° longitude) corresponds to the polar axis. As shown in Figure 4(a), a point P on the earth at $\alpha°$ E longitude and $\beta°$ N latitude is projected onto the point $P'(r, \theta)$ whose polar coordinates are

$$r = 2 R \tan\left(\frac{\beta}{2} + 45°\right)$$

$$\theta = \alpha$$

Figure 4(b) shows how the first of these formulas is obtained

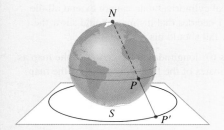

FIGURE 3

Point P on the earth's surface is projected onto point P' on the plane by a ray from the north pole.

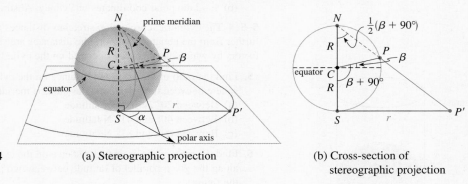

FIGURE 4   (a) Stereographic projection   (b) Cross-section of stereographic projection

Figure 5 shows a stereographic map of the southern hemisphere.

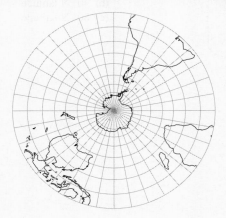

FIGURE 5

Stereographic projection of the southern hemisphere

Problems

1. A map maker wishes to map the earth using a cylindrical projection. The map is to be 36 inches wide. Thus, the equator is mapped onto a horizontal 36-inch line segment. The radius of the earth is 3960 miles.
   (a) What value of R should he use in the cylindrical projection formulas?
   (b) How many miles does one inch on the map represent at the equator?

2. To map the entire world using the cylindrical projection, the cylinder must extend infinitely far in the vertical direction. So a practical cylindrical map cannot extend all the way to the poles. The map maker in Problem 1 decides that his map should show the earth between 70° N and 70° S latitudes. How tall should his map be?

3. The map maker in Problem 1 places the y-axis (0° longitude) at the center of the map as shown in Figure 2(b). Find the x- and y-coordinates of the following cities on the map.
   (a) Seattle, Washington; 47.6° N, 122.3° W
   (b) Moscow, Russia; 55.8° N, 37.6° E
   (c) Sydney, Australia; 33.9° S, 151.2° E
   (d) Rio de Janeiro, Brazil; 22.9° S, 43.1° W

4. A map maker makes a stereographic projection of the southern hemisphere, from the south pole to the equator. The map is to have a radius of 20 in.
   (a) What value of R should he use in the stereographic projection formulas?
   (b) Find the polar coordinates of Sydney, Australia (33.9° S, 151.2° E) on his map.

5–6 ■ The cylindrical projection stretches distances between points not on the equator—the further from the equator, the more the distances are stretched. In these problems we find the factors by which distances are distorted on the cylindrical projection at various locations.

5. Find the ratio of the projected distance on the cylinder to the actual distance on the sphere between the given latitudes along a meridian (see the figure at the left).
   (a) Between 20° and 21° N latitude
   (b) Between 40° and 41° N latitude
   (c) Between 80° and 81° N latitude

6. Find the ratio of the projected distance on the cylinder to the distance on the sphere along the given parallel of latitude between two points that are 1° longitude apart (see the figure).
   (a) 20° N latitude
   (b) 40° N latitude
   (c) 80° N latitude

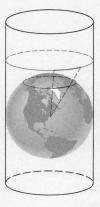

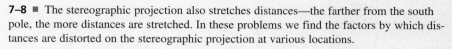

7–8 ■ The stereographic projection also stretches distances—the farther from the south pole, the more distances are stretched. In these problems we find the factors by which distances are distorted on the stereographic projection at various locations.

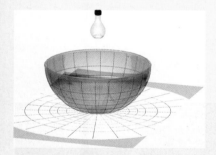

7. Find the ratio of the projected distance on the plane to the actual distance on the sphere between the given latitudes along a meridian (see the figure at the left).
   (a) Between 20° and 21° S latitude
   (b) Between 40° and 41° S latitude
   (c) Between 80° and 81° S latitude

8. Find the ratio of the projected distance on the plane to the distance on the sphere along the given parallel of latitude between two points that are 1° longitude apart (see the figure).
   (a) 20° S latitude
   (b) 40° S latitude
   (c) 80° S latitude

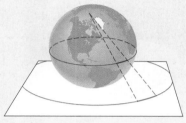

9. In this project we see how projection transfers lines of latitude and longitude from a sphere to a flat surface. You will need a round glass bowl, tracing paper, and a light source (a small transparent light bulb). Use a black marker to draw equally spaced lines of latitude and longitude on the outside of the bowl.
   (a) To model the stereographic projection, place the bowl on a sheet of tracing paper and use the light source as shown in the figure at the left.
   (b) To model the cylindrical projection, wrap the tracing paper around the bowl and use the light source as shown in the figure below.

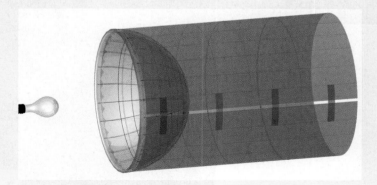

10. There are many other map projections, such as the Albers Conic Projection, the Azimuthal Projection, the Behrmann Cylindrical Equal-Area Projection, the Gall Isographic and Orthographic Projections, the Gnomonic Projection, the Lambert Equal-Area Projection, the Mercator Projection, the Mollweide Projection, the Rectangular Projection, and the Sinusoidal Projection. Research one of these projections in your library or on the Internet and write a report explaining how the map is constructed, and describing its advantages and disadvantages.

6 Analytic Geometry

The path of an object moving under the gravitational pull of another is a conic section. For instance, the trajectory of a basketball is a parabola; the orbit of a planet around the sun is an ellipse.

In studying the procedures of geometric thought we may hope to reach what is most essential in the human mind.

HENRI POINCARÉ

In this chapter we study the geometry of **conic sections** (or simply **conics**). Conic sections are the curves formed by the intersection of a plane with a pair of circular cones. These curves have four basic shapes, called **circles**, **ellipses**, **parabolas**, and **hyperbolas**, as illustrated in the figure.

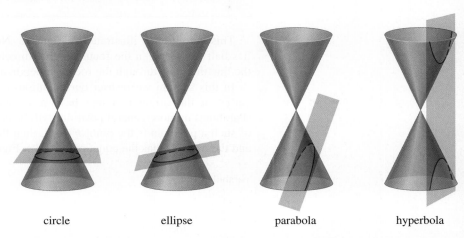

circle   ellipse   parabola   hyperbola

We also study the rotation of axes formulas and parametric equations. these topics utilize trigonometry in an essential way.

6.1 PARABOLAS

The graph of a quadratic equation $y = ax^2 + bx + c$ is a U-shaped curve called a *parabola* that opens either upward or downward, depending on whether the sign of a is positive or negative (see Figure 1). The lowest or highest point of the parabola is called the **vertex**, and the parabola is symmetric about its **axis** (or **axis of symmetry**).

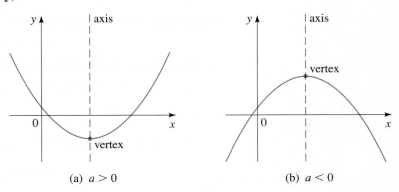

FIGURE 1
$y = ax^2 + bx + c$

(a) $a > 0$

(b) $a < 0$

In this section we study parabolas from a geometric rather than an algebraic point of view. We begin with the geometric definition of a parabola and show how this leads to the algebraic formula that we are already familiar with.

GEOMETRIC DEFINITION OF A PARABOLA

A **parabola** is the set of points in the plane equidistant from a fixed point F (called the **focus**) and a fixed line l (called the **directrix**).

This definition is illustrated in Figure 2. Note that the vertex V of the parabola lies halfway between the focus and the directrix and that the axis of symmetry is the line that runs through the focus perpendicular to the directrix.

In this section we restrict our attention to parabolas that are situated with the vertex at the origin and that have a vertical or horizontal axis of symmetry. (Parabolas in more general positions will be considered in Section 6.4.) If the focus of such a parabola is the point $F(0, p)$, then the axis of symmetry must be vertical and the directrix has the equation $y = -p$. Figure 3 illustrates the case $p > 0$.

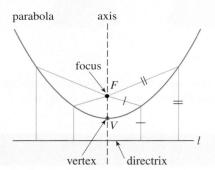

FIGURE 2

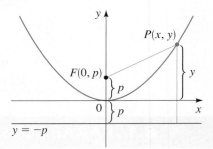

FIGURE 3

If $P(x, y)$ is any point on the parabola, then the distance from P to the focus F (using the Distance Formula) is

$$\sqrt{x^2 + (y - p)^2}$$

The distance from P to the directrix is

$$|y - (-p)| = |y + p|$$

By the definition of a parabola, these two distances must be equal:

$$\sqrt{x^2 + (y - p)^2} = |y + p|$$

$$x^2 + (y - p)^2 = |y + p|^2 = (y + p)^2 \qquad \text{Square both sides}$$

$$x^2 + y^2 - 2py + p^2 = y^2 + 2py + p^2 \qquad \text{Expand}$$

$$x^2 - 2py = 2py \qquad \text{Simplify}$$

$$x^2 = 4py$$

When x is replaced by $-x$, the equation remains unchanged, so the graph is symmetric about the y-axis. We summarize what we have proved in the following box.

PARABOLA WITH VERTICAL AXIS

The graph of the equation

$$x^2 = 4py$$

is a parabola with the following properties.

VERTEX	$V(0, 0)$
FOCUS	$F(0, p)$
DIRECTRIX	$y = -p$

The parabola opens upward if $p > 0$ or downward if $p < 0$.

$x^2 = 4py$ with $p > 0$ $x^2 = 4py$ with $p < 0$

EXAMPLE 1 ■ Finding the Equation of a Parabola

Find the equation of the parabola with vertex $V(0, 0)$ and focus $F(0, 2)$, and sketch its graph.

SOLUTION

Since the focus is $F(0, 2)$, we conclude that $p = 2$ (and so the directrix is $y = -2$). Thus, the equation of the parabola is

$$x^2 = 4(2)y \qquad \text{\small $x^2 = 4py$ with $p = 2$}$$

$$x^2 = 8y$$

Since $p = 2 > 0$, the parabola opens upward. See Figure 4. ■

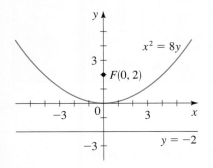

FIGURE 4

EXAMPLE 2 ■ Finding the Focus and Directrix of a Parabola from Its Equation

Find the focus and directrix of the parabola $y = -x^2$, and sketch the graph.

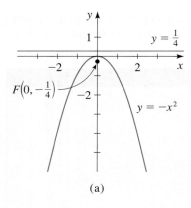

(a)

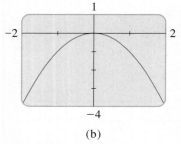

(b)

FIGURE 5

SOLUTION

To find the focus and directrix, we put the given equation in the standard form $x^2 = -y$. Comparing this to the general equation $x^2 = 4py$, we see that $4p = -1$, so $p = -\frac{1}{4}$. Thus, the focus is $F\left(0, -\frac{1}{4}\right)$ and the directrix is $y = \frac{1}{4}$. The graph of the parabola, together with the focus and the directrix, is shown in Figure 5(a). We can also draw the graph using a graphing calculator as shown in Figure 5(b). ■

Reflecting the graph in Figure 3 about the diagonal line $y = x$ has the effect of interchanging the roles of x and y. This results in a parabola with horizontal axis. By the same method as before, we can prove the following properties.

PARABOLA WITH HORIZONTAL AXIS

The graph of the equation

$$y^2 = 4px$$

is a parabola with the following properties.

VERTEX	$V(0, 0)$
FOCUS	$F(p, 0)$
DIRECTRIX	$x = -p$

The parabola opens to the right if $p > 0$ or to the left if $p < 0$.

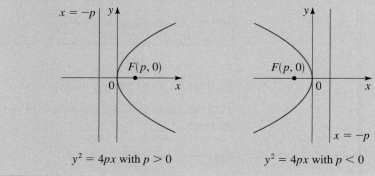

$y^2 = 4px$ with $p > 0$ $y^2 = 4px$ with $p < 0$

EXAMPLE 3 ■ A Parabola with Horizontal Axis

A parabola has the equation $6x + y^2 = 0$.

(a) Find the focus and directrix of the parabola, and sketch the graph.

(b) Use a graphing calculator to draw the graph.

SOLUTION

(a) To find the focus and directrix, we put the given equation in the standard form $y^2 = -6x$. Comparing this to the general equation $y^2 = 4px$, we see that $4p = -6$, so $p = -\frac{3}{2}$. Thus, the focus is $F\left(-\frac{3}{2}, 0\right)$ and the directrix is $x = \frac{3}{2}$.

Since $p < 0$, the parabola opens to the left. The graph of the parabola, together with the focus and the directrix, is shown in Figure 6(a).

 (b) To draw the graph using a graphing calculator, we need to solve for y.

$$6x + y^2 = 0$$

$$y^2 = -6x \qquad \text{Subtract } 6x$$

$$y = \pm\sqrt{-6x} \qquad \text{Take square roots}$$

To obtain the graph of the parabola, we graph both functions

$$y = \sqrt{-6x} \qquad \text{and} \qquad y = -\sqrt{-6x}$$

as shown in Figure 6(b).

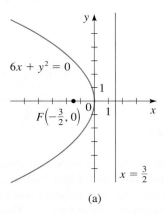

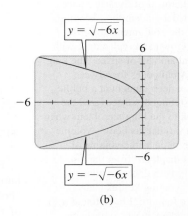

FIGURE 6   (a)   (b)   ■

The equation $y^2 = 4px$ does not define y as a function of x (see page 51). So, to use a graphing calculator to graph a parabola with horizontal axis, we must first solve for y. This leads to two functions, $y = \sqrt{4px}$ and $y = \sqrt{-4px}$. We must graph both functions to get the complete graph of the parabola. For example, in Figure 6(b) we had to graph both $y = \sqrt{-6x}$ and $y = -\sqrt{-6x}$ to graph the parabola $y^2 = -6x$.

We can use the coordinates of the focus to estimate the "width" of a parabola when sketching its graph. The line segment that runs through the focus perpendicular to the axis, with endpoints on the parabola, is called the **latus rectum**, and its length is the **focal diameter** of the parabola. From Figure 7 we can see that the distance from an endpoint Q of the latus rectum to the directrix is $|2p|$. Thus, the distance from Q to the focus must be $|2p|$ as well (by the definition of a parabola), and so the focal diameter is $|4p|$. In the next example we use the focal diameter to determine the "width" of a parabola when graphing it.

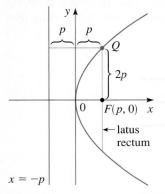

FIGURE 7

EXAMPLE 4 ■ Using the Focal Diameter to Sketch a Parabola

Find the focus, directrix, and focal diameter of the parabola $y = \frac{1}{2}x^2$, and sketch its graph.

SOLUTION

We first put the equation in the form $x^2 = 4py$.

$$y = \tfrac{1}{2}x^2$$

$$x^2 = 2y \qquad \text{Multiply each side by 2}$$

From this equation we see that $4p = 2$, so the focal diameter is 2. Solving for p gives $p = \frac{1}{2}$, so the focus is $\left(0, \frac{1}{2}\right)$ and the directrix is $y = -\frac{1}{2}$. Since the focal diameter is 2, the latus rectum extends 1 unit to the left and 1 unit to the right of the focus. This enables us to sketch the graph in Figure 8.

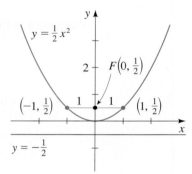

FIGURE 8

Parabolas have an important property that makes them useful as reflectors for lamps and telescopes. Light from a source placed at the focus of a surface with parabolic cross section will be reflected in such a way that it travels parallel to the axis of the parabola (see Figure 9). Thus, a parabolic mirror reflects the light into a beam of parallel rays. Conversely, light approaching the reflector in rays parallel to its axis of symmetry is concentrated to the focus. This *reflection property*, which can be proved using calculus, is used in the construction of reflecting telescopes.

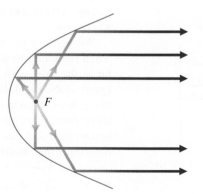

FIGURE 9
Parabolic reflector

EXAMPLE 5 ■ Finding the Focal Point of a Searchlight Reflector

A searchlight has a parabolic reflector that forms a "bowl," which is 12 in. wide from rim to rim and 8 in. deep, as shown in Figure 10. If the filament of the light bulb is located at the focus, how far from the vertex of the reflector is it?

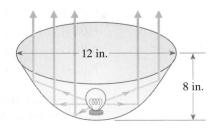

FIGURE 10
A parabolic reflector

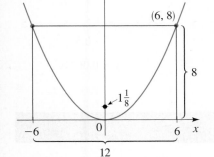

FIGURE 11

SOLUTION

We introduce a coordinate system and place a parabolic cross section of the reflector so that its vertex is at the origin and its axis is vertical (see Figure 11). Then the equation of this parabola has the form $x^2 = 4py$. From Figure 11 we see that the point $(6, 8)$ lies on the parabola. We use this to find p.

$$6^2 = 4p(8) \qquad \text{The point } (6, 8) \text{ satisfies the equation } x^2 = 4py$$

$$36 = 32p$$

$$p = \tfrac{9}{8}$$

The focus is $F\left(0, \tfrac{9}{8}\right)$, so the distance between the vertex and the focus is $\tfrac{9}{8} = 1\tfrac{1}{8}$ in. Because the filament is positioned at the focus, it is located $1\tfrac{1}{8}$ in. from the vertex of the reflector. ■

In the next example we graph a family of parabolas, to show how changing the distance between the focus and the vertex affects the "width" of a parabola.

EXAMPLE 6 ■ A Family of Parabolas

(a) Find equations for the parabolas with vertex at the origin and foci
    $F_1\left(0, \tfrac{1}{8}\right)$, $F_2\left(0, \tfrac{1}{2}\right)$, $F_3(0, 1)$, and $F_4(0, 4)$.
(b) Draw the graphs of the parabolas in part (a). What do you conclude?

SOLUTION

(a) Since the foci are on the positive y-axis, the parabolas open upward and have equations of the form $x^2 = 4py$. This leads to the following equations.

Focus	p	Equation $x^2 = 4py$	Form of the equation for graphing calculator
$F_1\left(0, \frac{1}{8}\right)$	$p = \frac{1}{8}$	$x^2 = \frac{1}{2}y$	$y = 2x^2$
$F_2\left(0, \frac{1}{2}\right)$	$p = \frac{1}{2}$	$x^2 = 2y$	$y = 0.5x^2$
$F_3(0, 1)$	$p = 1$	$x^2 = 4y$	$y = 0.25x^2$
$F_4(0, 4)$	$p = 4$	$x^2 = 16y$	$y = 0.0625x^2$

(b) The graphs are drawn in Figure 12. We see that the closer the focus to the vertex, the narrower the parabola.

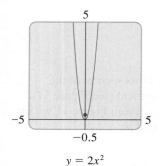

$y = 2x^2$

$y = 0.5x^2$

$y = 0.25x^2$

$y = 0.0625x^2$

FIGURE 12 A family of parabolas

6.1 EXERCISES

1–6 ■ Match the equation with the graphs labeled I–VI. Give reasons for your answers.

1. $y^2 = 2x$ **2.** $y^2 = -\frac{1}{4}x$ **3.** $x^2 = -6y$

4. $2x^2 = y$ **5.** $y^2 - 8x = 0$ **6.** $12y + x^2 = 0$

I
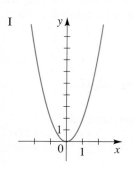

II
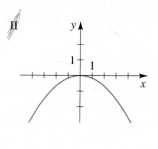

III
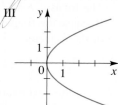

IV
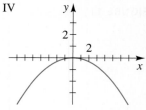

V
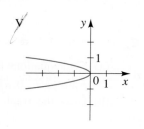

VI
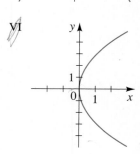

7–18 ■ Find the focus, directrix, and focal diameter of the parabola, and sketch its graph.

7. $y^2 = 4x$

8. $x^2 = y$

9. $x^2 = 9y$

10. $y^2 = 3x$

11. $y = 5x^2$

12. $y = -2x^2$

13. $x = -8y^2$

14. $x = \frac{1}{2}y^2$

15. $x^2 + 6y = 0$

16. $x - 7y^2 = 0$

17. $5x + 3y^2 = 0$

18. $8x^2 + 12y = 0$

19–24 ■ Use a graphing device to graph the parabola.

19. $x^2 = 16y$

20. $x^2 = -8y$

21. $y^2 = -\frac{1}{3}x$

22. $8y^2 = x$

23. $4x + y^2 = 0$

24. $x - 2y^2 = 0$

25–36 ■ Find an equation for the parabola that has its vertex at the origin and satisfies the given condition(s).

25. Focus $F(0, 2)$

26. Focus $F\left(0, -\frac{1}{2}\right)$

27. Focus $F(-8, 0)$

28. Focus $F(5, 0)$

29. Directrix $x = 2$

30. Directrix $y = 6$

31. Directrix $y = -10$

32. Directrix $x = -\frac{1}{8}$

33. Focus on the positive x-axis, 2 units away from the directrix

34. Directrix has y-intercept 6

35. Opens upward with focus 5 units from the vertex

36. Focal diameter 8 and focus on the negative y-axis

37–46 ■ Find an equation of the parabola whose graph is shown.

37.

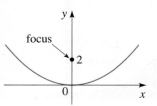

38.

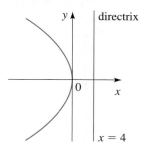

39.

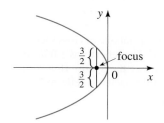

40.

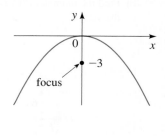

41.

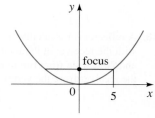

42.

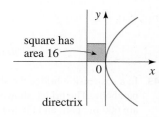

43.

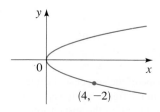

44.

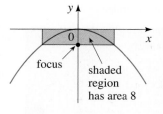

45.

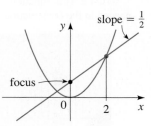

46.

47. A lamp with a parabolic reflector is shown in the figure on the following page. The bulb is placed at the focus and the focal diameter is 12 cm.

(a) Find an equation of the parabola.
(b) Find the diameter $d(C, D)$ of the opening, 20 cm from the vertex.

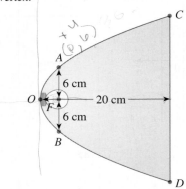

48. A reflector for a satellite dish is parabolic in cross section, with the receiver at the focus F. The reflector is 1 ft deep and 20 ft wide from rim to rim (see the figure). How far is the receiver from the vertex of the parabolic reflector?

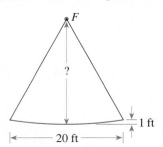

49. In a suspension bridge the shape of the suspension cables is parabolic. The bridge shown in the figure has towers that are 600 m apart, and the lowest point of the suspension cables is 150 m below the top of the towers. Find the equation of the parabolic part of the cables, placing the origin of the coordinate system at the vertex.

   NOTE This equation is used to find the length of cable needed in the construction of the bridge.

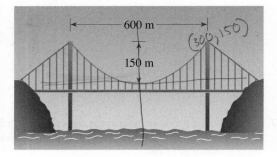

50. The Hale telescope at the Mount Palomar Observatory has a 200-in. mirror, as shown. The mirror is constructed in a parabolic shape that collects light from the stars and focuses it at the **prime focus**, that is, the focus of the parabola. The mirror is 3.79 in. deep at its center. Find the **focal length** of this parabolic mirror, that is, the distance from the vertex to the focus.

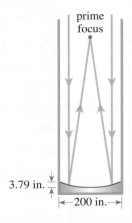

51. (a) Find equations for the family of parabolas with vertex at the origin and with directrixes $y = \frac{1}{2}$, $y = 1$, $y = 4$, and $y = 8$.
    (b) Draw the graphs. What do you conclude?

 DISCOVERY · DISCUSSION

52. **Parabolas in the Real World**   Several examples of the uses of parabolas are given in the text. Find other situations in real life where parabolas occur. Consult a scientific encyclopedia in the reference section of your library, or search the Internet.

53. **Light Cone from a Flashlight**   A flashlight is held to form a lighted area on the ground, as shown in the figure. Is it possible to angle the flashlight in such a way that the boundary of the lighted area is a parabola? Explain your answer.

Laboratory Project

Rolling Down a Ramp

Galileo (see page 427) was the first to show that the motion of a falling ball can be modeled by a parabola. To accomplish this, he rolled balls down a ramp and used his acute sense of timing to study the motion of the ball. In this project you will perform a similar experiment, using modern equipment. You will need the following:

- A wide board, about 6–8 ft long, to be used as a ramp
- A large ball, the size of a soccer or volleyball
- A calculator-based motion detector, such as the Texas Instruments CBR system (Calculator Based Ranger)

Use books to prop up the ramp at an angle of about 15°, clamp the motion detector to the top of the ramp, and connect it to the calculator, as shown in the figure. (Read the manual carefully to make sure you have set up the calculator and motion detector correctly.)

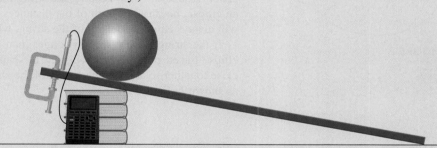

1. Mark a spot on the ramp about 2 ft from the top. Place the ball on the mark and release it to see how many seconds it takes to roll to the bottom. Adjust the motion detector to record the ball's position every 0.05 s over this length of time. Now let the ball roll down the ramp again, this time with the motion detector running. The calculator should record at least 50 data points that indicate the distance between the ball and the motion detector every 0.05 s.

2. Make a scatter plot of your data, plotting time on the x-axis and distance on the y-axis. Does the plot look like half of a parabola?

3. Use the quadratic regression command on your calculator (called **QuadReg** on the TI-83) to find the parabola equation $y = ax^2 + bx + c$ that best fits the data. Graph this equation on your scatter plot to see how well it fits. Do the data points really form part of a parabola?

4. Repeat the experiment with the ramp inclined at a shallower angle. How does reducing the angle of the ramp affect the shape of the parabola?

5. Try rolling the ball up the ramp from the bottom to the spot you marked in Step 1, so that it rolls up and then back down again. If you perform the experiment this way instead of just letting the ball roll down, how does your graph in Step 3 change?

6.2 ELLIPSES

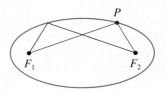

FIGURE 1

An ellipse is an oval curve that looks like an elongated circle. More precisely, we have the following definition.

GEOMETRIC DEFINITION OF AN ELLIPSE

An **ellipse** is the set of all points in the plane the sum of whose distances from two fixed points F_1 and F_2 is a constant. (See Figure 1.) These two fixed points are the **foci** (plural of **focus**) of the ellipse.

FIGURE 2

The geometric definition suggests a simple method for drawing an ellipse. Place a sheet of paper on a drawing board and insert thumbtacks at the two points that are to be the foci of the ellipse. Attach the ends of a string to the tacks, as shown in Figure 2. With the point of a pencil, hold the string taut. Then carefully move the pencil around the foci, keeping the string taut at all times. The pencil will trace out an ellipse, because the sum of the distances from the point of the pencil to the foci will always equal the length of the string, which is constant.

If the string is only slightly longer than the distance between the foci, then the ellipse traced out will be elongated in shape as in Figure 3(a), but if the foci are close together relative to the length of the string, the ellipse will be almost circular, as shown in Figure 3(b).

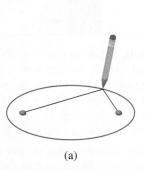 

FIGURE 3   (a)   (b)

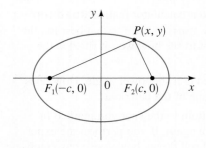

FIGURE 4

To obtain the simplest equation for an ellipse, we place the foci on the x-axis at $F_1(-c, 0)$ and $F_2(c, 0)$, so that the origin is halfway between them (see Figure 4).

For later convenience we let the sum of the distances from a point on the ellipse to the foci be $2a$. Then if $P(x, y)$ is any point on the ellipse, we have

$$d(P, F_1) + d(P, F_2) = 2a$$

So, from the Distance Formula

$$\sqrt{(x + c)^2 + y^2} + \sqrt{(x - c)^2 + y^2} = 2a$$

or

$$\sqrt{(x - c)^2 + y^2} = 2a - \sqrt{(x + c)^2 + y^2}$$

Squaring each side and expanding, we get

$$x^2 - 2cx + c^2 + y^2 = 4a^2 - 4a\sqrt{(x+c)^2 + y^2} + (x^2 + 2cx + c^2 + y^2)$$

which simplifies to

$$4a\sqrt{(x+c)^2 + y^2} = 4a^2 + 4cx$$

Dividing each side by 4 and squaring again, we get

$$a^2[(x+c)^2 + y^2] = (a^2 + cx)^2$$

$$a^2x^2 + 2a^2cx + a^2c^2 + a^2y^2 = a^4 + 2a^2cx + c^2x^2$$

$$(a^2 - c^2)x^2 + a^2y^2 = a^2(a^2 - c^2)$$

Since the sum of the distances from P to the foci must be larger than the distance between the foci, we have that $2a > 2c$, or $a > c$. Thus, $a^2 - c^2 > 0$, and we can divide each side of the preceding equation by $a^2(a^2 - c^2)$ to get

$$\frac{x^2}{a^2} + \frac{y^2}{a^2 - c^2} = 1$$

For convenience let $b^2 = a^2 - c^2$ (with $b > 0$). Since $b^2 < a^2$, it follows that $b < a$. The preceding equation then becomes

$$\frac{x^2}{a^2} + \frac{y^2}{b^2} = 1 \qquad \text{with } a > b$$

This is the equation of the ellipse. To graph it, we need to know the x- and y-intercepts. Setting $y = 0$, we get

$$\frac{x^2}{a^2} = 1$$

so $x^2 = a^2$, or $x = \pm a$. Thus, the ellipse crosses the x-axis at $(a, 0)$ and $(-a, 0)$. These points are called the **vertices** of the ellipse, and the segment that joins them is called the **major axis**. Its length is $2a$.

Similarly, if we set $x = 0$, we get $y = \pm b$, so the ellipse crosses the y-axis at $(0, b)$ and $(0, -b)$. The segment that joins these points is called the **minor axis**, and it has length $2b$. Note that $2a > 2b$, so the major axis is longer than the minor axis.

In Section 1.8 we studied several tests that detect symmetry in a graph. If we replace x by $-x$ or y by $-y$ in the ellipse equation, it remains unchanged. Thus, the ellipse is symmetric about both the x- and y-axes, and hence about the origin as well. For this reason the origin is called the **center** of the ellipse. The complete graph is shown in Figure 5.

If the foci of the ellipse are placed on the y-axis at $(0, \pm c)$ rather than on the x-axis, then the roles of x and y are reversed in the preceding discussion, and we get a vertical ellipse. Thus, we have the following description of ellipses.

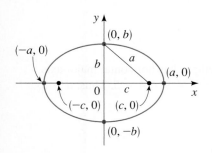

FIGURE 5

$$\frac{x^2}{a^2} + \frac{y^2}{b^2} = 1 \text{ with } a > b$$

ELLIPSE WITH CENTER AT THE ORIGIN

The graph of each of the following equations is an ellipse with center at the origin and having the given properties.

EQUATION	$\dfrac{x^2}{a^2} + \dfrac{y^2}{b^2} = 1$	$\dfrac{x^2}{b^2} + \dfrac{y^2}{a^2} = 1$
	$a > b > 0$	$a > b > 0$
VERTICES	$(\pm a, 0)$	$(0, \pm a)$
MAJOR AXIS	Horizontal, length $2a$	Vertical, length $2a$
MINOR AXIS	Vertical, length $2b$	Horizontal, length $2b$
FOCI	$(\pm c, 0), \quad c^2 = a^2 - b^2$	$(0, \pm c), \quad c^2 = a^2 - b^2$
GRAPH	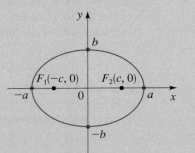	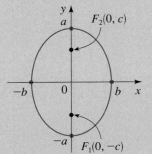

In the standard equation for an ellipse, a^2 is the *larger* denominator and b^2 is the *smaller*. To find c^2, we subtract: larger denominator minus smaller denominator.

EXAMPLE 1 ■ Sketching an Ellipse

An ellipse has the equation

$$\frac{x^2}{9} + \frac{y^2}{4} = 1$$

(a) Find the foci, vertices, and the lengths of the major and minor axes, and sketch the graph.

(b) Draw the graph using a graphing calculator.

SOLUTION

(a) Since the denominator of x^2 is larger, the ellipse has horizontal major axis. This gives $a^2 = 9$ and $b^2 = 4$, so $c^2 = a^2 - b^2 = 9 - 4 = 5$. Thus, $a = 3$, $b = 2$, and $c = \sqrt{5}$.

$$\text{FOCI} \quad (\pm \sqrt{5}, 0)$$

$$\text{VERTICES} \quad (\pm 3, 0)$$

$$\text{LENGTH OF MAJOR AXIS} \quad 6$$

$$\text{LENGTH OF MINOR AXIS} \quad 4$$

The graph is shown in Figure 6(a).

(b) To draw the graph using a graphing calculator, we need to solve for y.

$$\frac{x^2}{9} + \frac{y^2}{4} = 1$$

$$\frac{y^2}{4} = 1 - \frac{x^2}{9} \qquad \text{Subtract } x^2/9$$

$$y^2 = 4\left(1 - \frac{x^2}{9}\right) \qquad \text{Multiply by 4}$$

$$y = \pm 2 \sqrt{1 - \frac{x^2}{9}} \qquad \text{Take square roots}$$

Note that the equation of an ellipse does not define y as a function of x (see page 51). That's why we need to graph two functions to graph an ellipse.

To obtain the graph of the ellipse, we graph both functions

$$y = 2\sqrt{1 - x^2/9} \qquad \text{and} \qquad y = -2\sqrt{1 - x^2/9}$$

as shown in Figure 6(b).

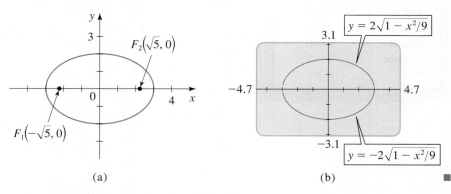

FIGURE 6

$$\frac{x^2}{9} + \frac{y^2}{4} = 1$$

(a)   (b)

EXAMPLE 2 ■ Finding the Equation of an Ellipse

The vertices of an ellipse are $(\pm 4, 0)$ and the foci are $(\pm 2, 0)$. Find its equation and sketch the graph.

SOLUTION

Since the vertices are $(\pm 4, 0)$, we have $a = 4$. The foci are $(\pm 2, 0)$, so $c = 2$. To write the equation, we need to find b. Since $c^2 = a^2 - b^2$, we have

$$2^2 = 4^2 - b^2$$

$$b^2 = 16 - 4 = 12$$

Thus, the equation of the ellipse is

$$\frac{x^2}{16} + \frac{y^2}{12} = 1$$

The graph is shown in Figure 7.

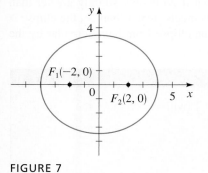

FIGURE 7

$$\frac{x^2}{16} + \frac{y^2}{12} = 1$$

EXAMPLE 3 ■ Finding the Foci of an Ellipse

Find the foci of the ellipse $16x^2 + 9y^2 = 144$, and sketch its graph.

SOLUTION

First we put the equation in standard form. Dividing by 144, we get

$$\frac{x^2}{9} + \frac{y^2}{16} = 1$$

Since $16 > 9$, this is an ellipse with its foci on the y-axis, and with $a = 4$ and $b = 3$. We have

$$c^2 = a^2 - b^2 = 16 - 9 = 7$$
$$c = \sqrt{7}$$

Thus, the foci are $(0, \pm\sqrt{7})$. The graph is shown in Figure 8(a).

We can also draw the graph using a graphing calculator as shown in Figure 8(b).

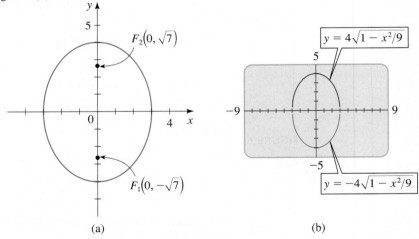

(a)   (b)

FIGURE 8
$16x^2 + 9y^2 = 144$

We saw earlier in this section (Figure 3) that if $2a$ is only slightly greater than $2c$, the ellipse is long and thin, whereas if $2a$ is much greater than $2c$, the ellipse is almost circular. We measure the deviation of an ellipse from being circular by the ratio of a and c.

DEFINITION OF ECCENTRICITY

For the ellipse $\dfrac{x^2}{a^2} + \dfrac{y^2}{b^2} = 1$ or $\dfrac{x^2}{b^2} + \dfrac{y^2}{a^2} = 1$ (with $a > b > 0$), the **eccentricity** e is the number

$$e = \frac{c}{a}$$

where $c = \sqrt{a^2 - b^2}$. The eccentricity of every ellipse satisfies $0 < e < 1$.

Johannes Kepler (1571–1630) was the first to give a correct description of the motion of the planets. The cosmology of his time postulated complicated systems of circles moving on circles to describe these motions. Kepler sought a simpler and more harmonious description. As official astronomer at the imperial court in Prague, he studied the astronomical observations of the Danish astronomer Tycho Brahe, whose data were the most accurate available at the time. After numerous attempts to find a theory, Kepler made the momentous discovery that the orbits of the planets are elliptical. His three great laws of planetary motion are

1. The orbit of each planet is an ellipse with the sun at one focus.
2. The line segment that joins the sun to a planet sweeps out equal areas in equal time (see the figure).
3. The square of the period of revolution of a planet is proportional to the cube of the length of the major axis of its orbit.

His formulation of these laws is perhaps the most impressive deduction from empirical data in the history of science.

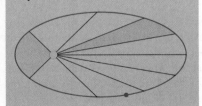

Thus, if e is close to 1, then c is almost equal to a, and the ellipse is elongated in shape, but if e is close to 0, then the ellipse is close to a circle in shape. The eccentricity is a measure of how "stretched" the ellipse is.

In Figure 9 we show a number of ellipses to demonstrate the effect of varying the eccentricity e.

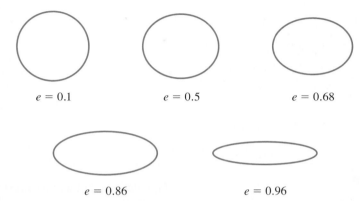

$e = 0.1$ $e = 0.5$ $e = 0.68$

$e = 0.86$ $e = 0.96$

FIGURE 9
Ellipses with various eccentricities

EXAMPLE 4 ■ **Finding the Equation of an Ellipse from Its Eccentricity and Foci**

Find the equation of the ellipse with foci $(0, \pm 8)$ and eccentricity $e = \frac{4}{5}$, and sketch its graph.

SOLUTION

We are given $e = \frac{4}{5}$ and $c = 8$. Thus

$$\frac{4}{5} = \frac{8}{a} \qquad \text{Eccentricity } e = \frac{c}{a}$$

$$4a = 40 \qquad \text{Cross multiply}$$

$$a = 10$$

To find b, we use the fact that $c^2 = a^2 - b^2$.

$$8^2 = 10^2 - b^2$$

$$b^2 = 10^2 - 8^2 = 36$$

$$b = 6$$

Thus, the equation of the ellipse is

$$\frac{x^2}{36} + \frac{y^2}{100} = 1$$

Because the foci are on the y-axis, the ellipse is oriented vertically. To sketch the ellipse, we find the intercepts: The x-intercepts are ± 6 and the y-intercepts are ± 10. The graph is sketched in Figure 10.

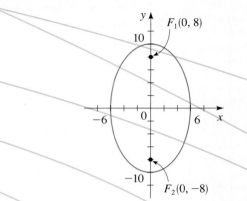

FIGURE 10

$$\frac{x^2}{36} + \frac{y^2}{100} = 1$$

Gravitational attraction causes the planets to move in elliptical orbits around the sun with the sun at one focus. This remarkable property was first observed by Johannes Kepler and was later deduced by Isaac Newton from his inverse square law of gravity, using calculus. The orbits of the planets have different eccentricities, but most are nearly circular (see the margin note on page 374).

Ellipses, like parabolas, have an interesting *reflection property* that leads to a number of practical applications. If a light source is placed at one focus of a reflecting surface with elliptical cross sections, then all the light will be reflected off the surface to the other focus, as shown in Figure 11. This principle, which works for sound waves as well as for light, is used in *lithotripsy*, a treatment for kidney stones. The patient is placed in a tub of water with elliptical cross sections in such a way that the kidney stone is accurately located at one focus. High-intensity sound waves generated at the other focus are reflected to the stone and destroy it with minimal damage to surrounding tissue. The patient is spared the trauma of surgery and recovers within days instead of weeks.

The reflection property of ellipses is also used in the construction of *whispering galleries*. Sound coming from one focus bounces off the walls and ceiling of an elliptical room and passes through the other focus. In these rooms even quiet whispers spoken at one focus can be heard clearly at the other. Famous whispering galleries include the National Statuary Gallery of the U.S. Capitol in Washington, D.C., and the Mormon Tabernacle in Salt Lake City, Utah.

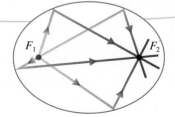

FIGURE 11

6.2 EXERCISES

1–4 ■ Match the equation with the graphs labeled I–IV. Give reasons for your answers.

1. $\dfrac{x^2}{16} + \dfrac{y^2}{4} = 1$

2. $x^2 + \dfrac{y^2}{9} = 1$

3. $4x^2 + y^2 = 4$

4. $16x^2 + 25y^2 = 400$

I

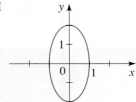

II

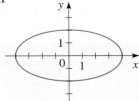

III

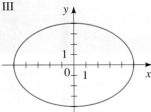

IV

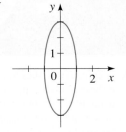

5–18 ■ Find the vertices, foci, and eccentricity of the ellipse. Determine the lengths of the major and minor axes, and sketch the graph.

5. $\dfrac{x^2}{25} + \dfrac{y^2}{9} = 1$

6. $\dfrac{x^2}{16} + \dfrac{y^2}{25} = 1$

7. $9x^2 + 4y^2 = 36$

8. $4x^2 + 25y^2 = 100$

9. $x^2 + 4y^2 = 16$

10. $4x^2 + y^2 = 16$

11. $2x^2 + y^2 = 3$

12. $5x^2 + 6y^2 = 30$

13. $x^2 + 4y^2 = 1$

14. $9x^2 + 4y^2 = 1$

15. $\frac{1}{2}x^2 + \frac{1}{8}y^2 = \frac{1}{4}$

16. $x^2 = 4 - 2y^2$

17. $y^2 = 1 - 2x^2$

18. $20x^2 + 4y^2 = 5$

19–24 ■ Find an equation for the ellipse whose graph is shown.

19.

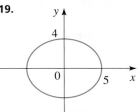

20.

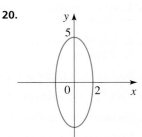

21.

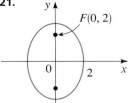

22.

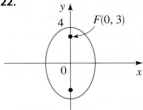

23.

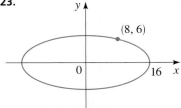

24.

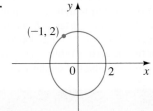

25–28 ■ Use a graphing device to graph the ellipse.

25. $\dfrac{x^2}{25} + \dfrac{y^2}{20} = 1$

26. $x^2 + \dfrac{y^2}{12} = 1$

27. $6x^2 + y^2 = 36$

28. $x^2 + 2y^2 = 8$

29–40 ■ Find an equation for the ellipse that satisfies the given conditions.

29. Foci $(\pm 4, 0)$, vertices $(\pm 5, 0)$

30. Foci $(0, \pm 3)$, vertices $(0, \pm 5)$

31. Length of major axis 4, length of minor axis 2, foci on y-axis

32. Length of major axis 6, length of minor axis 4, foci on x-axis

33. Foci $(0, \pm 2)$, length of minor axis 6

34. Foci $(\pm 5, 0)$, length of major axis 12

35. Endpoints of major axis $(\pm 10, 0)$, distance between foci 6

36. Endpoints of minor axis $(0, \pm 3)$, distance between foci 8

37. Length of major axis 10, foci on x-axis, ellipse passes through the point $(\sqrt{5}, 2)$

38. Eccentricity $\frac{1}{9}$, foci $(0, \pm 2)$

39. Eccentricity 0.8, foci $(\pm 1.5, 0)$

40. Eccentricity $\sqrt{3}/2$, foci on y-axis, length of major axis 4

41–42 ■ Find the intersection points of the pair of ellipses. Sketch the graphs of each pair of equations on the same coordinate axes and label the points of intersection.

41. $\begin{cases} 4x^2 + y^2 = 4 \\ 4x^2 + 9y^2 = 36 \end{cases}$

42. $\begin{cases} \dfrac{x^2}{16} + \dfrac{y^2}{9} = 1 \\ \dfrac{x^2}{9} + \dfrac{y^2}{16} = 1 \end{cases}$

43. The planets move around the sun in elliptical orbits with the sun at one focus. The point in the orbit at which the planet is closest to the sun is called **perihelion**, and the point at which it is farthest is called **aphelion**. These points are the vertices of the orbit. The earth's distance from the sun is 147,000,000 km at perihelion and 153,000,000 km at aphelion. Find an equation for the earth's orbit. (Place the origin at the center of the orbit with the sun on the x-axis.)

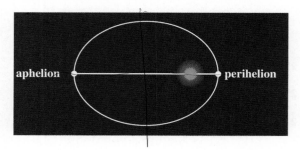

44. With an eccentricity of 0.25, Pluto's orbit is the most eccentric in the solar system. The length of the minor axis of its orbit is approximately 10,000,000,000 km. Find the distance between Pluto and the sun at perihelion and at aphelion. (See Exercise 43.)

45. For an object in an elliptical orbit around the moon, the points in the orbit that are closest to and farthest from the center of the moon are called **perilune** and **apolune**, respectively. These are the vertices of the orbit. The center of the moon is at one focus of the orbit. The *Apollo 11* spacecraft was placed in a lunar orbit with perilune at 68 mi and apolune at 195 mi above the surface of the moon. Assuming the moon is a sphere of radius 1075 mi, find an equation for the orbit of *Apollo 11*. (Place the coordinate axes so that the origin is at the center of the orbit and the foci are located on the x-axis.)

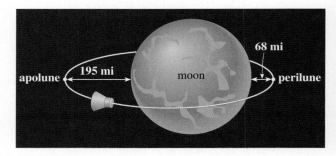

46. A carpenter wishes to construct an elliptical table top from a sheet of plywood, 4 ft by 8 ft. He will trace out the ellipse using the "thumbtack and string" method illustrated in Figures 2 and 3. What length of string should he use, and how far apart should the tacks be located, if the ellipse is to be the largest possible that can be cut out of the plywood sheet?

47. A "sunburst" window above a doorway is constructed in the shape of the top half of an ellipse, as shown in the

figure. The window is 20 in. tall at its highest point and 80 in. wide at the bottom. Find the height of the window 25 in. from the center of the base.

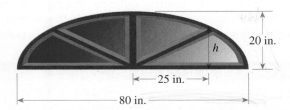

48. The **ancillary circle** of an ellipse is the circle with radius equal to half the length of the minor axis and center the same as the ellipse (see the figure). The ancillary circle is thus the largest circle that can fit within an ellipse.
  (a) Find an equation for the ancillary circle of the ellipse $x^2 + 4y^2 = 16$.
  (b) For the ellipse and ancillary circle of part (a), show that if (s, t) is a point on the ancillary circle, then $(2s, t)$ is a point on the ellipse.

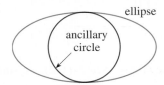

49. A **latus rectum** for an ellipse is a line segment perpendicular to the major axis at a focus, with endpoints on the ellipse, as shown. Show that the length of a latus rectum is $2b^2/a$ for the ellipse

$$\frac{x^2}{a^2} + \frac{y^2}{b^2} = 1 \qquad \text{with } a > b$$

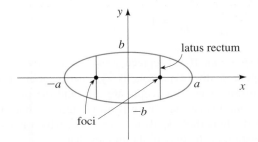

50. If $k > 0$, the following equation represents an ellipse:

$$\frac{x^2}{k} + \frac{y^2}{4+k} = 1$$

Show that all the ellipses represented by this equation have the same foci, no matter what the value of k.

 51. (a) Use a graphing device to sketch the top half (the portion in the first and second quadrants) of the family of ellipses $x^2 + ky^2 = 100$ for $k = 4, 10, 25,$ and 50.
  (b) What do the members of this family of ellipses have in common? How do they differ?

DISCOVERY · DISCUSSION

52. Drawing an Ellipse on a Blackboard Try drawing an ellipse as accurately as possible on a blackboard. How would a piece of string and two friends help this process?

53. Light Cone from a Flashlight A flashlight shines on a wall, as shown in the figure. What is the shape of the boundary of the lighted area? Explain your answer.

54. Is It an Ellipse? A piece of paper is wrapped around a cylindrical bottle, and then a compass is used to draw a circle on the paper, as shown in the figure. When the paper is laid flat, is the shape drawn on the paper an ellipse? (You don't need to prove your answer, but you may want to do the experiment and see what you get.)

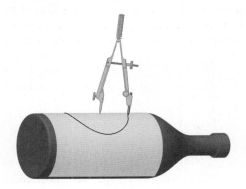

6.3 HYPERBOLAS

Although ellipses and hyperbolas have completely different shapes, their definitions and equations are similar. Instead of using the *sum* of distances from two fixed foci, as in the case of an ellipse, we use the *difference* to define a hyperbola.

GEOMETRIC DEFINITION OF A HYPERBOLA

A **hyperbola** is the set of all points in the plane, the difference of whose distances from two fixed points F_1 and F_2 is a constant. (See Figure 1.) These two fixed points are the **foci** of the hyperbola.

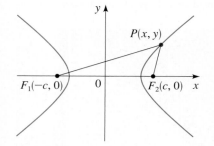

FIGURE 1
P is on the hyperbola if
$|d(P, F_1) - d(P, F_2)| = 2a$

As in the case of the ellipse, we get the simplest equation for the hyperbola by placing the foci on the x-axis at $(\pm c, 0)$, as shown in Figure 1. By definition, if $P(x, y)$ lies on the hyperbola, then either $d(P, F_1) - d(P, F_2)$ or $d(P, F_2) - d(P, F_1)$ must equal some positive constant, which we call $2a$. Thus, we have

$$d(P, F_1) - d(P, F_2) = \pm 2a$$

or

$$\sqrt{(x + c)^2 + y^2} - \sqrt{(x - c)^2 + y^2} = \pm 2a$$

Proceeding as we did in the case of the ellipse (Section 6.2), we simplify this to

$$(c^2 - a^2)x^2 - a^2y^2 = a^2(c^2 - a^2)$$

From triangle PF_1F_2 in Figure 1 we see that $\left| d(P, F_1) - d(P, F_2) \right| < 2c$. It follows that $2a < 2c$, or $a < c$. Thus, $c^2 - a^2 > 0$, so we can set $b^2 = c^2 - a^2$. We then simplify the last displayed equation to get

$$\frac{x^2}{a^2} - \frac{y^2}{b^2} = 1$$

This is the *equation of the hyperbola*. If we replace x by $-x$ or y by $-y$ in this equation, it remains unchanged, so the hyperbola is symmetric about both the x- and y-axes and about the origin. The x-intercepts are $\pm a$, and the points $(a, 0)$ and $(-a, 0)$ are the **vertices** of the hyperbola. There is no y-intercept, because setting $x = 0$ in the equation of the hyperbola leads to $-y^2 = b^2$, which has no real solution. Furthermore, the equation of the hyperbola implies that

$$\frac{x^2}{a^2} = \frac{y^2}{b^2} + 1 \geq 1$$

so $x^2/a^2 \geq 1$; thus, $x^2 \geq a^2$, and hence $x \geq a$ or $x \leq -a$. This means that the hyperbola consists of two parts, called its **branches**. The segment joining the two vertices on the separate branches is the **transverse axis** of the hyperbola, and the origin is called its **center**.

If we place the foci of the hyperbola on the *y*-axis rather than on the *x*-axis, then this has the effect of reversing the roles of *x* and *y* in the derivation of the equation of the hyperbola. This leads to a hyperbola with a vertical transverse axis.

The main properties of hyperbolas are listed in the following box.

HYPERBOLA WITH CENTER AT THE ORIGIN

The graph of each of the following equations is a hyperbola with center at the origin and having the given properties.

EQUATION	$\dfrac{x^2}{a^2} - \dfrac{y^2}{b^2} = 1 \quad (a > 0, b > 0)$	$\dfrac{y^2}{a^2} - \dfrac{x^2}{b^2} = 1 \quad (a > 0, b > 0)$
VERTICES	$(\pm a, 0)$	$(0, \pm a)$
TRANSVERSE AXIS	Horizontal, length $2a$	Vertical, length $2a$
ASYMPTOTES	$y = \pm\dfrac{b}{a}x$	$y = \pm\dfrac{a}{b}x$
FOCI	$(\pm c, 0), \qquad c^2 = a^2 + b^2$	$(0, \pm c), \qquad c^2 = a^2 + b^2$
GRAPH	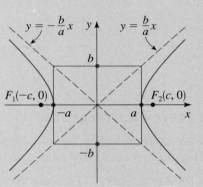	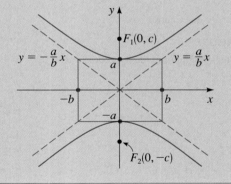

The *asymptotes* mentioned in this box are lines that the hyperbola approaches for large values of *x* and *y*. To find the asymptotes in the first case in the box, we solve the equation for *y* to get

$$y = \pm\frac{b}{a}\sqrt{x^2 - a^2}$$

$$= \pm\frac{b}{a}x\sqrt{1 - \frac{a^2}{x^2}}$$

As *x* gets large, a^2/x^2 gets closer to zero. In other words, as $x \to \infty$ we have $a^2/x^2 \to 0$. So, for large *x* the value of *y* can be approximated as $y = \pm(b/a)x$. This shows that these lines are asymptotes of the hyperbola.

Asymptotes are an essential aid for graphing a hyperbola; they help us determine its shape. A convenient way to find the asymptotes, for a parabola with horizontal transverse axis, is to first plot the points $(a, 0)$, $(-a, 0)$, $(0, b)$, and $(0, -b)$. Then sketch horizontal and vertical segments through these points to construct a rectangle, as shown in Figure 2(a). We call this rectangle the **central box** of the hyperbola. The slopes of the diagonals of the central box are $\pm b/a$, so by extending them we obtain the asymptotes $y = \pm(b/a)x$, as sketched in part (b) of the figure. Finally, we plot the vertices and use the asymptotes as a guide in sketching the hyperbola shown in part (c). (A similar procedure applies to graphing a hyperbola that has a vertical transverse axis.)

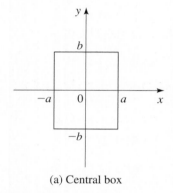

(a) Central box

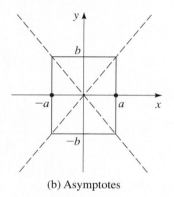

(b) Asymptotes

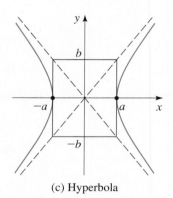

(c) Hyperbola

FIGURE 2

Steps in graphing the hyperbola $\dfrac{x^2}{a^2} - \dfrac{y^2}{b^2} = 1$

HOW TO SKETCH A HYPERBOLA

1. SKETCH THE CENTRAL BOX.   This is the rectangle centered at the origin, with sides parallel to the axes, that crosses one axis at $\pm a$, the other at $\pm b$.

2. SKETCH THE ASYMPTOTES.   These are the lines obtained by extending the diagonals of the central box.

3. PLOT THE VERTICES.   These are the two x-intercepts or the two y-intercepts.

4. SKETCH THE HYPERBOLA.   Start at a vertex and sketch a branch of the hyperbola, approaching the asymptotes. Sketch the other branch in the same way.

EXAMPLE 1 ■ A Hyperbola with Horizontal Transverse Axis

A hyperbola has the equation

$$9x^2 - 16y^2 = 144$$

(a) Find the vertices, foci, and asymptotes, and sketch the graph.

(b) Draw the graph using a graphing calculator.

SOLUTION

(a) First we divide both sides of the equation by 144 to put it into standard form:

$$\frac{x^2}{16} - \frac{y^2}{9} = 1$$

Because the x^2-term is positive, the hyperbola has a horizontal transverse axis; its vertices and foci are on the x-axis. Since $a^2 = 16$ and $b^2 = 9$, we get $a = 4$, $b = 3$, and $c = \sqrt{16 + 9} = 5$. Thus, we have

VERTICES	$(\pm 4, 0)$
FOCI	$(\pm 5, 0)$
ASYMPTOTES	$y = \pm \frac{3}{4}x$

After sketching the central box and asymptotes, we complete the sketch of the hyperbola as in Figure 3(a).

 (b) To draw the graph using a graphing calculator, we need to solve for y.

$$9x^2 - 16y^2 = 144$$

$$-16y^2 = -9x^2 + 144 \qquad \text{Subtract } 9x^2$$

$$y^2 = 9\left(\frac{x^2}{16} - 1\right) \qquad \text{Divide by } -16 \text{ and factor } 9$$

$$y = \pm 3 \sqrt{\frac{x^2}{16} - 1} \qquad \text{Take square roots}$$

To obtain the graph of the hyperbola, we graph the functions

$$y = 3\sqrt{(x^2/16) - 1} \qquad \text{and} \qquad y = -3\sqrt{(x^2/16) - 1}$$

as shown in Figure 3(b).

Note that the equation of a hyperbola does not define y as a function of x (see page 51). That's why we need to graph two functions to graph a hyperbola.

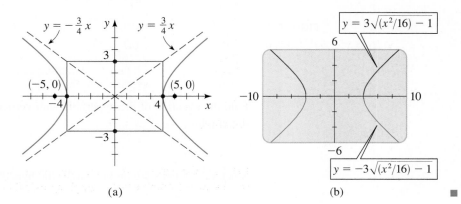

FIGURE 3

$9x^2 - 16y^2 = 144$

(a)

(b)

EXAMPLE 2 ■ A Hyperbola with Vertical Transverse Axis

Find the vertices, foci, and asymptotes of the hyperbola, and sketch its graph.

$$x^2 - 9y^2 + 9 = 0$$

SOLUTION

We begin by writing the equation in the standard form for a hyperbola.

$$x^2 - 9y^2 = -9$$

$$y^2 - \frac{x^2}{9} = 1 \qquad \text{Divide by } -9$$

Because the y^2-term is positive, the hyperbola has a vertical transverse axis; its foci and vertices are on the y-axis. Since $a^2 = 1$ and $b^2 = 9$, we get $a = 1$, $b = 3$, and $c = \sqrt{1 + 9} = \sqrt{10}$. Thus, we have

VERTICES	$(0, \pm 1)$
FOCI	$(0, \pm\sqrt{10})$
ASYMPTOTES	$y = \pm\frac{1}{3}x$

We sketch the central box and asymptotes, then complete the graph, as shown in Figure 4(a).

We can also draw the graph using a graphing calculator, as shown in Figure 4(b).

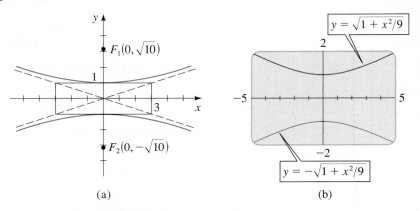

FIGURE 4
$x^2 - 9y^2 + 9 = 0$

(a)   (b)

EXAMPLE 3 ■ Finding the Equation of a Hyperbola from Its Vertices and Foci

Find the equation of the hyperbola with vertices $(\pm 3, 0)$ and foci $(\pm 4, 0)$. Sketch the graph.

SOLUTION

Since the vertices are on the x-axis, the hyperbola has a horizontal transverse axis.

Its equation is of the form

$$\frac{x^2}{3^2} - \frac{y^2}{b^2} = 1$$

We have $a = 3$ and $c = 4$. To find b, we use the relation $a^2 + b^2 = c^2$:

$$3^2 + b^2 = 4^2$$

$$b^2 = 4^2 - 3^2 = 7$$

$$b = \sqrt{7}$$

Thus, the equation of the hyperbola is

$$\frac{x^2}{9} - \frac{y^2}{7} = 1$$

The graph is shown in Figure 5. ∎

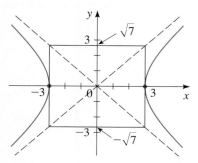

FIGURE 5
$$\frac{x^2}{9} - \frac{y^2}{7} = 1$$

EXAMPLE 4 ■ Finding the Equation of a Hyperbola from Its Vertices and Asymptotes

Find the equation and the foci of the hyperbola with vertices $(0, \pm2)$ and asymptotes $y = \pm2x$. Sketch the graph.

SOLUTION

Since the vertices are on the y-axis, the hyperbola has a vertical transverse axis with $a = 2$. From the asymptote equation we see that

$$\frac{a}{b} = 2$$

$$\frac{2}{b} = 2 \qquad \text{Since } a = 2$$

$$b = \frac{2}{2} = 1$$

Thus, the equation of the hyperbola is

$$\frac{y^2}{4} - x^2 = 1$$

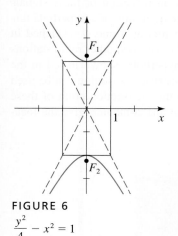

FIGURE 6
$$\frac{y^2}{4} - x^2 = 1$$

To find the foci, we calculate $c^2 = a^2 + b^2 = 2^2 + 1^2 = 5$, so $c = \sqrt{5}$. Thus, the foci are $(0, \pm\sqrt{5})$. The graph is shown in Figure 6. ∎

Like parabolas and ellipses, hyperbolas have an interesting *reflection property*. Light aimed at one focus of a hyperbolic mirror is reflected toward the other focus, as shown in Figure 7. This property is used in the construction of Cassegrain-type telescopes. A hyperbolic mirror is placed in the telescope tube so that light reflected from the primary parabolic reflector is aimed at one focus of the hyperbolic mirror. The light is then refocused at a more accessible point below the primary reflector (Figure 8).

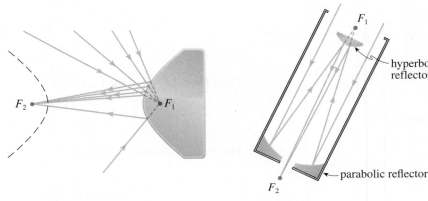

FIGURE 7

Reflection property of hyperbolas

FIGURE 8

Cassegrain-type telescope

The LORAN (LOng RAnge Navigation) system was used until the early 1990s; it has now been superseded by the GPS system (see page 408). In the LORAN system, hyperbolas are used onboard a ship to determine its location. In Figure 9 radio stations at A and B transmit signals simultaneously for reception by the ship at P. The onboard computer converts the time difference in reception of these signals into a distance difference $d(P, A) - d(P, B)$. From the definition of a hyperbola this locates the ship on one branch of a hyperbola with foci at A and B (sketched in black in the figure). The same procedure is carried out with two other radio stations at C and D, and this locates the ship on a second hyperbola (shown in red in the figure). (In practice, only three stations are needed because one station can be used as a focus for both hyperbolas.) The coordinates of the intersection point of these two hyperbolas, which can be calculated precisely by the computer, give the location of P.

FIGURE 9

LORAN system for finding the location of a ship

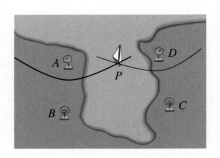

6.3 EXERCISES

1–4 ■ Match the equation with the graphs labeled I–IV. Give reasons for your answers.

1. $\dfrac{x^2}{4} - y^2 = 1$

2. $y^2 - \dfrac{x^2}{9} = 1$

3. $16y^2 - x^2 = 144$

4. $9x^2 - 25y^2 = 225$

I

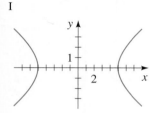

II

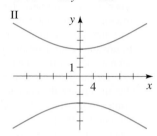

III

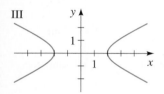

IV

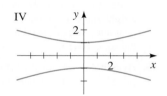

5–16 ■ Find the vertices, foci, and asymptotes of the hyperbola, and sketch its graph.

5. $\dfrac{x^2}{4} - \dfrac{y^2}{16} = 1$

6. $\dfrac{y^2}{9} - \dfrac{x^2}{16} = 1$

7. $y^2 - \dfrac{x^2}{25} = 1$

8. $\dfrac{x^2}{2} - y^2 = 1$

9. $x^2 - y^2 = 1$

10. $9x^2 - 4y^2 = 36$

11. $25y^2 - 9x^2 = 225$

12. $x^2 - y^2 + 4 = 0$

13. $x^2 - 4y^2 - 8 = 0$

14. $x^2 - 2y^2 = 3$

15. $4y^2 - x^2 = 1$

16. $9x^2 - 16y^2 = 1$

17–22 ■ Find the equation for the hyperbola whose graph is shown.

17.

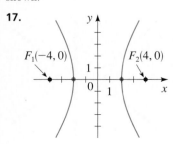

18.

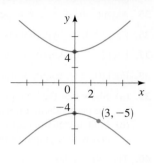

19.

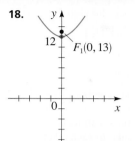

20.

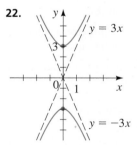

21.

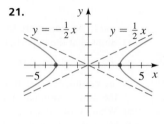

22.

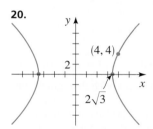

 23–26 ■ Use a graphing device to graph the hyperbola.

23. $x^2 - 2y^2 = 8$

24. $3y^2 - 4x^2 = 24$

25. $\dfrac{y^2}{2} - \dfrac{x^2}{6} = 1$

26. $\dfrac{x^2}{100} - \dfrac{y^2}{64} = 1$

27–38 ■ Find an equation for the hyperbola that satisfies the given conditions.

27. Foci $(\pm 5, 0)$, vertices $(\pm 3, 0)$

28. Foci $(0, \pm 10)$, vertices $(0, \pm 8)$

29. Foci $(0, \pm 2)$, vertices $(0, \pm 1)$

30. Foci $(\pm 6, 0)$, vertices $(\pm 2, 0)$

31. Vertices $(\pm 1, 0)$, asymptotes $y = \pm 5x$

32. Vertices $(0, \pm 6)$, asymptotes $y = \pm \frac{1}{3}x$

33. Foci $(0, \pm 8)$, asymptotes $y = \pm \frac{1}{2}x$

34. Vertices $(0, \pm 6)$, hyperbola passes through $(-5, 9)$

35. Asymptotes $y = \pm x$, hyperbola passes through $(5, 3)$

36. Foci $(\pm 3, 0)$, hyperbola passes through $(4, 1)$

37. Foci $(\pm 5, 0)$, length of transverse axis 6

38. Foci $(0, \pm 1)$, length of transverse axis 1

39. (a) Show that the asymptotes of the hyperbola $x^2 - y^2 = 5$ are perpendicular to each other.
   (b) Find an equation for the hyperbola with foci $(\pm c, 0)$ and with asymptotes perpendicular to each other.

40. The hyperbolas

$$\frac{x^2}{a^2} - \frac{y^2}{b^2} = 1 \quad \text{and} \quad \frac{x^2}{a^2} - \frac{y^2}{b^2} = -1$$

are said to be **conjugate** to each other.
   (a) Show that the hyperbolas

$$x^2 - 4y^2 + 16 = 0 \quad \text{and} \quad 4y^2 - x^2 + 16 = 0$$

are conjugate to each other, and sketch their graphs on the same coordinate axes.
   (b) What do the hyperbolas of part (a) have in common?
   (c) Show that any pair of conjugate hyperbolas have the relationship you discovered in part (b).

41. In the derivation of the equation of the hyperbola at the beginning of this section, we said that the equation

$$\sqrt{(x + c)^2 + y^2} - \sqrt{(x - c)^2 + y^2} = \pm 2a$$

simplifies to

$$(c^2 - a^2)x^2 - a^2 y^2 = a^2(c^2 - a^2)$$

Supply the steps needed to show this.

42. (a) For the hyperbola

$$\frac{x^2}{9} - \frac{y^2}{16} = 1$$

determine the values of a, b, and c, and find the coordinates of the foci F_1 and F_2.
   (b) Show that the point $P\left(5, \frac{16}{3}\right)$ lies on this hyperbola.
   (c) Find $d(P, F_1)$ and $d(P, F_2)$.
   (d) Verify that the difference between $d(P, F_1)$ and $d(P, F_2)$ is $2a$.

43. Refer to Figure 9 in the text. Suppose that the radio stations at A and B are 500 mi apart, and that the ship at P receives Station A's signal 2640 microseconds (μs) before it receives the signal from B.
   (a) Assuming that radio signals travel at 980 ft/μs, find $d(P, A) - d(P, B)$.

(b) Find an equation for the branch of the hyperbola indicated in black in the figure. (Place A and B on the y-axis with the origin halfway between them. Use miles as the unit of distance.)
   (c) If A is due north of B, and if P is due east of A, how far is P from A?

44. Some comets, such as Halley's comet, are a permanent part of the solar system, traveling in elliptical orbits around the sun. Others pass through the solar system only once, following a hyperbolic path with the sun at a focus. The figure shows the path of such a comet. Find an equation for the path, assuming that the closest the comet comes to the sun is 2×10^9 mi and that the path the comet was taking before it neared the solar system is at a right angle to the path it continues on after leaving the solar system.

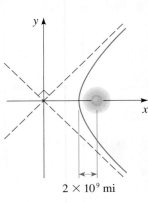

45. Hyperbolas are called **confocal** if they have the same foci.
   (a) Show that the hyperbolas

$$\frac{y^2}{k} - \frac{x^2}{16 - k} = 1 \quad \text{with } 0 < k < 16$$

are confocal.
   (b) Use a graphing device to draw the top branches of the family of hyperbolas in part (a) for $k = 1, 4, 8,$ and 12. How does the shape of the graph change as k increases?

46. Two stones are dropped simultaneously in a calm pool of water. The crests of the resulting waves form equally spaced concentric circles, as shown in the figures. The waves interact with each other to create cetain interference patterns.
   (a) Explain why the red dots lie on an ellipse.
   (b) Explain why the blue dots lie on a hyperbola.

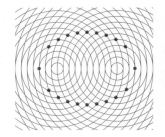 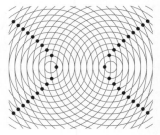

DISCOVERY · DISCUSSION

47. **Hyperbolas in the Real World**   Several examples of the uses of hyperbolas are given in the text. Find other situations in real life where hyperbolas occur. Consult a scientific encyclopedia in the reference section of your library, or search the Internet.

48. **Light from a Lamp**   The light from a lamp forms a lighted area on a wall, as shown in the figure. Why is the boundary of this lighted area a hyperbola? How can one hold a flashlight so that its beam forms a hyperbola on the ground?

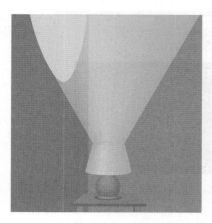

6.4   SHIFTED CONICS

In the preceding sections we studied parabolas with vertices at the origin and ellipses and hyperbolas with centers at the origin. We restricted ourselves to these cases because these equations have the simplest form. In this section we consider conics whose vertices and centers are not necessarily at the origin, and we determine how this affects their equations.

In Section 1.5 we studied transformations of functions that have the effect of shifting their graphs. In general, for any equation in x and y, if we replace x by $x - h$ or by $x + h$, the graph of the new equation is simply the old graph shifted horizontally; if y is replaced by $y - k$ or by $y + k$, the graph is shifted vertically. The following box gives the details.

SHIFTING GRAPHS OF EQUATIONS

If h and k are positive real numbers, then replacing x by $x - h$ or by $x + h$ and replacing y by $y - k$ or by $y + k$ has the following effect(s) on the graph of any equation in x and y.

Replacement	How the graph is shifted
1. x replaced by $x - h$	Right h units
2. x replaced by $x + h$	Left h units
3. y replaced by $y - k$	Upward k units
4. y replaced by $y + k$	Downward k units

For example, consider the ellipse with equation

$$\frac{x^2}{a^2} + \frac{y^2}{b^2} = 1$$

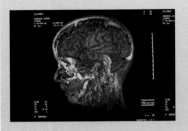
which is shown in Figure 1. If we shift it so that its center is at the point (h, k) instead of at the origin, then its equation becomes

$$\frac{(x-h)^2}{a^2} + \frac{(y-k)^2}{b^2} = 1$$

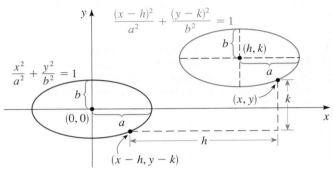

FIGURE 1
Shifted ellipse

EXAMPLE 1 ■ Sketching the Graph of a Shifted Ellipse

Sketch the graph of the ellipse

$$\frac{(x+1)^2}{4} + \frac{(y-2)^2}{9} = 1$$

and determine the coordinates of the foci.

SOLUTION

The ellipse

$$\frac{(x+1)^2}{4} + \frac{(y-2)^2}{9} = 1 \qquad \text{Shifted ellipse}$$

is shifted so that its center is at $(-1, 2)$. It is obtained from the ellipse

$$\frac{x^2}{4} + \frac{y^2}{9} = 1 \qquad \text{Ellipse with center at origin}$$

by shifting it left 1 unit and upward 2 units. The endpoints of the minor and major axes of the unshifted ellipse are $(2, 0)$, $(-2, 0)$, $(0, 3)$, $(0, -3)$. We apply the required shifts to these points to obtain the corresponding points on the shifted ellipse:

$$(2, 0) \quad \rightarrow \quad (2 - 1, 0 + 2) = (1, 2)$$

$$(-2, 0) \quad \rightarrow \quad (-2 - 1, 0 + 2) = (-3, 2)$$

$$(0, 3) \quad \rightarrow \quad (0 - 1, 3 + 2) = (-1, 5)$$

$$(0, -3) \quad \rightarrow \quad (0 - 1, -3 + 2) = (-1, -1)$$

This helps us sketch the graph in Figure 2.

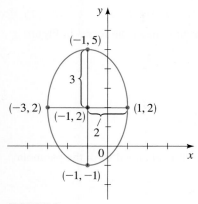

FIGURE 2

$$\frac{(x + 1)^2}{4} + \frac{(y - 2)^2}{9} = 1$$

To find the foci of the shifted ellipse, we first find the foci of the ellipse with center at the origin. Since $a^2 = 9$ and $b^2 = 4$, we have $c^2 = 9 - 4 = 5$, so $c = \sqrt{5}$. So the foci are $\left(0, \pm\sqrt{5}\right)$. Shifting left 1 unit and upward 2 units, we get

$$\left(0, \sqrt{5}\right) \quad \to \quad \left(0 - 1, \sqrt{5} + 2\right) = \left(-1, 2 + \sqrt{5}\right)$$

$$\left(0, -\sqrt{5}\right) \quad \to \quad \left(0 - 1, -\sqrt{5} + 2\right) = \left(-1, 2 - \sqrt{5}\right)$$

Thus, the foci of the shifted ellipse are

$$\left(-1, 2 + \sqrt{5}\right) \qquad \text{and} \qquad \left(-1, 2 - \sqrt{5}\right) \qquad\qquad ■$$

Applying shifts to parabolas and hyperbolas leads to the equations and graphs shown in Figures 3 and 4.

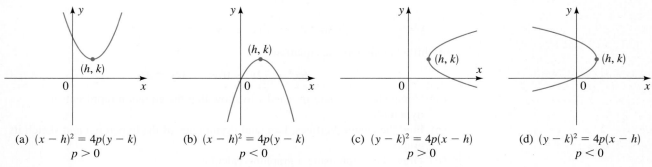

(a) $(x - h)^2 = 4p(y - k)$
$p > 0$

(b) $(x - h)^2 = 4p(y - k)$
$p < 0$

(c) $(y - k)^2 = 4p(x - h)$
$p > 0$

(d) $(y - k)^2 = 4p(x - h)$
$p < 0$

FIGURE 3
Shifted parabolas

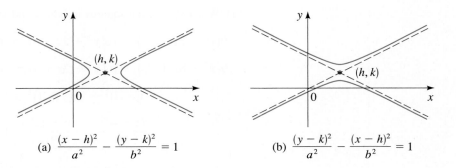

FIGURE 4
Shifted hyperbolas

(a) $\dfrac{(x - h)^2}{a^2} - \dfrac{(y - k)^2}{b^2} = 1$

(b) $\dfrac{(y - k)^2}{a^2} - \dfrac{(x - h)^2}{b^2} = 1$

EXAMPLE 2 ■ Graphing a Shifted Parabola

Determine the vertex, focus, and directrix and sketch the graph of the parabola.

$$x^2 - 4x = 8y - 28$$

SOLUTION

We complete the square in x to put this equation into one of the forms in Figure 3.

$$x^2 - 4x + 4 = 8y - 28 + 4 \qquad \text{Add 4 to complete the square}$$

$$(x - 2)^2 = 8y - 24$$

$$(x - 2)^2 = 8(y - 3) \qquad \text{Shifted parabola}$$

This parabola opens upward with vertex at $(2, 3)$. It is obtained from the parabola

$$x^2 = 8y \qquad \text{Parabola with vertex at origin}$$

by shifting right 2 units and upward 3 units. Since $4p = 8$, we have $p = 2$, so the focus is 2 units above the vertex and the directrix is 2 units below the vertex. Thus, the focus is $(2, 5)$ and the directrix is $y = 1$. The graph is shown in Figure 5. ∎

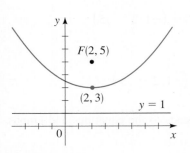

FIGURE 5

$x^2 - 4x = 8y - 28$

EXAMPLE 3 ■ **Graphing a Shifted Hyperbola**

A shifted conic has the equation

$$9x^2 - 72x - 16y^2 - 32y = 16$$

(a) Complete the square in x and y to show that the equation represents a hyperbola.

(b) Find the center, vertices, foci, and asymptotes of the hyperbola and sketch its graph.

 (c) Draw the graph using a graphing calculator.

SOLUTION

(a) We complete the squares in both x and y:

$$9(x^2 - 8x \quad) - 16(y^2 + 2y \quad) = 16$$

$$9(x^2 - 8x + 16) - 16(y^2 + 2y + 1) = 16 + 9 \cdot 16 - 16 \cdot 1 \qquad \text{Complete the squares}$$

$$9(x - 4)^2 - 16(y + 1)^2 = 144 \qquad \text{Divide this by 144}$$

$$\frac{(x - 4)^2}{16} - \frac{(y + 1)^2}{9} = 1 \qquad \text{Shifted hyperbola}$$

Comparing this to Figure 4(a), we see that this is the equation of a shifted hyperbola.

(b) The shifted hyperbola has center $(4, -1)$ and a horizontal transverse axis.

CENTER $(4, -1)$

Its graph will have the same shape as the unshifted hyperbola

$$\frac{x^2}{16} - \frac{y^2}{9} = 1 \qquad \text{Hyperbola with center at origin}$$

Since $a^2 = 16$ and $b^2 = 9$, we have $a = 4$, $b = 3$, and $c = \sqrt{a^2 + b^2} = \sqrt{16 + 9} = 5$. Thus, the foci lie 5 units to the left and to the right of the center, and the vertices lie 4 units to either side of the center.

$$\text{FOCI} \quad (-1, -1) \text{ and } (9, -1)$$

$$\text{VERTICES} \quad (0, -1) \text{ and } (8, -1)$$

The asymptotes of the unshifted hyperbola are $y = \pm\frac{3}{4}x$, so the asymptotes of the shifted parabola are found as follows.

$$\text{ASYMPTOTES} \quad y + 1 = \pm\tfrac{3}{4}(x - 4)$$

$$y + 1 = \pm\tfrac{3}{4}x \mp 3$$

$$y = \tfrac{3}{4}x - 4 \quad \text{and} \quad y = -\tfrac{3}{4}x + 2$$

To help us sketch the hyperbola, we draw the central box; it extends 4 units left and right from the center and 3 units upward and downward from the center. We then draw the asymptotes and complete the graph of the shifted hyperbola as shown in Figure 6(a) on the following page.

 (c) To draw the graph using a graphing calculator, we need to solve for y. The given equation is a quadratic equation in y, so we use the quadratic formula to solve for y. Writing the equation in the form

$$16y^2 + 32y - 9x^2 + 72x + 16 = 0$$

we get

$$y = \frac{-32 \pm \sqrt{32^2 - 4(16)(-9x^2 + 72x + 16)}}{2(16)} \qquad \text{Quadratic formula}$$

$$= \frac{-32 \pm \sqrt{576x^2 - 4608x}}{32} \qquad \text{Expand}$$

$$= \frac{-32 \pm 24\sqrt{x^2 - 8x}}{32} \qquad \text{Factor 576 from under the radical}$$

$$= -1 \pm \tfrac{3}{4}\sqrt{x^2 - 8x} \qquad \text{Simplify}$$

To obtain the graph of the hyperbola, we graph the functions

$$y = -1 + 0.75\sqrt{x^2 - 8x} \quad \text{and} \quad y = -1 - 0.75\sqrt{x^2 - 8x}$$

as shown in Figure 6(b).

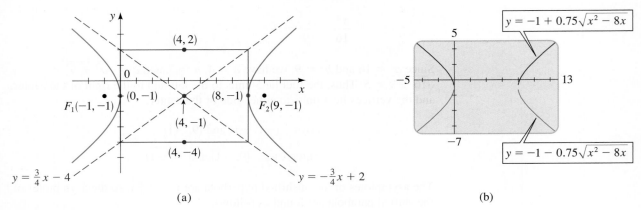

(a)   (b)

FIGURE 6
$9x^2 - 72x - 16y^2 - 32y = 16$

If we expand and simplify the equations of any of the shifted conics illustrated in Figures 1, 3, and 4, then we will always obtain an equation of the form

$$Ax^2 + Cy^2 + Dx + Ey + F = 0$$

where A and C are not both 0. Conversely, if we begin with an equation of this form, then we can complete the square in x and y to see which type of conic section the equation represents. In some cases, the graph of the equation turns out to be just a pair of lines, a single point, or there may be no graph at all. These cases are called **degenerate conics**. The next example illustrates such a case.

EXAMPLE 4 ■ **An Equation That Leads to a Degenerate Conic**

Sketch the graph of the equation

$$9x^2 - y^2 + 18x + 6y = 0$$

SOLUTION

Because the coefficients of x^2 and y^2 are of opposite sign, this equation looks as if it should represent a hyperbola (like the equation of Example 3). To see whether this is in fact the case, we complete the squares:

$$9(x^2 + 2x \quad) - (y^2 - 6y \quad) = 0$$

$$9(x^2 + 2x + 1) - (y^2 - 6y + 9) = 0 + 9 - 9$$

$$9(x + 1)^2 - (y - 3)^2 = 0$$

$$(x + 1)^2 - \frac{(y - 3)^2}{9} = 0 \qquad \text{Divide by 9}$$

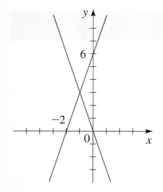

FIGURE 7
$9x^2 - y^2 + 18x + 6y = 0$

For this to fit the form of the equation of a hyperbola, we would need a nonzero constant to the right of the equal sign. In fact, further analysis shows that this is the equation of a pair of intersecting lines:

$$(y - 3)^2 = 9(x + 1)^2$$

$$y - 3 = \pm 3(x + 1) \qquad \text{Take square roots}$$

$$y = 3(x + 1) + 3 \qquad \text{or} \qquad y = -3(x + 1) + 3$$

$$y = 3x + 6 \qquad\qquad\qquad y = -3x$$

These lines are graphed in Figure 7. ∎

Because the equation in Example 4 looked at first glance like the equation of a hyperbola but, in fact, turned out to represent simply a pair of lines, we refer to its graph as a **degenerate hyperbola**. Degenerate ellipses and parabolas can also arise when we complete the square(s) in an equation that seems to represent a conic. For example, the equation

$$4x^2 + y^2 - 8x + 2y + 6 = 0$$

looks as if it should represent an ellipse, because the coefficients of x^2 and y^2 have the same sign. But completing the squares leads to

$$(x - 1)^2 + \frac{(y + 1)^2}{4} = -\frac{1}{4}$$

which has no solution at all (since the sum of two squares cannot be negative). This equation is therefore degenerate.

To summarize, we have the following theorem.

GENERAL EQUATION OF A SHIFTED CONIC

The graph of the equation

$$Ax^2 + Cy^2 + Dx + Ey + F = 0$$

where A and C are not both 0, is a conic or a degenerate conic. In the nondegenerate cases, the graph is

1. a parabola if A or C is 0.

2. an ellipse if A and C have the same sign (or a circle if $A = C$).

3. a hyperbola if A and C have opposite signs.

6.4 EXERCISES

1–4 ■ Find the center, foci, and vertices of the ellipse, and determine the lengths of the major and minor axes. Then sketch the graph.

1. $\dfrac{(x-2)^2}{9} + \dfrac{(y-1)^2}{4} = 1$ **2.** $\dfrac{(x-3)^2}{16} + (y+3)^2 = 1$

3. $\dfrac{x^2}{9} + \dfrac{(y+5)^2}{25} = 1$ **4.** $\dfrac{(x+2)^2}{4} + y^2 = 1$

5–8 ■ Find the vertex, focus, and directrix of the parabola, and sketch the graph.

5. $(x-3)^2 = 8(y+1)$ **6.** $(y+5)^2 = -6x + 12$

7. $-4\left(x + \tfrac{1}{2}\right)^2 = y$ **8.** $y^2 = 16x - 8$

9–12 ■ Find the center, foci, vertices, and asymptotes of the hyperbola. Then sketch the graph.

9. $\dfrac{(x+1)^2}{9} - \dfrac{(y-3)^2}{16} = 1$ **10.** $(x-8)^2 - (y+6)^2 = 1$

11. $y^2 - \dfrac{(x+1)^2}{4} = 1$ **12.** $\dfrac{(y-1)^2}{25} - (x+3)^2 = 1$

13–18 ■ Find an equation for the conic whose graph is shown.

13.

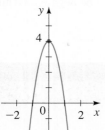

14.

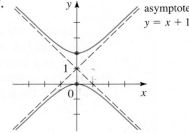

directrix
$y = -12$

15.

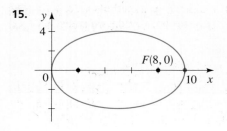

$F(8, 0)$

16.

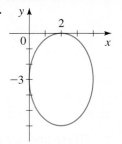

17.

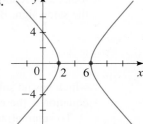

asymptote
$y = x + 1$

18.

19–30 ■ Complete the square to determine whether the equation represents an ellipse, a parabola, a hyperbola, or a degenerate conic. If the graph is an ellipse, find the center, foci, vertices, and lengths of the major and minor axes. If it is a parabola, find the vertex, focus, and directrix. If it is a hyperbola, find the center, foci, vertices, and asymptotes. Then sketch the graph of the equation. If the equation has no graph, explain why.

19. $9x^2 - 36x + 4y^2 = 0$

20. $y^2 = 4(x + 2y)$

21. $x^2 - 4y^2 - 2x + 16y = 20$

22. $x^2 + 6x + 12y + 9 = 0$

23. $4x^2 + 25y^2 - 24x + 250y + 561 = 0$

24. $2x^2 + y^2 = 2y + 1$

25. $16x^2 - 9y^2 - 96x + 288 = 0$

26. $4x^2 - 4x - 8y + 9 = 0$

27. $x^2 + 16 = 4(y^2 + 2x)$

28. $x^2 - y^2 = 10(x - y) + 1$

29. $3x^2 + 4y^2 - 6x - 24y + 39 = 0$

30. $x^2 + 4y^2 + 20x - 40y + 300 = 0$

 31–34 ■ Use a graphing device to graph the conic.

31. $2x^2 - 4x + y + 5 = 0$

32. $4x^2 + 9y^2 - 36y = 0$

33. $9x^2 + 36 = y^2 + 36x + 6y$

34. $x^2 - 4y^2 + 4x + 8y = 0$

35. Determine what the value of F must be if the graph of the equation

$$4x^2 + y^2 + 4(x - 2y) + F = 0$$

is (a) an ellipse, (b) a single point, or (c) the empty set.

36. Find an equation for the ellipse that shares a vertex and a focus with the parabola $x^2 + y = 100$ and has its other focus at the origin.

 37. This exercise deals with **confocal parabolas**, that is, families of parabolas that have the same focus.
(a) Draw graphs of the family of parabolas

$$x^2 = 4p(y + p)$$

for $p = -2, -\frac{3}{2}, -1, -\frac{1}{2}, \frac{1}{2}, 1, \frac{3}{2}, 2$.

(b) Show that each parabola in this family has its focus at the origin.
(c) Describe the effect on the graph of moving the vertex closer to the origin.

◆ **DISCOVERY · DISCUSSION**

38. A Family of Confocal Conics   Conics that share a focus are called **confocal**. Consider the family of conics that have a focus at $(0, 1)$ and a vertex at the origin (see the figure).
(a) Find equations of two different ellipses that have these properties.
(b) Find equations of two different hyperbolas that have these properties.
(c) Explain why only one parabola satisfies these properties. Find its equation.
(d) Sketch the conics you found in parts (a), (b), and (c) on the same coordinate axes (for the hyperbolas, sketch the top branches only).
(e) How are the ellipses and hyperbolas related to the parabola?

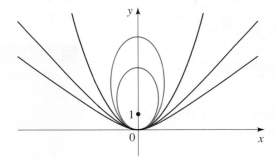

6.5   ROTATION OF AXES

In Section 6.4 we studied conics with equations of the form

$$Ax^2 + Cy^2 + Dx + Ey + F = 0$$

We saw that the graph is always an ellipse, parabola, or hyperbola with horizontal or vertical axes (except in the degenerate cases). In this section we study the most general second-degree equation

$$Ax^2 + Bxy + Cy^2 + Dx + Ey + F = 0$$

We will see that the graph of an equation of this form is also a conic. In fact, by rotating the coordinate axes through an appropriate angle, we can eliminate the term Bxy and then use our knowledge of conic sections to analyze the graph.

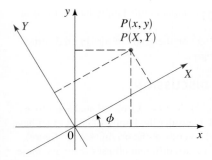

FIGURE 1

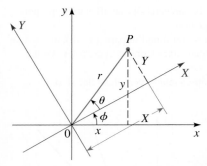

FIGURE 2

In Figure 1 the x- and y-axes have been rotated through an acute angle ϕ about the origin to produce a new pair of axes, which we call the X- and Y-axes. A point P that has coordinates (x, y) in the old system has coordinates (X, Y) in the new system. If we let r denote the distance of P from the origin and let θ be the angle that the segment OP makes with the new X-axis, then we can see from Figure 2 (by considering the two right triangles in the figure) that

$$X = r \cos \theta \qquad\qquad Y = r \sin \theta$$
$$x = r \cos(\theta + \phi) \qquad\qquad y = r \sin(\theta + \phi)$$

Using the addition formula for cosine, we see that

$$
\begin{aligned}
x &= r \cos(\theta + \phi) \\
&= r(\cos \theta \cos \phi - \sin \theta \sin \phi) \\
&= (r \cos \theta) \cos \phi - (r \sin \theta) \sin \phi \\
&= X \cos \phi - Y \sin \phi
\end{aligned}
$$

Similarly, we can apply the addition formula for sine to the expression for y to obtain $y = X \sin \phi + Y \cos \phi$. By treating these equations for x and y as a system of linear equations in the variables X and Y (see Exercise 33), we obtain expressions for X and Y in terms of x and y, as detailed in the following box.

ROTATION OF AXES FORMULAS

Suppose the x- and y-axes in a coordinate plane are rotated through the acute angle ϕ to produce the X- and Y-axes, as shown in Figure 1. Then the coordinates (x, y) and (X, Y) of a point in the xy- and the XY-planes are related as follows:

$$x = X \cos \phi - Y \sin \phi \qquad X = x \cos \phi + y \sin \phi$$
$$y = X \sin \phi + Y \cos \phi \qquad Y = -x \sin \phi + y \cos \phi$$

EXAMPLE 1 ■ Rotation of Axes

If the coordinate axes are rotated through $30°$, find the XY-coordinates of the point with xy-coordinates $(2, -4)$.

SOLUTION

Using the Rotation of Axes Formulas with $x = 2$, $y = -4$, and $\phi = 30°$, we get

$$X = 2 \cos 30° + (-4) \sin 30° = 2\left(\frac{\sqrt{3}}{2}\right) - 4\left(\frac{1}{2}\right) = \sqrt{3} - 2$$

$$Y = -2 \sin 30° + (-4) \cos 30° = -2\left(\frac{1}{2}\right) - 4\left(\frac{\sqrt{3}}{2}\right) = -1 - 2\sqrt{3}$$

The XY-coordinates are $(-2 + \sqrt{3}, -1 - 2\sqrt{3})$. ■

EXAMPLE 2 ■ Rotating a Hyperbola

Rotate the coordinate axes through $45°$ to show that the graph of the equation $xy = 2$ is a hyperbola.

SOLUTION

We use the Rotation of Axes Formulas with $\phi = 45°$ to obtain

$$x = X \cos 45° - Y \sin 45° = \frac{X}{\sqrt{2}} - \frac{Y}{\sqrt{2}}$$

$$y = X \sin 45° + Y \cos 45° = \frac{X}{\sqrt{2}} + \frac{Y}{\sqrt{2}}$$

Substituting these expressions into the original equation gives

$$\left(\frac{X}{\sqrt{2}} - \frac{Y}{\sqrt{2}} \right)\left(\frac{X}{\sqrt{2}} + \frac{Y}{\sqrt{2}} \right) = 2$$

$$\frac{X^2}{2} - \frac{Y^2}{2} = 2$$

$$\frac{X^2}{4} - \frac{Y^2}{4} = 1$$

We recognize this as a hyperbola with vertices $(\pm 2, 0)$ in the XY-coordinate system. Its asymptotes are $Y = \pm X$, which correspond to the coordinate axes in the xy-system (see Figure 3). ■

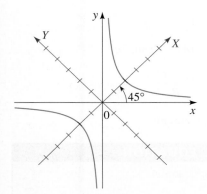

FIGURE 3
$xy = 2$

The method of Example 2 can be used to transform any equation of the form

$$Ax^2 + Bxy + Cy^2 + Dx + Ey + F = 0$$

into an equation in X and Y that doesn't contain an XY-term by choosing an appropriate angle of rotation. To find the angle that works, we rotate the axes through an angle ϕ and substitute for x and y using the Rotation of Axes Formulas:

$$A(X \cos \phi - Y \sin \phi)^2 + B(X \cos \phi - Y \sin \phi)(X \sin \phi + Y \cos \phi)$$

$$+ C(X \sin \phi + Y \cos \phi)^2 + D(X \cos \phi - Y \sin \phi)$$

$$+ E(X \sin \phi + Y \cos \phi) + F = 0$$

If we expand this and collect like terms, we obtain an equation of the form

$$A'X^2 + B'XY + C'Y^2 + D'X + E'Y + F' = 0$$

where

$$A' = A \cos^2\phi + B \sin\phi\cos\phi + C \sin^2\phi$$

$$B' = 2(C - A) \sin\phi\cos\phi + B(\cos^2\phi - \sin^2\phi)$$

$$C' = A \sin^2\phi - B \sin\phi\cos\phi + C \cos^2\phi$$

$$D' = D \cos\phi + E \sin\phi$$

$$E' = -D \sin\phi + E \cos\phi$$

$$F' = F$$

Double-angle formulas

$$\sin 2\phi = 2 \sin\phi\cos\phi$$
$$\cos 2\phi = \cos^2\phi - \sin^2\phi$$

To eliminate the XY-term, we would like to choose ϕ so that $B' = 0$, that is,

$$2(C - A) \sin\phi\cos\phi + B(\cos^2\phi - \sin^2\phi) = 0$$

$$(C - A) \sin 2\phi + B \cos 2\phi = 0 \qquad \text{Double-angle formulas for sine and cosine}$$

$$B \cos 2\phi = (A - C) \sin 2\phi$$

$$\cot 2\phi = \frac{A - C}{B} \qquad \text{Divide by } B \sin 2\phi$$

The preceding calculation proves the following theorem.

SIMPLIFYING THE GENERAL CONIC EQUATION

To eliminate the xy-term in the general conic equation

$$Ax^2 + Bxy + Cy^2 + Dx + Ey + F = 0$$

rotate the axes through the acute angle ϕ that satisfies

$$\cot 2\phi = \frac{A - C}{B}$$

EXAMPLE 3 ■ Eliminating the xy-Term

Use a rotation of axes to eliminate the xy-term in the equation

$$6\sqrt{3}\, x^2 + 6xy + 4\sqrt{3}\, y^2 = 21\sqrt{3}$$

Identify and sketch the curve.

SOLUTION

To eliminate the xy-term, we rotate the axes through an angle ϕ that satisfies

$$\cot 2\phi = \frac{A - C}{B} = \frac{6\sqrt{3} - 4\sqrt{3}}{6} = \frac{\sqrt{3}}{3}$$

Thus, $2\phi = 60°$ and hence $\phi = 30°$. With this value of ϕ, we get

$$x = X\left(\frac{\sqrt{3}}{2}\right) - Y\left(\frac{1}{2}\right)$$ Rotation of Axes Formulas

$$y = X\left(\frac{1}{2}\right) + Y\left(\frac{\sqrt{3}}{2}\right)$$ $\cos\phi = \frac{\sqrt{3}}{2}$, $\sin\phi = \frac{1}{2}$

Substituting these values for x and y into the given equation leads to

$$6\sqrt{3}\left(\frac{X\sqrt{3}}{2} - \frac{Y}{2}\right)^2 + 6\left(\frac{X\sqrt{3}}{2} - \frac{Y}{2}\right)\left(\frac{X}{2} + \frac{Y\sqrt{3}}{2}\right) + 4\sqrt{3}\left(\frac{X}{2} + \frac{Y\sqrt{3}}{2}\right)^2 = 21\sqrt{3}$$

Expanding and collecting like terms, we get

$$7\sqrt{3}\,X^2 + 3\sqrt{3}\,Y^2 = 21\sqrt{3}$$

$$\frac{X^2}{3} + \frac{Y^2}{7} = 1$$ Divide by $21\sqrt{3}$

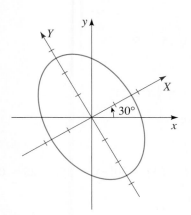

This is the equation of an ellipse in the XY-coordinate system. The foci lie on the Y-axis. Because $a^2 = 7$ and $b^2 = 3$, the length of the major axis is $2\sqrt{7}$, and the length of the minor axis is $2\sqrt{3}$. The ellipse is sketched in Figure 4.   ∎

FIGURE 4
$6\sqrt{3}\,x^2 + 6xy + 4\sqrt{3}\,y^2 = 21\sqrt{3}$

In the preceding example we were able to determine ϕ without difficulty, since we remembered that $\cot 60° = \sqrt{3}/3$. In general, finding ϕ is not quite so easy. The next example illustrates how the following half-angle formulas, which are valid for $0 < \phi < \pi/2$, are useful in determining ϕ (see Section 4.3):

$$\cos\phi = \sqrt{\frac{1 + \cos 2\phi}{2}} \qquad \sin\phi = \sqrt{\frac{1 - \cos 2\phi}{2}}$$

EXAMPLE 4 ■ **Graphing a Rotated Conic**

A conic has the equation

$$64x^2 + 96xy + 36y^2 - 15x + 20y - 25 = 0$$

(a) Use a rotation of axes to eliminate the xy-term.
(b) Identify and sketch the graph.
(c) Draw the graph using a graphing calculator.

SOLUTION

(a) To eliminate the xy-term, we rotate the axes through an angle ϕ that satisfies

$$\cot 2\phi = \frac{A - C}{B} = \frac{64 - 36}{96} = \frac{7}{24}$$

In Figure 5 we sketch a triangle with $\cot 2\phi = \frac{7}{24}$. We see that

$$\cos 2\phi = \frac{7}{25}$$

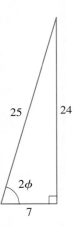

FIGURE 5

so, using the half-angle formulas, we get

$$\cos \phi = \sqrt{\frac{1 + \frac{7}{25}}{2}} = \sqrt{\frac{16}{25}} = \frac{4}{5}$$

$$\sin \phi = \sqrt{\frac{1 + \frac{7}{25}}{2}} = \sqrt{\frac{9}{25}} = \frac{3}{5}$$

The Rotation of Axes Formulas then give

$$x = \tfrac{4}{5}X - \tfrac{3}{5}Y \qquad \text{and} \qquad y = \tfrac{3}{5}X + \tfrac{4}{5}Y$$

Substituting into the given equation, we have

$$64\left(\tfrac{4}{5}X - \tfrac{3}{5}Y\right)^2 + 96\left(\tfrac{4}{5}X - \tfrac{3}{5}Y\right)\left(\tfrac{3}{5}X + \tfrac{4}{5}Y\right)$$
$$+ 36\left(\tfrac{3}{5}X + \tfrac{4}{5}Y\right)^2 - 15\left(\tfrac{4}{5}X - \tfrac{3}{5}Y\right) + 20\left(\tfrac{3}{5}X + \tfrac{4}{5}Y\right) - 25 = 0$$

Expanding and collecting like terms, we get

$$100X^2 + 25Y - 25 = 0$$

$$-4X^2 = Y - 1 \qquad \text{Simplify}$$

$$X^2 = -\tfrac{1}{4}(Y - 1) \qquad \text{Divide by 4}$$

(b) We recognize this as the equation of a parabola that opens along the negative Y-axis and has vertex $(0, 1)$ in XY-coordinates. Since $4p = -\frac{1}{4}$, we have $p = -\frac{1}{16}$, so the focus is $\left(0, \frac{15}{16}\right)$ and the directrix is $Y = \frac{17}{16}$. Using

$$\phi = \cos^{-1}\tfrac{4}{5} \approx 37°$$

we sketch the graph in Figure 6(a).

(c) To draw the graph using a graphing calculator, we need to solve for y. The given equation is a quadratic equation in y, so we can use the quadratic formula to solve for y. Writing the equation in the form

$$36y^2 + (96x + 20)y + (64x^2 - 15x - 25) = 0$$

we get

$$y = \frac{-(96x + 20) \pm \sqrt{(96x + 20)^2 - 4(36)(64x^2 - 15x - 25)}}{2(36)} \qquad \text{Quadratic formula}$$

$$= \frac{-(96x + 20) \pm \sqrt{6000x + 4000}}{72} \qquad \text{Expand}$$

$$= \frac{-96x - 20 \pm 20\sqrt{15x + 10}}{72} \qquad \text{Simplify}$$

$$= \frac{-24x - 5 \pm 5\sqrt{15x + 10}}{18} \qquad \text{Simplify}$$

To obtain the graph of the parabola, we graph the functions

$$y = (-24x - 5 + 5\sqrt{15x + 10})/18 \quad \text{and} \quad y = (-24x - 5 - 5\sqrt{15x + 10})/18$$

as shown in Figure 6(b).

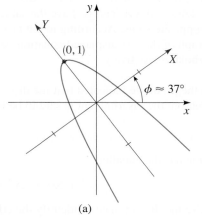

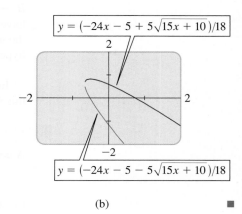

FIGURE 6

$64x^2 + 96xy + 36y^2 - 15x + 20y - 25 = 0$

(a)   (b)

In Examples 3 and 4 we were able to identify the type of conic by rotating the axes. The next theorem gives rules for identifying the type of conic directly from the equation, without rotating axes.

IDENTIFYING CONICS BY THE DISCRIMINANT

The graph of the equation

$$Ax^2 + Bxy + Cy^2 + Dx + Ey + F = 0$$

is either a conic or a degenerate conic. In the nondegenerate cases, the graph is

1. a parabola if $B^2 - 4AC = 0$.

2. an ellipse if $B^2 - 4AC < 0$.

3. a hyperbola if $B^2 - 4AC > 0$.

The quantity $B^2 - 4AC$ is called the **discriminant** of the equation.

■ **Proof**   If we rotate the axes through an angle ϕ, we get an equation of the form

$$A'X^2 + B'XY + C'Y^2 + D'X + E'Y + F' = 0$$

where $A', B', C', \ldots$ are given by the formulas on page 400. A straightforward calculation shows that

$$(B')^2 - 4A'C' = B^2 - 4AC$$

Thus, the expression $B^2 - 4AC$ remains unchanged for any rotation. In particular, if we choose a rotation that eliminates the xy-term $(B' = 0)$, we get

$$A'X^2 + C'Y^2 + D'X + E'Y + F' = 0$$

In this case, $B^2 - 4AC = -4A'C'$. So $B^2 - 4AC = 0$ if either A' or C' is zero; $B^2 - 4AC < 0$ if A' and C' have the same sign; and $B^2 - 4AC > 0$ if A' and C' have opposite signs. According to the box on page 403, these cases correspond to the graph of the last displayed equation being a parabola, an ellipse, or a hyperbola, respectively.　　□

In the proof we indicated that the discriminant is unchanged by any rotation; for this reason, the discriminant is said to be **invariant** under rotation.

EXAMPLE 5 ■ **Identifying a Conic by the Discriminant**

A conic has the equation

$$3x^2 + 5xy - 2y^2 + x - y + 4 = 0$$

(a) Use the discriminant to identify the conic.

(b) Confirm your answer to part (a) by graphing the conic with a graphing calculator.

SOLUTION

(a) Since $A = 3$, $B = 5$, and $C = -2$, the discriminant is

$$B^2 - 4AC = 5^2 - 4(3)(-2) = 49 > 0$$

So the conic is a hyperbola.

(b) Using the quadratic formula, we solve for y to get

$$y = \frac{5x - 1 \pm \sqrt{49x^2 - 2x + 33}}{4}$$

We graph these functions in Figure 7. The graph confirms that this is a hyperbola.　■

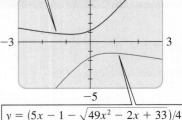

FIGURE 7

6.5 EXERCISES

1–6 ■ Determine the XY-coordinates of the given point if the coordinate axes are rotated through the indicated angle.

1. $(1, 1)$,　$\phi = 45°$

2. $(-2, 1)$,　$\phi = 30°$

3. $(3, -\sqrt{3})$,　$\phi = 60°$

4. $(2, 0)$,　$\phi = 15°$

5. $(0, 2)$,　$\phi = 55°$

6. $(\sqrt{2}, 4\sqrt{2})$,　$\phi = 45°$

7–12 ■ Determine the equation of the given conic in XY-coordinates when the coordinate axes are rotated through the indicated angle.

7. $x^2 - 3y^2 = 4$,　$\phi = 60°$

8. $y = (x - 1)^2$,　$\phi = 45°$

9. $x^2 - y^2 = 2y$,　$\phi = \cos^{-1}\frac{3}{5}$

10. $x^2 + 2y^2 = 16,\quad \phi = \sin^{-1}\frac{3}{5}$

11. $x^2 + 2\sqrt{3}\,xy - y^2 = 4,\quad \phi = 30°$

12. $xy = x + y,\quad \phi = \pi/4$

13–26 ■ (a) Use the discriminant to determine whether the graph of the equation is a parabola, an ellipse, or a hyperbola. (b) Use a rotation of axes to eliminate the xy-term. (c) Sketch the graph.

13. $xy = 8$

14. $xy + 4 = 0$

15. $x^2 + 2xy + y^2 + x - y = 0$

16. $13x^2 + 6\sqrt{3}\,xy + 7y^2 = 16$

17. $x^2 + 2\sqrt{3}\,xy - y^2 + 2 = 0$

18. $21x^2 + 10\sqrt{3}\,xy + 31y^2 = 144$

19. $11x^2 - 24xy + 4y^2 + 20 = 0$

20. $25x^2 - 120xy + 144y^2 - 156x - 65y = 0$

21. $\sqrt{3}\,x^2 + 3xy = 3$

22. $153x^2 + 192xy + 97y^2 = 225$

23. $2\sqrt{3}\,x^2 - 6xy + \sqrt{3}\,x + 3y = 0$

24. $9x^2 - 24xy + 16y^2 = 100(x - y - 1)$

25. $52x^2 + 72xy + 73y^2 = 40x - 30y + 75$

26. $(7x + 24y)^2 = 600x - 175y + 25$

27–30 ■ (a) Use the discriminant to identify the conic. (b) Confirm your answer by graphing the conic using a graphing device.

27. $2x^2 - 4xy + 2y^2 - 5x - 5 = 0$

28. $x^2 - 2xy + 3y^2 = 8$

29. $6x^2 + 10xy + 3y^2 - 6y = 36$

30. $9x^2 - 6xy + y^2 + 6x - 2y = 0$

31. (a) Use rotation of axes to show that the following equation represents a hyperbola:

$$7x^2 + 48xy - 7y^2 - 200x - 150y + 600 = 0$$

(b) Find the XY- and xy-coordinates of the center, vertices, and foci.

(c) Find the equations of the asymptotes in XY- and xy-coordinates.

32. (a) Use rotation of axes to show that the following equation represents a parabola:

$$2\sqrt{2}\,(x + y)^2 = 7x + 9y$$

(b) Find the XY- and xy-coordinates of the vertex and focus.

(c) Find the equation of the directrix in XY- and xy-coordinates.

33. Solve the equations:

$$x = X\cos\phi - Y\sin\phi$$
$$y = X\sin\phi + Y\cos\phi$$

for X and Y in terms of x and y. [*Hint:* To begin, multiply the first equation by $\cos\phi$ and the second by $\sin\phi$, and then add the two equations to solve for X.]

34. Show that the graph of the equation

$$\sqrt{x} + \sqrt{y} = 1$$

is part of a parabola by rotating the axes through an angle of 45°. [*Hint:* First convert the equation to one that does not involve radicals.]

● **DISCOVERY · DISCUSSION**

35. Algebraic Invariants   A quantity is invariant under rotation if it does not change when the axes are rotated. It was stated in the text that for the general equation of a conic, the quantity

$$B^2 - 4AC$$

is invariant under rotation.

(a) Use the formulas for A', B', and C' on page 400 to prove that the quantity $B^2 - 4AC$ is invariant under rotation; that is, show that

$$B^2 - 4AC = B'^2 - 4A'C'$$

(b) Prove that $A + C$ is invariant under rotation.

(c) Is the quantity F invariant under rotation?

36. Geometric Invariants   Do you expect that the distance between two points is invariant under rotation? Prove your answer by comparing the distance $d(P, Q)$ and $d(P', Q')$ where P' and Q' are the images of P and Q under a rotation of axes.

6.6 POLAR EQUATIONS OF CONICS

Earlier in this chapter we defined a parabola in terms of a focus and directrix, but we defined the ellipse and hyperbola in terms of two foci. In this section we give a more unified treatment of all three types of conics in terms of a focus and directrix. If we place the focus at the origin, then a conic section has a simple polar equation. Moreover, in polar form, rotation of conics becomes a simple matter. Polar equations of ellipses are crucial in the derivation of Kepler's laws of motion (see page 375).

EQUIVALENT DESCRIPTION OF CONICS

Let F be a fixed point (the **focus**), ℓ a fixed line (the **directrix**), and e a fixed positive number (the **eccentricity**). The set of all points P such that the ratio of the distance from P to F to the distance from P to ℓ is the constant e is a conic. That is, the set of all points P such that

$$\frac{d(P, F)}{d(P, \ell)} = e$$

is a conic. The conic is a parabola if $e = 1$, an ellipse if $e < 1$, or a hyperbola if $e > 1$.

■ **Proof**   If $e = 1$, then $d(P, F) = d(P, \ell)$, and so the given condition becomes the definition of a parabola as given in Section 6.1.

Now, suppose $e \neq 1$. Let's place the focus F at the origin and the directrix parallel to the y-axis and d units to the right. Thus, the directrix has equation $x = d$ and is perpendicular to the polar axis. If the point P has polar coordinates (r, θ), we see from Figure 1 that $d(P, F) = r$ and $d(P, \ell) = d - r \cos \theta$. Thus, the condition $d(P, F)/d(P, \ell) = e$, or $d(P, F) = e \cdot d(P, \ell)$, becomes

$$r = e(d - r \cos \theta)$$

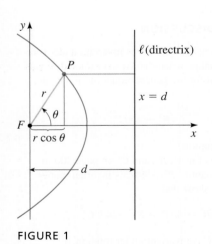

FIGURE 1

If we square both sides of this polar equation and convert to rectangular coordinates, we get

$$x^2 + y^2 = e^2(d - x)^2$$

$$(1 - e^2)x^2 + 2de^2x + y^2 = e^2d^2 \qquad \text{Expand and simplify}$$

$$\left(x + \frac{e^2d}{1 - e^2}\right)^2 + \frac{y^2}{1 - e^2} = \frac{e^2d^2}{(1 - e^2)^2} \qquad \text{Divide by } 1 - e^2 \text{ and complete the square}$$

If $e < 1$, then dividing both sides of this equation by $e^2d^2/(1 - e^2)^2$ gives an equation of the form

$$\frac{(x - h)^2}{a^2} + \frac{y^2}{b^2} = 1$$

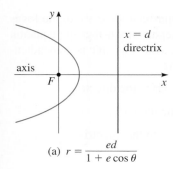

(a) $r = \dfrac{ed}{1 + e \cos \theta}$

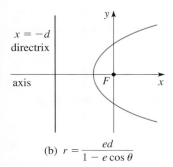

(b) $r = \dfrac{ed}{1 - e \cos \theta}$

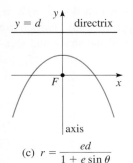

(c) $r = \dfrac{ed}{1 + e \sin \theta}$

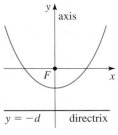

(d) $r = \dfrac{ed}{1 - e \sin \theta}$

FIGURE 2

The form of the polar equation of a conic indicates the location of the directrix

where

$$h = \frac{-e^2 d}{1 - e^2} \qquad a^2 = \frac{e^2 d^2}{(1 - e^2)^2} \qquad b^2 = \frac{e^2 d^2}{1 - e^2}$$

This is the equation of an ellipse with center $(h, 0)$. In Section 6.2 we found that the foci of an ellipse are a distance c from the center, where $c^2 = a^2 - b^2$. In our case

$$c^2 = a^2 - b^2 = \frac{e^4 d^2}{(1 - e^2)^2}$$

Thus, $c = e^2 d / (1 - e^2) = -h$, which confirms that the focus defined in the theorem is the same as the focus defined in Section 6.2. It also follows that

$$e = \frac{c}{a}$$

If $e > 1$, a similar proof shows that the conic is a hyperbola with $e = c/a$, where $c^2 = a^2 + b^2$. ◻

In the proof we saw that the polar equation of the conic in Figure 1 is $r = e(d - r \cos \theta)$. Solving for r, we get

$$r = \frac{ed}{1 + e \cos \theta}$$

If the directrix is chosen to be to the *left* of the focus $(x = -d)$, then we get the equation $r = ed/(1 - e \cos \theta)$. If the directrix is *parallel* to the polar axis $(y = d$ or $y = -d)$, then we get $\sin \theta$ instead of $\cos \theta$ in the equation. These observations are summarized in the following box and in Figure 2.

POLAR EQUATIONS OF CONICS

A polar equation of the form

$$r = \frac{ed}{1 \pm e \cos \theta} \qquad \text{or} \qquad r = \frac{ed}{1 \pm e \sin \theta}$$

represents a conic with one focus at the origin and with eccentricity e. The conic is

1. a parabola if $e = 1$.

2. an ellipse if $0 < e < 1$.

3. a hyperbola if $e > 1$.

To graph the polar equation of a conic, we first determine the location of the directrix from the form of the equation. The four cases that arise are shown in

Figure 2. (The figure shows only the parts of the graphs that are close to the focus at the origin. The shape of the rest of the graph depends on whether the equation represents a parabola, an ellipse, or a hyperbola.) The axis of a conic is perpendicular to the directrix—specifically we have the following:

1. For a parabola, the axis of symmetry is perpendicular to the directrix.

2. For an ellipse, the major axis is perpendicular to the directrix.

3. For a hyperbola, the transverse axis is perpendicular to the directrix.

EXAMPLE 1 ■ Finding a Polar Equation for a Conic

Find a polar equation for the parabola that has its focus at the origin and whose directrix is the line $y = -6$.

SOLUTION

Using $e = 1$ and $d = 6$, and using part (d) of Figure 2, we see that the polar equation of the parabola is

$$r = \frac{6}{1 - \sin \theta} \qquad ■$$

   To graph a polar conic, it is helpful to plot the points for which $\theta = 0$, $\pi/2$, π, and $3\pi/2$. Using these points and a knowledge of the type of conic (which we obtain from the eccentricity), we can easily get a rough idea of the shape and location of the graph.

EXAMPLE 2 ■ Identifying and Sketching a Conic

A conic is given by the polar equation

$$r = \frac{10}{3 - 2 \cos \theta}$$

(a) Show that the conic is an ellipse and sketch the graph.
(b) Find the center of the ellipse, and the lengths of the major and minor axes.

SOLUTION

(a) Dividing the numerator and denominator by 3, we have

$$r = \frac{\frac{10}{3}}{1 - \frac{2}{3} \cos \theta}$$

Since $e = \frac{2}{3} < 1$, the equation represents an ellipse. For a rough graph we plot the points for which $\theta = 0$, $\pi/2$, π, $3\pi/2$ (see Figure 3).

this system 24 satellites are strategi-cally located above the surface of the earth. A hand-held GPS device measures distance from a satellite using the travel time of radio sig-nals emitted from the satellite. Knowing the distance to three dif-ferent satellites tells us that we are at the point of intersection of three different spheres. This uniquely determines our position.

θ	F
0	10
$\pi/2$	$\frac{10}{3}$
π	2
$3\pi/2$	$\frac{10}{3}$

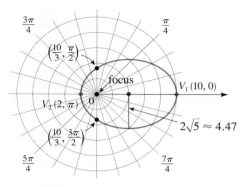

FIGURE 3

$$r = \frac{10}{3 - 2\cos\theta}$$

(b) Comparing the equation to those in Figure 2, we see that the major axis is hor-izontal. Thus, the endpoints of the major axis are $V_1(10, 0)$ and $V_1(2, \pi)$. So the center of the ellipse is at $C(4, 0)$, the midpoint of $V_1 V_2$.

The distance between the vertices V_1 and V_2 is 12; thus the length of the major axis is $2a = 12$, and so $a = 6$. To determine the length of the minor axis we need to find b. From page 407 we have $c = ae = 6\left(\frac{2}{3}\right) = 4$, so

$$b^2 = a^2 - c^2 = 6^2 - 4^2 = 20$$

Thus, $b = \sqrt{20} = 2\sqrt{5} \approx 4.47$, and the length of the minor axis is $2b = 4\sqrt{5} \approx 8.94$. ∎

θ	r
0	6
$\pi/2$	2
π	6
$3\pi/2$	-6

EXAMPLE 3 ■ Identifying and Sketching a Conic

A conic is given by the polar equation

$$r = \frac{12}{2 + 4\sin\theta}$$

(a) Show that the conic is a hyperbola and sketch the graph.
(b) Find the center of the hyperbola and sketch the asymptotes.

SOLUTION

(a) Dividing the numerator and denominator by 2, we have

$$r = \frac{6}{1 + 2\sin\theta}$$

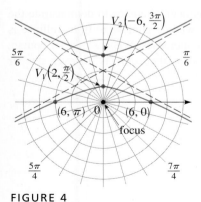

FIGURE 4

$$r = \frac{12}{2 + 4\sin\theta}$$

Since $e = 2 > 1$, the equation represents a hyperbola. For a rough graph we plot the points for which $\theta = 0$, $\pi/2$, π, $3\pi/2$ (see Figure 4).

(b) Comparing the equation to those in Figure 2, we see that the transverse axis is vertical. Thus, the endpoints of the transverse axis (the vertices of the hyperbola) are $V_1(2, \pi/2)$ and $V_2(-6, 3\pi/2) = V_2(6, \pi/2)$. So the center of the hyperbola is $C(4, \pi/2)$, the midpoint of V_1V_2.

To sketch the asymptotes, we need to find a and b. The distance between V_1 and V_2 is 4; thus, the length of the transverse axis is $2a = 4$, and so $a = 2$. To find b, we first find c. From page 407 we have $c = ae = 2 \cdot 2 = 4$, so

$$b^2 = c^2 - a^2 = 4^2 - 2^2 = 12$$

Thus, $b = \sqrt{12} = 2\sqrt{3} \approx 3.46$. Knowing a and b allows us to sketch the central box, from which we obtain the asymptotes shown in Figure 4. ∎

When we rotate conic sections, it is much more convenient to use polar equations than Cartesian equations. We use the fact that the graph of $r = f(\theta - \alpha)$ is the graph of $r = f(\theta)$ rotated counterclockwise about the origin through an angle α (see Exercise 52 in Section 5.2).

 EXAMPLE 4 ∎ **Rotating an Ellipse**

Suppose the ellipse of Example 2 is rotated through an angle $\pi/4$ about the origin. Find a polar equation for the resulting ellipse, and draw its graph.

SOLUTION

We get the equation of the rotated ellipse by replacing θ with $\theta - \pi/4$ in the equation given in Example 2. So the new equation is

$$r = \frac{10}{3 - 2\cos(\theta - \pi/4)}$$

We use this equation to graph the rotated ellipse in Figure 5. Notice that the ellipse has been rotated about the focus at the origin. ∎

In Figure 6 we use a computer to sketch a number of conics to demonstrate the effect of varying the eccentricity e. Notice that when e is close to 0, the ellipse is nearly circular and becomes more elongated as e increases. When $e = 1$, of course, the conic is a parabola. As e increases beyond 1, the conic is an ever steeper hyperbola.

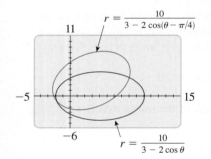

$r = \dfrac{10}{3 - 2\cos(\theta - \pi/4)}$

$r = \dfrac{10}{3 - 2\cos\theta}$

FIGURE 5

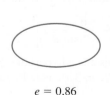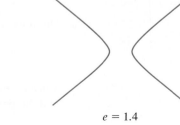

$e = 0.5$ $e = 0.86$ $e = 1$ $e = 1.4$ $e = 4$

FIGURE 6

6.6   EXERCISES

1–8 ■ Write a polar equation of a conic that has its focus at the origin and satisfies the given conditions.

1. Ellipse, eccentricity $\frac{2}{3}$, directrix $x = 3$

2. Hyperbola, eccentricity $\frac{4}{3}$, directrix $x = -3$

3. Parabola, directrix $y = 2$

4. Ellipse, eccentricity $\frac{1}{2}$, directrix $y = -4$

5. Hyperbola, eccentricity 4, directrix $r = 5 \sec \theta$

6. Ellipse, eccentricity 0.6, directrix $r = 2 \csc \theta$

7. Parabola, vertex at $(5, \pi/2)$

8. Ellipse, eccentricity 0.4, vertex at $(2, 0)$

9–14 ■ Match the polar equations with the graphs labeled I–VI. Give reasons for your answer.

9. $r = \dfrac{6}{1 + \cos \theta}$

10. $r = \dfrac{2}{2 - \cos \theta}$

11. $r = \dfrac{3}{1 - 2 \sin \theta}$

12. $r = \dfrac{5}{3 - 3 \sin \theta}$

13. $r = \dfrac{12}{3 + 2 \sin \theta}$

14. $r = \dfrac{12}{2 + 3 \cos \theta}$

I
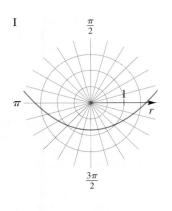

II
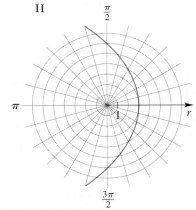

III
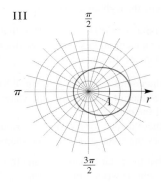

IV
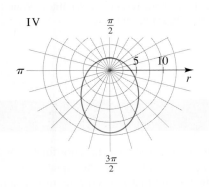

V
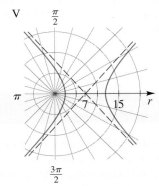

VI
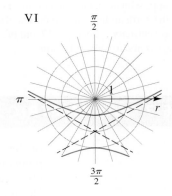

15–22 ■ (a) Find the eccentricity and identify the conic.
(b) Sketch the conic and label the vertices.

15. $r = \dfrac{4}{1 + 3 \cos \theta}$

16. $r = \dfrac{8}{3 + 3 \cos \theta}$

17. $r = \dfrac{2}{1 - \cos \theta}$

18. $r = \dfrac{10}{3 - 2 \sin \theta}$

19. $r = \dfrac{6}{2 + \sin \theta}$

20. $r = \dfrac{5}{2 - 3 \sin \theta}$

21. $r = \dfrac{7}{2 - 5 \sin \theta}$

22. $r = \dfrac{8}{3 + \cos \theta}$

 23. (a) Find the eccentricity and directrix of the conic $r = 1/(4 - 3 \cos \theta)$ and graph the conic and its directrix.
  (b) If this conic is rotated about the origin through an angle $\pi/3$, write the resulting equation and draw its graph.

 24. Graph the parabola $r = 5/(2 + 2 \sin \theta)$ and its directrix. Also graph the curve obtained by rotating this parabola about its focus through an angle $\pi/6$.

 25. Graph the conics $r = e/(1 - e \cos \theta)$ with $e = 0.4, 0.6, 0.8$, and 1.0 on a common screen. How does the value of e affect the shape of the curve?

 26. (a) Graph the conics $r = ed/(1 + e \sin \theta)$ for $e = 1$ and various values of d. How does the value of d affect the shape of the conic?
  (b) Graph these conics for $d = 1$ and various values of e. How does the value of e affect the shape of the conic?

27. (a) Show that the polar equation of an ellipse with directrix $x = -d$ can be written in the form
$$r = \frac{a(1 - e^2)}{1 - e \cos \theta}$$
  (b) Find an approximate polar equation for the elliptical orbit of the earth around the sun (at one focus) given that the eccentricity is about 0.017 and the length of the major axis is about 2.99×10^8 km.

28. (a) The planets move around the sun in elliptical orbits with the sun at one focus. The positions of a planet that are closest to, and farthest from, the sun are called its **perihelion** and **aphelion**, respectively. Use Exercise 27(a) to show that the perihelion distance from a planet to the sun is $a(1 - e)$ and the aphelion distance is $a(1 + e)$.

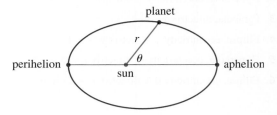

  (b) Use the data of Exercise 27(b) to find the distances from the earth to the sun at perihelion and at aphelion.

29. The distance from the planet Pluto to the sun is 4.43×10^9 km at perihelion and 7.37×10^9 km at aphelion. Use Exercise 28 to find the eccentricity of Pluto's orbit.

 DISCOVERY · DISCUSSION

30. Distance to a Focus When we found polar equations for the conics, we placed one focus at the pole. It's easy to find the distance from that focus to any point on the conic. Explain how the polar equation gives us this distance.

31. Polar Equations of Orbits When a satellite orbits the earth, its path is an ellipse with one focus at the center of the earth. Why do scientists use polar (rather than rectangular) coordinates to track the position of satellites? Your answer to Exercise 30 is relevant here.

6.7 PARAMETRIC EQUATIONS

So far we've described a curve by giving an equation that the coordinates of all points on the curve must satisfy. For example, we know that the equation $y = x^2$ represents a parabola in rectangular coordinates and that $r = \sin \theta$ represents a circle in polar coordinates. We now study another method for describing a curve in the plane, which in many situations turns out to be more useful and natural than either rectangular or polar equations. In this method, the x- and y-coordinates of points on the curve are given separately as functions of an additional variable t, called the **parameter**:

$$x = f(t) \qquad y = g(t)$$

These are called **parametric equations** for the curve. Substituting a value of t into each equation determines the coordinates of a point (x, y). As t varies, the point $(x, y) = (f(t), g(t))$ varies and traces out the curve. If we think of t as representing time, then as t increases, we can imagine a particle at $(x, y) = (f(t), g(t))$ moving along the curve.

EXAMPLE 1 ■ Sketching a Parametric Curve

Sketch the curve defined by the parametric equations

$$x = t^2 - 3t \qquad y = t - 1$$

Eliminate the parameter t to obtain a single equation for the curve in the variables x and y.

SOLUTION

For every value of t, we get a point on the curve. For example, if $t = 0$, then $x = 0$ and $y = -1$, so the corresponding point is $(0, -1)$. In Figure 1 we plot the points (x, y) determined by the values of t shown in the following table.

t	x	y
-2	10	-3
-1	4	-2
0	0	-1
1	-2	0
2	-2	1
3	0	2
4	4	3
5	10	4

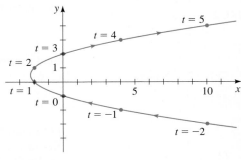

FIGURE 1

As t increases, a particle whose position is given by the parametric equations moves along the curve in the direction of the arrows. The curve seems to be a parabola. We can confirm this by eliminating the parameter t from the parametric equations and reducing them to a single equation as follows. First we solve for t in the second equation to get $t = y + 1$. Substituting this into the first equation, we get

$$x = (y + 1)^2 - 3(y + 1) = y^2 - y - 2$$

The curve is the parabola $x = y^2 - y - 2$. ■

Notice that we would obtain the same graph as in Example 1 from the parametrization

$$x = t^2 - t - 2 \qquad y = t$$

because the points on this curve also satisfy the equation $x = y^2 - y - 2$. But the same value of t produces different points on the curve in these two parametrizations. For example, when $t = 0$, the particle that traces out the curve in Figure 1 is at $(0, -1)$, whereas in the parametrization of the preceding equations, the particle is already at $(-2, 0)$ when $t = 0$. *Thus, a parametrization contains more information than just the shape of the curve; it also indicates how the curve is being traced out.*

EXAMPLE 2 ■ Eliminating the Parameter

Describe and graph the curve represented by the parametric equations

$$x = \cos t \qquad y = \sin t \qquad 0 \leq t \leq 2\pi$$

SOLUTION

To identify the curve, we eliminate the parameter. Since $\cos^2 t + \sin^2 t = 1$ and since $x = \cos t$ and $y = \sin t$ for every point (x, y) on the curve, we have

$$x^2 + y^2 = (\cos t)^2 + (\sin t)^2 = 1$$

This means that all points on the curve satisfy the equation $x^2 + y^2 = 1$, so the graph is a circle of radius 1 centered at the origin. As t increases from 0 to 2π, the point given by the parametric equations starts at $(1, 0)$ and moves counterclockwise once around the circle, as shown in Figure 2. Notice that the parameter t can be interpreted as the angle shown in the figure. ■

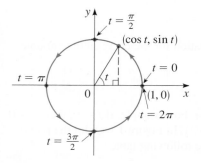

FIGURE 2

EXAMPLE 3 ■ Finding Parametric Equations for a Graph

Find parametric equations for the line of slope 3 that passes through the point $(2, 6)$.

SOLUTION

Let's start at the point $(2, 6)$ and move up and to the right along this line. Because the line has slope 3, for every 1 unit we move to the right, we must move up 3 units. In other words, if we increase the x-coordinate by t units, we must correspondingly increase the y-coordinate by $3t$ units. This leads to the parametric equations

$$x = 2 + t \qquad y = 6 + 3t$$

To confirm that these equations give the desired line, we eliminate the parameter. We solve for t in the first equation and substitute into the second to get

$$y = 6 + 3(x - 2) = 3x$$

Thus, the slope-intercept form of the equation of this line is $y = 3x$, which is a line of slope 3 that does pass through $(2, 6)$ as required. The graph is shown in Figure 3. ■

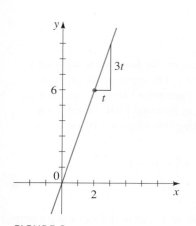

FIGURE 3

EXAMPLE 4 ■ Sketching a Parametric Curve

Sketch the curve with parametric equations

$$x = \sin t \qquad y = 2 - \cos^2 t$$

SOLUTION

To eliminate the parameter, we first use the trigonometric identity $\cos^2 t = 1 - \sin^2 t$ to change the second equation:

$$y = 2 - \cos^2 t = 2 - (1 - \sin^2 t) = 1 + \sin^2 t$$

Now we can substitute $\sin t = x$ from the first equation to get

$$y = 1 + x^2$$

and so the point (x, y) moves along the parabola $y = 1 + x^2$. However, since $-1 \leq \sin t \leq 1$, we have $-1 \leq x \leq 1$, so the parametric equations represent only the part of the parabola between $x = -1$ and $x = 1$. Since $\sin t$ is periodic, the point $(x, y) = (\sin t, 2 - \cos^2 t)$ moves back and forth infinitely often along the parabola between the points $(-1, 2)$ and $(1, 2)$ as shown in Figure 4. ■

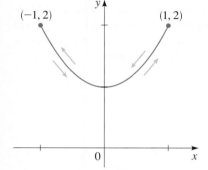

FIGURE 4

EXAMPLE 5 ■ Parametric Equations for the Cycloid

As a circle rolls along a straight line, the curve traced out by a fixed point P on the circumference of the circle is called a **cycloid** (see Figure 5). If the circle has radius a and rolls along the x-axis, with one position of the point P being at the origin, find parametric equations for the cycloid.

FIGURE 5

SOLUTION

Figure 6 shows the circle and the point P after the circle has rolled through an angle θ (in radians). The distance $d(O, T)$ that the circle has rolled must be the same as the length of the arc PT, which, by the arc length formula, is $a\theta$ (see Section 6.1). This means that the center of the circle is $C(a\theta, a)$.

Let the coordinates of P be (x, y). Then from Figure 6 (which illustrates the case $0 < \theta < \pi/2$), we see that

$$x = d(O, T) - d(P, Q) = a\theta - a \sin \theta = a(\theta - \sin \theta)$$
$$y = d(T, C) - d(Q, C) = a - a \cos \theta = a(1 - \cos \theta)$$

so parametric equations for the cycloid are

$$x = a(\theta - \sin \theta) \qquad y = a(1 - \cos \theta)$$ ■

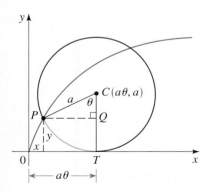

FIGURE 6

The cycloid has a number of interesting physical properties. It is the "curve of quickest descent" in the following sense. Let's choose two points P and Q that are not directly above each other, and join them with a wire. Suppose we allow a bead to slide down the wire under the influence of gravity (ignoring friction). Of all possible shapes that the wire can be bent into, the bead will slide from P to Q the fastest when the shape is half of an arch of an inverted cycloid (see Figure 7). The cycloid is also the "curve of equal descent" in the sense that no matter where we place a bead B on a cycloid-shaped wire, it takes the same time to slide to the bottom (see Figure 8). These rather surprising properties of the cycloid were proved (using calculus) in the 17th century by several mathematicians and physicists, including Johann Bernoulli, Blaise Pascal, and Christiaan Huygens.

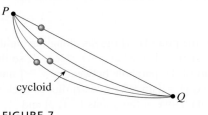

FIGURE 7

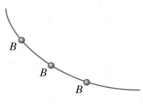

FIGURE 8

Using Graphing Devices to Graph Parametric Curves

Most graphing calculators and computer graphing programs can be used to graph parametric equations. Such devices are particularly useful when sketching complicated curves like the one shown in Figure 9.

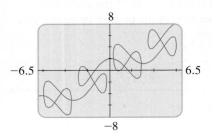

FIGURE 9

$x = t + 2 \sin 2t$, $y = t + 2 \cos 5t$

EXAMPLE 6 ■ Graphing Parametric Curves

Use a graphing device to draw the following parametric curves. Discuss their similarities and differences.

(a) $x = \sin 2t$
    $y = 2 \cos t$

(b) $x = \sin 3t$
    $y = 2 \cos t$

SOLUTION

In both parts (a) and (b), the graph will lie inside the rectangle given by $-1 \le x \le 1$, $-2 \le y \le 2$, since both the sine and the cosine of any number will be between -1 and 1. Thus, we may use the viewing rectangle $[-1.5, 1.5]$ by $[-2.5, 2.5]$.

(a) Since $2 \cos t$ is periodic with period 2π (see Section 2.3), and since $\sin 2t$ has period π, letting t vary over the interval $0 \le t \le 2\pi$ gives us the complete graph, which is shown in Figure 10(a).

(b) Again, letting t take on values between 0 and 2π gives the complete graph shown in Figure 10(b).

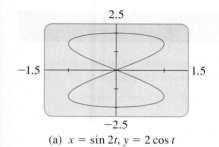

2.5

−1.5   1.5

−2.5

(a) $x = \sin 2t$, $y = 2 \cos t$

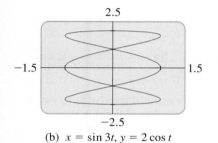

2.5

−1.5   1.5

−2.5

(b) $x = \sin 3t$, $y = 2 \cos t$

FIGURE 10

Both graphs are *closed curves*, which means they form loops with the same starting and ending point; also, both graphs cross over themselves. However, the graph in Figure 10(a) has two loops, like a figure eight, whereas the graph in Figure 10(b) has three loops. ∎

The curves graphed in Example 6 are called Lissajous figures. A **Lissajous figure** is the graph of a pair of parametric equations of the form

$$x = A \sin \omega_1 t \qquad y = B \cos \omega_2 t$$

where A, B, ω_1, and ω_2 are real constants. Since $\sin \omega_1 t$ and $\cos \omega_2 t$ are both between -1 and 1, a Lissajous figure will lie inside the rectangle determined by $-A \leq x \leq A$, $-B \leq y \leq B$. This fact can be used to choose a viewing rectangle when graphing a Lissajous figure, as in Example 6.

Recall from Section 5.1 that rectangular coordinates (x, y) and polar coordinates (r, θ) are related by the equations $x = r \cos \theta$, $y = r \sin \theta$. Thus, we can graph the polar equation $r = f(\theta)$ by changing it to parametric form as follows:

$$x = r \cos \theta = f(\theta) \cos \theta \qquad \text{Since } r = f(\theta)$$

$$y = r \sin \theta = f(\theta) \sin \theta$$

Replacing θ by the standard parametric variable t, we have the following result.

POLAR EQUATIONS IN PARAMETRIC FORM

The graph of the polar equation $r = f(\theta)$ is the same as the graph of the parametric equations

$$x = f(t) \cos t \qquad y = f(t) \sin t$$

EXAMPLE 7 ∎ **Parametric Form of a Polar Equation**

Consider the polar equation $r = \theta$, $1 \leq \theta \leq 10\pi$.

(a) Express the equation in parametric form.
(b) Draw a graph of the parametric equations from part (a).

SOLUTION

(a) The given polar equation is equivalent to the parametric equation

$$x = t \cos t \qquad y = t \sin t$$

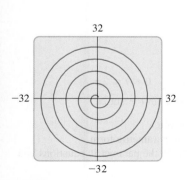

32

−32   32

−32

FIGURE 11

$x = t \cos t$, $y = t \sin t$

(b) Since $10\pi \approx 31.42$, we use the viewing rectangle $[-32, 32]$ by $[-32, 32]$, and we let t vary from 1 to 10π. The resulting graph shown in Figure 11 is a *spiral*. ∎

6.7 EXERCISES

1–22 ■ A pair of parametric equations is given.
(a) Sketch the curve represented by the parametric equations.
(b) Find a rectangular-coordinate equation for the curve by eliminating the parameter.

1. $x = 2t$, $y = t + 6$

2. $x = 6t - 4$, $y = 3t$, $t \geq 0$

3. $x = t^2$, $y = t - 2$, $2 \leq t \leq 4$

4. $x = 2t + 1$, $y = \left(t + \frac{1}{2}\right)^2$

5. $x = \sqrt{t}$, $y = 1 - t$ **6.** $x = t^2$, $y = t^4 + 1$

7. $x = \dfrac{1}{t}$, $y = t + 1$ **8.** $x = t + 1$, $y = \dfrac{t}{t+1}$

9. $x = 4t^2$, $y = 8t^3$

10. $x = |t|$, $y = |1 - |t||$

11. $x = 2 \sin t$, $y = 2 \cos t$, $0 \leq t \leq \pi$

12. $x = 2 \cos t$, $y = 3 \sin t$, $0 \leq t \leq 2\pi$

13. $x = \sin^2 t$, $y = \sin^4 t$

14. $x = \sin^2 t$, $y = \cos t$

15. $x = \cos t$, $y = \cos 2t$

16. $x = \cos 2t$, $y = \sin 2t$

17. $x = \sec t$, $y = \tan t$, $0 \leq t < \pi/2$

18. $x = \cot t$, $y = \csc t$, $0 < t < \pi$

19. $x = \tan t$, $y = \cot t$, $0 < t < \pi/2$

20. $x = \sec t$, $y = \tan^2 t$, $0 \leq t < \pi/2$

21. $x = \cos^2 t$, $y = \sin^2 t$

22. $x = \cos^3 t$, $y = \sin^3 t$, $0 \leq t \leq 2\pi$

23–26 ■ Find parametric equations for the line with the given properties.

23. Slope $\frac{1}{2}$, passing through $(4, -1)$

24. Slope -2, passing through $(-10, -20)$

25. Passing through $(6, 7)$ and $(7, 8)$

26. Passing through $(12, 7)$ and the origin

27. Find parametric equations for the circle $x^2 + y^2 = a^2$.

28. Find parametric equations for the ellipse

$$\frac{x^2}{a^2} + \frac{y^2}{b^2} = 1$$

29. Show by eliminating the parameter θ that the following parametric equations represent a hyperbola:

$$x = a \tan \theta \qquad y = b \sec \theta$$

30. Show that the following parametric equations represent a part of the hyperbola of Exercise 29:

$$x = a \sqrt{t} \qquad y = b \sqrt{t + 1}$$

31–34 ■ Stretch the curve given by the parametric equations.

31. $x = t \cos t$, $y = t \sin t$, $t \geq 0$

32. $x = \sin t$, $y = \sin 2t$ **33.** $x = \dfrac{3t}{1 + t^3}$, $y = \dfrac{3t^2}{1 + t^3}$

34. $x = \cot t$, $y = 2 \sin^2 t$, $0 < t < \pi$

35. If a projectile is fired with an initial speed of v_0 ft/s at an angle α above the horizontal, then its position after t seconds is given by the parametric equations

$$x = (v_0 \cos \alpha)t \qquad y = (v_0 \sin \alpha)t - 16t^2$$

(where x and y are measured in feet). Show that the path of the projectile is a parabola by eliminating the parameter t.

36. Referring to Exercise 35, suppose a gun fires a bullet into the air with an initial speed of 2048 ft/s at an angle of 30° to the horizontal.
(a) After how many seconds will the bullet hit the ground?
(b) How far from the gun will the bullet hit the ground?
(c) What is the maximum height attained by the bullet?

37–42 ■ Use a graphing device to draw the curve represented by the parametric equations.

37. $x = \sin t$, $y = 2 \cos 3t$

38. $x = 2 \sin t$, $y = \cos 4t$

39. $x = 3 \sin 5t$, $y = 5 \cos 3t$

40. $x = \sin 4t$, $y = \cos 3t$

41. $x = \sin(\cos t)$, $y = \cos(t^{3/2})$, $0 \leq t \leq 2\pi$

42. $x = 2 \cos t + \cos 2t$, $y = 2 \sin t - \sin 2t$

43–46 ■ A polar equation is given.
(a) Express the polar equation in parametric form.
(b) Use a graphing device to graph the parametric equations you found in part (a).

43. $r = 2^{\theta/12}$, $0 \leq \theta \leq 4\pi$ **44.** $r = \sin \theta + 2 \cos \theta$

45. $r = \dfrac{4}{2 - \cos \theta}$ **46.** $r = 2^{\sin \theta}$

47–50 ■ Match the parametric equations with the graphs labeled I–IV. Give reasons for your answers.

47. $x = t^3 - 2t, \quad y = t^2 - t$

48. $x = \sin 3t, \quad y = \sin 4t$

49. $x = t + \sin 2t, \quad y = t + \sin 3t$

50. $x = \sin(t + \sin t), \quad y = \cos(t + \cos t)$

I
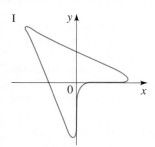

II
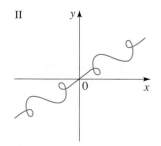

III
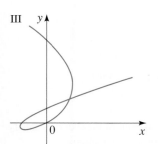

IV
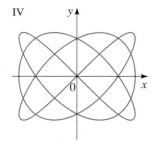

51. In Example 5 suppose the point P that traces out the curve lies not on the edge of the circle, but rather at a fixed point inside the rim, at a distance b from the center (with $b < a$). The curve traced out by P is called a **curtate cycloid** (or **trochoid**). Show that parametric equations for the curtate cycloid are

$$x = a\theta - b \sin \theta \qquad y = a - b \cos \theta$$

Sketch the graph.

52. In Exercise 51 if the point P lies *outside* the circle at a distance b from the center (with $b > a$), then the curve traced out by P is called a **prolate cycloid**. Show that parametric equations for the prolate cycloid are the same as the equations for the curtate cycloid, and sketch the graph for the case where $a = 1$ and $b = 2$.

53. A circle C of radius b rolls on the inside of a larger circle of radius a centered at the origin. Let P be a fixed point on

the smaller circle, with initial position at the point $(a, 0)$, as shown in the figure. The curve traced out by P is called a **hypocycloid**.

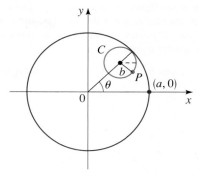

(a) Show that parametric equations for the hypocycloid are

$$x = (a - b) \cos \theta + b \cos\left(\frac{a - b}{b}\,\theta\right)$$

$$y = (a - b) \sin \theta - b \sin\left(\frac{a - b}{b}\,\theta\right)$$

(b) If $a = 4b$, the hypocycloid is called an **astroid**. Show that in this case the parametric equations can be reduced to

$$x = a \cos^3\theta \qquad y = a \sin^3\theta$$

Sketch the curve and eliminate the parameter to obtain an equation for the astroid in rectangular coordinates.

54. If the circle C of Exercise 53 rolls on the *outside* of the larger circle, the curve traced out by P is called an **epicycloid**. Find parametric equations for the epicycloid.

55. In the figure, the circle of radius a is stationary and, for every θ, the point P is the midpoint of the segment QR. The curve traced out by P for $0 < \theta < \pi$ is called the **longbow curve**. Find parametric equations for this curve.

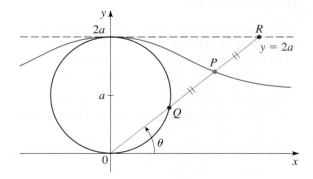

56. A string is wound around a circle and then unwound while being held taut. The curve traced out by the point P at the end of the string is called the **involute** of the circle, as shown in the figure. If the circle has radius a and is centered at the origin, and if the initial position of P is $(a, 0)$, show that parametric equations for the involute in terms of the parameter θ are

$$x = a(\cos \theta + \theta \sin \theta) \qquad y = a(\sin \theta - \theta \cos \theta)$$

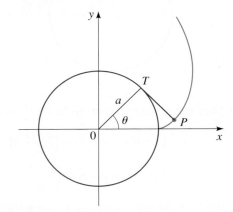

57. Eliminate the parameter θ in the parametric equations for the cycloid (Example 5) to obtain a rectangular coordinate equation for the section of the curve given by $0 \leqslant \theta \leqslant \pi$.

 DISCOVERY · DISCUSSION

58. More Information in Parametric Equations   In this section we stated that parametric equations contain more information than just the shape of a curve. Write a short paragraph explaining this statement. Use the following example and your answers to questions (a) and (b) in your explanation.

The position of a particle is given by the parametric equations

$$x = \sin t \qquad y = \cos t$$

where t represents time. We know that the shape of the path of the particle is a circle.

(a) How long does it take the particle to go once around the circle? Find parametric equations if the particle moves twice as fast around the circle.

(b) Does the particle travel clockwise or counterclockwise around the circle? Find parametric equations if the particle moves in the opposite direction around the circle.

59. Different Ways of Tracing Out a Curve   The curves C, D, E, and F are defined parametrically as follows, where the parameter t takes on all real values unless otherwise stated:

$$C: \quad x = t, \quad y = t^2$$
$$D: \quad x = \sqrt{t}, \quad y = t, \quad t \geqslant 0$$
$$E: \quad x = \sin t, \quad y = \sin^2 t$$
$$F: \quad x = 3^t, \quad y = 3^{2t}$$

(a) Show that the points on all four of these curves satisfy the same rectangular coordinate equation.

(b) Draw the graph of each curve and explain how the curves differ from one another.

6   REVIEW

CONCEPT CHECK

1. (a) Give the geometric definition of a parabola. What are the focus and directrix of the parabola?

(b) Sketch the parabola $x^2 = 4py$ for the case $p > 0$. Identify on your diagram the vertex, focus, and directrix. What happens if $p < 0$?

(c) Sketch the parabola $y^2 = 4px$, together with its vertex, focus, and directrix, for the case $p > 0$. What happens if $p < 0$?

2. (a) Give the geometric definition of an ellipse. What are the foci of the ellipse?

(b) For the ellipse with equation

$$\frac{x^2}{a^2} + \frac{y^2}{b^2} = 1$$

where $a > b > 0$, what are the coordinates of the vertices and the foci? What are the major and minor axes? Illustrate with a graph.

(c) Give an expression for the eccentricity of the ellipse in part (b).

(d) State the equation of an ellipse with foci on the y-axis.

3. (a) Give the geometric definition of a hyperbola. What are the foci of the hyperbola?

(b) For the hyperbola with equation

$$\frac{x^2}{a^2} - \frac{y^2}{b^2} = 1$$

what are the coordinates of the vertices and foci? What are the equations of the asymptotes? What is the transverse axis? Illustrate with a graph.

(c) State the equation of a hyperbola with foci on the y-axis.

(d) What steps would you take to sketch a hyperbola with a given equation?

4. Suppose h and k are positive numbers. What is the effect on the graph of an equation in x and y if

(a) x is replaced by $x - h$? By $x + h$?

(b) y is replaced by $y - k$? By $y + k$?

5. How can you tell whether the following nondegenerate conic is a parabola, an ellipse, or a hyperbola?

$$Ax^2 + Cy^2 + Dx + Ey + F = 0$$

6. Suppose the x- and y-axes are rotated through an acute angle ϕ to produce the X- and Y-axes. Write equations that relate the coordinates (x, y) and (X, Y) of a point in the xy-plane and XY-plane, respectively.

7. (a) How do you eliminate the xy-term in this equation?

$$Ax^2 + Bxy + Cy^2 + Dx + Ey + F = 0$$

(b) What is the discriminant of the conic in part (a)? How can you use the discriminant to determine whether the conic is a parabola, an ellipse, or a hyperbola?

8. (a) Write polar equations that represent a conic with eccentricity e.

(b) For what values of e is the conic an ellipse? A hyperbola? A parabola?

9. How do you sketch a curve with parametric equations $x = f(t)$, $y = g(t)$?

EXERCISES

1–4 ■ Find the vertex, focus, and directrix of the parabola, and sketch the graph.

1. $x^2 + 8y = 0$

2. $2x - y^2 = 0$

3. $x - y^2 + 4y - 2 = 0$

4. $2x^2 + 6x + 5y + 10 = 0$

5–8 ■ Find the center, vertices, foci, and the lengths of the major and minor axes of the ellipse, and sketch the graph.

5. $x^2 + 4y^2 = 16$

6. $9x^2 + 4y^2 = 1$

7. $4x^2 + 9y^2 = 36y$

8. $2x^2 + y^2 = 2 + 4(x - y)$

9–12 ■ Find the center, vertices, foci, and asymptotes of the hyperbola, and sketch the graph.

9. $x^2 - 2y^2 = 16$

10. $x^2 - 4y^2 + 16 = 0$

11. $9y^2 + 18y = x^2 + 6x + 18$

12. $y^2 = x^2 + 6y$

13–18 ■ Find an equation for the conic whose graph is shown.

13.

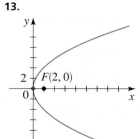

14.

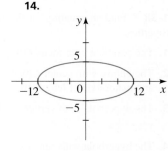

15.

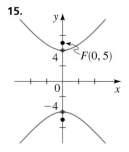

16.

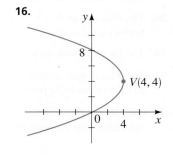

17.

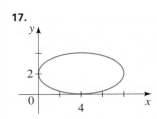

18.

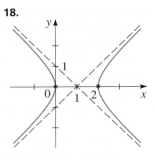

19–30 ■ Determine the type of curve represented by the equation. Find the foci and vertices (if any), and sketch the graph.

19. $\dfrac{x^2}{12} + y = 1$

20. $\dfrac{x^2}{12} + \dfrac{y^2}{144} = \dfrac{y}{12}$

21. $x^2 - y^2 + 144 = 0$

22. $x^2 + 6x = 9y^2$

23. $4x^2 + y^2 = 8(x + y)$

24. $3x^2 - 6(x + y) = 10$

25. $x = y^2 - 16y$

26. $2x^2 + 4 = 4x + y^2$

27. $2x^2 - 12x + y^2 + 6y + 26 = 0$

28. $36x^2 - 4y^2 - 36x - 8y = 31$

29. $9x^2 + 8y^2 - 15x + 8y + 27 = 0$

30. $x^2 + 4y^2 = 4x + 8$

31–38 ■ Find an equation for the conic section with the given properties.

31. The parabola with focus $F(0, 1)$ and directrix $y = -1$

32. The ellipse with center $C(0, 4)$, foci $F_1(0, 0)$ and $F_2(0, 8)$, and major axis of length 10

33. The hyperbola with vertices $V(0, \pm 2)$ and asymptotes $y = \pm\frac{1}{2}x$

34. The hyperbola with center $C(2, 4)$, foci $F_1(2, 1)$ and $F_2(2, 7)$, and vertices $V_1(2, 6)$ and $V_2(2, 2)$

35. The ellipse with foci $F_1(1, 1)$ and $F_2(1, 3)$, and with one vertex on the x-axis

36. The parabola with vertex $V(5, 5)$ and directrix the y-axis

37. The ellipse with vertices $V_1(7, 12)$ and $V_2(7, -8)$, and passing through the point $P(1, 8)$

38. The parabola with vertex $V(-1, 0)$ and horizontal axis of symmetry, and crossing the y-axis at $y = 2$

39. A cannon fires a cannonball as shown in the figure. The path of the cannonball is a parabola with vertex at the highest point of the path. If the cannonball lands 1600 ft from the cannon and the highest point it reaches is 3200 ft above the ground, find an equation for the path of the cannonball. Place the origin at the location of the cannon.

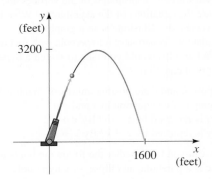

40. A satellite is in an elliptical orbit around the earth with the center of the earth at one focus. The height of the satellite above the earth varies between 140 mi and 440 mi. Assume the earth is a sphere with radius 3960 mi. Find an equation for the path of the satellite with the origin at the center of the earth.

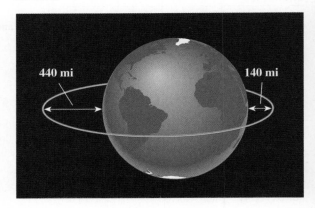

41. The path of the earth around the sun is an ellipse with the sun at one focus. The ellipse has major axis 186,000,000 mi and eccentricity 0.017. Find the distance between the earth and the sun when the earth is **(a)** closest to the sun and **(b)** farthest from the sun.

42. A ship is located 40 mi from a straight shoreline. LORAN stations A and B are located on the shoreline, 300 mi apart. From the LORAN signals, the captain determines that his ship is 80 mi closer to A than to B. Find the location of the ship. (Place A and B on the y-axis with the x-axis halfway between them. Find the x- and y-coordinates of the ship.)

43. 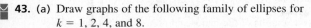 (a) Draw graphs of the following family of ellipses for $k = 1, 2, 4,$ and 8.

$$\frac{x^2}{16 + k^2} + \frac{y^2}{k^2} = 1$$

(b) Prove that all the ellipses in part (a) have the same foci.

44. (a) Draw graphs of the following family of parabolas for $k = \frac{1}{2}, 1, 2,$ and 4.

$$y = kx^2$$

(b) Find the foci of the parabolas in part (a).
(c) How does the location of the focus change as k increases?

45–48 ■ An equation of a conic is given.
(a) Use the discriminant to determine whether the graph of the equation is a parabola, an ellipse, or a hyperbola.
(b) Use a rotation of axes to eliminate the xy-term.
(c) Sketch the graph.

45. $x^2 + 4xy + y^2 = 1$

46. $5x^2 - 6xy + 5y^2 - 8x + 8y - 8 = 0$

47. $7x^2 - 6\sqrt{3}\,xy + 13y^2 - 4\sqrt{3}\,x - 4y = 0$

48. $9x^2 + 24xy + 16y^2 = 25$

49–52 ■ Use a graphing device to graph the conic. Identify the type of conic from the graph.

49. $5x^2 + 3y^2 = 60$ **50.** $9x^2 - 12y^2 + 36 = 0$

51. $6x + y^2 - 12y = 30$ **52.** $52x^2 - 72xy + 73y^2 = 100$

53–56 ■ A polar equation of a conic is given.
(a) Find the eccentricity and identify the conic.
(b) Sketch the conic and label the vertices.

53. $r = \dfrac{1}{1 - \cos \theta}$ **54.** $r = \dfrac{2}{1 + 2 \sin \theta}$

55. $r = \dfrac{4}{1 + 2 \sin \theta}$ **56.** $r = \dfrac{12}{1 - 4 \cos \theta}$

57–60 ■ A pair of parametric equations is given.
(a) Sketch the curve represented by the parametric equations.
(b) Find a rectangular-coordinate equation for the curve by eliminating the parameter.

57. $x = 1 - t^2, \quad y = 1 + t$

58. $x = t^2 - 1, \quad y = t^2 + 1$

59. $x = 1 + \cos t, \quad y = 1 - \sin t, \quad 0 \le t \le \pi/2$

60. $x = \dfrac{1}{t} + 2, \quad y = \dfrac{2}{t^2}, \quad 0 < t \le 2$

61–62 ■ Use a graphing device to draw the parametric curve.

61. $x = \cos 2t, \quad y = \sin 3t$

62. $x = \sin(t + \cos 2t), \quad y = \cos(t + \sin 3t)$

63. In the figure the point P is the midpoint of the segment QR and $0 \le \theta < \pi/2$. Using θ as the parameter, find a parametric representation for the curve traced out by P.

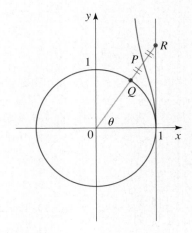

6 TEST

1. Find the focus and directrix of the parabola $x^2 = -12y$, and sketch its graph.

2. Find the vertices, foci, and the lengths of the major and minor axes for the ellipse $\dfrac{x^2}{16} + \dfrac{y^2}{4} = 1$. Then sketch its graph.

3. Find the vertices, foci, and asymptotes of the hyperbola $\dfrac{y^2}{9} - \dfrac{x^2}{16} = 1$. Then sketch its graph.

4–6 ■ Find an equation for the conic whose graph is shown.

4.

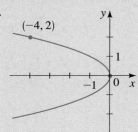

5.

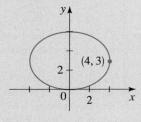

6.

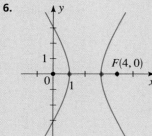

7–9 ■ Sketch the graph of the equation.

7. $16x^2 + 36y^2 - 96x + 36y + 9 = 0$

8. $9x^2 - 8y^2 + 36x + 64y = 164$

9. $2x + y^2 + 8y + 8 = 0$

10. Find an equation for the hyperbola with foci $(0, \pm 5)$ and with asymptotes $y = \pm \frac{3}{4}x$.

11. Find an equation for the parabola with focus $(2, 4)$ and directrix the x-axis.

12. A parabolic reflector for a car headlight forms a bowl shape that is 6 in. wide at its opening and 3 in. deep, as shown in the figure at the left. How far from the vertex should the filament of the bulb be placed if it is to be located at the focus?

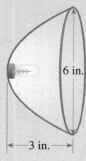

13. (a) Use the discriminant to determine whether the graph of this equation is a parabola, an ellipse, or a hyperbola:

$$5x^2 + 4xy + 2y^2 = 18$$

(b) Use rotation of axes to eliminate the xy-term in the equation.

(c) Sketch the graph of the equation.

(d) Find the coordinates of the vertices of this conic (in the xy-coordinate system).

14. (a) Find the polar equation of the conic that has a focus at the origin, eccentricity $e = \frac{1}{2}$, and directrix $x = 2$. Sketch the graph.

(b) What type of conic is represented by the following equation? Sketch its graph.

$$r = \frac{3}{2 - \sin \theta}$$

15. (a) Sketch the graph of the parametric curve

$$x = 3 \sin \theta + 3 \qquad y = 2 \cos \theta \qquad 0 \leqslant \theta \leqslant \pi$$

(b) Eliminate the parameter θ in part (a) to obtain an equation for this curve in rectangular coordinates.

Focus on Modeling
The Path of a Projectile

Modeling motion is one of the most important ideas in both classical and modern physics. Much of Isaac Newton's work dealt with creating a mathematical model for how objects move and interact—this was the main reason for his invention of calculus. Albert Einstein developed his Special Theory of Relativity in the early 1900s to refine Newton's laws of motion.

In this section we use coordinate geometry to model the motion of a projectile, such as a ball thrown upward into the air, a bullet fired from a gun, or any other sort of missile. A similar model was created by Galileo (see the margin), but we have the advantage of using our modern mathematical notation to make describing the model much easier than it was for Galileo!

Suppose that we fire a projectile into the air from ground level, with an initial speed v_0 and at an angle θ upward from the ground. The initial *velocity* of the projectile is a vector (see Section 5.5) with horizontal component $v_0 \cos \theta$ and vertical component $v_0 \sin \theta$, as shown in Figure 1.

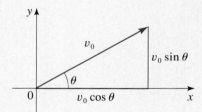

FIGURE 1

If there were no gravity (and no air resistance), the projectile would just keep moving indefinitely at the same speed and in the same direction. Since distance = speed × time, the projectile's position at time t would therefore be given by the following parametric equations (assuming the origin of our coordinate system is placed at the initial location of the projectile):

$$x = (v_0 \cos \theta)t \qquad y = (v_0 \sin \theta)t \qquad \text{No gravity}$$

But, of course, we know that gravity will pull the projectile back to ground level. Using calculus, it can be shown that the effect of gravity can be accounted for by subtracting $\frac{1}{2} gt^2$ from the vertical position of the projectile. In this expression, g is the gravitational acceleration: $g \approx 32 \text{ ft/s}^2 \approx 9.8 \text{ m/s}^2$.

Thus, we have the following parametric equations for the path of the projectile:

$$x = (v_0 \cos \theta)t \qquad y = (v_0 \sin \theta)t - \tfrac{1}{2}gt^2 \qquad \text{With gravity}$$

EXAMPLE ■ The Path of a Cannonball

Find parametric equations that model the path of a cannonball fired into the air with an initial speed of 150.0 m/s at a 30° angle of elevation. Sketch the path of the cannonball. How far from the cannon does the ball hit the ground, and for how long is it in the air?

SOLUTION

Substituting the given initial speed and angle into the general parametric equations of the path of a projectile, we get

$$x = (150.0 \cos 30°)t \qquad y = (150.0 \sin 30°)t - \tfrac{1}{2}(9.8)t^2 \qquad \text{Substitute } v_0 = 150.0, \theta = 30°$$

$$x = 129.9t \qquad y = 75.0t - 4.9t^2 \qquad \text{Simplify}$$

This path is graphed in Figure 2.

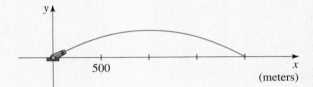

FIGURE 2
Path of a cannonball

How can we tell where and when the cannonball hits the ground? Since ground level corresponds to $y = 0$, we substitute this value for y and solve for t.

$$0 = 75.0t - 4.9t^2 \qquad \text{Set } y = 0$$

$$0 = t(75.0 - 4.9t) \qquad \text{Factor}$$

$$t = 0 \quad \text{or} \quad t = \frac{75.0}{4.9} \approx 15.3 \qquad \text{Solve for } t$$

The first solution, $t = 0$, is the time when the cannon was fired; the second solution means that the cannonball hits the ground after 15.3 s of flight. To see *where* this happens, we substitute this value into the equation for x, the horizontal location of the cannonball.

$$x = 129.9(15.3) \approx 1987.5 \text{ m}$$

The cannonball travels almost 2 km before hitting the ground.   ■

Galileo Galilei (1564–1642) was born in Pisa, Italy. He studied medicine, but later abandoned this in favor of science and mathematics. At the age of 25 he demonstrated that light objects fall at the same rate as heavier ones, by dropping cannonballs of various sizes from the Leaning Tower of Pisa. This contradicted the then-accepted view of Aristotle that heavier objects fall more quickly. He also showed that the distance an object falls is proportional to the square of the time it has been falling, and from this was able to prove that the path of a projectile is a parabola. Galileo constructed the first telescope, and using it, discovered the moons of Jupiter. His advocacy of the Copernican view that the earth revolves around the sun (rather than being stationary) led to his being called before the Inquisition. By then an old man, he was forced to recant his views, but he is said to have muttered under his breath "the earth nevertheless does move." Galileo revolutionized science by expressing scientific principles in the language of mathematics. He said, "The great book of nature is written in mathematical symbols."

Figure 3 shows the paths of several projectiles, all fired with the same initial speed but at different angles. From the graphs we see that if the firing angle is too high or too low, the projectile doesn't travel very far.

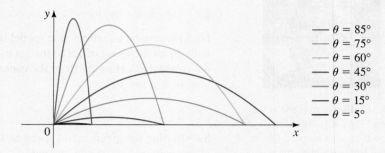

FIGURE 3
Paths of projectiles

Let's try to find the optimal firing angle—the angle that shoots the projectile as far as possible. We'll go through the same steps as we did in the preceding example, but we'll use the general parametric equations instead. First, we solve for the time when the projectile hits the ground by substituting $y = 0$.

$$0 = (v_0 \sin \theta)t - \tfrac{1}{2} gt^2 \qquad \text{Substitute } y = 0$$

$$0 = t(v_0 \sin \theta - \tfrac{1}{2} gt) \qquad \text{Factor}$$

$$0 = v_0 \sin \theta - \tfrac{1}{2} gt \qquad \text{Set second factor equal to 0}$$

$$t = \frac{2v_0 \sin \theta}{g} \qquad \text{Solve for } t$$

Now we substitute this into the equation for x to see how far the projectile has traveled horizontally when it hits the ground.

$$x = (v_0 \cos \theta)t \qquad \text{Parametric equation for } x$$

$$= (v_0 \cos \theta) \left(\frac{2v_0 \sin \theta}{g} \right) \qquad \text{Substitute } t = (2v_0 \sin \theta)/g$$

$$= \frac{2v_0^2 \sin \theta \cos \theta}{g} \qquad \text{Simplify}$$

$$= \frac{v_0^2 \sin 2\theta}{g} \qquad \text{Use identity } \sin 2\theta = 2 \sin \theta \cos \theta$$

We want to choose θ so that x is as large as possible. The largest value that the sine of any angle can have is 1, the sine of 90°. Thus, we want $2\theta = 90°$, or $\theta = 45°$. So to send the projectile as far as possible, it should be shot up at an angle of 45°. From the last equation in the preceding display, we can see that it will then travel a distance $x = v_0^2/g$.

Problems

1. From the graphs in Figure 3 the paths of projectiles appear to be parabolas that open downward. Eliminate the parameter t from the general parametric equations to verify that these are indeed parabolas.

2. Suppose a baseball is thrown at 30 ft/s at a 60° angle to the horizontal, from a height of 4 ft above the ground. Find parametric equations for the path of the baseball, and sketch its graph. How far does the baseball travel, and when does it hit the ground?

3. Suppose that a rocket is fired at an angle of 5° from the vertical, with an initial speed of 1000 ft/s.
  (a) Find the length of time the rocket is in the air.
  (b) Find the greatest height it reaches.
  (c) Find the horizontal distance it has traveled when it hits the ground.
  (d) Graph the rocket's path.

4. The initial speed of a missile is 330 m/s. At what angle should it be fired so that it hits a target 10 km away? You should find that there are two possible angles. Graph the missile paths for both angles. For which angle is the target hit sooner?

5. Find the maximum height reached by a projectile as a function of its initial speed v_0 and its firing angle θ.

6. Suppose that a projectile is fired into a headwind that pushes it back so as to reduce its horizontal speed by a constant amount w. Find parametric equations for the path of the projectile.

7. Using the parametric equations you derived in Problem 6, draw graphs of the path of a projectile with initial speed $v_0 = 32$ ft/s, fired into a headwind of $w = 24$ ft/s, for the angles $\theta = 5°, 15°, 30°, 40°, 45°, 55°, 60°,$ and 75°. Is it still true that the greatest range is attained when firing at 45°? Draw some more graphs for different angles, and use these graphs to estimate the optimal firing angle.

8. The path of a projectile can be simulated on a graphing calculator. On the TI-83 use the "Path" graph style to graph the general parametric equations for the path of a projectile and watch as the circular cursor moves, simulating the motion of the projectile. Selecting the size of the **Tstep** determines the speed of the "projectile."
  (a) Simulate the path of a projectile. Experiment with various values of θ. Use $v_0 = 10$ ft/s and **Tstep** = 0.02. Part (a) of the figure shows one such path.
  (b) Simulate the path of two projectiles, fired simultaneously, one at $\theta = 30°$ and the other at $\theta = 60°$. This can be done on the TI-83 using **Simul** mode ("simultaneous" mode). Use $v_0 = 10$ ft/s and **Tstep** = 0.02. See part (b) of the figure. Where do the projectiles land? Which lands first?
  (c) Simulate the path of a ball thrown straight up ($\theta = 90°$). Experiment with values of v_0 between 5 and 20 ft/s. Use the "Animate" graph style and **Tstep** = 0.02. Simulate the path of two balls thrown simultaneously at different speeds. To better distinguish the two balls, place them at different x-coordinates (for example, $x = 1$ and $x = 2$). See part (c) of the figure. How does doubling v_0 change the maximum height the ball reaches?

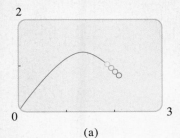

(a)

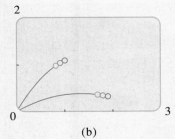

(b)

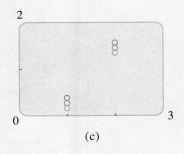

(c)

7

Exponential and Logarithmic Functions

Population growth—such as the growth of a herd of zebras in the wild—is modeled by exponential functions. These same functions describe such diverse phenomena as temperature change, compound interest, or the decay of radioisotopes such as those used in medical testing and treatment.

Mathematics compares the most diverse phenomena, and discovers the secret analogies which unite them.

JOSEPH FOURIER

So far we have studied relatively simple functions such as polynomial and rational functions. We now turn our attention to two of the most important functions in mathematics, the *exponential function* and its inverse function, the *logarithmic function*. We use these functions to describe exponential growth in biology and economics and radioactive decay in physics and chemistry, and other phenomena.

7.1 EXPONENTIAL FUNCTIONS

We know what a^x means if $a > 0$ and x is rational (see Appendix A.2). But what does a^x mean when x is irrational? For instance, what does $2^{\sqrt{3}}$ or 5^{π} mean? To help us answer these questions, we first look at the graph of the function $f(x) = 2^x$, where x is rational. A very crude representation of this graph is shown in Figure 1(a). The graph has a hole wherever x is irrational, and we want to fill in these holes with a smooth curve. To do this, we must define irrational powers of 2 appropriately. For example, to define $2^{\sqrt{3}}$ we use rational approximations of $\sqrt{3}$. Since

$$\sqrt{3} \approx 1.73205 \ldots$$

we successively approximate $2^{\sqrt{3}}$ by the following rational powers:

$$2^{1.7}, \quad 2^{1.73}, \quad 2^{1.732}, \quad 2^{1.7320}, \quad 2^{1.73205}, \ldots$$

Using advanced mathematics, it can be shown that there is exactly one number that these powers approach. We define $2^{\sqrt{3}}$ to be this number. Intuitively, these rational powers of 2 are getting closer and closer to $2^{\sqrt{3}}$. By this process we can approximate $2^{\sqrt{3}}$ to as many decimal places as we want:

$$2^{\sqrt{3}} \approx 3.321997 \ldots$$

Similarly, we can define 2^x (or a^x if $a > 0$) where x is any irrational number.

Using this definition of irrational powers, we can graph $f(x) = 2^x$ on all of $\mathbb{R}$, as shown in Figure 1(b). It is an increasing function and, in fact, it increases very rapidly when $x > 0$ (see the margin note).

To demonstrate just how quickly $f(x) = 2^x$ increases, let's perform the following thought experiment. Suppose we start with a piece of paper a thousandth of an inch thick, and we fold it in half 50 times. Each time we fold the paper, the thickness of the paper stack doubles, so the thickness of the resulting stack would be $2^{50}/1000$ inches. How thick do you think that is? It works out to be more than 17 million miles!

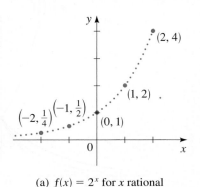

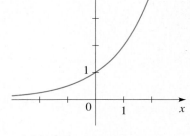

FIGURE 1   (a) $f(x) = 2^x$ for x rational   (b) $f(x) = 2^x$ for x real

It can be proved that *the Laws of Exponents are still true when the exponents are real numbers.*

EXAMPLE 1 ■ Graphing Exponential Functions by Plotting Points

Draw the graph of each function.

(a) $f(x) = 3^x$
(b) $g(x) = \left(\dfrac{1}{3}\right)^x$

SOLUTION

We calculate values of $f(x)$ and $g(x)$ and plot points to sketch the graphs in Figure 2.

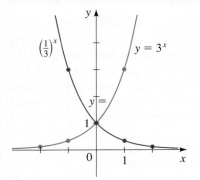

FIGURE 2

x	$f(x) = 3^x$	$g(x) = \left(\frac{1}{3}\right)^x$
-3	$\frac{1}{27}$	27
-2	$\frac{1}{9}$	9
-1	$\frac{1}{3}$	3
0	1	1
1	3	$\frac{1}{3}$
2	9	$\frac{1}{9}$
3	27	$\frac{1}{27}$

Notice that

$$g(x) = \left(\frac{1}{3}\right)^x = \frac{1}{3^x} = 3^{-x} = f(-x)$$

Reflecting graphs is explained in Section 1.5.

and so we could have obtained the graph of g from the graph of f by reflecting in the y-axis.   ■

Figure 3 shows the graphs of the family of exponential functions $f(x) = a^x$ for various values of the base a. All of these graphs pass through the point $(0, 1)$

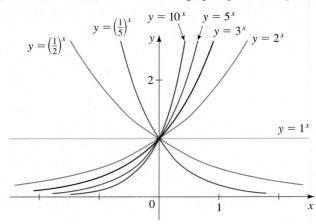

FIGURE 3

A family of exponential functions

because $a^0 = 1$ for $a \neq 0$. You can see from Figure 3 that there are three kinds of exponential functions $y = a^x$: If $0 < a < 1$, the exponential function decreases rapidly. If $a = 1$, it is constant. If $a > 1$, the function increases rapidly, and the larger the base, the more rapid the increase.

If $a > 1$, then the graph of $y = a^x$ approaches $y = 0$ as x decreases through negative values, and so the x-axis is a *horizontal asymptote* (that is, a line that the graph of the function gets close to). If $0 < a < 1$, the graph approaches $y = 0$ as x increases indefinitely and, again, the x-axis is a horizontal asymptote. In either case the graph never touches the x-axis because $a^x > 0$ for all x. Thus, for $a \neq 1$, the exponential function $f(x) = a^x$ has domain $\mathbb{R}$ and range $(0, \infty)$. Let's summarize the preceding discussion.

The **Gateway Arch** in St. Louis, Missouri, is shaped in the form of the graph of a combination of exponential functions (*not* a parabola, as it might first appear). Specifically, it is a **catenary**, which is the graph of an equation of the form

$$y = a(e^{bx} + e^{-bx})$$

(see Exercise 65). This shape was chosen because it is optimal for distributing the internal structural forces of the arch. Chains and cables suspended between two points (for example, the stretches of cable between pairs of telephone poles) hang in the shape of a catenary.

EXPONENTIAL FUNCTIONS

For $a > 0$, the **exponential function with base a** is defined by

$$f(x) = a^x$$

For $a \neq 1$, the domain of f is $\mathbb{R}$, the range of f is $(0, \infty)$, and the graph of f has one of the following shapes:

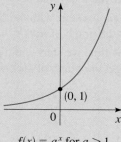

$f(x) = a^x$ for $a > 1$ $f(x) = a^x$ for $0 < a < 1$

The x-axis is a horizontal asymptote of the graph.

EXAMPLE 2 ■ Identifying Graphs of Exponential Functions

Find the exponential function $f(x) = a^x$ whose graph is given.

(a)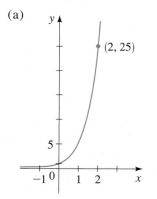

(b)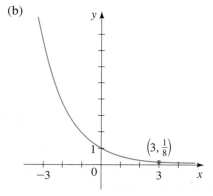

SOLUTION

(a) Since $f(2) = a^2 = 25$, we see by inspection that the base is $a = 5$. So $f(x) = 5^x$.

(b) Since $f(3) = a^3 = \frac{1}{8}$, we see by inspection that the base is $a = \frac{1}{2}$. So $f(x) = \left(\frac{1}{2}\right)^x$.   ∎

In the next two examples we see how to graph certain functions, not by plotting points, but by taking the basic graphs of the exponential functions in Figure 3 and applying the shifting and reflecting transformations of Section 1.5.

EXAMPLE 3 ■ **Transformations of Exponential Functions**

Use the graph $f(x) = 2^x$ to sketch the graph of each function.

(a) $g(x) = 1 + 2^x$ (b) $h(x) = -2^x$ (c) $k(x) = 2^{x-1}$

SOLUTION

Shifting and reflecting of graphs is explained in Section 1.5.

(a) To obtain the graph of $g(x) = 1 + 2^x$, we start with the graph of $f(x) = 2^x$ and shift it upward 1 unit. Notice from Figure 4(a) that the line $y = 1$ is now a horizontal asymptote.

(b) Again we start with the graph of $f(x) = 2^x$, but here we reflect in the x-axis to get the graph of $h(x) = -2^x$ shown in Figure 4(b).

(c) This time we start with the graph of $f(x) = 2^x$ and shift it to the right by 1 unit, to get the graph of $k(x) = 2^{x-1}$ shown in Figure 4(c).

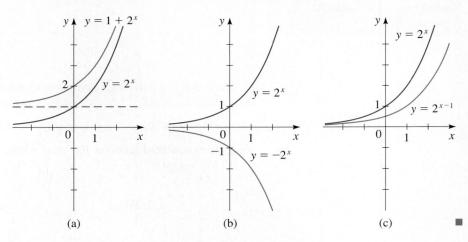

FIGURE 4   (a)   (b)   (c)   ∎

EXAMPLE 4 ■ **Comparing Exponential and Power Functions**

Compare the rates of growth of the exponential function $f(x) = 2^x$ and the power function $g(x) = x^2$ by drawing the graphs of both functions in the following viewing rectangles.

(a) $[0, 3]$ by $[0, 8]$ (b) $[0, 6]$ by $[0, 25]$ (c) $[0, 20]$ by $[0, 1000]$

SOLUTION

(a) Figure 5(a) shows that the graph of $g(x) = x^2$ catches up with, and becomes higher than, the graph of $f(x) = 2^x$ at $x = 2$.

(b) The larger viewing rectangle in Figure 5(b) shows that the graph of $f(x) = 2^x$ overtakes that of $g(x) = x^2$ when $x = 4$.

(c) Figure 5(c) gives a more global view and shows that, when x is large, $f(x) = 2^x$ is much larger than $g(x) = x^2$.

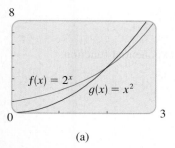

(a)

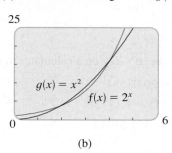

(b)

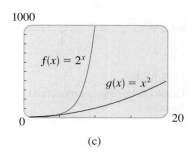

(c)

FIGURE 5

The Natural Exponential Function

Any positive number can be used as the base for an exponential function, but some bases are used more frequently than others. We will see in the remaining sections of this chapter that the bases 2 and 10 are convenient for certain applications, but the most important base is the number denoted by the letter e.

n	$\left(1 + \dfrac{1}{n}\right)^n$
1	2.00000
5	2.48832
10	2.59374
100	2.70481
1000	2.71692
10,000	2.71815
100,000	2.71827
1,000,000	2.71828
10,000,000	2.71828

The number e is defined as the value that $(1 + 1/n)^n$ approaches as n becomes large. (In calculus this idea is made more precise through the concept of a limit. See Exercise 63.) The table in the margin shows the values of the expression $(1 + 1/n)^n$ for increasingly large values of n. It appears that, correct to five decimal places, $e \approx 2.71828$; in fact, the approximate value to 20 decimal places is

$$e \approx 2.71828182845904523536$$

It can be shown that e is an irrational number, so we cannot write its exact value.

Why use such a strange base for an exponential function? It may seem at first that a base such as 10 is easier to work with. We will see, however, that in certain applications the number e is the best possible base. In this section we study how e occurs in the description of compound interest and population growth.

The notation e for the base of the natural exponential function was chosen by the Swiss mathematician Leonhard Euler (see page 323), probably because it is the first letter of the word *exponential*.

THE NATURAL EXPONENTIAL FUNCTION

The **natural exponential function** is the exponential function

$$f(x) = e^x$$

with base e. It is often referred to as *the* exponential function.

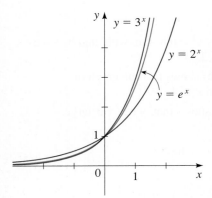

FIGURE 6

Graph of the natural exponential function

Since $2 < e < 3$, the graph of the natural exponential function lies between the graphs of $y = 2^x$ and $y = 3^x$, as shown in Figure 6.

Scientific calculators have a special key for the function $f(x) = e^x$. We use this key in the next example.

EXAMPLE 5 ■ **Evaluating the Exponential Function**

Evaluate each expression correct to five decimal places.

(a) e^3 (b) $2e^{-0.53}$ (c) $e^{4.8}$

SOLUTION

We use the $\boxed{e^x}$ key on a calculator to evaluate the exponential function.

(a) $e^3 \approx 20.08554$

(b) $2e^{-0.53} \approx 1.17721$

(c) $e^{4.8} \approx 121.51042$ ■

EXAMPLE 6 ■ **Transformations of the Exponential Function**

Sketch the graph of each function.

(a) $f(x) = e^{-x}$ (b) $g(x) = 3e^{0.5x}$

SOLUTION

Reflecting graphs is explained in Section 1.5.

(a) We start with the graph of $y = e^x$ and reflect in the y-axis to obtain the graph of $y = e^{-x}$ as in Figure 7.

(b) We calculate several values, plot the resulting points, then connect the points with a smooth curve. The graph is shown in Figure 8.

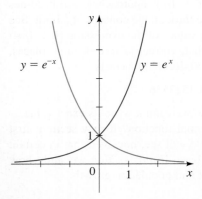

FIGURE 7

x	$f(x) = 3e^{0.5x}$
-3	0.67
-2	1.10
-1	1.82
0	3.00
1	4.95
2	8.15
3	13.45

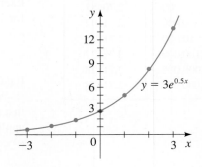

FIGURE 8   ■

EXAMPLE 7 ■ **An Exponential Model for the Spread of a Virus**

An infectious disease begins to spread in a small city of population 10,000. After t days, the number of persons who have succumbed to the virus is modeled by the function

$$v(t) = \frac{10,000}{5 + 1245e^{-0.97t}}$$

(a) How many infected people are there initially (at time $t = 0$)?

(b) Determine the number of infected people after one day, two days, and five days.

(c) Graph the function v and describe its behavior.

SOLUTION

(a) Since $v(0) = 10,000/(5 + 1245e^0) = 10,000/1250 = 8$, we conclude that 8 people initially have the disease.

(b) Using a calculator, we evaluate $v(1)$, $v(2)$, and $v(5)$, and then round off to obtain the following values.

Days	Infected people
1	21
2	54
5	678

(c) From the graph in Figure 9, we see that the number of infected people first rises slowly; then between day 3 and day 8 rises quickly, and then levels off when about 2000 people are infected. ∎

3000

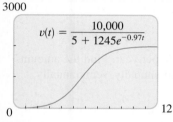

0   12

FIGURE 9

The graph in Figure 9 is called a *logistic curve* or a *logistic growth model*. Curves like it occur frequently in the study of population growth. (See Exercises 47 and 48.)

Compound Interest

Exponential functions occur in calculating compound interest. If an amount of money P, called the **principal**, is invested at an interest rate i per time period, then after one time period the interest is Pi, and the amount A of money is

$$A = P + Pi = P(1 + i)$$

If the interest is reinvested, then the new principal is $P(1 + i)$, and the amount after another time period is $A = P(1 + i)(1 + i) = P(1 + i)^2$. Similarly, after a third time period the amount is $A = P(1 + i)^3$. In general, after k periods the amount is

$$A = P(1 + i)^k$$

Notice that this is an exponential function with base $1 + i$.

If the annual interest rate is r and if interest is compounded n times per year, then in each time period the interest rate is $i = r/n$, and there are nt time periods in t years. This leads to the following formula for the amount after t years.

COMPOUND INTEREST

Compound interest is calculated by the formula

$$A(t) = P\left(1 + \frac{r}{n}\right)^{nt}$$

where $A(t)$ = amount after t years

P = principal

r is often referred to as the nominal annual interest rate.

r = interest rate per year

n = number of times interest is compounded per year

t = number of years

EXAMPLE 8 ■ Calculating Compound Interest

A sum of \$1000 is invested at an interest rate of 12% per year. Find the amounts in the account after 3 years if interest is compounded annually, semiannually, quarterly, monthly, and daily.

SOLUTION

We use the compound interest formula with $P = \$1000$, $r = 0.12$, and $t = 3$.

Compounding	n	Amount after 3 years	
Annual	1	$1000\left(1 + \dfrac{0.12}{1}\right)^{1(3)}$	$= \$1404.93$
Semiannual	2	$1000\left(1 + \dfrac{0.12}{2}\right)^{2(3)}$	$= \$1418.52$
Quarterly	4	$1000\left(1 + \dfrac{0.12}{4}\right)^{4(3)}$	$= \$1425.76$
Monthly	12	$1000\left(1 + \dfrac{0.12}{12}\right)^{12(3)}$	$= \$1430.77$
Daily	365	$1000\left(1 + \dfrac{0.12}{365}\right)^{365(3)}$	$= \$1433.24$

We see from Example 8 that the interest paid increases as the number of compounding periods n increases. Let's see what happens as n increases indefinitely. If we let $m = n/r$, then

$$A(t) = P\left(1 + \frac{r}{n}\right)^{nt} = P\left[\left(1 + \frac{r}{n}\right)^{n/r}\right]^{rt} = P\left[\left(1 + \frac{1}{m}\right)^{m}\right]^{rt}$$

Recall that as m becomes large, the quantity $(1 + 1/m)^m$ approaches the number e. Thus, the amount approaches $A = Pe^{rt}$. This expression gives the amount when the interest is compounded at "every instant."

CONTINUOUSLY COMPOUNDED INTEREST

Continuously compounded interest is calculated by the formula

$$A(t) = Pe^{rt}$$

where $A(t)$ = amount after t years

P = principal

r = interest rate per year

t = number of years

EXAMPLE 9 ■ Calculating Continuously Compounded Interest

Find the amount after 3 years if $1000 is invested at an interest rate of 12% per year, compounded continuously.

SOLUTION

We use the formula for continuously compounded interest with $P = \$1000$, $r = 0.12$, and $t = 3$ to get

$$A(3) = 1000e^{(0.12)3} = 1000e^{0.36} = \$1433.33$$

Compare this amount with the amounts in Example 8.   ■

7.1 EXERCISES

1–6 ■ Sketch the graph of the function by making a table of values. Use a calculator if necessary.

1. $f(x) = 2^x$

2. $g(x) = 8^x$

3. $f(x) = \left(\frac{1}{3}\right)^x$

4. $h(x) = (1.1)^x$

5. $g(x) = 3e^x$

6. $h(x) = 2e^{-0.5x}$

7–8 ■ Graph both functions on one set of axes.

7. $y = 4^x$ and $y = 7^x$

8. $y = \left(\frac{2}{3}\right)^x$ and $y = \left(\frac{4}{3}\right)^x$

9–12 ■ Find the exponential function $f(x) = a^x$ whose graph is given.

9.

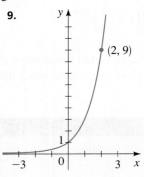

$(2, 9)$

10.

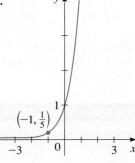

$\left(-1, \frac{1}{5}\right)$

11.

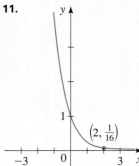

$\left(2, \frac{1}{16}\right)$

12.

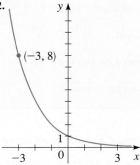

$(-3, 8)$

13–18 ■ Match the exponential function with one of the graphs labeled I–VI.

13. $f(x) = 5^x$ **14.** $f(x) = -5^x$

15. $f(x) = 5^{-x}$ **16.** $f(x) = 5^x + 3$

17. $f(x) = 5^{x-3}$ **18.** $f(x) = 5^{x+1} - 4$

I

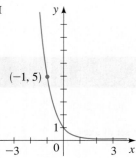

$(-1, 5)$

II

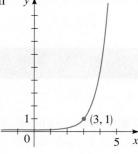

$(3, 1)$

III

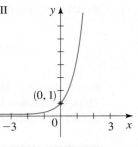

$(0, 1)$

IV

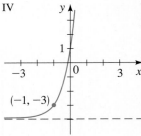

$(-1, -3)$

V

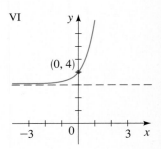

$(0, -1)$

VI

$(0, 4)$

19–32 ■ Graph the function, not by plotting points, but by starting from the graphs in Figures 3 and 6. State the domain, range, and asymptote.

19. $f(x) = -3^x$

20. $f(x) = 10^{-x}$

21. $g(x) = 2^x - 3$

22. $g(x) = 2^{x-3}$

23. $h(x) = 4 + \left(\frac{1}{2}\right)^x$

24. $h(x) = 6 - 3^x$

25. $f(x) = 10^{x+3}$

26. $f(x) = -\left(\frac{1}{5}\right)^x$

27. $f(x) = -e^x$

28. $y = 1 - e^x$

29. $y = e^{-x} - 1$

30. $f(x) = -e^{-x}$

31. $f(x) = e^{x-2}$

32. $y = e^{x-3} + 4$

33–34 ■ Find the function of the form $f(x) = Ca^x$ whose graph is given.

33.

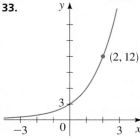

(2, 12)

34.

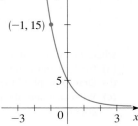

(−1, 15)

5

35. (a) Sketch the graphs of $f(x) = 2^x$ and $g(x) = 3(2^x)$.
(b) How are the graphs related?

36. (a) Sketch the graphs of $f(x) = 9^{x/2}$ and $g(x) = 3^x$.
(b) Use the Laws of Exponents to explain the relationship between these graphs.

37. If $f(x) = 10^x$, show that

$$\frac{f(x + h) - f(x)}{h} = 10^x\left(\frac{10^h - 1}{h}\right)$$

38. Compare the functions $f(x) = x^3$ and $g(x) = 3^x$ by evaluating both of them for $x = 0, 1, 2, 3, 4, 5, 6, 7, 8, 9, 10, 15,$ and 20. Then draw the graphs of f and g on the same set of axes.

39. (a) Compare the rates of growth of the functions $f(x) = 2^x$ and $g(x) = x^5$ by drawing the graphs of both functions in the following viewing rectangles.
   (i) $[0, 5]$ by $[0, 20]$
   (ii) $[0, 25]$ by $[0, 10^7]$
   (iii) $[0, 50]$ by $[0, 10^8]$
(b) Find the solutions of the equation $2^x = x^5$, correct to one decimal place.

40. (a) Compare the rates of growth of the functions $f(x) = 3^x$ and $g(x) = x^4$ by drawing the graphs of both functions in the following viewing rectangles:
   (i) $[-4, 4]$ by $[0, 20]$
   (ii) $[0, 10]$ by $[0, 5000]$
   (iii) $[0, 20]$ by $[0, 10^5]$
(b) Find the solutions of the equation $3^x = x^4$, correct to two decimal places.

41–42 ■ Draw graphs of the given family of functions for $c = 0.25, 0.5, 1, 2, 4$. How are the graphs related?

41. $f(x) = c2^x$

42. $f(x) = 2^{cx}$

43. A radioactive substance decays in such a way that the amount of mass remaining after t days is given by the function

$$m(t) = 13e^{-0.015t}$$

where $m(t)$ is measured in kilograms.
(a) Find the mass at time $t = 0$.
(b) How much of the mass remains after 45 days?

44. Radioactive iodine is used by doctors as a tracer in diagnosing certain thyroid gland disorders. This type of iodine decays in such a way that the mass remaining after t days is given by the function

$$m(t) = 6e^{-0.087t}$$

where $m(t)$ is measured in grams.
(a) Find the mass at time $t = 0$.
(b) How much of the mass remains after 20 days?

45. A sky diver jumps from a reasonable height above the ground. The air resistance she experiences is proportional to her velocity, and the constant of proportionality is 0.2. It can be shown that the downward velocity of the sky diver at time t is given by

$$v(t) = 80(1 - e^{-0.2t})$$

where t is measured in seconds and $v(t)$ is measured in feet per second (ft/s).
(a) Find the initial velocity of the sky diver.
(b) Find the velocity after 5 s and after 10 s.
(c) Draw a graph of the velocity function $v(t)$.
(d) The maximum velocity of a falling object with wind resistance is called its *terminal velocity*. From the graph in part (c) find the terminal velocity of this sky diver.

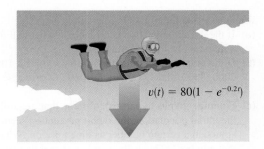

$v(t) = 80(1 - e^{-0.2t})$

46. A 50-gallon barrel is filled completely with pure water. Salt water with a concentration of 0.3 lb/gal is then pumped into the barrel, and the resulting mixture overflows at the same rate. The amount of salt in the barrel at time t is given by

$$Q(t) = 15(1 - e^{-0.04t})$$

where t is measured in minutes and $Q(t)$ is measured in pounds.
(a) How much salt is in the barrel after 5 min?
(b) How much salt is in the barrel after 10 min?
(c) Draw a graph of the function $Q(t)$.
(d) Use the graph in part (c) to determine the value that the amount of salt in the barrel approaches as t becomes large. Is this what you would expect?

$$Q(t) = 15(1 - e^{-0.04t})$$

47. Assume that a population of rabbits behaves according to the *logistic growth model*

$$n(t) = \frac{300}{0.05 + \left(\dfrac{300}{n_0} - 0.05\right)e^{-0.55t}}$$

where n_0 is the initial rabbit population.
(a) If the initial population is 50 rabbits, what will the population be after 12 years?
(b) Draw graphs of the function $n(t)$ for $n_0 = 50, 500, 2000, 8000$, and $12{,}000$ in the viewing rectangle $[0, 15]$ by $[0, 12{,}000]$.
(c) From the graphs in part (b), observe that, regardless of the initial population, the rabbit population seems to approach a certain number as time goes on. What is that number? (This is the number of rabbits that the island can support.)

48. The population of a certain species of bird is limited by the type of habitat required for nesting. The population behaves according to the *logistic growth model*

$$n(t) = \frac{5600}{0.5 + 27.5e^{-0.044t}}$$

where t is measured in years.
(a) Find the initial bird population.
(b) Draw a graph of the function $n(t)$.
(c) What size does the population approach as time goes on?

49. If $10,000 is invested at an interest rate of 10% per year, compounded semiannually, find the value of the investment after the given number of years.
(a) 5 years   (b) 10 years   (c) 15 years

50. If $4000 is borrowed at a rate of 16% interest per year, compounded quarterly, find the amount due at the end of the given number of years.
(a) 4 years   (b) 6 years   (c) 8 years

51. If $3000 is invested at an interest rate of 9% per year, find the amount of the investment at the end of 5 years for the following compounding methods.
(a) Annual   (b) Semiannual
(c) Monthly   (d) Weekly
(e) Daily   (f) Hourly
(g) Continuously

52. If $4000 is invested in an account for which interest is compounded quarterly, find the amount of the investment at the end of 5 years for the following interest rates.
(a) 6%   (b) $6\frac{1}{2}$%   (c) 7%   (d) 8%

53. Which of the given interest rates and compounding periods would provide the best investment?
(i) $8\frac{1}{2}$% per year, compounded semiannually
(ii) $8\frac{1}{4}$% per year, compounded quarterly
(iii) 8% per year, compounded continuously

54. Which of the given interest rates and compounding periods would provide the better investment?
(i) $9\frac{1}{4}$% per year, compounded semiannually
(ii) 9% per year, compounded continuously

55. The **present value** of a sum of money is the amount that must be invested now, at a given rate of interest, to produce the desired sum at a later date.
(a) Find the present value of $10,000 if interest is paid at a rate of 9% per year, compounded semiannually, for 3 years.

(b) Find the present value of $100,000 if interest is paid at a rate of 8% per year, compounded monthly, for 5 years.

56. A sum of $5000 is invested at an interest rate of 9% per year, compounded semiannually.
(a) Find the value $A(t)$ of the investment after t years.
(b) Draw a graph of $A(t)$.
(c) Use the graph of $A(t)$ to determine when this investment will amount to $25,000.

57. The *hyperbolic cosine function* is defined by

$$\cosh(x) = \frac{e^x + e^{-x}}{2}$$

Sketch the graphs of the functions $y = \frac{1}{2}e^x$ and $y = \frac{1}{2}e^{-x}$ on the same axes and use graphical addition (see Section 1.6) to sketch the graph of $y = \cosh(x)$.

58. The *hyperbolic sine function* is defined by

$$\sinh(x) = \frac{e^x - e^{-x}}{2}$$

Sketch the graph of this function using graphical addition as in Exercise 57.

59–62 ■ Use the definitions in Exercises 57 and 58 to prove the identity.

59. $\cosh(-x) = \cosh(x)$

60. $\sinh(-x) = -\sinh(x)$

61. $[\cosh(x)]^2 - [\sinh(x)]^2 = 1$

62. $\sinh(x + y) = \sinh(x)\cosh(y) + \cosh(x)\sinh(y)$

63. Illustrate the definition of the number e by graphing the curve $y = (1 + 1/x)^x$ and the line $y = e$ on the same screen using the viewing rectangle $[0, 40]$ by $[0, 4]$.

64. Investigate the behavior of the function

$$f(x) = \left(1 - \frac{1}{x}\right)^x$$

as $x \to \infty$ by graphing f and the line $y = 1/e$ on the same screen using the viewing rectangle $[0, 20]$ by $[0, 1]$.

65. (a) Draw the graphs of the family of functions

$$f(x) = \frac{a}{2}(e^{x/a} + e^{-x/a})$$

for $a = 0.5, 1, 1.5,$ and 2.
(b) How does a larger value of a affect the graph?

 **66–67** ■ Graph the function and comment on vertical and horizontal asymptotes.

66. $y = 2^{1/x}$

67. $y = \dfrac{e^x}{x}$

68–69 ■ Find the local maximum and minimum values of the function and the value of x at which each occurs. State each answer correct to two decimal places.

68. $g(x) = x^x$ $(x > 0)$

69. $g(x) = e^x + e^{-3x}$

70–71 ■ Find, correct to two decimal places, (a) the intervals on which the function is increasing or decreasing, and (b) the range of the function.

70. $y = 10^{x-x^2}$

71. $y = xe^{-x}$

● **DISCOVERY · DISCUSSION**

72. Growth of an Exponential Function Suppose you are offered a job that lasts one month, and you are to be very well paid. Which of the following methods of payment is more profitable for you?
(a) One million dollars at the end of the month
(b) Two cents on the first day of the month, 4 cents on the second day, 8 cents on the third day, and, in general, 2^n cents on the nth day

73. The Height of the Graph of an Exponential Function Your mathematics instructor asks you to sketch a graph of the exponential function

$$f(x) = 2^x$$

for x between 0 and 40, using a scale of 10 units to one inch. What are the dimensions of the sheet of paper you will need to sketch this graph?

Discovery Project

Exponential Explosion

To see how difficult it is to comprehend exponential growth, let's try a thought experiment.

Suppose you put a penny in your piggy bank today, two pennies tomorrow, four pennies the next day, and so on, doubling the number of pennies you add to the bank each day (see the table). How many pennies will you put in your piggy bank on day 30? The answer is 2^{30} pennies. That's simple, but can you guess how many dollars that is? 2^{30} pennies is more than 10 million dollars!

Day	Pennies
0	1
1	2
2	4
3	8
4	16
.	.
.	.
.	.
n	2^n
.	.
.	.
.	.

As you can see, the exponential function $f(x) = 2^x$ grows extremely fast. This is the principle behind atomic explosions. An atom splits releasing two neutrons which cause two atoms to split, each releasing two neutrons, causing four atoms to split, and so on. At the nth stage 2^n atoms split—an exponential explosion!

As we know, populations grow exponentially. Let's see what this means for a type of bacteria that splits every minute. Suppose that at 12:00 noon a single bacterium colonizes a discarded food can. The bacterium and his descendants are all happy, but they fear the time when the can is completely full of bacteria—doomsday.

1. How many bacteria are in the can at 12:05? at 12:10?

2. The can is completely full of bacteria at 1:00 P.M. At what time was the can only half full of bacteria?

3. When the can is exactly half full, the president of the bacteria colony reassures his constituents that doomsday is far away—after all, there is as much room left in the can as has been used in the entire previous history of the colony. Is the president correct? How much time is left before doomsday?

4. When the can is one-quarter full, how much time remains till doomsday?

5. A wise bacterium decides to start a new colony in another can and slow down splitting time to 2 minutes. How much time does this new colony have?

7.2 LOGARITHMIC FUNCTIONS

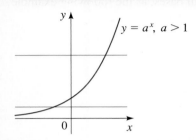

FIGURE 1
$f(x) = a^x$ is one-to-one

We read $\log_a x = y$ as "log base a of x is y."

Every exponential function $f(x) = a^x$, with $a > 0$ and $a \neq 1$, is a one-to-one function by the Horizontal Line Test (see Figure 1 for the case $a > 1$) and therefore has an inverse function. The inverse function f^{-1} is called the *logarithmic function with base a* and is denoted by $\log_a$. Recall from Section 1.7 that f^{-1} is defined by

$$f^{-1}(x) = y \quad \Leftrightarrow \quad f(y) = x$$

This leads to the following definition of the logarithmic function.

DEFINITION OF THE LOGARITHMIC FUNCTION

Let a be a positive number with $a \neq 1$. The **logarithmic function with base a**, denoted by **$\log_a$**, is defined by

$$\log_a x = y \quad \Leftrightarrow \quad a^y = x$$

In words, this says that

$\log_a x$ is the exponent to which the base a must be raised to give x.

By tradition, the name of the logarithmic function is $\log_a$, not just a single letter. Also, we usually omit the parentheses in the function notation and write

$$\log_a(x) = \log_a x$$

When we use the definition of logarithms to switch back and forth between the **logarithmic form** $\log_a x = y$ and the **exponential form** $a^y = x$, it's helpful to notice that, in both forms, the base is the same:

Logarithmic form	Exponential form
exponent	exponent
↓	↓
$\log_a x = y$	$a^y = x$
↑	↑
base	base

The following examples illustrate how to change an equation from one of these forms to the other.

EXAMPLE 1 ■ Logarithmic and Exponential Forms

The logarithmic and exponential forms are equivalent equations—if one is true, then so is the other. So, we can switch from one form to the other as in the following illustrations.

Logarithmic form	Exponential form
$\log_{10} 100{,}000 = 5$	$10^5 = 100{,}000$
$\log_2 8 = 3$	$2^3 = 8$
$\log_2\left(\frac{1}{8}\right) = -3$	$2^{-3} = \frac{1}{8}$
$\log_5 s = r$	$5^r = s$

■

x	$\log_{10} x$
10^4	4
10^3	3
10^2	2
10	1
1	0
10^{-1}	-1
10^{-2}	-2
10^{-3}	-3
10^{-4}	-4

It's important to understand that $\log_a x$ is an *exponent*. For example, the numbers in the right column of the table in the margin are the logarithms (base 10) of the numbers in the left column. This is the case for all bases, as the following example illustrates.

EXAMPLE 2 ■ Evaluating Logarithms

(a) $\log_{10} 1000 = 3$ because $10^3 = 1000$
(b) $\log_2 32 = 5$ because $2^5 = 32$
(c) $\log_{10} 0.1 = -1$ because $10^{-1} = 0.1$
(d) $\log_{16} 4 = \frac{1}{2}$ because $16^{1/2} = 4$ ■

■ Graphs of Logarithmic Functions

Recall that if a one-to-one function f has domain A and range B, then its inverse function f^{-1} has domain B and range A. Since the exponential function $f(x) = a^x$ with $a \neq 1$ has domain $\mathbb{R}$ and range $(0, \infty)$, we conclude that its inverse function, $f^{-1}(x) = \log_a x$, has domain $(0, \infty)$ and range $\mathbb{R}$.

The graph of $f^{-1}(x) = \log_a x$ is obtained by reflecting the graph of $f(x) = a^x$ in the line $y = x$. Figure 2 shows the case $a > 1$. The fact that $y = a^x$ (for $a > 1$) is a very rapidly increasing function for $x > 0$ implies that $y = \log_a x$ is a very slowly increasing function for $x > 1$ (see Exercise 76).

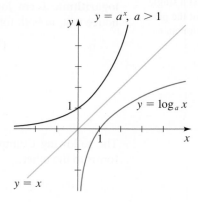

FIGURE 2

Graph of the logarithmic function
$f(x) = \log_a x$

Notice that since $a^0 = 1$, we have

$$\log_a 1 = 0$$

and so the x-intercept of the function $y = \log_a x$ is 1. Notice also that because the x-axis is a horizontal asymptote of $y = a^x$, the y-axis is a *vertical asymptote* of $y = \log_a x$. (Recall that an asymptote is a line that the graph of a function approaches.)

EXAMPLE 3 ■ **Graphing a Logarithmic Function by Plotting Points**

Sketch the graph of $f(x) = \log_2 x$.

SOLUTION

To make a table of values, we choose the x-values to be powers of 2 so that we can easily find their logarithms. We plot these points and connect them with a smooth curve as in Figure 3.

x	$\log_2 x$
2^4	4
2^3	3
2^2	2
2	1
1	0
2^{-1}	-1
2^{-2}	-2
2^{-3}	-3
2^{-4}	-4

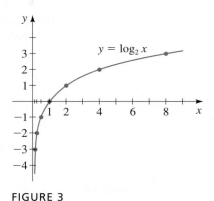

FIGURE 3   ■

Figure 4 shows the graphs of the family of logarithmic functions with bases 2, 3, 5, and 10. These graphs are drawn by reflecting the graphs of $y = 2^x$, $y = 3^x$, $y = 5^x$, and $y = 10^x$ (see Figure 3 in Section 7.1) in the line $y = x$. We can also plot points as an aid to sketching these graphs, as illustrated in Example 3.

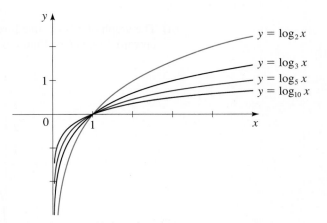

FIGURE 4

A family of logarithmic functions

In the next two examples we graph logarithmic functions by starting with the basic graphs in Figure 4 and using the transformations of Section 1.5.

EXAMPLE 4 ■ **Reflecting Graphs of Logarithmic Functions**

Sketch the graph of each function.

(a) $f(x) = -\log_2 x$ (b) $g(x) = \log_2(-x)$

SOLUTION

Reflecting graphs is explained in Section 1.5.

(a) We start with the graph of $y = \log_2 x$ in Figure 5(a) and reflect in the x-axis to get the graph of $f(x) = -\log_2 x$ in Figure 5(b).

(b) To obtain the graph of $g(x) = \log_2(-x)$, we reflect the graph of $y = \log_2 x$ in the y-axis. See Figure 5(c).

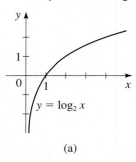   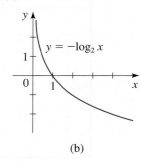   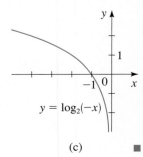

FIGURE 5   (a)   (b)   (c)   ■

EXAMPLE 5 ■ **Shifting Graphs of Logarithmic Functions**

Find the domain of each function, and sketch the graph.

(a) $f(x) = 2 + \log_5 x$ (b) $g(x) = \log_{10}(x - 3)$

SOLUTION

(a) The graph of f is obtained from the graph of $y = \log_5 x$ (Figure 4) by shifting upward 2 units (see Figure 6). The domain of f is $(0, \infty)$.

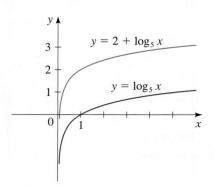

FIGURE 6

(b) The graph of g is obtained from the graph of $y = \log_{10} x$ (Figure 4) by shifting to the right 3 units (see Figure 7). The line $x = 3$ is a vertical asymptote. Since

$\log_{10} x$ is defined only when $x > 0$, the domain of $g(x) = \log_{10}(x - 3)$ is

$$\{x \mid x - 3 > 0\} = \{x \mid x > 3\} = (3, \infty)$$

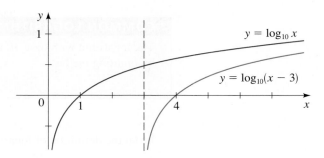

FIGURE 7

In Section 1.7 we saw that a function f and its inverse function f^{-1} satisfy the equations

$$f^{-1}(f(x)) = x \qquad \text{for } x \text{ in the domain of } f$$

$$f(f^{-1}(x)) = x \qquad \text{for } x \text{ in the domain of } f^{-1}$$

When applied to $f(x) = a^x$ and $f^{-1}(x) = \log_a x$, these equations become

$$\log_a(a^x) = x \qquad x \in \mathbb{R}$$

$$a^{\log_a x} = x \qquad x > 0$$

We list these and other properties of logarithms discussed in this section.

PROPERTIES OF LOGARITHMS

Property	Reason
1. $\log_a 1 = 0$	We must raise a to the power 0 to get 1.
2. $\log_a a = 1$	We must raise a to the power 1 to get a.
3. $\log_a a^x = x$	We must raise a to the power x to get a^x.
4. $a^{\log_a x} = x$	$\log_a x$ is the power to which a must be raised to get x.

EXAMPLE 6 ■ **Applying Properties of Logarithms**

We illustrate the properties of logarithms when the base is 5.

$$\log_5 1 = 0 \qquad \text{Property 1} \qquad\qquad \log_5 5 = 1 \qquad \text{Property 2}$$

$$\log_5 5^8 = 8 \qquad \text{Property 3} \qquad\qquad 5^{\log_5 12} = 12 \qquad \text{Property 4}$$

■ Common Logarithms

We now study logarithms with base 10.

> **COMMON LOGARITHM**
>
> The logarithm with base 10 is called the **common logarithm** and is denoted by omitting the base:
> $$\log x = \log_{10} x$$

From the definition of logarithms we can easily find that

$$\log 10 = 1 \qquad \text{and} \qquad \log 100 = 2$$

But how do we find log 50? We need to find the exponent y such that $10^y = 50$. Clearly, 1 is too small and 2 is too large. So

$$1 < \log 50 < 2$$

To get a better approximation, we can experiment to find a power of 10 closer to 50. Fortunately, scientific calculators are equipped with a $\boxed{\text{LOG}}$ key that directly gives values of common logarithms.

EXAMPLE 7 ■ Evaluating Common Logarithms

Use a calculator to find appropriate values of $f(x) = \log x$ and use the values to sketch the graph.

SOLUTION

We make a table of values, using a calculator to evaluate the function at those values of x that are not powers of 10. We plot those points and connect them by a smooth curve as in Figure 8.

x	$\log x$
0.01	-2
0.1	-1
0.5	-0.301
1	0
4	0.602
5	0.699
10	1
15	1.176

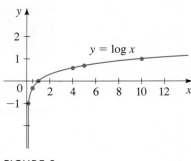

FIGURE 8

■

Natural Logarithms

Of all possible bases a for logarithms, it turns out that the most convenient choice for the purposes of calculus is the number e, which we defined in Section 7.1.

The notation ln is an abbreviation for the Latin name *logarithmus naturalis*.

NATURAL LOGARITHM

The logarithm with base e is called the **natural logarithm** and is denoted by **ln**:

$$\ln x = \log_e x$$

The natural logarithmic function $y = \ln x$ is the inverse function of the exponential function $y = e^x$. Both functions are graphed in Figure 9. By the definition of inverse functions we have

$$\ln x = y \quad \Leftrightarrow \quad e^y = x$$

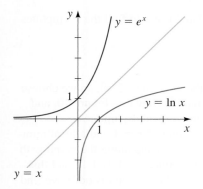

$y = x$

FIGURE 9

Graph of the natural logarithmic function

If we substitute $a = e$ and write "ln" for "$\log_e$" in the properties of logarithms mentioned earlier, we obtain the following properties of natural logarithms.

PROPERTIES OF NATURAL LOGARITHMS

Property	Reason
1. $\ln 1 = 0$	We must raise e to the power 0 to get 1.
2. $\ln e = 1$	We must raise e to the power 1 to get e.
3. $\ln e^x = x$	We must raise e to the power x to get e^x.
4. $e^{\ln x} = x$	$\ln x$ is the power to which e must be raised to get x.

Calculators are equipped with an $\boxed{\text{LN}}$ key that directly gives the values of natural logarithms.

EXAMPLE 8 ■ Evaluating the Natural Logarithm Function

(a) $\ln e^8 = 8$ Definition of natural logarithm

(b) $\ln\left(\dfrac{1}{e^2}\right) = \ln e^{-2} = -2$ Definition of natural logarithm

(c) $\ln 5 \approx 1.609$ Use the $\boxed{\text{LN}}$ key on a calculator ■

EXAMPLE 9 ■ Finding the Domain of a Logarithmic Function

Find the domain of the function $f(x) = \ln(4 - x^2)$.

SOLUTION

As with any logarithmic function, $\ln x$ is defined when $x > 0$.
Thus, the domain of f is

$$\{x \mid 4 - x^2 > 0\} = \{x \mid x^2 < 4\} = \{x \mid |x| < 2\}$$
$$= \{x \mid -2 < x < 2\} = (-2, 2) \qquad \blacksquare$$

EXAMPLE 10 ■ Drawing the Graph of a Logarithmic Function

Draw the graph of the function $y = x \ln(4 - x^2)$ and use it to find the asymptotes
and local maximum and minimum values.

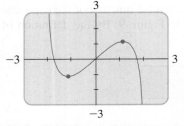

FIGURE 10
$y = x \ln(4 - x^2)$

SOLUTION

As in Example 9 the domain of this function is the interval $(-2, 2)$, so we choose
the viewing rectangle $[-3, 3]$ by $[-3, 3]$. The graph is shown in Figure 10, and
from it we see that the lines $x = -2$ and $x = 2$ are vertical asymptotes.
   The function has a local maximum point to the right of $x = 1$ and a local minimum point to the left of $x = -1$. By zooming in and tracing along the graph with
the cursor, we find that the local maximum value is approximately 1.13 and this
occurs when $x \approx 1.15$. Similarly (or by noticing that the function is odd), we find
that the local minimum value is about -1.13, and it occurs when $x \approx -1.15$. ■

7.2 EXERCISES

1–6 ■ Express the equation in exponential form.

1. (a) $\log_5 25 = 2$ (b) $\log_5 1 = 0$

2. (a) $\log_{10} 0.1 = -1$ (b) $\log_8 512 = 3$

3. (a) $\log_8 2 = \frac{1}{3}$ (b) $\log_2\!\left(\frac{1}{8}\right) = -3$

4. (a) $\log_3 81 = 4$ (b) $\log_8 4 = \frac{2}{3}$

5. (a) $\ln 5 = x$ (b) $\ln y = 5$

6. (a) $\ln(x + 1) = 2$ (b) $\ln(x - 1) = 4$

7–12 ■ Express the equation in logarithmic form.

7. (a) $5^3 = 125$ (b) $10^{-4} = 0.0001$

8. (a) $10^3 = 1000$ (b) $81^{1/2} = 9$

9. (a) $8^{-1} = \frac{1}{8}$ (b) $2^{-3} = \frac{1}{8}$

10. (a) $4^{-3/2} = 0.125$ (b) $7^3 = 343$

11. (a) $e^x = 2$ (b) $e^3 = y$

12. (a) $e^{x+1} = 0.5$ (b) $e^{0.5x} = t$

13–22 ■ Evaluate the expression.

13. (a) $\log_3 3$ (b) $\log_3 1$ (c) $\log_3 3^2$

14. (a) $\log_5 5^4$ (b) $\log_4 64$ (c) $\log_9 9$

15. (a) $\log_6 36$ (b) $\log_9 81$ (c) $\log_7 7^{10}$

16. (a) $\log_2 32$ (b) $\log_8 8^{17}$ (c) $\log_6 1$

17. (a) $\log_3\!\left(\frac{1}{27}\right)$ (b) $\log_{10} \sqrt{10}$ (c) $\log_5 0.2$

18. (a) $\log_5 125$ (b) $\log_{49} 7$ (c) $\log_9 \sqrt{3}$

19. (a) $2^{\log_2 37}$ (b) $3^{\log_3 8}$ (c) $e^{\ln \sqrt{5}}$

20. (a) $e^{\ln \pi}$ (b) $10^{\log 5}$ (c) $10^{\log 87}$

21. (a) $\log_8 0.25$ (b) $\ln e^4$ (c) $\ln(1/e)$

22. (a) $\log_4 \sqrt{2}$ (b) $\log_4\!\left(\frac{1}{2}\right)$ (c) $\log_4 8$

23–30 ■ Use the definition of the logarithmic function to find x.

23. (a) $\log_2 x = 5$ (b) $\log_2 16 = x$

24. (a) $\log_5 x = 4$ (b) $\log_{10} 0.1 = x$

25. (a) $\log_3 243 = x$ (b) $\log_3 x = 3$

26. (a) $\log_4 2 = x$ (b) $\log_4 x = 2$

27. (a) $\log_{10} x = 2$ (b) $\log_5 x = 2$

28. (a) $\log_x 1000 = 3$ (b) $\log_x 25 = 2$

29. (a) $\log_x 16 = 4$ (b) $\log_x 8 = \frac{3}{2}$

30. (a) $\log_x 6 = \frac{1}{2}$ (b) $\log_x 3 = \frac{1}{3}$

31–34 ■ Use a calculator to evaluate the expression, correct to four decimal places.

31. (a) $\log 2$ (b) $\log 35.2$ (c) $\log\left(\frac{2}{3}\right)$

32. (a) $\log 50$ (b) $\log \sqrt{2}$ (c) $\log\left(3\sqrt{2}\right)$

33. (a) $\ln 5$ (b) $\ln 25.3$ (c) $\ln\left(1 + \sqrt{3}\right)$

34. (a) $\ln 27$ (b) $\ln 7.39$ (c) $\ln 54.6$

35–38 ■ Find the function of the form $y = \log_a x$ whose graph is given.

35.

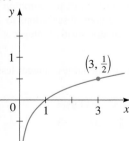

36.

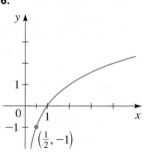

37.

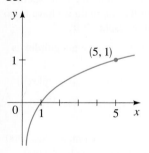

38.

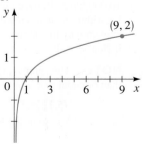

39–44 ■ Match the logarithmic function with one of the graphs labeled I–VI.

39. $f(x) = -\ln x$ **40.** $f(x) = \ln(x - 2)$

41. $f(x) = 2 + \ln x$ **42.** $f(x) = \ln(-x)$

43. $f(x) = \ln(2 - x)$ **44.** $f(x) = -\ln(-x)$

I
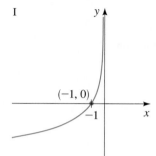

II
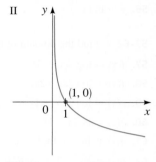

III
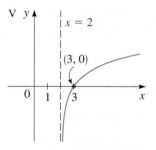

IV
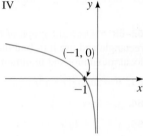

V

VI
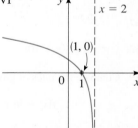

45. Draw the graph of $y = 4^x$, then use it to draw the graph of $y = \log_4 x$.

46. Draw the graph of $y = 3^x$, then use it to draw the graph of $y = \log_3 x$.

47–56 ■ Graph the function, not by plotting points, but by starting from the graphs in Figures 4 and 9. State the domain, range, and asymptote.

47. $f(x) = \log_2(x - 4)$ **48.** $f(x) = -\log_{10} x$

49. $g(x) = \log_5(-x)$ **50.** $g(x) = \ln(x + 2)$

51. $y = 2 + \log_3 x$

52. $y = \log_3(x - 1) - 2$

53. $y = 1 - \log_{10} x$

54. $y = 1 + \ln(-x)$

55. $y = |\ln x|$

56. $y = \ln |x|$

57–62 ■ Find the domain of the function.

57. $f(x) = \log_{10}(x + 3)$

58. $f(x) = \log_5(8 - 2x)$

59. $g(x) = \log_3(x^2 - 1)$

60. $g(x) = \ln(2x - 1)$

61. $h(x) = \ln x + \ln(2 - x)$

62. $h(x) = \sqrt{x - 2} - \log_5(10 - x)$

63–68 ■ Draw the graph of the function in a suitable viewing rectangle and use it to find the domain, the asymptotes, and the local maximum and minimum values.

63. $y = \log_{10}(1 - x^2)$

64. $y = \ln(x^2 - x)$

65. $y = x + \ln x$

66. $y = x(\ln x)^2$

67. $y = \dfrac{\ln x}{x}$

68. $y = x \log_{10}(x + 10)$

69. Compare the rates of growth of the functions

$$f(x) = \ln x \quad \text{and} \quad g(x) = \sqrt{x}$$

by drawing their graphs on a common screen using the viewing rectangle $[-1, 30]$ by $[-1, 6]$.

70. (a) By drawing the graphs of the functions

$$f(x) = 1 + \ln(1 + x) \quad \text{and} \quad g(x) = \sqrt{x}$$

in a suitable viewing rectangle, show that even when a logarithmic function starts out higher than a root function, it is ultimately overtaken by the root function.

(b) Find, correct to two decimal places, the solutions of the equation $\sqrt{x} = 1 + \ln(1 + x)$.

71–72 ■ A family of functions is given.
(a) Draw graphs of the family for $c = 1, 2, 3,$ and 4.
(b) How are the graphs in part (a) related?

71. $f(x) = \log(cx)$

72. $f(x) = c \log x$

73–74 ■ A function $f(x)$ is given.
(a) Find the domain of the function f.
(b) Find the inverse function of f.

73. $f(x) = \log_2(\log_{10} x)$

74. $f(x) = \ln(\ln(\ln x))$

75. (a) Find the inverse of the function

$$f(x) = \frac{2^x}{1 + 2^x}$$

(b) What is the domain of the inverse function?

DISCOVERY • DISCUSSION

76. The Height of the Graph of a Logarithmic Function Suppose that the graph of $y = 2^x$ is drawn on a coordinate plane where the unit of measurement is an inch.
(a) Show that at a distance 2 ft to the right of the origin the height of the graph is about 265 mi.
(b) If the graph of $y = \log_2 x$ is drawn on the same set of axes, how far to the right of the origin do we have to go before the height of the curve reaches 2 ft?

77. The Googolplex A **googol** is 10^{100}, and a **googolplex** is 10^{googol}. Find

$$\log(\log(\text{googol})) \quad \text{and} \quad \log(\log(\log(\text{googolplex})))$$

78. Comparing Logarithms Which is larger, $\log_4 17$ or $\log_5 24$? Explain your reasoning.

79. The Number of Digits in an Integer Compare log 1000 to the number of digits in 1000. Do the same for 10,000. How many digits does any number between 1000 and 10,000 have? Between what two values must the common logarithm of such a number lie? Use your observations to explain why the number of digits in any positive integer x is $[\![\log x]\!] + 1$.

NOTE The symbol $[\![x]\!]$ represents the largest integer less than or equal to x. For instance:

$$[\![5.7]\!] = 5 \qquad [\![5.0]\!] = 5 \qquad [\![4.9]\!] = 4$$
$$[\![0.9913]\!] = 0 \qquad [\![-2.3]\!] = -3$$

7.3 LAWS OF LOGARITHMS

Since logarithms are exponents, the Laws of Exponents give rise to the Laws of Logarithms. These properties give logarithmic functions a wide range of applications, as we will see in Section 7.5.

LAWS OF LOGARITHMS

Let a be a positive number, with $a \neq 1$. Let $A > 0$, $B > 0$, and C be any real numbers.

Law	Description
1. $\log_a(AB) = \log_a A + \log_a B$	The logarithm of a product of numbers is the sum of the logarithms of the numbers.
2. $\log_a\left(\dfrac{A}{B}\right) = \log_a A - \log_a B$	The logarithm of a quotient of numbers is the difference of the logarithms of the numbers.
3. $\log_a(A^C) = C \log_a A$	The logarithm of a power of a number is the exponent times the logarithm of the number.

■ **Proof**   We make use of the property $\log_a a^x = x$ from Section 7.2.

Law 1. Let
$$\log_a A = u \quad \text{and} \quad \log_a B = v$$

When written in exponential form, these equations become

$$a^u = A \quad \text{and} \quad a^v = B$$

Thus
$$\log_a(AB) = \log_a(a^u a^v) = \log_a(a^{u+v})$$
$$= u + v = \log_a A + \log_a B$$

Law 2. Using Law 1, we have

$$\log_a A = \log_a\left[\left(\frac{A}{B}\right)B\right] = \log_a\left(\frac{A}{B}\right) + \log_a B$$

so
$$\log_a\left(\frac{A}{B}\right) = \log_a A - \log_a B$$

Law 3. Let $\log_a A = u$. Then $a^u = A$, so

$$\log_a(A^C) = \log_a(a^u)^C = \log_a(a^{uC}) = uC = C \log_a A \qquad \Box$$

As the following examples illustrate, these laws are used in both directions. Since the domain of any logarithmic function is the interval $(0, \infty)$, we assume that all quantities whose logarithms occur are positive.

EXAMPLE 1 ■ Using the Laws of Logarithms to Expand Expressions

Use the Laws of Logarithms to rewrite each expression.

(a) $\log_2(6x)$

(b) $\log \sqrt{5}$

(c) $\log_5(x^3 y^6)$

(d) $\ln\left(\dfrac{ab}{\sqrt[3]{c}}\right)$

SOLUTION

(a) $\log_2(6x) = \log_2 6 + \log_2 x$ Law 1

(b) $\log \sqrt{5} = \log 5^{1/2} = \frac{1}{2} \log 5$ Law 3

(c) $\log_5(x^3 y^6) = \log_5 x^3 + \log_5 y^6$ Law 1

$\qquad\qquad = 3 \log_5 x + 6 \log_5 y$ Law 3

(d) $\ln\left(\dfrac{ab}{\sqrt[3]{c}}\right) = \ln(ab) - \ln \sqrt[3]{c}$ Law 2

$\qquad\qquad = \ln a + \ln b - \ln c^{1/3}$ Law 1

$\qquad\qquad = \ln a + \ln b - \frac{1}{3} \ln c$ Law 3   ∎

EXAMPLE 2 ■ Using the Laws of Logarithms to Evaluate Expressions

Evaluate each expression.

(a) $\log_4 2 + \log_4 32$ (b) $\log_2 80 - \log_2 5$ (c) $-\frac{1}{3} \log 8$

SOLUTION

(a) $\log_4 2 + \log_4 32 = \log_4(2 \cdot 32)$ Law 1

$\qquad\qquad\qquad = \log_4 64 = 3$ Because $4^3 = 64$

(b) $\log_2 80 - \log_2 5 = \log_2\left(\frac{80}{5}\right)$ Law 2

$\qquad\qquad\qquad = \log_2 16 = 4$ Because $2^4 = 16$

(c) $-\frac{1}{3} \log 8 = \log 8^{-1/3}$ Law 3

$\qquad\qquad = \log\left(\frac{1}{2}\right)$ Property of negative exponents

$\qquad\qquad \approx -0.301$ Use a calculator   ∎

EXAMPLE 3 ■ Writing an Expression as a Single Logarithm

Express $3 \log x + \frac{1}{2} \log(x + 1)$ as a single logarithm.

John Napier (1550–1617) was a Scottish landowner for whom mathematics was a hobby. We know him today because of his key invention—logarithms, which he published in 1614 under the title *A Description of the Marvelous Rule of Logarithms*. In Napier's time, logarithms were used exclusively for simplifying complicated calculations. For example, to multiply two large numbers we would write them as powers of 10. The exponents are simply the logarithms of the numbers. For instance,

$$4532 \times 57783$$
$$\approx 10^{3.65629} \times 10^{4.76180}$$
$$= 10^{8.41809}$$
$$\approx 261{,}872{,}564$$

The idea is that multiplying powers of 10 is easy (we simply add their exponents). Napier produced extensive tables giving the logarithms (or exponents) of numbers. Since the advent of calculators and computers, logarithms are no longer used for this purpose. The logarithmic functions, however, have found many applications, some of which are described in this chapter.

Napier wrote on many topics. One of his most colorful works is a book entitled *A Plaine Discovery of the Whole Revelation of Saint John*, in which he predicted that the world would end in the year 1700.

SOLUTION

$$3 \log x + \tfrac{1}{2} \log(x + 1) = \log x^3 + \log(x + 1)^{1/2} \qquad \text{Law 3}$$

$$= \log(x^3(x + 1)^{1/2}) \qquad \text{Law 1} \qquad \blacksquare$$

EXAMPLE 4 ■ Writing an Expression as a Single Logarithm

Express $3 \ln s + \tfrac{1}{2} \ln t - 4 \ln(t^2 + 1)$ as a single logarithm.

SOLUTION

$$3 \ln s + \tfrac{1}{2} \ln t - 4 \ln(t^2 + 1) = \ln s^3 + \ln t^{1/2} - \ln(t^2 + 1)^4 \qquad \text{Law 3}$$

$$= \ln(s^3 t^{1/2}) - \ln(t^2 + 1)^4 \qquad \text{Law 1}$$

$$= \ln\left(\frac{s^3 \sqrt{t}}{(t^2 + 1)^4}\right) \qquad \text{Law 2} \qquad \blacksquare$$

   WARNING Although the Laws of Logarithms tell us how to compute the logarithm of a product or a quotient, *there is no corresponding rule for the logarithm of a sum or a difference*. For instance,

$$\log_a(x + y) \neq \log_a x + \log_a y$$

In fact, we know that the right side is equal to $\log_a(xy)$.

   Also, don't improperly simplify quotients or powers of logarithms. For instance,

$$\frac{\log 6}{\log 2} \neq \log\left(\frac{6}{2}\right)$$

$$(\log_2 x)^3 \neq 3 \log_2 x$$

Change of Base

For some purposes, we find it useful to change from logarithms in one base to logarithms in another base. Suppose we are given $\log_a x$ and want to find $\log_b x$. Let

$$y = \log_b x$$

We write this in exponential form and take the logarithm, with base a, of each side.

$$b^y = x \qquad \text{Exponential form}$$

$$\log_a(b^y) = \log_a x \qquad \text{Take } \log_a \text{ of each side}$$

$$y \log_a b = \log_a x \qquad \text{Law 3}$$

$$y = \frac{\log_a x}{\log_a b} \qquad \text{Divide by } \log_a b$$

This proves the following formula.

We may write the Change of Base Formula as

$$\log_b x = \left(\frac{1}{\log_a b}\right)\log_a x$$

So, $\log_b x$ is just a constant multiple of $\log_a x$; the constant is $\frac{1}{\log_a b}$.

CHANGE OF BASE FORMULA

$$\log_b x = \frac{\log_a x}{\log_a b}$$

In particular, if we put $x = a$, then $\log_a a = 1$ and this formula becomes

$$\log_b a = \frac{1}{\log_a b}$$

We can now evaluate a logarithm to *any* base by using the Change of Base Formula to express the logarithm in terms of common logarithms or natural logarithms and then using a calculator.

EXAMPLE 5 ■ **Using the Change of Base Formula to Evaluate Logarithms**

Use the Change of Base Formula and common or natural logarithms to evaluate each logarithm, correct to five decimal places.

(a) $\log_8 5$ 　　　　　　　　　　　　　(b) $\log_9 20$

SOLUTION

(a) We use the Change of Base Formula with $b = 8$ and $a = 10$:

$$\log_8 5 = \frac{\log_{10} 5}{\log_{10} 8} \approx 0.77398$$

(b) We use the Change of Base Formula with $b = 9$ and $a = e$:

$$\log_9 20 = \frac{\ln 20}{\ln 9} \approx 1.36342$$

■

 EXAMPLE 6 ■ **Using the Change of Base Formula to Graph a Logarithmic Function**

Use a graphing calculator to graph $f(x) = \log_6 x$.

SOLUTION

Calculators don't have a key for $\log_6$, so we use the Change of Base Formula to write

$$f(x) = \log_6 x = \frac{\ln x}{\ln 6}$$

Since calculators do have an ☐LN☐ key, we can enter this new form of the function and graph it. The graph is shown in Figure 1.

■

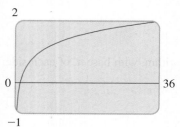

FIGURE 1

$$f(x) = \log_6 x = \frac{\ln x}{\ln 6}$$

7.3 EXERCISES

1–26 ■ Use the Laws of Logarithms to rewrite the expression in a form with no logarithm of a product, quotient, root, or power.

1. $\log_2 (2x)$

2. $\log_3 (5y)$

3. $\log_2(x(x-1))$

4. $\log_5\left(\dfrac{x}{2}\right)$

5. $\log 6^{10}$

6. $\ln\left(\sqrt{z}\right)$

7. $\log_2(AB^2)$

8. $\log_6 \sqrt[4]{17}$

9. $\log_3\!\left(x\sqrt{y}\right)$

10. $\log_2(xy)^{10}$

11. $\log_5 \sqrt[3]{x^2+1}$

12. $\log_a\!\left(\dfrac{x^2}{yz^3}\right)$

13. $\ln\sqrt{ab}$

14. $\ln\sqrt[3]{3r^2s}$

15. $\log\!\left(\dfrac{x^3y^4}{z^6}\right)$

16. $\log\!\left(\dfrac{a^2}{b^4\sqrt{c}}\right)$

17. $\log_2\!\left(\dfrac{x(x^2+1)}{\sqrt{x^2-1}}\right)$

18. $\log_5 \sqrt{\dfrac{x-1}{x+1}}$

19. $\ln\!\left(x\sqrt{\dfrac{y}{z}}\right)$

20. $\ln \dfrac{3x^2}{(x+1)^{10}}$

21. $\log \sqrt[4]{x^2+y^2}$

22. $\log\!\left(\dfrac{x}{\sqrt[3]{1-x}}\right)$

23. $\log \sqrt{\dfrac{x^2+4}{(x^2+1)(x^3-7)^2}}$

24. $\log \sqrt{x\sqrt{y}\sqrt{z}}$

25. $\ln\!\left(\dfrac{x^3\sqrt{x-1}}{3x+4}\right)$

26. $\log\!\left(\dfrac{10^x}{x(x^2+1)(x^4+2)}\right)$

27–38 ■ Evaluate the expression.

27. $\log_5 \sqrt{125}$

28. $\log_2 112 - \log_2 7$

29. $\log 2 + \log 5$

30. $\log \sqrt{0.1}$

31. $\log_4 192 - \log_4 3$

32. $\log_{12} 9 + \log_{12} 16$

33. $\ln 6 - \ln 15 + \ln 20$

34. $e^{3\ln 5}$

35. $10^{2\log 4}$

36. $\log_2 8^{33}$

37. $\log(\log 1000^{10,000})$

38. $\ln(\ln(\ln e^{e^{200}}))$

39–48 ■ Rewrite the expression as a single logarithm.

39. $\log_3 5 + 5\log_3 2$

40. $\log 12 + \tfrac{1}{2}\log 7 - \log 2$

41. $\log_2 A + \log_2 B - 2\log_2 C$

42. $\log_5(x^2-1) - \log_5(x-1)$

43. $4\log x - \tfrac{1}{3}\log(x^2+1) + 2\log(x-1)$

44. $\ln(a+b) + \ln(a-b) - 2\ln c$

45. $\ln 5 + 2\ln x + 3\ln(x^2+5)$

46. $2(\log_5 x + 2\log_5 y - 3\log_5 z)$

47. $\tfrac{1}{3}\log(2x+1) + \tfrac{1}{2}\left[\log(x-4) - \log(x^4-x^2-1)\right]$

48. $\log_a b + c\log_a d - r\log_a s$

49–56 ■ Use the Change of Base Formula and a calculator to evaluate the logarithm, correct to six decimal places. Use either natural or common logarithms.

49. $\log_2 5$

50. $\log_5 2$

51. $\log_3 16$

52. $\log_6 92$

53. $\log_7 2.61$

54. $\log_6 532$

55. $\log_4 125$

56. $\log_{12} 2.5$

 57. Use the Change of Base Formula to show that

$$\log_3 x = \frac{\ln x}{\ln 3}$$

Then use this fact to draw the graph of the function $f(x) = \log_3 x$.

 58. Draw graphs of the family of functions $y = \log_a x$ for $a = 2, e, 5$, and 10 on the same screen, using the viewing rectangle $[0, 5]$ by $[-3, 3]$. How are these graphs related?

59. Use the Change of Base Formula to show that

$$\log e = \frac{1}{\ln 10}$$

60. Simplify: $(\log_2 5)(\log_5 7)$

61. Show that $-\ln\!\left(x - \sqrt{x^2-1}\right) = \ln\!\left(x + \sqrt{x^2-1}\right)$.

▲ DISCOVERY · DISCUSSION

62. Is the Equation an Identity?   Discuss each equation and determine whether it is true for all possible values of the variables. (Ignore values of the variables for which any term is undefined.)

(a) $\log\!\left(\dfrac{x}{y}\right) = \dfrac{\log x}{\log y}$

(b) $\log_2(x - y) = \log_2 x - \log_2 y$

(c) $\log_5\left(\dfrac{a}{b^2}\right) = \log_5 a - 2\log_5 b$

(d) $\log 2^z = z \log 2$

(e) $(\log P)(\log Q) = \log P + \log Q$

(f) $\dfrac{\log a}{\log b} = \log a - \log b$

(g) $(\log_2 7)^x = x \log_2 7$

(h) $\log_a a^a = a$

(i) $\log(x - y) = \dfrac{\log x}{\log y}$

(j) $-\ln\left(\dfrac{1}{A}\right) = \ln A$

63. **Find the Error** What is wrong with the following argument?

$$\log 0.1 < 2 \log 0.1$$
$$= \log(0.1)^2$$
$$= \log 0.01$$
$$\log 0.1 < \log 0.01$$
$$0.1 < 0.01$$

64. **Shifting, Shrinking, and Stretching Graphs of Functions** Let $f(x) = x^2$. Show that $f(2x) = 4f(x)$, and explain how this shows that shrinking the graph of f horizontally has the same effect as stretching it vertically. Then use the identities $e^{2+x} = e^2 e^x$ and $\ln(2x) = \ln 2 + \ln x$ to show that for $g(x) = e^x$, a horizontal shift is the same as a vertical stretch and for $h(x) = \ln x$, a horizontal shrinking is the same as a vertical shift.

7.4 EXPONENTIAL AND LOGARITHMIC EQUATIONS

In this section we solve equations that involve exponential or logarithmic functions. The techniques we develop here will be used in the next section for solving applied problems.

Exponential Equations

An exponential equation is one in which the variable occurs in the exponent. For example,

$$2^x = 7$$

The variable x presents a difficulty because it is in the exponent. To deal with this difficulty, we take the logarithm of each side and then use the Laws of Logarithms to "bring down x" from the exponent.

$$2^x = 7$$

$$\ln 2^x = \ln 7 \qquad \text{Take ln of each side}$$

$$x \ln 2 = \ln 7 \qquad \text{Law 3 (bring down the exponent)}$$

$$x = \frac{\ln 7}{\ln 2} \qquad \text{Solve for } x$$

$$\approx 2.807 \qquad \text{Use a calculator}$$

Recall that Law 3 of the Laws of Logarithms says that $\log_a A^C = C \log_a A$.

The method we used to solve $2^x = 7$ is typical of the methods we use to solve all exponential equations, and it can be summarized as follows.

GUIDELINES FOR SOLVING EXPONENTIAL EQUATIONS

1. Isolate the exponential expression on one side of the equation.

2. Take the logarithm of each side, then use the Laws of Logarithms to "bring down the exponent."

3. Solve for the variable.

EXAMPLE 1 ■ Solving an Exponential Equation

Find the solution of the equation $3^{x+2} = 7$, correct to six decimal places.

SOLUTION

We take the common logarithm of each side and use Law 3.

$$3^{x+2} = 7$$

$$\log(3^{x+2}) = \log 7 \qquad \text{Take log of each side}$$

$$(x+2)\log 3 = \log 7 \qquad \text{Law 3 (bring down the exponent)}$$

$$x + 2 = \frac{\log 7}{\log 3} \qquad \text{Divide by log 3}$$

$$x = \frac{\log 7}{\log 3} - 2 \qquad \text{Subtract 2}$$

$$\approx -0.228756 \qquad \text{Use a calculator}$$

We could have used natural logarithms instead of common logarithms. In fact, using the same steps, we get

$$x = \frac{\ln 7}{\ln 3} - 2 \approx -0.228756$$

CHECK YOUR ANSWER ■ Substituting $x = -0.228756$ into the original equation and using a calculator, we get

$$3^{(-0.228756)+2} \approx 7 \quad \checkmark$$

■

EXAMPLE 2 ■ Solving an Exponential Equation

Solve the equation $8e^{2x} = 20$.

SOLUTION

We first divide by 8 in order to isolate the exponential term on one side of the equation.

$$8e^{2x} = 20$$

$$e^{2x} = \frac{20}{8} \qquad \text{Divide by 8}$$

$$\ln e^{2x} = \ln 2.5 \qquad \text{Take ln of each side}$$

$$2x = \ln 2.5 \qquad \text{Property of ln}$$

$$x = \frac{\ln 2.5}{2} \qquad \text{Divide by 2}$$

$$\approx 0.458 \qquad \text{Use a calculator}$$

■

CHECK YOUR ANSWER

Substituting $x = 0.458$ into the original equation and using a calculator, we get

$$8e^{2(0.458)} \approx 20 \quad \checkmark$$

EXAMPLE 3 ■ **Solving an Exponential Equation Algebraically and Graphically**

Solve the equation $e^{3-2x} = 4$ algebraically and graphically.

SOLUTION 1: ALGEBRAIC

Since the base of the exponential term is e, we use natural logarithms to solve this equation.

$$\ln(e^{3-2x}) = \ln 4 \qquad \text{Take ln of each side}$$

$$3 - 2x = \ln 4 \qquad \text{Property of ln}$$

$$2x = 3 - \ln 4$$

$$x = \tfrac{1}{2}(3 - \ln 4) \approx 0.807$$

You should check that this answer satisfies the original equation.

SOLUTION 2: GRAPHICAL

We graph the equations $y = e^{3-2x}$ and $y = 4$ in the same viewing rectangle as in Figure 1. The solutions occur where the graphs intersect. Zooming in on the point of intersection of the two graphs, we see that $x \approx 0.81$.

We can also solve the equation by graphing $y = e^{3-2x} - 4$ and finding the x-intercepts.

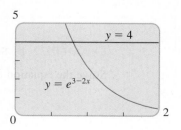

FIGURE 1

■

EXAMPLE 4 ■ **Solving an Exponential Equation**

Solve the equation $e^{2x} - e^x - 6 = 0$.

SOLUTION

To isolate the exponential term, we factor.

$$e^{2x} - e^x - 6 = 0$$

$$(e^x)^2 - e^x - 6 = 0 \qquad \text{Law of Exponents}$$

$$(e^x - 3)(e^x + 2) = 0 \qquad \text{Factor (a quadratic in } e^x)$$

$$e^x - 3 = 0 \quad \text{or} \quad e^x + 2 = 0 \qquad \text{Zero-Product Property}$$

$$e^x = 3 \qquad\qquad e^x = -2$$

The equation $e^x = 3$ leads to $x = \ln 3$. But the equation $e^x = -2$ has no solution because $e^x > 0$ for all x. Thus, $x = \ln 3 \approx 1.0986$ is the only solution. You should check that this answer satisfies the original equation. ■

EXAMPLE 5 ■ **Solving an Exponential Equation**

Solve the equation $3x^2 e^x + x^3 e^x = 0$.

SOLUTION

First we factor the left side of the equation.

$$3x^2 e^x + x^3 e^x = 0$$

$$(3x^2 + x^3)e^x = 0 \qquad \text{Factor out } e^x$$

$$x^2(3 + x)e^x = 0 \qquad \text{Factor out } x^2$$

$$x^2 = 0 \quad \text{or} \quad 3 + x = 0 \quad \text{or} \quad e^x = 0 \qquad \text{Zero-Product Property}$$

$$x = 0 \qquad\qquad x = -3$$

The equation $e^x = 0$ has no solution because $e^x > 0$ for all x. Thus, $x = 0$ and $x = -3$ are the only solutions. ■

Logarithmic Equations

A *logarithmic equation* is one in which a logarithm of the variable occurs. For example,

$$\log_2(x + 2) = 5$$

To solve for x, we write the equation in exponential form.

$$x + 2 = 2^5 \qquad \text{Exponential form}$$

$$x = 32 - 2 = 30 \qquad \text{Solve for } x$$

Radiocarbon dating is a method archeologists use to determine the age of ancient objects. The carbon dioxide in the atmosphere always contains a fixed fraction of radioactive carbon, carbon-14 (^{14}C), with a half-life of about 5730 years. Plants absorb carbon dioxide from the atmosphere, which then makes its way to animals through the food chain. Thus, all living creatures contain the same fixed proportions of ^{14}C to nonradioactive ^{12}C as the atmosphere.

After an organism dies, it stops assimilating ^{14}C, and the amount of ^{14}C in it begins to decay exponentially. We can then determine the time elapsed since the death of the organism by measuring the amount of ^{14}C left in it.

For example, if a donkey bone contains 73% as much ^{14}C as a living donkey and it died t years ago, then by the formula for radioactive decay (Section 7.5),

$$0.73 = (1.00)e^{-(t\ln 2)/5730}$$

We solve this exponential equation to find $t \approx 2600$, so the bone is about 2600 years old.

Another way of looking at the first step is to raise the base, 2, to each side of the equation.

$$2^{\log_2(x+2)} = 2^5 \qquad \text{Raise 2 to each side}$$
$$x + 2 = 2^5 \qquad \text{Property of logarithms}$$
$$x = 32 - 2 = 30 \qquad \text{Solve for } x$$

The methods used to solve this simple problem are typical. We summarize the steps as follows.

GUIDELINES FOR SOLVING LOGARITHMIC EQUATIONS

1. Isolate the logarithmic term on one side of the equation; you may need to first combine the logarithmic terms.

2. Write the equation in exponential form (or raise the base to each side of the equation).

3. Solve for the variable.

EXAMPLE 6 ■ Solving Logarithmic Equations

Solve each equation for x.

(a) $\ln x = 8$ (b) $\log_2(25 - x) = 3$

SOLUTION

(a)
$$\ln x = 8$$
$$x = e^8 \qquad \text{Exponential form}$$

Therefore, $x = e^8 \approx 2981$.

We can also solve this problem another way:

$$\ln x = 8$$
$$e^{\ln x} = e^8 \qquad \text{Raise } e \text{ to each side}$$
$$x = e^8 \qquad \text{Property of ln}$$

(b) The first step is to rewrite the equation in exponential form.

$$\log_2(25 - x) = 3$$
$$25 - x = 2^3 \qquad \text{Exponential form (or raise 2 to each side)}$$
$$25 - x = 8$$
$$x = 25 - 8 = 17$$

■

CHECK YOUR ANSWER

If $x = 17$, we get
$$\log_2(25 - 17) = \log_2 8 = 3 \qquad \checkmark$$

EXAMPLE 7 ■ Solving a Logarithmic Equation

Solve the equation $4 + 3 \log(2x) = 16$.

SOLUTION

We first isolate the logarithmic term. This allows us to write the equation in exponential form.

$$4 + 3 \log(2x) = 16$$

$$3 \log(2x) = 12 \qquad \text{Subtract 4}$$

$$\log(2x) = 4 \qquad \text{Divide by 3}$$

$$2x = 10^4 \qquad \text{Exponential form (or raise 10 to each side)}$$

$$x = 5000 \qquad \text{Divide by 2} \qquad\blacksquare$$

CHECK YOUR ANSWER

If $x = 5000$, we get

$$4 + 3 \log 2(5000) = 4 + 3 \log 10{,}000$$

$$= 4 + 3(4)$$

$$= 16 \qquad \checkmark$$

EXAMPLE 8 ■ Solving a Logarithmic Equation Algebraically and Graphically

Solve the equation $\log(x + 2) + \log(x - 1) = 1$ algebraically and graphically.

SOLUTION 1: ALGEBRAIC

We first combine the logarithmic terms using the Laws of Logarithms.

$$\log[(x + 2)(x - 1)] = 1 \qquad \text{Law 1}$$

$$(x + 2)(x - 1) = 10 \qquad \text{Exponential form (or raise 10 to each side)}$$

$$x^2 + x - 2 = 10 \qquad \text{Expand left side}$$

$$x^2 + x - 12 = 0 \qquad \text{Subtract 10}$$

$$(x + 4)(x - 3) = 0 \qquad \text{Factor}$$

$$x = -4 \qquad \text{or} \qquad x = 3$$

We check these potential solutions in the original equation and find that $x = -4$ is not a solution (because logarithms of negative numbers are undefined), but $x = 3$ is a solution. (See *Check Your Answers*.)

CHECK YOUR ANSWERS

$x = -4$:

$$\log(-4 + 2) + \log(-4 - 1)$$
$$= \log(-2) + \log(-5)$$
$$\text{undefined} \qquad \times$$

$x = 3$:

$$\log(3 + 2) + \log(3 - 1)$$
$$= \log 5 + \log 2 = \log(5 \cdot 2)$$
$$= \log 10 = 1 \qquad \checkmark$$

SOLUTION 2: GRAPHICAL

We first move all terms to one side of the equation:

$$\log(x + 2) + \log(x - 1) - 1 = 0$$

Then we graph

$$y = \log(x + 2) + \log(x - 1) - 1$$

as in Figure 2. The solutions are the x-intercepts of the graph. Thus, the only solution is $x \approx 3$. $\blacksquare$

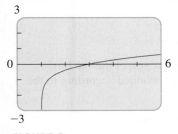

FIGURE 2

EXAMPLE 9 ■ Solving a Logarithmic Equation Graphically

Solve the equation $x^2 = 2 \ln(x + 2)$.

SOLUTION

In Example 9, it's not possible to isolate x algebraically, so we must solve the equation graphically.

We first move all terms to one side of the equation

$$x^2 - 2 \ln(x + 2) = 0$$

Then we graph

$$y = x^2 - 2 \ln(x + 2)$$

as in Figure 3. The solutions are the x-intercepts of the graph. Zooming in on the x-intercepts, we see that there are two solutions:

$$x \approx -0.71 \qquad \text{and} \qquad x \approx 1.60$$

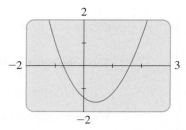

FIGURE 3   ■

Compound Interest

Recall the formulas for interest that we found in Section 7.1. If a principal P is invested at an interest rate r for a period of t years, then the amount A of the investment is given by

$$A = P(1 + r)$$ Simple interest (for one year)

$$A(t) = P\left(1 + \frac{r}{n}\right)^{nt}$$ Interest compounded n times per year

$$A(t) = Pe^{rt}$$ Interest compounded continuously

We can use logarithms to determine the time it takes for the principal to increase to a given amount.

EXAMPLE 10 ■ Finding the Term for an Investment to Double

A sum of $5000 is invested at an interest rate of 9% per year. Find the time required for the money to double if the interest is compounded according to the following method.

(a) Semiannual   (b) Continuous

SOLUTION

(a) We use the formula for compound interest with $P = \$5000$, $A(t) = \$10,000$, $r = 0.09$, $n = 2$, and solve the resulting exponential equation for t.

$$5000\left(1 + \frac{0.09}{2}\right)^{2t} = 10,000$$

$(1.045)^{2t} = 2$ Divide by 5000

$\log 1.045^{2t} = \log 2$ Take log of each side

$2t \log 1.045 = \log 2$ Law 3 (bring down the exponent)

$t = \dfrac{\log 2}{2 \log 1.045}$ Divide by 2 log 1.045

$t \approx 7.9$ Use a calculator

The money will double in 7.9 years.

(b) We use the formula for continuously compounded interest with $P = \$5000$, $A(t) = \$10,000$, $r = 0.09$, and solve the resulting exponential equation for t.

$$5000e^{0.09t} = 10,000$$

$e^{0.09t} = 2$ Divide by 5000

$\ln e^{0.09t} = \ln 2$ Take ln of each side

$0.09t = \ln 2$ Property of ln

$t = \dfrac{\ln 2}{0.09}$ Divide by 0.09

$t \approx 7.702$ Use a calculator

The money will double in 7.7 years. ∎

EXAMPLE 11 ■ Time Required to Grow an Investment

A sum of $1000 is invested at an interest rate of 8% per year. Find the time required for the amount to grow to $4000 if interest is compounded continuously.

SOLUTION

We use the formula for continuously compounded interest with $P = \$1000$, $A(t) = \$4000$, $r = 0.08$, and solve the resulting exponential equation for t.

$$1000e^{0.08t} = 4000$$

$$e^{0.08t} = 4 \qquad \text{Divide by 1000}$$

$$0.08t = \ln 4 \qquad \text{Take ln of each side}$$

$$t = \frac{\ln 4}{0.08} \qquad \text{Divide by 0.08}$$

$$t \approx 17.33 \qquad \text{Use a calculator}$$

The amount will be \$4000 in about 17 years and 4 months.   ∎

If an investment earns compound interest, then the **annual percentage yield** (APY) is the *simple* interest rate that yields the same amount at the end of one year.

EXAMPLE 12 ∎ Calculating the Annual Percentage Yield

Find the annual percentage yield for an investment that earns interest at a rate of 6% per year, compounded daily.

SOLUTION

After one year, a principal P will grow to the amount

$$A = P\left(1 + \frac{0.06}{365}\right)^{365} = P(1.06183)$$

The formula for simple interest is

$$A = P(1 + r)$$

Comparing, we see that $r = 0.06183$, so the annual percentage yield is 6.183%.   ∎

7.4 EXERCISES

1–26 ∎ Find the solution of the exponential equation, correct to four decimal places.

1. $e^x = 16$

2. $10^{-x} = 2$

3. $10^{2x} = 5$

4. $e^{-2x} = \frac{1}{10}$

5. $2^{1-x} = 3$

6. $3^{2x-1} = 5$

7. $3e^x = 10$

8. $2e^{12x} = 17$

9. $e^{1-4x} = 2$

10. $4(1 + 10^{5x}) = 9$

11. $4 + 3^{5x} = 8$

12. $2^{3x} = 34$

13. $8^{0.4x} = 5$

14. $3^{x/14} = 0.1$

15. $5^{-x/100} = 2$

16. $e^{3-5x} = 16$

17. $e^{2x+1} = 200$

18. $\left(\frac{1}{4}\right)^x = 75$

19. $5^x = 4^{x+1}$

20. $10^{1-x} = 6^x$

21. $2^{3x+1} = 3^{x-2}$

22. $7^{x/2} = 5^{1-x}$

23. $\dfrac{50}{1 + e^{-x}} = 4$

24. $\dfrac{10}{1 + e^{-x}} = 2$

25. $100(1.04)^{2t} = 300$

26. $(1.00625)^{12t} = 2$

27–34 ∎ Solve the equation.

27. $x^2 2^x - 2^x = 0$

28. $x^2 10^x - x 10^x = 2(10^x)$

29. $4x^3 e^{-3x} - 3x^4 e^{-3x} = 0$

30. $x^2 e^x + xe^x - e^x = 0$

31. $e^{2x} - 3e^x + 2 = 0$

32. $e^{2x} - e^x - 6 = 0$

33. $e^{4x} + 4e^{2x} - 21 = 0$

34. $e^x - 12e^{-x} - 1 = 0$

35–50 ∎ Solve the logarithmic equation for x.

35. $\ln x = 10$

36. $\ln(2 + x) = 1$

37. $\log x = -2$

38. $\log(x - 4) = 3$

39. $\log(3x + 5) = 2$

40. $\log_3(2 - x) = 3$

41. $2 - \ln(3 - x) = 0$

42. $\log_2(x^2 - x - 2) = 2$

43. $\log_2 3 + \log_2 x = \log_2 5 + \log_2(x - 2)$

44. $2 \log x = \log 2 + \log(3x - 4)$

45. $\log x + \log(x - 1) = \log(4x)$

46. $\log_5 x + \log_5(x + 1) = \log_5 20$

47. $\log_5(x + 1) - \log_5(x - 1) = 2$

48. $\log x + \log(x - 3) = 1$

49. $\log_9(x - 5) + \log_9(x + 3) = 1$

50. $\ln(x - 1) + \ln(x + 2) = 1$

51. For what value of x is the following true?

$$\log(x + 3) = \log x + \log 3$$

52. For what value of x is it true that $(\log x)^3 = 3 \log x$?

53. Solve for x: $2^{2/\log_5 x} = \frac{1}{16}$

54. Solve for x: $\log_2(\log_3 x) = 4$

55. A man invests $5000 in an account that pays 8.5% interest per year, compounded quarterly.
(a) Find the amount after 3 years.
(b) How long will it take for the investment to double?

56. A man invests $6500 in an account that pays 6% interest per year, compounded continuously.
(a) What is the amount after 2 years?
(b) How long will it take for the amount to be $8000?

57. Find the time required for an investment of $5000 to grow to $8000 at an interest rate of 7.5% per year, compounded quarterly.

58. Nancy wants to invest $4000 in saving certificates that bear an interest rate of 9.75% per year, compounded semiannually. How long a time period should she choose in order to save an amount of $5000?

59. How long will it take for an investment of $1000 to double in value if the interest rate is 8.5% per year, compounded continuously?

60. A sum of $1000 was invested for 4 years, and the interest was compounded semiannually. If this sum amounted to $1435.77 in the given time, what was the interest rate?

61. Find the annual percentage yield for an investment that earns 8% per year, compounded monthly.

62. Find the annual percentage yield for an investment that earns $5\frac{1}{2}$% per year, compounded continuously.

63. A 15-g sample of radioactive iodine decays in such a way that the mass remaining after t days is given by $m(t) = 15e^{-0.087t}$ where $m(t)$ is measured in grams. After how many days is there only 5 g remaining?

64. The velocity of a sky diver t seconds after jumping is given by $v(t) = 80(1 - e^{-0.2t})$. After how many seconds is the velocity 70 ft/s?

65. A small lake is stocked with a certain species of fish. The fish population is modeled by the function

$$P = \frac{10}{1 + 4e^{-0.8t}}$$

where P is the number of fish in thousands and t is measured in years since the lake was stocked.
(a) Find the fish population after 3 years.
(b) After how many years will the fish population reach 5000 fish?

66. Environmental scientists measure the intensity of light at various depths in a lake to find the "transparency" of the water. Certain levels of transparency are required for the biodiversity of the submerged macrophyte population. In a certain lake the intensity of light at depth x is given by

$$I = 4e^{-0.6x}$$

where I is measured in lux (a measure of light intensity) and x in cm.
(a) Find the intensity at a depth of 3 cm.
(b) At what depth has the light intensity dropped to $I = 2$?

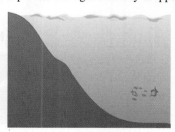

67. An electric circuit contains a battery that produces a voltage of 60 volts (V), a resistor with a resistance of 13 ohms (Ω), and an inductor with an inductance of 5 henrys (H), as shown in the figure. Using calculus, it can be shown that the current $I = I(t)$ (in amperes, A) t seconds after the switch is closed is $I = \frac{60}{13}(1 - e^{-13t/5})$.

(a) Use this equation to express the time t as a function of the current I.

(b) After how many seconds is the current 2 A?

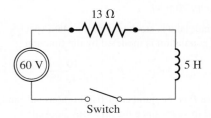

68. A *learning curve* is a graph of a function $P(t)$ that measures the performance of someone learning a skill as a function of the training time t. At first, the rate of learning is rapid. Then, as performance increases and approaches a maximal value M, the rate of learning decreases. It has been found that the function $P(t) = M - Ce^{-kt}$, where k and C are positive constants and $C < M$, is a reasonable model for learning.

(a) Express the learning time t as a function of the performance level P.

(b) For a pole-vaulter in training, the learning curve is given by $P(t) = 20 - 14e^{-0.024t}$, where $P(t)$ is the height he is able to pole-vault after t months. After how many months of training is he able to vault 12 ft?

 (c) Draw a graph of the learning curve in part (b).

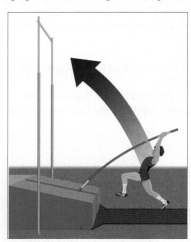

 69–76 ■ Use a graphing device to find all solutions of the equation, correct to two decimal places.

69. $\ln x = 3 - x$

70. $\log x = x^2 - 2$

71. $x^3 - x = \log(x + 1)$

72. $x = \ln(4 - x^2)$

73. $e^x = -x$

74. $2^{-x} = x - 1$

75. $4^{-x} = \sqrt{x}$

76. $e^{x^2} - 2 = x^3 - x$

77–80 ■ Solve the inequality.

77. $\log 2 + \log(9 - x) < 1$

78. $3 \leq \log_2 x \leq 4$

79. $2 < 10^x < 5$

80. $x^2 e^x - 2e^x < 0$

81–83 ■ Solve the equation.

81. $(x - 1)^{\log(x-1)} = 100(x - 1)$

82. $\log_2 x + \log_4 x + \log_8 x = 11$

83. $4^x - 2^{x+1} = 3$
[*Hint:* First write the equation as a quadratic equation in 2^x.]

■ **DISCOVERY · DISCUSSION**

84. **Estimating a Solution**   Without actually solving the equation, find two whole numbers between which the solution of $9^x = 20$ must lie. Do the same for $9^x = 100$. Explain how you reached your conclusions.

85. **A Surprising Equation**   Take logarithms to show that the equation

$$x^{1/\log x} = 5$$

has no solution. For what values of k does the equation

$$x^{1/\log x} = k$$

have a solution? What does this tell us about the graph of the function $f(x) = x^{1/\log x}$? Confirm your answer using a graphing device.

7.5   MODELING WITH EXPONENTIAL AND LOGARITHMIC FUNCTIONS

Many processes that occur in nature, such as population growth, radioactive decay, heat diffusion, and numerous others, can be modeled using exponential functions. Logarithmic functions are used in models for the loudness of sounds, the intensity of earthquakes, and many other phenomena. In this section we study exponential and logarithmic models.

■ Exponential Models of Population Growth

Biologists have observed that the population of a species doubles its size in a fixed period of time. For example, under ideal conditions a certain population of bacteria doubles in size every 3 hours. If the culture is started with 1000 bacteria, then after 3 hours there will be 2000 bacteria, after another 3 hours there will be 4000, and so on. If we let $n = n(t)$ be the number of bacteria after t hours, then

$$n(0) = 1000$$

$$n(3) = 1000 \cdot 2$$

$$n(6) = (1000 \cdot 2) \cdot 2 = 1000 \cdot 2^2$$

$$n(9) = (1000 \cdot 2^2) \cdot 2 = 1000 \cdot 2^3$$

$$n(12) = (1000 \cdot 2^3) \cdot 2 = 1000 \cdot 2^4$$

From this pattern it appears that the number of bacteria after t hours is modeled by the function

$$n(t) = 1000 \cdot 2^{t/3}$$

In general, suppose that the initial size of a population is n_0 and the doubling period is a. Then the size of the population at time t is modeled by

$$n(t) = n_0 2^{ct}$$

where $c = 1/a$. If we knew the tripling time b, then the formula would be $n(t) = n_0 3^{ct}$ where $c = 1/b$. These formulas indicate that the growth of the bacteria is modeled by an exponential function. But what base should we use? The answer is e, because then it can be shown (using calculus) that the population is modeled by

$$n(t) = n_0 e^{rt}$$

where r is the *relative rate of growth of population, expressed as a proportion of the population at any time*. For instance, if $r = 0.02$, then at any time t the growth rate is 2% of the population at time t.

rates at which predator eats prey and the rates of growth of each population. Notice that as predator eats prey, the prey population decreases; this means less food supply for the predators, so their population begins to decrease; with fewer predators the prey population begins to increase, and so on. (See the *Discovery Project* on page 146.) Normally, a state of equilibrium develops, and the two populations alternate between a minimum and a maximum. Notice that if the predators eat the prey too fast they will be left without food and ensure their own extinction.

Notice that the formula for population growth is the same as that for continuously compounded interest. In fact, the same principle is at work in both cases: The growth of a population (or an investment) per time period is proportional to the size of the population (or the amount of the investment). A population of 1,000,000 will increase more in one year than a population of 1000; in exactly the same way, an investment of $1,000,000 will increase more in one year than an investment of $1000.

EXPONENTIAL GROWTH MODEL

A population that experiences **exponential growth** increases according to the model

$$n(t) = n_0 e^{rt}$$

where $n(t)$ = population at time t

n_0 = initial size of the population

r = relative rate of growth (expressed as a proportion of the population)

t = time

In the following examples we assume that the populations grow exponentially.

EXAMPLE 1 ■ Predicting the Size of a Population

The initial bacterium count in a culture is 500. A biologist later makes a sample count of bacteria in the culture and finds that the relative rate of growth is 40% per hour.

(a) Find a function that models the number of bacteria after t hours.
(b) What is the estimated count after 10 hours?
(c) Sketch the graph of the function $n(t)$.

SOLUTION

(a) We use the exponential growth model with $n_0 = 500$ and $r = 0.4$ to get

$$n(t) = 500 e^{0.4t}$$

where t is measured in hours.

(b) Using the function in part (a), we find that the bacterium count after 10 hours is

$$n(10) = 500 e^{0.4(10)} = 500 e^4 \approx 27,300$$

(c) The graph is shown in Figure 1.

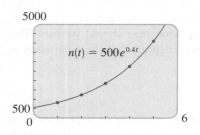

FIGURE 1

EXAMPLE 2 ■ Comparing Effects of Different Rates of Population Growth

In 2000 the population of the world was 6.1 billion and the relative rate of growth was 1.4% per year. It is claimed that a rate of 1.0% per year would make a significant difference in the total population in just a few decades. Test this claim by estimating the population of the world in the year 2050 using a relative rate of growth of (a) 1.4% per year and (b) 1.0% per year.

Graph the population functions for the next 100 years for the two relative growth rates in the same viewing rectangle.

SOLUTION

(a) By the exponential growth model, we have

$$n(t) = 6.1e^{0.014t}$$

where $n(t)$ is measured in billions and t is measured in years since 2000. Because the year 2050 is 50 years after 2000, we find

$$n(50) = 6.1e^{0.014(50)} = 6.1e^{0.7} \approx 12.3$$

Thus, the estimated population in the year 2050 is about 12.3 billion.

(b) We use the function

$$n(t) = 6.1e^{0.010t}$$

and find

$$n(50) = 6.1e^{0.010(50)} = 6.1e^{0.50} \approx 10.1$$

So, the estimated population in the year 2050 is about 10.1 billion.

The graphs in Figure 2 show that a small change in the relative rate of growth will, over time, make a large difference in population size.   ■

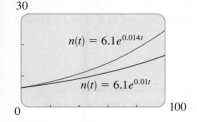

FIGURE 2

EXAMPLE 3 ■ Finding the Initial Population

A certain breed of rabbit was introduced onto a small island about 8 years ago. The current rabbit population on the island is estimated to be 4100, with a relative growth rate of 55% per year.

(a) What was the initial size of the rabbit population?
(b) Estimate the population 12 years from now.

SOLUTION

(a) From the exponential growth model, we have

$$n(t) = n_0 e^{0.55t}$$

and we know that the population at time $t = 8$ is $n(8) = 4100$.

We substitute what we know into the equation and solve for n_0:

$$4100 = n_0 e^{0.55(8)}$$

$$n_0 = \frac{4100}{e^{0.55(8)}} \approx \frac{4100}{81.45} \approx 50$$

Thus, we estimate that 50 rabbits were introduced onto the island.

Another way to solve part (b) is to let t be the number of years from now. In this case, $n_0 = 4100$ (the current population), and the population 12 years from now will be

$$n(12) = 4100e^{0.55(12)} \approx 3 \text{ million}$$

(b) Now that we know n_0, we can write a formula for population growth:

$$n(t) = 50e^{0.55t}$$

Twelve years from now, $t = 20$ and

$$n(20) = 50e^{0.55(20)} \approx 2,993,707$$

So, we estimate that the rabbit population on the island 12 years from now will be about 3 million. ∎

Can the rabbit population in Example 3(b) actually reach such a high number? In reality, as the island becomes overpopulated with rabbits, the rabbit population growth will be slowed due to food shortage and other factors. One model that takes into account such factors is the *logistic growth model* described in *Focus on Modeling*, Problem 10, page 509.

EXAMPLE 4 ■ World Population Projections

The population of the world in 2000 was 6.1 billion, and the estimated relative growth rate was 1.4% per year. If the population continues to grow at this rate, when will it reach 122 billion?

SOLUTION

Standing Room Only

The population of the world was about 6.1 billion in 2000, and was increasing at 1.4% per year. Using the exponential model for population growth, and assuming that each person occupies an average of 4 ft² of the surface of the earth, we find that by the year 2801 there will be standing room only! (The total land surface area of the world is about 1.8×10^{15} ft².)

We use the population growth function with $n_0 = 6.1$ billion, $r = 0.014$, and $n(t) = 122$ billion. This leads to an exponential equation, which we solve for t.

$$6.1e^{0.014t} = 122$$

$$e^{0.014t} = 20 \qquad \text{Divide by 6.1}$$

$$\ln e^{0.014t} = \ln 20 \qquad \text{Take ln of each side}$$

$$0.014t = \ln 20 \qquad \text{Property of ln}$$

$$t = \frac{\ln 20}{0.014} \qquad \text{Divide by 0.014}$$

$$t \approx 213.98 \qquad \text{Use a calculator}$$

Thus, the population will reach 122 billion in approximately 214 years, that is, in the year $2000 + 214 = 2214$. ∎

EXAMPLE 5 ■ **The Number of Bacteria in a Culture**

A culture starts with 10,000 bacteria, and the number doubles every 40 min.

(a) Find a function that models the number of bacteria at time t.
(b) Find the number of bacteria after one hour.
(c) After how many minutes will there be 50,000 bacteria?
(d) Sketch a graph of the number of bacteria at time t.

SOLUTION

(a) To find the function that models this population growth, we need to find the rate r. To do this, we use the formula for population growth with $n_0 = 10{,}000$, $t = 40$, and $n(t) = 20{,}000$, and then solve for r.

$$10{,}000 \cdot e^{r(40)} = 20{,}000$$

$$e^{40r} = 2 \qquad \text{Divide by 10,000}$$

$$\ln e^{40r} = \ln 2 \qquad \text{Take ln of each side}$$

$$40r = \ln 2 \qquad \text{Property of ln}$$

$$r = \frac{\ln 2}{40} \qquad \text{Divide by 40}$$

$$r \approx 0.01733 \qquad \text{Use a calculator}$$

Now that we know $r \approx 0.01733$, we can write the function for the population growth:

$$n(t) = 10{,}000 \cdot e^{0.01733t}$$

(b) Using the function we found in part (a) with $t = 60$ min (one hour), we get

$$n(60) = 10{,}000 \cdot e^{0.01733(60)} \approx 28{,}287$$

Thus, the number of bacteria after one hour is approximately 28,000.

(c) We use the function we found in part (a) with $n(t) = 50{,}000$ and solve the resulting exponential equation for t.

$$10{,}000 \cdot e^{0.01733t} = 50{,}000$$

$$e^{0.01733t} = 5 \qquad \text{Divide by 10,000}$$

$$\ln e^{0.01733t} = \ln 5 \qquad \text{Take ln of each side}$$

$$0.01733t = \ln 5 \qquad \text{Property of ln}$$

$$t = \frac{\ln 5}{0.01733} \qquad \text{Divide by 0.01733}$$

$$t \approx 92.9 \qquad \text{Use a calculator}$$

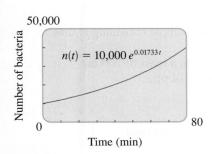

FIGURE 3

The bacterium count will reach 50,000 in approximately 93 min.

(d) The graph of the function $n(t) = 10{,}000 \cdot e^{0.01733t}$ is shown in Figure 3. ■

■ Radioactive Decay

Radioactive substances decay by spontaneously emitting radiation. The rate of decay is directly proportional to the mass of the substance. This is analogous to population growth, except that the mass of radioactive material *decreases*. It can be shown that the mass $m(t)$ remaining at time t is modeled by the function

$$m(t) = m_0 e^{-rt}$$

where r is the rate of decay expressed as a proportion of the mass and m_0 is the initial mass. Physicists express the rate of decay in terms of **half-life**, the time required for half the mass to decay. We can obtain the rate r from this as follows. If h is the half-life, then a mass of 1 unit becomes $\frac{1}{2}$ unit when $t = h$. Substituting this into the model, we get

$$\tfrac{1}{2} = 1 \cdot e^{-rh}$$

$$\ln\!\left(\tfrac{1}{2}\right) = -rh \qquad\qquad \text{Take ln of each side}$$

$$r = -\frac{1}{h}\ln(2^{-1}) \qquad\qquad \text{Solve for } r$$

$$r = \frac{\ln 2}{h} \qquad\qquad \ln 2^{-1} = -\ln 2 \text{ by Law 3}$$

This last equation allows us to find the rate r from the half-life h.

Half-lives of **radioactive elements** vary from very long to very short. Here are some examples.

Element	Half-life
Thorium-232	14.5 billion years
Uranium-235	4.5 billion years
Thorium-230	80,000 years
Plutonium-239	24,360 years
Carbon-14	5,730 years
Radium-226	1,600 years
Cesium-137	30 years
Strontium-90	28 years
Polonium-210	140 days
Thorium-234	25 days
Iodine-135	8 days
Radon-222	3.8 days
Lead-211	3.6 minutes
Krypton-91	10 seconds

RADIOACTIVE DECAY MODEL

If m_0 is the initial mass of a radioactive substance with half-life h, then the mass remaining at time t is modeled by the function

$$m(t) = m_0 e^{-rt}$$

where $r = \dfrac{\ln 2}{h}$.

EXAMPLE 6 ■ Radioactive Decay

Polonium-210 (^{210}Po) has a half-life of 140 days. Suppose a sample of this substance has a mass of 300 mg.

(a) Find a function that models the amount of the sample remaining at time t.
(b) Find the mass remaining after one year.
(c) How long will it take for the sample to decay to a mass of 200 mg?
 (d) Draw a graph of the sample mass as a function of time.

SOLUTION

(a) Using the model for radioactive decay with $m_0 = 300$ and $r = (\ln 2/140) \approx 0.00495$, we have

$$m(t) = 300e^{-0.00495t}$$

(b) We use the function we found in part (a) with $t = 365$ (one year).

$$m(365) = 300e^{-0.00495(365)} \approx 49.256$$

Thus, approximately 49 mg of ^{210}Po remains after one year.

(c) We use the function we found in part (a) with $m(t) = 200$ and solve the resulting exponential equation for t.

$$300e^{-0.00495t} = 200$$

$$e^{-0.00495t} = \tfrac{2}{3} \qquad \text{Divide by 300}$$

$$\ln e^{-0.00495t} = \ln \tfrac{2}{3} \qquad \text{Take ln of each side}$$

$$-0.00495t = \ln \tfrac{2}{3} \qquad \text{Property of ln}$$

$$t = -\frac{\ln \tfrac{2}{3}}{0.00495} \qquad \text{Divide by } -0.00495$$

$$t \approx 81.9 \qquad \text{Use a calculator}$$

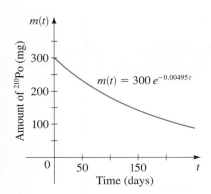

The time required for the sample to decay to 200 mg is about 82 days.

(d) A graph of the function $m(t) = 300e^{-0.00495t}$ is shown in Figure 4. ∎

FIGURE 4

Newton's Law of Cooling

Newton's Law of Cooling states that the rate of cooling of an object is proportional to the temperature difference between the object and its surroundings, provided that the temperature difference is not too large. Using calculus, the following model can be deduced from this law.

NEWTON'S LAW OF COOLING

If D_0 is the initial temperature difference between an object and its surroundings, and if its surroundings have temperature T_s, then the temperature of the object at time t is modeled by the function

$$T(t) = T_s + D_0 e^{-kt}$$

where k is a positive constant that depends on the type of object.

EXAMPLE 7 ■ Newton's Law of Cooling

A cup of coffee has a temperature of 200°F and is placed in a room that has a temperature of 70°F. After 10 min the temperature of the coffee is 150°F.

(a) Find a function that models the temperature of the coffee at time t.
(b) Find the temperature of the coffee after 15 min.
(c) When will the coffee have cooled to 100°F?

(d) Illustrate by drawing a graph of the temperature function.

Radioactive Waste

Harmful radioactive isotopes are produced whenever a nuclear reaction occurs, whether as the result of an atomic bomb test, a nuclear accident such as the one at Chernobyl in 1986, or the uneventful production of electricity at a nuclear power plant.

One radioactive material produced in atomic bombs is the isotope strontium-90 (^{90}Sr), with a half-life of 28 years. This is deposited like calcium in human bone tissue, where it can cause leukemia and other cancers. However, in the decades since atmospheric testing of nuclear weapons was halted, ^{90}Sr levels in the environment have fallen to a level that no longer poses a threat to health.

Nuclear power plants produce radioactive plutonium-239 (^{239}Pu), which has a half-life of 24,360 years. Because of its long half-life, ^{239}Pu could pose a threat to the environment for thousands of years. So, great care must be taken to dispose of it properly. The difficulty of ensuring the safety of the disposed radioactive waste is one reason that nuclear power plants remain controversial.

SOLUTION

(a) The temperature of the room is $T_s = 70°F$, and the initial temperature difference is

$$D_0 = 200 - 70 = 130°F$$

So, by Newton's Law of Cooling, the temperature after t minutes is modeled by the function

$$T(t) = 70 + 130e^{-kt}$$

We need to find the constant k associated with this cup of coffee. To do this, we use the fact that when $t = 10$, the temperature is $T(10) = 150$. So we have

$$70 + 130e^{-10k} = 150$$

$$130e^{-10k} = 80 \qquad \text{Subtract 70}$$

$$e^{-10k} = \tfrac{8}{13} \qquad \text{Divide by 130}$$

$$-10k = \ln \tfrac{8}{13} \qquad \text{Take ln of each side}$$

$$k = -\tfrac{1}{10} \ln \tfrac{8}{13} \qquad \text{Divide by } -10$$

$$k \approx 0.04855 \qquad \text{Use a calculator}$$

Substituting this value of k into the expression for $T(t)$, we get

$$T(t) = 70 + 130e^{-0.04855t}$$

(b) We use the function we found in part (a) with $t = 15$.

$$T(15) = 70 + 130e^{-0.04855(15)} \approx 133°F$$

(c) We use the function we found in part (a) with $T(t) = 100$ and solve the resulting exponential equation for t.

$$70 + 130e^{-0.04855t} = 100$$

$$130e^{-0.04855t} = 30 \qquad \text{Subtract 70}$$

$$e^{-0.04855t} = \tfrac{3}{13} \qquad \text{Divide by 130}$$

$$-0.04855t = \ln \tfrac{3}{13} \qquad \text{Take ln of each side}$$

$$t = \frac{\ln \tfrac{3}{13}}{-0.04855} \qquad \text{Divide by 0.04855}$$

$$t \approx 30.2 \qquad \text{Use a calculator}$$

The coffee will have cooled to 100°F after about half an hour.

(d) The graph of the temperature function is sketched in Figure 5. Notice that the line $t = 70$ is a horizontal asymptote. (Why?)

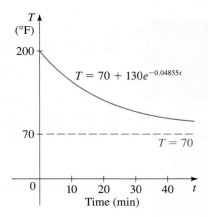

FIGURE 5

Temperature of coffee after t minutes

Logarithmic Scales

When a physical quantity varies over a very large range, it is often convenient to take its logarithm in order to have a more manageable set of numbers. We discuss three such situations: the pH scale, which measures acidity; the Richter scale, which measures the intensity of earthquakes; and the decibel scale, which measures the loudness of sounds. Other quantities that are measured on logarithmic scales are light intensity, information capacity, and radiation.

THE pH SCALE   Chemists measured the acidity of a solution by giving its hydrogen ion concentration until Sorensen, in 1909, proposed a more convenient measure. He defined

$$pH = -\log[H^+]$$

where $[H^+]$ is the concentration of hydrogen ions measured in moles per liter (M). He did this to avoid very small numbers and negative exponents. For instance,

$$\text{if} \quad [H^+] = 10^{-4} \text{ M}, \qquad \text{then} \qquad pH = -\log_{10}(10^{-4}) = -(-4) = 4$$

Solutions with a pH of 7 are defined as *neutral*, those with pH < 7 are *acidic*, and those with pH > 7 are *basic*. Notice that when the pH increases by one unit, $[H^+]$ decreases by a factor of 10.

EXAMPLE 8 ■ **pH Scale and Hydrogen Ion Concentration**

(a) The hydrogen ion concentration of a sample of human blood was measured to be $[H^+] = 3.16 \times 10^{-8}$ M. Find the pH and classify the blood as acidic or basic.

Law Enforcement
Mathematics aids law enforcement in numerous and surprising ways, from the reconstruction of bullet trajectories, to determining the time of death, to calculating the probability that a DNA sample is from a particular person. One interesting use is in the search for missing persons. If a person has been missing for several years, that person may look quite different than their most recent available photograph. This is particularly true if the missing person is a child. Have you ever wondered what you will look like 5, 10, or 15 years from now?

Researchers have found that different parts of the body grow at different rates. For example, you no doubt noticed that a baby's head is much larger relative to its body than an adult's. As another example, the ratio of arm length to height is $\frac{1}{3}$ in a child but about $\frac{2}{5}$ in an adult. By collecting data and analyzing the graphs, researchers are able to determine the functions that model growth. As in all growth phenomena, exponential and logarithmic functions play a crucial role. For instance, the formula that relates arm length l to height h is $l = ae^{kh}$ where a and k are constants. By studying various physical characteristics of a person, mathematical biologists model each characteristic by a function that describes how it

(continued)

(b) The most acidic rainfall ever measured occurred in Scotland in 1974; its pH was 2.4. Find the hydrogen ion concentration.

SOLUTION

(a) A calculator gives

$$\text{pH} = -\log[\text{H}^+] = -\log(3.16 \times 10^{-8}) \approx 7.5$$

Since this is greater than 7, the blood is basic.

(b) To find the hydrogen ion concentration, we need to solve for $[\text{H}^+]$ in the logarithmic equation

$$\log[\text{H}^+] = -\text{pH}$$

So, we write it in exponential form.

$$[\text{H}^+] = 10^{-\text{pH}}$$

In this case, pH = 2.4, so

$$[\text{H}^+] = 10^{-2.4} \approx 4.0 \times 10^{-3} \text{ M} \qquad \blacksquare$$

THE RICHTER SCALE In 1935 the American geologist Charles Richter (1900–1984) defined the magnitude M of an earthquake to be

$$M = \log \frac{I}{S}$$

where I is the intensity of the earthquake (measured by the amplitude of a seismograph reading taken 100 km from the epicenter of the earthquake) and S is the intensity of a "standard" earthquake (whose amplitude is 1 micron = 10^{-4} cm). The magnitude of a standard earthquake is

$$M = \log \frac{S}{S} = \log 1 = 0$$

Richter studied many earthquakes that occurred between 1900 and 1950. The largest had magnitude 8.9 on the Richter scale, and the smallest had magnitude 0. This corresponds to a ratio of intensities of 800,000,000, so the Richter scale provides more manageable numbers to work with. For instance, an earthquake of magnitude 6 is ten times stronger than an earthquake of magnitude 5.

EXAMPLE 9 ■ **Magnitude of Earthquakes**

The 1906 earthquake in San Francisco had an estimated magnitude of 8.3 on the Richter scale. In the same year the strongest earthquake ever recorded occurred on

changes over time. Models of facial characteristics can be programmed into a computer to give a picture of how a person's appearance changes over time. These pictures aid law enforcement agencies in locating missing persons.

the Colombia-Ecuador border and was four times as intense. What was the magnitude of the Colombia-Ecuador earthquake on the Richter scale?

SOLUTION

If I is the intensity of the San Francisco earthquake, then from the definition of magnitude we have

$$M = \log \frac{I}{S} = 8.3$$

The intensity of the Colombia-Ecuador earthquake was $4I$, so its magnitude was

$$M = \log \frac{4I}{S} = \log 4 + \log \frac{I}{S} = \log 4 + 8.3 \approx 8.9 \qquad \blacksquare$$

EXAMPLE 10 ■ Intensity of Earthquakes

The 1989 Loma Prieta earthquake that shook San Francisco had a magnitude of 7.1 on the Richter scale. How many times more intense was the 1906 earthquake (see Example 9) than the 1989 event?

SOLUTION

If I_1 and I_2 are the intensities of the 1906 and 1989 earthquakes, then we are required to find I_1/I_2. To relate this to the definition of magnitude, we divide numerator and denominator by S.

$$\log \frac{I_1}{I_2} = \log \frac{I_1/S}{I_2/S} \qquad \text{Divide numerator and denominator by } S$$

$$= \log \frac{I_1}{S} - \log \frac{I_2}{S} \qquad \text{Law 2 of Logarithms}$$

$$= 8.3 - 7.1 = 1.2 \qquad \text{Definition of earthquake magnitude}$$

Therefore

$$\frac{I_1}{I_2} = 10^{\log(I_1/I_2)} = 10^{1.2} \approx 16$$

The 1906 earthquake was about 16 times as intense as the 1989 earthquake. ■

THE DECIBEL SCALE   The ear is sensitive to an extremely wide range of sound intensities. We take as a reference intensity $I_0 = 10^{-12}$ W/m² (watts per square meter) at a frequency of 1000 hertz, which measures a sound that is just barely audible (the threshold of hearing). The psychological sensation of loudness varies with the logarithm of the intensity (the Weber-Fechner Law) and so the **intensity level** β, measured in decibels (dB), is defined as

$$\beta = 10 \log \frac{I}{I_0}$$

The intensity level of the barely audible reference sound is

$$\beta = 10 \log \frac{I_0}{I_0} = 10 \log 1 = 0 \text{ dB}$$

The **intensity levels of sounds** that we can hear vary from very loud to very soft. Here are some examples of the decibel levels of commonly heard sounds.

Source of sound	β (dB)
Jet takeoff	140
Jackhammer	130
Rock concert	120
Subway	100
Heavy traffic	80
Ordinary traffic	70
Normal conversation	50
Whisper	30
Rustling leaves	10–20
Threshold of hearing	0

EXAMPLE 11 ■ Sound Intensity of a Jet Takeoff

Find the decibel intensity level of a jet engine during takeoff if the intensity was measured at 100 W/m^2.

SOLUTION

From the definition of intensity level we see that

$$\beta = 10 \log \frac{I}{I_0} = 10 \log \frac{10^2}{10^{-12}} = 10 \log 10^{14} = 140 \text{ dB}$$

Thus, the intensity level is 140 dB. ■

The table in the margin lists decibel intensity levels for some common sounds ranging from the threshold of hearing to the jet takeoff of Example 11. The threshold of pain is about 120 dB.

7.5 EXERCISES

1–13 ■ These exercises use the population growth model.

1. The number of bacteria in a culture is modeled by the function

$$n(t) = 500e^{0.45t}$$

where t is measured in hours.
(a) What is the initial number of bacteria?
(b) What is the relative rate of growth of this bacterium population? Express your answer as a percentage.
(c) How many bacteria are in the culture after 3 hours?
(d) After how many hours will the number of bacteria reach 10,000?

2. The number of a certain species of fish is modeled by the function

$$n(t) = 12e^{0.012t}$$

where t is measured in years and $n(t)$ is measured in millions.
(a) What is the relative rate of growth of the fish population? Express your answer as a percentage.
(b) What will the fish population be after 5 years?
(c) After how many years will the number of fish reach 30 million?

(d) Sketch a graph of the fish population function $n(t)$.

3. The fox population in a certain region has a relative growth rate of 8% per year. It is estimated that the population in 2000 was 18,000.
(a) Find a function that models the population t years after 2000.
(b) Use the function from part (a) to estimate the fox population in the year 2008.
(c) Sketch a graph of the fox population function for the years 2000–2008.

4. The population of a country has relative growth rate of 3% per year. The government is trying to reduce the growth rate to 2%. The population in 1995 was approximately 110 million. Find the projected population for the year 2020 for the following conditions.
(a) The relative growth rate remains at 3% per year.
(b) The relative growth rate is reduced to 2% per year.

5. The population of a certain city was 112,000 in 1998, and the observed relative growth rate is 4% per year.
(a) Find a function that models the population after t years.
(b) Find the projected population in the year 2004.
(c) In what year will the population reach 200,000?

6. The frog population in a small pond grows exponentially. The current population is 85 frogs, and the relative growth rate is 18% per year.
(a) Find a function that models the population after t years.
(b) Find the projected population after 3 years.
(c) Find the number of years required for the frog population to reach 600.

7. The graph shows the deer population in a Pennsylvania county between 1996 and 2000. Assume that the population grows exponentially.
(a) What was the deer population in 1996?
(b) Find a function that models the deer population t years after 1996.
(c) What is the projected deer population in 2004?
(d) In what year will the deer population reach 100,000?

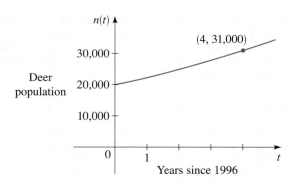

8. A culture contains 1500 bacteria initially and doubles every 30 min.
(a) Find a function that models the number of bacteria $n(t)$ after t minutes.
(b) Find the number of bacteria after 2 hours.
(c) After how many minutes will the culture contain 4000 bacteria?

9. A culture starts with 8600 bacteria. After one hour the count is 10,000.
(a) Find a function that models the number of bacteria $n(t)$ after t hours.
(b) Find the number of bacteria after 2 hours.
(c) After how many hours will the number of bacteria double?

10. The count in a culture of bacteria was 400 after 2 hours and 25,600 after 6 hours.
(a) What is the relative rate of growth of the bacterium population? Express your answer as a percentage.
(b) What was the initial size of the culture?
(c) Find a function that models the number of bacteria $n(t)$ after t hours.
(d) Find the number of bacteria after 4.5 hours.
(e) When will the number of bacteria be 50,000?

11. The population of the world was 5.7 billion in 1995 and the observed relative growth rate was 2% per year.
(a) By what year will the population have doubled?
(b) By what year will the population have tripled?

12. The population of California was 10,586,223 in 1950 and 23,668,562 in 1980. Assume the population grows exponentially.
(a) Find a function that models the population t years after 1950.
(b) Find the time required for the population to double.
(c) Use the function from part (a) to predict the population of California in the year 2000. Look up the actual California population in 2000, and compare.

13. An infectious strain of bacteria increases in number at a relative growth rate of 200% per hour. When a certain critical number of bacteria are present in the bloodstream, a person becomes ill. If a single bacterium infects a person, the critical level is reached in 24 hours. How long will it take for the critical level to be reached if the same person is infected with 10 bacteria?

14–22 ■ These exercises use the radioactive decay model.

14. The half-life of radium-226 is 1600 years. Suppose we have a 22-mg sample.
(a) Find a function that models the mass remaining after t years.
(b) How much of the sample will remain after 4000 years?
(c) After how long will only 18 mg of the sample remain?

15. The half-life of cesium-137 is 30 years. Suppose we have a 10-g sample.
   (a) Find a function that models the mass remaining after t years.
   (b) How much of the sample will remain after 80 years?
   (c) After how long will only 2 g of the sample remain?

16. The mass $m(t)$ remaining after t days from a 40-g sample of thorium-234 is given by

$$m(t) = 40e^{-0.0277t}$$

   (a) How much of the sample will remain after 60 days?
   (b) After how long will only 10 g of the sample remain?
   (c) Find the half-life of thorium-234.

17. The half-life of strontium-90 is 28 years. How long will it take a 50-mg sample to decay to a mass of 32 mg?

18. Radium-221 has a half-life of 30 s. How long will it take for 95% of a sample to decay?

19. If 250 mg of a radioactive element decays to 200 mg in 48 hours, find the half-life of the element.

20. After 3 days a sample of radon-222 has decayed to 58% of its original amount.
   (a) What is the half-life of radon-222?
   (b) How long will it take the sample to decay to 20% of its original amount?

21. A wooden artifact from an ancient tomb contains 65% of the carbon-14 that is present in living trees. How long ago was the artifact made? (The half-life of carbon-14 is 5730 years.)

22. The burial cloth of an Egyptian mummy is estimated to contain 59% of the carbon-14 it contained originally. How long ago was the mummy buried? (The half-life of carbon-14 is 5730 years.)

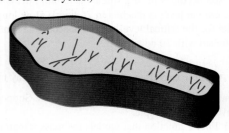

23–26 ■ These exercises use Newton's Law of Cooling.

23. A hot bowl of soup is served at a dinner party. It starts to cool according to Newton's Law of Cooling so that its temperature at time t is given by

$$T(t) = 65 + 145e^{-0.05t}$$

   where t is measured in minutes and T is measured in °F.
   (a) What is the initial temperature of the soup?
   (b) What is the temperature after 10 min?
   (c) After how long will the temperature be 100°F?

24. Newton's Law of Cooling is used in homicide investigations to determine the time of death. The normal body temperature is 98.6°F. Immediately following death, the body begins to cool. It has been determined experimentally that the constant in Newton's Law of Cooling is approximately $k = 0.1947$, assuming time is measured in hours. Suppose that the temperature of the surroundings is 60°F.
   (a) Find a function $T(t)$ that models the temperature t hours after death.
   (b) If the temperature of the body is now 72°F, how long ago was the time of death?

25. A roasted turkey is taken from an oven when its temperature has reached 185°F and is placed on a table in a room where the temperature is 75°F.
   (a) If the temperature of the turkey is 150°F after half an hour, what is its temperature after 45 min?
   (b) When will the turkey cool to 100°F?

26. A kettle full of water is brought to a boil in a room with temperature 20°C. After 15 min the temperature of the water has decreased from 100°C to 75°C. Find the temperature after another 10 min. Illustrate by sketching a graph of the temperature function.

27–41 ■ These exercises are about logarithmic scales.

27. The hydrogen ion concentration of a sample of each substance is given. Calculate the pH of the substance.
   (a) Lemon juice: $[H^+] = 5.0 \times 10^{-3}$ M
   (b) Tomato juice: $[H^+] = 3.2 \times 10^{-4}$ M
   (c) Seawater: $[H^+] = 5.0 \times 10^{-9}$ M

28. An unknown substance has a hydrogen ion concentration of $[H^+] = 3.1 \times 10^{-8}$ M. Find the pH and classify the substance as acidic or basic.

29. The pH reading of a sample of each substance is given. Calculate the hydrogen ion concentration of the substance.
(a) Vinegar: pH = 3.0
(b) Milk: pH = 6.5

30. The pH reading of a glass of liquid is given. Find the hydrogen ion concentration of the liquid.
(a) Beer: pH = 4.6
(b) Water: pH = 7.3

31. The hydrogen ion concentrations in cheeses range from 4.0×10^{-7} M to 1.6×10^{-5} M. Find the corresponding range of pH readings.

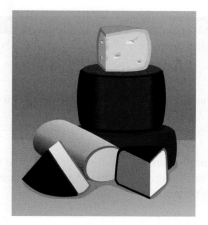

32. The pH readings for wines vary from 2.8 to 3.8. Find the corresponding range of hydrogen ion concentrations.

33. If one earthquake is 20 times as intense as another, how much larger is its magnitude on the Richter scale?

34. The 1906 earthquake in San Francisco had a magnitude of 8.3 on the Richter scale. At the same time in Japan an earthquake with magnitude 4.9 caused only minor damage. How many times more intense was the San Francisco earthquake than the Japanese earthquake?

35. The Alaska earthquake of 1964 had a magnitude of 8.6 on the Richter scale. How many times more intense was this than the 1906 San Francisco earthquake? (See Exercise 34.)

36. The Northridge, California, earthquake of 1994 had a magnitude of 6.8 on the Richter scale. A year later, a 7.2-magnitude earthquake struck Kobe, Japan. How many times more intense was the Kobe earthquake than the Northridge earthquake?

37. The 1985 Mexico City earthquake had a magnitude of 8.1 on the Richter scale. The 1976 earthquake in Tangshan, China, was 1.26 times as intense. What was the magnitude of the Tangshan earthquake?

38. The intensity of the sound of traffic at a busy intersection was measured at 2.0×10^{-5} W/m². Find the intensity level in decibels.

39. The intensity level of the sound of a subway train was measured at 98 dB. Find the intensity in W/m².

40. The noise from a power mower was measured at 106 dB. The noise level at a rock concert was measured at 120 dB. Find the ratio of the intensity of the rock music to that of the power mower.

41. A law of physics states that the intensity of sound is inversely proportional to the square of the distance d from the source:

$$I = \frac{k}{d^2}$$

(a) Use this model and the equation

$$\beta = 10 \log \frac{I}{I_0}$$

(described in this section) to show that the decibel levels β_1 and β_2 at distances d_1 and d_2 from a sound source are related by the equation

$$\beta_2 = \beta_1 + 20 \log \frac{d_1}{d_2}$$

(b) The intensity level at a rock concert is 120 dB at a distance 2 m from the speakers. Find the intensity level at a distance of 10 m.

7.6   DAMPED HARMONIC MOTION

In Section 2.5 we learned about modeling harmonic motion using sine and cosine functions. For instance, we saw that a mass suspended on a spring from the ceiling and then set into motion will move up and down, with its vertical displacement given by a function of the form $y = k \cos \omega t$. Of course, we know that in real life this motion won't continue forever. Air resistance and friction in the spring will cause the amplitude of the motion to decline and eventually become imperceptible. Motion of this kind is called *damped harmonic motion*. Using the laws of physics and a branch of mathematics called Differential Equations, it can be shown that damped harmonic motion can be described as in the following box.

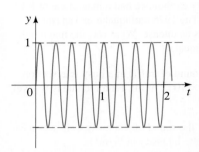

(a) Harmonic motion: $y = \sin 8\pi t$

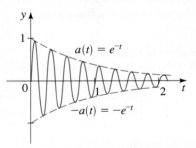

(b) Damped harmonic motion:
$y = e^{-t} \sin 8\pi t$

FIGURE 1

> ### DAMPED HARMONIC MOTION
>
> If the equation describing the displacement y of an object at time t is
>
> $$y = ke^{-ct} \sin \omega t \qquad \text{or} \qquad y = ke^{-ct} \cos \omega t \qquad (c > 0)$$
>
> then the object is in **damped harmonic motion**. The constant c is the **damping constant**.

Damped harmonic motion is simply harmonic motion for which the amplitude is governed by the function $a(t) = ke^{-ct}$. Figure 1 shows the difference between harmonic motion and damped harmonic motion.

EXAMPLE 1 ■ Modeling Damped Harmonic Motion

Two mass-spring systems are experiencing damped harmonic motion, both at 0.5 cycles per second, and both with an initial maximum displacement of 10 cm. The first has a damping constant of 0.5 and the second has a damping constant of 0.1.

(a) Find functions of the form $g(t) = ke^{-ct} \cos \omega t$ to model the motion in each case.

(b) Graph the two functions you found in part (a). How do they differ?

SOLUTION

(a) At time $t = 0$, the displacement is 10 cm. Thus $g(0) = ke^{-c \cdot 0} \cos(\omega \cdot 0) = k$, and so $k = 10$. Also, the frequency is $f = 0.5$ Hz, and since $\omega = 2\pi f$ (see Section 2.5), we get $\omega = 2\pi(0.5) = \pi$. Using the given damping constants, we find that the motions of the two springs are given by the functions

$$g_1(t) = 10e^{-0.5t} \cos \pi t \qquad \text{and} \qquad g_2(t) = 10e^{-0.1t} \cos \pi t$$

Hz is the abbreviation for hertz. One hertz is one cycle per second.

(b) The functions g_1 and g_2 are graphed in Figure 2. From the graphs we see that in the first case (where the damping constant is larger) the motion dies down quickly, whereas in the second case, perceptible motion continues much longer.

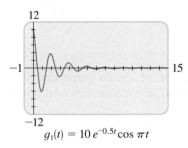

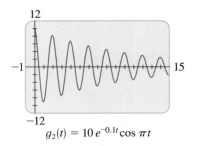

FIGURE 2

$g_1(t) = 10\, e^{-0.5t} \cos \pi t$

$g_2(t) = 10\, e^{-0.1t} \cos \pi t$ ■

As the preceding example indicates, the larger the damping constant c, the quicker the oscillation dies down. When a guitar string is plucked and then allowed to vibrate freely, a point on that string undergoes damped harmonic motion. We can hear the damping of the motion as the sound produced by the vibration of the string fades. How fast the damping of the string occurs (as measured by the size of the constant c) is a property of the size of the string and the material it is made of. Another example of damped harmonic motion is the motion that a shock absorber on a car undergoes when the car hits a bump in the road. In this case, the shock absorber is engineered to damp the motion as quickly as possible (large c) and to have the frequency as small as possible (small ω). On the other hand, the sound produced by a tuba player playing a note is undamped as long as the player can maintain the loudness of the note. The electromagnetic waves that produce light move in simple harmonic motion that is not damped.

EXAMPLE 2 ■ A Vibrating Violin String

The G-string on a violin is pulled a distance of 0.5 cm above its rest position, then released and allowed to vibrate. The damping constant c for this string is determined to be 1.4. Suppose that the note produced is a pure G (frequency = 200 cycles per second). Find an equation that describes the motion of the point at which the string was plucked.

SOLUTION

Let P be the point at which the string was plucked. We will find a function $f(t)$ that gives the distance at time t of the point P from its original rest position. Since the maximum displacement occurs at $t = 0$, we find an equation in the form

$$y = ke^{-ct} \cos \omega t$$

From this equation, we see that $f(0) = k$. But we know that the original displacement of the string is 0.5 cm. Thus, $k = 0.5$. Since the frequency of the vibration is 200, we have $\omega = 2\pi f = 2\pi(200) = 400\pi$. Finally, since we know that the damping constant is 1.4, we get

$$f(t) = 0.5e^{-1.4t} \cos 400\pi t$$ ■

EXAMPLE 3 ■ Modeling Damped Harmonic Motion from its Graph

The motion of a mass suspended from the ceiling by a spring is graphed in Figure 3. Find an equation to model this damped harmonic motion.

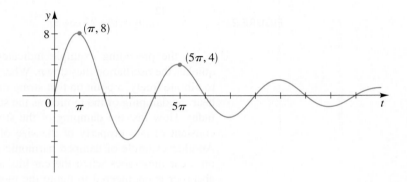

FIGURE 3

SOLUTION

This is a damped sine function, so we are looking for a function of the form $y = ke^{-ct} \sin \omega t$. First, we find the value of ω. One complete cycle of the motion occurs between $t = 0$ and $t = 4\pi$, so the period* is $p = 4\pi$. Thus, $\omega = 2\pi/p = (2\pi)/(4\pi) = 0.5$.

Now we determine the value of c. When $t = \pi$, the displacement is $y = 8$, and when $t = 5\pi$, the displacement is 4. Thus, we have

$$8 = ke^{-c\pi} \sin(0.5\pi) \qquad \text{Set } t = \pi \text{ and } \omega = 0.5$$

$$8 = ke^{-c\pi} \qquad \text{sin}(0.5\pi) = 1$$

and

$$4 = ke^{-c5\pi} \sin(2.5\pi) \qquad \text{Set } t = 5\pi \text{ and } \omega = 0.5$$

$$4 = ke^{-c5\pi} \qquad \text{sin}(2.5\pi) = 1$$

---

*In the case of damped harmonic motion, the term *quasi-period* is often used instead of *period* because the motion is not actually periodic—it diminishes with time. However, we will continue to use the term *period* to avoid confusion.

Dividing these two equations, we get

$$\frac{8}{4} = \frac{ke^{-c\pi}}{ke^{-5c\pi}} \qquad \text{Divide}$$

$$2 = e^{5c\pi - c\pi} = e^{4c\pi} \qquad \text{Simplify}$$

$$\ln 2 = 4c\pi \qquad \text{Take natural logarithms}$$

$$c = \frac{\ln 2}{4\pi} \approx 0.05516 \qquad \text{Solve for } c$$

Finally, we must find k. Using the fact that when $t = \pi$ we have $y = 8$, we get

$$8 = ke^{-0.05516\pi} \sin(0.5\pi) \qquad \text{Set } t = \pi, c = 0.05516, \text{ and } \omega = 0.5$$

$$k = \frac{8}{e^{-0.05516\pi} \sin(0.5\pi)} \approx 9.51 \qquad \text{Solve for } k$$

Thus, the function that models this damped harmonic motion is
$y = 9.51e^{-0.05516t} \sin(0.5t)$. ∎

EXAMPLE 4 ■ Ripples on a Pond

A stone is dropped in a calm lake, causing waves to form. The up-and-down motion of a point on the surface of the water is modeled by damped harmonic motion. At some time the amplitude of the wave is measured, and 20 s later it is found that the amplitude has dropped to $\frac{1}{10}$ of this value. Find the damping constant c.

SOLUTION

The amplitude is governed by the coefficient ke^{-ct} in the equations for damped harmonic motion. Thus, the amplitude at time t is ke^{-ct}, and 20 s later, it is $ke^{-c(t+20)}$. So, from the given information

$$ke^{-c(t+20)} = \tfrac{1}{10} ke^{-ct}$$

We now solve this equation for c. Canceling k and using the Laws of Exponents, we get

$$e^{-ct} \cdot e^{-20c} = \tfrac{1}{10} e^{-ct}$$

$$e^{-20c} = \tfrac{1}{10} \qquad \text{Cancel } e^{-ct}$$

$$e^{20c} = 10 \qquad \text{Take reciprocals}$$

Taking the natural logarithm of each side gives

$$20c = \ln(10)$$

$$c = \tfrac{1}{20} \ln(10) \approx \tfrac{1}{20}(2.30) \approx 0.12$$

Thus, the damping constant is $c \approx 0.12$. ∎

7.6 EXERCISES

1–4 ■ An initial amplitude k, damping constant c, and frequency f or period p are given. (Recall from Section 2.5 that frequency and period are related by the equation $f = 1/p$.)
(a) Find a function of the form $y = ke^{-ct} \cos \omega t$ that models damped harmonic motion.
(b) Graph the function.

1. $k = 2$, $c = 1.5$, $f = 3$

2. $k = 15$, $c = 0.25$, $f = 0.6$

3. $k = 100$, $c = 0.05$, $p = 4$

4. $k = 0.75$, $c = 3$, $p = 3\pi$

5–8 ■ An initial amplitude k, damping constant c, and frequency f or period p are given. (Recall from Section 2.5 that period and frequency are related by the equation $p = 1/f$.)
(a) Find a function of the form $y = ke^{-ct} \sin \omega t$ that models damped harmonic motion.
(b) Graph the function.

5. $k = 7$, $c = 10$, $p = \pi/6$

6. $k = 1$, $c = 1$, $p = 1$

7. $k = 0.3$, $c = 0.2$, $f = 20$

8. $k = 12$, $c = 0.01$, $f = 8$

9–12 ■ Find a function of the form $y = ke^{-ct} \sin \omega t$ or $y = ke^{-ct} \cos \omega t$ that models the damped harmonic motion whose graph is shown.

9.

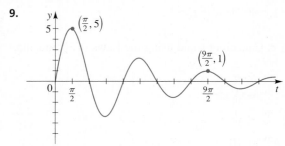

10.

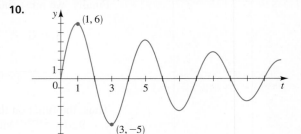

11.

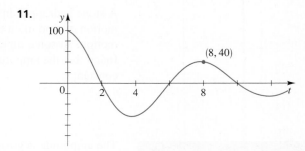

12.

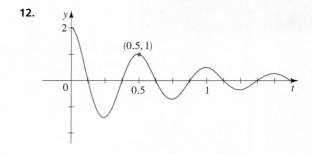

13. A strong gust of wind strikes a tall building, causing it to sway back and forth in damped harmonic motion. The frequency of the oscillation is 0.5 cycle per second and the damping constant is $c = 0.9$. Find an equation that describes the motion of the building. (Assume $k = 1$ and take $t = 0$ to be the instant when the gust of wind strikes the building.)

14. When a car hits a certain bump on the road, a shock absorber on the car is compressed a distance of 6 in., then released (see the figure). The shock absorber vibrates in damped harmonic motion with a frequency of 2 cycles per second. The damping constant for this particular shock absorber is 2.8.

(a) Find an equation that describes the displacement of the shock absorber from its rest position as a function of time. Take $t = 0$ to be the instant that the shock absorber is released.

(b) How long does it take for the amplitude of the vibration to decrease to 0.5 in?

15. A tuning fork is struck and oscillates in damped harmonic motion. The amplitude of the motion is measured, and 3 s later it is found that the amplitude has dropped to $\frac{1}{4}$ of this value. Find the damping constant c for this tuning fork.

16. A guitar string is pulled at point P a distance of 3 cm above its rest position. It is then released and vibrates in damped harmonic motion with a frequency of 165 cycles per second. After 2 s, it is observed that the amplitude of the vibration at point P is 0.6 cm.

(a) Find the damping constant c.

(b) Find an equation that describes the position of point P above its rest position as a function of time. Take $t = 0$ to be the instant that the string is released.

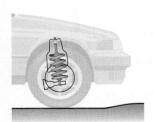 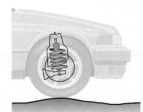 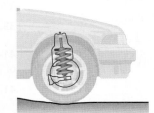

7 REVIEW

CONCEPT CHECK

1. (a) Write an equation that defines the exponential function with base a.

(b) What is the domain of this function?

(c) If $a \neq 1$, what is the range of this function?

(d) Sketch the general shape of the graph of the exponential function for each of the following cases.

    (i) $a > 1$ (ii) $a = 1$ (iii) $a < 1$

2. If x is large, which function grows faster, $y = 2^x$ or $y = x^2$?

3. (a) How is the number e defined?

(b) What is the natural exponential function?

4. (a) How is the logarithmic function $y = \log_a x$ defined?

(b) What is the domain of this function?

(c) What is the range of this function?

(d) Sketch the general shape of the graph of the function $y = \log_a x$ if $a > 1$.

(e) What is the natural logarithm?

(f) What is the common logarithm?

5. State the three Laws of Logarithms.

6. State the Change of Base Formula.

7. (a) How do you solve an exponential equation?
   (b) How do you solve a logarithmic equation?

8. Suppose an amount P is invested at an interest rate r and A is the amount after t years.
   (a) Write an expression for A if the interest is compounded n times per year.
   (b) Write an expression for A if the interest is compounded continuously.

9. If the initial size of a population is n_0 and the population grows exponentially with relative growth rate r, write an expression for the population $n(t)$ at time t.

10. (a) What is the half-life of a radioactive substance?
   (b) If a radioactive substance has initial mass m_0 and half-life h, write an expression for the mass $m(t)$ remaining at time t.

11. What does Newton's Law of Cooling say?

12. What do the pH scale, the Richter scale, and the decibel scale have in common? What do they measure?

13. What are the equations used to model damped harmonic motion? What is the damping constant?

EXERCISES

1–12 ■ Sketch the graph of the function. State the domain, range, and asymptote.

1. $f(x) = 3^{-x}$

2. $g(x) = 2^{x-1}$

3. $y = 5 - 10^x$

4. $y = 1 + 5^{-x}$

5. $f(x) = \log_3(x - 1)$

6. $g(x) = \log(-x)$

7. $y = 2 - \log_2 x$

8. $y = 3 + \log_5(x + 4)$

9. $F(x) = e^x - 1$

10. $G(x) = \frac{1}{2}e^{x-1}$

11. $y = 2 \ln x$

12. $y = \ln(x^2)$

13–16 ■ Find the domain of the function.

13. $f(x) = 10^{x^2} + \log(1 - 2x)$

14. $g(x) = \ln(2 + x)$

15. $h(x) = \ln(x^2 - 4)$

16. $k(x) = \ln |x|$

17–20 ■ Write the equation in exponential form.

17. $\log_2 1024 = 10$

18. $\log_6 37 = x$

19. $\log x = y$

20. $\ln c = 17$

21–24 ■ Write the equation in logarithmic form.

21. $2^6 = 64$

22. $49^{-1/2} = \frac{1}{7}$

23. $10^x = 74$

24. $e^k = m$

25–40 ■ Evaluate the expression without using a calculator.

25. $\log_2 128$

26. $\log_8 1$

27. $10^{\log 45}$

28. $\log 0.000001$

29. $\ln(e^6)$

30. $\log_4 8$

31. $\log_3\left(\frac{1}{27}\right)$

32. $2^{\log_2 13}$

33. $\log_5 \sqrt{5}$

34. $e^{2\ln 7}$

35. $\log 25 + \log 4$

36. $\log_3 \sqrt{243}$

37. $\log_2 16^{23}$

38. $\log_5 250 - \log_5 2$

39. $\log_8 6 - \log_8 3 + \log_8 2$

40. $\log \log 10^{100}$

41–46 ■ Rewrite the expression in a form with no logarithms of products, quotients, or powers.

41. $\log(AB^2C^3)$

42. $\log_2\left(x\sqrt{x^2 + 1}\right)$

43. $\ln \sqrt{\dfrac{x^2 - 1}{x^2 + 1}}$

44. $\log\left(\dfrac{4x^3}{y^2(x - 1)^5}\right)$

45. $\log_5\left(\dfrac{x^2(1 - 5x)^{3/2}}{\sqrt{x^3 - x}}\right)$

46. $\ln\left(\dfrac{\sqrt[3]{x^4 + 12}}{(x + 16)\sqrt{x - 3}}\right)$

47–52 ■ Rewrite the expression as a single logarithm.

47. $\log 6 + 4 \log 2$

48. $\log x + \log(x^2 y) + 3 \log y$

49. $\frac{3}{2}\log_2(x - y) - 2 \log_2(x^2 + y^2)$

50. $\log_5 2 + \log_5(x + 1) - \frac{1}{3}\log_5(3x + 7)$

51. $\log(x - 2) + \log(x + 2) - \frac{1}{2}\log(x^2 + 4)$

52. $\frac{1}{2}[\ln(x - 4) + 5 \ln(x^2 + 4x)]$

53–62 ■ Use a calculator to find the solution of the equation, correct to two decimal places.

53. $\log_2(1 - x) = 4$

54. $2^{3x-5} = 7$

55. $5^{5-3x} = 26$

56. $\ln(2x - 3) = 14$

57. $e^{3x/4} = 10$ **58.** $2^{1-x} = 3^{2x+5}$

59. $\log x + \log(x + 1) = \log 12$

60. $\log_8(x + 5) - \log_8(x - 2) = 1$

61. $x^2 e^{2x} + 2xe^{2x} = 8e^{2x}$

62. $2^{3^x} = 5$

63–66 ■ Use a calculator to find the solution of the equation, correct to six decimal places.

63. $5^{-2x/3} = 0.63$ **64.** $2^{3x-5} = 7$

65. $5^{2x+1} = 3^{4x-1}$ **66.** $e^{-15k} = 10,000$

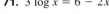
67–70 ■ Draw a graph of the function and use it to determine the asymptotes and the local maximum and minimum values.

67. $y = e^{x/(x+2)}$ **68.** $y = 2x^2 - \ln x$

69. $y = \log(x^3 - x)$ **70.** $y = 10^x - 5^x$

71–72 ■ Find the solutions of the equation, correct to two decimal places.

71. $3 \log x = 6 - 2x$ **72.** $4 - x^2 = e^{-2x}$

73–74 ■ Solve the inequality graphically.

73. $\ln x > x - 2$ **74.** $e^x < 4x^2$

75. Use a graph of $f(x) = e^x - 3e^{-x} - 4x$ to find, approximately, the intervals on which f is increasing and on which f is decreasing.

76. Find an equation of the line shown in the figure.

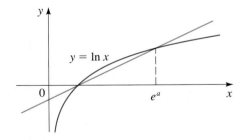

77. Evaluate $\log_4 15$, correct to six decimal places.

78. Solve the inequality: $0.2 \leqslant \log x < 2$

79. Which is larger, $\log_4 258$ or $\log_5 620$?

80. Find the inverse of the function $f(x) = 2^{3^x}$ and state its domain and range.

81. If $12,000 is invested at an interest rate of 10% per year, find the amount of the investment at the end of 3 years for each compounding method.
(a) Semiannual   (b) Monthly
(c) Daily   (d) Continuous

82. A sum of $5000 is invested at an interest rate of $8\frac{1}{2}$% per year, compounded semiannually.
(a) Find the amount of the investment after $1\frac{1}{2}$ years.
(b) After what period of time will the investment amount to $7000?

83. The stray-cat population in a small town grows exponentially. In 1999, the town had 30 stray cats and the relative growth rate was 15% per year.
(a) Find a function that models the stray-cat population $n(t)$ after t years.
(b) Find the projected population after 4 years.
(c) Find the number of years required for the stray-cat population to reach 500.

84. A culture contains 10,000 bacteria initially. After an hour the bacteria count is 25,000.
(a) Find the doubling period.
(b) Find the number of bacteria after 3 hours.

85. Uranium-234 has a half-life of 2.7×10^5 years.
(a) Find the amount remaining from a 10-mg sample after a thousand years.
(b) How long will it take this sample to decompose until its mass is 7 mg?

86. A sample of bismuth-210 decayed to 33% of its original mass after 8 days.
(a) Find the half-life of this element.
(b) Find the mass remaining after 12 days.

87. The half-life of radium-226 is 1590 years.
(a) If a sample has a mass of 150 mg, find a function that models the mass that remains after t years.
(b) Find the mass that will remain after 1000 years.
(c) After how many years will only 50 mg remain?

88. The half-life of palladium-100 is 4 days. After 20 days a sample has been reduced to a mass of 0.375 g.
(a) What was the initial mass of the sample?
(b) Find a function that models the mass remaining after t days.
(c) What is the mass after 3 days?
(d) After how many days will only 0.15 g remain?

89. The graph shows the population of a rare species of bird, where t represents years since 1994 and $n(t)$ is measured in thousands.
   (a) Find a function that models the bird population at time t in the form $n(t) = n_0 e^{rt}$.
   (b) What is the bird population expected to be in the year 2005?

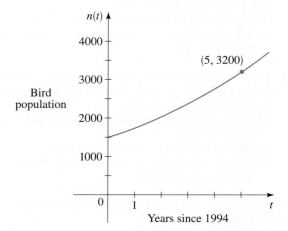

90. A car engine runs at a temperature of 190°F. When the engine is turned off, it cools according to Newton's Law of Cooling with constant $k = 0.0341$, where the time is measured in minutes. Find the time needed for the engine to cool to 90°F if the surrounding temperature is 60°F.

91. The hydrogen ion concentration of fresh egg whites was measured as

$$[H^+] = 1.3 \times 10^{-8} \text{ M}$$

Find the pH, and classify the substance as acidic or basic.

92. The pH of lime juice is 1.9. Find the hydrogen ion concentration.

93. If one earthquake has magnitude 6.5 on the Richter scale, what is the magnitude of another quake that is 35 times as intense?

94. The drilling of a jackhammer was measured at 132 dB. The sound of whispering was measured at 28 dB. Find the ratio of the intensity of the drilling to that of the whispering.

95. The top floor of a building undergoes damped harmonic motion after a sudden brief earthquake. At time $t = 0$ the displacement is at a maximum, 16 cm from the normal position. The damping constant is $c = 0.72$ and the building vibrates at 1.4 cycles per second.
   (a) Find a function of the form $y = ke^{-ct} \cos \omega t$ to model the motion.
   (b) Graph the function you found in part (a).
   (c) What is the displacement at time $t = 10$ s?

7 TEST

1. Graph the functions $y = 2^x$ and $y = \log_2 x$ on the same axes.

2. Sketch the graph of the function $f(x) = \log(x + 2)$ and state the domain, range, and asymptote.

3. Evaluate each logarithmic expression.
   (a) $\log_5 \sqrt{125}$
   (b) $\log_2 56 - \log_2 7$
   (c) $\log_8 4$
   (d) $\log_6 4 + \log_6 9$

4. Use the Laws of Logarithms to rewrite the expression without logarithms of products, quotients, powers, or roots.

$$\log \sqrt{\frac{x + 2}{x^4(x^2 + 4)}}$$

5. Write as a single logarithm: $\ln x - 2 \ln(x^2 + 1) + \frac{1}{2} \ln(3 - x^4)$

6. Find the solution of the equation, correct to two decimal places.
   (a) $2^{x-1} = 10$
   (b) $5 \ln(3 - x) = 4$
   (c) $10^{x+3} = 6^{2x}$
   (d) $\log_2(x + 2) + \log_2(x - 1) = 2$

7. The initial size of a culture of bacteria is 1000. After one hour the bacterium count is 8000.
   (a) Find a function that models the population after t hours.
   (b) Find the population after 1.5 hours.
   (c) When will the population reach 15,000?
   (d) Sketch the graph of the population function.

8. Suppose that $12,000 is invested in a savings account paying 5.6% interest per year.
   (a) Write the formula for the amount in the account after t years if interest is compounded monthly.
   (b) Find the amount in the account after 3 years if interest is compounded daily.
   (c) How long will it take for the amount in the account to grow to $20,000 if interest is compounded semiannually?

9. Let $f(x) = \dfrac{e^x}{x^3}$.

   (a) Graph f in an appropriate viewing rectangle.
   (b) Find, correct to two decimal places, the local minimum value of f and the value of x at which it occurs.
   (c) Find the range of f.
   (d) Solve the equation $\dfrac{e^x}{x^3} = 2x + 1$. State each solution correct to two decimal places.

10. An object is moving up and down in damped harmonic motion. Its displacement at time $t = 0$ is 16 in; this is its maximum displacement. The damping constant is $c = 0.1$ and the frequency is 12 Hz.
    (a) Find a function that models this motion.
    (b) Graph the function.

Focus on Modeling

Fitting Exponential and Power Functions to Data

In *Focus on Modeling* (pages 102–111), we learned how to construct linear models from data. Figure 1 shows some scatter plots of data; the first plot appears to be linear but the others are not. What do we do when the data we are studying are not linear? In this case, our model would be some other type of function that best fits the data. The type of function we choose is determined by the shape of the scatter plot or by some physical principle that underlies the data. In this *Focus* we learn how to construct exponential, power, and polynomial models. Most graphing calculators are capable of applying the method of least squares (see page 104) to obtain the exponential, power, or polynomial function that best fits the data.

We use the symbols for the various regression commands as they are given on the TI-83. On other calculators, the commands have slightly different names. Consult your calculator manual.

FIGURE 1

■ Modeling with Exponential Functions

To model data, we first draw a scatter plot. The shape of the scatter plot can help us decide on the type of function we need to model the data. If the scatter plot increases rapidly, we might seek an *exponential model*, that is, a function of the form

$$y = Ce^{kx}$$

where C and k are constants.

In the first example we model world population. Recall from Section 7.5 that population tends to increase exponentially.

EXAMPLE 1 ■ An Exponential Model for World Population

Table 1 gives the population of the world in the 20th century.
(a) Draw a scatter plot and note that the population grows too rapidly for a linear model to be appropriate.
(b) Find an exponential function that models population growth.
(c) Draw a graph of the function you found together with the scatter plot. How well does the model fit the data?

TABLE 1 World population

Year (t)	World population (P, in millions)
1900	1650
1910	1750
1920	1860
1930	2070
1940	2300
1950	2520
1960	3020
1970	3700
1980	4450
1990	5300
2000	6060

(d) Use the model you found to predict world population in the year 2020.

SOLUTION

(a) The scatter plot is shown in Figure 2. The plotted points do not appear to lie along a straight line, so a linear model is not appropriate.

The population of the world increases exponentially.

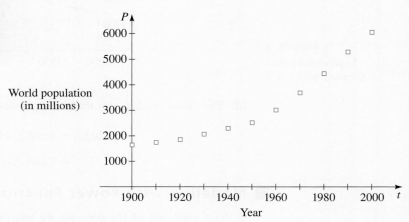

FIGURE 2
Scatter plot of world population

(b) Using a graphing calculator and the **ExpReg** command, we get the exponential model

```
ExpReg
y=a*b^x
a=.0082543035
b=1.013718645
```

$$P(t) = (0.0082543) \cdot (1.0137186)^t$$

This is a model of the form $y = Cb^t$. To convert this to the form $y = Ce^{kt}$, we need to find a value of k so that $b = e^k$, that is,

$$1.0137186 = e^k$$

$$k = \ln 1.0137186 \approx 0.013625 \qquad \text{Solve for } k$$

So $$P(t) = 0.0082543e^{0.013625t}$$

(c) From the graph in Figure 3, we see that the model appears to fit the data fairly well. The period of relatively slow population growth is explained by the depression of the 1930s and the two world wars.

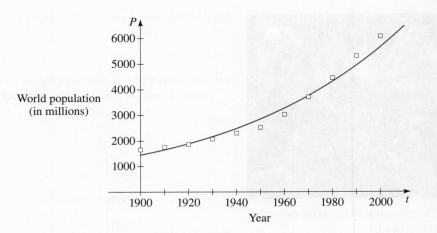

FIGURE 3

Exponential model
for world population

(d) The model predicts that the world population in 2020 will be

$$P(2020) = 0.0082543e^{(0.013625)(2020)}$$

$$\approx 7,405,400,000$$ ∎

◼ Modeling with Power Functions

If the scatter plot of the data we are studying resembles the graph of $y = ax^2$, $y = ax^{1.32}$, or some other power function, then we seek a *power model*, that is, a function of the form

$$y = ax^n$$

where a is a positive constant and n is any real number.

In the next example we seek a power model for some astronomical data. In astronomy, distance in the solar system is often measured in astronomical units. An *astronomical unit* (AU) is the mean distance from the earth to the sun. The *period* of a planet is the time it takes the planet to make a complete revolution around the sun (measured in earth years). In this example we derive the remarkable relationship, first discovered by Johannes Kepler (see page 375), between the mean distance of a planet from the sun and its period.

TABLE 2 Distances and
periods of the planets

Planet	d	T
Mercury	0.387	0.241
Venus	0.723	0.615
Earth	1.000	1.000
Mars	1.523	1.881
Jupiter	5.203	11.861
Saturn	9.541	29.457
Uranus	19.190	84.008
Neptune	30.086	164.784
Pluto	39.507	248.350

EXAMPLE 2 ◼ A Power Model for Planetary Periods

Table 2 gives the mean distance d of each planet from the sun in astronomical units and its period T in years.

(a) Sketch a scatter plot. Is a linear model appropriate?
(b) Find a power function that models the data.
(c) Draw a graph of the function you found and the scatter plot on the same graph. How well does the model fit the data?
(d) Use the model you found to find the period of an asteroid whose mean distance from the sun is 5 AU.

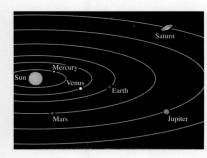

SOLUTION

(a) The scatter plot shown in Figure 4 indicates that the plotted points do not lie along a straight line, so a linear model is not appropriate.

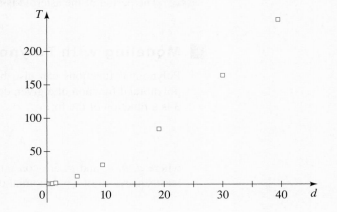

FIGURE 4

```
PwrReg
 y=a*x^b
 a=1.000396048
 b=1.499661718
```

(b) Using a graphing calculator and the **PwrReg** command, we get the power model

$$T = 1.000396d^{1.49966}$$

If we round both the coefficient and the exponent to three significant figures, we can write the model as

$$T = d^{1.5}$$

This is the relationship discovered by Kepler (see page 375). Sir Isaac Newton later used his Law of Gravity to derive this relationship theoretically, thereby providing strong scientific evidence that the Law of Gravity must be true.

(c) The graph is shown in Figure 5. The model appears to fit the data very well.

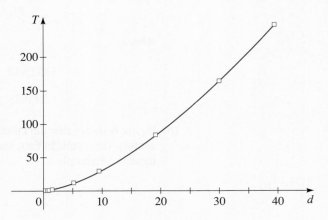

FIGURE 5

(d) In this case, $d = 5$ AU and so our model gives

$$T = 1.00039 \cdot 5^{1.49966} \approx 11.22$$

The period of the asteroid is about 11.2 years.   ∎

Modeling with Polynomial Functions

Polynomial functions can also be used to model data. A *polynomial model* is a polynomial function of a given degree. For example, a polynomial model of degree 3 is a function of the form

$$y = ax^3 + bx^2 + cx + d$$

where a, b, c, and d, are constants. Most graphing calculators use the method of least squares to fit a polynomial of specified degree to a given set of data.

EXAMPLE 3 ■ A Polynomial Model

Consider the world population data in Table 1 on page 496.

(a) Find a polynomial function of degree 3 that models the data.
(b) Draw a graph of the function you found and the scatter plot on the same graph. How well does this model fit the data?
(c) Use the model you found to estimate the population in the year 1975.
(d) Would it be appropriate to use the model to predict the population in 2100?

SOLUTION

(a) Using the `CubicReg` command on a graphing calculator, we obtain the cubic model

$$P(t) = at^3 + bt^2 + ct + d$$

where

$$a = 1252.914 \qquad\qquad b = -6.817424 \times 10^6$$

$$c = 1.233675 \times 10^{10} \qquad\qquad d = -7.420959 \times 10^{12}$$

(b) Figure 6 shows that the cubic function models the world population of the 20th century very well. In fact, this model seems even better than the exponential model of Example 1.

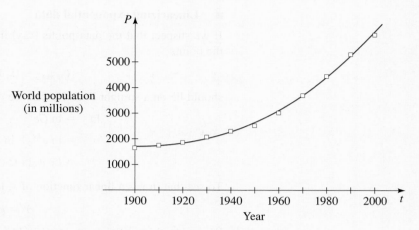

FIGURE 6
Cubic model for world population

(c) For 1975, the population estimate provided by the model is

$$P(1975) \approx 4,024,400,000$$

This is very close to the official U.N. estimate for 1975.

(d) The cubic model is not likely to be accurate for dates outside the 20th century, because we know that the physical mechanism of population growth is inherently exponential. For instance, the model gives the following estimate for 1650:

$$P(1650) \approx 2,488,000,000$$

But historical records indicate that the world's population in 1650 was only about 550,000,000. In fact, this model gives negative populations for dates earlier than about 1550. [Try evaluating $P(1500)$.] So the model's prediction of $P(2100) \approx 24,600,000,000$ is extremely unlikely to be anywhere near the correct figure. ∎

Linearizing Data

We have used the shape of a scatter plot to decide which type of model to use—linear, exponential, or power. This works well if the data points lie on a straight line. But it's difficult to distinguish a scatter plot that is exponential from one that requires a power model. So, to help decide which model to use, we can *linearize* the data, that is, apply a function to the data that results in "straightening" the scatter plot. The inverse of the linearizing function is then an appropriate model. We now describe how to linearize data that can be modeled by exponential or power functions.

■ Linearizing exponential data

If we suspect that the data points (x, y) lie on an exponential curve $y = Ce^{kx}$, then the points

$$(x, \ln y)$$

should lie on a straight line. We can see this from the following calculations:

$$\ln y = \ln Ce^{kx} \qquad \text{Assume } y = Ce^{kx}$$
$$= \ln e^{kx} + \ln C \qquad \text{Property of ln}$$
$$= kx + \ln C \qquad \text{Property of ln}$$

To see that $\ln y$ is a linear function of x, let $Y = \ln y$ and $A = \ln C$; then

$$Y = kx + A$$

We apply this technique to the world population data (t, P) to obtain the points $(t, \ln P)$ in Table 3. The scatter plot in Figure 7 shows that the linearized data lie approximately on a straight line, so an exponential model should be appropriate.

TABLE 3 World population data

t	Population P (in millions)	$\ln P$
1900	1650	21.224
1910	1750	21.283
1920	1860	21.344
1930	2070	21.451
1940	2300	21.556
1950	2520	21.648
1960	3020	21.829
1970	3700	22.032
1980	4450	22.216
1990	5300	22.391
2000	6060	22.525

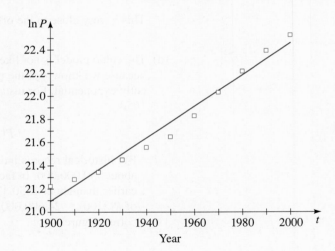

FIGURE 7

■ Linearizing power data

If we suspect that the data points (x, y) lie on a power curve $y = ax^n$, then the points

$$(\ln x, \ln y)$$

should be on a straight line. We can see this from the following calculations:

$$\ln y = \ln ax^n \qquad \text{Assume } y = ax^n$$
$$= \ln a + \ln x^n \qquad \text{Property of ln}$$
$$= \ln a + n \ln x \qquad \text{Property of ln}$$

To see that $\ln y$ is a linear function of $\ln x$, let $Y = \ln y$, $X = \ln x$, and $A = \ln a$; then

$$Y = nX + A$$

We apply this technique to the planetary data (d, T) in Table 2, to obtain the points $(\ln d, \ln T)$ in Table 4. The scatter plot in Figure 8 shows that the data lie on a straight line, so a power model seems appropriate.

TABLE 4 Log-log table

ln *d*	ln *T*
−0.94933	−1.4230
−0.32435	−0.48613
0	0
0.42068	0.6318
1.6492	2.4733
2.2556	3.3829
2.9544	4.4309
3.4041	5.1046
3.6765	5.5148

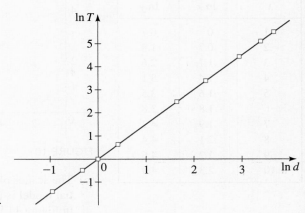

FIGURE 8
Log-log plot of data in Table 4

EXAMPLE 4 ■ **An Exponential or Power Model?**

Data points (x, y) are shown in Table 5.

(a) Draw a scatter plot of the data.
(b) Draw scatter plots of $(x, \ln y)$ and $(\ln x, \ln y)$.
(c) Is an exponential function or a power function appropriate for modeling this data?
(d) Find an appropriate function to model the data.

SOLUTION

(a) The scatter plot of the data is shown in Figure 9.

TABLE 5

x	*y*
1	2
2	6
3	14
4	22
5	34
6	46
7	64
8	80
9	102
10	130

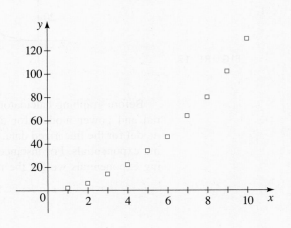

FIGURE 9

TABLE 6

x	$\ln x$	$\ln y$
1	0	0.7
2	0.7	1.8
3	1.1	2.6
4	1.4	3.1
5	1.6	3.5
6	1.8	3.8
7	1.9	4.2
8	2.1	4.4
9	2.2	4.6
10	2.3	4.9

(b) We use the values from Table 6 to graph the scatter plots in Figures 10 and 11.

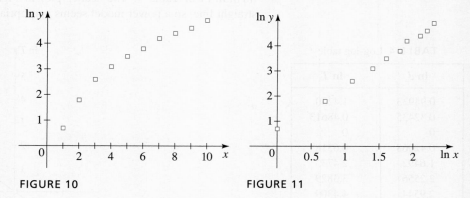

FIGURE 10   FIGURE 11

(c) The scatter plot of $(x, \ln y)$ in Figure 10 does not appear linear, so an exponential model is not appropriate. On the other hand, the scatter plot of $(\ln x, \ln y)$ in Figure 11 is very nearly linear, so a power model is appropriate.

(d) Using the **PwrReg** command on a calculator, we find that the power function that best fits the data point is

$$y = 1.85x^{1.82}$$

The graph of this function and the original data points are shown in Figure 12.

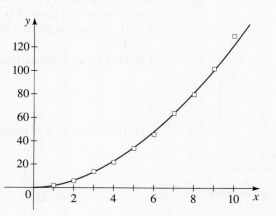

FIGURE 12

Before graphing calculators and statistical software became common, exponential and power models for data were often constructed by first finding a linear model for the linearized data. Then the model for the actual data was found by taking exponentials. For instance, if it was found that $\ln y = A \ln x + B$, then by taking exponentials we get the model $y = e^B \cdot e^{A \ln x}$, or $y = Cx^A$ (where $C = e^B$).

Special graphing paper called "log paper" or "log-log paper" was used to facilitate this process.

We can also construct models from data using other types of functions. In Problems 9 and 10, for instance, we use logarithmic and logistic functions to model data.

■ Problems

1. The U.S. Constitution requires a census every 10 years. The census data for 1790–1990 is given in the table.
   (a) Make a scatter plot of the data.
   (b) Use a calculator to find an exponential model for the data.
   (c) Use your model to predict the population at the 2000 census.
   (d) Use your model to estimate the population in 1965.
   (e) Compare your answers from parts (c) and (d) to the values in the table. Do you think an exponential model is appropriate for these data?

Year	Population (in millions)	Year	Population (in millions)	Year	Population (in millions)
1790	3.9	1860	31.4	1930	123.2
1800	5.3	1870	38.6	1940	132.2
1810	7.2	1880	50.2	1950	151.3
1820	9.6	1890	63.0	1960	179.3
1830	12.9	1900	76.2	1970	203.3
1840	17.1	1910	92.2	1980	226.5
1850	23.2	1920	106.0	1990	248.7

2. In a physics experiment a lead ball is dropped from a height of 5 m. The students record the distance the ball has fallen every one-tenth of a second. (This can be done using a camera and a strobe light.)
   (a) Make a scatter plot of the data.
   (b) Use a calculator to find a power model.
   (c) Use the model you found to predict how far a dropped ball would fall in 3 s.

Time (s)	Distance (m)
0.1	0.048
0.2	0.197
0.3	0.441
0.4	0.882
0.5	1.227
0.6	1.765
0.7	2.401
0.8	3.136
0.9	3.969
1.0	4.902

3. The U.S. health-care expenditures for 1960–1993 are given in the table, and a scatter plot of the data is shown in the figure.

(a) Does the scatter plot shown suggest an exponential model?

(b) Make a table of the values $(t, \ln E)$ and a scatter plot. Does the scatter plot appear to be linear?

(c) Find the regression line for the data in part (b).

(d) Use the results of part (b) to find an exponential model for the growth of health-care expenditures.

(e) Use the model you found in part (d) to predict the total health-care expenditures in 1996.

Year	Health expenditures (in billions of dollars)
1960	27.1
1970	74.3
1980	251.1
1985	434.5
1987	506.2
1989	623.9
1990	696.6
1991	755.8
1992	820.3
1993	884.2

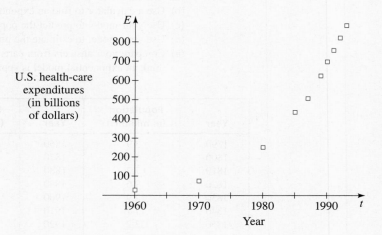

U.S. health-care expenditures (in billions of dollars)

4. A student is trying to determine the half-life of radioactive iodine-131. He measures the amount of iodine-131 in a sample solution every 8 hours. His data are shown in the table.

(a) Make a scatter plot of the data.

(b) Use a calculator to find an exponential model.

(c) Use your model to find the half-life of iodine-131.

Time (h)	Amount (g)
0	4.80
8	4.66
16	4.51
24	4.39
32	4.29
40	4.14
48	4.04

Year	Lead emissions
1970	199.1
1975	143.8
1980	68.0
1985	18.3
1988	5.9
1989	5.5
1990	5.1
1991	4.5
1992	4.7

5. The table at the left gives U.S. lead emissions into the environment in millions of metric tons for 1970–1992.
  (a) Find an exponential model for these data.
  (b) Find a fourth-degree polynomial model for these data.
  (c) Which of these curves gives a better model for the data? Use graphs of the two models to decide.
  (d) Use each model to estimate the lead emissions in 1972 and 1982.

6. A study of the U.S. Office of Science and Technology in 1972 estimated the cost of reducing automobile emissions by certain percentages. Find a model that captures the "diminishing returns" trend of these data.

Reduction in emissions (%)	Cost per car ($)
50	45
55	55
60	62
65	70
70	80
75	90
80	100
85	200
90	375
95	600

7. Data points (x, y) are shown in the table.
  (a) Draw a scatter plot of the data.
  (b) Draw scatter plots of $(x, \ln y)$ and $(\ln x, \ln y)$.
  (c) Is an exponential function or a power function appropriate for modeling this data?
  (d) Find an appropriate function to model the data.

x	y
2	0.08
4	0.12
6	0.18
8	0.25
10	0.36
12	0.52
14	0.73
16	1.06

8. Data points (x, y) are shown in the table.
   (a) Draw a scatter plot of the data.
   (b) Draw scatter plots of $(x, \ln y)$ and $(\ln x, \ln y)$.
   (c) Is an exponential function or a power function appropriate for modeling this data?
   (d) Find an appropriate function to model the data.

x	y
10	29
20	82
30	151
40	235
50	330
60	430
70	546
80	669
90	797

9. A **logarithmic model** is a function of the form

$$y = a + b \ln x$$

Many relationships between variables in the real world can be modeled by this type of function. The table and the scatter plot show the coal production (in metric tons) from a small mine in northern British Columbia.
   (a) Use the **LnReg** command on your calculator to find a logarithmic model for these production figures.
   (b) Use the model to predict coal production from this mine in 2005.

Year	Metric tons of coal
1950	882
1960	889
1970	894
1980	899
1990	905
2000	909

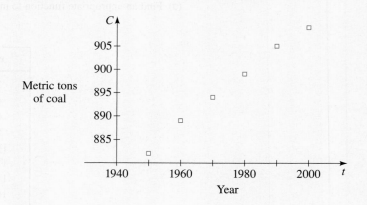

10. A **logistic model** is a function of the form

$$y = \frac{c}{1 + ae^{-bx}}$$

Logistic functions are appropriate for modeling population growth where the growth is limited by available resources. The table and scatter plot give the population of black flies in a closed laboratory container over an 18-day period.

(a) Use the `Logistic` command on your calculator to find a logistic model for these data.

(b) Use the model to estimate the time when there were 400 flies in the container.

Time (days)	Number of flies
0	10
2	25
4	66
6	144
8	262
10	374
12	446
16	492
18	498

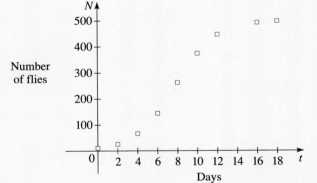

Appendix A
Algebra Review

The different types of real numbers were invented to meet specific needs. For example, natural numbers are needed for counting, negative numbers for describing debt or below-zero temperatures, rational numbers for concepts like "half a gallon of milk," and irrational numbers for measuring certain distances, like the diagonal of a square.

Let's recall the types of numbers that make up the real number system. We start with the **natural numbers**:

$$1, 2, 3, 4, \ldots$$

The **integers** consist of the natural numbers together with their negatives and 0:

$$\ldots, -3, -2, -1, 0, 1, 2, 3, 4, \ldots$$

We construct the **rational numbers** by taking ratios of integers. Thus, any rational number r can be expressed as

$$r = \frac{m}{n} \qquad \text{where } m \text{ and } n \text{ are integers and } n \neq 0$$

Examples are: $\quad \frac{1}{2} \qquad -\frac{3}{7} \qquad 46 = \frac{46}{1} \qquad 0.17 = \frac{17}{100}$

(Recall that division by 0 is always ruled out, so expressions like $\frac{3}{0}$ and $\frac{0}{0}$ are undefined.) There are also real numbers, such as $\sqrt{2}$, that cannot be expressed as a ratio of integers and are therefore called **irrational numbers**. It can be shown, with varying degrees of difficulty, that these numbers are also irrational:

$$\sqrt{3} \qquad \sqrt{5} \qquad \sqrt[3]{2} \qquad \pi \qquad \frac{3}{\pi^2}$$

The set of all real numbers is usually denoted by the symbol $\mathbb{R}$. When we use the word *number* without qualification, we will mean "real number." Figure 1 is a diagram of the types of real numbers that we work with in this book.

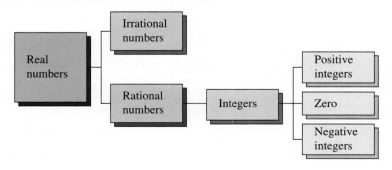

FIGURE 1
The real number system

A repeating decimal such as
$$x = 3.5474747\ldots$$
is a rational number. To convert it to a ratio of two integers, we write
$$1000x = 3547.47474747\ldots$$
$$\underline{\quad 10x = \quad\;\; 35.47474747\ldots}$$
$$990x = 3512.0$$
Thus, $x = \frac{3512}{990}$. (The idea is to multiply x by appropriate powers of 10, and then subtract to eliminate the repeating part.)

Every real number has a decimal representation. If the number is rational, then its corresponding decimal is repeating. For example,

$$\frac{1}{2} = 0.5000\ldots = 0.5\overline{0} \qquad\qquad \frac{2}{3} = 0.66666\ldots = 0.\overline{6}$$

$$\frac{157}{495} = 0.3171717\ldots = 0.3\overline{17} \qquad \frac{9}{7} = 1.285714285714\ldots = 1.\overline{285714}$$

(The bar indicates that the sequence of digits repeats forever.) If the number is irrational, the decimal representation is nonrepeating:

$$\sqrt{2} = 1.414213562373095\ldots \qquad\qquad \pi = 3.141592653589793\ldots$$

If we stop the decimal expansion of any number at a certain place, we get an approximation to the number. For instance, we can write

$$\pi \approx 3.14159265$$

where the symbol $\approx$ is read "is approximately equal to." The more decimal places we retain, the better the approximation we get.

■ Properties of Real Numbers

In combining real numbers using the familiar operations of addition and multiplication, we use the following properties of real numbers.

PROPERTIES OF REAL NUMBERS	
Property	**Example**
Commutative Properties	
$a + b = b + a$	$7 + 3 = 3 + 7$
$ab = ba$	$3 \cdot 5 = 5 \cdot 3$
Associative Properties	
$(a + b) + c = a + (b + c)$	$(2 + 4) + 7 = 2 + (4 + 7)$
$(ab)c = a(bc)$	$(3 \cdot 7) \cdot 5 = 3 \cdot (7 \cdot 5)$
Distributive Property	
$a(b + c) = ab + ac$	$2 \cdot (3 + 5) = 2 \cdot 3 + 2 \cdot 5$
$(b + c)a = ab + ac$	$(3 + 5) \cdot 2 = 2 \cdot 3 + 2 \cdot 5$

EXAMPLE 1 ■ **Using the Properties of the Real Numbers**

Let x, y, z, and w be real numbers.

(a) $(x + y)(2zw) = (2zw)(x + y)$ Commutative Property for multiplication

(b) $(x + y)(z + w) = (x + y)z + (x + y)w$ Distributive Property (with $a = x + y$)

$$= (zx + zy) + (wx + wy)$$ Distributive Property

$$= zx + zy + wx + wy$$ Associative Property of addition

In the last step we removed the parentheses because, according to the Associative Property, the order of addition doesn't matter. ■

The Real Line

The real numbers can be represented by points on a line, as shown in Figure 2. The positive direction (toward the right) is indicated by an arrow. We choose an arbitrary reference point O, called the **origin**, which corresponds to the real number 0. Given any convenient unit of measurement, each positive number x is represented by the point on the line a distance of x units to the right of the origin, and each negative number $-x$ is represented by the point x units to the left of the origin. Thus, every real number is represented by a point on the line, and every point P on the line corresponds to exactly one real number. The number associated with the point P is called the coordinate of P, and the line is then called a **coordinate line**, or a **real number line**, or simply a **real line**. Often we identify the point with its coordinate and think of a number as being a point on the real line.

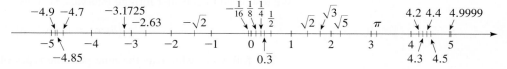

FIGURE 2
The real line

The real numbers are *ordered*. We say that **a is less than b** and write $a < b$ if $b - a$ is a positive number. Geometrically, this means that a lies to the left of b on the number line. (Equivalently, we can say that **b is greater than a** and write $b > a$.) The symbol $a \leq b$ (or $b \geq a$) means that either $a < b$ or $a = b$ and is read "a is less than or equal to b." For instance, the following are true inequalities (see Figure 3):

$$7 < 7.4 < 7.5 \qquad -\pi < -3 \qquad \sqrt{2} < 2 \qquad 2 \leq 2$$

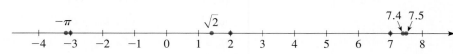

FIGURE 3

Sets and Intervals

In the discussion that follows, we need to use set notation. A **set** is a collection of objects, and these objects are called the **elements** of the set. If S is a set, the notation $a \in S$ means that a is an element of S, and $b \notin S$ means that b is not an element of S. For example, if Z represents the set of integers, then $-3 \in Z$ but $\pi \notin Z$.

Some sets can be described by listing their elements within braces. For instance, the set A that consists of all positive integers less than 7 can be written as

$$A = \{1, 2, 3, 4, 5, 6\}$$

We could also write A in **set-builder notation** as

$$A = \{x \mid x \text{ is an integer and } 0 < x < 7\}$$

which is read "A is the set of all x such that x is an integer and $0 < x < 7$."

If S and T are sets, then their **union** $S \cup T$ is the set that consists of all elements that are in S *or* T (or in both). The **intersection** of S and T is the set $S \cap T$ consisting of all elements that are in both S *and* T. In other words, $S \cap T$ is the common part of S and T. The **empty set**, denoted by $\varnothing$, is the set that contains no element.

Certain sets of real numbers, called **intervals**, occur frequently in calculus and correspond geometrically to line segments. For example, if $a < b$, then the **open interval** from a to b consists of all numbers between a and b and is denoted by the symbol (a, b). Using set-builder notation, we can write

$$(a, b) = \{x \mid a < x < b\}$$

The **closed interval** from a to b is the set

$$[a, b] = \{x \mid a \le x \le b\}$$

We also need to consider infinite intervals, such as

$$(a, \infty) = \{x \mid x > a\}$$

The following table lists the nine possible types of intervals. When these intervals are discussed, we will always assume that $a < b$.

Notation	Set description	Graph
(a, b)	$\{x \mid a < x < b\}$	
$[a, b]$	$\{x \mid a \le x \le b\}$	
$[a, b)$	$\{x \mid a \le x < b\}$	
$(a, b]$	$\{x \mid a < x \le b\}$	
(a, ∞)	$\{x \mid a < x\}$	
$[a, \infty)$	$\{x \mid a \le x\}$	
$(-\infty, b)$	$\{x \mid x < b\}$	
$(-\infty, b]$	$\{x \mid x \le b\}$	
$(-\infty, \infty)$	$\mathbb{R}$ (set of all real numbers)	

EXAMPLE 2 ■ Finding Unions and Intersections of Intervals

Graph each set.

(a) $(1, 3) \cap [2, 7]$ (b) $(1, 3) \cup [2, 7]$

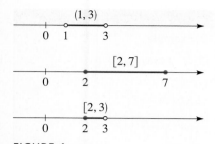

FIGURE 4
$(1, 3) \cap [2, 7]$

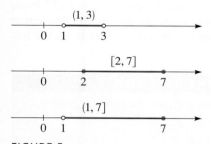

FIGURE 5
$(1, 3) \cup [2, 7]$

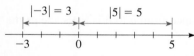

FIGURE 6

SOLUTION

(a) The intersection of two intervals consists of the numbers that are in both intervals. Therefore

$$(1, 3) \cap [2, 7] = \{x \mid 1 < x < 3 \text{ and } 2 \leqslant x \leqslant 7\}$$
$$= \{x \mid 2 \leqslant x < 3\}$$
$$= [2, 3)$$

This set is illustrated in Figure 4.

(b) The union of two intervals consists of the numbers that are in either one interval or the other (or both). Therefore

$$(1, 3) \cup [2, 7] = \{x \mid 1 < x < 3 \text{ or } 2 \leqslant x \leqslant 7\}$$
$$= \{x \mid 1 < x \leqslant 7\}$$
$$= (1, 7]$$

This set is illustrated in Figure 5.   ■

■ Absolute Value and Distance

The **absolute value** of a number a, denoted by $|a|$, is the distance from a to 0 on the real number line (see Figure 6). Distance is always positive or zero, so we have $|a| \geqslant 0$ for every number a. Remembering that $-a$ is positive when a is negative, we have the following definition.

DEFINITION OF ABSOLUTE VALUE

If a is a real number, then the **absolute value** of a is

$$|a| = \begin{cases} a & \text{if } a \geqslant 0 \\ -a & \text{if } a < 0 \end{cases}$$

EXAMPLE 3 ■ Evaluating Absolute Values of Numbers

(a) $|3| = 3$

(b) $|-3| = -(-3) = 3$

(c) $|0| = 0$

(d) $|\sqrt{2} - 1| = \sqrt{2} - 1$ (since $\sqrt{2} > 1 \Rightarrow \sqrt{2} - 1 > 0$)

(e) $|3 - \pi| = -(3 - \pi) = \pi - 3$ (since $\pi > 3 \Rightarrow 3 - \pi < 0$)   ■

When working with absolute values, we use the following properties.

PROPERTIES OF ABSOLUTE VALUE

Property	Example
1. $|a| \geqslant 0$	$|-3| = 3 \geqslant 0$
2. $|a| = |-a|$	$|5| = |-5|$
3. $|ab| = |a||b|$	$|-2 \cdot 5| = |-2||5|$
4. $\left|\dfrac{a}{b}\right| = \dfrac{|a|}{|b|}$	$\left|\dfrac{12}{-3}\right| = \dfrac{|12|}{|-3|}$

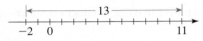

FIGURE 7

What is the distance on the real line between the numbers -2 and 11? From Figure 7 we see that the distance is 13. We arrive at this by finding either $|11 - (-2)| = 13$ or $|(-2) - 11| = 13$. From this observation we make the following definition (see Figure 8).

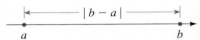

FIGURE 8
Length of a line segment $= |b - a|$

DISTANCE BETWEEN POINTS ON THE REAL LINE

If a and b are real numbers, then the **distance** between the points a and b on the real line is

$$d(a, b) = |b - a|$$

From Property 2 of absolute values it follows that

$$|b - a| = |-(a - b)| = |a - b|$$

This confirms that, as we would expect, the distance from a to b is the same as the distance from b to a.

EXAMPLE 4 ■ **Distance between Points on the Real Line**

The distance between the numbers -8 and 2 is

$$d(a, b) = |-8 - 2| = |-10| = 10$$

FIGURE 9

We can check this calculation geometrically, as shown in Figure 9.　　　　■

A.1 EXERCISES

1–6 ■ State the property of real numbers being used.

1. $3x + 4y = 4y + 3x$

2. $c(a + b) = (a + b)c$

3. $(x + 2y) + 3z = x + (2y + 3z)$

4. $2(A + B) = 2A + 2B$

5. $(5x + 1)3 = 15x + 3$

6. $(x + a)(x + b) = (x + a)x + (x + a)b$

7–12 ■ Use properties of real numbers to write the expression without parentheses.

7. $3(x + y)$　　　　　　**8.** $(a - b)8$

9. $4(2m)$

10. $\frac{4}{3}(-6y)$

11. $-\frac{5}{2}(2x - 4y)$

12. $(3a)(b + c - 2d)$

13–16 ■ State whether each inequality is true or false.

13. (a) $-6 < -10$　　　　(b) $\sqrt{2} > 1.41$

14. (a) $\dfrac{10}{11} < \dfrac{12}{13}$　　　(b) $-\dfrac{1}{2} < -1$

15. (a) $-\pi > -3$　　　　(b) $8 \leqslant 9$

16. (a) $1.1 > 1.\overline{1}$　　　　(b) $8 \leqslant 8$

17–18 ■ Write each statement in terms of inequalities.

17. (a) x is positive
(b) t is less than 4
(c) a is greater than or equal to π
(d) x is less than $\frac{1}{3}$ and is greater than -5
(e) The distance from p to 3 is at most 5

18. (a) y is negative
(b) z is greater than 1
(c) b is at most 8
(d) w is positive and is less than or equal to 17
(e) y is at least 2 units from π

19–22 ■ Find the indicated set if $A = \{x \mid x \geqslant -2\}$, $B = \{x \mid x < 4\}$, and $C = \{x \mid -1 < x \leqslant 5\}$.

19. (a) $A \cup B$　　　　(b) $A \cap B$

20. (a) $A \cup C$　　　　(b) $A \cap C$

21. (a) $B \cup C$　　　　(b) $B \cap C$

22. (a) $A \cup B \cup C$　　　(b) $A \cap B \cap C$

23–28 ■ Express the interval in terms of inequalities, and then graph the interval.

23. $(-3, 0)$　　　　**24.** $(2, 8]$

25. $[2, 8)$　　　　**26.** $[-6, -\frac{1}{2}]$

27. $[2, \infty)$　　　　**28.** $(-\infty, 1)$

29–34 ■ Express the inequality in interval notation, and then graph the corresponding interval.

29. $x \leqslant 1$

30. $1 \leqslant x \leqslant 2$

31. $-2 < x \leqslant 1$

32. $x \geqslant -5$

33. $x > -1$

34. $-5 < x < 2$

35–40 ■ Graph the set.

35. $(-2, 0) \cup (-1, 1)$

36. $(-2, 0) \cap (-1, 1)$

37. $[-4, 6] \cap [0, 8)$

38. $[-4, 6) \cup [0, 8)$

39. $(-\infty, -4) \cup (4, \infty)$

40. $(-\infty, 6] \cap (2, 10)$

41–46 ■ Evaluate each expression.

41. (a) $|100|$　　　　(b) $|-73|$

42. (a) $|\sqrt{5} - 5|$　　　(b) $|10 - \pi|$

43. (a) $\big||-6| - |-4|\big|$　　(b) $\dfrac{-1}{|-1|}$

44. (a) $\big|2 - |-12|\big|$　　(b) $-1 - \big|1 - |-1|\big|$

45. (a) $|(-2) \cdot 6|$　　　(b) $\big|(-\frac{1}{3})(-15)\big|$

46. (a) $\left|\dfrac{-6}{24}\right|$　　　(b) $\left|\dfrac{7 - 12}{12 - 7}\right|$

47–48 ■ Find the distance between the given numbers.

47. (a) 2 and 17
(b) -3 and 21
(c) $\frac{11}{8}$ and $-\frac{3}{10}$

48. (a) $\frac{7}{15}$ and $-\frac{1}{21}$
(b) -38 and -57
(c) -2.6 and -1.8

A.2   EXPONENTS AND RADICALS

In this section we give meaning to expressions such as $a^{m/n}$ in which the exponent m/n is a rational number. To do this, we need to recall some facts about integer exponents, radicals, and nth roots.

■ Integer Exponents

A product of identical numbers is usually written in exponential notation. For example, $5 \cdot 5 \cdot 5$ is written as 5^3. In general, we have the following definition.

EXPONENTIAL NOTATION

If a is any real number and n is a positive integer, then the **nth power** of a is

$$a^n = \underbrace{a \cdot a \cdot \cdots \cdot a}_{n \text{ factors}}$$

The number a is called the **base** and n is called the **exponent**.

EXAMPLE 1 ■ Exponential Notation

Note the distinction between $(-3)^4$ and -3^4. In $(-3)^4$ the exponent applies to -3, but in -3^4 the exponent applies only to 3.

(a) $\left(\frac{1}{2}\right)^5 = \left(\frac{1}{2}\right)\left(\frac{1}{2}\right)\left(\frac{1}{2}\right)\left(\frac{1}{2}\right)\left(\frac{1}{2}\right) = \frac{1}{32}$

(b) $(-3)^4 = (-3) \cdot (-3) \cdot (-3) \cdot (-3) = 81$

(c) $-3^4 = -(3 \cdot 3 \cdot 3 \cdot 3) = -81$ ■

ZERO AND NEGATIVE EXPONENTS

If $a \neq 0$ is any real number and n is a positive integer, then

$$a^0 = 1 \qquad \text{and} \qquad a^{-n} = \frac{1}{a^n}$$

EXAMPLE 2 ■ Zero and Negative Exponents

(a) $\left(\frac{4}{7}\right)^0 = 1$

(b) $x^{-1} = \frac{1}{x^1} = \frac{1}{x}$

(c) $(-2)^{-3} = \frac{1}{(-2)^3} = \frac{1}{-8} = -\frac{1}{8}$ ■

Familiarity with the following rules is essential for our work with exponents and bases. In the table the bases a and b are real numbers, and the exponents m and n are integers.

LAWS OF EXPONENTS

Law	Example
1. $a^m a^n = a^{m+n}$	$3^2 \cdot 3^5 = 3^{2+5} = 3^7$
2. $\dfrac{a^m}{a^n} = a^{m-n}$	$\dfrac{3^5}{3^2} = 3^{5-2} = 3^3$
3. $(a^m)^n = a^{mn}$	$(3^2)^5 = 3^{2\cdot5} = 3^{10}$
4. $(ab)^n = a^n b^n$	$(3 \cdot 4)^2 = 3^2 \cdot 4^2$
5. $\left(\dfrac{a}{b}\right)^n = \dfrac{a^n}{b^n}$	$\left(\dfrac{3}{4}\right)^2 = \dfrac{3^2}{4^2}$
6. $\left(\dfrac{a}{b}\right)^{-n} = \left(\dfrac{b}{a}\right)^n$	$\left(\dfrac{3}{4}\right)^{-2} = \left(\dfrac{4}{3}\right)^2$
7. $\dfrac{a^{-n}}{b^{-m}} = \dfrac{b^m}{a^n}$	$\dfrac{3^{-2}}{4^{-5}} = \dfrac{4^5}{3^2}$

EXAMPLE 3 ■ Simplifying Expressions with Exponents

Simplify: (a) $(2a^3b^2)(3ab^4)^3$ (b) $\left(\dfrac{x}{y}\right)^3 \left(\dfrac{y^2x}{z}\right)^4$

SOLUTION

(a) $(2a^3b^2)(3ab^4)^3 = (2a^3b^2)[3^3a^3(b^4)^3]$ Law 4

$\qquad\qquad\qquad = (2a^3b^2)(27a^3b^{12})$ Law 3

$\qquad\qquad\qquad = (2)(27)a^3a^3b^2b^{12}$ Group factors with the same base

$\qquad\qquad\qquad = 54a^6b^{14}$ Law 1

(b) $\left(\dfrac{x}{y}\right)^3 \left(\dfrac{y^2x}{z}\right)^4 = \dfrac{x^3}{y^3}\,\dfrac{(y^2)^4x^4}{z^4}$ Laws 5 and 4

$\qquad\qquad\qquad = \dfrac{x^3}{y^3}\,\dfrac{y^8x^4}{z^4}$ Law 3

$\qquad\qquad\qquad = (x^3x^4)\left(\dfrac{y^8}{y^3}\right)\dfrac{1}{z^4}$ Group factors with the same base

$\qquad\qquad\qquad = \dfrac{x^7y^5}{z^4}$ Laws 1 and 2

■

EXAMPLE 4 ■ Simplifying Expressions with Negative Exponents

Eliminate negative exponents and simplify each expression.

(a) $\dfrac{6st^{-4}}{2s^{-2}t^2}$ (b) $\left(\dfrac{y}{3z^2}\right)^{-2}$

SOLUTION

(a) We use Law 7, which allows us to move a number raised to a power from the numerator to the denominator (or vice versa) by changing the sign of the exponent.

$$\frac{6st^{-4}}{2s^{-2}t^2} = \frac{6ss^2}{2t^4t^2} \qquad \text{Law 7}$$

$$= \frac{3s^3}{t^6} \qquad \text{Law 1}$$

(b) We use Law 6, which allows us to change the sign of the exponent of a fraction by inverting the fraction.

$$\left(\frac{y}{3z^2}\right)^{-2} = \left(\frac{3z^2}{y}\right)^2 \qquad \text{Law 6}$$

$$= \frac{9z^4}{y^2} \qquad \text{Laws 5 and 4}$$

∎

▮ Radicals

We know what 2^n means whenever n is an integer. To give meaning to a power, such as $2^{4/5}$, whose exponent is a rational number, we need to discuss radicals.

The symbol $\sqrt{}$ means "the positive square root of." Thus

It is true that the number 9 has two square roots, 3 and -3, but the notation $\sqrt{9}$ is reserved for the *positive* square root of 9 (sometimes called the *principal square root* of 9). If we want the negative root, we *must* write $-\sqrt{9}$, which is -3.

$$\boxed{\quad \sqrt{a} = b \qquad \text{means} \qquad b^2 = a \quad \text{and} \quad b \geq 0 \quad}$$

Since $a = b^2 \geq 0$, the symbol $\sqrt{a}$ makes sense only when $a \geq 0$. For instance,

$$\sqrt{9} = 3 \qquad \text{because} \qquad 3^2 = 9 \quad \text{and} \quad 3 \geq 0$$

Square roots are special cases of nth roots. The nth root of x is the number that, when raised to the nth power, gives x.

DEFINITION OF nth ROOT

If n is any positive integer, then the **principal nth root** of a is defined as follows:

$$\sqrt[n]{a} = b \qquad \text{means} \qquad b^n = a$$

If n is even, we must have $a \geq 0$ and $b \geq 0$.

Thus

$$\sqrt[4]{81} = 3 \qquad \text{because} \qquad 3^4 = 81 \quad \text{and} \quad 3 \geq 0$$

$$\sqrt[3]{-8} = -2 \qquad \text{because} \qquad (-2)^3 = -8$$

But $\sqrt{-8}$, $\sqrt[4]{-8}$, and $\sqrt[6]{-8}$ are not defined. (For instance, $\sqrt{-8}$ is not defined because the square of every real number is nonnegative.)

Notice that

$$\sqrt{4^2} = \sqrt{16} = 4 \qquad \text{but} \qquad \sqrt{(-4)^2} = \sqrt{16} = 4 = |-4|$$

Thus, the equation $\sqrt{a^2} = a$ is not always true; it is true only when $a \geq 0$. However, we can always write $\sqrt{a^2} = |a|$. This last equation is true not only for square roots, but for any even root. This and other rules used in working with nth roots are listed in the following box. In each property we assume that all the given roots exist.

PROPERTIES OF nth ROOTS

Property	Example
1. $\sqrt[n]{ab} = \sqrt[n]{a}\,\sqrt[n]{b}$	$\sqrt[3]{-8 \cdot 27} = \sqrt[3]{-8}\,\sqrt[3]{27} = (-2)(3) = -6$
2. $\sqrt[n]{\dfrac{a}{b}} = \dfrac{\sqrt[n]{a}}{\sqrt[n]{b}}$	$\sqrt[4]{\dfrac{16}{81}} = \dfrac{\sqrt[4]{16}}{\sqrt[4]{81}} = \dfrac{2}{3}$
3. $\sqrt[m]{\sqrt[n]{a}} = \sqrt[mn]{a}$	$\sqrt{\sqrt[3]{729}} = \sqrt[6]{729} = 3$
4. $\sqrt[n]{a^n} = a$ if n is odd	$\sqrt[3]{(-5)^3} = -5, \ \sqrt[5]{2^5} = 2$
5. $\sqrt[n]{a^n} = |a|$ if n is even	$\sqrt[4]{(-3)^4} = |-3| = 3$

EXAMPLE 5 ■ Simplifying Expressions Involving nth Roots

(a) $\sqrt[3]{x^4} = \sqrt[3]{x^3 x}$ Factor out the largest cube

$\qquad\quad = \sqrt[3]{x^3}\,\sqrt[3]{x}$ Property 1

$\qquad\quad = x\,\sqrt[3]{x}$ Property 4

(b) $\sqrt[4]{81x^8 y^4} = \sqrt[4]{81}\,\sqrt[4]{x^8}\,\sqrt[4]{y^4}$ Property 1

$\qquad\qquad\quad = 3\,\sqrt[4]{(x^2)^4}\,|y|$ Property 5

$\qquad\qquad\quad = 3x^2\,|y|$ Property 5   ■

It is frequently useful to combine like radicals in an expression such as $2\sqrt{3} + 5\sqrt{3}$. This can be done by using the Distributive Property. Thus

$$2\sqrt{3} + 5\sqrt{3} = (2 + 5)\sqrt{3} = 7\sqrt{3}$$

The next example further illustrates this process.

⊘ Avoid making the following error:

$$\sqrt{a + b} \neq \sqrt{a} + \sqrt{b}$$

For instance, if we let $a = 9$ and $b = 16$, then we see the error:

$$\sqrt{9 + 16} \overset{?}{=} \sqrt{9} + \sqrt{16}$$

$$\sqrt{25} \overset{?}{=} 3 + 4$$

$$5 \overset{?}{=} 7 \quad \text{Wrong!}$$

EXAMPLE 6 ■ Combining Radicals

(a) $\sqrt{32} + \sqrt{200} = \sqrt{16 \cdot 2} + \sqrt{100 \cdot 2}$ Factor out the largest squares

$\qquad\qquad\qquad\ = \sqrt{16}\,\sqrt{2} + \sqrt{100}\,\sqrt{2}$ Property 1

$\qquad\qquad\qquad\ = 4\sqrt{2} + 10\sqrt{2} = 14\sqrt{2}$ Distributive Property

(b) If $b > 0$, then

$$\sqrt{25b} - \sqrt{b^3} = \sqrt{25}\,\sqrt{b} - \sqrt{b^2}\,\sqrt{b} \qquad \text{Property 1}$$

$$= 5\,\sqrt{b} - b\,\sqrt{b} \qquad \text{Property 5, } b > 0$$

$$= (5 - b)\,\sqrt{b} \qquad \text{Distributive Property} \qquad \blacksquare$$

■ Rational Exponents

To define what is meant by a *rational exponent* or, equivalently, a *fractional exponent* such as $a^{1/3}$, we need to use radicals. In order to give meaning to the symbol $a^{1/n}$ in a way that is consistent with the Laws of Exponents, we would have to have

$$(a^{1/n})^n = a^{(1/n)n} = a^1 = a$$

So, by the definition of nth root,

$$\boxed{a^{1/n} = \sqrt[n]{a}}$$

In general, we define rational exponents as follows.

DEFINITION OF RATIONAL EXPONENTS

For any rational exponent m/n in lowest terms, where m and n are integers and $n > 0$, we define

$$a^{m/n} = \left(\sqrt[n]{a}\right)^m$$

or equivalently

$$a^{m/n} = \sqrt[n]{a^m}$$

If n is even, then we require that $a \geq 0$.

With this definition it can be proved that *the Laws of Exponents also hold for rational exponents.*

EXAMPLE 7 ■ Using the Definition of Rational Exponents

(a) $4^{1/2} = \sqrt{4} = 2$

(b) $8^{2/3} = (\sqrt[3]{8})^2 = 2^2 = 4$ Alternative solution: $8^{2/3} = \sqrt[3]{8^2} = \sqrt[3]{64} = 4$

(c) $(125)^{-1/3} = \dfrac{1}{125^{1/3}} = \dfrac{1}{\sqrt[3]{125}} = \dfrac{1}{5}$ $\blacksquare$

EXAMPLE 8 ■ Using the Laws of Exponents with Rational Exponents

(a) $a^{1/3}a^{7/3} = a^{8/3}$ $\qquad$ Law 1

(b) $\dfrac{a^{2/5}a^{7/5}}{a^{3/5}} = a^{2/5+7/5-3/5} = a^{6/5}$ $\qquad$ Laws 1 and 2

(c) $\left(\dfrac{2x^{3/4}}{y^{1/3}}\right)^3 \left(\dfrac{y^4}{x^{-1/2}}\right) = \dfrac{2^3(x^{3/4})^3}{(y^{1/3})^3} \cdot (y^4 x^{1/2})$ $\qquad$ Laws 5, 4, and 7

$\qquad\qquad\qquad\quad = \dfrac{8x^{9/4}}{y} \cdot y^4 x^{1/2}$ $\qquad$ Law 3

$\qquad\qquad\qquad\quad = 8x^{11/4}y^3$ $\qquad$ Laws 1 and 2 $\qquad$ ■

EXAMPLE 9 ■ Simplifying by Writing Radicals as Rational Exponents

(a) $(2\sqrt{x})(3\sqrt[3]{x}) = (2x^{1/2})(3x^{1/3})$ $\qquad$ Definition of rational exponents

$\qquad\qquad\qquad = 6x^{1/2+1/3} = 6x^{5/6}$ $\qquad$ Law 1

(b) $\sqrt{x\sqrt{x}} = (xx^{1/2})^{1/2}$ $\qquad$ Definition of rational exponents

$\qquad\quad = (x^{3/2})^{1/2}$ $\qquad$ Law 1

$\qquad\quad = x^{3/4}$ $\qquad$ Law 3 $\qquad$ ■

■ Rationalizing the Denominator

It is often useful to eliminate the radical in a denominator by multiplying both numerator and denominator by an appropriate expression. This procedure is called **rationalizing the denominator**. If the denominator is of the form $\sqrt{a}$, we multiply numerator and denominator by $\sqrt{a}$. In doing so we multiply the given quantity by 1, so we do not change its value. For instance,

$$\frac{1}{\sqrt{a}} = \frac{1}{\sqrt{a}} \cdot 1 = \frac{1}{\sqrt{a}} \cdot \frac{\sqrt{a}}{\sqrt{a}} = \frac{\sqrt{a}}{a}$$

Note that the denominator in the last fraction contains no radical. In general, if the denominator is of the form $\sqrt[n]{a^m}$ with $m < n$, then multiplying numerator and denominator by $\sqrt[n]{a^{n-m}}$ will rationalize the denominator, because (for $a > 0$)

$$\sqrt[n]{a^m}\sqrt[n]{a^{n-m}} = \sqrt[n]{a^{m+n-m}} = \sqrt[n]{a^n} = a$$

EXAMPLE 10 ■ Rationalizing Denominators

(a) $\dfrac{2}{\sqrt{3}} = \dfrac{2}{\sqrt{3}} \cdot \dfrac{\sqrt{3}}{\sqrt{3}} = \dfrac{2\sqrt{3}}{3}$

(b) $\dfrac{1}{\sqrt[3]{x^2}} = \dfrac{1}{\sqrt[3]{x^2}}\dfrac{\sqrt[3]{x}}{\sqrt[3]{x}} = \dfrac{\sqrt[3]{x}}{\sqrt[3]{x^3}} = \dfrac{\sqrt[3]{x}}{x}$ $\qquad$ ■

A.2 EXERCISES

1–6 ■ Write each radical expression using exponents, and each exponential expression using radicals.

1. $\dfrac{1}{\sqrt{17}}$ **2.** $\sqrt[4]{7^3}$ **3.** $4^{2/3}$

4. $\sqrt[3]{b^5}$ **5.** $a^{3/5}$ **6.** $w^{-3/2}$

7–14 ■ Evaluate each number.

7. (a) $(-2)^4$ (b) -2^4 (c) $(-2)^0$

8. (a) $\left(\frac{1}{2}\right)^4 4^{-2}$ (b) $\left(\frac{1}{4}\right)^{-2}$ (c) $\left(\frac{1}{4}\right)^0 2^{-1}$

9. (a) $2^4 5^{-2}$ (b) $\dfrac{10^7}{10^4}$ (c) $(2^3 \cdot 2^2)^2$

10. (a) $\sqrt{64}$ (b) $\sqrt[3]{-64}$ (c) $\sqrt[5]{-32}$

11. (a) $\sqrt{\frac{4}{9}}$ (b) $\sqrt[4]{256}$ (c) $\sqrt[6]{\frac{1}{64}}$

12. (a) $\sqrt{7}\sqrt{28}$ (b) $\dfrac{\sqrt{48}}{\sqrt{3}}$ (c) $\sqrt[4]{24}\sqrt[4]{54}$

13. (a) $\left(\frac{4}{9}\right)^{-1/2}$ (b) $(-32)^{2/5}$ (c) $(-125)^{-1/3}$

14. (a) $1024^{-0.1}$ (b) $\left(-\frac{27}{8}\right)^{2/3}$ (c) $\left(\frac{25}{64}\right)^{3/2}$

15–18 ■ Evaluate the expression using $x = 3$, $y = 4$, and $z = -1$.

15. $\sqrt{x^2 + y^2}$ **16.** $\sqrt[4]{x^3 + 14y + 2z}$

17. $(9x)^{2/3} + (2y)^{2/3} + z^{2/3}$ **18.** $(xy)^{2z}$

19–22 ■ Simplify the expression.

19. $\sqrt[3]{108} - \sqrt[3]{32}$ **20.** $\sqrt{8} + \sqrt{50}$

21. $\sqrt{245} - \sqrt{125}$ **22.** $\sqrt[3]{54} - \sqrt[3]{16}$

23–40 ■ Simplify the expression and eliminate any negative exponent(s).

23. $a^9 a^{-5}$ **24.** $(3y^2)(4y^5)$

25. $(12x^2 y^4)\left(\frac{1}{2}x^5 y\right)$ **26.** $(6y)^3$

27. $\dfrac{x^9(2x)^4}{x^3}$ **28.** $\dfrac{a^{-3}b^4}{a^{-5}b^5}$

29. $b^4\left(\frac{1}{3}b^2\right)(12b^{-8})$ **30.** $(2s^3 t^{-1})\left(\frac{1}{4}s^6\right)(16t^4)$

31. $(rs)^3(2s)^{-2}(4r)^4$ **32.** $(2u^2 v^3)^3(3u^3 v)^{-2}$

33. $\dfrac{(6y^3)^4}{2y^5}$ **34.** $\dfrac{(2x^3)^2(3x^4)}{(x^3)^4}$

35. $\dfrac{(x^2 y^3)^4 (xy^4)^{-3}}{x^2 y}$ **36.** $\left(\dfrac{c^4 d^3}{cd^2}\right)\left(\dfrac{d^2}{c^3}\right)^3$

37. $\dfrac{(xy^2 z^3)^4}{(x^3 y^2 z)^3}$ **38.** $\left(\dfrac{xy^{-2}z^{-3}}{x^2 y^3 z^{-4}}\right)^{-3}$

39. $\left(\dfrac{q^{-1}rs^{-2}}{r^{-5}sq^{-8}}\right)^{-1}$ **40.** $(3ab^2 c)\left(\dfrac{2a^2 b}{c^3}\right)^{-2}$

41–56 ■ Simplify the expression and eliminate any negative exponent(s). Assume that all letters denote positive numbers.

41. $x^{2/3} x^{1/5}$ **42.** $(-2a^{3/4})(5a^{3/2})$

43. $(4b)^{1/2}(8b^{2/5})$ **44.** $(8x^6)^{-2/3}$

45. $(c^2 d^3)^{-1/3}$ **46.** $(4x^6 y^8)^{3/2}$

47. $(y^{3/4})^{2/3}$ **48.** $(a^{2/5})^{-3/4}$

49. $(2x^4 y^{-4/5})^3 (8y^2)^{2/3}$ **50.** $(x^{-5} y^3 z^{10})^{-3/5}$

51. $\left(\dfrac{x^6 y}{y^4}\right)^{5/2}$ **52.** $\left(\dfrac{-2x^{1/3}}{y^{1/2} z^{1/6}}\right)^4$

53. $\left(\dfrac{3a^{-2}}{4b^{-1/3}}\right)^{-1}$ **54.** $\dfrac{(y^{10} z^{-5})^{1/5}}{(y^{-2} z^3)^{1/3}}$

55. $\dfrac{(9st)^{3/2}}{(27s^3 t^{-4})^{2/3}}$ **56.** $\left(\dfrac{a^2 b^{-3}}{x^{-1} y^2}\right)^3 \left(\dfrac{x^{-2} b^{-1}}{a^{3/2} y^{1/3}}\right)$

57–64 ■ Simplify the expression. Assume the letters denote any real numbers.

57. $\sqrt[4]{x^4}$ **58.** $\sqrt[3]{x^3 y^6}$

59. $\sqrt[3]{x^3 y}$ **60.** $\sqrt{x^4 y^4}$

61. $\sqrt[5]{a^6 b^7}$ **62.** $\sqrt[3]{a^2 b}\,\sqrt[3]{a^4 b}$

63. $\sqrt[3]{\sqrt{64x^6}}$ **64.** $\sqrt[4]{x^4 y^2 z^2}$

65–68 ■ Rationalize the denominator.

65. (a) $\dfrac{1}{\sqrt{6}}$ (b) $\sqrt{\dfrac{x}{3y}}$ (c) $\sqrt{\dfrac{3}{20}}$

66. (a) $\sqrt{\dfrac{x^5}{2}}$ (b) $\sqrt{\dfrac{2}{3}}$ (c) $\sqrt{\dfrac{1}{2x^3 y^5}}$

67. (a) $\dfrac{1}{\sqrt[3]{x}}$ (b) $\dfrac{1}{\sqrt[5]{x^2}}$ (c) $\dfrac{1}{\sqrt[7]{x^3}}$

68. (a) $\dfrac{1}{\sqrt[3]{x^2}}$ (b) $\dfrac{1}{\sqrt[4]{x^3}}$ (c) $\dfrac{1}{\sqrt[3]{x^4}}$

A.3   ALGEBRAIC EXPRESSIONS

Algebraic expressions such as

$$2x^2 - 3x + 4 \qquad ax + b$$

$$\frac{y - 1}{y^2 + 2} \qquad \frac{cx^2y + dy^2z}{\sqrt{x^2 + y^2 + z^2}}$$

are obtained by starting with variables such as x, y, and z and constants such as 2, -3, a, b, c, and d, and combining them using addition, subtraction, multiplication, division, and roots. A **variable** is a letter that can represent any number in a given set of numbers, whereas a **constant** represents a fixed (or specific) number. The **domain** of a variable is the set of numbers that the variable is permitted to have. For instance, in the expression $\sqrt{x}$ the domain of x is $\{x \mid x \geq 0\}$, whereas in the expression $2/(x - 3)$ the domain of x is $\{x \mid x \neq 3\}$.

The simplest types of algebraic expressions use only addition, subtraction, and multiplication. Such expressions are called **polynomials**. The general form of a polynomial of degree n (where n is a nonnegative integer) in the variable x is

$$a_nx^n + a_{n-1}x^{n-1} + \cdots + a_1x + a_0$$

where $a_0, a_1 \ldots, a_n$ are constants and $a_n \neq 0$. The **degree** of a polynomial is the highest power of the variable. Any polynomial is a sum of **terms** of the form ax^k, called **monomials**, where a is a constant and k is a nonnegative integer. A **binomial** is a sum of two monomials, a **trinomial** is the sum of three monomials, and so on. Thus, $2x^2 - 3x + 4$, $ax + b$, and $x^4 + 2x^3$ are polynomials of degree 2, 1, and 4, respectively; the first is a trinomial, the other two are binomials.

Monomials:

$$5, \quad 6x, \quad ax^2, \quad -10ab$$

Binomials:

$$2 + 3x, \quad 6x^2 - 5, \quad ax + b$$

Trinomials:

$$x^2 + x + 1, \quad ax + by + cz,$$
$$x^5 + 2x^3 + 3x$$

Combining Algebraic Expressions

We **add** and **subtract** polynomials using the properties of real numbers that were discussed in Appendix A.1. The idea is to combine **like terms** (that is, terms with the same variables raised to the same powers) using the Distributive Property. For instance,

Distributive Property

$$ac + bc = (a + b)c$$

$$5x^7 + 3x^7 = (5 + 3)x^7 = 8x^7$$

EXAMPLE 1 ■ Adding and Subtracting Polynomials

(a) Find the sum $(x^3 - 6x^2 + 2x + 4) + (x^3 + 5x^2 - 7x)$.

(b) Find the difference $(x^3 - 6x^2 + 2x + 4) - (x^3 + 5x^2 - 7x)$.

SOLUTION

(a) $(x^3 - 6x^2 + 2x + 4) + (x^3 + 5x^2 - 7x)$

$= (x^3 + x^3) + (-6x^2 + 5x^2) + (2x - 7x) + 4$ Group like terms

$= 2x^3 - x^2 - 5x + 4$ Combine like terms

(b) $(x^3 - 6x^2 + 2x + 4) - (x^3 + 5x^2 - 7x)$

$$= x^3 - 6x^2 + 2x + 4 - x^3 - 5x^2 + 7x \qquad \text{Distributive Property}$$

$$= (x^3 - x^3) + (-6x^2 - 5x^2) + (2x + 7x) + 4 \qquad \text{Group like terms}$$

$$= -11x^2 + 9x + 4 \qquad \text{Combine like terms} \qquad \blacksquare$$

To find the **product** of polynomials or other algebraic expressions, we need to use the Distributive Property repeatedly. In particular, using it three times on the product of two binomials, we get

$$(a + b)(c + d) = a(c + d) + b(c + d) = ac + ad + bc + bd$$

This says that we multiply the two factors by multiplying each term in one factor by each term in the other factor and adding these products. Schematically we have

The acronym **FOIL** helps us remember that the product of two binomials is the sum of the products of the **F**irst terms, the **O**uter terms, the **I**nner terms, and the **L**ast terms.

$$(a + b)(c + d) = ac + ad + bc + bd$$
$$\qquad\qquad\qquad \uparrow \quad \uparrow \quad \uparrow \quad \uparrow$$
$$\qquad\qquad\qquad \text{F} \quad \text{O} \quad \text{I} \quad \text{L}$$

In general, we can multiply two algebraic expressions by using the Distributive Property and the Laws of Exponents.

EXAMPLE 2 ■ Multiplying Algebraic Expressions

(a) $(2x + 1)(3x - 5) = 6x^2 - 10x + 3x - 5 \qquad \text{Distributive Property}$

$$= 6x^2 - 7x - 5 \qquad \text{Combine like terms}$$

(b) $(1 + \sqrt{x})(2 - 3\sqrt{x}) = 2 - 3\sqrt{x} + 2\sqrt{x} - 3(\sqrt{x})^2 \qquad \text{Distributive Property}$

$$= 2 - \sqrt{x} - 3x \qquad \text{Combine like terms} \qquad \blacksquare$$

Certain types of products occur so frequently that you should memorize them. You can verify the following formulas by performing the multiplications.

SPECIAL PRODUCT FORMULAS

1. $(A - B)(A + B) = A^2 - B^2$

2. $(A + B)^2 = A^2 + 2AB + B^2$

3. $(A - B)^2 = A^2 - 2AB + B^2$

4. $(A + B)^3 = A^3 + 3A^2B + 3AB^2 + B^3$

5. $(A - B)^3 = A^3 - 3A^2B + 3AB^2 - B^3$

The key idea in using these formulas (or any other formula in algebra) is the **Principle of Substitution**: We may substitute any algebraic expression for any letter in a formula. For example, to find $(x^2 + y^3)^2$ we use Product Formula 2:

$$(A + B)^2 = A^2 + 2AB + B^2$$

We substitute x^2 for A and y^3 for B to get

$$(x^2 + y^3)^2 = (x^2)^2 + 2(x^2)(y^3) + (y^3)^2$$

This type of substitution is valid because every algebraic expression (in this case, x^2 or y^3) represents a number.

EXAMPLE 3 ■ Using the Special Product Formulas

Use the Special Product Formulas to find each product.

(a) $(3x + 5)^2$ 　　　　　　　　　　　(b) $(2x - \sqrt{y})(2x + \sqrt{y})$

SOLUTION

(a) Product Formula 2, with $A = 3x$ and $B = 5$, gives

$$(3x + 5)^2 = (3x)^2 + 2(3x)(5) + 5^2 = 9x^2 + 30x + 25$$

(b) Using Product Formula 1 with $A = 2x$ and $B = \sqrt{y}$, we have

$$(2x - \sqrt{y})(2x + \sqrt{y}) = (2x)^2 - (\sqrt{y})^2 = 4x^2 - y$$ ■

■ Factoring

We used the Distributive Property to expand algebraic expressions. We sometimes need to reverse this process (again using the Distributive Property) by **factoring** an expression as a product of simpler ones. For example, we can write

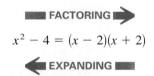

$$x^2 - 4 = (x - 2)(x + 2)$$

We say that $x - 2$ and $x + 2$ are **factors** of $x^2 - 4$. The easiest type of factoring occurs when the terms have a common factor.

EXAMPLE 4 ■ Factoring Out Common Factors

Factor each expression.

(a) $3x^2 - 6x$ 　　　　　　　　　　　(b) $8x^4y^2 + 6x^3y^3 - 2xy^4$

SOLUTION

(a) The greatest common factor of the terms $3x^2$ and $-6x$ is $3x$, so we have

$$3x^2 - 6x = 3x(x - 2)$$

(b) The greatest common factor of the three terms in the polynomial is $2xy^2$, so

$$8x^4y^2 + 6x^3y^3 - 2xy^4 = (2xy^2)(4x^3) + (2xy^2)(3x^2y) + (2xy^2)(-y^2)$$
$$= 2xy^2(4x^3 + 3x^2y - y^2)$$ ■

CHECK YOUR ANSWER

Multiplying gives

$$3x(x - 2) = 3x^2 - 6x \quad \checkmark$$

CHECK YOUR ANSWER

Multiplying gives

$$2xy^2(4x^3 + 3x^2y - y^2) =$$
$$8x^4y^2 + 6x^3y^3 - 2xy^4 \quad \checkmark$$

To factor a **quadratic** $x^2 + bx + c$, we look for factors of the form $x + r$ and $x + s$:

$$x^2 + bx + c = (x + r)(x + s) = x^2 + (r + s)x + rs$$

So we need to find numbers r and s so that $r + s = b$ and $rs = c$.

EXAMPLE 5 ■ Factoring $x^2 + bx + c$ by Trial and Error

Factor: $x^2 + 7x + 12$

SOLUTION

We need to find two integers whose product is 12 and whose sum is 7. By trial and error we find that the two integers are 3 and 4. Thus, the factorization is

$$x^2 + 7x + 12 = (x + 3)(x + 4)$$ ■

CHECK YOUR ANSWER

Multiplying gives

$(x + 3)(x + 4) = x^2 + 7x + 12$ ✓

To factor a quadratic $ax^2 + bx + c$ with $a \neq 1$, we look for factors of the form $px + r$ and $qx + s$:

$$ax^2 + bx + c = (px + r)(qx + s) = pqx^2 + (ps + qr)x + rs$$

Therefore, we try to find numbers p, q, r, and s such that $pq = a$, $rs = c$, $ps + qr = b$. If these numbers are all integers, then we will have a limited number of possibilities to try for p, q, r, and s.

$$\text{factors of } a$$
$$\downarrow \qquad \downarrow$$
$$ax^2 + bx + c = (px + r)(qx + s)$$
$$\uparrow \qquad \uparrow$$
$$\text{factors of } c$$

EXAMPLE 6 ■ Factoring $ax^2 + bx + c$ by Trial and Error

Factor: $6x^2 + 7x - 5$

SOLUTION

We can factor 6 as $6 \cdot 1$ or $3 \cdot 2$, and -5 as $-5 \cdot 1$ or $5 \cdot (-1)$. By trying these possibilities, we arrive at the factorization

$$6x^2 + 7x - 5 = (3x + 5)(2x - 1)$$ ■

CHECK YOUR ANSWER

Multiplying gives

$(3x + 5)(2x - 1) = 6x^2 + 7x - 5$
   ✓

Some special algebraic expressions can be factored using the following formulas. The first three are simply the Special Product Formulas written backward.

FACTORING FORMULAS	
Formula	**Name**
1. $A^2 - B^2 = (A - B)(A + B)$	Difference of squares
2. $A^2 + 2AB + B^2 = (A + B)^2$	Perfect square
3. $A^2 - 2AB + B^2 = (A - B)^2$	Perfect square
4. $A^3 - B^3 = (A - B)(A^2 + AB + B^2)$	Difference of cubes
5. $A^3 + B^3 = (A + B)(A^2 - AB + B^2)$	Sum of cubes

EXAMPLE 7 ■ Factoring Differences of Squares

Factor each polynomial.

(a) $4x^2 - 25$ (b) $(x + y)^2 - z^2$

SOLUTION

(a) Using the formula for a difference of squares with $A = 2x$ and $B = 5$, we have

$$4x^2 - 25 = (2x)^2 - 5^2$$
$$= (2x - 5)(2x + 5)$$

(b) We use the formula for the difference of squares with $A = x + y$ and $B = z$.

$$(x + y)^2 - z^2 = (x + y - z)(x + y + z)$$ ■

A trinomial is a perfect square if it is of the form

$$A^2 + 2AB + B^2 \qquad \text{or} \qquad A^2 - 2AB + B^2$$

So, we **recognize a perfect square** if the middle term ($2AB$ or $-2AB$) is plus or minus twice the product of the square roots of the outer two terms.

EXAMPLE 8 ■ Recognizing Perfect Squares

Factor each trinomial: (a) $x^2 + 6x + 9$ (b) $4x^2 - 4xy + y^2$

SOLUTION

(a) Here $A = x$ and $B = 3$, so $2AB = 2 \cdot x \cdot 3 = 6x$. Since the middle term is $6x$, the trinomial is a perfect square. By Formula 2 we have

$$x^2 + 6x + 9 = (x + 3)^2$$

(b) Here $A = 2x$ and $B = y$, so $2AB = 2 \cdot 2x \cdot y = 4xy$. Since the middle term is $-4xy$, the trinomial is a perfect square. By Formula 2 we have

$$4x^2 - 4xy + y^2 = (2x - y)^2$$ ■

■ Fractional Expressions

A quotient of two algebraic expressions is called a **fractional expression**. We assume that all fractions are defined; that is, *we deal only with values of the variables such that the denominators are not zero.*

To **simplify fractional expressions**, we factor both numerator and denominator and use the following property of fractions:

$$\frac{AC}{BC} = \frac{A}{B}$$

This says that we can **cancel** common factors from numerator and denominator.

EXAMPLE 9 ■ **Simplifying Fractional Expressions by Cancellation**

Simplify: $\dfrac{x^2 - 1}{x^2 + x - 2}$

SOLUTION

$$\frac{x^2 - 1}{x^2 + x - 2} = \frac{(x - 1)(x + 1)}{(x - 1)(x + 2)} \qquad \text{Factor}$$

$$= \frac{x + 1}{x + 2} \qquad \text{Cancel common factors}$$ ■

⊘ We can't cancel the x^2's in

$\dfrac{x^2 - 1}{x^2 + x - 2}$ because x^2 is not a factor.

■ Multiplying and Dividing Fractional Expressions

To **multiply fractional expressions**, we use the following property of fractions:

$$\frac{A}{B} \cdot \frac{C}{D} = \frac{AC}{BD}$$

This says that to multiply two fractions we multiply their numerators and multiply their denominators.

EXAMPLE 10 ■ **Multiplying Fractional Expressions**

Perform the indicated multiplication and simplify: $\dfrac{x^2 + 2x - 3}{x^2 + 8x + 16} \cdot \dfrac{3x + 12}{x - 1}$

SOLUTION

We first factor.

$$\frac{x^2 + 2x - 3}{x^2 + 8x + 16} \cdot \frac{3x + 12}{x - 1} = \frac{(x - 1)(x + 3)}{(x + 4)^2} \cdot \frac{3(x + 4)}{x - 1} \qquad \text{Factor}$$

$$= \frac{3(x + 3)}{x + 4} \qquad \text{Cancel common factors}$$ ■

To **divide fractional expressions**, we use the following property of fractions:

$$\frac{A}{B} \div \frac{C}{D} = \frac{A}{B} \cdot \frac{D}{C}$$

This says that to divide a fraction by another fraction we invert the divisor and multiply.

Diophantus lived in Alexandria about 250 A.D. His book *Arithmetica* is considered the first book on algebra. In it he gives methods for finding integer solutions of algebraic equations. *Arithmetica* was read and studied for more than a thousand years. Fermat (see page 532) made some of his most important discoveries while studying this book. Diophantus' major contribution is the use of symbols to stand for the unknowns in a problem. Although his symbolism is not as simple as what we use today, it was a major advance over writing everything in words. In Diophantus' notation the equation

$$x^5 - 7x^2 + 8x - 5 = 24$$

is written

$$\Delta \mathrm{K}^{\gamma} \alpha \varsigma \eta \mathring{\phi} \Delta^{\gamma} \zeta \mathring{M} \varepsilon \iota^{\sigma} \kappa \delta$$

Our modern algebraic notation did not come into common use until the 17th century.

EXAMPLE 11 ■ **Dividing Fractional Expressions**

Perform the indicated division and simplify: $\dfrac{x-4}{x^2-4} \div \dfrac{x^2-3x-4}{x^2+5x+6}$

SOLUTION

$$\frac{x-4}{x^2-4} \div \frac{x^2-3x-4}{x^2+5x+6} = \frac{x-4}{x^2-4} \cdot \frac{x^2+5x+6}{x^2-3x-4} \qquad \text{Invert and multiply}$$

$$= \frac{(x-4)(x+2)(x+3)}{(x-2)(x+2)(x-4)(x+1)} \qquad \text{Factor}$$

$$= \frac{x+3}{(x-2)(x+1)} \qquad \text{Cancel common factors} \qquad ■$$

■ Adding and Subtracting Fractional Expressions

To **add or subtract fractional expressions**, we first find a common denominator and then use the following property of fractions:

$$\boxed{\frac{A}{C} + \frac{B}{C} = \frac{A+B}{C}}$$

⊘ Avoid making the following error:

$$\frac{A}{B+C} \;\cancel{\neq}\; \frac{A}{B} + \frac{A}{C}$$

For instance, if we let $A = 2$, $B = 1$, and $C = 1$, then we see the error:

$$\frac{2}{1+1} \overset{?}{=} \frac{2}{1} + \frac{2}{1}$$

$$\frac{2}{2} \overset{?}{=} 2 + 2$$

$$1 \overset{?}{=} 4 \quad \text{Wrong!}$$

Although any common denominator will work, it is best to use the **least common denominator** (LCD). The LCD is found by factoring each denominator and taking the product of the distinct factors, using the highest power that appears in any of the factors.

EXAMPLE 12 ■ **Subtracting Fractional Expressions**

Simplify: $\dfrac{1}{x^2-1} - \dfrac{2}{(x+1)^2}$

SOLUTION

The LCD of $x^2 - 1 = (x-1)(x+1)$ and $(x+1)^2$ is $(x-1)(x+1)^2$, so we have

$$\frac{1}{x^2-1} - \frac{2}{(x+1)^2} = \frac{1}{(x-1)(x+1)} - \frac{2}{(x+1)^2} \qquad \text{Factor}$$

$$= \frac{(x+1) - 2(x-1)}{(x-1)(x+1)^2} \qquad \begin{array}{l}\text{Combine fractions}\\ \text{using LCD}\end{array}$$

$$= \frac{x+1-2x+2}{(x-1)(x+1)^2} \qquad \text{Distributive Property}$$

$$= \frac{3-x}{(x-1)(x+1)^2} \qquad \begin{array}{l}\text{Combine terms}\\ \text{in numerator}\end{array} \qquad ■$$

Compound Fractions

A **compound fraction** is a fraction in which the numerator, the denominator, or both, are themselves fractional expressions.

EXAMPLE 13 ■ Simplifying a Compound Fraction

Simplify: $\dfrac{\dfrac{x}{y} + 1}{1 - \dfrac{y}{x}}$

SOLUTION 1

We combine the terms in the numerator into a single fraction. We do the same in the denominator. Then we invert and multiply.

$$\frac{\dfrac{x}{y} + 1}{1 - \dfrac{y}{x}} = \frac{\dfrac{x + y}{y}}{\dfrac{x - y}{x}} = \frac{x + y}{y} \cdot \frac{x}{x - y}$$

$$= \frac{x(x + y)}{y(x - y)}$$

SOLUTION 2

We find the LCD of all the fractions in the expression, then multiply numerator and denominator by it. In this example the LCD of all the fractions is xy. Thus

$$\frac{\dfrac{x}{y} + 1}{1 - \dfrac{y}{x}} = \frac{\dfrac{x}{y} + 1}{1 - \dfrac{y}{x}} \cdot \frac{xy}{xy} \qquad \text{Multiply numerator and denominator by } xy$$

$$= \frac{x^2 + xy}{xy - y^2} \qquad \text{Simplify}$$

$$= \frac{x(x + y)}{y(x - y)} \qquad \text{Factor}$$

Rationalizing the Denominator or the Numerator

If a fraction has a denominator of the form $A + B \sqrt{C}$, we may rationalize the denominator by multiplying numerator and denominator by the **conjugate radical** $A - B \sqrt{C}$. This is effective because, by Product Formula 1 on page 526, the product of the denominator and its conjugate radical does not contain a radical:

$$\left(A + B \sqrt{C}\right)\left(A - B \sqrt{C}\right) = A^2 - B^2C$$

EXAMPLE 14 ■ Rationalizing the Denominator

Rationalize the denominator: $\dfrac{1}{1 + \sqrt{2}}$

SOLUTION

We multiply both the numerator and the denominator by the conjugate radical of $1 + \sqrt{2}$, which is $1 - \sqrt{2}$.

$$\frac{1}{1 + \sqrt{2}} = \frac{1}{1 + \sqrt{2}} \cdot \frac{1 - \sqrt{2}}{1 - \sqrt{2}}$$

Multiply numerator and denominator by the conjugate radical

Product Formula 1
$$(a + b)(a - b) = a^2 - b^2$$

$$= \frac{1 - \sqrt{2}}{1^2 - \left(\sqrt{2}\right)^2}$$

Product Formula 1

$$= \frac{1 - \sqrt{2}}{1 - 2} = \frac{1 - \sqrt{2}}{-1} = \sqrt{2} - 1$$

■

EXAMPLE 15 ■ Rationalizing the Numerator

Rationalize the numerator: $\dfrac{\sqrt{4 + h} - 2}{h}$

SOLUTION

We multiply numerator and denominator by the conjugate radical $\sqrt{4 + h} + 2$.

$$\frac{\sqrt{4 + h} - 2}{h} = \frac{\sqrt{4 + h} - 2}{h} \cdot \frac{\sqrt{4 + h} + 2}{\sqrt{4 + h} + 2}$$

Multiply numerator and denominator by the conjugate radical

$$= \frac{\left(\sqrt{4 + h}\right)^2 - 2^2}{h\left(\sqrt{4 + h} + 2\right)}$$

Product Formula 1

$$= \frac{4 + h - 4}{h\left(\sqrt{4 + h} + 2\right)}$$

$$= \frac{h}{h\left(\sqrt{4 + h} + 2\right)} = \frac{1}{\sqrt{4 + h} + 2}$$

Property 5 of fractions (cancel common factors)

■

A.3 EXERCISES

1–26 ■ Perform the indicated operations and simplify.

1. $(3x^2 + x + 1) + (2x^2 - 3x - 5)$

2. $(3x^2 + x + 1) - (2x^2 - 3x - 5)$

3. $8(2x + 5) - 7(x - 9)$

4. $4(x^2 - 3x + 5) - 3(x^2 - 2x + 1)$

5. $2(2 - 5t) + t^2(t - 1) - (t^4 - 1)$

6. $5(3t - 4) - (t^2 + 2) - 2t(t - 3)$

7. $\sqrt{x}\,(x - \sqrt{x})$

8. $x^{3/2}\left(\sqrt{x} - 1/\sqrt{x}\right)$

9. $(x + 2y)(3x - y)$

10. $(4x - 3y)(2x + 5y)$

11. $(1 - 2y)^2$

12. $(3x + 4)^2$

13. $(2x^2 + 3y^2)^2$

14. $\left(c + \dfrac{1}{c}\right)^2$

15. $(2x - 5)(x^2 - x + 1)$

16. $(1 + 2x)(x^2 - 3x + 1)$

17. $(x^2 - a^2)(x^2 + a^2)$

18. $(x^{1/2} + y^{1/2})(x^{1/2} - y^{1/2})$

19. $\left(\sqrt{a} - \dfrac{1}{b}\right)\left(\sqrt{a} + \dfrac{1}{b}\right)$

20. $(1 - 2y)^3$

21. $(x^2 + x - 2)(x^3 - x + 1)$

22. $(1 + x + x^2)(1 - x + x^2)$

23. $(1 + x^{4/3})(1 - x^{2/3})$

24. $(1 - b)^2(1 + b)^2$

25. $(3x^2y + 7xy^2)(x^2y^3 - 2y^2)$

26. $(x^4y - y^5)(x^2 + xy + y^2)$

27–60 ▪ Factor the expression completely.

27. $12x^3 + 18x$

28. $30x^3 + 15x^4$

29. $6y^4 - 15y^3$

30. $5ab - 8abc$

31. $x^2 - 2x - 8$

32. $x^2 - 14x + 48$

33. $y^2 - 8y + 15$

34. $z^2 + 6z - 16$

35. $2x^2 + 5x + 3$

36. $2x^2 + 7x - 4$

37. $9x^2 - 36x - 45$

38. $8x^2 + 10x + 3$

39. $6x^2 - 5x - 6$

40. $6 + 5t - 6t^2$

41. $4t^2 - 12t + 9$

42. $4x^2 + 4xy + y^2$

43. $r^2 - 6rs + 9s^2$

44. $25s^2 - 10st + t^2$

45. $x^2 - 36$

46. $4x^2 - 25$

47. $49 - 4y^2$

48. $4t^2 - 9s^2$

49. $(a + b)^2 - (a - b)^2$

50. $\left(1 + \dfrac{1}{x}\right)^2 - \left(1 - \dfrac{1}{x}\right)^2$

51. $x^2(x^2 - 1) - 9(x^2 - 1)$

52. $(a^2 - 1)b^2 - 4(a^2 - 1)$

53. $t^3 + 1$

54. $x^3 - 27$

55. $x^3 + 2x^2 + x$

56. $3x^3 - 27x$

57. $(x - 1)(x + 2)^2 - (x - 1)^2(x + 2)$

58. $(x + 1)^3x - 2(x + 1)^2x^2 + x^3(x + 1)$

59. $y^4(y + 2)^3 + y^5(y + 2)^4$

60. $n(x - y) + (n - 1)(y - x)$

61–100 ▪ Simplify the expression.

61. $\dfrac{x - 2}{x^2 - 4}$

62. $\dfrac{x^2 - x - 2}{x^2 - 1}$

63. $\dfrac{x^2 + 6x + 8}{x^2 + 5x + 4}$

64. $\dfrac{x^2 - x - 12}{x^2 + 5x + 6}$

65. $\dfrac{y^2 + y}{y^2 - 1}$

66. $\dfrac{y^2 - 3y - 18}{2y^2 + 5y + 3}$

67. $\dfrac{2x^3 - x^2 - 6x}{2x^2 - 7x + 6}$

68. $\dfrac{1 - x^2}{x^3 - 1}$

69. $\dfrac{t - 3}{t^2 + 9} \cdot \dfrac{t + 3}{t^2 - 9}$

70. $\dfrac{x^2 - x - 6}{x^2 + 2x} \cdot \dfrac{x^3 + x^2}{x^2 - 2x - 3}$

71. $\dfrac{x^2 + 7x + 12}{x^2 + 3x + 2} \cdot \dfrac{x^2 + 5x + 6}{x^2 + 6x + 9}$

72. $\dfrac{x^2 + 2xy + y^2}{x^2 - y^2} \cdot \dfrac{2x^2 - xy - y^2}{x^2 - xy - 2y^2}$

73. $\dfrac{2x^2 + 3x + 1}{x^2 + 2x - 15} \div \dfrac{x^2 + 6x + 5}{2x^2 - 7x + 3}$

74. $\dfrac{4y^2 - 9}{2y^2 + 9y - 18} \div \dfrac{2y^2 + y - 3}{y^2 + 5y - 6}$

75. $\dfrac{x/y}{z}$

76. $\dfrac{x}{y/z}$

77. $\dfrac{1}{x + 5} + \dfrac{2}{x - 3}$

78. $\dfrac{1}{x + 1} + \dfrac{1}{x - 1}$

79. $\dfrac{1}{x + 1} - \dfrac{1}{x + 2}$

80. $\dfrac{x}{x - 4} - \dfrac{3}{x + 6}$

81. $\dfrac{x}{(x + 1)^2} + \dfrac{2}{x + 1}$

82. $\dfrac{5}{2x - 3} - \dfrac{3}{(2x - 3)^2}$

83. $u + 1 + \dfrac{u}{u + 1}$

84. $\dfrac{2}{a^2} - \dfrac{3}{ab} + \dfrac{4}{b^2}$

85. $\dfrac{1}{x^2} + \dfrac{1}{x^2 + x}$

86. $\dfrac{1}{x} + \dfrac{1}{x^2} + \dfrac{1}{x^3}$

87. $\dfrac{2}{x + 3} - \dfrac{1}{x^2 + 7x + 12}$

88. $\dfrac{x}{x^2 - 4} + \dfrac{1}{x - 2}$

89. $\dfrac{1}{x + 3} + \dfrac{1}{x^2 - 9}$

90. $\dfrac{x}{x^2 + x - 2} - \dfrac{2}{x^2 - 5x + 4}$

91. $\dfrac{2}{x} + \dfrac{3}{x - 1} - \dfrac{4}{x^2 - x}$

92. $\dfrac{x}{x^2 - x - 6} - \dfrac{1}{x + 2} - \dfrac{2}{x - 3}$

93. $\dfrac{1}{x^2 + 3x + 2} - \dfrac{1}{x^2 - 2x - 3}$

94. $\dfrac{1}{x + 1} - \dfrac{2}{(x + 1)^2} + \dfrac{3}{x^2 - 1}$

95. $\dfrac{\dfrac{x}{y} - \dfrac{y}{x}}{\dfrac{1}{x^2} - \dfrac{1}{y^2}}$

96. $x - \dfrac{y}{\dfrac{x}{y} + \dfrac{y}{x}}$

97. $\dfrac{1 + \dfrac{1}{c-1}}{1 - \dfrac{1}{c-1}}$

98. $1 + \dfrac{1}{1 + \dfrac{1}{1+x}}$

99. $\dfrac{x^{-2} - y^{-2}}{x^{-1} + y^{-1}}$

100. $\dfrac{\dfrac{1}{a+h} - \dfrac{1}{a}}{h}$

101–104 ■ Rationalize the denominator.

101. $\dfrac{2}{3 + \sqrt{5}}$

102. $\dfrac{1}{\sqrt{x} + 1}$

103. $\dfrac{2}{\sqrt{2} + \sqrt{7}}$

104. $\dfrac{y}{\sqrt{3} + \sqrt{y}}$

105–110 ■ Rationalize the numerator.

105. $\dfrac{1 - \sqrt{5}}{3}$

106. $\dfrac{\sqrt{3} + \sqrt{5}}{2}$

107. $\dfrac{\sqrt{r} + \sqrt{2}}{5}$

108. $\dfrac{\sqrt{x} - \sqrt{x+h}}{h\sqrt{x}\sqrt{x+h}}$

109. $\sqrt{x^2 + 1} - x$

110. $\sqrt{x+1} - \sqrt{x}$

A.4 EQUATIONS

An equation is a statement that two mathematical expressions are equal. For example,

$$3 + 5 = 8$$

is an equation. Most equations that we study in algebra contain variables, which are symbols (usually letters) that stand for numbers. In the equation

$$4x + 7 = 19$$

the letter x is the variable. We think of x as the "unknown" in the equation, and our goal is to find the value of x that makes the equation true. The values of the unknown that make the equation true are called the **solutions** or **roots** of the equation, and the process of finding the solutions is called **solving the equation**.

Two equations with exactly the same solutions are called **equivalent equations**. To solve an equation, we try to find a simpler, equivalent equation in which the variable stands alone on one side of the "equal" sign. Here are the properties that we use to solve an equation. (In these properties, A, B, and C stand for any algebraic expressions, and the symbol $\Leftrightarrow$ means "is equivalent to.")

PROPERTIES OF EQUALITY

Property	Description
1. $A = B \Leftrightarrow A + C = B + C$	Adding the same quantity to both sides of an equation gives an equivalent equation.
2. $A = B \Leftrightarrow CA = CB \quad (C \neq 0)$	Multiplying both sides of an equation by the same nonzero quantity gives an equivalent equation.

These properties require that you *perform the same operation on both sides of an equation* when solving it. Thus, if we say "*add* -7" when solving an equation, that is just a short way of saying "*add* -7 to each side of the equation."

■ Linear Equations

The simplest type of equation is a **linear equation**, or first-degree equation, which is an equation in which each term is either a constant or a nonzero multiple of the variable. This means that it is equivalent to an equation of the form $ax + b = 0$. Here a and b represent real numbers with $a \neq 0$, and x is the unknown variable that we are solving for. The equation in the following example is linear.

EXAMPLE 1 ■ Solving a Linear Equation

Solve the equation $7x - 4 = 3x + 8$.

SOLUTION

We solve this by changing it to an equivalent equation with all terms that have the variable x on one side and all constant terms on the other.

$$7x - 4 = 3x + 8$$
$$7x = 3x + 12 \qquad \text{Add 4}$$
$$4x = 12 \qquad \text{Subtract } 3x$$
$$x = 3 \qquad \text{Multiply by } \tfrac{1}{4}$$

LHS stands for "left-hand side" and RHS stands for "right-hand side."

CHECK YOUR ANSWER

$x = 3$:   LHS $= 7(3) - 4$ RHS $= 3(3) + 8$
                     $= 17$ $= 17$

LHS = RHS   ✓

Many formulas in the sciences involve several variables, and it is often necessary to express one of the variables in terms of the others, as in the next example.

EXAMPLE 2 ■ Solving for One Variable in Terms of Others

The surface area A of the closed rectangular box shown in Figure 1 can be calculated from the length l, the width w, and the height h according to the formula

$$A = 2lw + 2wh + 2lh$$

Solve for w in terms of the other variables in this equation.

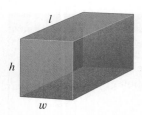

FIGURE 1

A closed rectangular box

Euclid (circa 300 B.C.) taught in Alexandria. His *Elements* is the most widely influential scientific book in history. For 2000 years it was the standard introduction to geometry in the schools, and for many generations it was considered the best way to develop logical reasoning. Abraham Lincoln, for instance, studied the *Elements* as a way to sharpen his mind. The story is told that King Ptolemy once asked Euclid if there was a faster way to learn geometry than through the *Elements*. Euclid replied that there is "no royal road to geometry"—meaning by this that mathematics does not respect wealth or social status. Euclid was revered in his own time and was referred to by the title "The Geometer" or "The Writer of the *Elements*." The greatness of the *Elements* stems from its precise, logical, and systematic treatment of geometry. For dealing with equality, Euclid lists the following rules, which he calls "common notions."

1. Things that are equal to the same thing are equal to each other.

2. If equals are added to equals, the sums are equal.

3. If equals are subtracted from equals, the remainders are equal.

4. Things that coincide with one another are equal.

5. The whole is greater than the part.

SOLUTION

Although this equation involves more than one variable, we solve it as usual by isolating w on one side, treating the other variables as we would numbers.

$$A = (2lw + 2wh) + 2lh \qquad \text{Collect terms involving } w$$

$$A - 2lh = 2lw + 2wh \qquad \text{Subtract } 2lh$$

$$A - 2lh = (2l + 2h)w \qquad \text{Factor } w \text{ from RHS}$$

$$\frac{A - 2lh}{2l + 2h} = w \qquad \text{Divide by } 2l + 2h$$

The solution is $w = \dfrac{A - 2lh}{2l + 2h}$. ∎

Quadratic Equations

Linear equations are first-degree equations of the form $ax + b = 0$. Quadratic equations are second-degree equations; they contain an additional term involving the square of the variable.

QUADRATIC EQUATIONS

A **quadratic equation** is an equation of the form

$$ax^2 + bx + c = 0$$

where a, b, and c are real numbers with $a \neq 0$.

Some quadratic equations can be solved by factoring and using the following basic property of real numbers.

ZERO-PRODUCT PROPERTY

$$AB = 0 \qquad \text{if and only if} \qquad A = 0 \quad \text{or} \quad B = 0$$

This means that if we can factor the left-hand side of a quadratic (or other) equation, then we can solve it by setting each factor equal to 0 in turn. This method works only when the right-hand side of the equation is 0.

EXAMPLE 3 ■ Solving a Quadratic Equation by Factoring

Solve the equation $x^2 + 5x = 24$.

SOLUTION

We must first rewrite the equation so that the right-hand side is 0.

$$x^2 + 5x = 24$$

$$x^2 + 5x - 24 = 0 \qquad \text{Subtract 24}$$

$$(x - 3)(x + 8) = 0 \qquad \text{Factor}$$

$$x - 3 = 0 \quad \text{or} \quad x + 8 = 0 \qquad \text{Zero-Product Property}$$

$$x = 3 \qquad\qquad x = -8 \quad \text{Solve}$$

The solutions are $x = 3$ and $x = -8$. ∎

A quadratic equation of the form $x^2 - c = 0$, where c is a positive constant, factors as $(x - \sqrt{c})(x + \sqrt{c}) = 0$, and so the solutions are $x = \sqrt{c}$ and $x = -\sqrt{c}$. We often abbreviate this as $x = \pm\sqrt{c}$.

SOLVING A SIMPLE QUADRATIC EQUATION

The solutions of the equation $x^2 = c$ are $x = \sqrt{c}$ and $x = -\sqrt{c}$.

EXAMPLE 4 ■ **Solving Simple Quadratics**

Solve each equation: (a) $x^2 = 5$ (b) $(x - 4)^2 = 5$

SOLUTION

(a) From the principle in the preceding box, we get $x = \pm\sqrt{5}$.

(b) We can take the square root of each side of this equation as well.

$$(x - 4)^2 = 5$$

$$x - 4 = \pm\sqrt{5} \qquad \text{Take the square root}$$

$$x = 4 \pm \sqrt{5} \quad \text{Add 4}$$

The solutions are $x = 4 + \sqrt{5}$ and $x = 4 - \sqrt{5}$. ∎

See page 529 for how to recognize when a quadratic expression is a perfect square.

As we saw in Example 4, if a quadratic equation is of the form $(x \pm a)^2 = c$, then we can solve it by taking the square root of each side. In an equation of this form the left-hand side is a *perfect square*: the square of a linear expression in x. So, if a quadratic equation does not factor readily, then we can solve it using the technique of **completing the square**. This means that we add a constant to an expression to make it a perfect square. For example, to make $x^2 - 6x$ a perfect square we must add 9, since $x^2 - 6x + 9 = (x - 3)^2$.

Completing the Square

Area of blue region is

$$x^2 + 2\left(\frac{b}{2}\right)x = x^2 + bx$$

Add a small square of area $(b/2)^2$ to "complete" the square.

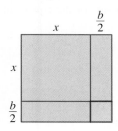

COMPLETING THE SQUARE

To make $x^2 + bx$ a perfect square, add $\left(\dfrac{b}{2}\right)^2$, the square of half the coefficient of x. This gives the perfect square

$$x^2 + bx + \left(\frac{b}{2}\right)^2 = \left(x + \frac{b}{2}\right)^2$$

EXAMPLE 5 ■ Solving Quadratic Equations by Completing the Square

Solve each equation.

(a) $x^2 - 8x + 13 = 0$ (b) $3x^2 - 12x + 6 = 0$

SOLUTION

(a)
$$x^2 - 8x + 13 = 0$$

$$\begin{aligned} x^2 - 8x &= -13 && \text{Subtract 13} \\ x^2 - 8x + 16 &= -13 + 16 && \text{Complete the square: add } \left(\tfrac{-8}{2}\right)^2 = 16 \\ (x - 4)^2 &= 3 && \text{Perfect square} \\ x - 4 &= \pm\sqrt{3} && \text{Take square root} \\ x &= 4 \pm \sqrt{3} && \text{Add 4} \end{aligned}$$

⊘ When completing the square, make sure the coefficient of x^2 is 1. If it isn't, you must factor this coefficient from both terms that contain x:

$$ax^2 + bx = a\left(x^2 + \frac{b}{a}x\quad\right)$$

Then complete the square inside the parentheses. Remember that the term added inside the parentheses is multiplied by a.

(b) After subtracting 6 from each side of the equation, we must factor the coefficient of x^2 (the 3) from the left side to put the equation in the correct form for completing the square.

$$\begin{aligned} 3x^2 - 12x + 6 &= 0 \\ 3x^2 - 12x &= -6 && \text{Subtract 6} \\ 3(x^2 - 4x\quad) &= -6 && \text{Factor 3 from LHS} \end{aligned}$$

Now we complete the square by adding $(-2)^2 = 4$ inside the parentheses. Since everything inside the parentheses is multiplied by 3, this means that we are actually adding $3 \cdot 4 = 12$ to the left side of the equation. Thus, we must add 12 to the right side as well.

$$\begin{aligned} 3(x^2 - 4x + 4) &= -6 + 3 \cdot 4 && \text{Complete the square: add 4} \\ 3(x - 2)^2 &= 6 && \text{Perfect square} \\ (x - 2)^2 &= 2 && \text{Divide by 3} \\ x - 2 &= \pm\sqrt{2} && \text{Take square root} \\ x &= 2 \pm \sqrt{2} && \text{Add 2} \end{aligned}$$

■

François Viète (1540–1603) had a successful political career before taking up mathematics late in life. He became one of the most famous French mathematicians of the 16th century. Viète introduced a new level of abstraction in algebra by using letters to stand for *known* quantities in an equation. Before Viète's time, each equation had to be solved on its own. For instance, the quadratic equations

$$3x^2 + 2x + 8 = 0$$

and $$5x^2 - 6x + 4 = 0$$

had to be solved separately for the unknown *x*. Viète's idea was to consider all quadratic equations at once by writing

$$ax^2 + bx + c = 0$$

where *a*, *b*, and *c* are known quantities. Thus, he made it possible to write a *formula* (in this case, the quadratic formula) involving *a*, *b*, and *c* that can be used to solve all such equations in one fell swoop. Viète's mathematical genius proved valuable during a war between France and Spain. To communicate with their troops, the Spaniards used a complicated code which Viète managed to decipher. Unaware of Viète's accomplishment, King Philip II of Spain protested to the Pope, claiming that the French were using witchcraft to read his messages.

We can use the technique of completing the square to derive a formula for the roots of the general quadratic equation $ax^2 + bx + c = 0$. First, we divide each side of the equation by *a* and move the constant to the right side, giving

$$x^2 + \frac{b}{a}x = -\frac{c}{a}$$

We now complete the square by adding $(b/2a)^2$ to each side of the equation:

$$x^2 + \frac{b}{a}x + \left(\frac{b}{2a}\right)^2 = -\frac{c}{a} + \left(\frac{b}{2a}\right)^2 \qquad \text{Complete the square:} \atop \text{Add } \left(\frac{b}{2a}\right)^2$$

$$\left(x + \frac{b}{2a}\right)^2 = \frac{-4ac + b^2}{4a^2} \qquad \text{Perfect square}$$

$$x + \frac{b}{2a} = \pm\sqrt{\frac{-4ac + b^2}{4a^2}} = \pm\frac{\sqrt{b^2 - 4ac}}{2a} \qquad \text{Take square root}$$

$$x = \frac{-b \pm \sqrt{b^2 - 4ac}}{2a} \qquad \text{Subtract } \frac{b}{2a}$$

This is the quadratic formula.

THE QUADRATIC FORMULA

The roots of the quadratic equation $ax^2 + bx + c = 0$, where $a \neq 0$, are

$$x = \frac{-b \pm \sqrt{b^2 - 4ac}}{2a}$$

The quadratic formula could be used to solve the equations in Example 5. You should carry out the details of these calculations.

EXAMPLE 6 ■ Using the Quadratic Formula

Find all solutions of each equation.

(a) $3x^2 - 5x - 1 = 0$ (b) $4x^2 + 12x + 9 = 0$ (c) $x^2 + 2x + 2 = 0$

SOLUTION

(a) Using the quadratic formula with $a = 3$, $b = -5$, and $c = -1$, we get

$$x = \frac{-(-5) \pm \sqrt{(-5)^2 - 4(3)(-1)}}{2(3)} = \frac{5 \pm \sqrt{37}}{6}$$

If approximations are desired, we use a calculator and obtain

$$x = \frac{5 + \sqrt{37}}{6} \approx 1.8471 \qquad \text{and} \qquad x = \frac{5 - \sqrt{37}}{6} \approx -0.1805$$

(b) Using the quadratic formula with $a = 4$, $b = 12$, and $c = 9$ gives

$$x = \frac{-12 \pm \sqrt{(12)^2 - 4 \cdot 4 \cdot 9}}{2 \cdot 4} = \frac{-12 \pm 0}{8} = -\frac{3}{2}$$

This equation has only one solution, $x = -\frac{3}{2}$.

(c) Using the quadratic formula with $a = 1$, $b = 2$, and $c = 2$ gives

$$x = \frac{-2 \pm \sqrt{2^2 - 4 \cdot 2}}{2} = \frac{-2 \pm \sqrt{-4}}{2} = \frac{-2 \pm 2\sqrt{-1}}{2} = -1 \pm \sqrt{-1}$$

Since the square of any real number is nonnegative, $\sqrt{-1}$ is undefined in the real number system. The equation has no real solution. ∎

In Section 5.3 we study the complex number system, in which the square roots of negative numbers do exist. The equation in Example 6(c) does have solutions in the complex number system.

The quantity $b^2 - 4ac$ that appears under the square root sign in the quadratic formula is called the *discriminant* of the equation $ax^2 + bx + c = 0$ and is given the symbol D. If $D < 0$, then $\sqrt{b^2 - 4ac}$ is undefined, and the quadratic equation has no real solution, as in Example 6(c). If $D = 0$, then the equation has only one real solution, as in Example 6(b). Finally, if $D > 0$, then the equation has two distinct real solutions, as in Example 6(a). The following box summarizes these observations.

THE DISCRIMINANT

The **discriminant** of the general quadratic $ax^2 + bx + c = 0$ $(a \neq 0)$ is $D = b^2 - 4ac$.

1. If $D > 0$, then the equation has two distinct real solutions.

2. If $D = 0$, then the equation has exactly one real solution.

3. If $D < 0$, then the equation has no real solution.

EXAMPLE 7 ■ Using the Discriminant

Use the discriminant to determine how many real solutions each equation has.

(a) $x^2 + 4x - 1 = 0$ (b) $4x^2 - 12x + 9 = 0$ (c) $\frac{1}{3}x^2 - 2x + 4 = 0$

SOLUTION

(a) The discriminant is $D = 4^2 - 4(1)(-1) = 20 > 0$, so the equation has two distinct real solutions.

(b) The discriminant is $D = (-12)^2 - 4 \cdot 4 \cdot 9 = 0$, so the equation has exactly one real solution.

(c) The discriminant is $D = (-2)^2 - 4\left(\frac{1}{3}\right)4 = -\frac{4}{3} < 0$, so the equation has no real solution. ∎

■ Other Equations

So far we have learned how to solve linear and quadratic equations. Now we study other types of equations, including those that involve fractional expressions, radicals, and higher powers.

EXAMPLE 8 ■ An Equation Involving Fractional Expressions

Solve the equation $\dfrac{3}{x} + \dfrac{5}{x + 2} = 2$.

SOLUTION

To simplify the equation, we multiply each side by the common denominator.

$$\left(\frac{3}{x} + \frac{5}{x + 2}\right)x(x + 2) = 2x(x + 2) \qquad \text{Multiply by LCD } x(x + 2)$$

$$3(x + 2) + 5x = 2x^2 + 4x \qquad \text{Expand}$$

$$8x + 6 = 2x^2 + 4x \qquad \text{Expand LHS}$$

$$0 = 2x^2 - 4x - 6 \qquad \text{Subtract } 8x + 6$$

$$0 = x^2 - 2x - 3 \qquad \text{Divide both sides by 2}$$

$$0 = (x - 3)(x + 1) \qquad \text{Factor}$$

$$x - 3 = 0 \quad \text{or} \quad x + 1 = 0 \qquad \text{Zero-Product Property}$$

$$x = 3 \qquad\qquad x = -1 \qquad \text{Solve}$$

CHECK YOUR ANSWERS

$x = 3$:

$$\text{LHS} = \frac{3}{3} + \frac{5}{3 + 2}$$

$$= 1 + 1 = 2$$

$$\text{RHS} = 2$$

$$\text{LHS} = \text{RHS} \qquad ✓$$

$x = -1$:

$$\text{LHS} = \frac{3}{-1} + \frac{5}{-1 + 2}$$

$$= -3 + 5 = 2$$

$$\text{RHS} = 2$$

$$\text{LHS} = \text{RHS} \qquad ✓$$

We must check our answers because multiplying by an expression that contains the variable can introduce extraneous solutions (see the *Warning* on the next page). From *Check Your Answers* we see that the solutions are $x = 3$ and -1. ∎

When you solve an equation that involves radicals, you must be especially careful to check your final answers. The next example demonstrates why.

EXAMPLE 9 ■ An Equation Involving a Radical

Solve the equation $2x = 1 - \sqrt{2 - x}$.

SOLUTION

To eliminate the square root, we first isolate it on one side of the equal sign, then square.

$$2x - 1 = -\sqrt{2 - x} \qquad \text{Subtract 1}$$

$$(2x - 1)^2 = 2 - x \qquad \text{Square each side}$$

$$4x^2 - 4x + 1 = 2 - x \qquad \text{Expand LHS}$$

$$4x^2 - 3x - 1 = 0 \qquad \text{Add } -2 + x$$

$$(4x + 1)(x - 1) = 0 \qquad \text{Factor}$$

$$4x + 1 = 0 \quad \text{or} \quad x - 1 = 0 \qquad \text{Zero-Product Property}$$

$$x = -\tfrac{1}{4} \qquad\qquad x = 1 \qquad \text{Solve}$$

The values $x = -\tfrac{1}{4}$ and $x = 1$ are only potential solutions. We must check them to see if they satisfy the original equation. From *Check Your Answers* we see that $x = -\tfrac{1}{4}$ is a solution but $x = 1$ is not. The only solution is

$$x = -\tfrac{1}{4} \qquad\qquad \blacksquare$$

CHECK YOUR ANSWERS

$x = -\tfrac{1}{4}$:

$\quad$ LHS $= 2\left(-\tfrac{1}{4}\right) = -\tfrac{1}{2}$

$\quad$ RHS $= 1 - \sqrt{2 - \left(-\tfrac{1}{4}\right)}$

$\qquad = 1 - \sqrt{\tfrac{9}{4}}$

$\qquad = 1 - \tfrac{3}{2} = -\tfrac{1}{2}$

$\quad$ LHS $=$ RHS $\qquad$ ✓

$x = 1$:

$\quad$ LHS $= 2(1) = 2$

$\quad$ RHS $= 1 - \sqrt{2 - 1}$

$\qquad = 1 - 1 = 0$

$\quad$ LHS $\neq$ RHS $\qquad$ ✗

When we solve an equation, we may end up with one or more **extraneous solutions**, that is, potential solutions that do not satisfy the original equation. In Example 3 the value $x = 1$ is an extraneous solution. Extraneous solutions may be introduced when we square each side of an equation because the operation of squaring can turn a false equation into a true one. For example, $-1 \neq 1$, but $(-1)^2 = 1^2$. Thus, the squared equation may be true for more values of the variable than the original equation. That is why you must always check your answers to make sure that each satisfies the original equation.

An equation of the form $aw^2 + bw + c = 0$, where w is an algebraic expression, is an equation of **quadratic type**. We solve equations of quadratic type by substituting for the algebraic expression, as we see in the next two examples.

EXAMPLE 10 ■ A Fourth-Degree Equation of Quadratic Type

Find all solutions of the equation $x^4 - 8x^2 + 8 = 0$.

SOLUTION

If we set $w = x^2$, then we get a quadratic equation in the new variable w:

$$(x^2)^2 - 8x^2 + 8 = 0 \qquad \text{Write } x^4 \text{ as } (x^2)^2$$

$$w^2 - 8w + 8 = 0 \qquad \text{Let } w = x^2$$

$$w = \frac{-(-8) \pm \sqrt{(-8)^2 - 4 \cdot 8}}{2} = 4 \pm 2\sqrt{2} \qquad \text{Quadratic formula}$$

$$x^2 = 4 \pm 2\sqrt{2} \qquad w = x^2$$

$$x = \pm\sqrt{4 \pm 2\sqrt{2}} \qquad \text{Take square roots}$$

So, there are four solutions:

$$\sqrt{4 + 2\sqrt{2}}, \qquad \sqrt{4 - 2\sqrt{2}}, \qquad -\sqrt{4 + 2\sqrt{2}}, \qquad -\sqrt{4 - 2\sqrt{2}}$$

Using a calculator, we obtain the approximations $x \approx 2.61, 1.08, -2.61, -1.08.$ ∎

EXAMPLE 11 ■ An Equation Involving Fractional Powers

Find all solutions of the equation $x^{1/3} + x^{1/6} - 2 = 0$.

SOLUTION

This equation is of quadratic type because if we let $w = x^{1/6}$, then $w^2 = x^{1/3}$.

$$x^{1/3} + x^{1/6} - 2 = 0$$

$$w^2 + w - 2 = 0 \qquad \text{Let } w = x^{1/6}$$

$$(w - 1)(w + 2) = 0 \qquad \text{Factor}$$

$$w - 1 = 0 \quad \text{or} \quad w + 2 = 0 \qquad \text{Zero-Product Property}$$

$$w = 1 \qquad\qquad w = -2 \qquad \text{Solve}$$

$$x^{1/6} = 1 \qquad\qquad x^{1/6} = -2 \qquad w = x^{1/6}$$

$$x = 1^6 = 1 \qquad\qquad x = (-2)^6 = 64 \qquad \text{Take the 6th power}$$

From *Check Your Answers* we see that $x = 1$ is a solution but $x = 64$ is not. The only solution is $x = 1$.

CHECK YOUR ANSWERS

$x = 1$:
$$\text{LHS} = 1^{1/3} + 1^{1/6} - 2 = 0$$

$$\text{RHS} = 0$$
$$\text{LHS} = \text{RHS}$$

$x = 64$:
$$\text{LHS} = 64^{1/3} + 64^{1/6} - 2$$
$$= 4 + 2 - 2 = 4$$

$$\text{RHS} = 0$$
$$\text{LHS} \neq \text{RHS}$$

∎

EXAMPLE 12 ■ An Equation Involving Absolute Value

Solve the equation $|2x - 5| = 3$.

SOLUTION

By the definition of absolute vaue, $|2x - 5| = 3$ is equivalent to

$$2x - 5 = 3 \quad \text{or} \quad 2x - 5 = -3$$

$$2x = 8 \qquad\qquad 2x = 2$$

$$x = 4 \qquad\qquad x = 1$$

The solutions are $x = 1, x = 4$. ∎

A.4 EXERCISES

1–4 ■ Determine whether the given value is a solution of the equation.

1. $3x + 7 = 5x - 1$
(a) $x = 4$
(b) $x = \frac{3}{2}$

2. $\frac{1}{x} - \frac{1}{x+3} = \frac{1}{6}$
(a) $x = -3$
(b) $x = 3$

3. $1 - [2 - (3 - x)] = 4x - (6 + x)$
(a) $x = 2$
(b) $x = 22$

4. $ax - 2b = 0$ $(a \neq 0, b \neq 0)$
(a) $x = 0$
(b) $x = \frac{2b}{a}$

5–16 ■ Solve the linear equation.

5. $3x - 5 = 7$
6. $4x + 12 = 28$

7. $x - 3 = 2x + 6$
8. $4x + 7 = 9x - 13$

9. $-7w = 15 - 2w$
10. $5t - 13 = 12 - 5t$

11. $\frac{1}{2}y - 2 = \frac{1}{3}y$
12. $\frac{z}{5} = \frac{3}{10}z + 7$

13. $2(1 - x) = 3(1 + 2x) + 5$

14. $5(x + 3) + 9 = -2(x - 2) - 1$

15. $4\left(y - \frac{1}{2}\right) - y = 6(5 - y)$ **16.** $\frac{2}{3}y + \frac{1}{2}(y - 3) = \frac{y+1}{4}$

17–22 ■ Solve the equation by factoring.

17. $x^2 + 2x - 8 = 0$
18. $x^2 + 6x + 8 = 0$

19. $2y^2 + 7y + 3 = 0$
20. $4w^2 = 4w + 3$

21. $6x^2 + 5x = 4$
22. $x^2 = 5(x + 100)$

23–28 ■ Solve the equation by completing the square.

23. $x^2 + 2x - 2 = 0$
24. $x^2 - 6x - 9 = 0$

25. $x^2 + x - \frac{3}{4} = 0$
26. $x^2 + 22x + 21 = 0$

27. $2x^2 + 8x + 1 = 0$
28. $3x^2 - 6x - 1 = 0$

29–38 ■ Find all real solutions of the quadratic equation. Use any method.

29. $x^2 + 12x - 27 = 0$
30. $8x^2 - 6x - 9 = 0$

31. $3x^2 + 6x - 5 = 0$
32. $x^2 - 6x + 1 = 0$

33. $2y^2 - y - \frac{1}{2} = 0$
34. $\theta^2 - \frac{3}{2}\theta + \frac{9}{16} = 0$

35. $10y^2 - 16y + 5 = 0$
36. $25x^2 + 70x + 49 = 0$

37. $3x^2 + 2x + 2 = 0$
38. $5x^2 - 7x + 5 = 0$

39–62 ■ Find all real solutions of the equation.

39. $\frac{1}{x-1} + \frac{1}{x+2} = \frac{5}{4}$
40. $\frac{10}{x} - \frac{12}{x-3} + 4 = 0$

41. $\frac{x^2}{x+100} = 50$
42. $\frac{1}{x-1} - \frac{2}{x^2} = 0$

43. $\frac{x+5}{x-2} = \frac{5}{x+2} + \frac{28}{x^2-4}$

44. $\frac{x}{2x+7} - \frac{x+1}{x+3} = 1$

45. $\sqrt{2x+1} + 1 = x$
46. $\sqrt{5-x} + 1 = x - 2$

47. $2x + \sqrt{x+1} = 8$
48. $\sqrt{\sqrt{x-5}+x} = 5$

49. $x^4 - 13x^2 + 40 = 0$
50. $x^4 - 5x^2 + 4 = 0$

51. $2x^4 + 4x^2 + 1 = 0$
52. $x^6 - 2x^3 - 3 = 0$

53. $x^{4/3} - 5x^{2/3} + 6 = 0$
54. $\sqrt{x} - 3\sqrt[4]{x} - 4 = 0$

55. $4(x+1)^{1/2} - 5(x+1)^{3/2} + (x+1)^{5/2} = 0$

56. $x^{1/2} + 3x^{-1/2} = 10x^{-3/2}$

57. $x^{1/2} - 3x^{1/3} = 3x^{1/6} - 9$
58. $x - 5\sqrt{x} + 6 = 0$

59. $|2x| = 3$
60. $|3x + 5| = 1$

61. $|x - 4| = 0.01$
62. $|x - 6| = -1$

63–74 ■ Solve the equation for the indicated variable.

63. $PV = nRT$;   for R
64. $F = G\frac{mM}{r^2}$;   for m

65. $\frac{1}{R} = \frac{1}{R_1} + \frac{1}{R_2}$;   for R_1
66. $P = 2l + 2w$;   for w

67. $\frac{ax+b}{cx+d} = 2$; for x

68. $a - 2[b - 3(c - x)] = 6$;   for x

69. $a^2x + (a - 1) = (a + 1)x$;   for x

70. $\frac{a+1}{b} = \frac{a-1}{b} + \frac{b+1}{a}$;   for a

71. $V = \frac{1}{3}\pi r^2 h$;   for r
72. $F = G\frac{mM}{r^2}$;   for r

73. $a^2 + b^2 = c^2$; for b **74.** $A = P\left(1 + \dfrac{i}{100}\right)^2$; for i

75–78 ■ Use the discriminant to determine the number of real solutions of the equation. Do not solve the equation.

75. $x^2 - 6x + 1 = 0$ **76.** $3x^2 = 6x - 9$

77. $x^2 + 2.20x + 1.21 = 0$ **78.** $x^2 + rx - s = 0$ $(s > 0)$

79–80 ■ Suppose an object is dropped from a height h_0 above the ground. Then its height after t seconds is given by $h = -16t^2 + h_0$, where h is measured in feet. Use this information to solve the problem.

79. If a ball is dropped from 288 ft above the ground, how long does it take to reach ground level?

80. A ball is dropped from the top of a building 96 ft tall.
  (a) How long will it take to fall half the distance to ground level?
  (b) How long will it take to fall to ground level?

81. The fish population in a certain lake rises and falls according to the formula

$$F = 1000(30 + 17t - t^2)$$

Here F is the number of fish at time t, where t is measured in years since January 1, 1992, when the fish population was first estimated.

(a) On what date will the fish population again be the same as on January 1, 1992?
(b) By what date will all the fish in the lake have died?

82. If an imaginary line segment is drawn between the centers of the earth and the moon, then the net gravitational force F acting on an object situated on this line segment is

$$F = \frac{-K}{x^2} + \frac{0.012K}{(239 - x)^2}$$

where $K > 0$ is a constant and x is the distance of the object from the center of the earth, measured in thousands of miles. How far from the center of the earth is the "dead spot" where no net gravitational force acts upon the object? (Express your answer to the nearest thousand miles.)

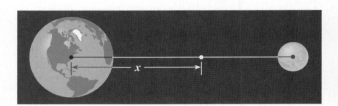

A.5 INEQUALITIES

Some problems in algebra lead to **inequalities** instead of equations. An inequality looks just like an equation, except that in the place of the equal sign is one of the symbols, $<$, $>$, $\le$, or $\ge$. Here is an example of an inequality:

$$4x + 7 \le 19$$

x	$4x + 7 \le 19$
1	$11 \le 19$ ✓
2	$15 \le 19$ ✓
3	$19 \le 19$ ✓
4	$23 \le 19$ ✗
5	$27 \le 19$ ✗

The table in the margin shows that some numbers satisfy the inequality and some numbers don't.

   To **solve** an inequality that contains a variable means to find all values of the variable that make the inequality true. Unlike an equation, an inequality generally has infinitely many solutions, which form an interval or a union of intervals on the real line. The following illustration shows how an inequality differs from its corresponding equation:

		Solution	Graph
Equation:	$4x + 7 = 19$	$x = 3$	
Inequality:	$4x + 7 \le 19$	$x \le 3$	

To solve inequalities, we use the following rules to isolate the variable on one side of the inequality sign. These rules tell us when two inequalities are *equivalent* (the symbol ⇔ means "is equivalent to"). In these rules the symbols *A*, *B*, and *C* stand for real numbers or algebraic expressions. Here we state the rules for inequalities involving the symbol ≤, but they apply to all four inequality symbols.

RULES FOR INEQUALITIES

Rule	Description
1. $A \leq B \iff A + C \leq B + C$	**Adding** the same quantity to each side of an inequality gives an equivalent inequality.
2. $A \leq B \iff A - C \leq B - C$	**Subtracting** the same quantity from each side of an inequality gives an equivalent inequality.
3. If $C > 0$, then $A \leq B \iff CA \leq CB$	**Multiplying** each side of an inequality by the same *positive* quantity gives an equivalent inequality.
4. If $C < 0$, then $A \leq B \iff CA \geq CB$	**Multiplying** each side of an inequality by the same *negative* quantity *reverses the direction* of the inequality.
5. If $A > 0$ and $B > 0$, then $A \leq B \iff \dfrac{1}{A} \geq \dfrac{1}{B}$	**Taking reciprocals** of each side of an inequality involving *positive* quantities *reverses the direction* of the inequality.
6. If $A \leq B$ and $C \leq D$, then $A + C \leq B + D$	Inequalities can be added.

 Pay special attention to Rules 3 and 4. Rule 3 says that we can multiply (or divide) each side of an inequality by a *positive* number, but Rule 4 says that if we multiply each side of an inequality by a *negative* number, then we reverse the direction of the inequality. For example, if we start with the inequality

$$3 < 5$$

and multiply by 2, we get

$$6 < 10$$

but if we multiply by −2, we get

$$-6 > -10$$

■ Linear Inequalities

An inequality is **linear** if each term is constant or a multiple of the variable.

EXAMPLE 1 ■ Solving a Linear Inequality

Solve the inequality $3x < 9x + 4$ and sketch the solution set.

SOLUTION

$$3x < 9x + 4$$

$$3x - 9x < 9x + 4 - 9x \qquad \text{Subtract } 9x$$

$$-6x < 4 \qquad \text{Simplify}$$

$$\left(-\tfrac{1}{6}\right)(-6x) > -\tfrac{1}{6}(4) \qquad \text{Multiply by } -\tfrac{1}{6} \text{ (or divide by } -6)$$

$$x > -\tfrac{2}{3} \qquad \text{Simplify}$$

The solution set consists of all numbers greater than $-\tfrac{2}{3}$. In other words the solution of the inequality is the interval $\left(-\tfrac{2}{3}, \infty\right)$. It is graphed in Figure 1. ■

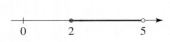

FIGURE 1

EXAMPLE 2 ■ **Solving a Pair of Simultaneous Inequalities**

Solve the inequalities $4 \leqslant 3x - 2 < 13$.

SOLUTION

The solution set consists of all values of x that satisfy both inequalities. Using Rules 1 and 3, we see that the following inequalities are equivalent:

$$4 \leqslant 3x - 2 < 13$$

$$6 \leqslant 3x < 15 \qquad \text{Add 2}$$

$$2 \leqslant x < 5 \qquad \text{Divide by 3}$$

Therefore, the solution set is $[2, 5)$, as shown in Figure 2. ■

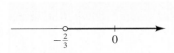

FIGURE 2

EXAMPLE 3 ■ **Relationship between Fahrenheit and Celsius Scales**

The instructions on a box of film indicate that the box should be stored at a temperature between 5°C and 30°C. What range of temperatures does this correspond to on the Fahrenheit scale?

SOLUTION

The relationship between degrees Celsius (C) and degrees Fahrenheit (F) is given by the equation $C = \tfrac{5}{9}(F - 32)$. Expressing the statement on the box in terms of inequalities, we have

$$5 < C < 30$$

so the corresponding Fahrenheit temperatures satisfy the inequalities

$$5 < \tfrac{5}{9}(F - 32) < 30$$

$$\tfrac{9}{5} \cdot 5 < F - 32 < \tfrac{9}{5} \cdot 30 \qquad \text{Multiply by } \tfrac{9}{5}$$

$$9 < F - 32 < 54 \qquad \text{Simplify}$$

$$9 + 32 < F < 54 + 32 \qquad \text{Add 32}$$

$$41 < F < 86 \qquad \text{Simplify}$$

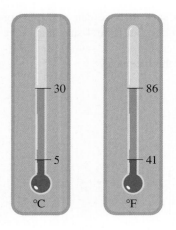

The film should be stored at a temperature between 41°F and 86°F. ■

■ Absolute Value Inequalities

We use the following properties to solve inequalities that involve absolute value.

PROPERTIES OF ABSOLUTE VALUE INEQUALITIES		
Inequality	**Equivalent form**	**Graph**
1. $\|x\| < c$	$-c < x < c$	
2. $\|x\| \leqslant c$	$-c \leqslant x \leqslant c$	
3. $\|x\| > c$	$x < -c$ or $c < x$	
4. $\|x\| \geqslant c$	$x \leqslant -c$ or $c \leqslant x$	

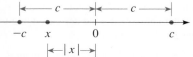

FIGURE 3

These properties can be proved using the definition of absolute value. To prove Property 1, for example, we see that the inequality $\|x\| < c$ says that the distance from x to 0 is less than c, and from Figure 3 you can see that this is true if and only if x is between c and $-c$.

EXAMPLE 4 ■ **Solving an Absolute Value Inequality**

Solve the inequality $\|x - 5\| < 2$.

SOLUTION 1

The inequality $\|x - 5\| < 2$ is equivalent to

$$-2 < x - 5 < 2 \qquad \text{Property 1}$$
$$3 < x < 7 \qquad \text{Add 5}$$

The solution set is the open interval $(3, 7)$.

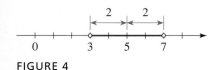

FIGURE 4

SOLUTION 2

Geometrically, the solution set consists of all numbers x whose distance from 5 is less than 2. From Figure 4 we see that this is the interval $(3, 7)$.   ■

EXAMPLE 5 ■ **Solving an Absolute Value Inequality**

Solve the inequality $\|3x + 2\| \geqslant 4$.

SOLUTION

By Property 4 the inequality $\|3x + 2\| \geqslant 4$ is equivalent to

$$3x + 2 \geqslant 4 \qquad \text{or} \qquad 3x + 2 \leqslant -4$$
$$3x \geqslant 2 \qquad\qquad 3x \leqslant -6 \qquad \text{Subtract 2}$$
$$x \geqslant \tfrac{2}{3} \qquad\qquad x \leqslant -2 \qquad \text{Divide by 3}$$

So the solution set is

FIGURE 5

$$\{x \mid x \leqslant -2 \quad \text{or} \quad x \geqslant \tfrac{2}{3}\} = (-\infty, -2] \cup [\tfrac{2}{3}, \infty)$$

The set is graphed in Figure 5.   ∎

A.5 EXERCISES

1–4 ■ Let $S = \{-1, 0, \tfrac{1}{2}, \sqrt{2}, 2\}$. Use substitution to determine which elements of S satisfy the inequality.

1. $2x + 10 > 8$ **2.** $4x + 1 \leqslant 2x$

3. $\dfrac{1}{x} \leqslant \dfrac{1}{2}$ **4.** $x^2 + 2 < 4$

5–24 ■ Solve the linear inequality. Express the solution using interval notation and graph the solution set.

5. $2x \leqslant 7$ **6.** $-4x \geqslant 10$

7. $2x - 5 > 3$ **8.** $3x + 11 < 5$

9. $7 - x \geqslant 5$ **10.** $5 - 3x \leqslant -16$

11. $2x + 1 < 0$ **12.** $0 < 5 - 2x$

13. $3x + 11 \leqslant 6x + 8$ **14.** $6 - x \geqslant 2x + 9$

15. $\tfrac{1}{2}x - \tfrac{2}{3} > 2$ **16.** $\tfrac{2}{5}x + 1 < \tfrac{1}{5} - 2x$

17. $4 - 3x \leqslant -(1 + 8x)$ **18.** $2(7x - 3) \leqslant 12x + 16$

19. $2 \leqslant x + 5 < 4$ **20.** $5 \leqslant 3x - 4 \leqslant 14$

21. $-1 < 2x - 5 < 7$ **22.** $1 < 3x + 4 \leqslant 16$

23. $-2 < 8 - 2x \leqslant -1$ **24.** $-3 \leqslant 3x + 7 \leqslant \tfrac{1}{2}$

25–36 ■ Solve the inequality. Express the solution using interval notation and graph the solution set.

25. $|x| < 7$ **26.** $|x| \geqslant 3$

27. $|x - 5| \leqslant 3$ **28.** $|x - 9| > 9$

29. $|x + 5| < 2$ **30.** $|x + 1| \geqslant 3$

31. $|2x - 3| \leqslant 0.4$ **32.** $|5x - 2| < 6$

33. $\left|\dfrac{x - 2}{3}\right| < 2$ **34.** $\left|\dfrac{x + 1}{2}\right| \geqslant 4$

35. $4|x + 2| - 3 < 13$ **36.** $3 - |2x + 4| \leqslant 1$

37. Use the relationship between C and F given in Example 3 to find the interval on the Fahrenheit scale corresponding to the temperature range $20 \leqslant C \leqslant 30$.

38. What interval on the Celsius scale corresponds to the temperature range $50 \leqslant F \leqslant 95$?

39. As dry air moves upward, it expands and in so doing cools at a rate of about 1°C for each 100 m rise, up to about 12 km.
   (a) If the ground temperature is 20°C, write a formula for the temperature at height h.
   (b) What range of temperatures can be expected if a plane takes off and reaches a maximum height of 5 km?

40. A coffee merchant sells a customer 3 lb of Hawaiian Kona at $6.50 per pound. His scale is accurate to within ±0.03 lb. By how much could the customer have been overcharged or undercharged because of possible inaccuracy in the scale?

Appendix B
Geometry Review

In this appendix we review the concepts of congruence and similarity, which are essential in the study of trigonometry.

■ Congruent Triangles

In general, two geometric figures are congruent if they have the same shape and size. In particular, two line segments are congruent if they have the same length, and two angles are congruent if they have the same measure. For triangles, we have the following definition.

CONGRUENT TRIANGLES

Two triangles are **congruent** if their vertices can be matched up so that corresponding sides and angles are congruent.

We write $\triangle ABC \cong \triangle PQR$ to mean that triangle ABC is congruent to triangle PQR and that the sides and angles correspond as follows:

$$AB = PQ \qquad \angle A = \angle P$$

$$BC = QR \qquad \angle B = \angle Q$$

$$AC = PR \qquad \angle C = \angle R$$

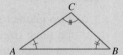 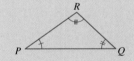

To prove that two triangles are congruent, we don't need to show that all six corresponding parts (side and angles) are congruent. For instance, if all three sides are congruent, then all three angles must also be congruent. You can easily see why the following properties lead to congruent triangles.

- Side-Side-Side (SSS). If each side of one triangle is congruent to the corresponding side of another triangle, then the two triangles are congruent. See Figure 1(a).

- Side-Angle-Side (SAS). If two sides and the included angle in one triangle are congruent to the corresponding sides and angle in another triangle, then the two triangles are congruent. See Figure 1(b).

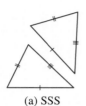

(a) SSS

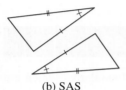

(b) SAS

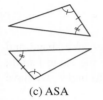

(c) ASA

FIGURE 1

- Angle-Side-Angle (ASA). If two angles and the included side in one triangle are congruent to the corresponding angles and side in another triangle, then the triangles are congruent. See Figure 1(c).

EXAMPLE 1 ■ Congruent Triangles

(a) $\triangle ADB \cong \triangle CBD$ by SSS.

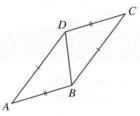

(b) $\triangle ABE \cong \triangle CBD$ by SAS.

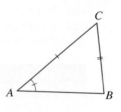

(c) $\triangle ABD \cong \triangle CBD$ by ASA.

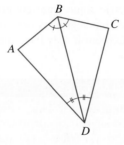

(d) These triangles are not necessarily congruent. "Side-side-angle" does *not* determine congruence.

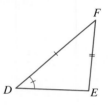

■

Similar Triangles

Two geometric figures are similar if they have the same shape, but not necessarily the same size. (See the Discovery Project on page 207.) In the case of triangles, we can define similarity as follows.

SIMILAR TRIANGLES

Two triangles are **similar** if their vertices can be matched up so that corresponding angles are congruent. In this case, corresponding sides are proportional.

We write $\triangle ABC \sim \triangle PQR$ to mean that triangle ABC is similar to triangle PQR and that the following conditions hold.

The angles correspond as follows:

$$\angle A = \angle P, \ \angle B = \angle Q, \ \angle C = \angle R$$

The sides are proportional as follows:

$$\frac{AB}{PQ} = \frac{BC}{QR} = \frac{AC}{PR}$$

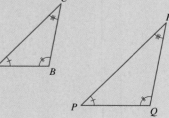

The sum of the angles in any triangle is 180°. So, if we know two angles in a triangle, the third is determined. Thus, to prove that two triangles are similar, we need only show that two angles in one are congruent to two angles in the other.

EXAMPLE 2 ■ Similar Triangles

Find all pairs of similar triangles in the figures.

(a)

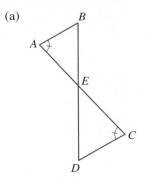

(b)

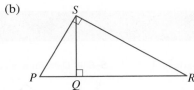

SOLUTION

(a) Since $\angle AEB$ and $\angle CED$ are opposite angles, they are equal. Thus, $\triangle AEB \sim \triangle CED$.

(b) Since all triangles in the figure are right triangles, we have

$$\angle QSR + \angle QRS = 90°$$
$$\angle QSR + \angle QSP = 90°$$

Subtracting these equations we find that $\angle QSP = \angle QRS$. Thus

$$\triangle PQS \sim \triangle SQR \sim \triangle PSR$$

■

EXAMPLE 3 ■ Proportional Sides in Similar Triangles

Given that the triangles in the figure are similar, find the lengths x and y.

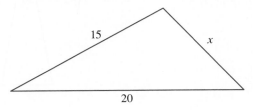

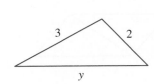

SOLUTION

By similarity, we know that the lengths of corresponding sides in the triangles are proportional. First we find x:

$$\frac{x}{2} = \frac{15}{3} \qquad \text{Corresponding sides are proportional}$$

$$x = \frac{2 \cdot 15}{3} = 10 \qquad \text{Solve for } x$$

Now we find y:

$$\frac{15}{3} = \frac{20}{y} \qquad \text{Corresponding sides are proportional}$$

$$y = \frac{20 \cdot 3}{15} = 4 \qquad \text{Solve for } y$$

∎

B.1 EXERCISES

1–4 ■ Determine whether the pair of triangles is congruent. If so, state the congruence principle you are using.

1.

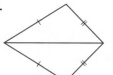

2.

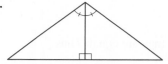

3.

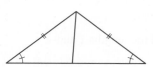

4.

5–8 ■ Determine whether the pair of triangles is similar.

5.

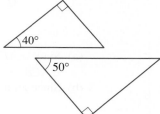

40°

50°

6.

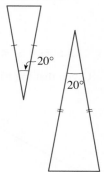

20°

20°

7.

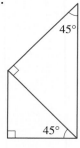

45°

45°

8.

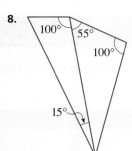

9–12 ■ Given that the pair of triangles is similar, find the length(s) x and/or y.

9.

10.

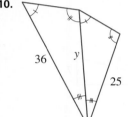

11.   **12.**

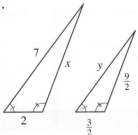   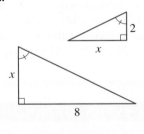

13–14 ■ Express x in terms of a, b, and c.

13.

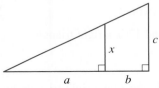

14.

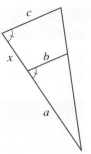

15. In the figure *CDEF* is a rectangle. Prove that
△*ABC* ~ △*AED* ~ △*EBF*.

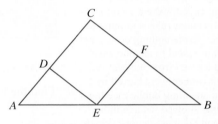

16. In the figure *DEFG* is a square. Prove the following:
  (a) △*ADG* ~ △*GCF*
  (b) △*ADG* ~ △*FEB*
  (c) *AD* · *EB* = *DG* · *FE*
  (d) *DE* = $\sqrt{AD \cdot EB}$

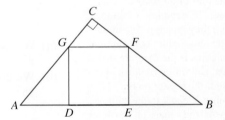

17. Two vertical poles, one 8 ft tall and the other 24 ft tall, have ropes stretched from the top of each to the base of the other (see the figure). How high above the ground is the point where the ropes cross?

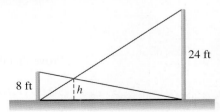

B.2 THE PYTHAGOREAN THEOREM

In a right triangle, the side opposite the right angle is called the **hypotenuse** and the other two sides are called the **legs**.

THE PYTHAGOREAN THEOREM

In a right triangle the square of the hypotenuse is equal to the sum of the squares of the legs. That is, in triangle ABC in the figure

$$a^2 + b^2 = c^2$$

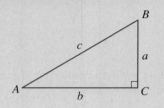

Pythagoras (circa 580–500 B.C.) founded a school in Croton in southern Italy, devoted to the study of arithmetic, geometry, music, and astronomy. The Pythagoreans, as they were called, were a secret society with peculiar rules and initiation rites. They wrote nothing down, and were not to reveal to anyone what they had learned from the Master. Although women were barred by law from attending public meetings, Pythagoras allowed women in his school, and his most famous student was Theano (whom he later married).

According to Aristotle, the Pythagoreans were convinced that "the principles of mathematics are the principles of all things." Their motto was "Everything is Number," by which they meant *whole* numbers. The outstanding contribution of Pythagoras is the theorem that bears his name: In a right triangle the area of the square on the hypotenuse is equal to the sum of the areas of the square on the other two sides.

EXAMPLE 1 ■ Using the Pythagorean Theorem

Find the lengths x and y in the right triangles shown.

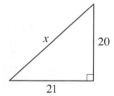

SOLUTION

(a) We use the Pythagorean theorem with $a = 20$, and $b = 21$, and $c = x$. Then $x^2 = 20^2 + 21^2 = 841$. So $x = \sqrt{841} = 29$.
(b) We use the Pythagorean theorem with $c = 25$, $a = 7$, and $b = y$. Then $25^2 = 7^2 + y^2$, so $y^2 = 25^2 - 7^2 = 576$. Thus, $y = \sqrt{576} = 24$. ■

The converse of the Pythagorean theorem is also true.

CONVERSE OF THE PYTHAGOREAN THEOREM

If the square of one side of a triangle is equal to the sum of the squares of the other two sides, then the triangle is a right triangle.

EXAMPLE 2 ■ Proving That a Triangle Is a Right Triangle

Prove that the triangle with sides of length 8, 15, and 17 is a right triangle.

SOLUTION

You can check that $8^2 + 15^2 = 17^2$. So the triangle must be a right triangle by the converse of the Pythagorean theorem. ■

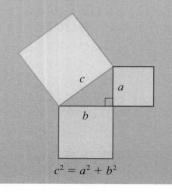

$c^2 = a^2 + b^2$

B.2   EXERCISES

1–6 ■ In the given right triangle, find the side labeled x.

1.

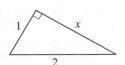

2.

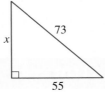

3.

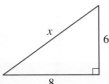

4.

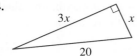

5.

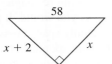

6.

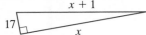

7–12 ■ The lengths of the sides of a triangle are given. Determine whether the triangle is a right triangle.

7. 5, 12, 13

8. 15, 20, 25

9. 8, 10, 12

10. 6, 17, 18

11. 48, 55, 73

12. 13, 84, 85

13. One leg of a right triangle measures 11 cm. The hypotenuse is 1 cm longer than the other leg. Find the length of the hypotenuse.

14. The length of a rectangle is 1 ft greater than its width. Each diagonal is 169 ft long. Find the dimensions of the rectangle.

15. Each of the diagonals of a quadrilateral is 27 cm long. Two adjacent sides measure 17 cm and 21 cm. Is the quadrilateral a rectangle?

16. Find the height h of the right triangle ABC shown in the figure. [*Hint*: Find the area of triangle ABC in two different ways.]

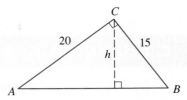

17. Find the length of the diagonal of the rectangular box shown in the figure.

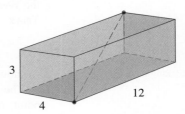

18. If a, b, c are positive integers such that $a^2 + b^2 = c^2$, then (a, b, c) is called a **Pythagorean triple**.
(a) Let m and n be positive integers with $m > n$. Let $a = m^2 - n^2$, $b = 2mn$, and $c = m^2 + n^2$. Show that (a, b, c) is a Pythagorean triple.
(b) Use part (a) to find the rest of the Pythagorean triples in the table.

m	n	(a, b, c)
2	1	(3, 4, 5)
3	1	(8, 6, 10)
3	2	
4	1	
4	2	
4	3	
5	1	
5	2	
5	3	
5	4	

Appendix C
Graphing Calculators

C.1 USING A GRAPHING CALCULATOR

FIGURE 1
The viewing rectangle $[a, b]$ by $[c, d]$

A graphing calculator or computer displays a rectangular portion of the graph of an equation in a display window or viewing screen, which we call a **viewing rectangle**. The default screen often gives an incomplete or misleading picture, so it is important to choose the viewing rectangle with care. If we choose the x-values to range from a minimum value of $\text{Xmin} = a$ to a maximum value of $\text{Xmax} = b$ and the y-values to range from a minimum value of $\text{Ymin} = c$ to a maximum value of $\text{Ymax} = d$, then the displayed portion of the graph lies in the rectangle

$$[a, b] \times [c, d] = \{(x, y) \mid a \leqslant x \leqslant b, c \leqslant x \leqslant d\}$$

as shown in Figure 1. We refer to this as the $[a, b]$ by $[c, d]$ viewing rectangle.

The graphing device draws the graph of an equation much as you would. It plots points of the form (x, y) for a certain number of values of x, equally spaced between a and b. If the equation is not defined for an x-value, or if the corresponding y-value lies outside the viewing rectangle, the device ignores this value and moves on to the next x-value. The machine connects each point to the preceding plotted point to form a representation of the graph of the equation.

EXAMPLE 1 ■ Choosing an Appropriate Viewing Rectangle

Graph the equation $y = x^2 + 3$ in an appropriate viewing rectangle.

SOLUTION

Let's experiment with different viewing rectangles. We'll start with the viewing rectangle $[-2, 2]$ by $[-2, 2]$, so we set

$$\text{Xmin} = -2 \qquad \text{Ymin} = -2$$

$$\text{Xmax} = 2 \qquad \text{Ymax} = 2$$

The resulting graph in Figure 2(a) is blank! This is because $x^2 \geqslant 0$, so $x^2 + 3 \geqslant 3$ for all x. Thus, the graph lies entirely above the viewing rectangle, so this viewing rectangle is not appropriate. If we enlarge the viewing rectangle to $[-4, 4]$ by $[-4, 4]$, as in Figure 2(b), we begin to see a portion of the graph.

Now let's try the viewing rectangle $[-10, 10]$ by $[-5, 30]$. The graph in Figure 2(c) seems to give a more complete view of the graph. If we enlarge the viewing rectangle even further, as in Figure 2(d), the graph doesn't show clearly that the y-intercept is 3.

So, the viewing rectangle $[-10, 10]$ by $[-5, 30]$ gives an appropriate representation of the graph.

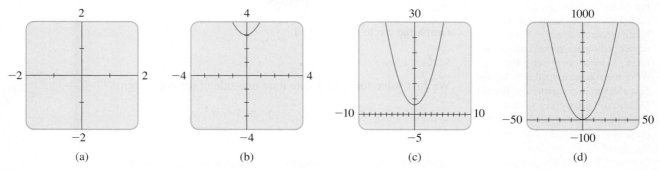

(a)   (b)   (c)   (d)

FIGURE 2

Graphs of $y = x^2 + 3$ ∎

Alan Turing (1912–1954) was at the center of two pivotal events of the 20th century—World War II and the invention of computers. At the age of 23 Turing made his mark on mathematics by solving an important problem in the foundations of mathematics that was posed by David Hilbert at the 1928 International Congress of Mathematicians. In this research he invented a theoretical machine, now called a Turing machine, which was the inspiration for modern digital computers. During World War II Turing was in charge of the British effort

(continued)

EXAMPLE 2 ■ **Two Graphs on the Same Screen**

Graph the equations $y = 3x^2 - 6x + 1$ and $y = 0.23x - 2.25$ together in the viewing rectangle $[-1, 3]$ by $[-2.5, 1.5]$. Do the graphs intersect in this viewing rectangle?

SOLUTION

Figure 3(a) shows the essential features of both graphs. One is a parabola and the other is a line. It looks as if the graphs intersect near the point $(1, -2)$. However, if we zoom in on the area around this point as shown in Figure 3(b), we see that although the graphs almost touch, they don't actually intersect.

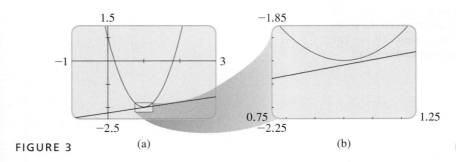

FIGURE 3   (a)   (b)   ∎

You can see from Examples 1 and 2 that the choice of a viewing rectangle makes a big difference in the appearance of a graph. If you want an overview of the essential features of a graph, you must choose a relatively large viewing rectangle to obtain a global view of the graph. If you want to investigate the details of a graph, you must zoom in to a small viewing rectangle that shows just the feature of interest.

to decipher secret German codes. His complete success in this endeavor played a decisive role in the Allies' victory. To carry out the numerous logical steps required to break a coded message, Turing developed decision procedures similar to modern computer programs. After the war he helped develop the first electronic computers in Britain. He also did pioneering work on artificial intelligence and computer models of biological processes. At the age of 42 Turing died of cyanide poisoning under mysterious circumstances.

Most graphing calculators can only graph equations in which y is isolated on one side of the equal sign. The next example shows how to graph equations that don't have this property.

EXAMPLE 3 ■ Graphing a Circle

Graph the circle $x^2 + y^2 = 1$.

SOLUTION

We first solve for y, to isolate it on one side of the equal sign.

$$y^2 = 1 - x^2$$
$$y = \pm\sqrt{1 - x^2}$$

Therefore, the circle is described by the graphs of *two* equations:

$$y = \sqrt{1 - x^2} \qquad \text{and} \qquad y = -\sqrt{1 - x^2}$$

The first equation represents the top half of the circle (because $y \geq 0$), and the second represents the bottom half of the circle (because $y \leq 0$). If we graph the first equation in the viewing rectangle $[-2, 2]$ by $[-2, 2]$, we get the semicircle shown in Figure 4(a). The graph of the second equation is the semicircle in Figure 4(b). Graphing these semicircles together on the same viewing screen, we get the full circle in Figure 4(c).

The graph in Figure 4(c) looks somewhat flattened. Most graphing calculators allow you to set the scales on the axes so that circles really look like circles. On the TI-82 and TI-83, from the ZOOM menu, choose **ZSquare** to set the scales appropriately. (On the TI-85 the command is **Zsq.**)

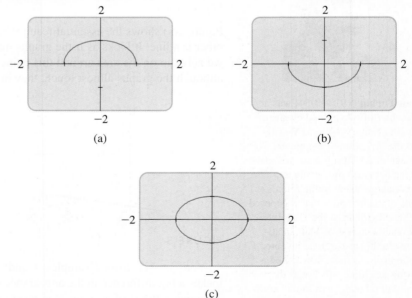

(a)

(b)

(c)

FIGURE 4
Graphing the equation $x^2 + y^2 = 1$

Other uses and capabilities of the graphing calculator are discussed in Appendix C.2 and throughout this textbook.

C.1 EXERCISES

1–6 ■ Use a graphing calculator or computer to decide which viewing rectangle (a)–(d) produces the most appropriate graph of the equation.

1. $y = x^4 + 2$
   (a) $[-2, 2]$ by $[-2, 2]$
   (b) $[0, 4]$ by $[0, 4]$
   (c) $[-8, 8]$ by $[-4, 40]$
   (d) $[-40, 40]$ by $[-80, 800]$

2. $y = x^2 + 7x + 6$
   (a) $[-5, 5]$ by $[-5, 5]$
   (b) $[0, 10]$ by $[-20, 100]$
   (c) $[-15, 8]$ by $[-20, 100]$
   (d) $[-10, 3]$ by $[-100, 20]$

3. $y = 100 - x^2$
   (a) $[-4, 4]$ by $[-4, 4]$
   (b) $[-10, 10]$ by $[-10, 10]$
   (c) $[-15, 15]$ by $[-30, 110]$
   (d) $[-4, 4]$ by $[-30, 110]$

4. $y = 2x^2 - 1000$
   (a) $[-10, 10]$ by $[-10, 10]$
   (b) $[-10, 10]$ by $[-100, 100]$
   (c) $[-10, 10]$ by $[-1000, 1000]$
   (d) $[-25, 25]$ by $[-1200, 200]$

5. $y = 10 + 25x - x^3$
   (a) $[-4, 4]$ by $[-4, 4]$
   (b) $[-10, 10]$ by $[-10, 10]$
   (c) $[-20, 20]$ by $[-100, 100]$
   (d) $[-100, 100]$ by $[-200, 200]$

6. $y = \sqrt{8x - x^2}$
   (a) $[-4, 4]$ by $[-4, 4]$
   (b) $[-5, 5]$ by $[0, 100]$
   (c) $[-10, 10]$ by $[-10, 40]$
   (d) $[-2, 10]$ by $[-2, 6]$

7–18 ■ Determine an appropriate viewing rectangle for the equation and use it to draw the graph.

7. $y = 100x^2$

8. $y = -100x^2$

9. $y = 4 + 6x - x^2$

10. $y = 0.3x^2 + 1.7x - 3$

11. $y = \sqrt[4]{256 - x^2}$

12. $y = \sqrt{12x - 17}$

13. $y = 0.01x^3 - x^2 + 5$

14. $y = x(x + 6)(x - 9)$

15. $y = x^4 - 4x^3$

16. $y = \dfrac{x}{x^2 + 25}$

17. $y = 1 + |x - 1|$

18. $y = 2x - |x^2 - 5|$

19. Graph the circle $x^2 + y^2 = 9$ by solving for y and graphing two equations as in Example 3.

20. Graph the circle $(y - 1)^2 + x^2 = 1$ by solving for y and graphing two equations as in Example 3.

21. Graph the equation $4x^2 + 2y^2 = 1$ by solving for y and graphing two equations corresponding to the negative and positive square roots. (This graph is called an *ellipse*.)

22. Graph the equation $y^2 - 9x^2 = 1$ by solving for y and graphing the two equations corresponding to the positive and negative square roots. (This graph is called a *hyperbola*.)

23–26 ■ Do the graphs intersect in the given viewing rectangle? If they do, how many points of intersection are there?

23. $y = -3x^2 + 6x - \frac{1}{2}$, $y = \sqrt{7 - \frac{7}{12}x^2}$; $[-4, 4]$ by $[-1, 3]$

24. $y = \sqrt{49 - x^2}$, $y = \frac{1}{5}(41 - 3x)$; $[-8, 8]$ by $[-1, 8]$

25. $y = 6 - 4x - x^2$, $y = 3x + 18$; $[-6, 2]$ by $[-5, 20]$

26. $y = x^3 - 4x$, $y = x + 5$; $[-4, 4]$ by $[-15, 15]$

27. When you enter the following equations into your calculator, how does what you see on the screen differ from the usual way of writing the equations? (Check your user's manual if you're not sure.)
   (a) $y = |x|$
   (b) $y = \sqrt[5]{x}$
   (c) $y = \dfrac{x}{x - 1}$
   (d) $y = x^3 + \sqrt[3]{x + 2}$

28. A student wishes to graph the equations

$$y = x^{1/3} \quad \text{and} \quad y = \frac{x}{x + 4}$$

on the same screen, so he enters the following information into his calculator:

$$Y_1 = X^1/3 \qquad Y_2 = X/X + 4$$

The calculator graphs two lines instead of the equations he wanted. What went wrong? Why are the graphs lines?

C.2 SOLVING EQUATIONS AND INEQUALITIES GRAPHICALLY

In Appendix A.4 and A.5 we solved equations and inequalities algebraically. In this appendix we use graphs to solve equations and inequalities.

■ Solving Equations Graphically

"Algebra is a merry science," Uncle Jakob would say. "We go hunting for a little animal whose name we don't know, so we call it *x*. When we bag our game we pounce on it and give it its right name."

ALBERT EINSTEIN

One way to solve an equation like

$$3x - 5 = 0$$

is to use the **algebraic method**. This means we use the rules of algebra to isolate *x* on one side of the equation. We view *x* as an *unknown* and we use the rules of algebra to hunt it down. Here are the steps in the solution:

$$3x - 5 = 0$$
$$3x = 5 \qquad \text{Add 5}$$
$$x = \tfrac{5}{3} \qquad \text{Divide by 3}$$

So the solution is $x = \tfrac{5}{3}$.

We can also solve this equation by the **graphical method**. In this method we view *x* as a *variable* and sketch the graph of the equation

$$y = 3x - 5$$

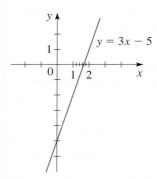

FIGURE 1

Different values for *x* give different values for *y*. Our goal is to find the value of *x* for which $y = 0$. From the graph in Figure 1 we see that $y = 0$ when $x \approx 1.7$. Thus, the solution is $x \approx 1.7$. Note that from the graph we obtain an approximate solution.

We summarize these methods in the following box.

SOLVING AN EQUATION	
Algebraic Method	**Graphical Method**
Use the rules of algebra to isolate the unknown *x* on one side of the equation.	Move all terms to one side and set equal to *y*. Sketch the graph to find the value of *x* where $y = 0$.
Example: $2x = 6 - x$ $\qquad 3x = 6 \quad \text{Add } x$ $\qquad\ \ x = 2 \quad \text{Divide by 3}$ The solution is $x = 2$.	**Example:** $2x = 6 - x$ $\qquad\ \ 0 = 6 - 3x.$ Set $y = 6 - 3x$ and graph.

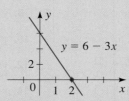

From the graph the solution is $x \approx 2$.

The advantage of the algebraic method is that it gives exact answers. Also, the process of unraveling the equation to arrive at the answer helps us understand the algebraic structure of the equation. On the other hand, for many equations it is difficult or impossible to isolate x.

The graphical method gives a numerical approximation to the answer. This is an advantage when a numerical answer is desired. (For example, an engineer might find an answer expressed as $x \approx 2.6$ more immediately useful than $x = \sqrt{7}$.) Also, graphing an equation helps us visualize how the solution is related to other values of the variable.

EXAMPLE 1 ■ Solving an Equation Algebraically and Graphically

Solve the equations algebraically and graphically.

(a) $x^2 - 4x + 2 = 0$ (b) $x^2 - 4x + 4 = 0$ (c) $x^2 - 4x + 6 = 0$

SOLUTION 1: ALGEBRAIC

We use the quadratic formula to solve each equation.

The quadratic formula is discussed on page 540.

(a) $x = \dfrac{-(-4) \pm \sqrt{(-4)^2 - 4 \cdot 1 \cdot 2}}{2} = \dfrac{4 \pm \sqrt{8}}{2} = 2 \pm \sqrt{2}$

There are two solutions, $x = 2 + \sqrt{2}$ and $x = 2 - \sqrt{2}$.

(b) $x = \dfrac{-(-4) \pm \sqrt{(-4)^2 - 4 \cdot 1 \cdot 4}}{2} = \dfrac{4 \pm \sqrt{0}}{2} = 2$

There is just one solution, $x = 2$.

(c) $x = \dfrac{-(-4) \pm \sqrt{(-4)^2 - 4 \cdot 1 \cdot 6}}{2} = \dfrac{4 \pm \sqrt{-8}}{2}$

There is no real solution.

SOLUTION 2: GRAPHICAL

We graph the equations $y = x^2 - 4x + 2$, $y = x^2 - 4x + 4$, and $y = x^2 - 4x + 6$ in Figure 2. By determining the x-intercepts of the graphs, we find the following solutions.

(a) $x \approx 0.6$ and $x \approx 3.4$ (b) $x = 2$

(c) There is no x-intercept, so the equation has no solution.

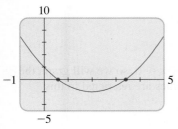

(a) $y = x^2 - 4x + 2$

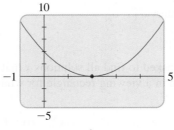

(b) $y = x^2 - 4x + 4$

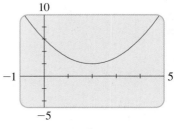

(c) $y = x^2 - 4x + 6$

FIGURE 2

The graphs in Figure 2 show visually why a quadratic equation may have two solutions, one solution, or no real solution. We proved this fact algebraically in Appendix A.4 when we studied the discriminant.

EXAMPLE 2 ■ Another Graphical Method

Solve the equation algebraically and graphically: $5 - 3x = 8x - 20$

SOLUTION 1: ALGEBRAIC

$$5 - 3x = 8x - 20$$

$$-3x = 8x - 25 \qquad \text{Subtract 5}$$

$$-11x = -25 \qquad \text{Subtract } 8x$$

$$x = \frac{-25}{-11} = 2\tfrac{3}{11} \qquad \text{Divide by } -11 \text{ and simplify}$$

SOLUTION 2: GRAPHICAL

We could move all terms to one side of the equal sign, set the result equal to y, and graph the resulting equation. But to avoid all this algebra, we graph two equations instead:

$$y_1 = 5 - 3x \qquad \text{and} \qquad y_2 = 8x - 20$$

The solution of the original equation will be the value of x that makes y_1 equal to y_2; that is, the solution is the x-coordinate of the intersection point of the two graphs. Using the $\boxed{\text{TRACE}}$ feature or the `intersect` command on a graphing calculator, we see from Figure 3 that the solution is $x \approx 2.27$. ■

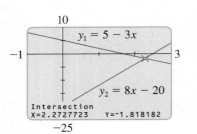

FIGURE 3

In the next example we use the graphical method to solve an equation that is extremely difficult to solve algebraically.

EXAMPLE 3 ■ Solving an Equation in an Interval

Solve the equation

$$x^3 - 6x^2 + 9x = \sqrt{x}$$

in the interval $[1, 6]$.

SOLUTION

We are asked to find all solutions x that satisfy $1 \le x \le 6$, so we will graph the equation in a viewing rectangle for which the x-values are restricted to this interval.

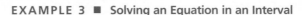

$$x^3 - 6x^2 + 9x = \sqrt{x}$$

$$x^3 - 6x^2 + 9x - \sqrt{x} = 0 \qquad \text{Subtract } \sqrt{x}$$

We can also use the `zero` command to find the solutions, as shown in Figures 4(a) and 4(b).

Figure 4 shows the graph of the equation $y = x^3 - 6x^2 + 9x - \sqrt{x}$ in the viewing rectangle $[1, 6]$ by $[-5, 5]$. There are two x-intercepts in this viewing rectangle; zooming in we see that the solutions are $x \approx 2.18$ and $x \approx 3.72$.

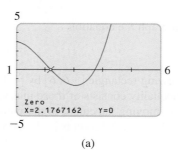

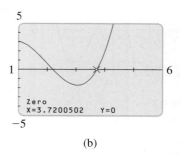

FIGURE 4   (a)   (b)

The equation in Example 3 actually has four solutions. You are asked to find the other two in Exercise 31.

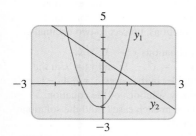

FIGURE 5
$x^2 - 5x + 6 \leq 0$

Solving Inequalities Graphically

Inequalities can be solved graphically. To describe the method we solve

$$x^2 - 5x + 6 \leq 0$$

To solve this inequality graphically, we draw the graph of

$$y = x^2 - 5x + 6$$

Our goal is to find those values of x for which $y \leq 0$. These are simply the x-values for which the graph lies below the x-axis. From Figure 5 we see that the solution of the inequality is the interval $[2, 3]$.

EXAMPLE 4 ■ Solving an Inequality Graphically

Solve the inequality $3.7x^2 + 1.3x - 1.9 \leq 2.0 - 1.4x$.

SOLUTION

We graph the equations

$$y_1 = 3.7x^2 + 1.3x - 1.9$$
$$y_2 = 2.0 - 1.4x$$

in the same viewing rectangle in Figure 6. We are interested in those values of x for which $y_1 \leq y_2$; these are points for which the graph of y_2 lies on or above the graph of y_1. To determine the appropriate interval, we look for the x-coordinates of points where the graphs intersect. We conclude that the solution is (approximately) the interval $[-1.45, 0.72]$.   ■

FIGURE 6
$y_1 = 3.7x^2 + 1.3x - 1.9$
$y_2 = 2.0 - 1.4x$

EXAMPLE 5 ■ Solving an Inequality Graphically

Solve the inequality $x^3 - 5x^2 \geq -8$.

SOLUTION

We write the inequality as

$$x^3 - 5x^2 + 8 \geqslant 0$$

and then graph the equation

$$y = x^3 - 5x^2 + 8$$

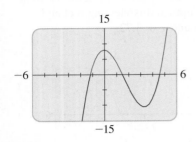

FIGURE 7
$x^3 - 5x^2 + 8 \geqslant 0$

in the viewing rectangle $[-6, 6]$ by $[-15, 15]$, as shown in Figure 7. The solution of the inequality consists of those intervals on which the graph lies on or above the x-axis. By moving the cursor to the x-intercepts we find that, correct to one decimal place, the solution is $[-1.1, 1.5] \cup [4.6, \infty)$. ∎

C.2 EXERCISES

1–10 ■ Solve the equation both algebraically and graphically.

1. $x - 4 = 5x + 12$

2. $\frac{1}{2}x - 3 = 6 + 2x$

3. $\frac{2}{x} + \frac{1}{2x} = 7$

4. $\frac{4}{x + 2} - \frac{6}{2x} = \frac{5}{2x + 4}$

5. $x^2 - 32 = 0$

6. $x^3 + 16 = 0$

7. $16x^4 = 625$

8. $2x^5 - 243 = 0$

9. $(x - 5)^4 - 80 = 0$

10. $6(x + 2)^5 = 64$

11–18 ■ Solve the equation graphically in the given interval. State each answer correct to two decimals.

11. $x^2 - 7x + 12 = 0;$ $[0, 6]$

12. $x^2 - 0.75x + 0.125 = 0;$ $[-2, 2]$

13. $x^3 - 6x^2 + 11x - 6 = 0;$ $[-1, 4]$

14. $16x^3 + 16x^2 = x + 1;$ $[-2, 2]$

15. $x - \sqrt{x + 1} = 0;$ $[-1, 5]$

16. $1 + \sqrt{x} = \sqrt{1 + x^2};$ $[-1, 5]$

17. $x^{1/3} - x = 0;$ $[-3, 3]$

18. $x^{1/2} + x^{1/3} - x = 0;$ $[-1, 5]$

19–22 ■ Find all real solutions of the equation, correct to two decimals.

19. $x^3 - 2x^2 - x - 1 = 0$

20. $x^4 - 8x^2 + 2 = 0$

21. $x(x - 1)(x + 2) = \frac{1}{6}x$

22. $x^4 = 16 - x^3$

23–30 ■ Find the solutions of the inequality by drawing appropriate graphs. State each answer correct to two decimals.

23. $x^2 - 3x - 10 \leqslant 0$

24. $0.5x^2 + 0.875x \leqslant 0.25$

25. $x^3 + 11x \leqslant 6x^2 + 6$

26. $16x^3 + 24x^2 > -9x - 1$

27. $x^{1/3} < x$

28. $\sqrt{0.5x^2 + 1} \leqslant 2|x|$

29. $(x + 1)^2 < (x - 1)^2$

30. $(x + 1)^2 \leqslant x^3$

31. In Example 3 we found two solutions of the equation $x^3 - 6x^2 + 9x = \sqrt{x}$, the solutions that lie between 1 and 6. Find two more solutions, correct to two decimals.

32. Consider the family of equations $x^3 - 3x = k$.
(a) Draw the graphs of $y_1 = x^3 - 3x$ and $y_2 = k$ in the same viewing rectangle, in the cases $k = -4, -2, 0, 2,$ and 4. How many solutions of the equation $x^3 - 3x = k$ are there in each case? Find the solutions correct to two decimals.
(b) For what ranges of values of k does the equation have one solution? two solutions? three solutions?

A ppendix D.1   Dividing Polynomials

So far in this chapter we have been studying polynomial functions *graphically*. In this section we begin to study polynomials *algebraically*. Most of our work will be concerned with factoring polynomials, and to factor, we need to know how to divide polynomials.

Long Division of Polynomials

Dividing polynomials is much like the familiar process of dividing numbers. When we divide 38 by 7, the quotient is 5 and the remainder is 3. We write

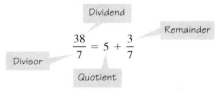

$$\frac{38}{7} = 5 + \frac{3}{7}$$

To divide polynomials, we use long division, as in the next example.

Example 1   Long Division of Polynomials

Divide $6x^2 - 26x + 12$ by $x - 4$.

Solution   The *dividend* is $6x^2 - 26x + 12$ and the *divisor* is $x - 4$. We begin by arranging them as follows:

$$x - 4\overline{)6x^2 - 26x + 12}$$

Next we divide the leading term in the dividend by the leading term in the divisor to get the first term of the quotient: $6x^2/x = 6x$. Then we multiply the divisor by $6x$ and subtract the result from the dividend.

$$
\begin{array}{r}
6x \phantom{{} - 26x + 12} \\
x - 4\overline{)6x^2 - 26x + 12} \\
6x^2 - 24x \phantom{{} + 12} \\
\hline
-2x + 12
\end{array}
$$

Divide leading terms: $\dfrac{6x^2}{x} = 6x$

Multiply: $6x(x - 4) = 6x^2 - 24x$

Subtract and "bring down" 12

We repeat the process using the last line $-2x + 12$ as the dividend.

$$
\begin{array}{r}
6x - 2 \phantom{{} + 12} \\
x - 4\overline{)6x^2 - 26x + 12} \\
6x^2 - 24x \phantom{{} + 12} \\
\hline
-2x + 12 \\
-2x + 8 \\
\hline
4
\end{array}
$$

Divide leading terms: $\dfrac{-2x}{x} = -2$

Multiply: $-2(x - 4) = -2x + 8$

Subtract

The division process ends when the last line is of lesser degree than the divisor. The last line then contains the *remainder*, and the top line contains the *quotient*. The result of the division can be interpreted in either of two ways.

$$\frac{6x^2 - 26x + 12}{x - 4} = 6x - 2 + \frac{4}{x - 4}$$

or

$$6x^2 - 26x + 12 = (x - 4)(6x - 2) + 4$$

Remainder

Dividend   Divisor   Quotient

We summarize the long division process in the following theorem.

Example 2   Long Division of Polynomials

Let $P(x) = 8x^4 + 6x^2 - 3x + 1$ and $D(x) = 2x^2 - x + 2$. Find polynomials $Q(x)$ and $R(x)$ such that $P(x) = D(x) \cdot Q(x) + R(x)$.

Solution   We use long division after first inserting the term $0x^3$ into the dividend to ensure that the columns line up correctly.

$$
\begin{array}{r}
4x^2 + 2x \phantom{{}- 3x + 1} \\
2x^2 - x + 2 \overline{)\, 8x^4 + 0x^3 + 6x^2 - 3x + 1} \\
\underline{8x^4 - 4x^3 + 8x^2} \phantom{{}- 3x + 1} \\
4x^3 - 2x^2 - 3x \phantom{{}+ 1} \\
\underline{4x^3 - 2x^2 + 4x} \phantom{{}+ 1} \\
-7x + 1
\end{array}
$$

Multiply divisor by $4x^2$

Subtract

Multiply divisor by $2x$

Subtract

The process is complete at this point because $-7x + 1$ is of lesser degree than the divisor $2x^2 - x + 2$. From the above long division we see that $Q(x) = 4x^2 + 2x$ and $R(x) = -7x + 1$, so

$$8x^4 + 6x^2 - 3x + 1 = (2x^2 - x + 2)(4x^2 + 2x) + (-7x + 1)$$

Division Algorithm

If $P(x)$ and $D(x)$ are polynomials, with $D(x) \neq 0$, then there exist unique polynomials $Q(x)$ and $R(x)$, where $R(x)$ is either 0 or of degree less than the degree of $D(x)$, such that

$$P(x) = D(x) \cdot Q(x) + R(x)$$

Remainder

Dividend   Divisor   Quotient

The polynomials $P(x)$ and $D(x)$ are called the **dividend** and **divisor**, respectively, $Q(x)$ is the **quotient**, and $R(x)$ is the **remainder**.

To write the division algorithm another way, divide through by $D(x)$:

$$\frac{P(x)}{D(x)} = Q(x) + \frac{R(x)}{D(x)}$$

Synthetic Division

Synthetic division is a quick method of dividing polynomials; it can be used when the divisor is of the form $x - c$. In synthetic division we write only the essential parts of the long division. Compare the following long and synthetic divisions, in which we divide $2x^3 - 7x^2 + 5$ by $x - 3$. (We'll explain how to perform the synthetic division in Example 3.)

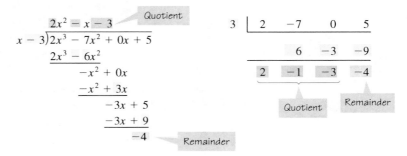

Long Division

Synthetic Division

Note that in synthetic division we abbreviate $2x^3 - 7x^2 + 5$ by writing only the coefficients: 2 -7 0   5, and instead of $x - 3$, we simply write 3. (Writing 3 instead of -3 allows us to add instead of subtract, but this changes the sign of all the numbers that appear in the gold boxes.)

The next example shows how synthetic division is performed.

Example 3   **Synthetic Division**

Use synthetic division to divide $2x^3 - 7x^2 + 5$ by $x - 3$.

Solution   We begin by writing the appropriate coefficients to represent the divisor and the dividend.

$$\text{Divisor } x - 3 \qquad 3 \;\big|\; 2 \quad -7 \quad 0 \quad 5 \qquad \begin{array}{l} \text{Dividend} \\ 2x^3 - 7x^2 + 0x + 5 \end{array}$$

We bring down the 2, multiply $3 \cdot 2 = 6$, and write the result in the middle row. Then we add:

$$
\begin{array}{c|cccc}
3 & 2 & -7 & 0 & 5 \\
  &   & 6 &   &   \\
\hline
  & \boxed{2} & -1 & & \\
\end{array}
\qquad
\begin{array}{l}
\text{Multiply: } 3 \cdot 2 = 6 \\
\text{Add: } -7 + 6 = -1
\end{array}
$$

We repeat this process of multiplying and then adding until the table is complete.

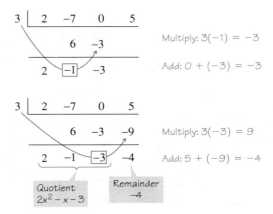

From the last line of the synthetic division, we see that the quotient is $2x^2 - x - 3$ and the remainder is -4. Thus

$$2x^3 - 7x^2 + 5 = (x - 3)(2x^2 - x - 3) - 4$$ ∎

The Remainder and Factor Theorems

The next theorem shows how synthetic division can be used to evaluate polynomials easily.

■ **Proof**   If the divisor in the Division Algorithm is of the form $x - c$ for some real number c, then the remainder must be a constant (since the degree of the remainder is less than the degree of the divisor). If we call this constant r, then

$$P(x) = (x - c) \cdot Q(x) + r$$

Setting $x = c$ in this equation, we get $P(c) = (c - c) \cdot Q(x) + r = 0 + r = r$, that is, $P(c)$ is the remainder r.   ∎

Example 4   **Using the Remainder Theorem to Find the Value of a Polynomial**

Let $P(x) = 3x^5 + 5x^4 - 4x^3 + 7x + 3$.

(a) Find the quotient and remainder when $P(x)$ is divided by $x + 2$.

(b) Use the Remainder Theorem to find $P(-2)$.

Solution

(a) Since $x + 2 = x - (-2)$, the synthetic division for this problem takes the following form.

Remainder Theorem

If the polynomial $P(x)$ is divided by $x - c$, then the remainder is the value $P(c)$.

$$\begin{array}{r|rrrrrr} -2 & 3 & 5 & -4 & 0 & 7 & 3 \\ & & -6 & 2 & 4 & -8 & 2 \\ \hline & 3 & -1 & -2 & 4 & -1 & 5 \end{array}$$

Remainder is 5, so
$P(-2) = 5$.

The quotient is $3x^4 - x^3 - 2x^2 + 4x - 1$ and the remainder is 5.

(b) By the Remainder Theorem, $P(-2)$ is the remainder when $P(x)$ is divided by $x - (-2) = x + 2$. From part (a) the remainder is 5, so $P(-2) = 5$. ■

The next theorem says that *zeros* of polynomials correspond to *factors*; we used this fact in Section 8.1 to graph polynomials.

Factor Theorem

c is a zero of P if and only if $x - c$ is a factor of $P(x)$.

■ **Proof**   If $P(x)$ factors as $P(x) = (x - c) \cdot Q(x)$, then

$$P(c) = (c - c) \cdot Q(c) = 0 \cdot Q(c) = 0$$

Conversely, if $P(c) = 0$, then by the Remainder Theorem

$$P(x) = (x - c) \cdot Q(x) + 0 = (x - c) \cdot Q(x)$$

so $x - c$ is a factor of $P(x)$. ■

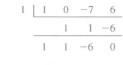

$$\begin{array}{r|rrrr} 1 & 1 & 0 & -7 & 6 \\ & & 1 & 1 & -6 \\ \hline & 1 & 1 & -6 & 0 \end{array}$$

$$\begin{array}{r} x^2 + x - 6 \\ x - 1 \overline{\smash{\big)}\ x^3 + 0x^2 - 7x + 6} \\ \underline{x^3 - x^2} \\ x^2 - 7x \\ \underline{x^2 - x} \\ -6x + 6 \\ \underline{-6x + 6} \\ 0 \end{array}$$

Example 5   Factoring a Polynomial Using the Factor Theorem

Let $P(x) = x^3 - 7x + 6$. Show that $P(1) = 0$, and use this fact to factor $P(x)$ completely.

Solution   Substituting, we see that $P(1) = 1^3 - 7 \cdot 1 + 6 = 0$. By the Factor Theorem, this means that $x - 1$ is a factor of $P(x)$. Using synthetic or long division (shown in the margin), we see that

$$\begin{aligned} P(x) &= x^3 - 7x + 6 \\ &= (x - 1)(x^2 + x - 6) \qquad \text{See margin} \\ &= (x - 1)(x - 2)(x + 3) \qquad \text{Factor quadratic } x^2 + x - 6 \end{aligned}$$ ■

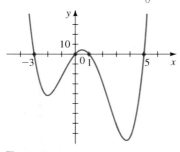

Example 6   Finding a Polynomial with Specified Zeros

Find a polynomial of degree 4 that has zeros $-3, 0, 1$, and 5.

Solution   By the Factor Theorem, $x - (-3), x - 0, x - 1$, and $x - 5$ must all be factors of the desired polynomial, so let

$$P(x) = (x + 3)(x - 0)(x - 1)(x - 5) = x^4 - 3x^3 - 13x^2 + 15x$$

Since $P(x)$ is of degree 4 it is a solution of the problem. Any other solution of the problem must be a constant multiple of $P(x)$, since only multiplication by a constant does not change the degree. ■

Figure 1
$P(x) = (x + 3)x(x - 1)(x - 5)$
has zeros $-3, 0, 1$, and 5.

The polynomial P of Example 6 is graphed in Figure 1. Note that the zeros of P correspond to the x-intercepts of the graph.

D.1 Exercises

1–6 ■ Two polynomials P and D are given. Use either synthetic or long division to divide $P(x)$ by $D(x)$, and express P in the form $P(x) = D(x) \cdot Q(x) + R(x)$.

1. $P(x) = 3x^2 + 5x - 4$, $D(x) = x + 3$

2. $P(x) = x^3 + 4x^2 - 6x + 1$, $D(x) = x - 1$

3. $P(x) = 2x^3 - 3x^2 - 2x$, $D(x) = 2x - 3$

4. $P(x) = 4x^3 + 7x + 9$, $D(x) = 2x + 1$

5. $P(x) = x^4 - x^3 + 4x + 2$, $D(x) = x^2 + 3$

6. $P(x) = 2x^5 + 4x^4 - 4x^3 - x - 3$, $D(x) = x^2 - 2$

7–12 ■ Two polynomials P and D are given. Use either synthetic or long division to divide $P(x)$ by $D(x)$, and express the quotient $P(x)/D(x)$ in the form

$$\frac{P(x)}{D(x)} = Q(x) + \frac{R(x)}{D(x)}$$

7. $P(x) = x^2 + 4x - 8$, $D(x) = x + 3$

8. $P(x) = x^3 + 6x + 5$, $D(x) = x - 4$

9. $P(x) = 4x^2 - 3x - 7$, $D(x) = 2x - 1$

10. $P(x) = 6x^3 + x^2 - 12x + 5$, $D(x) = 3x - 4$

11. $P(x) = 2x^4 - x^3 + 9x^2$, $D(x) = x^2 + 4$

12. $P(x) = x^5 + x^4 - 2x^3 + x + 1$, $D(x) = x^2 + x - 1$

13–22 ■ Find the quotient and remainder using long division.

13. $\dfrac{x^2 - 6x - 8}{x - 4}$

14. $\dfrac{x^3 - x^2 - 2x + 6}{x - 2}$

15. $\dfrac{4x^3 + 2x^2 - 2x - 3}{2x + 1}$

16. $\dfrac{x^3 + 3x^2 + 4x + 3}{3x + 6}$

17. $\dfrac{x^3 + 6x + 3}{x^2 - 2x + 2}$

18. $\dfrac{3x^4 - 5x^3 - 20x - 5}{x^2 + x + 3}$

19. $\dfrac{6x^3 + 2x^2 + 22x}{2x^2 + 5}$

20. $\dfrac{9x^2 - x + 5}{3x^2 - 7x}$

21. $\dfrac{x^6 + x^4 + x^2 + 1}{x^2 + 1}$

22. $\dfrac{2x^5 - 7x^4 - 13}{4x^2 - 6x + 8}$

23–36 ■ Find the quotient and remainder using synthetic division.

23. $\dfrac{x^2 - 5x + 4}{x - 3}$

24. $\dfrac{x^2 - 5x + 4}{x - 1}$

25. $\dfrac{3x^2 + 5x}{x - 6}$

26. $\dfrac{4x^2 - 3}{x + 5}$

27. $\dfrac{x^3 + 2x^2 + 2x + 1}{x + 2}$

28. $\dfrac{3x^3 - 12x^2 - 9x + 1}{x - 5}$

29. $\dfrac{x^3 - 8x + 2}{x + 3}$

30. $\dfrac{x^4 - x^3 + x^2 - x + 2}{x - 2}$

31. $\dfrac{x^5 + 3x^3 - 6}{x - 1}$

32. $\dfrac{x^3 - 9x^2 + 27x - 27}{x - 3}$

33. $\dfrac{2x^3 + 3x^2 - 2x + 1}{x - \frac{1}{2}}$

34. $\dfrac{6x^4 + 10x^3 + 5x^2 + x + 1}{x + \frac{2}{3}}$

35. $\dfrac{x^3 - 27}{x - 3}$

36. $\dfrac{x^4 - 16}{x + 2}$

37–49 ■ Use synthetic division and the Remainder Theorem to evaluate $P(c)$.

37. $P(x) = 4x^2 + 12x + 5$, $c = -1$

38. $P(x) = 2x^2 + 9x + 1$, $c = \frac{1}{2}$

39. $P(x) = x^3 + 3x^2 - 7x + 6$, $c = 2$

40. $P(x) = x^3 - x^2 + x + 5$, $c = -1$

41. $P(x) = x^3 + 2x^2 - 7$, $c = -2$

42. $P(x) = 2x^3 - 21x^2 + 9x - 200$, $c = 11$

43. $P(x) = 5x^4 + 30x^3 - 40x^2 + 36x + 14$, $c = -7$

44. $P(x) = 6x^5 + 10x^3 + x + 1$, $c = -2$

45. $P(x) = x^7 - 3x^2 - 1$, $c = 3$

46. $P(x) = -2x^6 + 7x^5 + 40x^4 - 7x^2 + 10x + 112$, $c = -3$

47. $P(x) = 3x^3 + 4x^2 - 2x + 1$, $c = \frac{2}{3}$

48. $P(x) = x^3 - x + 1$, $c = \frac{1}{4}$

49. $P(x) = x^3 + 2x^2 - 3x - 8$, $c = 0.1$

50. Let

$$P(x) = 6x^7 - 40x^6 + 16x^5 - 200x^4$$
$$- 60x^3 - 69x^2 + 13x - 139$$

Calculate $P(7)$ by **(a)** using synthetic division and **(b)** substituting $x = 7$ into the polynomial and evaluating directly.

51–54 ■ Use the Factor Theorem to show that $x - c$ is a factor of $P(x)$ for the given value(s) of c.

51. $P(x) = x^3 - 3x^2 + 3x - 1$, $c = 1$

52. $P(x) = x^3 + 2x^2 - 3x - 10$, $c = 2$

53. $P(x) = 2x^3 + 7x^2 + 6x - 5, \quad c = \frac{1}{2}$

54. $P(x) = x^4 + 3x^3 - 16x^2 - 27x + 63, \quad c = 3, -3$

55–56 ■ Show that the given value(s) of c are zeros of $P(x)$, and find all other zeros of $P(x)$.

55. $P(x) = x^3 - x^2 - 11x + 15, \quad c = 3$

56. $P(x) = 3x^4 - x^3 - 21x^2 - 11x + 6, \quad c = \frac{1}{3}, -2$

57–60 ■ Find a polynomial of the specified degree that has the given zeros.

57. Degree 3;   zeros $-1, 1, 3$

58. Degree 4;   zeros $-2, 0, 2, 4$

59. Degree 4;   zeros $-1, 1, 3, 5$

60. Degree 5;   zeros $-2, -1, 0, 1, 2$

61. Find a polynomial of degree 3 that has zeros $1, -2,$ and 3, and in which the coefficient of x^2 is 3.

62. Find a polynomial of degree 4 that has integer coefficients and zeros $1, -1, 2,$ and $\frac{1}{2}$.

63–66 ■ Find the polynomial of the specified degree whose graph is shown.

63. Degree 3

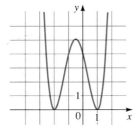

64. Degree 3

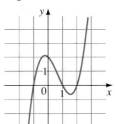

65. Degree 4

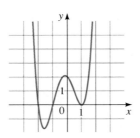

66. Degree 4

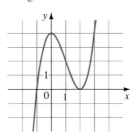

Discovery • Discussion

67. Impossible Division?   Suppose you were asked to solve the following two problems on a test:

   A.   Find the remainder when $6x^{1000} - 17x^{562} + 12x + 26$ is divided by $x + 1$.

   B.   Is $x - 1$ a factor of $x^{567} - 3x^{400} + x^9 + 2$?

Obviously, it's impossible to solve these problems by dividing, because the polynomials are of such large degree. Use one or more of the theorems in this section to solve these problems *without* actually dividing.

68. Nested Form of a Polynomial   Expand Q to prove that the polynomials P and Q are the same.

$$P(x) = 3x^4 - 5x^3 + x^2 - 3x + 5$$

$$Q(x) = (((3x - 5)x + 1)x - 3)x + 5$$

Try to evaluate $P(2)$ and $Q(2)$ in your head, using the forms given. Which is easier? Now write the polynomial $R(x) = x^5 - 2x^4 + 3x^3 - 2x^2 + 3x + 4$ in "nested" form, like the polynomial Q. Use the nested form to find $R(3)$ in your head.

   Do you see how calculating with the nested form follows the same arithmetic steps as calculating the value of a polynomial using synthetic division?

Section D.1 Answers ■

1. $(x + 3)(3x - 4) + 8$ **3.** $(2x - 3)(x^2 - 1) - 3$

5. $(x^2 + 3)(x^2 - x - 3) + (7x + 11)$

7. $x + 1 + \dfrac{-11}{x + 3}$

9. $2x - \frac{1}{2} + \dfrac{-\frac{15}{2}}{2x - 1}$ **11.** $2x^2 - x + 1 + \dfrac{4x - 4}{x^2 + 4}$

*In answers 13–36, the first polynomial given is the
quotient and the second is the remainder.*

13. $x - 2, -16$ **15.** $2x^2 - 1, -2$ **17.** $x + 2, 8x - 1$

19. $3x + 1, 7x - 5$ **21.** $x^4 + 1, 0$ **23.** $x - 2, -2$

25. $3x + 23, 138$ **27.** $x^2 + 2, -3$ **29.** $x^2 - 3x + 1, -1$

31. $x^4 + x^3 + 4x^2 + 4x + 4, -2$ **33.** $2x^2 + 4x, 1$

35. $x^2 + 3x + 9, 0$ **37.** -3 **39.** 12 **41.** -7 **43.** -483

45. 2159 **47.** $\frac{7}{3}$ **49.** -8.279 **55.** $-1 \pm \sqrt{6}$

57. $x^3 - 3x^2 - x + 3$ **59.** $x^4 - 8x^3 + 14x^2 + 8x - 15$

61. $-\frac{3}{2}x^3 + 3x^2 + \frac{15}{2}x - 9$ **63.** $(x + 1)(x - 1)(x - 2)$

65. $(x + 2)^2(x - 1)^2$

**Modeling with Exponential
and Logarithmic Functions**

Many processes that occur in nature, such as population growth, radioactive decay, heat diffusion, and numerous others, can be modeled using exponential functions. Logarithmic functions are used in models for the loudness of sounds, the intensity of earthquakes, and many other phenomena. In this section we study exponential and logarithmic models.

Exponential Models of Population Growth

Biologists have observed that the population of a species doubles its size in a fixed period of time. For example, under ideal conditions a certain population of bacteria doubles in size every 3 hours. If the culture is started with 1000 bacteria, then after 3 hours there will be 2000 bacteria, after another 3 hours there will be 4000, and so on. If we let $n = n(t)$ be the number of bacteria after t hours, then

$$n(0) = 1000$$

$$n(3) = 1000 \cdot 2$$

$$n(6) = (1000 \cdot 2) \cdot 2 = 1000 \cdot 2^2$$

$$n(9) = (1000 \cdot 2^2) \cdot 2 = 1000 \cdot 2^3$$

$$n(12) = (1000 \cdot 2^3) \cdot 2 = 1000 \cdot 2^4$$

From this pattern it appears that the number of bacteria after t hours is modeled by the function

$$n(t) = 1000 \cdot 2^{t/3}$$

In general, suppose that the initial size of a population is n_0 and the doubling period is a. Then the size of the population at time t is modeled by

$$n(t) = n_0 2^{ct}$$

where $c = 1/a$. If we knew the tripling time b, then the formula would be $n(t) = n_0 3^{ct}$ where $c = 1/b$. These formulas indicate that the growth of the bacteria is modeled by an exponential function. But what base should we use? The answer is e, because then it can be shown (using calculus) that the population is modeled by

$$n(t) = n_0 e^{rt}$$

where r is the *relative rate of growth of population, expressed as a proportion of the population at any time*. For instance, if $r = 0.02$, then at any time t the growth rate is 2% of the population at time t.

Notice that the formula for population growth is the same as that for continuously compounded interest. In fact, the same principle is at work in both cases: The growth of a population (or an investment) per time period is proportional to the size of the population (or the amount of the investment). A population of 1,000,000 will increase more in one year than a population of 1000; in exactly the same way, an investment of $1,000,000 will increase more in one year than an investment of $1000.

In the following examples we assume that the populations grow exponentially.

Example 1 Predicting the Size of a Population

The initial bacterium count in a culture is 500. A biologist later makes a sample count of bacteria in the culture and finds that the relative rate of growth is 40% per hour.

(a) Find a function that models the number of bacteria after t hours.

(b) What is the estimated count after 10 hours?

(c) Sketch the graph of the function $n(t)$.

Exponential Growth Model

A population that experiences **exponential growth** increases according to the model

$$n(t) = n_0 e^{rt}$$

where
$n(t) =$ population at time t

$n_0 =$ initial size of the population

$r =$ relative rate of growth (expressed as a proportion of the population)

$t =$ time

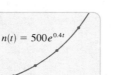

Figure 1

Solution

(a) We use the exponential growth model with $n_0 = 500$ and $r = 0.4$ to get

$$n(t) = 500e^{0.4t}$$

where t is measured in hours.

(b) Using the function in part (a), we find that the bacterium count after 10 hours is

$$n(10) = 500e^{0.4(10)} = 500e^4 \approx 27,300$$

(c) The graph is shown in Figure 1. ∎

Example 2 Comparing Different Rates of Population Growth

In 2000 the population of the world was 6.1 billion and the relative rate of growth was 1.4% per year. It is claimed that a rate of 1.0% per year would make a significant difference in the total population in just a few decades. Test this claim by estimating the population of the world in the year 2050 using a relative rate of growth of (a) 1.4% per year and (b) 1.0% per year.

Graph the population functions for the next 100 years for the two relative growth rates in the same viewing rectangle.

Solution

(a) By the exponential growth model, we have

$$n(t) = 6.1e^{0.014t}$$

where $n(t)$ is measured in billions and t is measured in years since 2000. Because the year 2050 is 50 years after 2000, we find

$$n(50) = 6.1e^{0.014(50)} = 6.1e^{0.7} \approx 12.3$$

The estimated population in the year 2050 is about 12.3 billion.

(b) We use the function

$$n(t) = 6.1e^{0.010t}$$

and find $\quad n(50) = 6.1e^{0.010(50)} = 6.1e^{0.50} \approx 10.1$

The estimated population in the year 2050 is about 10.1 billion.

The graphs in Figure 2 show that a small change in the relative rate of growth will, over time, make a large difference in population size. ∎

30

$n(t) = 6.1e^{0.014t}$

$n(t) = 6.1e^{0.01t}$

0   100

Figure 2

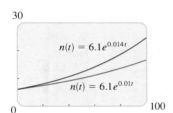

Example 3   **Finding the Initial Population**

A certain breed of rabbit was introduced onto a small island about 8 years ago. The current rabbit population on the island is estimated to be 4100, with a relative growth rate of 55% per year.

(a) What was the initial size of the rabbit population?

(b) Estimate the population 12 years from now.

Solution

(a) From the exponential growth model, we have

$$n(t) = n_0 e^{0.55t}$$

and we know that the population at time $t = 8$ is $n(8) = 4100$. We substitute what we know into the equation and solve for n_0:

$$4100 = n_0 e^{0.55(8)}$$

$$n_0 = \frac{4100}{e^{0.55(8)}} \approx \frac{4100}{81.45} \approx 50$$

Thus, we estimate that 50 rabbits were introduced onto the island.

(b) Now that we know n_0, we can write a formula for population growth:

$$n(t) = 50e^{0.55t}$$

Twelve years from now, $t = 20$ and

$$n(20) = 50e^{0.55(20)} \approx 2{,}993{,}707$$

Another way to solve part (b) is to let t be the number of years from now. In this case, $n_0 = 4100$ (the current population), and the population 12 years from now will be

$$n(12) = 4100e^{0.55(12)} \approx 3 \text{ million}$$

We estimate that the rabbit population on the island 12 years from now will be about 3 million. ∎

Can the rabbit population in Example 3(b) actually reach such a high number? In reality, as the island becomes overpopulated with rabbits, the rabbit population growth will be slowed due to food shortage and other factors. One model that takes into account such factors is the *logistic growth model* described in the *Focus on Modeling*, page 392.

Example 4 World Population Projections

The population of the world in 2000 was 6.1 billion, and the estimated relative growth rate was 1.4% per year. If the population continues to grow at this rate, when will it reach 122 billion?

Solution   We use the population growth function with $n_0 = 6.1$ billion, $r = 0.014$, and $n(t) = 122$ billion. This leads to an exponential equation, which we solve for t.

$$6.1e^{0.014t} = 122 \qquad \text{\small $n_0 e^{rt} = n(t)$}$$

$$e^{0.014t} = 20 \qquad \text{\small Divide by 6.1}$$

$$\ln e^{0.014t} = \ln 20 \qquad \text{\small Take ln of each side}$$

$$0.014t = \ln 20 \qquad \text{\small Property of ln}$$

$$t = \frac{\ln 20}{0.014} \qquad \text{\small Divide by 0.014}$$

$$t \approx 213.98 \qquad \text{\small Calculator}$$

Thus, the population will reach 122 billion in approximately 214 years, that is, in the year $2000 + 214 = 2214$. ∎

Standing Room Only

The population of the world was about 6.1 billion in 2000, and was increasing at 1.4% per year. Assuming that each person occupies an average of 4 ft^2 of the surface of the earth, the exponential model for population growth projects that by the year 2801 there will be standing room only! (The total land surface area of the world is about 1.8×10^{15} ft^2.)

Example 5 The Number of Bacteria in a Culture

A culture starts with 10,000 bacteria, and the number doubles every 40 min.

(a) Find a function that models the number of bacteria at time t.

(b) Find the number of bacteria after one hour.

(c) After how many minutes will there be 50,000 bacteria?

 (d) Sketch a graph of the number of bacteria at time t.

Solution

(a) To find the function that models this population growth, we need to find the rate r. To do this, we use the formula for population growth with $n_0 = 10,000$, $t = 40$, and $n(t) = 20,000$, and then solve for r.

$$10,000e^{r(40)} = 20,000 \qquad \text{\small $n_0 e^{rt} = n(t)$}$$

$$e^{40r} = 2 \qquad \text{\small Divide by 10,000}$$

$$\ln e^{40r} = \ln 2 \qquad \text{\small Take ln of each side}$$

$$40r = \ln 2 \qquad \text{Property of ln}$$

$$r = \frac{\ln 2}{40} \qquad \text{Divide by 40}$$

$$r \approx 0.01733 \qquad \text{Calculator}$$

Now that we know $r \approx 0.01733$, we can write the function for the population growth:

$$n(t) = 10,000e^{0.01733t}$$

(b) Using the function we found in part (a) with $t = 60$ min (one hour), we get

$$n(60) = 10,000e^{0.01733(60)} \approx 28,287$$

Thus, the number of bacteria after one hour is approximately 28,000.

(c) We use the function we found in part (a) with $n(t) = 50,000$ and solve the resulting exponential equation for t.

$$10,000e^{0.01733t} = 50,000 \qquad n_0 e^{rt} = n(t)$$

$$e^{0.01733t} = 5 \qquad \text{Divide by 10,000}$$

$$\ln e^{0.01733t} = \ln 5 \qquad \text{Take ln of each side}$$

$$0.01733t = \ln 5 \qquad \text{Property of ln}$$

$$t = \frac{\ln 5}{0.01733} \qquad \text{Divide by 0.01733}$$

$$t \approx 92.9 \qquad \text{Calculator}$$

The bacterium count will reach 50,000 in approximately 93 min.

(d) The graph of the function $n(t) = 10,000e^{0.01733t}$ is shown in Figure 3. ∎

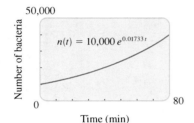

Figure 3

Element	Half-life
Thorium-232	14.5 billion years
Uranium-235	4.5 billion years
Thorium-230	80,000 years
Plutonium-239	24,360 years
Carbon-14	5,730 years
Radium-226	1,600 years
Cesium-137	30 years
Strontium-90	28 years
Polonium-210	140 days
Thorium-234	25 days
Iodine-135	8 days
Radon-222	3.8 days
Lead-211	3.6 minutes
Krypton-91	10 seconds

The half-lives of **radioactive elements** vary from very long to very short. Here are some examples.

Radioactive Decay

Radioactive substances decay by spontaneously emitting radiation. The rate of decay is directly proportional to the mass of the substance. This is analogous to population growth, except that the mass of radioactive material *decreases*. It can be shown that the mass $m(t)$ remaining at time t is modeled by the function

$$m(t) = m_0 e^{-rt}$$

where r is the rate of decay expressed as a proportion of the mass and m_0 is the initial mass. Physicists express the rate of decay in terms of **half-life**, the time required for half the mass to decay. We can obtain the rate r from this as follows. If h is the half-life, then a mass of 1 unit becomes $\frac{1}{2}$ unit when $t = h$. Substituting this into the model, we get

$$\tfrac{1}{2} = 1 \cdot e^{-rh} \qquad m(t) = m_0 e^{-rt}$$

Radioactive Waste

Harmful radioactive isotopes are produced whenever a nuclear reaction occurs, whether as the result of an atomic bomb test, a nuclear accident such as the one at Chernobyl in 1986, or the uneventful production of electricity at a nuclear power plant.

One radioactive material produced in atomic bombs is the isotope strontium-90 (^{90}Sr), with a half-life of 28 years. This is deposited like calcium in human bone tissue, where it can cause leukemia and other cancers. However, in the decades since atmospheric testing of nuclear weapons was halted, ^{90}Sr levels in the environment have fallen to a level that no longer poses a threat to health.

Nuclear power plants produce radioactive plutonium-239 (^{239}Pu), which has a half-life of 24,360 years. Because of its long half-life, ^{239}Pu could pose a threat to the environment for thousands of years. So, great care must be taken to dispose of it properly. The difficulty of ensuring the safety of the disposed radioactive waste is one reason that nuclear power plants remain controversial.

Joel W. Rogers/Corbis

$$\ln\left(\tfrac{1}{2}\right) = -rh \qquad \text{Take ln of each side}$$

$$r = -\frac{1}{h}\ln(2^{-1}) \qquad \text{Solve for } r$$

$$r = \frac{\ln 2}{h} \qquad \ln 2^{-1} = -\ln 2 \text{ by Law 3}$$

This last equation allows us to find the rate r from the half-life h.

Radioactive Decay Model

If m_0 is the initial mass of a radioactive substance with half-life h, then the mass remaining at time t is modeled by the function

$$m(t) = m_0 e^{-rt}$$

where $r = \dfrac{\ln 2}{h}$.

Example 6 Radioactive Decay

Polonium-210 (^{210}Po) has a half-life of 140 days. Suppose a sample of this substance has a mass of 300 mg.

(a) Find a function that models the amount of the sample remaining at time t.

(b) Find the mass remaining after one year.

(c) How long will it take for the sample to decay to a mass of 200 mg?

(d) Draw a graph of the sample mass as a function of time.

Solution

(a) Using the model for radioactive decay with $m_0 = 300$ and $r = (\ln 2/140) \approx 0.00495$, we have

$$m(t) = 300e^{-0.00495t}$$

(b) We use the function we found in part (a) with $t = 365$ (one year).

$$m(365) = 300e^{-0.00495(365)} \approx 49.256$$

Thus, approximately 49 mg of ^{210}Po remains after one year.

(c) We use the function we found in part (a) with $m(t) = 200$ and solve the resulting exponential equation for t.

$$300e^{-0.00495t} = 200 \qquad m(t) = m_0 e^{-rt}$$

$$e^{-0.00495t} = \tfrac{2}{3} \qquad \text{Divided by 300}$$

$$\ln e^{-0.00495t} = \ln \tfrac{2}{3} \qquad \text{Take ln of each side}$$

$$-0.00495t = \ln \tfrac{2}{3} \qquad \text{Property of ln}$$

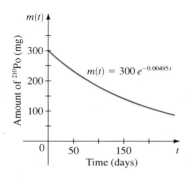

Figure 4

$$t = -\frac{\ln \frac{2}{3}}{0.00495} \qquad \text{Divide by } -0.00495$$

$$t \approx 81.9 \qquad \text{Calculator}$$

The time required for the sample to decay to 200 mg is about 82 days.

(d) A graph of the function $m(t) = 300e^{-0.00495t}$ is shown in Figure 4. ∎

Newton's Law of Cooling

Newton's Law of Cooling states that the rate of cooling of an object is proportional to the temperature difference between the object and its surroundings, provided that the temperature difference is not too large. Using calculus, the following model can be deduced from this law.

Newton's Law of Cooling

If D_0 is the initial temperature difference between an object and its surroundings, and if its surroundings have temperature T_s, then the temperature of the object at time t is modeled by the function

$$T(t) = T_s + D_0 e^{-kt}$$

where k is a positive constant that depends on the type of object.

Example 7   Newton's Law of Cooling

A cup of coffee has a temperature of 200 °F and is placed in a room that has a temperature of 70 °F. After 10 min the temperature of the coffee is 150 °F.

(a) Find a function that models the temperature of the coffee at time t.

(b) Find the temperature of the coffee after 15 min.

(c) When will the coffee have cooled to 100 °F?

(d) Illustrate by drawing a graph of the temperature function.

Solution

(a) The temperature of the room is $T_s = 70\,°F$, and the initial temperature difference is

$$D_0 = 200 - 70 = 130\,°F$$

So, by Newton's Law of Cooling, the temperature after t minutes is modeled by the function

$$T(t) = 70 + 130e^{-kt}$$

We need to find the constant k associated with this cup of coffee. To do this, we use the fact that when $t = 10$, the temperature is $T(10) = 150$.

So we have

$$70 + 130e^{-10k} = 150 \qquad \text{\small $T_s + D_0 e^{-kt} = T(t)$}$$

$$130e^{-10k} = 80 \qquad \text{\small Subtract 70}$$

$$e^{-10k} = \tfrac{8}{13} \qquad \text{\small Divide by 130}$$

$$-10k = \ln \tfrac{8}{13} \qquad \text{\small Take ln of each side}$$

$$k = -\tfrac{1}{10} \ln \tfrac{8}{13} \qquad \text{\small Divide by -10}$$

$$k \approx 0.04855 \qquad \text{\small Caculator}$$

Substituting this value of k into the expression for $T(t)$, we get

$$T(t) = 70 + 130e^{-0.04855t}$$

(b) We use the function we found in part (a) with $t = 15$.

$$T(15) = 70 + 130e^{-0.04855(15)} \approx 133\,°\mathrm{F}$$

(c) We use the function we found in part (a) with $T(t) = 100$ and solve the resulting exponential equation for t.

$$70 + 130e^{-0.04855t} = 100 \qquad \text{\small $T_s + D_0 e^{-kt} = T(t)$}$$

$$130e^{-0.04855t} = 30 \qquad \text{\small Subtract 70}$$

$$e^{-0.04855t} = \tfrac{3}{13} \qquad \text{\small Divide by 130}$$

$$-0.04855t = \ln \tfrac{3}{13} \qquad \text{\small Take ln of each side}$$

$$t = \frac{\ln \tfrac{3}{13}}{-0.04855} \qquad \text{\small Divide by -0.04855}$$

$$t \approx 30.2 \qquad \text{\small Calculator}$$

The coffee will have cooled to 100°F after about half an hour.

(d) The graph of the temperature function is sketched in Figure 5. Notice that the line $t = 70$ is a horizontal asymptote. (Why?) ∎

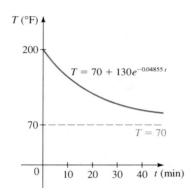

Figure 5

Temperature of coffee after t minutes

Logarithmic Scales

When a physical quantity varies over a very large range, it is often convenient to take its logarithm in order to have a more manageable set of numbers. We discuss three such situations: the pH scale, which measures acidity; the Richter scale, which measures the intensity of earthquakes; and the decibel scale, which measures the loudness of sounds. Other quantities that are measured on logarithmic scales are light intensity, information capacity, and radiation.

THE pH SCALE   Chemists measured the acidity of a solution by giving its hydrogen ion concentration until Sorensen, in 1909, proposed a more convenient measure. He defined

$$\mathrm{pH} = -\log[\mathrm{H}^+]$$

pH for Some Common Substances

Substance	pH
Milk of Magnesia	10.5
Seawater	8.0–8.4
Human blood	7.3–7.5
Crackers	7.0–8.5
Hominy (lye)	6.9–7.9
Cow's milk	6.4–6.8
Spinach	5.1–5.7
Tomatoes	4.1–4.4
Oranges	3.0–4.0
Apples	2.9–3.3
Limes	1.3–2.0
Battery acid	1.0

where $[H^+]$ is the concentration of hydrogen ions measured in moles per liter (M). He did this to avoid very small numbers and negative exponents. For instance,

$$\text{if} \quad [H^+] = 10^{-4}\,M, \quad \text{then} \quad pH = -\log_{10}(10^{-4}) = -(-4) = 4$$

Solutions with a pH of 7 are defined as *neutral*, those with pH < 7 are *acidic*, and those with pH > 7 are *basic*. Notice that when the pH increases by one unit, $[H^+]$ decreases by a factor of 10.

Example 8   pH Scale and Hydrogen Ion Concentration

(a) The hydrogen ion concentration of a sample of human blood was measured to be $[H^+] = 3.16 \times 10^{-8}$ M. Find the pH and classify the blood as acidic or basic.

(b) The most acidic rainfall ever measured occurred in Scotland in 1974; its pH was 2.4. Find the hydrogen ion concentration.

Solution

(a) A calculator gives

$$pH = -\log[H^+] = -\log(3.16 \times 10^{-8}) \approx 7.5$$

Since this is greater than 7, the blood is basic.

(b) To find the hydrogen ion concentration, we need to solve for $[H^+]$ in the logarithmic equation

$$\log[H^+] = -pH$$

So, we write it in exponential form.

$$[H^+] = 10^{-pH}$$

In this case, pH = 2.4, so

$$[H^+] = 10^{-2.4} \approx 4.0 \times 10^{-3}\,M \qquad \blacksquare$$

THE RICHTER SCALE   In 1935 the American geologist Charles Richter (1900–1984) defined the magnitude M of an earthquake to be

$$M = \log \frac{I}{S}$$

where I is the intensity of the earthquake (measured by the amplitude of a seismograph reading taken 100 km from the epicenter of the earthquake) and S is the intensity of a "standard" earthquake (whose amplitude is 1 micron $= 10^{-4}$ cm). The magnitude of a standard earthquake is

$$M = \log \frac{S}{S} = \log 1 = 0$$

Richter studied many earthquakes that occurred between 1900 and 1950. The largest had magnitude 8.9 on the Richter scale, and the smallest had magnitude 0. This corresponds to a ratio of intensities of 800,000,000, so the Richter scale provides more

Largest Earthquakes		
Location	Date	Magnitude
Chile	1960	9.5
Alaska	1964	9.2
Alaska	1957	9.1
Kamchatka	1952	9.0
Sumatra	2004	9.0
Ecuador	1906	8.8
Alaska	1965	8.7
Tibet	1950	8.6
Kamchatka	1923	8.5
Indonesia	1938	8.5
Kuril Islands	1963	8.5

manageable numbers to work with. For instance, an earthquake of magnitude 6 is ten times stronger than an earthquake of magnitude 5.

Example 9 Magnitude of Earthquakes

The 1906 earthquake in San Francisco had an estimated magnitude of 8.3 on the Richter scale. In the same year a powerful earthquake occurred on the Colombia-Ecuador border and was four times as intense. What was the magnitude of the Colombia-Ecuador earthquake on the Richter scale?

Solution If I is the intensity of the San Francisco earthquake, then from the definition of magnitude we have

$$M = \log \frac{I}{S} = 8.3$$

The intensity of the Colombia-Ecuador earthquake was $4I$, so its magnitude was

$$M = \log \frac{4I}{S} = \log 4 + \log \frac{I}{S} = \log 4 + 8.3 \approx 8.9 \qquad \blacksquare$$

Example 10 Intensity of Earthquakes

The 1989 Loma Prieta earthquake that shook San Francisco had a magnitude of 7.1 on the Richter scale. How many times more intense was the 1906 earthquake (see Example 9) than the 1989 event?

Solution If I_1 and I_2 are the intensities of the 1906 and 1989 earthquakes, then we are required to find I_1/I_2. To relate this to the definition of magnitude, we divide numerator and denominator by S.

$$\log \frac{I_1}{I_2} = \log \frac{I_1/S}{I_2/S} \qquad \text{Divide numerator and denominator by } S$$

$$= \log \frac{I_1}{S} - \log \frac{I_2}{S} \qquad \text{Law 2 of logarithms}$$

$$= 8.3 - 7.1 = 1.2 \qquad \text{Definition of earthquake magnitude}$$

Therefore

$$\frac{I_1}{I_2} = 10^{\log(I_1/I_2)} = 10^{1.2} \approx 16$$

The 1906 earthquake was about 16 times as intense as the 1989 earthquake. $\qquad \blacksquare$

THE DECIBEL SCALE The ear is sensitive to an extremely wide range of sound intensities. We take as a reference intensity $I_0 = 10^{-12}$ W/m^2 (watts per square meter) at a frequency of 1000 hertz, which measures a sound that is just barely audible (the threshold of hearing). The psychological sensation of loudness varies with the logarithm of the intensity (the Weber-Fechner Law) and so the **intensity level** B, measured in decibels (dB), is defined as

$$B = 10 \log \frac{I}{I_0}$$

Roger Ressmeyer/Corbis

The intensity level of the barely audible reference sound is

$$B = 10 \log \frac{I_0}{I_0} = 10 \log 1 = 0 \text{ dB}$$

The **intensity levels of sounds** that we can hear vary from very loud to very soft. Here are some examples of the decibel levels of commonly heard sounds.

Source of sound	B (dB)
Jet takeoff	140
Jackhammer	130
Rock concert	120
Subway	100
Heavy traffic	80
Ordinary traffic	70
Normal conversation	50
Whisper	30
Rustling leaves	10–20
Threshold of hearing	0

Example 11 Sound Intensity of a Jet Takeoff

Find the decibel intensity level of a jet engine during takeoff if the intensity was measured at 100 W/m^2.

Solution From the definition of intensity level we see that

$$B = 10 \log \frac{I}{I_0} = 10 \log \frac{10^2}{10^{-12}} = 10 \log 10^{14} = 140 \text{ dB}$$

Thus, the intensity level is 140 dB. ■

The table in the margin lists decibel intensity levels for some common sounds ranging from the threshold of human hearing to the jet takeoff of Example 11. The threshold of pain is about 120 dB.

D.2 Exercises

1–13 ■ These exercises use the population growth model.

1. **Bacteria Culture** The number of bacteria in a culture is modeled by the function

   $$n(t) = 500e^{0.45t}$$

   where t is measured in hours.
   (a) What is the initial number of bacteria?
   (b) What is the relative rate of growth of this bacterium population? Express your answer as a percentage.
   (c) How many bacteria are in the culture after 3 hours?
   (d) After how many hours will the number of bacteria reach 10,000?

2. **Fish Population** The number of a certain species of fish is modeled by the function

   $$n(t) = 12e^{0.012t}$$

   where t is measured in years and $n(t)$ is measured in millions.
   (a) What is the relative rate of growth of the fish population? Express your answer as a percentage.
   (b) What will the fish population be after 5 years?
   (c) After how many years will the number of fish reach 30 million?
   (d) Sketch a graph of the fish population function $n(t)$.

3. **Fox Population** The fox population in a certain region has a relative growth rate of 8% per year. It is estimated that the population in 2000 was 18,000.
   (a) Find a function that models the population t years after 2000.

   (b) Use the function from part (a) to estimate the fox population in the year 2008.
   (c) Sketch a graph of the fox population function for the years 2000–2008.

4. **Population of a Country** The population of a country has a relative growth rate of 3% per year. The government is trying to reduce the growth rate to 2%. The population in 1995 was approximately 110 million. Find the projected population for the year 2020 for the following conditions.
   (a) The relative growth rate remains at 3% per year.
   (b) The relative growth rate is reduced to 2% per year.

5. **Population of a City** The population of a certain city was 112,000 in 1998, and the observed relative growth rate is 4% per year.
   (a) Find a function that models the population after t years.
   (b) Find the projected population in the year 2004.
   (c) In what year will the population reach 200,000?

6. Frog Population   The frog population in a small pond grows exponentially. The current population is 85 frogs, and the relative growth rate is 18% per year.

   (a) Find a function that models the population after t years.

   (b) Find the projected population after 3 years.

   (c) Find the number of years required for the frog population to reach 600.

7. Deer Population   The graph shows the deer population in a Pennsylvania county between 1996 and 2000. Assume that the population grows exponentially.

   (a) What was the deer population in 1996?

   (b) Find a function that models the deer population t years after 1996.

   (c) What is the projected deer population in 2004?

   (d) In what year will the deer population reach 100,000?

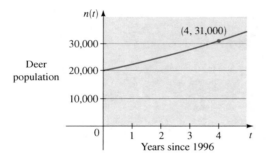

8. Bacteria Culture   A culture contains 1500 bacteria initially and doubles every 30 min.

   (a) Find a function that models the number of bacteria $n(t)$ after t minutes.

   (b) Find the number of bacteria after 2 hours.

   (c) After how many minutes will the culture contain 4000 bacteria?

9. Bacteria Culture   A culture starts with 8600 bacteria. After one hour the count is 10,000.

   (a) Find a function that models the number of bacteria $n(t)$ after t hours.

   (b) Find the number of bacteria after 2 hours.

   (c) After how many hours will the number of bacteria double?

10. Bacteria Culture   The count in a culture of bacteria was 400 after 2 hours and 25,600 after 6 hours.

   (a) What is the relative rate of growth of the bacteria population? Express your answer as a percentage.

   (b) What was the initial size of the culture?

   (c) Find a function that models the number of bacteria $n(t)$ after t hours.

   (d) Find the number of bacteria after 4.5 hours.

   (e) When will the number of bacteria be 50,000?

11. World Population   The population of the world was 5.7 billion in 1995 and the observed relative growth rate was 2% per year.

   (a) By what year will the population have doubled?

   (b) By what year will the population have tripled?

12. Population of California   The population of California was 10,586,223 in 1950 and 23,668,562 in 1980. Assume the population grows exponentially.

   (a) Find a function that models the population t years after 1950.

   (b) Find the time required for the population to double.

   (c) Use the function from part (a) to predict the population of California in the year 2000. Look up California's actual population in 2000, and compare.

13. Infectious Bacteria   An infectious strain of bacteria increases in number at a relative growth rate of 200% per hour. When a certain critical number of bacteria are present in the bloodstream, a person becomes ill. If a single bacterium infects a person, the critical level is reached in 24 hours. How long will it take for the critical level to be reached if the same person is infected with 10 bacteria?

14–22 ■ These exercises use the radioactive decay model.

14. Radioactive Radium   The half-life of radium-226 is 1600 years. Suppose we have a 22-mg sample.

   (a) Find a function that models the mass remaining after t years.

   (b) How much of the sample will remain after 4000 years?

   (c) After how long will only 18 mg of the sample remain?

15. Radioactive Cesium   The half-life of cesium-137 is 30 years. Suppose we have a 10-g sample.

   (a) Find a function that models the mass remaining after t years.

   (b) How much of the sample will remain after 80 years?

   (c) After how long will only 2 g of the sample remain?

16. Radioactive Thorium   The mass $m(t)$ remaining after t days from a 40-g sample of thorium-234 is given by

$$m(t) = 40e^{-0.0277t}$$

   (a) How much of the sample will remain after 60 days?

   (b) After how long will only 10 g of the sample remain?

   (c) Find the half-life of thorium-234.

17. Radioactive Strontium   The half-life of strontium-90 is 28 years. How long will it take a 50-mg sample to decay to a mass of 32 mg?

18. **Radioactive Radium** Radium-221 has a half-life of 30 s. How long will it take for 95% of a sample to decay?

19. **Finding Half-life** If 250 mg of a radioactive element decays to 200 mg in 48 hours, find the half-life of the element.

20. **Radioactive Radon** After 3 days a sample of radon-222 has decayed to 58% of its original amount.

    (a) What is the half-life of radon-222?

    (b) How long will it take the sample to decay to 20% of its original amount?

21. **Carbon-14 Dating** A wooden artifact from an ancient tomb contains 65% of the carbon-14 that is present in living trees. How long ago was the artifact made? (The half-life of carbon-14 is 5730 years.)

22. **Carbon-14 Dating** The burial cloth of an Egyptian mummy is estimated to contain 59% of the carbon-14 it contained originally. How long ago was the mummy buried? (The half-life of carbon-14 is 5730 years.)

23–26 ■ These exercises use Newton's Law of Cooling.

23. **Cooling Soup** A hot bowl of soup is served at a dinner party. It starts to cool according to Newton's Law of Cooling so that its temperature at time t is given by

    $$T(t) = 65 + 145e^{-0.05t}$$

    where t is measured in minutes and T is measured in °F.

    (a) What is the initial temperature of the soup?

    (b) What is the temperature after 10 min?

    (c) After how long will the temperature be 100°F?

24. **Time of Death** Newton's Law of Cooling is used in homicide investigations to determine the time of death. The normal body temperature is 98.6°F. Immediately following death, the body begins to cool. It has been determined experimentally that the constant in Newton's Law of Cooling is approximately $k = 0.1947$, assuming time is measured in hours. Suppose that the temperature of the surroundings is 60°F.

    (a) Find a function $T(t)$ that models the temperature t hours after death.

    (b) If the temperature of the body is now 72°F, how long ago was the time of death?

25. **Cooling Turkey** A roasted turkey is taken from an oven when its temperature has reached 185°F and is placed on a table in a room where the temperature is 75°F.

    (a) If the temperature of the turkey is 150°F after half an hour, what is its temperature after 45 min?

    (b) When will the turkey cool to 100°F?

26. **Boiling Water** A kettle full of water is brought to a boil in a room with temperature 20°C. After 15 min the temperature of the water has decreased from 100°C to 75°C. Find the temperature after another 10 min. Illustrate by graphing the temperature function.

27–41 ■ These exercises deal with logarithmic scales.

27. **Finding pH** The hydrogen ion concentration of a sample of each substance is given. Calculate the pH of the substance.

    (a) Lemon juice: $[H^+] = 5.0 \times 10^{-3}$ M

    (b) Tomato juice: $[H^+] = 3.2 \times 10^{-4}$ M

    (c) Seawater: $[H^+] = 5.0 \times 10^{-9}$ M

28. **Finding pH** An unknown substance has a hydrogen ion concentration of $[H^+] = 3.1 \times 10^{-8}$ M. Find the pH and classify the substance as acidic or basic.

29. **Ion Concentration** The pH reading of a sample of each substance is given. Calculate the hydrogen ion concentration of the substance.

    (a) Vinegar: pH = 3.0

    (b) Milk: pH = 6.5

30. **Ion Concentration** The pH reading of a glass of liquid is given. Find the hydrogen ion concentration of the liquid.

    (a) Beer: pH = 4.6

    (b) Water: pH = 7.3

31. **Finding pH** The hydrogen ion concentrations in cheeses range from 4.0×10^{-7} M to 1.6×10^{-5} M. Find the corresponding range of pH readings.

32. **Ion Concentration in Wine** The pH readings for wines vary from 2.8 to 3.8. Find the corresponding range of hydrogen ion concentrations.

33. **Earthquake Magnitudes** If one earthquake is 20 times as intense as another, how much larger is its magnitude on the Richter scale?

34. **Earthquake Magnitudes** The 1906 earthquake in San Francisco had a magnitude of 8.3 on the Richter scale. At the same time in Japan an earthquake with magnitude 4.9

caused only minor damage. How many times more intense was the San Francisco earthquake than the Japanese earthquake?

35. **Earthquake Magnitudes** The Alaska earthquake of 1964 had a magnitude of 8.6 on the Richter scale. How many times more intense was this than the 1906 San Francisco earthquake? (See Exercise 34.)

36. **Earthquake Magnitudes** The Northridge, California, earthquake of 1994 had a magnitude of 6.8 on the Richter scale. A year later, a 7.2-magnitude earthquake struck Kobe, Japan. How many times more intense was the Kobe earthquake than the Northridge earthquake?

37. **Earthquake Magnitudes** The 1985 Mexico City earthquake had a magnitude of 8.1 on the Richter scale. The 1976 earthquake in Tangshan, China, was 1.26 times as intense. What was the magnitude of the Tangshan earthquake?

38. **Traffic Noise** The intensity of the sound of traffic at a busy intersection was measured at 2.0×10^{-5} W/m^2. Find the intensity level in decibels.

39. **Subway Noise** The intensity of the sound of a subway train was measured at 98 dB. Find the intensity in W/m^2.

40. **Comparing Decibel Levels** The noise from a power mower was measured at 106 dB. The noise level at a rock concert was measured at 120 dB. Find the ratio of the intensity of the rock music to that of the power mower.

41. **Inverse Square Law for Sound** A law of physics states that the intensity of sound is inversely proportional to the square of the distance d from the source: $I = k/d^2$.

(a) Use this model and the equation

$$B = 10 \log \frac{I}{I_0}$$

(described in this section) to show that the decibel levels B_1 and B_2 at distances d_1 and d_2 from a sound source are related by the equation

$$B_2 = B_1 + 20 \log \frac{d_1}{d_2}$$

(b) The intensity level at a rock concert is 120 dB at a distance 2 m from the speakers. Find the intensity level at a distance of 10 m.

Section D.2 Answers ■

1. (a) 500 (b) 45% (c) 1929 (d) 6.66 h
3. (a) $n(t) = 18{,}000e^{0.08t}$ (b) 34,137

(c)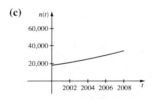

5. (a) $n(t) = 112{,}000e^{0.04t}$ (b) About 142,000
(c) 2008 7. (a) 20,000 (b) $n(t) = 20{,}000e^{0.1096t}$
(c) About 48,000 (d) 2010 9. (a) $n(t) = 8600e^{0.1508t}$
(b) About 11,600 (c) 4.6 h 11. (a) 2029
(b) 2049 13. 22.85 h 15. (a) $n(t) = 10e^{-0.0231t}$
(b) 1.6 g (c) 70 yr 17. 18 yr 19. 149 h
21. 3560 yr 23. (a) 210°F (b) 153°F
(c) 28 min 25. (a) 137°F (b) 116 min 27. (a) 2.3
(b) 3.5 (c) 8.3 29. (a) 10^{-3} M (b) 3.2×10^{-7} M
31. $4.8 \leq \text{pH} \leq 6.4$ 33. $\log 20 \approx 1.3$
35. Twice as intense 37. 8.2 39. 6.3×10^{-3} W/m^2
41. (b) 106 dB

Appendix D.3

Absolute Value Problems to Prepare for Calculus

In calculus, absolute values are often awkward to work with. So we look for an alternative way to write an absolute value expression.

Consider the expression $|a|$. We call the expression inside the absolute value bars the "argument." Let's try a few choices for the values of the argument, a, to see what effect the absolute value has on the argument.

> If a is 5, then $|a| = |5| = 5 = a$
>
> If a is -9, then $|a| = |-9| = 9 = -a$

To summarize, if the argument, a, of an absolute value is positive, then $|a| = a$. If the argument is negative, then $|a| = -a$. The special case where a is zero is most easily treated by grouping it with the positive case, since $|a| = |0| = 0 = a$.

We now have a way to summarize the effect of the absolute value operation, without using the absolute value bars. Instead, we use piecewise function notation:

$$|a| = \begin{cases} a, & \text{if } a \geq 0 \\ -a, & \text{if } a < 0 \end{cases}$$

Example #1   Write $|3x - 12|$ in an equivalent form without absolute value bars.

> **Solution** We must consider separately the cases when the argument is positive and when the argument is negative. You can find the "cut" point between these two cases by determining when the argument is zero:
>
> $$argument = 3x - 12 = 0 \quad \rightarrow \quad x = 4 \text{ is the "cut" point}$$
>
> The cut point represents the value of x where the argument might change sign, so we use the cut point to divide the number line into intervals. We know that the argument is zero at the cut point, but now we need to find the sign of the argument on either side of the cut point. We use a representative value (called a "test value") from each interval, substitute it for x in the argument, and see whether the argument is positive or negative on that interval.

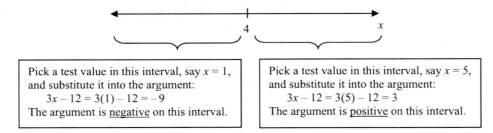

Pick a test value in this interval, say $x = 1$, and substitute it into the argument:
$3x - 12 = 3(1) - 12 = -9$
The argument is <u>negative</u> on this interval.

Pick a test value in this interval, say $x = 5$, and substitute it into the argument:
$3x - 12 = 3(5) - 12 = 3$
The argument is <u>positive</u> on this interval.

So, for values of x that are <u>less than</u> 4, the argument is negative. Therefore, the absolute value of $3x - 12$ is the same as taking the *opposite* of $3x - 12$, and we get:
$$|3x - 12| = -(3x - 12) = -3x + 12$$

For values of x that are <u>greater than</u> 4, the argument is positive. Therefore, the absolute value bars have no effect on the value of the argument:
$$|3x - 12| = 3x - 12$$

The simplest way to handle the case where x <u>equals</u> 4 is to observe that, at $x = 4$, the argument is zero, and the absolute value of zero is zero (i.e., the absolute value of zero is itself). Therefore, in this example, the case of $x = 4$ can be grouped with the interval $x > 4$, where the argument is positive. An alternative would be to group $x = 4$ with the interval $x < 4$.

We summarize these observations using piecewise function notation:

$$|3x - 12| = \begin{cases} -3x + 12 & \text{if } x < 4 \\ 3x - 12 & \text{if } x \geq 4 \end{cases} \quad \text{or} \quad |3x - 12| = \begin{cases} -3x + 12 & \text{if } x \leq 4 \\ 3x - 12 & \text{if } x > 4 \end{cases}$$

Example #2   Write $9x + |30 - 6x|$ in an equivalent form without absolute value bars.

Solution   Find the "cut" point by determining when the argument is zero:

$$argument = 30 - 6x = 0 \ \rightarrow \ x = 5 \text{ is the "cut" point}$$

Use a test value each interval, one on either side of the cut point:

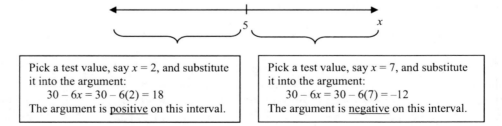

Pick a test value, say $x = 2$, and substitute it into the argument:	Pick a test value, say $x = 7$, and substitute it into the argument:
$30 - 6x = 30 - 6(2) = 18$	$30 - 6x = 30 - 6(7) = -12$
The argument is <u>positive</u> on this interval.	The argument is <u>negative</u> on this interval.

So, for values of x that are <u>less than</u> the cut point of 5, the argument will be positive, and the absolute value bars will have no effect on the argument:
$$9x + |30 - 6x| = 9x + (30 - 6x) = 9x + 30 - 6x = 3x + 30$$

When the argument is positive or zero, $|30 - 6x|$ is the same as $(30 - 6x)$.

For values of x that are <u>greater than</u> the cut point of 5, the argument will be negative, and the absolute value bars take the opposite of the argument:

$$9x + |30 - 6x| \;=\; 9x + (-30 + 6x) \;=\; 9x - 30 + 6x = 15x - 30$$

When the argument is negative, $|30 - 6x|$ is the same as the *opposite of* $(30 - 6x)$.

At the cut point of $x = 5$, the argument is zero. For convenience, we will group the case of $x = 5$ with the interval $x < 5$, where the argument is positive.

Summarize the results using piecewise function notation:

$$9x + |30 - 6x| = \begin{cases} 3x + 30 & \text{if } \; x \le 5 \\ 15x - 30 & \text{if } \; x > 5 \end{cases}$$

Let's try some numerical examples to check our work on the previous example. For the first interval ($x \le 5$), we can choose any value of x as long as it is less than 5...let's choose 4. Now, substitute 4 for x in the original absolute value expression:

$$9x + |30 - 6x| \;=\; 9(4) + |30 - 6(4)| \;=\; 36 + |6| = 36 + 6 = 42.$$

These are the same!

Now, substitute 4 for x in the expression we obtained as the simplified form:
$$3x + 30 = 3(4) + 30 = 12 + 30 = 42.$$

For the second interval ($x > 5$), we can choose any value of x as long as it is greater than 5...let's choose 10. Now, substitute 10 for x in the original absolute value expression:

$$9x + |30 - 6x| \;=\; 9(10) + |30 - 6(10)| \;=\; 90 + |-30| = 90 + 30 = 120.$$

These are the same!

Now, substitute 10 for x in the expression we obtained as the simplified form:
$$15x - 30 = 15(10) - 30 = 150 - 30 = 120.$$

So our work checks out.

Example #3 Write $|x - 8| + |2x + 10|$ in an equivalent form, without absolute value bars.

Solution Since there are two absolute values, we will have two cut points to consider. We find the cut points by setting each argument equal to zero:

$$argument = x - 8 = 0 \quad \rightarrow \quad x = 8 \text{ is one cut point}$$
$$argument = 2x + 10 = 0 \quad \rightarrow \quad x = -5 \text{ is the other cut point}$$

After placing the cut points on a number line, use a test value from each of the three resulting intervals. The test values must be substituted into each argument separately.

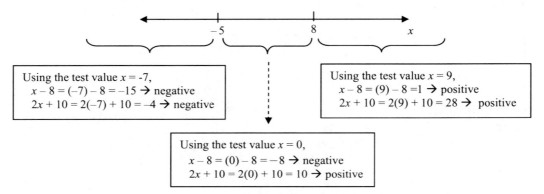

Using the test value $x = -7$,
$x - 8 = (-7) - 8 = -15 \rightarrow$ negative
$2x + 10 = 2(-7) + 10 = -4 \rightarrow$ negative

Using the test value $x = 9$,
$x - 8 = (9) - 8 = 1 \rightarrow$ positive
$2x + 10 = 2(9) + 10 = 28 \rightarrow$ positive

Using the test value $x = 0$,
$x - 8 = (0) - 8 = -8 \rightarrow$ negative
$2x + 10 = 2(0) + 10 = 10 \rightarrow$ positive

For the interval $x < -5$, both of the arguments are negative. Therefore,
$$|x - 8| + |2x + 10| = (-x + 8) + (-2x - 10) = -3x - 2$$

Since both arguments are negative, the absolute values take their opposites.

For the interval $-5 < x < 8$, the argument $x - 8$ is negative and the argument $2x + 10$ is positive. Therefore,
$$|x - 8| + |2x + 10| = (-x + 8) + (2x + 10) = x + 18$$

Since the first argument is negative, the absolute value takes its opposite.

The second argument is positive, so the absolute value has no effect.

For the interval $x > 8$, both arguments are positive. Therefore,
$$|x - 8| + |2x + 10| = (x - 8) + (2x + 10) = 3x + 2$$

Since both arguments are positive, the absolute values have no effect.

Finally, we must consider the cut points themselves. We have some flexibility on how to handle them, because we can group a cut point with either interval that uses that cut point as an endpoint. The reasoning behind this is that if the argument is zero (which is what happens at a cut point) and we remove the absolute value bars, then it doesn't make any difference whether we leave the argument unchanged or we take its opposite. In this example, therefore, we could group the cut point of $x = -5$ either with the interval $x < -5$ (making $x \leq -5$) or with $-5 < x < 8$ (making $-5 \leq x < 8$). Likewise, we could group the cut point of $x = 8$ either with the interval $-5 < x < 8$ or with $x > 8$. Just for convenience, this example will group both cut points with the middle interval to make $-5 \leq x \leq 8$.

We summarize the results using piecewise function notation:

$$|x - 8| + |2x + 10| = \begin{cases} -3x - 2 & if \ \ x < -5 \\ x + 18 & if \ -5 \leq x \leq 8 \\ 3x + 2 & if \ \ x > 8 \end{cases}$$

Example #4 Write $\dfrac{|6 - 2x|}{2x - 6}$ in an equivalent form, without absolute value bars.

Solution Find the cut point by setting the argument equal to zero:

$$argument = 6 - 2x = 0 \ \ \rightarrow \ \ x = 3 \ is \ the \ cut \ point$$

Use a test value from each interval on the number line to determine whether the argument is positive or negative on that interval:

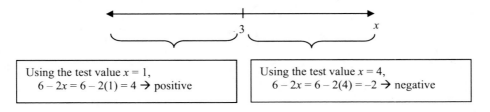

Using the test value $x = 1$,
$6 - 2x = 6 - 2(1) = 4 \rightarrow$ positive

Using the test value $x = 4$,
$6 - 2x = 6 - 2(4) = -2 \rightarrow$ negative

For the interval $x < 3$, the argument is positive. Therefore,
$$\frac{|6 - 2x|}{2x - 6} = \frac{6 - 2x}{2x - 6} = -1$$

For the interval $x > 3$, the argument is negative. Therefore,
$$\frac{|6 - 2x|}{2x - 6} = \frac{-(6 - 2x)}{2x - 6} = \frac{-6 + 2x}{2x - 6} = 1$$

At the cut point $x = 3$, the expression is indeterminate (since both the numerator and the denominator would be zero), so we exclude $x = 3$ as a possible value of x.

We summarize the results using piecewise function notation:

$$\frac{|6-2x|}{2x-6} = \begin{cases} -1 & \text{if } x < 3 \\ 1 & \text{if } x > 3 \end{cases}$$

Absolute Value Exercises

Find an equivalent way to write each expression, without absolute value bars. Many (but not all) answers will require piecewise notation.

1. $|x-1| - 2x, \ \ if \ \ x < 1$

2. $5x - |2x-3|, \ \ if \ \ x < \frac{3}{2}$

3. $|5x-2|$

4. $|x+1| - 3x + 1$

5. $4x - |2x-3|$

6. $|x+1| - |x-3|, \ \ if \ \ -1 < x < 3$

7. $|x-1| - |x+2|$

8. $|9-x| + |3x-5|$

9. $\dfrac{|2x-3|}{2x-3}$

10. $|1-\sqrt{2}| \ - \ \dfrac{5x+2}{|5x+2|}$

11. $|x^2 + 3x|$

Answers

1. $1 - 3x$

2. $7x - 3$

3. $\begin{cases} 5x - 2 & \text{if } x \geq \frac{2}{5} \\ 2 - 5x & \text{if } x < \frac{2}{5} \end{cases}$

4. $\begin{cases} 2 - 2x & \text{if } x \geq -1 \\ -4x & \text{if } x < -1 \end{cases}$

5. $\begin{cases} 2x + 3 & \text{if } x \geq \frac{3}{2} \\ 6x - 3 & \text{if } x < \frac{3}{2} \end{cases}$

6. $2x - 2$

7. $\begin{cases} 3 & \text{if } x < -2 \\ -2x - 1 & \text{if } -2 \leq x \leq 1 \\ -3 & \text{if } x > 1 \end{cases}$

8. $\begin{cases} -4x + 14 & \text{if } x < \frac{5}{3} \\ 2x + 4 & \text{if } \frac{5}{3} \leq x \leq 9 \\ 4x - 14 & \text{if } x > 9 \end{cases}$

9. $\begin{cases} 1 & \text{if } x > \frac{3}{2} \\ -1 & \text{if } x < \frac{3}{2} \\ \text{undefined} & \text{if } x = \frac{3}{2} \end{cases}$

10. $\begin{cases} \sqrt{2} - 2 & \text{if } x > \frac{-2}{5} \\ \sqrt{2} & \text{if } x < \frac{-2}{5} \\ \text{undefined} & \text{if } x = \frac{-2}{5} \end{cases}$

11. $\begin{cases} x^2 + 3x & \text{if } x \leq -3 \text{ or } x \geq 0 \\ -x^2 - 3x & \text{if } -3 < x < 0 \end{cases}$

Appendix D.4
Simplification Problems to Prepare for Calculus

In calculus, you will encounter some long expressions that will require strong factoring skills. This section is designed to help you develop those skills.

First, consider a simple simplifying problem. To simplify $4(x+2)+7(x+1)$, we distribute to remove the parentheses, then combine like terms:
$$4(x+2)+7(x+1) = 4x+8+7x+7 = 11x+15$$

To simplify $4(x+2)^2+7(x+1)$, we can still remove the parentheses and combine like terms:
$$4(x+2)^2+7(x+1) = 4(x^2+4x+4)+7x+7 = 4x^2+16x+16+7x+7 = 4x^2+23x+23$$

When simplifying $4(x+2)^3+7(x+1)^6$, removing the parentheses is cumbersome because of the large exponents. Similarly, when simplifying $4(x+2)^{-\frac{1}{2}}+7(x+1)^{\frac{1}{2}}$, removing the parentheses is impossible because of the fractional exponents. What do we do when removing parentheses is cumbersome or impossible? In these cases, we simplify by factoring.

Here is an example of what an expression from calculus might look like:
$$4(x+2)^3(x+1)^7+7(x+1)^6(x+2)^4$$

> This addition sign is the reason that this expression is NOT in factored form. We need to write the expression using ONLY multiplication, division, and powers of polynomials.

Simplifying an expression such as the one above by factoring requires that we find the greatest common factor (GCF). Before tackling this problem, we'll begin with two simpler examples.

Example #1 Factor $6x^7+15x^4$

> **Solution** The GCF for the two terms is $3x^4$ (remember to use the **lower** power of a variable when the variable appears in more than one term). We then write the GCF outside a set of grouping symbols (usually parentheses or brackets), and use the rules for exponents to determine what terms belong inside the grouping symbols.

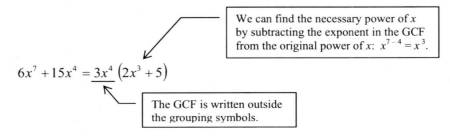

> We can find the necessary power of x by subtracting the exponent in the GCF from the original power of x: $x^{7-4}=x^3$.

$$6x^7+15x^4 = \underline{3x^4}\left(2x^3+5\right)$$

> The GCF is written outside the grouping symbols.

We can check our factoring by using the distributive property to be sure that we obtain the original expression.

Example #2 Factor $10x^4 y^5 - 15x^7 y^2$

Solution The GCF for the two terms is $5x^4 y^2$. We write the GCF outside a set of grouping symbols, and use the rules for exponents to determine what terms belong inside the grouping symbols.

Each of the new exponents is found by taking the exponent of the variable as found in the original expression, then subtracting the exponent used for that same variable in the GCF.

$$10x^4 y^5 - 15x^{10} y^2 = \underline{5x^4 y^2} \ (2x^{4-4} y^{5-2} - 3x^{10-4} y^{2-2}) = 5x^4 y^2 \ (2y^3 - 3x^6)$$

The GCF is written outside the grouping symbols.

Example #3 Simplify by factoring $4(x+2)^3 (x+1)^7 + 7(x+1)^6 (x+2)^4$

Solution Notice that $(x + 2)$ is a common base in this expression and that 3 is the *smaller* power to which this base appears. Also, $(x + 1)$ is a common base and 6 is the *smaller* power to which it appears. Therefore, the greatest common factor is $(x+2)^3 (x+1)^6$. The GCF can be factored out, as follows:

$4(x+2)^3 (x+1)^7 + 7(x+1)^6 (x+2)^4$
$$= \underline{(x+2)^3 (x+1)^6} \ [4(x+2)^{3-3} (x+1)^{7-6} + 7(x+1)^{6-6} (x+2)^{4-3}]$$

The GCF is placed outside the grouping symbols. Because the problem already had parentheses, this time the grouping symbols were written as brackets.

The remaining steps involve simplifying the polynomial inside the brackets:

$$= (x+2)^3 (x+1)^6 [\underline{4(x+1) + 7(x+2)}]$$

Simplifying the exponents.

$$= (x+2)^3 (x+1)^6 [\underline{4x+4+7x+14}]$$

Using the distributive property.

$$= (x+2)^3(x+1)^6\underline{(11x+18)}$$

Combining like terms.

The expression has now been simplified as much as possible, while retaining its factored form. Recall that factored form involves only multiplication, division, and powers of polynomials.

The next several examples involve negative exponents. There are two common ways to approach these simplifying problems. Each method will be described briefly, followed by two examples.

Method A: Use the usual rule of "lowest exponents" for the GCF, factor out the GCF, and simplify the expression inside the grouping symbols. As the last step, rewrite any expressions involving negative exponents as quotients.

Example #4A Simplify by factoring $-4(3x+1)(4x-1)^{-2} + 3(4x-1)^{-1}$

Solution Notice that there is a common base of $(4x-1)$ in this expression, appearing with exponents of -1 and -2. Since -2 is the *smaller* exponent to which $(4x-1)$ appears, the GCF is $(4x-1)^{-2}$.

The new exponents are found by taking the corresponding exponent of $(4x-1)$ as found in the original expression, and subtracting the exponent of $(4x-1)$ in the GCF.

$$-4(3x+1)(4x-1)^{-2} + 3(4x-1)^{-1}$$

$$= \underline{(4x-1)^{-2}} \, [-4(3x+1)\underline{(4x-1)^{-2-(-2)}} + 3\underline{(4x-1)^{-1-(-2)}}]$$

The GCF.

This factor simplifies to $(4x-1)^0 = 1$.

$$= (4x-1)^{-2} \, [-4(3x+1) + 3(4x-1)^1]$$

$$= (4x-1)^{-2}[-12x-4+12x-3]$$

$$= (4x-1)^{-2}[-7]$$

$$= -7(4x-1)^{-2}$$

Simplifying inside the brackets.

$$= \frac{-7}{(4x-1)^2}$$

Interpreting the negative exponent as a reciprocal.

Example #5A Simplify by factoring $x^2\left(\dfrac{-1}{2}\right)(x^2+1)^{-3/2}(2x) + 2x(x^2+1)^{-1/2}$.

Solution Before factoring, notice that the first half of the expression can be simplified:

The product of $-\frac{1}{2}$ and 2 is -1.

$$x^2\left(\dfrac{-1}{2}\right)(x^2+1)^{-3/2}(2x) = -x^3(x^2+1)^{-3/2}$$

The product of x^2 and x is x^3.

So the original expression simplifies to $-x^3(x^2+1)^{-3/2} + 2x(x^2+1)^{-1/2}$.

When we compare the two parts of the expression, the smaller exponent of the common base x is 1, and the smaller exponent of the common base (x^2+1) is $-\frac{3}{2}$. The common factor is therefore $x^1(x^2+1)^{-3/2}$, or, more simply, $x(x^2+1)^{-3/2}$.

$$x^2\left(\dfrac{-1}{2}\right)(x^2+1)^{-3/2}(2x) + 2x(x^2+1)^{-1/2}$$

$$= -x^3(x^2+1)^{-3/2} + 2x(x^2+1)^{-1/2} \quad \boxed{\text{Simplifying.}}$$

$$= x(x^2+1)^{-3/2}\left[-x^{3-1}(x^2+1)^{-3/2-(-3/2)} + 2x^{1-1}(x^2+1)^{-1/2-(-3/2)}\right]$$

This factor simplifies to $(x^2+1)^0 = 1$.

$\boxed{\begin{array}{l}\text{Factoring out the GCF and} \\ \text{subtracting exponents.}\end{array}}$

This factor simplifies to $x^0 = 1$.

$$= x(x^2+1)^{-3/2}\left[-x^2 + 2(x^2+1)\right]$$

$$= x(x^2+1)^{-3/2}\left[-x^2 + 2x^2 + 2\right]$$

$\left.\begin{array}{l}\\ \\ \\ \\ \\ \\ \end{array}\right\}$ $\boxed{\begin{array}{l}\text{Simplifying inside} \\ \text{the brackets.}\end{array}}$

$$= x(x^2+1)^{-3/2}\left[x^2+2\right]$$

$$= \dfrac{x(x^2+2)}{(x^2+1)^{3/2}} \quad \boxed{\begin{array}{l}\text{Interpreting the negative} \\ \text{exponent as a reciprocal.}\end{array}}$$

Method B: First, write expressions involving negative exponents as quotients. Find a common denominator, then combine and simplify the numerators.

Example #4B Simplify $-4(3x+1)(4x-1)^{-2} + 3(4x-1)^{-1}$.

> **Solution** $-4(3x+1)(4x-1)^{-2} + 3(4x-1)^{-1}$
>
> $$= \frac{-4(3x+1)}{(4x-1)^2} + \frac{3}{(4x-1)}$$
>
> | Rewriting the negative exponents using reciprocals. |
>
> $$= \frac{-4(3x+1)}{(4x-1)^2} + \frac{3(4x-1)}{(4x-1)^2}$$
>
> | The least common denominator is $(4x-1)^2$. The second fraction was multiplied by $\dfrac{4x-1}{4x-1}$. |
>
> $$= \frac{-4(3x+1) + 3(4x-1)}{(4x-1)^2}$$
>
> $$= \frac{-12x - 4 + 12x - 3}{(4x-1)^2}$$
>
> | Adding and simplifying in the numerator. |
>
> $$= \frac{-7}{(4x-1)^2}$$

Example #5B Simplify $x^2\left(\dfrac{-1}{2}\right)(x^2+1)^{-3/2}(2x) + 2x(x^2+1)^{-1/2}$.

Solution Before factoring, notice that the first half of the expression can be simplified:

The product of $-\frac{1}{2}$ and 2 is -1.

$$x^2\left(\frac{-1}{2}\right)(x^2+1)^{-3/2}(2x) = -x^3(x^2+1)^{-3/2}$$

The product of x^2 and x is x^3.

So the original expression simplifies to $-x^3(x^2+1)^{-3/2} + 2x(x^2+1)^{-1/2}$.

$$x^2\left(\frac{-1}{2}\right)(x^2+1)^{-3/2}(2x) + 2x(x^2+1)^{-1/2}$$

$$= -x^3(x^2+1)^{-3/2} + 2x(x^2+1)^{-1/2} \quad \boxed{\text{Simplifying}}$$

$$= \frac{-x^3}{(x^2+1)^{3/2}} + \frac{2x}{(x^2+1)^{1/2}}$$

> Writing the negative
> exponents using reciprocals.

$$= \frac{-x^3}{(x^2+1)^{3/2}} + \frac{2x(x^2+1)}{(x^2+1)^{3/2}}$$

> The least common denominator
> is $(x^2+1)^{3/2}$. The second fraction
> was multiplied by $\dfrac{x^2+1}{x^2+1}$

$$= \frac{-x^3 + 2x(x^2+1)}{(x^2+1)^{3/2}}$$

$$= \frac{-x^3 + 2x^3 + 2x}{(x^2+1)^{3/2}}$$

> Adding and simplifying
> the numerators.

$$= \frac{x^3 + 2x}{(x^2+1)^{3/2}}$$

$$= \frac{x(x^2+2)}{(x^2+1)^{3/2}}$$

> Factoring the numerator.

Simplification Exercises

Simplify each expression.

1. $(x-1)^3 4(x+2)^3 + 3(x-1)^2 (x+2)^4$

2. $(x+1)^2 (-3)(x^2+1)^{-4}(2x) + 2(x+1)(x^2+1)^{-3}$

3. $(2x+1)(-1)(x^2-1)^{-2}(2x) + 2(x^2-1)^{-1}$

4. $(2x+5)(-1)(3x-2)^{-2}(3) + 2(3x-2)^{-1}$

5. $2\left(\dfrac{x+1}{x-1}\right)[(x+1)(-1)(x-1)^{-2} + (x-1)^{-1}]$

6. $-x(x^2+1)^{-2}(2x) + (x^2+1)^{-1}$

7. $-x^2(x+1)^{-2} + 2x(x+1)^{-1}$

8. $-2x(3x^2+1)^{-2}(6x) + 2(3x^2+1)^{-1}$

9. $x\left(\dfrac{-1}{2}\right)(x^2-4)^{-\frac{3}{2}}(2x) + (x^2-4)^{-\frac{1}{2}}$

10. $\left(\sqrt[3]{x^2+3}\right)(-1)(x^{-2}) + \dfrac{1}{3}(x^2+3)^{-\frac{2}{3}}(2x)(x^{-1})$

11. $-2x(3+x^2)^{-2}(2x) + 2(3+x^2)^{-1}$

12. $\dfrac{1}{2}x(1-x^2)^{-\frac{1}{2}}(-2x) + \sqrt{1-x^2}$

13. $(x+1)(-1)(x^2-2x+4)^{-2}(2x-2) + (x^2-2x+4)^{-1}$

14. $(1-x)^3(-1)(2-3x)^{-2}(-3) + 3(1-x)^2(-1)(2-3x)^{-1}$

15. $x\left(\dfrac{-1}{2}\right)(1-x^2)^{-\frac{3}{2}}(-2x) + (1-x^2)^{-\frac{1}{2}}$

16. $(x+1)^2(-2)(x^2+2x)^{-3}(2x+2) + 2(x+1)(x^2+2x)^{-2}$

17. $(x+1)^{-5}(x+2)^{-6} + (x+1)^{-6}(x+2)^{-7}$

18. $(2x-1)^{-9}(x+5)^{-10} + (2x-1)^{-10}(x+5)^{-11}$

Answers

1. $(x-1)^2(x+2)^3(7x+2)$

2. $\dfrac{-2(2x^2+3x-1)(x+1)}{(x^2+1)^4}$

3. $\dfrac{-2(x^2+x+1)}{(x^2-1)^2}$

4. $\dfrac{-19}{(3x-2)^2}$

5. $\dfrac{-4(x+1)}{(x-1)^3}$

6. $\dfrac{(1-x^2)}{(x^2+1)^2}$

7. $\dfrac{x(x+2)}{(x+1)^2}$

8. $\dfrac{2(1-3x^2)}{(3x^2+1)^2}$

9. $\dfrac{-4}{(x^2-4)^{3/2}}$

10. $\dfrac{-(x^2+9)}{3x^2(x^2+3)^{-2/3}}$

11. $\dfrac{2(3-x^2)}{(3+x^2)^2}$

12. $\dfrac{1-2x^2}{\sqrt{1-x^2}}$

13. $\dfrac{6-2x-x^2}{(x^2-2x+4)^2}$

14. $\dfrac{3(1-x)^2(2x-1)}{(2-3x)^2}$

15. $\dfrac{1}{(1-x^2)^{3/2}}$

16. $\dfrac{-2(x+1)(x^2+2x+2)}{x^3(x+2)^3}$

17. $\dfrac{x^2+3x+3}{(x+1)^6(x+2)^7}$

18. $\dfrac{2x^2+9x-4}{(2x-1)^{10}(x+5)^{11}}$

Answers to Odd-Numbered Exercises and Chapter Tests

CHAPTER 1

Section 1.1 ■ page 14

1.

3. (a)

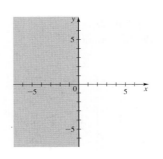

(b) $\sqrt{10}$

(c) $\left(\frac{7}{2}, \frac{5}{2}\right)$

5. (a)

(b) $\sqrt{74}$

(c) $\left(\frac{5}{2}, \frac{1}{2}\right)$

9. 24

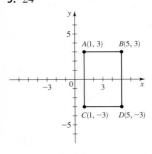

7. (a)

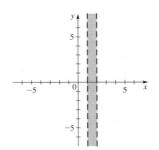

(b) 10

(c) $(0, 0)$

11. Trapezoid, area = 9

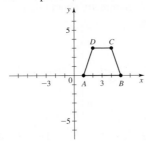

13.

15.

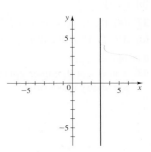

17.

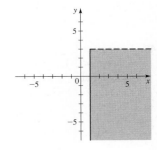

19.

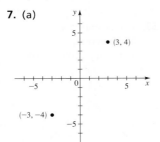

21.

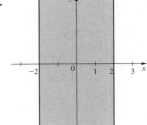

23. $A(6, 7)$ **25.** $Q(-1, 3)$ **29.** (b) 10
33. 6.02, 5.22, 6.08 (correct to two decimals)

35. (a)

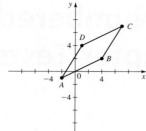

(b) $\left(\frac{5}{2}, 3\right), \left(\frac{5}{2}, 3\right)$

37. (a) $(8, 5)$ (b) $(a + 3, b + 2)$ (c) $(0, 2)$
(d) $A'(-2, 1), B'(0, 4), C'(5, 3)$ **39.** No, yes, no

41. No, yes, yes
43. x-intercept 0, y-intercept 0,
   symmetry about origin

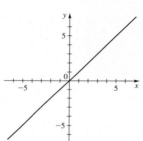

45. x-intercept 1,
   y-intercept -1,
   no symmetry

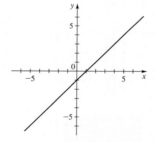

47. x-intercept $\frac{5}{3}$,
   y-intercept -5,
   no symmetry

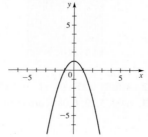

49. x-intercepts ± 1,
   y-intercept 1,
   symmetry about y-axis

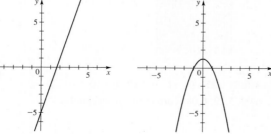

51. x-intercept 0,
   y-intercept 0,
   symmetry about y-axis

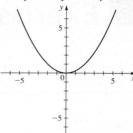

53. x-intercepts ± 3,
   y-intercept -9,
   symmetry about y-axis

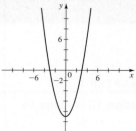

55. x-intercept 0,
   y-intercept 0,
   no symmetry

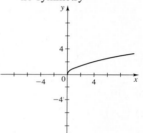

57. x-intercept 0,
   y-intercept 0,
   symmetry about y-axis

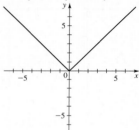

59. x-intercepts ± 4,
   y-intercept 4,
   symmetry about y-axis

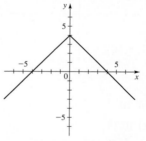

61. x-intercept 0,
   y-intercept 0,
   symmetry about y-axis

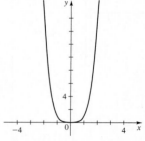

63. Symmetry about y-axis **65.** Symmetry about origin
67. Symmetry about origin
69.

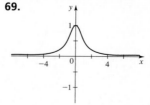

71.

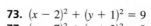

73. $(x - 2)^2 + (y + 1)^2 = 9$ **75.** $(x + 1)^2 + (y - 5)^2 = 130$
77. $(x - 7)^2 + (y + 3)^2 = 9$ **79.** $(x + 2)^2 + (y - 2)^2 = 4$

81. $(1, -2), 2$ **83.** $(0, -3), \sqrt{7}$ **85.** $\left(-1, -\frac{1}{2}\right), \frac{1}{2}$

87.

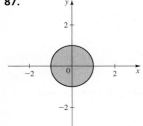

89. 12π

Section 1.2 ■ page 28

1. 2   **3.** $-\frac{1}{4}$ **5.** 4   **7.** $-\frac{9}{2}$

9. $-2, \frac{1}{2}, 3, -\frac{1}{4}$ **11.** $x + y - 4 = 0$ **13.** $3x - 2y - 6 = 0$

15. $x - y + 1 = 0$ **17.** $2x - 3y + 19 = 0$

19. $5x + y - 11 = 0$ **21.** $3x - y - 2 = 0$

23. $3x - y - 3 = 0$ **25.** $y = 5$ **27.** $x + 2y + 11 = 0$

29. $x = -1$ **31.** $5x - 2y + 1 = 0$ **33.** $x - y + 6 = 0$

35. (a)

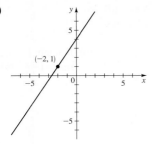

(b) $3x - 2y + 8 = 0$

37. All lines pass through $(3, 2)$

39. $-1, 3$ **41.** $-\frac{1}{3}, 0$

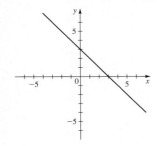
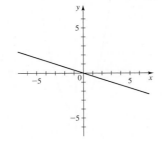

43. $\frac{3}{2}, 3$

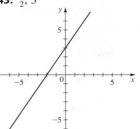

45. $0, 4$

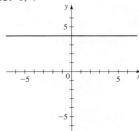

47. $\frac{3}{4}, -3$

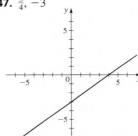

49. $-\frac{3}{4}, \frac{1}{4}$

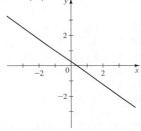

55. $x - y - 3 = 0$ **57.** (b) $4x - 3y - 24 = 0$

59. 16,667 ft

61. (a) 8.34; the slope represents the increase in dosage for a one-year increase in age.
(b) 8.34 mg

63. (a)

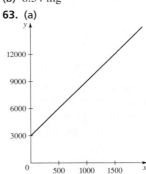

(b) The slope represents production cost per toaster; the y-intercept represents monthly fixed cost.

65. (a) $t = \frac{5}{24}n + 45$ (b) $76°F$

67. (a) $P = 0.434d + 15$, where P is pressure in lb/in^2 and d is depth in feet   (b) 196 ft

69. (a) $C = \frac{1}{4}d + 260$
(b) $635
(c) The slope represents cost per mile.
(d) The y-intercept represents annual fixed cost.

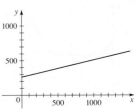

Section 1.3 ■ page 41

1. $f(x) = 7x + 2$ **3.** $f(x) = (x - 4)^2$ **5.** Divide by 2, then add 7 **7.** Square, multiply by 3, then subtract 2

9.

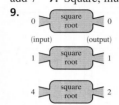

(input)   (output)

11.

x	$f(x)$
-1	3
0	1
1	3
2	9
3	19

13. $3, -3, 2, 2a + 1, -2a + 1, 2a + 2b + 1$

15. $-\dfrac{1}{3}, -3, \dfrac{1}{3}, \dfrac{1-a}{1+a}, \dfrac{2-a}{a}$, undefined

17. $-4, 10, -2, 3\sqrt{2}, 2x^2 + 7x + 1, 2x^2 - 3x - 4$

19. $6, 2, 1, 2, 2|x|, 2(x^2 + 1)$ **21.** $4, 1, 1, 2, 3$

23. $8, -\dfrac{3}{4}, -1, 0, 1$ **25.** $x^2 + 4x + 5, x^2 + 6$

27. $x^2 + 4, x^2 + 8x + 16$ **29.** $3a + 2, 3(a + h) + 2, 3$

31. $5, 5, 0$

33. $3 - 5a + 4a^2, 3 - 5a - 5h + 4a^2 + 8ah + 4h^2,$
$-5 + 8a + 4h$

35. (a) $C(10) = 1532.1, C(100) = 2100$ (b) The cost of producing 10 yd and 100 yd (c) $C(0) = 1500$

37. (a) $D(0.1) = 28.1, D(0.2) = 39.8$ (b) 41.3 mi (c) 235.6 mi

39. (a) $v(0.1) = 4440, v(0.4) = 1665$
(b) Flow is faster near central axis

(c)

r	$v(r)$
0	4625
0.1	4440
0.2	3885
0.3	2960
0.4	1665
0.5	0

41. (a) $T(5000) = 0, T(12,000) = 960, T(25,000) = 1975$
(b) The amount of tax paid on incomes of 5000, 12,000, and
25,000 **43.** $(-\infty, \infty)$ **45.** $[-1, 5]$ **47.** $\{x \mid x \neq 3\}$

49. $\{x \mid x \neq \pm1\}$ **51.** $[5, \infty)$ **53.** $(-\infty, \infty)$ **55.** $\left[\dfrac{5}{2}, \infty\right)$

57. $[-2, 3) \cup (3, \infty)$ **59.** $(-\infty, 0] \cup [6, \infty)$

61. This person's weight increases as he grows, then continues to increase; the person then goes on a crash diet (possibly) at age 30, then gains weight again, the weight gain eventually leveling off.

63.

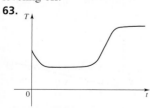

65. A won the race. All runners finished. Runner B fell, but got up again to finish second.

67.

69. (a) 500 MW, 725 MW (b) Between 3:00 A.M. and
4:00 A.M. (c) Just before noon

71.

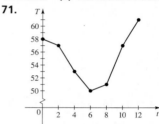

Section 1.4 ■ page 57

1. (a) $1, -1, 3, 4$ (b) Domain $[-3, 4]$, range $[-1, 4]$

3. (a) $f(0)$ (b) $g(-3)$ (c) $-2, 2$

5. (a) Yes (b) No (c) Yes (d) No

7. Function, domain $[-3, 2]$, range $[-2, 2]$

9. Not a function

11. (a)

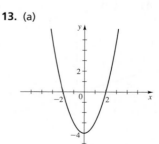

(b) Domain $(-\infty, \infty)$,
range $(-\infty, \infty)$

13. (a)

(b) Domain $(-\infty, \infty)$,
range $[-4, \infty)$

15. (a)

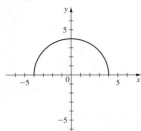

17. (a)

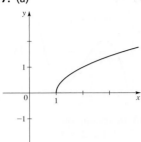

31.

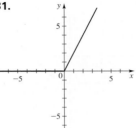

33.

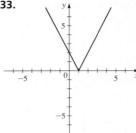

(b) Domain $[-4, 4]$, range $[0, 4]$

(b) Domain $[1, \infty)$, range $[0, \infty)$

35. Yes   **37.** No   **39.** Yes   **41.** Yes

43. (a)

$c = 6$ $c = 4$ $c = 2$ $c = 0$

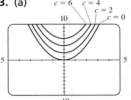

(b)

$c = 0$ $c = -2$ $c = -4$ $c = -6$

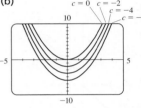

(c) If $c > 0$, then the graph of $f(x) = x^2 + c$ is the same as the graph of $y = x^2$ shifted upward c units. If $c < 0$, then the graph of $f(x) = x^2 + c$ is the same as the graph of $y = x^2$ shifted downward c units.

19.

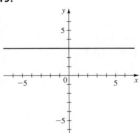

21.

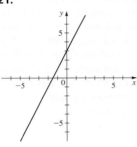

45. (a)

$c = 0$ $c = 2$ $c = 4$ $c = 6$

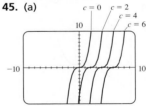

(b)

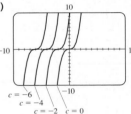

$c = -6$ $c = -4$ $c = -2$ $c = 0$

(c) If $c > 0$, then the graph of $f(x) = (x - c)^3$ is the same as the graph of $y = x^3$ shifted right c units. If $c < 0$, then the graph of $f(x) = (x - c)^3$ is the same as the graph of $y = x^3$ shifted left c units.

23.

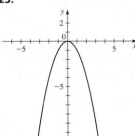

25.

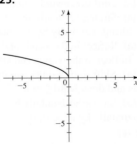

27.

29.

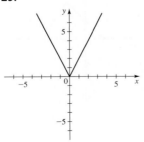

47. (a)

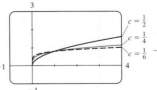

$c = \frac{1}{2}$
$c = \frac{1}{4}$
$c = \frac{1}{6}$

(b)

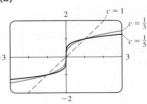

$c = 1$
$c = \frac{1}{3}$
$c = \frac{1}{5}$

(c) Graphs of even roots are similar to $\sqrt{x}$; graphs of odd roots are similar to $\sqrt[3]{x}$. As c increases, the graph of $y = \sqrt[c]{x}$ becomes steeper near 0 and flatter when $x > 1$.

49.

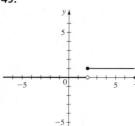

51.

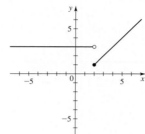

53.

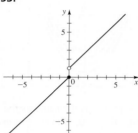

55.

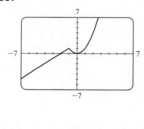

57.

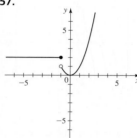

59.

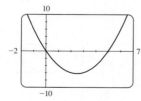

61. Increasing on $[-1, 1]$, $[2, 4]$; decreasing on $[1, 2]$
63. Increasing on $[-2, -1]$, $[1, 2]$; decreasing on $[-3, -2]$, $[-1, 1]$, $[2, 3]$
65. (a)

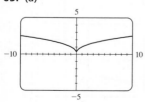

(b) Increasing on $[0, \infty)$; decreasing on $(-\infty, 0]$

67. (a)

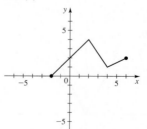

(b) Increasing on $[2.5, \infty)$; decreasing on $(-\infty, 2.5]$

69. (a)

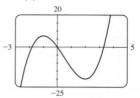

(b) Increasing on $(-\infty, -1]$, $[2, \infty)$; decreasing on $[-1, 2]$

71. (a)

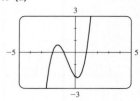

(b) Increasing on $(-\infty, -1.55]$, $[0.22, \infty)$; decreasing on $[-1.55, 0.22]$

73. Local minimum ≈ -4.01 when $x \approx -0.90$
75. Local maximum ≈ 0.38 when $x \approx -0.58$; local minimum ≈ -0.38 when $x \approx 0.58$
77. Local maximum ≈ 0 when $x = 0$; local minimum ≈ -13.61 when $x \approx -1.71$; local minimum ≈ -73.32 when $x \approx 3.21$
79. Local maximum ≈ 5.66 when $x \approx 4.00$
81. Local maximum ≈ 0.38 when $x \approx -1.73$; local minimum ≈ -0.38 when $x \approx 1.73$
83. (a) 55 ft   (b) 204.88 ft
85. 50 trees per acre
87. 7.5 mi/h

Section 1.5 ■ page 70

1. (a) Shift downward 3 units   (b) Shift right 3 units
3. (a) Stretch vertically by a factor of 3
(b) Shrink vertically by a factor of $\frac{1}{3}$
5. (a) Reflect in the x-axis and stretch vertically by a factor of 2
(b) Reflect in the x-axis and shrink vertically by a factor of $\frac{1}{2}$
7. (a) Shift right 4 units and upward $\frac{3}{4}$ unit   (b) Shift left 4 units and downward $\frac{3}{4}$ unit
9. (a) Shrink horizontally by a factor of $\frac{1}{4}$ (b) Stretch horizontally by a factor of 4
11. (a)   (b)

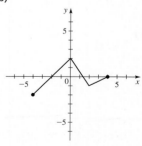

(c)

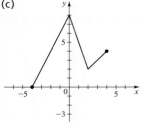

(d)

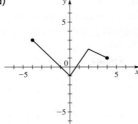

(e)

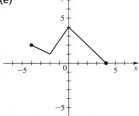

(f)

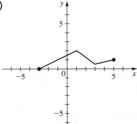

13. (a)

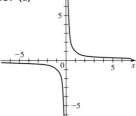

(b) (i)

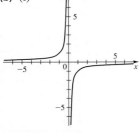

(ii)

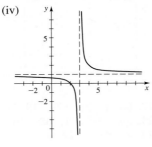

(iii)

(iv)

15. (a) Shift left 2 units   **(b)** Shift up 2 units

17. (a) Stretch vertically by a factor of 2

(b) Shift right 2 units, then shrink vertically by a factor of $\frac{1}{2}$

19. $g(x) = (x - 2)^2 + 3$ **21.** $g(x) = -5\sqrt{x + 3}$

23. $g(x) = 0.1 \left| x - \frac{1}{2} \right| - 2$

25.

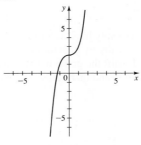

27.

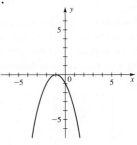

29.

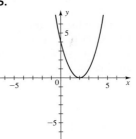

31.

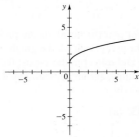

33.

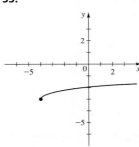

35.

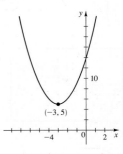

(−3, 5)

37.

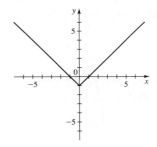

39.

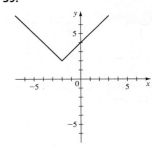

41.

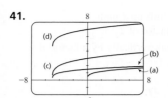

For part (b) shift the graph in (a) left 5 units; for part (c) shift the graph in (a) left 5 units and stretch vertically by a factor of 2; for part (d) shift the graph in (a) left 5 units, stretch vertically by a factor of 2, and then shift upward 4 units.

43.

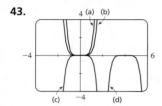

For part (b) shrink the graph in (a) vertically by a factor of $\frac{1}{3}$; for part (c) shrink the graph in (a) vertically by a factor of $\frac{1}{3}$ and reflect in the x-axis; for part (d) shift the graph in (a) right 4 units, shrink vertically by a factor of $\frac{1}{3}$, and then reflect in the x-axis.

45. (a)

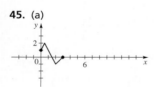

(b)

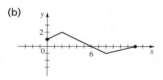

47.

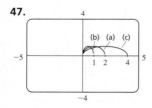

49. Even

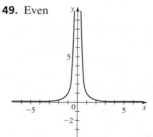

51. Neither

53. Odd

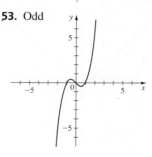

55. Neither
57. To obtain the graph of g, reflect in the x-axis the part of the graph of f that is below the x-axis.
59. (a)

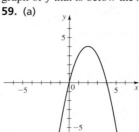

(b)

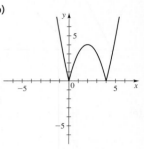

Section 1.6 ■ page 80

1. $(f + g)(x) = x^2 + x + 2, (-\infty, \infty)$;
$(f - g)(x) = x^2 - x - 2, (-\infty, \infty)$;
$(fg)(x) = x^3 + 2x^2, (-\infty, \infty)$;
$(f/g)(x) = x^2/(x + 2), (-\infty, -2) \cup (-2, \infty)$
3. $(f + g)(x) = \sqrt{1 + x^2} + \sqrt{1 - x}, (-\infty, 1]$;
$(f - g)(x) = \sqrt{1 + x^2} - \sqrt{1 - x}, (-\infty, 1]$;
$(fg)(x) = \sqrt{1 - x + x^2 - x^3}, (-\infty, 1]$;
$(f/g)(x) = \sqrt{\dfrac{1 + x^2}{1 - x}}, (-\infty, 1)$
5. $(f + g)(x) = 8/(x(x + 4)), x \neq -4, x \neq 0$;
$(f - g)(x) = 4(x + 2)/(x(x + 4)), x \neq -4, x \neq 0$;
$(fg)(x) = -4/(x(x + 4)), x \neq -4, x \neq 0$;
$(f/g)(x) = -(x + 4)/x, x \neq -4, x \neq 0$
7. $[0, 1]$ **9.** $[4, \infty)$

11.

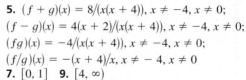

13.

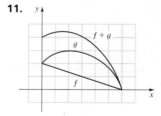

15.

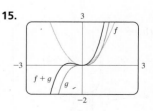

17. (a) 1   (b) -23 **19.** (a) -11 (b) -119
21. (a) $-3x^2 + 1$ (b) $-9x^2 + 30x - 23$
23. 4   **25.** 5   **27.** 4

29. $(f \circ g)(x) = 8x + 1, (-\infty, \infty);$
$(g \circ f)(x) = 8x + 11, (-\infty, \infty);$
$(f \circ f)(x) = 4x + 9, (-\infty, \infty);$
$(g \circ g)(x) = 16x - 5, (-\infty, \infty)$
31. $(f \circ g)(x) = (x + 1)^2, (-\infty, \infty)$
$(g \circ f)(x) = x^2 + 1, (-\infty, \infty)$
$(f \circ f)(x) = x^4, (-\infty, \infty)$
$(g \circ g)(x) = x + 2, (-\infty, \infty)$
33. $(f \circ g)(x) = \dfrac{1}{2x + 4}, x \neq -2$

$(g \circ f)(x) = \dfrac{2}{x} + 4, x \neq 0$

$(f \circ f)(x) = x, x \neq 0$
$(g \circ g)(x) = 4x + 12, (-\infty, \infty)$
35. $(f \circ g)(x) = |2x + 3|, (-\infty, \infty)$
$(g \circ f)(x) = 2|x| + 3, (-\infty, \infty)$
$(f \circ f)(x) = |x|, (-\infty, \infty)$
$(g \circ g)(x) = 4x + 9, (-\infty, \infty)$
37. $(f \circ g)(x) = \dfrac{2x - 1}{2x}, x \neq 0$

$(g \circ f)(x) = \dfrac{2x}{x + 1} - 1, x \neq -1$

$(f \circ f)(x) = \dfrac{x}{2x + 1}, x \neq -1, x \neq -\tfrac{1}{2}$

$(g \circ g)(x) = 4x - 3, (-\infty, \infty)$
39. $(f \circ g)(x) = \sqrt[12]{x}, [0, \infty)$
$(g \circ f)(x) = \sqrt[12]{x}, [0, \infty)$
$(f \circ f)(x) = \sqrt[9]{x}, (-\infty, \infty)$
$(g \circ g)(x) = \sqrt[16]{x}, [0, \infty)$
41. $(f \circ g \circ h)(x) = \sqrt{x - 1} - 1$
43. $(f \circ g \circ h)(x) = (\sqrt{x} - 5)^4 + 1$
45. $g(x) = x - 9, f(x) = x^5$ **47.** $g(x) = x^2, f(x) = x/(x + 4)$
49. $g(x) = 1 - x^3, f(x) = |x|$
51. $h(x) = x^2, g(x) = x + 1, f(x) = 1/x$
53. $h(x) = \sqrt[3]{x}, g(x) = 4 + x, f(x) = x^9$
55. $A(t) = 3600\pi t^2$ **57.** $A(t) = 16\pi t^2$ **59.** (a) $f(x) = 0.9x$
(b) $g(x) = x - 100$ (c) $f \circ g(x) = 0.9x - 90,$
$g \circ f(x) = 0.9x - 100, f \circ g:$ first rebate, then discount, $g \circ f:$
first discount, then rebate, $g \circ f$ is the better deal

Section 1.7 ▪ page 91

1. No **3.** Yes **5.** No **7.** Yes **9.** Yes **11.** Yes **13.** No
15. No **17.** (a) 2 (b) 3 **19.** 1
31. $f^{-1}(x) = \tfrac{1}{2}(x - 1)$ **33.** $f^{-1}(x) = \tfrac{1}{4}(x - 7)$
35. $f^{-1}(x) = 2x$ **37.** $f^{-1}(x) = (1/x) - 2$
39. $f^{-1}(x) = (5x - 1)/(2x + 3)$
41. $f^{-1}(x) = \tfrac{1}{5}(x^2 - 2), x \geq 0$

43. $f^{-1}(x) = \sqrt{4 - x}$ **45.** $f^{-1}(x) = (x - 4)^3$
47. $f^{-1}(x) = x^2 - 2x, x \geq 1$ **49.** $f^{-1}(x) = \sqrt[4]{x}$
51. (a) 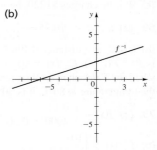 (b)

(c) $f^{-1}(x) = \tfrac{1}{3}(x + 6)$
53. (a) 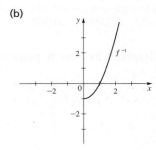 (b)

(c) $f^{-1}(x) = x^2 - 1, x \geq 0$
55. Not one-to-one **57.** One-to-one

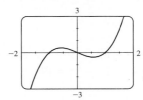 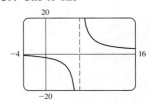

59. Not one-to-one **61.** $x \geq 0, f^{-1}(x) = \sqrt{4 - x}$
63. $x \geq -2, h^{-1}(x) = \sqrt{x} - 2$

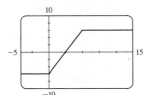

65.

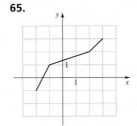

67. (a) $f(x) = 500 + 80x$ (b) $f^{-1}(x) = \frac{1}{80}(x - 500)$, the number of hours worked as a function of the fee
(c) 9; if he charges \$1220, he worked 9 h

69. (a) $v^{-1}(t) = \sqrt{0.25 - \dfrac{t}{18,500}}$
(b) 0.498; at a distance 0.498 from the central axis, the velocity is 30   **71.** (a) $F^{-1}(x) = \frac{5}{9}(x - 32)$; the Celsius temperature when the Fahrenheit temperature is x (b) $F^{-1}(86) = 30$; when the temperature is 86°F, it is 30°C

73. (a) $f(x) = \begin{cases} 0.1x & \text{if } x \leq 20,000 \\ 2000 + 0.2(x - 20,000) & \text{if } x > 20,000 \end{cases}$

(b) $f^{-1}(x) = \begin{cases} 10x & \text{if } x \leq 2000 \\ 10,000 + 5x & \text{if } x > 2000 \end{cases}$
If you pay x euros in taxes, your income is $f^{-1}(x)$
(c) $f^{-1}(10,000) = 60,000$

Chapter 1 Review ■ page 96

1. (a)

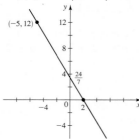

(b) $\sqrt{193}$ (c) $\left(-\frac{3}{2}, 6\right)$
(d) $y = -\frac{12}{7}x + \frac{24}{7}$ (e) $(x - 2)^2 + y^2 = 193$

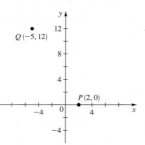

3.

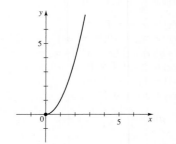

5. B
7. $(x + 5)^2 + (y + 1)^2 = 26$

9. Circle, center $(-1, 3)$, radius 1   **11.** No graph

13. No symmetry

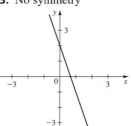

15. Symmetry about y-axis

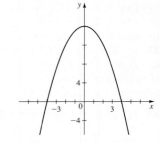

17. No symmetry

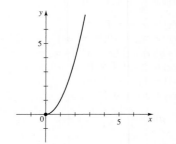

19. $2x - 3y - 16 = 0$ **21.** $3x + y - 12 = 0$
23. $x + 5y = 0$ **25.** $x^2 + y^2 = 169, 5x - 12y + 169 = 0$
27. $-4, 8, -16, a^3 + 2a - 4, -a^3 - 2a - 4,$
$x^3 + 3x^2 + 5x - 1, 8x^3 + 4x - 4, 2x^3 + 4x - 10$
29. (a) $-1, 2$ (b) $[-4, 5]$ (c) $[-4, 4]$ (d) Increasing on $[-4, -2]$ and $[-1, 4]$; decreasing on $[-2, -1]$ and $[4, 5]$
(e) No   **31.** Domain $[-3, \infty)$, range $[0, \infty)$ **33.** $(-\infty, \infty)$
35. $[-4, \infty)$ **37.** $\{x \mid x \neq -2, -1, 0\}$
39.

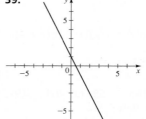

41.

43.

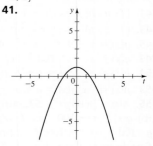

45.

47.

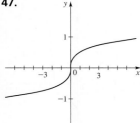

49.

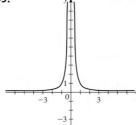

51.

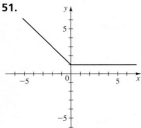

53.

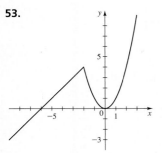

55. (iii)

57.

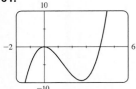

59.

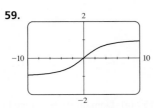

61.

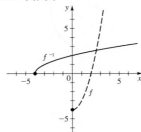

Increasing on $(-\infty, 0], [2.67, \infty)$; decreasing on $[0, 2.67]$

63. (a) Shift upward 8 units   (b) Shift left 8 units
(c) Stretch vertically by a factor of 2, then shift upward 1 unit

(d) Shift right 2 units and downward 2 units
(e) Reflect in y-axis
(f) Reflect in y-axis, then in x-axis
(g) Reflect in x-axis   (h) Reflect in line $y = x$
65. (a) Neither   (b) Odd   (c) Even   (d) Neither
67. 68 ft
69. Local maximum ≈ 3.79 when $x \approx 0.46$;
local minimum ≈ 2.81 when $x \approx -0.46$
71. (a) $(f + g)(x) = x^2 - 6x + 6$
(b) $(f - g)(x) = x^2 - 2$
(c) $(fg)(x) = -3x^3 + 13x^2 - 18x + 8$
(d) $(f/g)(x) = (x^2 - 3x + 2)/(4 - 3x)$
(e) $(f \circ g)(x) = 9x^2 - 15x + 6$
(f) $(g \circ f)(x) = -3x^2 + 9x - 2$
73. $(f \circ g)(x) = -3x^2 + 6x - 1, (-\infty, \infty)$;
$(g \circ f)(x) = -9x^2 + 12x - 3, (-\infty, \infty)$;
$(f \circ f)(x) = 9x - 4, (-\infty, \infty)$;
$(g \circ g)(x) = -x^4 + 4x^3 - 6x^2 + 4x, (-\infty, \infty)$
75. $(f \circ g \circ h)(x) = 1 + \sqrt{x}$ **77.** Yes   **79.** No   **81.** No

83. $f^{-1}(x) = \dfrac{x + 2}{3}$ **85.** $f^{-1}(x) = \sqrt[3]{x} - 1$

87. (a), (b)

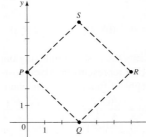

(c) $f^{-1}(x) = \sqrt{x + 4}$

Chapter 1 Test ■ page 100

1. (a) $S(3, 6)$ (b) 18

2. (a)

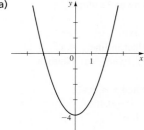

(b) x-intercepts $-2, 2$
y-intercept -4
(c) Symmetric about y-axis

3. (a) 20 **(b)** $(-1, -4)$ **(c)** $4x + 3y + 16 = 0$
(d) $3x - 4y - 13 = 0$ **(e)** $(x - 5)^2 + (y + 12)^2 = 169$
(f) $(x + 1)^2 + (y + 4)^2 = 100$

4. (a) Center $(0, 4)$; radius 3 **(b)** Center $(3, -5)$; radius 5

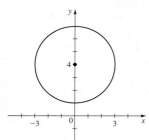 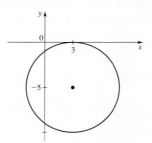

5. $y = \frac{3}{4}x + 6$, slope $\frac{3}{4}$, y-intercept 6

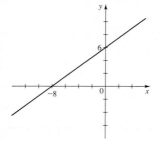

6. (a) $x + 3y - 7 = 0$ **(b)** $4x - y + 12 = 0$
7. (a) \$35,000
(b) The slope represents the cost of producing one more
blender. The C-intercept represents the fixed costs.
8. (a) and (b) are graphs of functions, (a) is one-to-one
9. (a) $f(4) = \dfrac{2}{3}$, $f(6) = \dfrac{\sqrt{6}}{5}$, $f(a + 1) = \dfrac{\sqrt{a + 1}}{a}$
(b) $[0, 1) \cup (1, \infty)$

10. (a) **(b)**

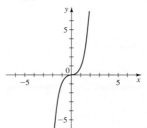 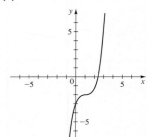

11. (a) Shift right 3 units, then shift upward 2 units
(b) Reflect in y-axis
12. (a) $-3, 3$ **(b)**

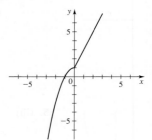

13. (a) $(f \circ g)(x) = 4x^2 - 8x + 2$
(b) $(g \circ f)(x) = 2x^2 + 4x - 5$ **(c)** 2 **(d)** 11
(e) $(g \circ g \circ g)(x) = 8x - 21$
14. (a) $f^{-1}(x) = 3 - x^2, x \geq 0$ **(b)**

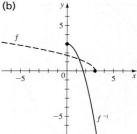

15. (a) Domain $[0, 6]$, range $[1, 7]$
(b) **(c)** $\frac{5}{4}$

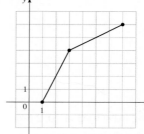

16. (a)

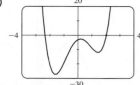

(b) No

(c) Local minimum ≈ -27.18 when $x \approx -1.61$;
local maximum ≈ -2.55 when $x \approx 0.18$;
local minimum ≈ -11.93 when $x \approx 1.43$
(d) $[-27.18, \infty)$ (e) Increasing on $[-1.61, 0.18] \cup [1.43, \infty)$;
decreasing on $(-\infty, -1.61] \cup [0.18, 1.43]$

Focus on Modeling ■ page 106

1. (a)

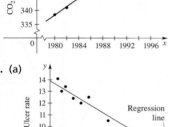

(b) $y = 1.5125x - 2656.4$
(c) 365.6 ppm

3. (a)

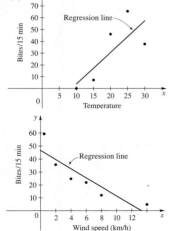

(b) $y = -0.0995x + 13.9$, x in thousands of dollars
(c) 11.4 per 100 population   (d) 5.8 per 100 population
5. (a)

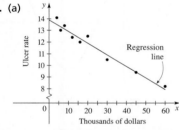

(b) $y = 2.6768x - 22.19$, $y = -3.5336x + 46.73$
(c) 0.77 is the correlation coefficient for the temperature-bites
data, so a linear model is not appropriate; -0.89 is the correlation coefficient for the wind/bites data, so a linear model is
more suitable in this case.
7. (a)

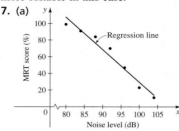

(b) $y = -3.9018x + 419.7$ (c) The correlation coefficient
is -0.98, so a linear model is appropriate.   (d) 53%
9. (a)

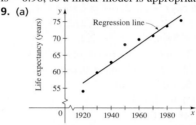

(b) $y = 0.29083x - 501.8$ (c) 79.9 years
11. (a) Men $y = -0.181x + 65.0$,
women $y = -0.288x + 79.5$
(b)

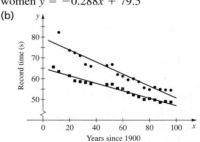

In the year 2036.

CHAPTER 2

Section 2.1 ■ page 120
5. $P\left(\frac{4}{5}, \frac{3}{5}\right)$ **7.** $P\left(-\sqrt{5}/3, \frac{2}{3}\right)$ **9.** $P(-\sqrt{2}/3, -\sqrt{7}/3)$
11. $t = \pi/4$, $(\sqrt{2}/2, \sqrt{2}/2)$; $t = \pi/2$, $(0, 1)$; $t = 3\pi/4$,
$(-\sqrt{2}/2, \sqrt{2}/2)$; $t = \pi$, $(-1, 0)$; $t = 5\pi/4$, $(-\sqrt{2}/2, -\sqrt{2}/2)$;
$t = 3\pi/2$, $(0, -1)$; $t = 7\pi/4$, $(\sqrt{2}/2, -\sqrt{2}/2)$; $t = 2\pi$, $(1, 0)$
13. $(0, 1)$ **15.** $\left(-\sqrt{3}/2, \frac{1}{2}\right)$ **17.** $\left(\frac{1}{2}, -\sqrt{3}/2\right)$
19. $\left(-\frac{1}{2}, \sqrt{3}/2\right)$ **21.** $(-\sqrt{2}/2, -\sqrt{2}/2)$
23. (a) $\left(-\frac{3}{5}, \frac{4}{5}\right)$ (b) $\left(\frac{3}{5}, -\frac{4}{5}\right)$ (c) $\left(-\frac{3}{5}, -\frac{4}{5}\right)$ (d) $\left(\frac{3}{5}, \frac{4}{5}\right)$

25. (a) $\pi/4$ (b) $\pi/3$ (c) $\pi/3$ (d) $\pi/6$
27. (a) $\pi/5$ (b) $\pi/6$ (c) $\pi/3$ (d) $\pi/6$
29. (a) $\pi/3$ (b) $\left(-\frac{1}{2}, \sqrt{3}/2\right)$
31. (a) $\pi/4$ (b) $\left(-\sqrt{2}/2, \sqrt{2}/2\right)$
33. (a) $\pi/3$ (b) $\left(-\frac{1}{2}, -\sqrt{3}/2\right)$
35. (a) $\pi/4$ (b) $\left(-\sqrt{2}/2, -\sqrt{2}/2\right)$
37. (a) $\pi/6$ (b) $\left(-\sqrt{3}/2, -\frac{1}{2}\right)$
39. (a) $\pi/3$ (b) $\left(\frac{1}{2}, \sqrt{3}/2\right)$
41. (a) $\pi/3$ (b) $\left(-\frac{1}{2}, -\sqrt{3}/2\right)$
43. $(0.5, 0.8)$
45. $(0.5, -0.9)$

Section 2.2 ■ page 130

1. $t = \pi/4$, $\sin t = \sqrt{2}/2$, $\cos t = \sqrt{2}/2$; $t = \pi/2$, $\sin t = 1$, $\cos t = 0$; $t = 3\pi/4$, $\sin t = \sqrt{2}/2$, $\cos t = -\sqrt{2}/2$; $t = \pi$, $\sin t = 0$, $\cos t = -1$; $t = 5\pi/4$, $\sin t = -\sqrt{2}/2$, $\cos t = -\sqrt{2}/2$; $t = 3\pi/2$, $\sin t = -1$, $\cos t = 0$; $t = 7\pi/4$, $\sin t = -\sqrt{2}/2$, $\cos t = \sqrt{2}/2$; $t = 2\pi$, $\sin t = 0$, $\cos t = 1$
3. (a) $-\sqrt{3}/2$ (b) $\frac{1}{2}$ **5.** (a) -1 (b) -1
7. (a) 1 (b) -1 **9.** (a) 0 (b) 0
11. (a) $\frac{1}{2}$ (b) 2 **13.** (a) $\frac{1}{2}$ (b) $\frac{1}{2}$
15. (a) $\sqrt{3}/3$ (b) $-\sqrt{3}/3$
17. (a) 2 (b) $-2\sqrt{3}/3$
19. (a) $\sqrt{2}/2$ (b) $\sqrt{2}$
21. (a) -1 (b) -1
23. $\sin 0 = 0$, $\cos 0 = 1$, $\tan 0 = 0$, $\sec 0 = 1$, others undefined
25. $\sin \pi = 0$, $\cos \pi = -1$, $\tan \pi = 0$, $\sec \pi = -1$, others undefined
27. $\frac{4}{5}, \frac{3}{5}, \frac{4}{3}$ **29.** $-\sqrt{11}/4, \sqrt{5}/4, -\sqrt{55}/5$ **31.** $\frac{9}{41}, \frac{40}{41}, \frac{9}{40}$
33. $-\frac{12}{13}, -\frac{5}{13}, \frac{12}{5}$ **35.** (a) 0.8 (b) 0.84147
37. (a) 0.9 (b) 0.93204 **39.** (a) 1 (b) 1.02964
41. (a) -0.6 (b) -0.57482 **43.** Negative
45. Negative **47.** II **49.** II
51. $\sin t = \sqrt{1 - \cos^2 t}$ **53.** $\tan t = (\sin t)/\sqrt{1 - \sin^2 t}$
55. $\sec t = -\sqrt{1 + \tan^2 t}$ **57.** $\tan t = \sqrt{\sec^2 t - 1}$
59. $\tan^2 t = (\sin^2 t)/(1 - \sin^2 t)$
61. $\cos t = -\frac{4}{5}$, $\tan t = -\frac{3}{4}$, $\csc t = \frac{5}{3}$, $\sec t = -\frac{5}{4}$, $\cot t = -\frac{4}{3}$
63. $\sin t = -2\sqrt{2}/3$, $\cos t = \frac{1}{3}$, $\tan t = -2\sqrt{2}$, $\csc t = -\frac{3}{4}\sqrt{2}$, $\cot t = -\sqrt{2}/4$
65. $\sin t = -\frac{3}{5}$, $\cos t = \frac{4}{5}$, $\csc t = -\frac{5}{3}$, $\sec t = \frac{5}{4}$, $\cot t = -\frac{4}{3}$
67. $\cos t = -\sqrt{15}/4$, $\tan t = \sqrt{15}/15$, $\csc t = -4$, $\sec t = -4\sqrt{15}/15$, $\cot t = \sqrt{15}$
69. Odd **71.** Odd **73.** Even **75.** Neither

Section 2.3 ■ page 143

1.
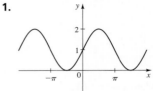

3.
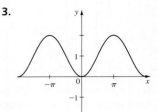

5.
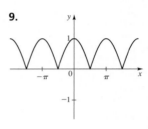

7.
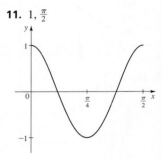

9.
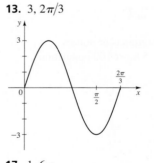

11. $1, \frac{\pi}{2}$
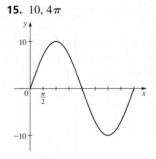

13. $3, 2\pi/3$
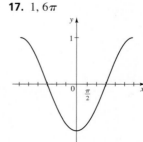

15. $10, 4\pi$
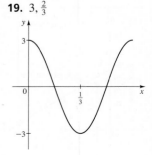

17. $1, 6\pi$

19. $3, \frac{2}{3}$

21. $1, 2\pi, \pi/2$

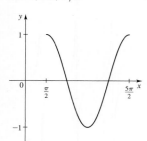

23. $2, 2\pi, \pi/6$

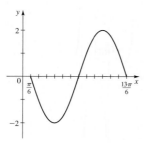

25. $5, 2\pi/3, \pi/12$

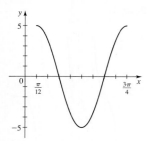

27. $2, 3\pi, \pi/4$

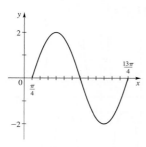

29. $3, 2, -\frac{1}{2}$

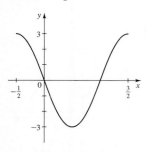

31. $\frac{1}{2}, \pi, \pi/6$

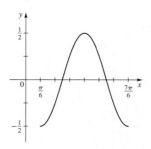

33. $1, 2\pi/3, -\pi/3$

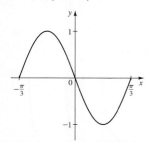

35. (a) $4, 2\pi, 0$ (b) $y = 4 \sin x$
37. (a) $3, 4\pi, 0$ (b) $y = 3 \sin \frac{1}{2} x$
39. (a) $\frac{1}{2}, \pi, -\pi/3$ (b) $y = -\frac{1}{2} \cos 2(x + \pi/3)$

41.

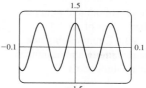

43.

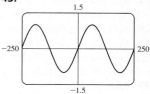

45.

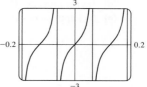

47.

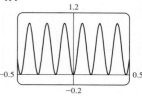

49. (a) 20 s   (b) 6 ft   **51.** (a) $\frac{1}{80}$ min   (b) 80
(c)   (d) 140/90; it is higher
                                            than normal

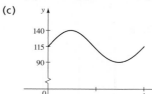

53.

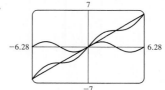

55.

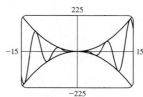

$y = x^2 \sin x$ is a sine curve that lies between the graphs of $y = x^2$ and $y = -x^2$

57.

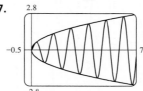

$y = \sqrt{x} \sin 5\pi x$ is a sine curve that lies between the graphs of $y = \sqrt{x}$ and $y = -\sqrt{x}$

59.

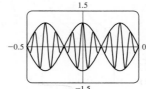

$y = \cos 3\pi x \cos 21\pi x$ is a cosine curve that lies between the graphs of $y = \cos 3\pi x$ and $y = -\cos 3\pi x$

61. Maximum value 1.76 when $x \approx 0.94$, minimum value
-1.76 when $x \approx -0.94$ (The same maximum and minimum
values occur at infinitely many other values of x.)
63. Maximum value 3.00 when $x \approx 1.57$, minimum value
-1.00 when $x \approx -1.57$ (The same maximum and minimum
values occur at infinitely many other values of x.)
65. 1.16   **67.** 0.34, 2.80
69. (a) Odd   (b) 0, $\pm 2\pi$, $\pm 4\pi$, $\pm 6\pi$, . . .
(c)   (d) $f(x)$ approaches 0
                                              (e) $f(x)$ approaches 0

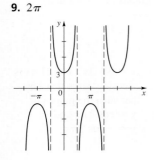

Section 2.4 ■ page 155

1. π

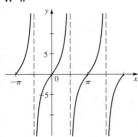

3. π

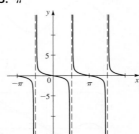

5. π

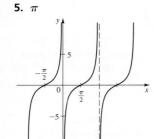

7. 2π

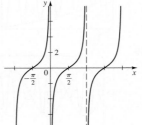

9. 2π

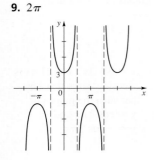

11. π

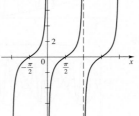

13. 2π

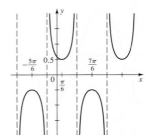

15. π

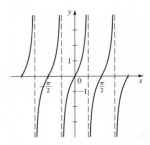

17. 2π

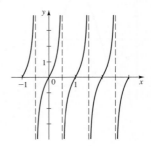

19. $\pi/2$

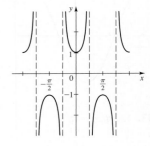

21. 1

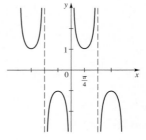

23. π

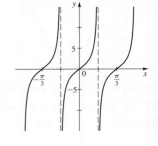

25. π

27. $\pi/3$

29. $2\pi/3$

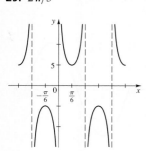

31. $\pi/2$

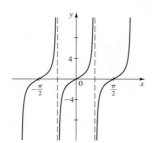

45. $\pi/2$

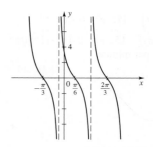

33. $\pi/2$

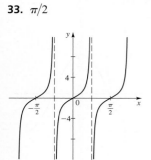

35. $\pi/2$

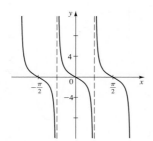

Section 2.5 ■ page 162

1. (a) 2, $2\pi/3$, $3/(2\pi)$ (b)

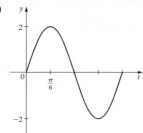

37. 2

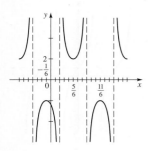

39. $2\pi/3$

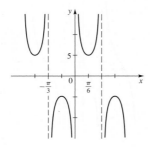

3. (a) 1, $20\pi/3$, $3/(20\pi)$ (b)

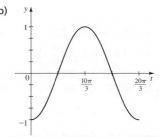

5. (a) $\frac{1}{4}$, $4\pi/3$, $3/(4\pi)$ (b)

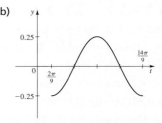

41. $3\pi/2$

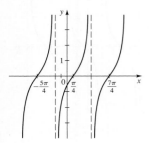

43. 2

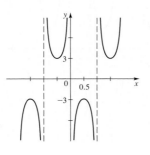

7. (a) 5, 3π, $1/(3\pi)$ (b)

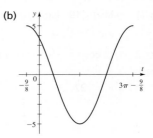

9. $y = 10 \sin\left(\dfrac{2\pi}{3} t\right)$ **11.** $y = 6 \sin(10t)$

13. $y = 60 \cos(4\pi t)$ **15.** $y = 2.4 \cos(1500\pi t)$

17. (a) 10 cycles per minute

(b)   (c) 0.4 m

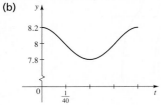

19. (a) 8900   (b) about 3.14 yr   **21.** $d(t) = 5 \sin(5\pi t)$

23. $y = 21 \sin\left(\dfrac{\pi}{6} t\right)$

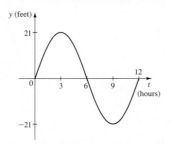

25. $y = 5 \cos(2\pi t)$ **27.** $y = 11 + 10 \sin\left(\dfrac{\pi t}{10}\right)$

29. $y = 3.8 + 0.2 \sin\left(\dfrac{\pi}{5} t\right)$

31. $E(t) = 310 \cos(200\pi t)$, 219.2 V

33. (a) 45 V   (b) 40   (c) 40   (d) $E(t) = 45 \cos(80\pi t)$

Chapter 2 Review ■ page 166

1. (b) $\frac{1}{2}$, $-\sqrt{3}/2$, $-\sqrt{3}/3$ **3.** (a) $\pi/3$ (b) $\left(-\frac{1}{2}, \sqrt{3}/2\right)$

(c) $\sin t = \sqrt{3}/2$, $\cos t = -\frac{1}{2}$, $\tan t = -\sqrt{3}$, $\csc t = 2\sqrt{3}/3$,

$\sec t = -2$, $\cot t = -\sqrt{3}/3$ **5.** (a) $\pi/4$ (b) $\left(-\sqrt{2}/2, -\sqrt{2}/2\right)$

(c) $\sin t = -\sqrt{2}/2$, $\cos t = -\sqrt{2}/2$, $\tan t = 1$, $\csc t = -\sqrt{2}$,

$\sec t = -\sqrt{2}$, $\cot t = 1$ **7.** (a) $\sqrt{2}/2$ (b) $-\sqrt{2}/2$

9. (a) 0.89121   (b) 0.45360   **11.** (a) 0   (b) Undefined

13. (a) Undefined   (b) 0   **15.** (a) $-\sqrt{3}/3$ (b) $-\sqrt{3}$

17. $(\sin t)/(1 - \sin^2 t)$ **19.** $(\sin t)/\sqrt{1 - \sin^2 t}$

21. $\tan t = -\frac{5}{12}$, $\csc t = \frac{13}{5}$, $\sec t = -\frac{13}{12}$, $\cot t = -\frac{12}{5}$

23. $\sin t = 2\sqrt{5}/5$, $\cos t = -\sqrt{5}/5$, $\tan t = -2$,

$\sec t = -\sqrt{5}$

25. $(16 - \sqrt{17})/4$ **27.** 3

29. (a) $10, 4\pi, 0$

(b)

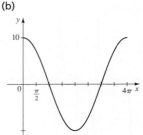

31. (a) $1, 4\pi, 0$

(b)

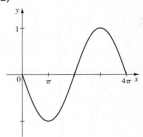

33. (a) $3, \pi, 1$

(b)

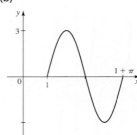

35. (a) $1, 4, -\frac{1}{3}$

(b)

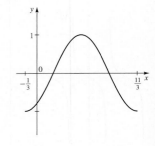

37. $y = 5 \sin 4x$ **39.** $y = \frac{1}{2} \sin 2\pi\left(x + \frac{1}{3}\right)$

41. π

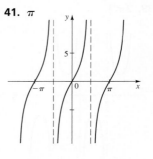

43. π

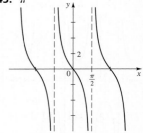

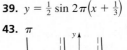

45. π

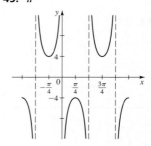

47. 2π

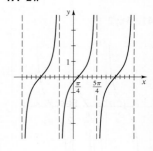

49. (a)
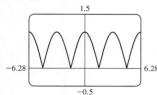

(b) Period π
(c) Even

51. (a)
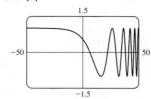

(b) Not periodic
(c) Neither

53. (a)
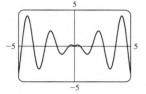

(b) Not periodic
(c) Even

55.
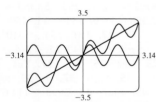

$y = x \sin x$ is a sine function whose graph lies between those of $y = x$ and $y = -x$

57.
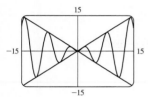

The graphs are related by graphical addition.

59. 1.76, -1.76 **61.** 0.30, 2.84
63. (a) Odd   (b) 0, $\pm\pi$, $\pm2\pi$, . . .
(c)
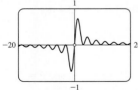

(d) $f(x)$ approaches 0
(e) $f(x)$ approaches 0

65. $y = 50 \cos (16\,\pi t)$ **67.** $y = 4 \cos \left(\dfrac{\pi}{6}t\right)$

Chapter 2 Test ■ page 168
1. $y = -\frac{5}{6}$ **2.** (a) $\frac{4}{5}$ (b) $-\frac{3}{5}$ (c) $-\frac{4}{3}$ (d) $-\frac{5}{3}$
3. (a) $-\frac{1}{2}$ (b) $-\sqrt{2}/2$ (c) $\sqrt{3}$ (d) -1
4. $\tan t = -(\sin t)/\sqrt{1 - \sin^2 t}$ **5.** $-\frac{2}{15}$

6. (a) 5, $\pi/2$, 0
(b)
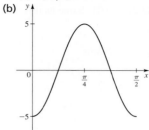

7. (a) 2, 4π, $\pi/3$
(b)
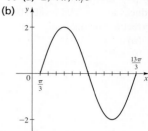

8. π
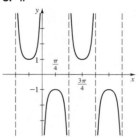

9. $\pi/2$
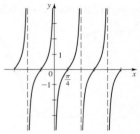

10. $y = 2 \sin 2(x + \pi/3)$
11. (a)
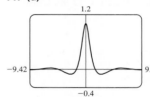

(b) Even
(c) Minimum value -0.11
when $x \approx \pm2.54$,
maximum value 1
when $x = 0$

12. $y = 5 \sin (4\pi t)$

Focus on Modeling ■ page 173
1. (a)
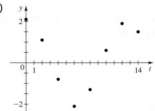

(b) $y = 2.1 \cos (0.52t)$

(c)
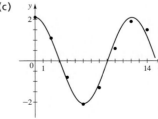

(d) $y = 2.05 \sin(0.50t + 1.55) - 0.01$ (e) The formula of (d) reduces to $y = 2.05 \cos(0.50t - 0.02) - 0.01$. Same as (b), correct to one decimal.

3. (a)
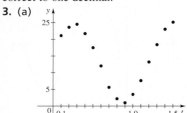

(b) $y = 12.05 \cos(5.2(t - 0.3)) + 13.05$

(c)
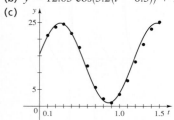

(d) $y = 11.72 \sin(5.05t + 0.24) + 12.96$ (e) The formula of (d) reduces to $y = 11.72 \cos(5.05(t - 0.26)) + 12.96$. Close, but not identical, to (b).

5. (a)
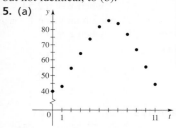

(b) $y = 22.9 \cos(0.52(t - 6)) + 62.9$ where y is temperature (°F) and t is months (January $= 0$)

(c)
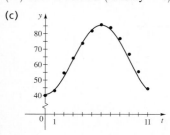

(d) $y = 23.4 \sin(0.48t - 1.36) + 62.2$

7. (a)
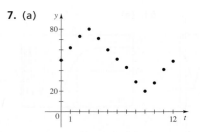

(b) $y = 30 \sin(0.52t) + 50$ where y is the owl population in year t

(c)
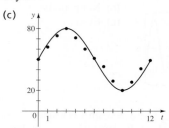

(d) $y = 25.8 \sin(0.52t - 0.02) + 50.6$

CHAPTER 3

Section 3.1 ■ page 184
1. $\pi/5 \approx 0.628$ rad   **3.** $-8\pi/3 \approx -8.378$ rad   **5.** $\pi/3 \approx 1.047$ rad   **7.** $-3\pi/4 \approx -2.356$ rad   **9.** $135°$ **11.** $150°$
13. $-270/\pi \approx 85.9°$ **15.** $-15°$ **17.** $410°, 770°, -310°, -670°$ **19.** $11\pi/4, 19\pi/4, -5\pi/4, -13\pi/4$ **21.** $7\pi/4, 15\pi/4, -9\pi/4, -17\pi/4$ **23.** Yes   **25.** Yes   **27.** Yes
29. $13°$ **31.** $30°$ **33.** $280°$ **35.** $5\pi/6$ **37.** π **39.** $\pi/4$
41. $55\pi/9 \approx 19.2$ **43.** 4 **45.** 4 mi   **47.** 2 rad $\approx 114.6°$
49. $36/\pi \approx 11.459$ m   **51.** $330\pi \approx 1037$ mi
53. 1.6 million mi   **55.** 1.15 mi   **57.** 50 m²   **59.** 4 m
61. 6 cm²   **63.** $32\pi/15$ ft/s ≈ 6.7 ft/s
65. (a) 2000π rad/min   (b) $50\pi/3$ ft/s ≈ 52.4 ft/s
67. 39.3 mi/h   **69.** 2.1 m/s

Section 3.2 ■ page 193
1. $\sin \theta = \frac{4}{5}$, $\cos \theta = \frac{3}{5}$, $\tan \theta = \frac{4}{3}$, $\csc \theta = \frac{5}{4}$, $\sec \theta = \frac{5}{3}$, $\cot \theta = \frac{3}{4}$ **3.** $\sin \theta = \frac{40}{41}$, $\cos \theta = \frac{9}{41}$, $\tan \theta = \frac{40}{9}$ $\csc \theta = \frac{41}{40}$, $\sec \theta = \frac{41}{9}$, $\cot \theta = \frac{9}{40}$ **5.** $\sin \theta = 2\sqrt{13}/13$, $\cos \theta = 3\sqrt{13}/13$, $\tan \theta = \frac{2}{3}$, $\csc \theta = \sqrt{13}/2$, $\sec \theta = \sqrt{13}/3$, $\cot \theta = \frac{3}{2}$ **7.** (a) $3\sqrt{34}/34, 3\sqrt{34}/34$ (b) $\frac{3}{5}, \frac{3}{5}$ (c) $\sqrt{34}/5, \sqrt{34}/5$ **9.** $\frac{25}{2}$ **11.** $13\sqrt{3}/2$ **13.** 16.51658

15. $x = 28 \cos \theta$, $y = 28 \sin \theta$

17. $\cos \theta = \frac{4}{5}$, $\tan \theta = \frac{3}{4}$, $\csc \theta = \frac{5}{3}$, $\sec \theta = \frac{5}{4}$, $\cot \theta = \frac{4}{3}$

19. $\sin \theta = \sqrt{2}/2$, $\cos \theta = \sqrt{2}/2$,
$\tan \theta = 1$, $\csc \theta = \sqrt{2}$,
$\sec \theta = \sqrt{2}$

21. $\sin \theta = 3\sqrt{5}/7$, $\cos \theta = \frac{2}{7}$, $\tan \theta = 3\sqrt{5}/2$, $\csc \theta = 7\sqrt{5}/15$,
$\cot \theta = 2\sqrt{5}/15$ **23.** $(1 + \sqrt{3})/2$ **25.** 1   **27.** $\frac{1}{2}$

29.   **31.**

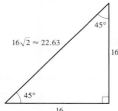   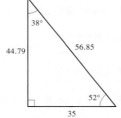

33. $\sin \theta \approx 0.45$, $\cos \theta \approx 0.89$, $\tan \theta = 0.50$, $\csc \theta \approx 2.24$,
$\sec \theta \approx 1.12$, $\cot \theta = 2.00$

35. 1026 ft   **37.** (a) 2100 mi   (b) No   **39.** 19 ft

41. 38.7°   **43.** 345 ft   **45.** 415 ft, 152 ft

47. 2570 ft   **49.** 5808 ft   **51.** 91.7 million mi

53. 3960 mi   **55.** 230.9   **57.** 63.7

59. $a = \sin \theta$, $b = \tan \theta$, $c = \sec \theta$, $d = \cos \theta$

Section 3.3 ■ page 205

1. (a) 30°   (b) 60°   (c) 60°   **3.** (a) $\pi/4$ (b) $\pi/6$ (c) $\pi/3$
5. (a) $\pi/5$ (b) $\pi - \frac{11}{5} \approx 0.94$ (c) $3\pi/7$ **7.** $\frac{1}{2}$ **9.** $-\sqrt{2}/2$
11. $-\sqrt{3}$ **13.** 1   **15.** $-\sqrt{3}/2$ **17.** $\sqrt{3}/3$ **19.** $\sqrt{3}/2$
21. -1 **23.** $\frac{1}{2}$ **25.** 2   **27.** -1 **29.** undefined
31. III   **33.** IV   **35.** $\tan \theta = -\sqrt{1 - \cos^2\theta}/\cos \theta$
37. $\cos \theta = \sqrt{1 - \sin^2\theta}$ **39.** $\sec \theta = -\sqrt{1 + \tan^2\theta}$
41. $\cos \theta = -\frac{4}{5}$, $\tan \theta = -\frac{3}{4}$, $\csc \theta = \frac{5}{3}$, $\sec \theta = -\frac{5}{4}$,
$\cot \theta = -\frac{4}{3}$
43. $\sin \theta = -\frac{3}{5}$, $\cos \theta = \frac{4}{5}$, $\csc \theta = -\frac{5}{3}$, $\sec \theta = \frac{5}{4}$,
$\cot \theta = -\frac{4}{3}$
45. $\sin \theta = \frac{1}{2}$, $\cos \theta = \sqrt{3}/2$, $\tan \theta = \sqrt{3}/3$,
$\sec \theta = 2\sqrt{3}/3$, $\cot \theta = \sqrt{3}$

47. $\sin \theta = 3\sqrt{5}/7$, $\tan \theta = -3\sqrt{5}/2$, $\csc \theta = 7\sqrt{5}/15$,
$\sec \theta = -\frac{7}{2}$, $\cot \theta = -2\sqrt{5}/15$
49. (a) $\sqrt{3}/2$, $\sqrt{3}$ (b) $\frac{1}{2}$, $\sqrt{3}/4$ (c) $\frac{3}{4}$, 0.88967
51. 19.1   **53.** 66.1°
55. (b)

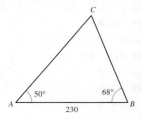

(c) 21.07
57. (a) $A(\theta) = 400 \sin \theta \cos \theta$

(b)

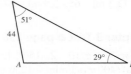

(c) width = depth ≈ 14.14 in.

Section 3.4 ■ page 214

1. 318.8   **3.** 24.8   **5.** 44°   **7.** $\angle C = 114°$, $a \approx 51$, $b \approx 24$
9. $\angle C = 62°$, $a \approx 200$, $b \approx 242$

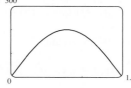

11. $\angle B = 85°$, $a \approx 5$,   **13.** $\angle A = 100°$, $a \approx 89$,
$c \approx 9$ $c \approx 71$

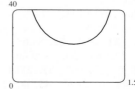

15. $\angle B \approx 30°$, $\angle C \approx 40°$, $c \approx 19$ **17.** No solution
19. $\angle A_1 \approx 125°$, $\angle C_1 \approx 30°$, $a_1 \approx 49$;
$\angle A_2 \approx 5°$, $\angle C_2 \approx 150°$, $a_2 \approx 5.6$
21. No solution   **23.** 219 ft
25. (a) 1018 mi   (b) 1017 mi   **27.** 155 m
29. 192 m   **31.** (a) 91.146°   (b) 14.427°

Section 3.5 ■ page 222

1. 28.9   **3.** 47   **5.** 29.89°   **7.** 15
9. $\angle A \approx 39.4°$, $\angle B \approx 20.6°$, $c \approx 24.6$
11. $\angle A \approx 48°$, $\angle B \approx 79°$, $c \approx 3.2$
13. $\angle A \approx 50°$, $\angle B \approx 73°$, $\angle C \approx 57°$
15. $\angle A_1 \approx 83.6°$, $\angle C_1 \approx 56.4°$, $a_1 \approx 193$;
$\angle A_2 \approx 16.4°$, $\angle C_2 \approx 123.6$, $a_2 \approx 54.9$
17. No such triangle   **19.** 2   **21.** 25.4   **23.** 84.6°
25. 24.3   **27.** 2.30 mi   **29.** 23.1 mi   **31.** 2179 mi
33. (a) 62.6 mi   (b) S 18.2° E   **35.** 96°   **37.** 211 ft
39. 3835 ft   **41.** 3.85 cm²   **43.** 104.6 m²   **45.** 40.77

Chapter 3 Review ■ page 225

1. (a) $\pi/3$ (b) $11\pi/6$ (c) $-3\pi/4$ (d) $-\pi/2$
3. (a) 450°   (b) −30°   (c) 405°   (d) $(558/\pi)° \approx 177.6°$
5. 8 m   **7.** 82 ft   **9.** 0.619 rad $\approx 35.4°$
11. 18,151 ft²   **13.** 300π rad/min ≈ 942.5 rad/min,
7539.8 in./min = 628.3 ft/min
15. $\sin \theta = 5/\sqrt{74}$, $\cos \theta = 7/\sqrt{74}$, $\tan \theta = \frac{5}{7}$, $\csc \theta = \sqrt{74}/5$,
$\sec \theta = \sqrt{74}/7$, $\cot \theta = \frac{7}{5}$
17. $x \approx 3.83$, $y \approx 3.21$ **19.** $x \approx 2.92$, $y \approx 3.11$
21.
23. $a = \cot \theta$, $b = \csc \theta$
25. 48 m   **27.** 1076 mi
29. $-\sqrt{2}/2$ **31.** 1
33. $-\sqrt{3}/3$ **35.** $-\sqrt{2}/2$ **37.** $2\sqrt{3}/3$ **39.** $-\sqrt{3}$
41. $\sin \theta = \frac{12}{13}$, $\cos \theta = -\frac{5}{13}$, $\tan \theta = -\frac{12}{5}$, $\csc \theta = \frac{13}{12}$,
$\sec \theta = -\frac{13}{5}$, $\cot \theta = -\frac{5}{12}$
43. 60°   **45.** $\tan \theta = -\sqrt{1 - \cos^2\theta}/\cos \theta$
47. $\tan^2\theta = \sin^2\theta/(1 - \sin^2\theta)$
49. $\sin \theta = \sqrt{7}/4$, $\cos \theta = \frac{3}{4}$, $\csc \theta = 4\sqrt{7}/7$,
$\cot \theta = 3\sqrt{7}/7$
51. $\cos \theta = -\frac{4}{5}$, $\tan \theta = -\frac{3}{4}$, $\csc \theta = \frac{5}{3}$, $\sec \theta = -\frac{5}{4}$,
$\cot \theta = -\frac{4}{3}$
53. $-\sqrt{5}/5$ **55.** 1   **57.** 5.32   **59.** 148.07   **61.** 77.82
63. 77.3 mi   **65.** 3.9 mi   **67.** 32.12

Chapter 3 Test ■ page 230

1. $5\pi/3$, $-\pi/10$ **2.** 150°, 137.5°
3. (a) 400π rad/min ≈ 1256.6 rad/min   (b) 31,416 ft/min
4. (a) $\sqrt{2}/2$ (b) $\sqrt{3}/3$ (c) 2   (d) 1
5. $(26 + 6\sqrt{13})/39$ **6.** $a = 24 \sin \theta$, $b = 24 \cos \theta$
7. $(4 - 3\sqrt{2})/4$ **8.** $-\frac{13}{12}$ **9.** $\tan \theta = -\sqrt{\sec^2\theta - 1}$
10. 19.6 ft   **11.** 9.1   **12.** 250.5   **13.** 8.4   **14.** 19.5
15. (a) 15.3 m²   (b) 24.3 m   **16.** (a) 129.9°   (b) 44.9
17. 554 ft

Focus on Modeling ■ page 234

1. 1.41 mi   **3.** 14.3 m   **5.** (c) 2349.8 ft
7.

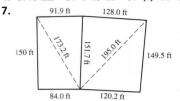

CHAPTER 4

Section 4.1 ■ page 242

1. $\cos t$ **3.** $\sec x$ **5.** −1   **7.** $\csc u$ **9.** 1   **11.** $\cos y$
13. $\sin^2 x$ **15.** $\sec x$ **17.** $2 \sec u$ **19.** $\cos^2 x$
21. $\cos \theta$ **23.** LHS $= \sin \theta \dfrac{\cos \theta}{\sin \theta} = $ RHS
25. LHS $= \cos u \dfrac{1}{\cos u} \cot u = $ RHS
27. LHS $= \dfrac{\sin y}{\cos y} \sin y = \dfrac{1 - \cos^2 y}{\cos y} = \sec y - \cos y = $ RHS
29. LHS $= \sin B + \cos B \dfrac{\cos B}{\sin B}$
$= \dfrac{\sin^2 B + \cos^2 B}{\sin B} = \dfrac{1}{\sin B} = $ RHS
31. LHS $= -\dfrac{\cos \alpha}{\sin \alpha} \cos \alpha - \sin \alpha = \dfrac{-\cos^2 \alpha - \sin^2 \alpha}{\sin \alpha}$
$= \dfrac{-1}{\sin \alpha} = $ RHS
33. LHS $= \dfrac{\sin \theta}{\cos \theta} + \dfrac{\cos \theta}{\sin \theta} = \dfrac{\sin^2 \theta + \cos^2 \theta}{\cos \theta \sin \theta}$
$= \dfrac{1}{\cos \theta \sin \theta} = $ RHS
35. LHS $= 1 - \cos^2 \beta = \sin^2 \beta = $ RHS
37. LHS $= \dfrac{(\sin x + \cos x)^2}{(\sin x + \cos x)(\sin x - \cos x)} = \dfrac{\sin x + \cos x}{\sin x - \cos x}$
$= \dfrac{(\sin x + \cos x)(\sin x - \cos x)}{(\sin x - \cos x)(\sin x - \cos x)} = $ RHS
39. LHS $= \dfrac{\dfrac{1}{\cos t} - \cos t}{\dfrac{1}{\cos t}} \cdot \dfrac{\cos t}{\cos t} = \dfrac{1 - \cos^2 t}{1} = $ RHS
41. LHS $= \dfrac{1}{\cos^2 y} = \sec^2 y = $ RHS

43. LHS $= \cot x \cos x + \cot x - \csc x \cos x - \csc x$

$= \dfrac{\cos^2 x}{\sin x} + \dfrac{\cos x}{\sin x} - \dfrac{\cos x}{\sin x} - \dfrac{1}{\sin x} = \dfrac{\cos^2 x - 1}{\sin x}$

$= \dfrac{-\sin^2 x}{\sin x} = $ RHS

45. LHS $= \sin^2 x \left(1 + \dfrac{\cos^2 x}{\sin^2 x}\right) = \sin^2 x + \cos^2 x = $ RHS

47. LHS $= 2(1 - \sin^2 x) - 1 = 2 - 2\sin^2 x - 1 = $ RHS

49. LHS $= \dfrac{1 - \cos \alpha}{\sin \alpha} \cdot \dfrac{1 + \cos \alpha}{1 + \cos \alpha} = \dfrac{1 - \cos^2 \alpha}{\sin \alpha(1 + \cos \alpha)}$

$= \dfrac{\sin^2 \alpha}{\sin \alpha(1 + \cos \alpha)} = $ RHS

51. LHS $= \dfrac{\sin x - 1}{\sin x + 1} \cdot \dfrac{\sin x + 1}{\sin x + 1} = \dfrac{\sin^2 x - 1}{(\sin x + 1)^2} = $ RHS

53. LHS $= \dfrac{\sin^2 t + 2\sin t \cos t + \cos^2 t}{\sin t \cos t}$

$= \dfrac{\sin^2 t + \cos^2 t}{\sin t \cos t} + \dfrac{2\sin t \cos t}{\sin t \cos t} = \dfrac{1}{\sin t \cos t} + 2$

$= $ RHS

55. LHS $= \dfrac{1 + \frac{\sin^2 u}{\cos^2 u}}{1 - \frac{\sin^2 u}{\cos^2 u}} \cdot \dfrac{\cos^2 u}{\cos^2 u} = \dfrac{\cos^2 u + \sin^2 u}{\cos^2 u - \sin^2 u} = $ RHS

57. LHS $= \dfrac{\sec x}{\sec x - \tan x} \cdot \dfrac{\sec x + \tan x}{\sec x + \tan x}$

$= \dfrac{\sec x(\sec x + \tan x)}{\sec^2 x - \tan^2 x} = $ RHS

59. LHS $= (\sec v - \tan v) \cdot \dfrac{\sec v + \tan v}{\sec v + \tan v}$

$= \dfrac{\sec^2 v - \tan^2 v}{\sec v + \tan v} = $ RHS

61. LHS $= \dfrac{\sin x + \cos x}{\frac{1}{\cos x} + \frac{1}{\sin x}} = \dfrac{\sin x + \cos x}{\frac{\sin x + \cos x}{\cos x \sin x}}$

$= (\sin x + \cos x)\dfrac{\cos x \sin x}{\sin x + \cos x} = $ RHS

63. LHS $= \dfrac{\frac{1}{\sin x} - \frac{\cos x}{\sin x}}{\frac{1}{\cos x} - 1} \cdot \dfrac{\sin x \cos x}{\sin x \cos x} = \dfrac{\cos x(1 - \cos x)}{\sin x(1 - \cos x)}$

$= \dfrac{\cos x}{\sin x} = $ RHS

65. LHS $= \dfrac{\sin^2 u}{\cos^2 u} - \dfrac{\sin^2 u \cos^2 u}{\cos^2 u} = \dfrac{\sin^2 u}{\cos^2 u}(1 - \cos^2 u) = $ RHS

67. LHS $= (\sec^2 x - \tan^2 x)(\sec^2 x + \tan^2 x) = $ RHS

69. RHS $= \dfrac{\sin \theta - \frac{1}{\sin \theta}}{\cos \theta - \frac{\cos \theta}{\sin \theta}} = \dfrac{\frac{\sin^2 \theta - 1}{\sin \theta}}{\frac{\cos \theta \sin \theta - \cos \theta}{\sin \theta}}$

$= \dfrac{\cos^2 \theta}{\cos \theta(\sin \theta - 1)} = $ LHS

71. LHS $= \dfrac{-\sin^2 t + \tan^2 t}{\sin^2 t} = -1 + \dfrac{\sin^2 t}{\cos^2 t} \cdot \dfrac{1}{\sin^2 t}$

$= -1 + \sec^2 t = $ RHS

73. LHS $= \dfrac{\sec x - \tan x + \sec x + \tan x}{(\sec x + \tan x)(\sec x - \tan x)}$

$= \dfrac{2\sec x}{\sec^2 x - \tan^2 x} = $ RHS

75. LHS $= \tan^2 x + 2\tan x \cot x + \cot^2 x = \tan^2 x + 2 + \cot^2 x$

$= (\tan^2 x + 1) + (\cot^2 x + 1) = $ RHS

77. LHS $= \dfrac{\frac{1}{\cos u} - 1}{\frac{1}{\cos u} + 1} \cdot \dfrac{\cos u}{\cos u} = $ RHS

79. LHS $= \dfrac{(\sin x + \cos x)(\sin^2 x - \sin x \cos x + \cos^2 x)}{\sin x + \cos x}$

$= \sin^2 x - \sin x \cos x + \cos^2 x = $ RHS

81. LHS $= \dfrac{1 + \sin x}{1 - \sin x} \cdot \dfrac{1 + \sin x}{1 + \sin x} = \dfrac{(1 + \sin x)^2}{1 - \sin^2 x}$

$= \dfrac{(1 + \sin x)^2}{\cos^2 x} = \left(\dfrac{1 + \sin x}{\cos x}\right)^2 = $ RHS

83. LHS $= \left(\dfrac{\sin x}{\cos x} + \dfrac{\cos x}{\sin x}\right)^4 = \left(\dfrac{\sin^2 x + \cos^2 x}{\sin x \cos x}\right)^4$

$= \left(\dfrac{1}{\sin x \cos x}\right)^4 = $ RHS

85. $\tan \theta$ **87.** $\tan \theta$ **89.** $3\cos \theta$

91.

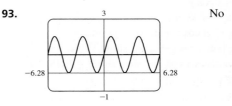

Yes

93.

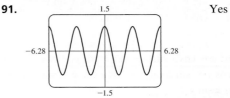

No

Section 4.2 ■ page 250

1. $\dfrac{\sqrt{6}+\sqrt{2}}{4}$ **3.** $\dfrac{\sqrt{6}-\sqrt{2}}{4}$ **5.** $2+\sqrt{3}$

7. $\dfrac{\sqrt{6}-\sqrt{2}}{4}$ **9.** $\dfrac{\sqrt{6}+\sqrt{2}}{4}$ **11.** $\sqrt{2}/2$

13. $1/2$ **15.** $\sqrt{3}$

17. LHS $= \dfrac{\sin\left(\frac{\pi}{2}-u\right)}{\cos\left(\frac{\pi}{2}-u\right)} = \dfrac{\sin\frac{\pi}{2}\cos u - \cos\frac{\pi}{2}\sin u}{\cos\frac{\pi}{2}\cos u + \sin\frac{\pi}{2}\sin u}$

$= \dfrac{\cos u}{\sin u} = $ RHS

19. LHS $= \dfrac{1}{\cos\left(\frac{\pi}{2}-u\right)} = \dfrac{1}{\cos\frac{\pi}{2}\cos u + \sin\frac{\pi}{2}\sin u}$

$= \dfrac{1}{\sin u} = $ RHS

21. LHS $= \sin x \cos\frac{\pi}{2} - \cos x \sin\frac{\pi}{2} = $ RHS
23. LHS $= \sin x \cos \pi - \cos x \sin \pi = $ RHS
25. LHS $= \dfrac{\tan x - \tan \pi}{1 + \tan x \tan \pi} = $ RHS
27. LHS $=$

$\cos x \cos\frac{\pi}{6} - \sin x \sin\frac{\pi}{6} + \sin x \cos\frac{\pi}{3} - \cos x \sin\frac{\pi}{3}$
$= \frac{\sqrt{3}}{2}\cos x - \frac{1}{2}\sin x + \frac{1}{2}\sin x - \frac{\sqrt{3}}{2}\cos x = $ RHS

29. LHS $= \sin x \cos y + \cos x \sin y$
$-(\sin x \cos y - \cos x \sin y) = $ RHS

31. LHS $= \dfrac{1}{\tan(x-y)} = \dfrac{1+\tan x \tan y}{\tan x - \tan y}$

$= \dfrac{1+\frac{1}{\cot x}\frac{1}{\cot y}}{\frac{1}{\cot x}-\frac{1}{\cot y}} \cdot \dfrac{\cot x \cot y}{\cot x \cot y} = $ RHS

33. LHS $= \dfrac{\sin x}{\cos x} - \dfrac{\sin y}{\cos y} = \dfrac{\sin x \cos y - \cos x \sin y}{\cos x \cos y} = $ RHS

35. LHS $=$

$\dfrac{\sin x \cos y + \cos x \sin y - (\sin x \cos y - \cos x \sin y)}{\cos x \cos y - \sin x \sin y + \cos x \cos y + \sin x \sin y}$
$= \dfrac{2\cos x \sin y}{2\cos x \cos y} = $ RHS

37. LHS $= \sin((x+y)+z)$
$= \sin(x+y)\cos z + \cos(x+y)\sin z$
$= \cos z\,[\sin x \cos y + \cos x \sin y]$
$\quad + \sin z\,[\cos x \cos y - \sin x \sin y] = $ RHS

39. $2\sin\left(x+\dfrac{5\pi}{6}\right)$

41. $5\sqrt{2}\sin\left(2x+\dfrac{7\pi}{4}\right)$

43. $f(x) = \sqrt{2}\sin\left(x+\dfrac{\pi}{4}\right)$

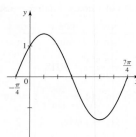

47. $\tan \gamma = \dfrac{17}{6}$

49. (a)

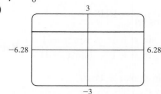

$\sin^{2}\left(x+\dfrac{\pi}{4}\right) + \sin^{2}\left(x-\dfrac{\pi}{4}\right) = 1$

51. (a)

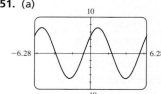

(b) $k = 5\sqrt{2}$,
$\theta = \pi/4$

Section 4.3 ■ page 259

1. $\frac{120}{169}, \frac{119}{169}, \frac{120}{119}$ **3.** $-\frac{24}{25}, \frac{7}{25}, -\frac{24}{7}$ **5.** $\frac{24}{25}, \frac{7}{25}, \frac{24}{7}$
7. $-\frac{3}{5}, \frac{4}{5}, -\frac{3}{4}$ **9.** $\frac{1}{2}\left(\frac{3}{4}-\cos 2x + \frac{1}{4}\cos 4x\right)$
11. $\frac{1}{32}\left(\frac{3}{4}-\cos 4x + \frac{1}{4}\cos 8x\right)$
13. $\frac{1}{16}(1 - \cos 2x - \cos 4x + \cos 2x \cos 4x)$
15. $\frac{1}{2}\sqrt{2-\sqrt{3}}$ **17.** $\frac{1}{2}\sqrt{2+\sqrt{2}}$ **19.** $\sqrt{2}-1$
21. $\frac{1}{2}\sqrt{2-\sqrt{3}}$ **23.** (a) $\sin 36°$ (b) $\sin 6\theta$
25. (a) $\cos 68°$ (b) $\cos 10\theta$ **27.** (a) $\tan 4°$ (b) $\tan 2\theta$
29. $\sqrt{10}/10, 3\sqrt{10}/10, \frac{1}{3}$
31. $\sqrt{(3+2\sqrt{2})/6}, \sqrt{(3-2\sqrt{2})/6}, 3+2\sqrt{2}$
33. $\sqrt{6}/6, -\sqrt{30}/6, -\sqrt{5}/5$
35. $\frac{1}{2}(\sin 5x - \sin x)$ **37.** $\frac{1}{2}(\sin 5x + \sin 3x)$
39. $\frac{3}{2}(\cos 11x + \cos 3x)$ **41.** $2\sin 4x \cos x$
43. $2\sin 5x \sin x$ **45.** $-2\cos\frac{9}{2}x \sin\frac{5}{2}x$
47. $(\sqrt{2}+\sqrt{3})/2$ **49.** $\frac{1}{4}(\sqrt{2}-1)$ **51.** $\sqrt{2}/2$
53. LHS $= \cos(2 \cdot 5x) = $ RHS
55. LHS $= \sin^{2}x + 2\sin x \cos x + \cos^{2}x = 1 + 2\sin x \cos x$
$\quad\quad = $ RHS

57. LHS $= \dfrac{(2 \sin 2x \cos 2x)}{\sin x} = \dfrac{2(2 \sin x \cos x)(\cos 2x)}{\sin x}$

$= $ RHS

59. LHS $= \dfrac{2(\tan x - \cot x)}{(\tan x + \cot x)(\tan x - \cot x)} = \dfrac{2}{\tan x + \cot x}$

$= \dfrac{2}{\frac{\sin x}{\cos x} + \frac{\cos x}{\sin x}} \cdot \dfrac{\sin x \cos x}{\sin x \cos x} = \dfrac{2 \sin x \cos x}{\sin^2 x + \cos^2 x}$

$= 2 \sin x \cos x = $ RHS

61. LHS $= \tan(2x + x) = \dfrac{\tan 2x + \tan x}{1 - \tan 2x \tan x}$

$= \dfrac{\frac{2 \tan x}{1 - \tan^2 x} + \tan x}{1 - \frac{2 \tan x}{1 - \tan^2 x} \tan x}$

$= \dfrac{2 \tan x + \tan x(1 - \tan^2 x)}{1 - \tan^2 x - 2 \tan x \tan x} = $ RHS

63. LHS $= (\cos^2 x + \sin^2 x)(\cos^2 x - \sin^2 x)$

$= \cos^2 x - \sin^2 x = $ RHS

65. LHS $= \dfrac{2 \sin 3x \cos 2x}{2 \cos 3x \cos 2x} = \dfrac{\sin 3x}{\cos 3x} = $ RHS

67. LHS $= \dfrac{2 \sin 5x \cos 5x}{2 \sin 5x \cos 4x} = $ RHS

69. LHS $= \dfrac{2 \sin\left(\frac{x+y}{2}\right) \cos\left(\frac{x-y}{2}\right)}{2 \cos\left(\frac{x+y}{2}\right) \cos\left(\frac{x-y}{2}\right)}$

$= \dfrac{\sin\left(\frac{x+y}{2}\right)}{\cos\left(\frac{x+y}{2}\right)} = $ RHS

73. LHS $=$

$\dfrac{(\sin x + \sin 5x) + (\sin 2x + \sin 4x) + \sin 3x}{(\cos x + \cos 5x) + (\cos 2x + \cos 4x) + \cos 3x}$

$= \dfrac{2 \sin 3x \cos 2x + 2 \sin 3x \cos x + \sin 3x}{2 \cos 3x \cos 2x + 2 \cos 3x \cos x + \cos 3x}$

$= \dfrac{\sin 3x(2 \cos 2x + 2 \cos x + 1)}{\cos 3x(2 \cos 2x + 2 \cos x + 1)} = $ RHS

75. (a)

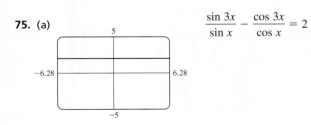

$\dfrac{\sin 3x}{\sin x} - \dfrac{\cos 3x}{\cos x} = 2$

77. (a)

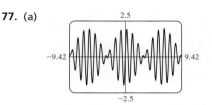

(c)

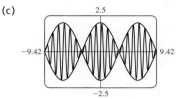

The graph of $y = f(x)$ lies between the two other graphs.

83. (a) $P(t) = 8t^4 - 8t^2 + 1$
(b) $Q(t) = 16t^5 - 20t^3 + 5t$

Section 4.4 ■ page 269

1. (a) $\pi/6$ (b) $\pi/3$ (c) Not defined
3. (a) $\pi/4$ (b) $\pi/4$ (c) $-\pi/4$
5. (a) $\pi/2$ (b) 0 (c) π
7. (a) $\pi/6$ (b) $-\pi/6$ (c) Not defined
9. (a) 0.13889 (b) 2.75876 **11.** (a) 0.88998
(b) Not defined **13.** $\frac{1}{4}$ **15.** 5 **17.** $\pi/3$ **19.** $-\pi/6$
21. $-\pi/3$ **23.** $\sqrt{3}/3$ **25.** $\frac{1}{2}$ **27.** $\pi/3$ **29.** $\frac{4}{5}$
31. $\frac{12}{13}$ **33.** $\frac{13}{5}$ **35.** $\sqrt{5}/5$ **37.** $\frac{24}{25}$ **39.** 1
41. $\sqrt{1 - x^2}$ **43.** $x/\sqrt{1 - x^2}$ **45.** $\dfrac{1 - x^2}{1 + x^2}$ **47.** 0
49. (a) $h = 2 \tan \theta$ (b) $\theta = \tan^{-1}\left(\frac{h}{2}\right)$
51. (a) $\theta = \sin^{-1}\left(\frac{h}{680}\right)$ (b) $\theta = 0.826$ rad
53. (a)

Conjecture: $y = \pi/2$ for $-1 \le x \le 1$
55. (a) 0.28 (b) $(-3 + \sqrt{17})/4$

Section 4.5 ■ page 281

1. $\dfrac{\pi}{2} + 2k\pi$ **3.** $\dfrac{\pi}{3} + 2k\pi, \dfrac{5\pi}{3} + 2k\pi$

5. $\dfrac{4\pi}{3} + 2k\pi, \dfrac{5\pi}{3} + 2k\pi$

7. $\dfrac{\pi}{3} + 2k\pi, \dfrac{2\pi}{3} + 2k\pi, \dfrac{4\pi}{3} + 2k\pi, \dfrac{5\pi}{3} + 2k\pi$

9. $\dfrac{(2k + 1)\pi}{4}$ **11.** $\dfrac{\pi}{2} + k\pi, \dfrac{7\pi}{6} + 2k\pi, \dfrac{11\pi}{6} + 2k\pi$

13. $-\dfrac{\pi}{3} + k\pi$ **15.** $\dfrac{\pi}{2} + k\pi$

17. $\dfrac{\pi}{3} + 2k\pi, \dfrac{5\pi}{3} + 2k\pi$

19. $\dfrac{3\pi}{2} + 2k\pi$ **21.** No solution

23. $\dfrac{7\pi}{18} + \dfrac{2k\pi}{3}, \dfrac{11\pi}{18} + \dfrac{2k\pi}{3}$

25. $\dfrac{1}{4}\left(\dfrac{\pi}{3} + 2k\pi\right), \dfrac{1}{4}\left(-\dfrac{\pi}{3} + 2k\pi\right)$ **27.** $\dfrac{1}{2}\left(\dfrac{\pi}{6} + k\pi\right)$

29. $4k\pi$ **31.** $4\left(\dfrac{2\pi}{3} + k\pi\right)$ **33.** $\dfrac{k\pi}{3}$

35. $\dfrac{\pi}{6} + 2k\pi, \dfrac{2\pi}{3} + 2k\pi, \dfrac{5\pi}{6} + 2k\pi, \dfrac{4\pi}{3} + 2k\pi$

37. $\dfrac{\pi}{8} + \dfrac{k\pi}{2}, \dfrac{3\pi}{8} + \dfrac{k\pi}{2}$ **39.** $\dfrac{\pi}{9}, \dfrac{5\pi}{9}, \dfrac{7\pi}{9}, \dfrac{11\pi}{9}, \dfrac{13\pi}{9}, \dfrac{17\pi}{9}$

41. $\dfrac{\pi}{6}, \dfrac{3\pi}{4}, \dfrac{5\pi}{6}, \dfrac{7\pi}{4}$ **43.** $\dfrac{\pi}{3}, \dfrac{2\pi}{3}, \dfrac{4\pi}{3}, \dfrac{5\pi}{3}$

45. $0, \dfrac{2\pi}{3}, \dfrac{4\pi}{3}$ **47.** (a) $1.15928 + 2k\pi, 5.12391 + 2k\pi$

(b) $1.15928, 5.12391$

49. (a) $1.36944 + 2k\pi, 4.91375 + 2k\pi$

(b) $1.36944, 4.91375$

51. (a) $0.46365 + k\pi, 2.67795 + k\pi$

(b) $0.46365, 2.67795, 3.60524, 5.81954$

53. (a) $0.33984 + 2k\pi, 2.80176 + 2k\pi$

(b) $0.33984, 2.80176$

55. $((2k + 1)\pi, -2)$ **57.** $\left(\dfrac{\pi}{3} + k\pi, \sqrt{3}\right)$

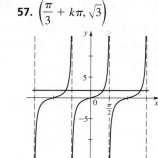

59. $0.94721°$ or $89.05279°$ **61.** $44.95°$

63. $\dfrac{\pi}{8}, \dfrac{3\pi}{8}, \dfrac{5\pi}{8}, \dfrac{7\pi}{8}, \dfrac{9\pi}{8}, \dfrac{11\pi}{8}, \dfrac{13\pi}{8}, \dfrac{15\pi}{8}$

65. $\dfrac{\pi}{9}, \dfrac{2\pi}{9}, \dfrac{7\pi}{9}, \dfrac{8\pi}{9}, \dfrac{13\pi}{9}, \dfrac{14\pi}{9}$

67. $\dfrac{\pi}{2}, \dfrac{7\pi}{6}, \dfrac{3\pi}{2}, \dfrac{11\pi}{6}$ **69.** 0 **71.** $\dfrac{k\pi}{2}$

73. $\dfrac{\pi}{9} + \dfrac{2k\pi}{3}, \dfrac{\pi}{2} + k\pi, \dfrac{5\pi}{9} + \dfrac{2k\pi}{3}$

75. $0, \pm0.95$ **77.** 1.92 **79.** ±0.71

Chapter 4 Review ■ page 283

1. LHS $= \sin\theta\left(\dfrac{\cos\theta}{\sin\theta} + \dfrac{\sin\theta}{\cos\theta}\right) = \cos\theta + \dfrac{\sin^2\theta}{\cos\theta}$

$= \dfrac{\cos^2\theta + \sin^2\theta}{\cos\theta} = $ RHS

3. LHS $= (1 - \sin^2x)\csc x - \csc x = \csc x - \sin^2x\csc x - \csc x$

$= -\sin^2x\dfrac{1}{\sin x} = $ RHS

5. LHS $= \dfrac{\cos^2x}{\sin^2x} - \dfrac{\tan^2x}{\sin^2x} = \cot^2x - \dfrac{1}{\cos^2x} = $ RHS

7. LHS $= \dfrac{\cos x}{\frac{1}{\cos x}(1 - \sin x)} = \dfrac{\cos x}{\frac{1}{\cos x} - \frac{\sin x}{\cos x}} = $ RHS

9. LHS $= \sin^2x\dfrac{\cos^2x}{\sin^2x} + \cos^2x\dfrac{\sin^2x}{\cos^2x} = \cos^2x + \sin^2x = $ RHS

11. LHS $= \dfrac{2\sin x\cos x}{1 + 2\cos^2x - 1} = \dfrac{2\sin x\cos x}{2\cos^2x} = \dfrac{2\sin x}{2\cos x} = $ RHS

13. LHS $= \dfrac{1 - \cos x}{\sin x} = \dfrac{1}{\sin x} - \dfrac{\cos x}{\sin x} = $ RHS

15. LHS $= \frac{1}{2}[\cos((x + y) - (x - y)) - \cos((x + y) + (x - y))]$

$= \frac{1}{2}(\cos 2y - \cos 2x) = \frac{1}{2}[1 - 2\sin^2y - (1 - 2\sin^2x)]$

$= \frac{1}{2}(2\sin^2x - 2\sin^2y) = $ RHS

17. LHS $= 1 + \dfrac{\sin x}{\cos x} \cdot \dfrac{1 - \cos x}{\sin x} = 1 + \dfrac{1 - \cos x}{\cos x}$

$= 1 + \dfrac{1}{\cos x} - 1 = $ RHS

19. LHS $= \cos^2\frac{x}{2} - 2\sin\frac{x}{2}\cos\frac{x}{2} + \sin^2\frac{x}{2} = 1 - \sin\left(2 \cdot \frac{x}{2}\right) = $ RHS

21. LHS $= \dfrac{2\sin x\cos x}{\sin x} - \dfrac{2\cos^2x - 1}{\cos x}$

$= 2\cos x - 2\cos x + \dfrac{1}{\cos x} = $ RHS

23. LHS $= \dfrac{\tan x + \tan\frac{\pi}{4}}{1 - \tan x\tan\frac{\pi}{4}} = $ RHS

25. (a) 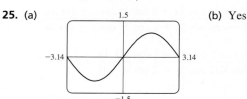 (b) Yes

27. (a) 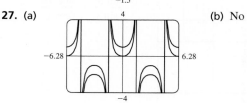 (b) No

29. (a) $2\sin^2 3x + \cos 6x = 1$

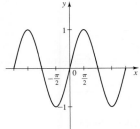

31. $0, \pi$ **33.** $\dfrac{\pi}{6}, \dfrac{5\pi}{6}$ **35.** $\dfrac{\pi}{3}, \dfrac{5\pi}{3}$ **37.** $\dfrac{2\pi}{3}, \dfrac{4\pi}{3}$

39. $\dfrac{\pi}{3}, \dfrac{2\pi}{3}, \dfrac{3\pi}{4}, \dfrac{4\pi}{3}, \dfrac{5\pi}{3}, \dfrac{7\pi}{4}$

41. $\dfrac{\pi}{6}, \dfrac{\pi}{2}, \dfrac{5\pi}{6}, \dfrac{7\pi}{6}, \dfrac{3\pi}{2}, \dfrac{11\pi}{6}$ **43.** $\dfrac{\pi}{6}$ **45.** 1.18

49. $\frac{1}{2}\sqrt{2 + \sqrt{3}}$ **51.** $\sqrt{2} - 1$ **53.** $\sqrt{2}/2$

55. $\sqrt{2}/2$ **57.** $\dfrac{\sqrt{2} + \sqrt{3}}{4}$ **59.** $2\dfrac{\sqrt{10} + 1}{9}$

61. $\frac{2}{3}\left(\sqrt{2} + \sqrt{5}\right)$ **63.** $\sqrt{(3 + 2\sqrt{2})/6}$ **65.** $\pi/3$

67. $\frac{1}{2}$ **69.** $2/\sqrt{21}$ **71.** $\frac{7}{9}$ **73.** $x/\sqrt{1 + x^2}$

75. $\theta = \cos^{-1}\dfrac{x}{3}$ **77. (a)** $\theta = \tan^{-1}\left(\dfrac{10}{x}\right)$ **(b)** 286.4 ft

Chapter 4 Test ■ page 286

1. (a) $\text{LHS} = \dfrac{\sin\theta}{\cos\theta}\sin\theta + \cos\theta = \dfrac{\sin^2\theta + \cos^2\theta}{\cos\theta} = \text{RHS}$

(b) $\text{LHS} = \dfrac{\tan x}{1 - \cos x} \cdot \dfrac{1 + \cos x}{1 + \cos x} = \dfrac{\tan x(1 + \cos x)}{1 - \cos^2 x}$

$= \dfrac{\frac{\sin x}{\cos x}(1 + \cos x)}{\sin^2 x} = \dfrac{1}{\sin x} \cdot \dfrac{1 + \cos x}{\cos x} = \text{RHS}$

(c) $\text{LHS} = \dfrac{2\tan x}{\sec^2 x} = \dfrac{2\sin x}{\cos x} \cdot \cos^2 x = 2\sin x\cos x = \text{RHS}$

2. $\tan\theta$ **3. (a)** $\frac{1}{2}$ **(b)** $\dfrac{\sqrt{2} + \sqrt{6}}{4}$ **(c)** $\frac{1}{2}\sqrt{2 - \sqrt{3}}$

4. $(10 - 2\sqrt{5})/15$

5. (a) $\frac{1}{2}(\sin 8x - \sin 2x)$ **(b)** $-2\cos\frac{7}{2}x\sin\frac{3}{2}x$ **6.** -2

7.

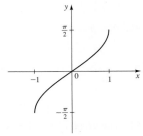

Domain $\mathbb{R}$ Domain $[-1, 1]$

8. (a) $\theta = \tan^{-1}\dfrac{x}{4}$ **(b)** $\theta = \cos^{-1}\dfrac{3}{x}$

9. (a) $\dfrac{2\pi}{3}, \dfrac{4\pi}{3}$ **(b)** $\dfrac{\pi}{6}, \dfrac{\pi}{2}, \dfrac{5\pi}{6}, \dfrac{3\pi}{2}$

10. 0.57964, 2.56195, 3.72123, 5.70355

11. $\frac{40}{41}$

Focus on Modeling ■ page 290

1. (a) $y = -5\sin\left(\dfrac{\pi}{2}t\right)$ **(b)**

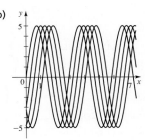

(c) $v = \pi/4$

Yes, it is a traveling wave.

3. $y(x, t) = 2.7\sin(0.68x - 4.10t)$

5. $y(x, t) = 0.6\sin(\pi x)\cos(40\pi t)$

7. (a) 1, 2, 3, 4

(b) 5:

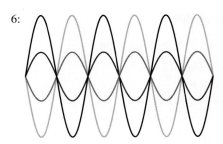

6:

(c) 880π

(d) $y(x, t) = \sin t\,\cos(880\pi t)$;

$y(x, t) = \sin(2t)\,\cos(880\pi t)$;

$y(x, t) = \sin(3t)\,\cos(880\pi t)$;

$y(x, t) = \sin(4t)\,\cos(880\pi t)$

CHAPTER 5

Section 5.1 ■ page 300

1. **3.**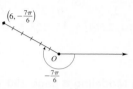

5. **7.** 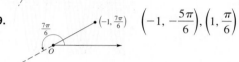 $\left(-3, \dfrac{3\pi}{2}\right), \left(3, \dfrac{5\pi}{2}\right)$

9. 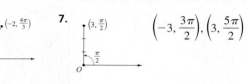 $\left(-1, -\dfrac{5\pi}{6}\right), \left(1, \dfrac{\pi}{6}\right)$

11. $(-5, 2\pi), (5, \pi)$

13. Q **15.** Q **17.** P **19.** P **21.** $\left(3\sqrt{2}, \dfrac{3\pi}{4}\right)$

23. $\left(-\dfrac{5}{2}, -\dfrac{5\sqrt{3}}{2}\right)$ **25.** $(2\sqrt{3}, 2)$ **27.** $(1, -1)$ **29.** $(-5, 0)$

31. $\left(3\sqrt{6}, -3\sqrt{2}\right)$ **33.** $\left(\sqrt{2}, \dfrac{3\pi}{4}\right)$ **35.** $\left(4, \dfrac{\pi}{4}\right)$

37. $\left(5, \tan^{-1}\dfrac{4}{3}\right)$ **39.** $(6, \pi)$ **41.** $\theta = \dfrac{\pi}{4}$ **43.** $r = \tan\theta\sec\theta$

45. $r = 4\sec\theta$ **47.** $x^2 + y^2 = 49$ **49.** $x = 6$

51. $x^2 + y^2 = \dfrac{y}{x}$ **53.** $y - x = 1$

55. $x^2 + y^2 = (x^2 + y^2 - x)^2$ **57.** $x = 2$ **59.** $y = \pm\sqrt{3}x$

Section 5.2 ■ page 309

1. VI   **3.** II   **5.** I   **7.** Symmetric about $\theta = \dfrac{\pi}{2}$

9. Symmetric about the polar axis

11. Symmetric about $\theta = \dfrac{\pi}{2}$

13. All three types of symmetry

15. 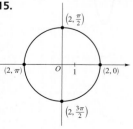   **17.**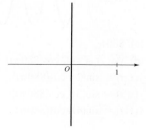

19. 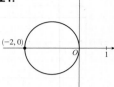   **21.**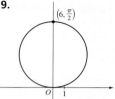

23 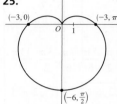   **25.**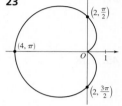

27. 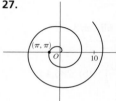   **29.**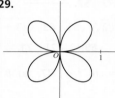

31. 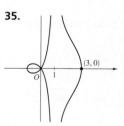   **33.**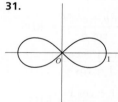

35. 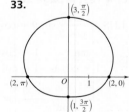   **37.** $0 \le \theta \le 4\pi$

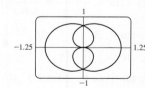

39. $0 \le \theta \le 4\pi$

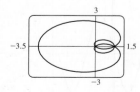

41. The graph of $r = 1 + \sin n\theta$ has n loops.

43. IV   **45.** III

Section 5.3 ■ page 316

1. Real part 5, imaginary part -7 **3.** Real part $-\frac{2}{3}$,
imaginary part $-\frac{5}{3}$ **5.** Real part 3, imaginary part 0
7. Real part 0, imaginary part $-\frac{2}{3}$
9. Real part $\sqrt{3}$, imaginary part 2
11. $5 - i$ **13.** $3 + 5i$ **15.** $2 - 2i$ **17.** $-19 + 4i$
19. $-4 + 8i$ **21.** $30 + 10i$ **23.** $-33 - 56i$ **25.** $27 - 8i$
27. $-i$ **29.** $\frac{8}{5} + \frac{1}{5}i$ **31.** $-5 + 12i$ **33.** $-4 + 2i$
35. $2 - \frac{4}{3}i$ **37.** $-i$ **39.** $-i$ **41.** 1   **43.** $5i$ **45.** -6
47. $(3 + \sqrt{5}) + (3 - \sqrt{5})i$ **49.** 2   **51.** $-i\sqrt{2}$ **53.** $\pm 3i$
55. $2 \pm i$ **57.** $-\dfrac{1}{2} \pm \dfrac{\sqrt{3}}{2}i$ **59.** $\frac{1}{2} \pm \frac{1}{2}i$ **61.** $-\dfrac{3}{2} \pm \dfrac{\sqrt{3}}{2}i$
63. $\dfrac{-6 \pm \sqrt{6}\,i}{6}$ **65.** $1 \pm 3i$

Section 5.4 ■ page 327

1. 4

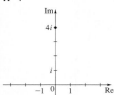

3. $\sqrt{29}$

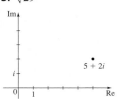

5. 2

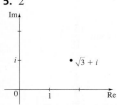

7. 1

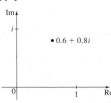

9.

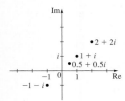

11.

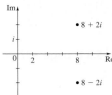

13.

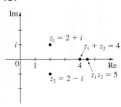

15.

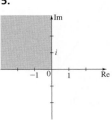

17.

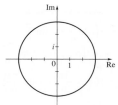

19.

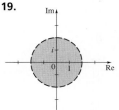

21.

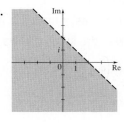

23. $\sqrt{2}\left(\cos\dfrac{\pi}{4} + i\sin\dfrac{\pi}{4}\right)$ **25.** $2\left(\cos\dfrac{7\pi}{4} + i\sin\dfrac{7\pi}{4}\right)$

27. $4\left(\cos\dfrac{11\pi}{6} + i\sin\dfrac{11\pi}{6}\right)$ **29.** $3\left(\cos\dfrac{3\pi}{2} + i\sin\dfrac{3\pi}{2}\right)$

31. $5\sqrt{2}\left(\cos\dfrac{\pi}{4} + i\sin\dfrac{\pi}{4}\right)$ **33.** $8\left(\cos\dfrac{11\pi}{6} + i\sin\dfrac{11\pi}{6}\right)$

35. $20(\cos \pi + i\sin \pi)$ **37.** $5\left[\cos\left(\tan^{-1}\frac{4}{3}\right) + i\sin\left(\tan^{-1}\frac{4}{3}\right)\right]$

39. $3\sqrt{2}\left(\cos\dfrac{3\pi}{4} + i\sin\dfrac{3\pi}{4}\right)$ **41.** $8\left(\cos\dfrac{\pi}{6} + i\sin\dfrac{\pi}{6}\right)$

43. $\sqrt{5}\left[\cos\left(\tan^{-1}\frac{1}{2}\right) + i\sin\left(\tan^{-1}\frac{1}{2}\right)\right]$

45. $2\left(\cos\dfrac{\pi}{4} + i\sin\dfrac{\pi}{4}\right)$

47. $z_1 z_2 = \cos\dfrac{4\pi}{3} + i\sin\dfrac{4\pi}{3}$ $\dfrac{z_1}{z_2} = \cos\dfrac{2\pi}{3} + i\sin\dfrac{2\pi}{3}$

49. $z_1 z_2 = 15\left(\cos\dfrac{3\pi}{2} + i\sin\dfrac{3\pi}{2}\right)$
$\dfrac{z_1}{z_2} = \dfrac{3}{5}\left(\cos\dfrac{7\pi}{6} - i\sin\dfrac{7\pi}{6}\right)$

51. $z_1 z_2 = 8(\cos 150° + i\sin 150°)$ **53.** $z_1 z_2 = 100(\cos 350° + i\sin 350°)$
$\dfrac{z_1}{z_2} = 2(\cos 90° + i\sin 90°)$ $\dfrac{z_1}{z_2} = \dfrac{4}{25}(\cos 50° + i\sin 50°)$

55. $z_1 = 2\left(\cos\dfrac{\pi}{6} + i\sin\dfrac{\pi}{6}\right)$ **57.** $z_1 = 4\left(\cos\dfrac{11\pi}{6} + i\sin\dfrac{11\pi}{6}\right)$

$z_2 = 2\left(\cos\dfrac{\pi}{3} + i\sin\dfrac{\pi}{3}\right)$ $z_2 = \sqrt{2}\left(\cos\dfrac{3\pi}{4} + i\sin\dfrac{3\pi}{4}\right)$

$z_1 z_2 = 4\left(\cos\dfrac{\pi}{2} + i\sin\dfrac{\pi}{2}\right)$ $z_1 z_2 = 4\sqrt{2}\left(\cos\dfrac{7\pi}{12} + i\sin\dfrac{7\pi}{12}\right)$

$\dfrac{z_1}{z_2} = \cos\dfrac{\pi}{6} - i\sin\dfrac{\pi}{6}$ $\dfrac{z_1}{z_2} = 2\sqrt{2}\left(\cos\dfrac{13\pi}{12} + i\sin\dfrac{13\pi}{12}\right)$

$\dfrac{1}{z_1} = \dfrac{1}{2}\left(\cos\dfrac{\pi}{6} - i\sin\dfrac{\pi}{6}\right)$ $\dfrac{1}{z_1} = \dfrac{1}{4}\left(\cos\dfrac{11\pi}{6} - i\sin\dfrac{11\pi}{6}\right)$

59. $z_1 = 5\sqrt{2}\left(\cos\dfrac{\pi}{4} + i\sin\dfrac{\pi}{4}\right)$ **61.** $z_1 = 20(\cos\pi + i\sin\pi)$

$z_2 = 4(\cos 0 + i\sin 0)$ $z_2 = 2\left(\cos\dfrac{\pi}{6} + i\sin\dfrac{\pi}{6}\right)$

$z_1 z_2 = 20\sqrt{2}\left(\cos\dfrac{\pi}{4} + i\sin\dfrac{\pi}{4}\right)$ $z_2 z_2 = 40\left(\cos\dfrac{7\pi}{6} + i\sin\dfrac{7\pi}{6}\right)$

$\dfrac{z_1}{z_2} = \dfrac{5\sqrt{2}}{4}\left(\cos\dfrac{\pi}{4} + i\sin\dfrac{\pi}{4}\right)$ $\dfrac{z_1}{z_2} = 10\left(\cos\dfrac{5\pi}{6} + i\sin\dfrac{5\pi}{6}\right)$

$\dfrac{1}{z_1} = \dfrac{\sqrt{2}}{10}\left(\cos\dfrac{\pi}{4} - i\sin\dfrac{\pi}{4}\right)$ $\dfrac{1}{z_1} = \tfrac{1}{20}(\cos\pi - i\sin\pi)$

63. -1024 **65.** $512(-\sqrt{3} + i)$ **67.** -1

69. 4096 **71.** $8(-1 + i)$ **73.** $\dfrac{1}{2048}(-\sqrt{3} - i)$

75. $2\sqrt{2}\left(\cos\dfrac{\pi}{12} + i\sin\dfrac{\pi}{12}\right)$,

$2\sqrt{2}\left(\cos\dfrac{13\pi}{12} + i\sin\dfrac{13\pi}{12}\right)$

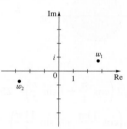

77. $3\left(\cos\dfrac{3\pi}{8} + i\sin\dfrac{3\pi}{8}\right)$,

$3\left(\cos\dfrac{7\pi}{8} + i\sin\dfrac{7\pi}{8}\right)$,

$3\left(\cos\dfrac{11\pi}{8} + i\sin\dfrac{11\pi}{8}\right)$,

$3\left(\cos\dfrac{15\pi}{8} + i\sin\dfrac{15\pi}{8}\right)$

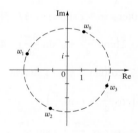

79. $\pm 1,\ \pm i,\ \pm\dfrac{\sqrt{2}}{2} \pm \dfrac{\sqrt{2}}{2}i$

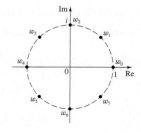

81. $\dfrac{\sqrt{3}}{2} + \dfrac{1}{2}i,\ -\dfrac{\sqrt{3}}{2} + \dfrac{1}{2}i,\ -i$

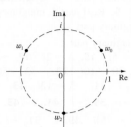

83. $\pm\dfrac{\sqrt{2}}{2} \pm \dfrac{\sqrt{2}}{2}i$

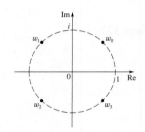

85. $\pm\dfrac{\sqrt{2}}{2} \pm \dfrac{\sqrt{2}}{2}i$

87. $2\left(\cos\dfrac{\pi}{18} + i\sin\dfrac{\pi}{18}\right),\ 2\left(\cos\dfrac{13\pi}{18} + i\sin\dfrac{13\pi}{18}\right)$,

$2\left(\cos\dfrac{25\pi}{18} + i\sin\dfrac{25\pi}{18}\right)$

89. $2^{1/6}\left(\cos\dfrac{5\pi}{12} + i\sin\dfrac{5\pi}{12}\right),\ 2^{1/6}\left(\cos\dfrac{13\pi}{12} + i\sin\dfrac{13\pi}{12}\right)$,

$2^{1/6}\left(\cos\dfrac{21\pi}{12} + i\sin\dfrac{21\pi}{12}\right)$

Section 5.5 ■ page 337

1.

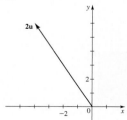

3.

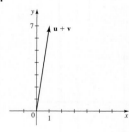

5.

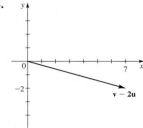

7. $\langle 3, 3 \rangle$ **9.** $\langle 3, -1 \rangle$ **11.** $\langle 5, 7 \rangle$ **13.** $\langle -4, -3 \rangle$
15. $\langle 0, 2 \rangle$ **17.** $\langle 4, 14 \rangle, \langle -9, -3 \rangle, \langle 5, 8 \rangle, \langle -6, 17 \rangle$
19. $\langle 0, -2 \rangle, \langle 6, 0 \rangle, \langle -2, -1 \rangle, \langle 8, -3 \rangle$
21. $4\mathbf{i}, -9\mathbf{i} + 6\mathbf{j}, 5\mathbf{i} - 2\mathbf{j}, -6\mathbf{i} + 8\mathbf{j}$
23. $\sqrt{5}, \sqrt{13}, 2\sqrt{5}, \frac{1}{2}\sqrt{13}, \sqrt{26}, \sqrt{10}, \sqrt{5} - \sqrt{13}$
25. $\sqrt{101}, 2\sqrt{2}, 2\sqrt{101}, \sqrt{2}, \sqrt{73}, \sqrt{145}, \sqrt{101} - 2\sqrt{2}$
27. $20\sqrt{3}\,\mathbf{i} + 20\mathbf{j}$ **29.** $-\frac{\sqrt{2}}{2}\mathbf{i} - \frac{\sqrt{2}}{2}\mathbf{j}$
31. $4\cos 10°\mathbf{i} + 4\sin 10°\mathbf{j} \approx 3.94\mathbf{i} + 0.69\mathbf{j}$
33. $15\sqrt{3}, -15$ **35.** $5, 53.13°$ **37.** $13, 157.38°$
39. $2, 60°$ **41.** $2\mathbf{i} - 3\mathbf{j}$ **43.** (a) $40\mathbf{j}$ (b) $425\mathbf{i}$
(c) $425\mathbf{i} + 40\mathbf{j}$ (d) 427 mi/h, N 84.6° E
45. 794 mi/h, N 26.6° W **47.** (a) $10\mathbf{i}$ (b) $10\mathbf{i} + 17.32\mathbf{j}$
(c) $20\mathbf{i} + 17.32\mathbf{j}$ (d) 26.5 mi/h, N 49.1° E
49. (a) $22.8\mathbf{i} + 7.4\mathbf{j}$ (b) 7.4 mi/h, 22.8 mi/h
51. (a) $\langle 5, -3 \rangle$ (b) $\langle -5, 3 \rangle$ **53.** (a) $-4\mathbf{j}$ (b) $4\mathbf{j}$
55. (a) $\langle -7.57, 10.61 \rangle$ (b) $\langle 7.57, -10.61 \rangle$
57. $\mathbf{T}_1 \approx -56.5\mathbf{i} + 67.4\mathbf{j}, \mathbf{T}_2 \approx 56.5\mathbf{i} + 32.6\mathbf{j}$

Section 5.6 ■ page 347

1. (a) 2 (b) 45° **3.** (a) 13 (b) 56° **5.** (a) −1
(b) 97° **7.** (a) $5\sqrt{3}$ (b) 30° **9.** Yes **11.** No
13. Yes **15.** 9 **17.** −5 **19.** $-\frac{12}{5}$ **21.** −24
23. (a) $\langle 1, 1 \rangle$ (b) $\mathbf{u}_1 = \langle 1, 1 \rangle, \mathbf{u}_2 = \langle -3, 3 \rangle$
25. (a) $\langle -\frac{1}{2}, \frac{3}{2} \rangle$ (b) $\mathbf{u}_1 = \langle -\frac{1}{2}, \frac{3}{2} \rangle, \mathbf{u}_2 = \langle \frac{3}{2}, \frac{1}{2} \rangle$
27. (a) $\langle -\frac{18}{5}, \frac{24}{5} \rangle$ (b) $\mathbf{u}_1 = \langle -\frac{18}{5}, \frac{24}{5} \rangle, \mathbf{u}_2 = \langle \frac{28}{5}, \frac{21}{5} \rangle$
29. −28 **31.** 25 **33.** 16 ft-lb **35.** 8660 ft-lb
37. 1164 lb **39.** 23.6°

Chapter 5 Review ■ page 350

1. (a)

(b) $(6\sqrt{3}, 6)$

3. (a)

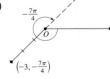

(b) $\left(-\frac{3\sqrt{2}}{2}, -\frac{3\sqrt{2}}{2} \right)$

5. (a)

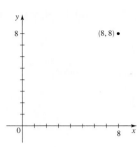

(b) $\left(8\sqrt{2}, \frac{\pi}{4} \right)$

(c) $\left(-8\sqrt{2}, \frac{5\pi}{4} \right)$

7. (a)

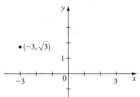

(b) $\left(2\sqrt{3}, \frac{5\pi}{6} \right)$

(c) $\left(-2\sqrt{3}, -\frac{\pi}{6} \right)$

9. (a) $r = \dfrac{4}{\cos \theta + \sin \theta}$ (b)

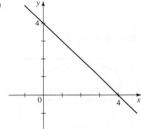

11. (a) $r = 4(\cos \theta + \sin \theta)$ (b)

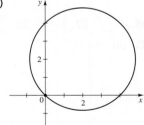

13. (a)

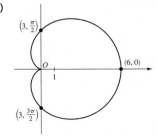

(b) $(x^2 + y^2 - 3x)^2 = 9(x^2 + y^2)$

15. (a)

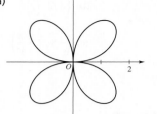

(b) $(x^2 + y^2)^3 = 16x^2y^2$

39. (a)

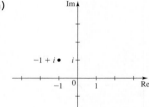

(b) $\sqrt{2}, \dfrac{3\pi}{4}$ (c) $\sqrt{2}\left(\cos\dfrac{3\pi}{4} + i\sin\dfrac{3\pi}{4}\right)$

41. $8(-1 + i\sqrt{3})$ **43.** $-\dfrac{1}{32}(1 + i\sqrt{3})$

45. $\pm 2\sqrt{2}(1 - i)$ **47.** $\pm 1, \pm\dfrac{1}{2} \pm \dfrac{\sqrt{3}}{2}i$

49. $\sqrt{13}, \langle 6, 4 \rangle, \langle -10, 2 \rangle, \langle -4, 6 \rangle, \langle -22, 7 \rangle$

51. $3\mathbf{i} - 4\mathbf{j}$ **53.** $(10, -2)$ **55.** (a) $(4.8\mathbf{i} + 0.4\mathbf{j}) \times 10^4$

(b) 4.8×10^4 lb, N 85.2° E   **57.** 5, 25, 60

59. $2\sqrt{2}, 8, 0$ **61.** Yes   **63.** No, 45°

65. (a) $17\sqrt{37}/37$ (b) $\langle \tfrac{102}{37}, -\tfrac{17}{37} \rangle$ (c) $\mathbf{u}_1 = \langle \tfrac{102}{37}, -\tfrac{17}{37} \rangle,$

$\mathbf{u}_2 = \langle \tfrac{9}{37}, \tfrac{54}{37} \rangle$ **67.** -6

17. (a)

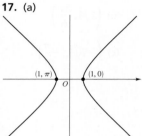

19. (a)

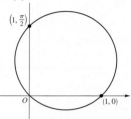

(b) $x^2 - y^2 = 1$ (b) $x^2 + y^2 = x + y$

21. $0 \le \theta \le 6\pi$ **23.** $0 \le \theta \le 6\pi$

25. $3 + i$ **27.** $8 - i$ **29.** $\dfrac{6}{5} + \dfrac{8}{5}i$ **31.** i **33.** 2

35. (a)

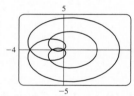

(b) $4\sqrt{2}, \dfrac{\pi}{4}$

(c) $4\sqrt{2}\left(\cos\dfrac{\pi}{4} + i\sin\dfrac{\pi}{4}\right)$

37. (a)

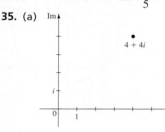

(b) $\sqrt{34}, \tan^{-1}\left(\tfrac{3}{5}\right)$ (c) $\sqrt{34}\left[\cos\left(\tan^{-1}\tfrac{3}{5}\right) + i\sin\left(\tan^{-1}\tfrac{3}{5}\right)\right]$

Chapter 5 Test ■ page 353

1. (a) $(-4\sqrt{2}, -4\sqrt{2})$ (b) $(4\sqrt{3}, 5\pi/6), (-4\sqrt{3}, 11\pi/6)$

2. (a)

, circle

(b) $(x - 4)^2 + y^2 = 16$

3. (a) $-1 - \tfrac{3}{2}i$ (b) $5 + i$ (c) $-1 + 2i$ (d) -1

(e) $(16 - 2\sqrt{2}) - (4 + 8\sqrt{2})i$

4. (a)

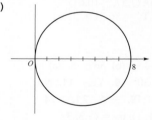

(b) $2\left(\cos\dfrac{\pi}{3} + i\sin\dfrac{\pi}{3}\right)$ (c) -512 **5.** $-8, \sqrt{3} + i$

6. $-3i,\ 3\left(\pm\dfrac{\sqrt{3}}{2}+\dfrac{1}{2}i\right)$

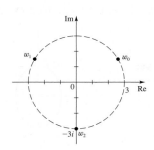

7. (a) $-6\mathbf{i}+10\mathbf{j}$ (b) $2\sqrt{34}$
8. (a) $\langle 19,\ -3\rangle$ (b) $5\sqrt{2}$ (c) 0 (d) Yes
9. (a) $14\mathbf{i}+6\sqrt{3}\,\mathbf{j}$ (b) 17.4 mi/h, N $53.4°$ E

10. (a) $45°$ (b) $\sqrt{26}/2$ (c) $\dfrac{5}{2}\mathbf{i}-\dfrac{1}{2}\mathbf{j}$

11. 90

Focus on Modeling ■ page 356

1. (a) $R=\dfrac{18}{\pi}\approx 5.73$ (b) 691.2 mi
3. (a) $x\approx -12.23,\ y\approx 6.27$
(b) $x\approx 3.76,\ y\approx 8.43$
(c) $x\approx 15.12,\ y\approx -3.85$
(d) $x\approx -4.31,\ y\approx -2.42$
5. (a) 1.14 (b) 1.73 (c) 36.81
7. (a) 1.48 (b) 1.21 (c) 1.007

CHAPTER 6

Section 6.1 ■ page 366

1. III   **3.** II   **5.** VI

Order of answers: focus; directrix; focal diameter

7. $F(1,0);\ x=-1;\ 4$ **9.** $F\left(0,\frac{9}{4}\right);\ y=-\frac{9}{4};\ 9$

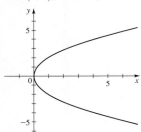

11. $F\left(0,\frac{1}{20}\right);\ y=-\frac{1}{20};\ \frac{1}{5}$ **13.** $F\left(-\frac{1}{32},0\right);\ x=\frac{1}{32};\ \frac{1}{8}$

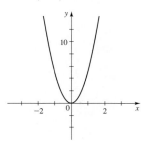

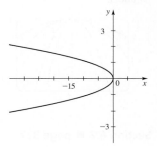

15. $F\left(0,-\frac{3}{2}\right);\ y=\frac{3}{2};\ 6$ **17.** $F\left(-\frac{5}{12},0\right);\ x=\frac{5}{12};\ \frac{5}{3}$

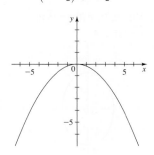

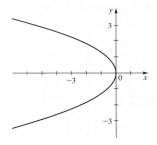

19.   **21.**

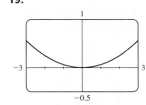

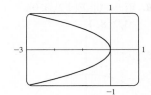

23.

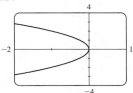

25. $x^2=8y$ **27.** $y^2=-32x$ **29.** $y^2=-8x$
31. $x^2=40y$ **33.** $y^2=4x$ **35.** $x^2=20y$
37. $x^2=8y$ **39.** $y^2=-16x$ **41.** $y^2=-3x$
43. $x=y^2$ **45.** $x^2=-4\sqrt{2}\,y$
47. (a) $y^2=12x$ (b) $8\sqrt{15}\approx 31$ cm
49. $x^2=600y$
51. (a) $x^2=-4py,\ p=\frac{1}{2},\ 1,\ 4,\ \text{and}\ 8$

(b) The closer the directrix to the vertex, the steeper the parabola.

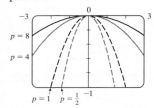

Section 6.2 ■ page 377

1. II   **3.** I

Order of answers: vertices; foci; eccentricity; major axis and minor axis

5. $V(\pm 5, 0)$; $F(\pm 4, 0)$; $\frac{4}{5}$; 10, 6

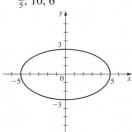

7. $V(0, \pm 3)$; $F(0, \pm\sqrt{5})$; $\sqrt{5}/3$; 6, 4

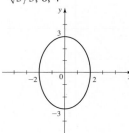

9. $V(\pm 4, 0)$; $F(\pm 2\sqrt{3}, 0)$; $\sqrt{3}/2$; 8, 4

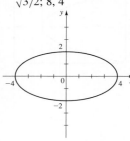

11. $V(0, \pm\sqrt{3})$; $F(0, \pm\sqrt{3/2})$; $1/\sqrt{2}$; $2\sqrt{3}$, $\sqrt{6}$

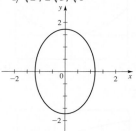

13. $V(\pm 1, 0)$; $F(\pm\sqrt{3}/2, 0)$; $\sqrt{3}/2$; 2, 1

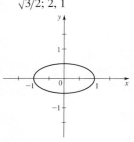

15. $V(0, \pm\sqrt{2})$; $F(0, \pm\sqrt{3/2})$; $\sqrt{3}/2$; $2\sqrt{2}$, $\sqrt{2}$

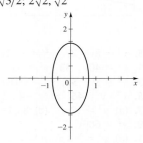

17. $V(0, \pm 1)$; $F(0, \pm 1/\sqrt{2})$; $1/\sqrt{2}$; 2, $\sqrt{2}$

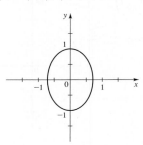

19. $\dfrac{x^2}{25} + \dfrac{y^2}{16} = 1$ **21.** $\dfrac{x^2}{4} + \dfrac{y^2}{8} = 1$ **23.** $\dfrac{x^2}{256} + \dfrac{y^2}{48} = 1$

25.

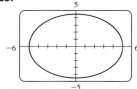

27.

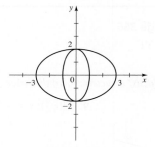

29. $\dfrac{x^2}{25} + \dfrac{y^2}{9} = 1$ **31.** $x^2 + \dfrac{y^2}{4} = 1$ **33.** $\dfrac{x^2}{9} + \dfrac{y^2}{13} = 1$

35. $\dfrac{x^2}{100} + \dfrac{y^2}{91} = 1$ **37.** $\dfrac{x^2}{25} + \dfrac{y^2}{5} = 1$

39. $\dfrac{64x^2}{225} + \dfrac{64y^2}{81} = 1$

41. $(0, \pm 2)$

43. $\dfrac{x^2}{2.2500 \times 10^{16}} + \dfrac{y^2}{2.2491 \times 10^{16}} = 1$

45. $\dfrac{x^2}{1{,}455{,}642} + \dfrac{y^2}{1{,}451{,}610} = 1$

47. $5\sqrt{39}/2 \approx 15.6$ in.

51. (a)

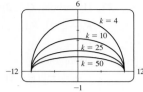

(b) Common major axes and vertices; eccentricity increases as k increases

Section 6.3 ■ page 387

1. III   **3.** II

Order of answers: vertices; foci; asymptotes

5. $V(\pm2, 0)$; $F(\pm2\sqrt{5}, 0)$; $y = \pm2x$

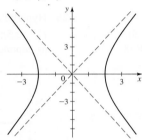

7. $V(0, \pm1)$; $F(0, \pm\sqrt{26})$; $y = \pm\frac{1}{5}x$

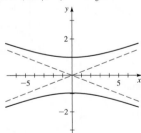

9. $V(\pm1, 0)$; $F(\pm\sqrt{2}, 0)$; $y = \pm x$

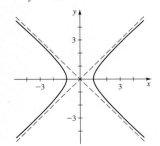

11. $V(0, \pm3)$; $F(0, \pm\sqrt{34})$; $y = \pm\frac{3}{5}x$

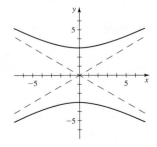

13. $V(\pm2\sqrt{2}, 0)$; $F(\pm\sqrt{10}, 0)$; $y = \pm\frac{1}{2}x$

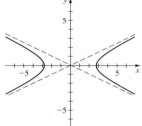

15. $V\left(0, \pm\frac{1}{2}\right)$; $F(0, \pm\sqrt{5}/2)$; $y = \pm\frac{1}{2}x$

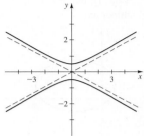

17. $\dfrac{x^2}{4} - \dfrac{y^2}{12} = 1$ **19.** $\dfrac{y^2}{16} - \dfrac{x^2}{16} = 1$ **21.** $\dfrac{x^2}{9} - \dfrac{4y^2}{9} = 1$

23.

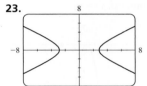

25.

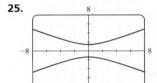

27. $\dfrac{x^2}{9} - \dfrac{y^2}{16} = 1$ **29.** $y^2 - \dfrac{x^2}{3} = 1$

31. $x^2 - \dfrac{y^2}{25} = 1$ **33.** $\dfrac{5y^2}{64} - \dfrac{5x^2}{256} = 1$

35. $\dfrac{x^2}{16} - \dfrac{y^2}{16} = 1$ **37.** $\dfrac{x^2}{9} - \dfrac{y^2}{16} = 1$

39. (b) $x^2 - y^2 = c^2/2$

43. (a) 490 mi   **(b)** $\dfrac{y^2}{60,025} - \dfrac{x^2}{2475} = 1$ **(c)** 10.1 mi

45. (b)

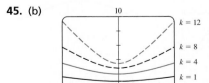

Section 6.4 ■ page 396

1. Center $C(2, 1)$;
foci $F(2 \pm \sqrt{5}, 1)$;
vertices $V_1(-1, 1)$,
$V_2(5, 1)$; major axis 6,
minor axis 4

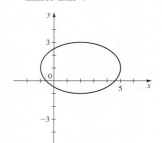

3. Center $C(0, -5)$;
foci $F_1(0, -1)$, $F_2(0, -9)$;
vertices $V_1(0, 0)$, $V_2(0, -10)$;
major axis 10, minor axis 6

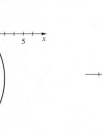

19. Ellipse; $C(2, 0)$;
$F(2, \pm\sqrt{5})$; $V(2, \pm3)$;
major axis 6,
minor axis 4

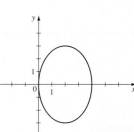

21. Hyperbola; $C(1, 2)$;
$F_1\left(-\frac{3}{2}, 2\right)$, $F_2\left(\frac{7}{2}, 2\right)$;
$V(1 \pm \sqrt{5}, 2)$;
asymptotes
$y = \pm\frac{1}{2}(x - 1) + 2$

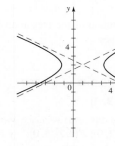

5. Vertex $V(3, -1)$;
focus $F(3, 1)$;
directrix $y = -3$

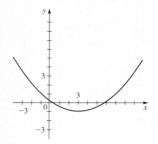

7. Vertex $V\left(-\frac{1}{2}, 0\right)$;
focus $F\left(-\frac{1}{2}, -\frac{1}{16}\right)$;
directrix $y = \frac{1}{16}$

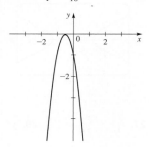

23. Ellipse; $C(3, -5)$;
$F(3 \pm \sqrt{21}, -5)$;
$V_1(-2, -5)$, $V_1(8, -5)$;
major axis 10,
minor axis 4

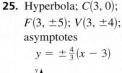

25. Hyperbola; $C(3, 0)$;
$F(3, \pm5)$; $V(3, \pm4)$;
asymptotes
$y = \pm\frac{4}{3}(x - 3)$

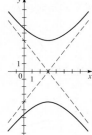

9. Center $C(-1, 3)$;
foci $F_1(-6, 3)$, $F_2(4, 3)$;
vertices $V_1(-4, 3)$, $V_2(2, 3)$;
asymptotes
$y = \pm\frac{4}{3}(x + 1) + 3$

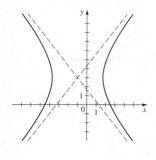

11. Center $C(-1, 0)$;
foci $F(-1, \pm\sqrt{5})$;
vertices $V(-1, \pm1)$;
asymptotes
$y = \pm\frac{1}{2}(x + 1)$

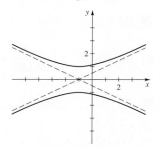

27. Degenerate conic
(pairs of lines),
$y = \pm\frac{1}{2}(x - 4)$

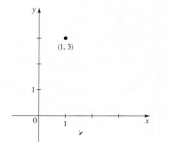

29. Point $(1, 3)$

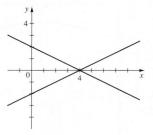

13. $x^2 = -\frac{1}{4}(y - 4)$

15. $\dfrac{(x - 5)^2}{25} + \dfrac{y^2}{16} = 1$

17. $(y - 1)^2 - x^2 = 1$

31.

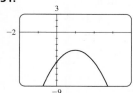

33.

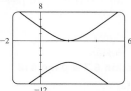

35. (a) $F < 17$ (b) $F = 17$ (c) $F > 17$

37. (a)

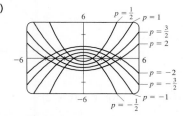

(c) The parabolas become narrower.

Section 6.5 ■ page 404

1. $(\sqrt{2}, 0)$ **3.** $(0, -2\sqrt{3})$ **5.** $(1.6383, 1.1472)$
7. $X^2 + \sqrt{3}\,XY + 2 = 0$
9. $7Y^2 - 48XY - 7X^2 - 40X - 30Y = 0$
11. $X^2 - Y^2 = 2$
13. (a) Hyberbola   **15.** (a) Parabola
(b) $X^2 - Y^2 = 16$ (b) $Y = \sqrt{2}X^2$
(c) $\phi = 45°$ (c) $\phi = 45°$

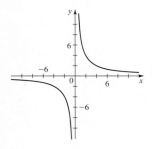

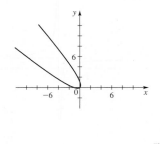

17. (a) Hyberbola

(b) $Y^2 - X^2 = 1$

(c) $\phi = 30°$

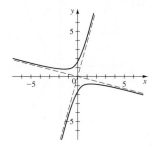

19. (a) Hyberbola

(b) $\dfrac{X^2}{4} - Y^2 = 1$

(c) $\phi \approx 53°$

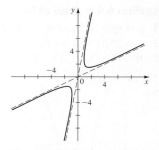

21. (a) Hyberbola   **23.** (a) Hyberbola
(b) $3X^2 - Y^2 = 2\sqrt{3}$ (b) $(X - 1)^2 - 3Y^2 = 1$
(c) $\phi = 30°$ (c) $\phi = 60°$

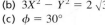

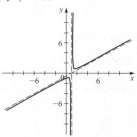

25. (a) Ellipse

(b) $X^2 + \dfrac{(Y + 1)^2}{4} = 1$

(c) $\phi \approx 53°$
See graph at right.

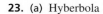

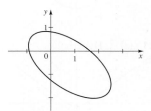

27. (a) Parabola   (b)

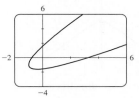

29. (a) Hyperbola   (b)

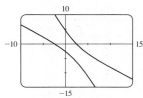

31. (a) $(X - 5)^2 - Y^2 = 1$
(b) XY-coordinates: $C(5, 0)$; $V_1(6, 0)$, $V_2(4, 0)$; $F(5 \pm \sqrt{2}, 0)$;
xy-coordinates: $C(4, 3)$; $V_1\left(\frac{24}{5}, \frac{18}{5}\right)$, $V_2\left(\frac{16}{5}, \frac{12}{5}\right)$;
$F_1\left(4 + \frac{4}{5}\sqrt{2}, 3 + \frac{3}{5}\sqrt{2}\right)$, $F_2\left(4 - \frac{4}{5}\sqrt{2}, 3 - \frac{3}{5}\sqrt{2}\right)$
(c) $Y = \pm(X - 5)$; $7x - y - 25 = 0$, $x + 7y - 25 = 0$
33. $X = x \cos \phi + y \sin \phi$; $Y = -x \sin \phi + y \cos \phi$

Section 6.6 ■ page 411

1. $r = 6/(3 + 2\cos\theta)$ **3.** $r = 2/(1 + \sin\theta)$
5. $r = 20/(1 + 4\cos\theta)$ **7.** $r = 10/(1 + \sin\theta)$
9. II **11.** VI **13.** IV

15. (a) 3, Hyperbola
(b)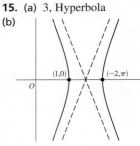

17. (a) 1, Parabola
(b)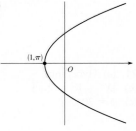

19. (a) $\frac{1}{2}$, Ellipse
(b)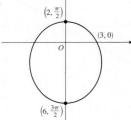

21. (a) $\frac{5}{2}$, Hyperbola
(b)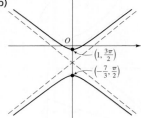

23. (a) $e = \frac{3}{4}$, directrix $x = -\frac{1}{3}$

(b) $r = \dfrac{1}{4 - 3\cos\left(\theta - \dfrac{\pi}{3}\right)}$

25. The ellipse is nearly circular when e is close to 0 and becomes more elongated as $e \to 1^-$. At $e = 1$, the curve becomes a parabola.

27. (b) $r = (1.49 \times 10^8)/(1 - 0.017\cos\theta)$
29. 0.25

Section 6.7 ■ page 418

1. (a)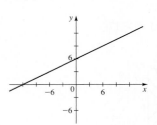
(b) $x - 2y + 12 = 0$

3. (a)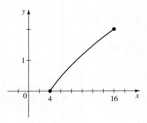
(b) $x = (y + 2)^2$

5. (a)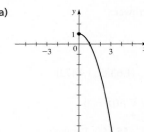
(b) $x = \sqrt{1 - y}$

7. (a)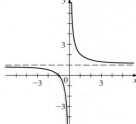
(b) $y = \dfrac{1}{x} + 1$

9. (a)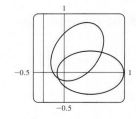
(b) $x^3 = y^2$

11. (a)

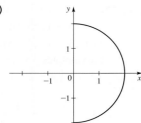

(b) $x^2 + y^2 = 4$

13. (a)

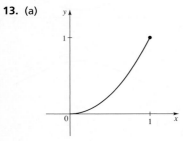

(b) $y = x^2$

15. (a)

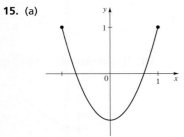

(b) $y = 2x^2 - 1$

17. (a)

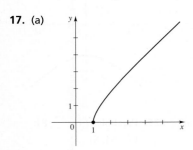

(b) $x^2 - y^2 = 1$

19. (a)

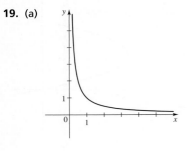

(b) $xy = 1$

21. (a)

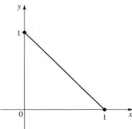

(b) $x + y = 1$

23. $x = 4 + t$, $y = -1 + \frac{1}{2}t$ **25.** $x = 6 + t$, $y = 7 + t$

27. $x = a \cos t$, $y = a \sin t$

31.

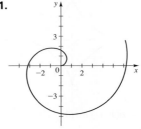

33.

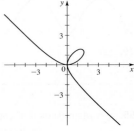

37.

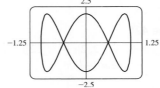

39.

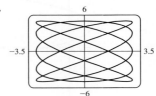

41.

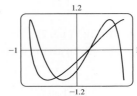

43. (a) $x = 2^{t/12} \cos t$, $y = 2^{t/12} \sin t$

(b)

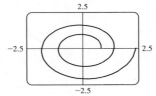

45. (a) $x = \dfrac{4 \cos t}{2 - \cos t}$, $y = \dfrac{4 \sin t}{2 - \cos t}$

(b)

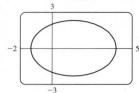

47. III   **49.** II

51.

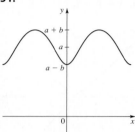

53. (b) $x^{2/3} + y^{2/3} = a^{2/3}$

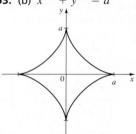

55. $x = a(\sin \theta \cos \theta + \cot \theta)$, $y = a(1 + \sin^2\theta)$

57. $y = a - a \cos\left(\dfrac{x + \sqrt{2ay - y^2}}{a}\right)$

Chapter 6 Review ■ page 421

1. $V(0, 0)$; $F(0, -2)$; $y = 2$

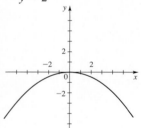

3. $V(-2, 2)$; $F\left(-\frac{7}{4}, 2\right)$; $x = -\frac{9}{4}$

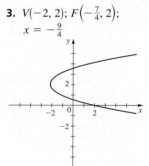

5. $C(0, 0)$; $V(\pm 4, 0)$; $F(\pm 2\sqrt{3}, 0)$; axes 8, 4

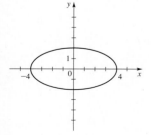

7. $C(0, 2)$; $V(\pm 3, 2)$; $F(\pm\sqrt{5}, 2)$; axes 6, 4

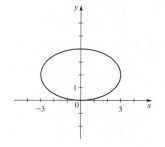

9. $C(0, 0)$; $V(\pm 4, 0)$; $F(\pm 2\sqrt{6}, 0)$; asymptotes $y = \pm\dfrac{1}{\sqrt{2}}x$

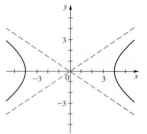

11. $C(-3, -1)$; $V(-3, -1 \pm \sqrt{2})$; $F(-3, -1 \pm 2\sqrt{5})$; asymptotes $y = \frac{1}{3}x$, $y = -\frac{1}{3}x - 2$

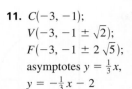
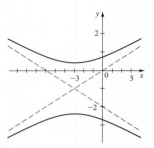

13. $y^2 = 8x$ **15.** $\dfrac{y^2}{16} - \dfrac{x^2}{9} = 1$

17. $\dfrac{(x-4)^2}{16} + \dfrac{(y-2)^2}{4} = 1$

19. Parabola; $F(0, -2)$; $V(0, 1)$

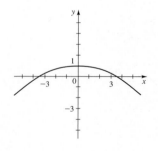

21. Hyperbola; $F(0, \pm 12\sqrt{2})$; $V(0, \pm 12)$

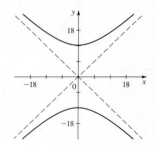

23. Ellipse; $F(1, 4 \pm \sqrt{15})$; $V(1, 4 \pm 2\sqrt{5})$

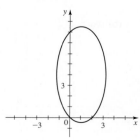

25. Parabola; $F\left(-\frac{255}{4}, 8\right)$; $V(-64, 8)$

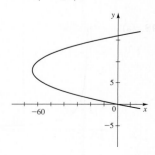

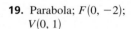

27. Ellipse;
$F(3, -3 \pm 1/\sqrt{2})$;
$V_1(3, -4)$, $V_2(3, -2)$

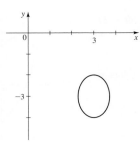

29. Has no graph   **31.** $x^2 = 4y$ **33.** $\dfrac{y^2}{4} - \dfrac{x^2}{16} = 1$

35. $\dfrac{(x-1)^2}{3} + \dfrac{(y-2)^2}{4} = 1$ **37.** $\dfrac{4(x-7)^2}{225} + \dfrac{(y-2)^2}{100} = 1$

39. $(x - 800)^2 = -200(y - 3200)$

41. (a) 91,419,000 mi   (b) 94,581,000 mi

43. (a)

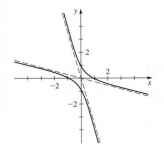

45. (a) Hyperbola
(b) $3X^2 - Y^2 = 1$
(c) $\phi = 45°$

47. (a) Ellipse
(b) $(X - 1)^2 + 4Y^2 = 1$
(c) $\phi = 30°$

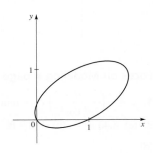

49. Ellipse

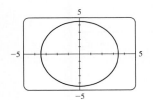

51. Parabola

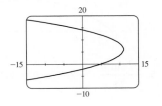

53. (a) $e = 1$, parabola
(b)

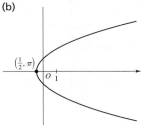

55. (a) $e = 2$, hyperbola
(b)

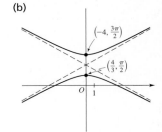

$\left(-4, \frac{3\pi}{2}\right)$
$\left(\frac{4}{3}, \frac{\pi}{2}\right)$

57. (a)

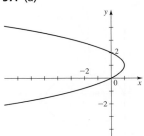

(b) $x = 2y - y^2$

59. (a)

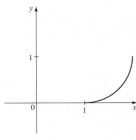

(b) $(x - 1)^2 + (y - 1)^2 = 1$

61.

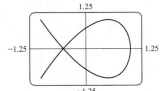

63. $x = \frac{1}{2}(1 + \cos\theta)$, $y = \frac{1}{2}(\sin\theta + \tan\theta)$

Chapter 6 Test ■ page 424

1. $F(0, -3)$, $y = 3$ **2.** $V(\pm 4, 0)$; $F(\pm 2\sqrt{3}, 0)$; 8, 4

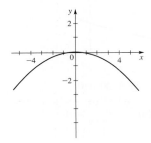

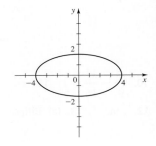

3. $V(0, \pm 3)$; $F(0, \pm 5)$; $y = \pm \frac{3}{4}x$

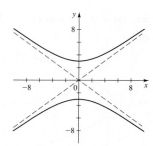

(c) $\phi \approx 27°$

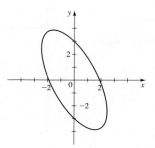

4. $y^2 = -x$ **5.** $\dfrac{x^2}{16} + \dfrac{(y-3)^2}{9} = 1$ **6.** $(x-2)^2 - \dfrac{y^2}{3} = 1$

(d) $(-3\sqrt{2/5},\, 6\sqrt{2/5}),\ (3\sqrt{2/5},\, -6\sqrt{2/5})$

14. (a) $r = \dfrac{1}{1 + 0.5\cos\theta}$ **(b)** Ellipse

7. $\dfrac{(x-3)^2}{9} + \dfrac{\left(y+\frac{1}{2}\right)^2}{4} = 1$

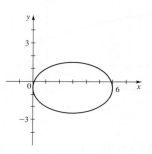

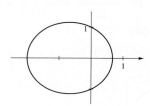

15. (a)

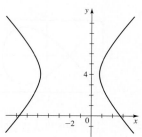

(b) $\dfrac{(x-3)^2}{9} + \dfrac{y^2}{4} = 1$

8. $9(x+2)^2 - 8(y-4)^2 = 72$

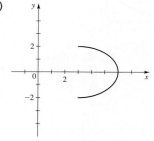

Focus on Modeling ■ **page 429**

9. $(y+4)^2 = -2(x-4)$

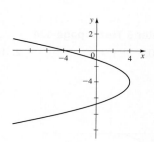

1. $y = -\left(\dfrac{g}{2v_0^2\cos^2\theta}\right)x^2 + (\tan\theta)x$

3. (a) 5.45 s   **(b)** 118.7 ft   **(c)** 5426.5 ft

(d)

10. $\dfrac{y^2}{9} - \dfrac{x^2}{16} = 1$ **11.** $x^2 - 4x - 8y + 20 = 0$

12. $\frac{3}{4}$ in.   **13. (a)** Ellipse   **(b)** $\dfrac{X^2}{3} + \dfrac{Y^2}{18} = 1$

5. $\dfrac{v_0^2\sin^2\theta}{2g}$ **7.** No, $\theta \approx 23°$

CHAPTER 7

Section 7.1 ■ page 439

1.
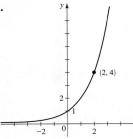
(2, 4)

3.
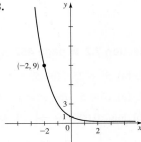
(−2, 9)

5.
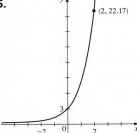
(2, 22.17)

7.
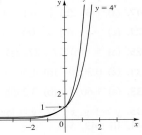
$y = 7^x$
$y = 4^x$

9. $f(x) = 3^x$ **11.** $f(x) = \left(\frac{1}{4}\right)^x$ **13.** III **15.** I **17.** II
19. $\mathbb{R}, (-\infty, 0), y = 0$ **21.** $\mathbb{R}, (-3, \infty), y = -3$

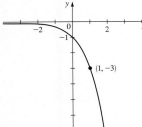
(1, −3)

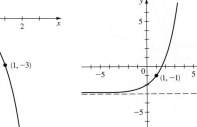
(1, −1)

23. $\mathbb{R}, (4, \infty), y = 4$ **25.** $\mathbb{R}, (0, \infty), y = 0$

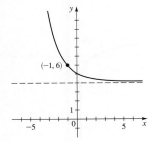
(−1, 6)

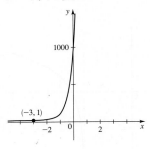
(−3, 1)

27.
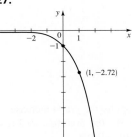
(1, −2.72)

29.
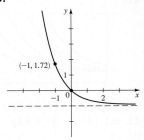
(−1, 1.72)

31.
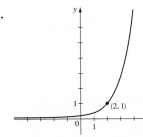
(2, 1)

33. $y = 3(2^x)$
35. (a)
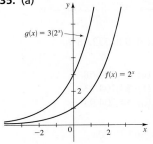
$g(x) = 3(2^x)$
$f(x) = 2^x$

(b) The graph of g is steeper than that of f.
39. (a)
(i) 20
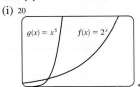
$g(x) = x^5$ $f(x) = 2^x$
0   5

(ii) 10^7
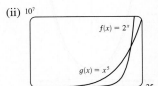
$f(x) = 2^x$
$g(x) = x^5$
0   25

(iii) 10^8
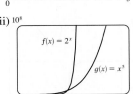
$f(x) = 2^x$
$g(x) = x^5$
0   50

The graph of f ultimately
increases much more
quickly than g.

(b) 1.2, 22.4

41.

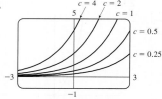

The larger the value of c, the more rapidly the graph increases.
43. (a) 13 kg   (b) 6.6 kg   **45.** (a) 0   (b) 50.6 ft/s, 69.2 ft/s
(c) 100
(d) 80 ft/s

47. (a) 5164   (b)

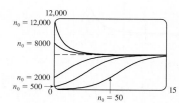

(c) 6000
49. (a) \$16,288.95   (b) \$26,532.98
(c) \$43,219.42

51. (a) \$4,615.87   (e) \$4,704.68
(b) \$4,658.91   (f) \$4,704.93
(c) \$4,697.04   (g) \$4,704.94
(d) \$4,703.11

53. (i)   **55.** (a) \$7,678.96   (b) \$67,121.04
57.

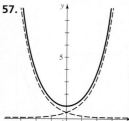

63. 4

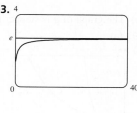

65.

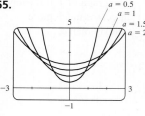

67.

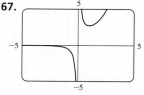

Vertical asymptote $x = 0$,
horizontal asymptote $y = 0$

69. Local minimum $\approx (0.27, 1.75)$
71. (a) Increasing on $(-\infty, 1.00]$, decreasing on $[1.00, \infty)$
(b) $(-\infty, 0.37]$

Section 7.2 ■ **page 452**

1. (a) $5^2 = 25$ (b) $5^0 = 1$ **3.** (a) $8^{1/3} = 2$ (b) $2^{-3} = \dfrac{1}{8}$
5. (a) $e^x = 5$ (b) $e^5 = y$ **7.** (a) $\log_5 125 = 3$
(b) $\log_{10} 0.0001 = -4$ **9.** (a) $\log_8 \dfrac{1}{8} = -1$
(b) $\log_2 \dfrac{1}{8} = -3$ **11.** (a) $\ln 2 = x$ (b) $\ln y = 3$
13. (a) 1   (b) 0   (c) 2   **15.** (a) 2   (b) 2   (c) 10
17. (a) -3 (b) $\frac{1}{2}$ (c) -1 **19.** (a) 37   (b) 8   (c) $\sqrt{5}$
21. (a) $-\frac{2}{3}$ (b) 4   (c) -1 **23.** (a) 32   (b) 4
25. (a) 5   (b) 27   **27.** (a) 100   (b) 25   **29.** (a) 2   (b) 4
31. (a) 0.3010   (b) 1.5465   (c) -0.1761
33. (a) 1.6094   (b) 3.2308   (c) 1.0051
35. $y = \log_5 x$ **37.** $y = \log_9 x$ **39.** II
41. III   **43.** VI

45.

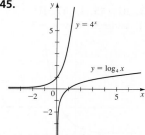

47. $(4, \infty)$, $\mathbb{R}$, $x = 4$ **49.** $(-\infty, 0)$, $\mathbb{R}$, $x = 0$

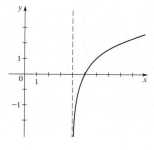
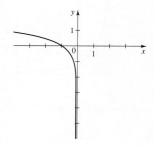

51. $(0, \infty)$, $\mathbb{R}$, $x = 0$

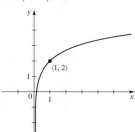

53. $(0, \infty)$, $\mathbb{R}$, $x = 0$

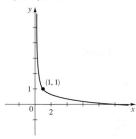

55. $(0, \infty)$, $[0, \infty)$, $x = 0$

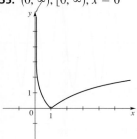

57. $\left(-3, \infty\right)$ **59.** $(-\infty, -1) \cup (1, \infty)$ **61.** $(0, 2)$

63.

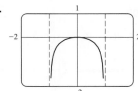

domain $= (-1, 1)$
vertical asymptotes
$x = 1$, $x = -1$
local maximum $(0, 0)$

65.

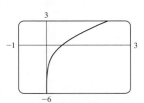

domain $= (0, \infty)$
vertical asymptote $x = 0$
no maximum or minimum

67.

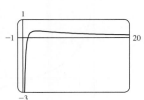

domain $= (0, \infty)$
vertical asymptote $x = 0$
horizontal asymptote $y = 0$
local maximum
$\approx (2.72, 0.37)$

69. The graph of f grows more slowly than g.

71. (a)

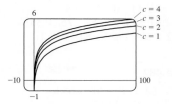

(b) The graph of $f(x) = \log(cx)$ is the graph of $f(x) = \log x$ shifted upward $\log c$ units.
73. (a) $(1, \infty)$ (b) $f^{-1}(x) = 10^{2^x}$

75. (a) $f^{-1}(x) = \log_2\!\left(\dfrac{x}{1 - x}\right)$ (b) $(0, 1)$

Section 7.3 ■ page 459
1. $1 + \log_2 x$ **3.** $\log_2 x + \log_2 (x - 1)$ **5.** $10 \log 6$
7. $\log_2 A + 2 \log_2 B$ **9.** $\log_3 x + \frac{1}{2} \log_3 y$
11. $\frac{1}{3} \log_5(x^2 + 1)$ **13.** $\frac{1}{2}(\ln a + \ln b)$
15. $3 \log x + 4 \log y - 6 \log z$
17. $\log_2 x + \log_2(x^2 + 1) - \frac{1}{2} \log_2(x^2 - 1)$
19. $\ln x + \frac{1}{2}(\ln y - \ln z)$ **21.** $\frac{1}{4} \log(x^2 + y^2)$
23. $\frac{1}{2}[\log(x^2 + 4) - \log(x^2 + 1) - 2 \log(x^3 - 7)]$
25. $3 \ln x + \frac{1}{2} \ln (x - 1) - \ln (3x + 4)$
27. $\frac{3}{2}$ **29.** 1   **31.** 3   **33.** $\ln 8$ **35.** 16   **37.** $4 + \log 3$
39. $\log_3 160$ **41.** $\log_2(AB/C^2)$ **43.** $\log\left[\dfrac{x^4(x - 1)^2}{\sqrt[3]{x^2 + 1}}\right]$
45. $\ln[5x^2(x^2 + 5)^3]$
47. $\log\left[\sqrt[3]{2x + 1} \sqrt{(x - 4)/(x^4 - x^2 - 1)}\right]$
49. 2.321928   **51.** 2.523719   **53.** 0.493008
55. 3.482892
57.

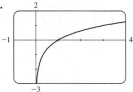

Section 7.4 ■ page 468
1. 2.7726   **3.** 0.3495   **5.** -0.5850 **7.** 1.2040   **9.** 0.0767
11. 0.2524   **13.** 1.9349   **15.** -43.0677 **17.** 2.1492
19. 6.2126   **21.** -2.9469 **23.** -2.4423 **25.** 14.0055
27. ± 1 **29.** $0, \frac{4}{3}$ **31.** $\ln 2 \approx 0.6931, 0$
33. $\frac{1}{2} \ln 3 \approx 0.5493$ **35.** $e^{10} \approx 22026$ **37.** 0.01   **39.** $\frac{95}{3}$
41. $3 - e^2 \approx -4.3891$ **43.** 5   **45.** 5   **47.** $\frac{13}{12}$
49. 6   **51.** $\frac{3}{2}$ **53.** $1/\sqrt{5} \approx 0.4472$ **55.** (a) \$6435.09
(b) 8.24 yr   **57.** 6.33 yr   **59.** 8.15 yr   **61.** 8.30%
63. 13 days   **65.** (a) 7337   (b) 1.73 yr

67. (a) $t = -\frac{5}{13} \ln\left(1 - \frac{13}{60} I\right)$ (b) 0.218 s
69. 2.21   **71.** 0.00, 1.14   **73.** -0.57 **75.** 0.36
77. $x > 4$ **79.** $\log 2 < x < \log 5$ **81.** 101, 1.1
83. $\log_2 3 \approx 1.58$

Section 7.5 ■ page 482

1. (a) 500   (b) 45%   (c) 1929   (d) 6.66 h
3. (a) $n(t) = 18{,}000 e^{0.08t}$ (b) 34,137

(c)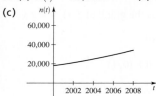

5. (a) $n(t) = 112{,}000 e^{0.04t}$ (b) About 142,000   (c) 2008
7. (a) 20,000   (b) $n(t) = 20{,}000 e^{0.1096t}$
(c) About 48,000   (d) 2010
9. (a) $n(t) = 8600 e^{0.1508t}$ (b) About 11,600   (c) 4.6 h
11. (a) 2029   (b) 2049   **13.** 22.85 h
15. (a) $n(t) = 10 e^{-0.0231t}$ (b) 1.6 g   (c) 70 yr
17. 18 yr   **19.** 149 h   **21.** 3560 yr
23. (a) 210°F   (b) 153°F   (c) 28 min
25. (a) 137°F   (b) 116 min   **27.** (a) 2.3   (b) 3.5   (c) 8.3
29. (a) 10^{-3} M   (b) 3.2×10^{-7} M   **31.** $4.8 \leqslant \text{pH} \leqslant 6.4$
33. $\log 20 \approx 1.3$ **35.** Twice as intense   **37.** 8.2
39. 6.3×10^{-3} W/m²   **41.** (b) 106 dB

Section 7.6 ■ page 490

1. (a) $y = 2e^{-1.5t} \cos 6\pi t$ (b)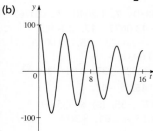

3. (a) $y = 100 e^{-0.05t} \cos \dfrac{\pi}{2} t$
(b)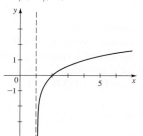

5. (a) $y = 7 e^{-10t} \sin 12 t$ (b)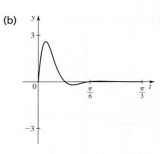

7. (a) $y = 0.3 e^{-0.2t} \sin 40 \pi t$ (b)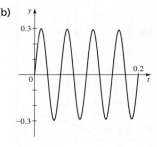

9. $y = 6.114 e^{-0.128t} \sin t$ **11.** $y = 100 e^{-0.115t} \cos \dfrac{\pi}{4} t$
13. $f(t) = e^{-0.9t} \sin \pi t$ **15.** $c = \dfrac{1}{3} \ln 4 \approx 0.46$

Chapter 7 Review ■ page 492

1. $\mathbb{R}$, $(0, \infty)$, $y = 0$ **3.** $\mathbb{R}$, $(-\infty, 5)$, $y = 5$

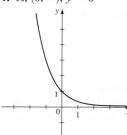   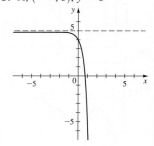

5. $(1, \infty)$, $\mathbb{R}$, $x = 1$ **7.** $(0, \infty)$, $\mathbb{R}$, $x = 0$

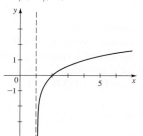   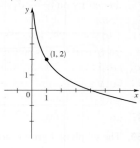

9. $\mathbb{R}, (-1, \infty), y = -1$

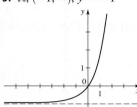

11. $(0, \infty), \mathbb{R}, x = 0$

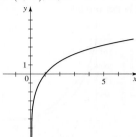

95. (a) $y = 16e^{-0.72t} \cos 2.8\pi t$
(b)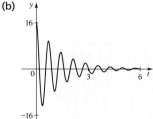
(c) 0.012 cm

13. $\left(-\infty, \frac{1}{2}\right)$　**15.** $(-\infty, -2) \cup (2, \infty)$　**17.** $2^{10} = 1024$
19. $10^y = x$　**21.** $\log_2 64 = 6$　**23.** $\log 74 = x$　**25.** 7
27. 45　**29.** 6　**31.** -3　**33.** $\frac{1}{2}$　**35.** 2　**37.** 92　**39.** $\frac{2}{3}$
41. $\log A + 2 \log B + 3 \log C$
43. $\frac{1}{2}\left[\ln(x^2 - 1) - \ln(x^2 + 1)\right]$
45. $2 \log_5 x + \frac{3}{2} \log_5(1 - 5x) - \frac{1}{2} \log_5(x^3 - x)$
47. $\log 96$　**49.** $\log_2\left[\dfrac{(x - y)^{3/2}}{(x^2 + y^2)^2}\right]$　**51.** $\log\left(\dfrac{x^2 - 4}{\sqrt{x^2 + 4}}\right)$
53. -15　**55.** $\frac{1}{3}(5 - \log_5 26) \approx 0.99$
57. $\frac{4}{3} \ln 10 \approx 3.07$　**59.** 3　**61.** $-4, 2$　**63.** 0.430618
65. 2.303600
67.

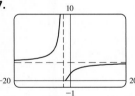

vertical asymptote
$x = -2$
horizontal asymptote
$y = 2.72$
no maximum or minimum

69.

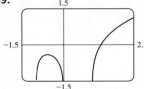

vertical asymptotes
$x = -1, x = 0, x = 1$
local maximum
$\approx (-0.58, -0.41)$

71. 2.42　**73.** $0.16 < x < 3.15$
75. Increasing on $(-\infty, 0]$ and $[1.10, \infty)$,
decreasing on $[0, 1.10]$
77. 1.953445　**79.** $\log_4 258$
81. (a) \$16,081.15　**(b)** \$16,178.18　**(c)** \$16,197.64
(d) \$16,198.31　**83. (a)** $n(t) = 30e^{0.15t}$　**(b)** 55　**(c)** 19 yr
85. (a) 9.97 mg　**(b)** 1.39×10^5 yr
87. (a) $n(t) = 150e^{-0.0004359t}$　**(b)** 97.0 mg　**(c)** 2520 yr
89. (a) $n(t) = 1500e^{0.1515t}$　**(b)** 7940　**91.** 7.9, basic
93. 8.0

Chapter 7 Test ■ page 495

1.

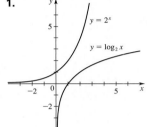

2.

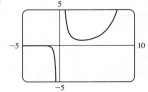

$(-2, \infty), \mathbb{R}, x = -2$

3. (a) $\frac{3}{2}$　**(b)** 3　**(c)** $\frac{2}{3}$　**(d)** 2
4. $\frac{1}{2}\left[\log(x + 2) - 4 \log x - \log(x^2 + 4)\right]$
5. $\ln\left(\dfrac{x\sqrt{3 - x^4}}{(x^2 + 1)^2}\right)$　**6. (a)** 4.32　**(b)** 0.77　**(c)** 5.39　**(d)** 2
7. (a) $n(t) = 1000e^{2.07944t}$　**(b)** 22,627　**(c)** 1.3 h
(d)

8. (a) $A(t) = 12{,}000\left(1 + \dfrac{0.056}{12}\right)^{12t}$
(b) \$14,195.06　**(c)** 9.249 yr
9. (a)

(b) Local minimum $\approx (3.00, 0.74)$
(c) $(-\infty, 0) \cup [0.74, \infty)$
(d) $-0.85, 0.96, 9.92$

10. $y = 16e^{-0.1t} \cos 24\pi t$

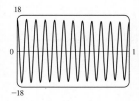

Focus on Modeling ■ page 505

1. (a)

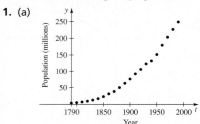

(b) $y = ab^t$, where $a = 4.041807 \times 10^{-16}$ and $b = 1.021003194$, and y is the population in millions in the year t.   (c) 457.9 million   (d) 221.2 million   (e) No
3. (a) Yes   (b) Yes, the scatter plot appears linear.

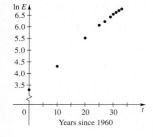

(c) $\ln E = 3.30161 \times 0.10769t$, where t is years since 1960 and E is expenditure in billions of dollars.
(d) $E = 27.15633e^{0.10769t}$ (e) 1310.9 billion dollars

5. (a) $y = ab^t$, where $a = 301.813054$, $b = 0.819745$, and t is the number of years since 1970
(b) $y = at^4 + bt^3 + ct^2 + dt + e$, where $a = -0.002430$, $b = 0.135159$, $c = -2.014322$, $d = -4.055294$, $e = 199.092227$, and t is the number of years since 1970

(c) From the graphs we see that the fourth-degree polynomial is a better model.

(d) 202.8, 27.8; 184.0, 43.5

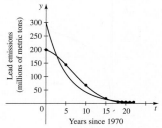

7. (a)

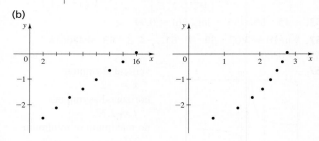

(b)

(c) Exponential Function
(d) $y = a \cdot b^x$ where $a = 0.057697$ and $b = 1.200236$
9. (a) $y = a + b \ln t$ where $a = -7154.888$, $b = 1016.007$, and y is metric tons of coal produced in the year t
(b) 912 metric tons

Appendix A.1 ■ page 516

1. Commutative Property for addition
3. Associative Property for addition   **5.** Distributive Property
7. $3x + 3y$ **9.** $8m$ **11.** $-5x + 10y$
13. (a) False   (b) True   **15.** (a) False   (b) True
17. (a) $x > 0$ (b) $t < 4$ (c) $a \geq \pi$ (d) $-5 < x < \frac{1}{3}$
(e) $|p - 3| \leq 5$
19. (a) $\mathbb{R}$ (b) $\{x \mid -2 \leq x < 4\}$
21. (a) $\{x \mid x \leq 5\}$ (b) $\{x \mid -1 < x < 4\}$
23. $-3 < x < 0$ **25.** $2 \leq x < 8$

27. $x \ge 2$

29. $(-\infty, 1]$

31. $(-2, 1]$

33. $(-1, \infty)$

35.

37.

39.

41. (a) 100 (b) 73 **43.** (a) 2 (b) -1
45. (a) 12 (b) 5 **47.** (a) 15 (b) 24 (c) $\frac{67}{40}$

Appendix A.2 ■ page 524

1. $17^{1/2}$ **3.** $\sqrt[3]{4^2}$ **5.** $\sqrt[5]{a^3}$ **7.** (a) 16 (b) -16 (c) 1
9. (a) $\frac{16}{25}$ (b) 1000 (c) 1024 **11.** (a) $\frac{2}{3}$ (b) 4 (c) $\frac{1}{2}$
13. (a) $\frac{3}{2}$ (b) 4 (c) $-\frac{1}{5}$ **15.** 5 **17.** 14 **19.** $\sqrt[3]{4}$
21. $2\sqrt{5}$ **23.** a^4 **25.** $6x^7y^5$ **27.** $16x^{10}$ **29.** $4/b^2$
31. $64r^7s$ **33.** $648y^7$ **35.** $\dfrac{x^3}{y}$ **37.** $\dfrac{y^2z^9}{x^5}$ **39.** $\dfrac{s^3}{q^7r^6}$
41. $x^{13/15}$ **43.** $16b^{9/10}$ **45.** $\dfrac{1}{c^{2/3}d}$ **47.** $y^{1/2}$ **49.** $\dfrac{32x^{12}}{y^{16/15}}$
51. $\dfrac{x^{15}}{y^{15/2}}$ **53.** $\dfrac{4a^2}{3b^{1/3}}$ **55.** $\dfrac{3t^{25/6}}{s^{1/2}}$ **57.** $|x|$ **59.** $x\sqrt[3]{y}$
61. $ab\sqrt[5]{ab^2}$ **63.** $2|x|$ **65.** (a) $\dfrac{\sqrt{6}}{6}$ (b) $\dfrac{\sqrt{3xy}}{3y}$ (c) $\dfrac{\sqrt{15}}{10}$
67. (a) $\dfrac{\sqrt[3]{x^2}}{x}$ (b) $\dfrac{\sqrt[5]{x^3}}{x}$ (c) $\dfrac{\sqrt[7]{x^4}}{x}$

Appendix A.3 ■ page 533

1. $5x^2 - 2x - 4$ **3.** $9x + 103$
5. $-t^4 + t^3 - t^2 - 10t + 5$ **7.** $x^{3/2} - x$
9. $3x^2 + 5xy - 2y^2$ **11.** $1 - 4y + 4y^2$
13. $4x^4 + 12x^2y^2 + 9y^4$ **15.** $2x^3 - 7x^2 + 7x - 5$
17. $x^4 - a^4$ **19.** $a - \dfrac{1}{b^2}$ **21.** $x^5 + x^4 - 3x^3 + 3x - 2$
23. $1 - x^{2/3} + x^{4/3} - x^2$
25. $3x^4y^4 + 7x^3y^5 - 6x^2y^3 - 14xy^4$
27. $6x(2x^2 + 3)$ **29.** $3y^3(2y - 5)$ **31.** $(x - 4)(x + 2)$
33. $(y - 3)(y - 5)$ **35.** $(2x + 3)(x + 1)$ **37.** $9(x - 5)(x + 1)$
39. $(3x + 2)(2x - 3)$ **41.** $(2t - 3)^2$ **43.** $(r - 3s)^2$
45. $(x + 6)(x - 6)$ **47.** $(7 + 2y)(7 - 2y)$
49. $4ab$ **51.** $(x + 3)(x - 3)(x + 1)(x - 1)$
53. $(t + 1)(t^2 - t + 1)$ **55.** $x(x + 1)^2$
57. $3(x - 1)(x + 2)$ **59.** $y^4(y + 2)^3(y + 1)^2$

61. $\dfrac{1}{x + 2}$ **63.** $\dfrac{x + 2}{x + 1}$ **65.** $\dfrac{y}{y - 1}$ **67.**
69. $\dfrac{1}{t^2 + 9}$ **71.** $\dfrac{x + 4}{x + 1}$ **73.** $\dfrac{(2x + 1)(2\ldots}{(x + 5)^2}$
75. $\dfrac{x}{yz}$ **77.** $\dfrac{3x + 7}{(x - 3)(x + 5)}$ **79.** $\dfrac{1}{(x + 1)(x + 2)}$
81. $\dfrac{3x + 2}{(x + 1)^2}$ **83.** $\dfrac{u^2 + 3u + 1}{u + 1}$ **85.** $\dfrac{2x + 1}{x^2(x + 1)}$
87. $\dfrac{2x + 7}{(x + 3)(x + 4)}$ **89.** $\dfrac{x - 2}{(x + 3)(x - 3)}$
91. $\dfrac{5x - 6}{x(x - 1)}$ **93.** $\dfrac{-5}{(x + 1)(x + 2)(x - 3)}$ **95.** $-xy$
97. $\dfrac{c}{c - 2}$ **99.** $\dfrac{y - x}{xy}$ **101.** $\dfrac{3 - \sqrt{5}}{2}$ **103.** $\dfrac{2(\sqrt{7} - \sqrt{2})}{5}$
105. $\dfrac{-4}{3(1 + \sqrt{5})}$ **107.** $\dfrac{r - 2}{5(\sqrt{r} - \sqrt{2})}$ **109.** $\dfrac{1}{\sqrt{x^2 + 1} + x}$

Appendix A.4 ■ page 545

1. (a) Yes (b) No **3.** (a) Yes (b) No **5.** 4 **7.** -9
9. -3 **11.** 12 **13.** $-\frac{3}{4}$ **15.** $\frac{32}{9}$ **17.** $-4, 2$
19. $-3, -\dfrac{1}{2}$ **21.** $-\dfrac{4}{3}, \dfrac{1}{2}$ **23.** $-1 \pm \sqrt{3}$ **25.** $-\dfrac{3}{2}, \dfrac{1}{2}$
27. $-2 \pm \dfrac{\sqrt{14}}{2}$ **29.** $-6 \pm 3\sqrt{7}$ **31.** $\dfrac{-3 \pm 2\sqrt{6}}{3}$
33. $\dfrac{1 \pm \sqrt{5}}{4}$ **35.** $\dfrac{8 \pm \sqrt{14}}{10}$ **37.** No real solution **39.** $-\dfrac{7}{5}, 2$
41. $-50, 100$ **43.** -4 **45.** 4 **47.** 3 **49.** $\pm 2\sqrt{2}, \pm\sqrt{5}$
51. No real solution **53.** $\pm 3\sqrt{3}, \pm 2\sqrt{2}$ **55.** $-1, 0, 3$
57. 27, 729 **59.** $-\dfrac{3}{2}, \dfrac{3}{2}$ **61.** 3.99, 4.01 **63.** $R = \dfrac{PV}{nT}$
65. $R_1 = \dfrac{RR_2}{R_2 - R}$ **67.** $x = \dfrac{2d - b}{a - 2c}$ **69.** $x = \dfrac{1 - a}{a^2 - a - 1}$
71. $r = \pm\sqrt{\dfrac{3V}{\pi h}}$ **73.** $b = \pm\sqrt{c^2 - a^2}$ **75.** 2 **77.** 1
79. 4.24 s **81.** (a) After 17 yr, on Jan. 1, 2009
(b) After 18.612 yr, on Aug. 12, 2010

Appendix A.5 ■ page 550

1. $\left\{0, \frac{1}{2}, \sqrt{2}, 2\right\}$ **3.** $\{-1, 2\}$ **5.** $\left(-\infty, \frac{7}{2}\right]$

7. $(4, \infty)$

9. $(-\infty, 2]$

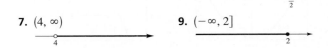

13. $[1, \infty)$

$\left(-\infty, -\frac{1}{2}\right)$

$-\frac{1}{2}$

15. $\left(\frac{16}{3}, \infty\right)$

$\frac{16}{3}$

17. $(-\infty, -1]$

-1 0

19. $[-3, -1)$

-3 -1

21. $(2, 6)$

2 6

23. $\left[\frac{9}{2}, 5\right)$

$\frac{9}{2}$ 5

25. $(-7, 7)$

-7 7

27. $[2, 8]$

2 8

29. $(-7, -3)$

-7 -3

31. $[1.3, 1.7]$

1.3 1.7

33. $(-4, 8)$

-4 8

35. $(-6, 2)$

-6 2

37. $68 \leqslant F \leqslant 86$

39. (a) $T = -0.01h + 20$ (b) $-30 \leqslant T \leqslant 20$

11.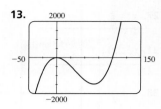

13.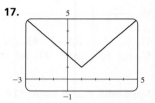

15.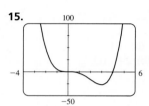

17.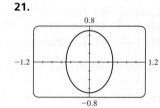

19.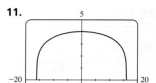

21.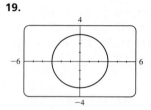

23. No   **25.** Yes, 2

Appendix B.1 ■ page 554

1. Congruent, ASA   **3.** Not necessarily congruent

5. Similar   **7.** Similar   **9.** $x = 125$ **11.** $x = 6, y = \frac{21}{4}$

13. $x = \dfrac{ac}{a + b}$ **17.** $h = 6$

Appendix B.2 ■ page 557

1. $x = 10$ **3.** $x = \sqrt{3}$ **5.** $x = 40$ **7.** Yes   **9.** No
11. Yes   **13.** 61   **15.** No   **17.** 13

Appendix C.1 ■ page 561

1. (c)   **3.** (c)   **5.** (c)

7.

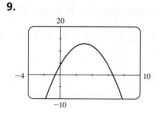

9.

Appendix C.2 ■ page 566

1. -4 **3.** $\dfrac{5}{14}$ **5.** $\pm 4\sqrt{2} \approx \pm 5.7$ **7.** $2.5, -2.5$

9. $5 + 2\sqrt[4]{5} \approx 7.99, 5 - 2\sqrt[4]{5} \approx 2.01$ **11.** $3.00, 4.00$

13. $1.00, 2.00, 3.00$ **15.** 1.62 **17.** $-1.00, 0.00, 1.00$

19. 2.55 **21.** $-2.05, 0, 1.05$ **23.** $[-2.00, 5.00]$

25. $(-\infty, 1.00] \cup [2.00, 3.00]$ **27.** $(-1.00, 0) \cup (1.00, \infty)$

29. $(-\infty, 0)$ **31.** $0, 0.01$

Index

Photo Credits

This page constitutes an extension of the copyright page. We have made every effort to trace the ownership of all copyrighted material and to secure permission from copyright holders. In the event of any question arising as to the use of any material, we will be pleased to make the necessary corrections in future printings. Thanks are due to the following authors, publishers, and agents for permission to use the material indicated.

Chapter 1

2: left, Lori Adamski Peck/ Stone/ Getty Images
2: right, Staffan Windstrand, Kevin Morris/ Corbis
51: Stanford University News Service
67: The Granger Collection
103: Kevin R. Morris/ Corbis
105: Eric & David Hosking/ Corbis
109: Phil Shemeister/ Corbis

Chapter 2

112: left, Michael Busselle/ Stone/ Getty Images
112: right, Bob Krist/ Corbis
146: © Jeff Lepore/ Photo Researchers Inc.
150: Courtesy of NASA

Chapter 3

176: left, Science Photo Library/ Photo Researchers Inc.
176: right, Alan Oddie/ PhotoEdit
220: NASA
234: British Library

Chapter 4

236: left, Corbis
236: right, NASA
276: © USA Today, reprinted with permission

Chapter 5

294: left, George Hall/ Corbis
294: right, J. L. Amos/ SuperStock
314: Bill Ross/ Corbis
317: Courtesy of David Dewey
349: J. L. Amos/ SuperStock

Chapter 6

358: left, Corbis
358: right, Lew Long/ The Stock Market/ Corbis
390: Roger Ressmeyer/ Corbis
408: NASA
427: The Granger Collection

Chapter 7

430: left, Joe McDonal/ Corbis
430: right, Owen Franken/ Corbis
433: Garry McMichael/ Photo Researchers Inc.

471: Art Wolfe/ Stone/ Getty Images
478: Joel W. Rogers/ Corbis
480: left, Bettmann/ Corbis
480: right, Hulton-Deutsch Collection/ Corbis
481: Roger Ressmeyer/ Corbis
497: The Image Bank/ Getty Images

Appendix

559: National Portrait Gallery

EXPONENTS AND RADICALS

$x^m x^n = x^{m+n}$

$(x^m)^n = x^{mn}$

$(xy)^n = x^n y^n$

$x^{1/n} = \sqrt[n]{x}$

$\sqrt[n]{xy} = \sqrt[n]{x}\,\sqrt[n]{y}$

$\sqrt[m]{\sqrt[n]{x}} = \sqrt[n]{\sqrt[m]{x}} = \sqrt[mn]{x}$

$\dfrac{x^m}{x^n} = x^{m-n}$

$x^{-n} = \dfrac{1}{x^n}$

$\left(\dfrac{x}{y}\right)^n = \dfrac{x^n}{y^n}$

$x^{m/n} = \sqrt[n]{x^m} = \left(\sqrt[n]{x}\right)^m$

$\sqrt[n]{\dfrac{x}{y}} = \dfrac{\sqrt[n]{x}}{\sqrt[n]{y}}$

SPECIAL PRODUCTS

$(x + y)^2 = x^2 + 2xy + y^2$

$(x - y)^2 = x^2 - 2xy + y^2$

$(x + y)^3 = x^3 + 3x^2 y + 3xy^2 + y^3$

$(x - y)^3 = x^3 - 3x^2 y + 3xy^2 - y^3$

FACTORING FORMULAS

$x^2 - y^2 = (x + y)(x - y)$

$x^2 + 2xy + y^2 = (x + y)^2$

$x^2 - 2xy + y^2 = (x - y)^2$

$x^3 + y^3 = (x + y)(x^2 - xy + y^2)$

$x^3 - y^3 = (x - y)(x^2 + xy + y^2)$

QUADRATIC FORMULA

If $ax^2 + bx + c = 0$, then

$$x = \frac{-b \pm \sqrt{b^2 - 4ac}}{2a}$$

INEQUALITIES AND ABSOLUTE VALUE

If $a < b$ and $b < c$, then $a < c$.

If $a < b$, then $a + c < b + c$.

If $a < b$ and $c > 0$, then $ca < cb$.

If $a < b$ and $c < 0$, then $ca > cb$.

If $a > 0$, then

$|x| = a$ means $x = a$ or $x = -a$.

$|x| < a$ means $-a < x < a$.

$|x| > a$ means $x > a$ or $x < -a$.

DISTANCE AND MIDPOINT FORMULAS

Distance between $P_1(x_1, y_1)$ and $P_2(x_2, y_2)$:

$$d = \sqrt{(x_2 - x_1)^2 + (y_2 - y_1)^2}$$

Midpoint of $P_1 P_2$: $\left(\dfrac{x_1 + x_2}{2}, \dfrac{y_1 + y_2}{2}\right)$

LINES

Slope of line through
$P_1(x_1, y_1)$ and $P_2(x_2, y_2)$

$m = \dfrac{y_2 - y_1}{x_2 - x_1}$

Point-slope equation of line
through $P_1(x_1, y_1)$ with slope m

$y - y_1 = m(x - x_1)$

Slope-intercept equation of
line with slope m and y-intercept b

$y = mx + b$

Two-intercept equation of line
with x-intercept a and y-intercept b

$\dfrac{x}{a} + \dfrac{y}{b} = 1$

LOGARITHMS

$y = \log_a x$ means $a^y = x$

$\log_a a^x = x$

$\log_a 1 = 0$

$\log x = \log_{10} x$

$\log_a xy = \log_a x + \log_a y$

$\log_a x^b = b \log_a x$

$a^{\log_a x} = x$

$\log_a a = 1$

$\ln x = \log_e x$

$\log_a \left(\dfrac{x}{y}\right) = \log_a x - \log_a y$

$\log_b x = \dfrac{\log_a x}{\log_a b}$

EXPONENTIAL AND LOGARITHMIC FUNCTIONS

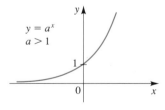

$y = a^x$
$a > 1$

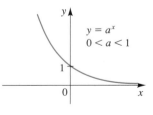

$y = a^x$
$0 < a < 1$

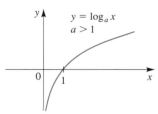

$y = \log_a x$
$a > 1$

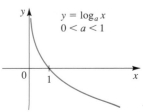

$y = \log_a x$
$0 < a < 1$